blank_____

Architecture, apartheid and after

Hilton Judin and Ivan Vladislavić

NAi Publishers, Rotterdam

Landscapes of exclusion

Foreword

This book is not simply a catalogue for an exhibition. It tells a story about the architecture of South Africa, a country where architecture and urban planning are inextricably connected with politics and culture.

Everybody knows something about apartheid, but here in Europe we know little of its direct consequences for the urban environment, and we are unfamiliar with the built manifestation of its political programme. Before we started work on this project I studied everything that had been published about architecture in South Africa. The results of my initial research were discouraging, because I found that there was very little literature extant. The few articles that I did find were about specific buildings, and were primarily concerned with their built form.

During the half century of apartheid, South Africa was subject to an academic and cultural boycott. In the country itself there were few critics or historians of architecture to examine the complex relationship between architecture and politics. There was no critical analysis of these issues except within the architecture profession itself; there was no public forum for discussion or debate about architecture. And within the universities, the discussions were predominantly of a technical or professional nature. This situation is to a large degree the same today.

On my first trip to South Africa I was concerned about this lack of critical awareness and wondered how it would even be possible to begin on such a project. It became clear to me that if we were to proceed, the project would not be like the exhibition projects that we are accustomed to; it would be an enormous and complex task involving research, analysis and detailed examination. It would be an incredible logistical challenge as well as a daring and innovative venture.

It was also obvious to me that this project could only be seriously and responsibly realized with the close collaboration of a South African curator. After many meetings with potential candidates we kept encountering conceptual or pragmatic differences that marred the success of our quest. I was ready to give up. However, my final meeting was different. In fact, in my initial discussions with Hilton Judin, a young architect and philosopher, we both had the intense and immediate sense that we were already involved in the project. This was just the beginning.

Back in the Netherlands, after a number of meetings with various government ministries, it became clear that there was considerable interest in increasing contact with South Africa, especially in the cultural and social realm. This interest was determined in part by the strong historical connection between the two countries over the last three centuries. This relationship not only includes a close interweaving of language, culture and religion, but also encompasses the strong anti-apartheid movement in the Netherlands: solidarity and boycott, a sense of guilt and pride, and dialogue and reflection have all characterized relations between the two countries at different points in history.

Thanks to the generous support of the government of the Netherlands and other institutions we have been able to complete an extensive and wide-ranging project and produce this book as well as the exhibition. This support made it possible for more than sixty people from South Africa to work with us on this project over the last year and a half: four researchers, ten photographers, six film makers, and more than thirty writers from different disciplines. Because there is no archive for architecture in South Africa, this team had to bring together material which had previously been dispersed, and sometimes even hidden, from all over the country. Without the strong personal engagement of all these people it would have been impossible to complete such an enormous and pressing task.

I hope that this book and the exhibition will initiate a process of study and debate in a country where architecture is emerging as a critical component in the construction of a new nation from the remnants of the past.

Kristin Feireiss
Director Netherlands Architecture Institute

Directions

This book had its origins in a conceptual map. The map itself was an attempt to organize the vast and relatively unexplored field of architecture in South Africa. An attempt was made to represent key architectural concepts in geographical terms, in the context of apartheid and thereafter. In this map, affinities were represented as proximity, tendencies by direction and intensities by accumulation. The map showed the major conceptual positions as landmarks, as well as some minor features. The edges of the map indicated connections between points at the top and bottom and on the left and right.

The essays in the book, both written and photographic, developed in response to the map. Each of the writers, photographers and artists was given the map in order to gain an overview of the terrain. The diverse disciplines and interests of the contributors ensured that much of the terrain was covered. Essays were positioned on the map according to their main focus. In addition to the conceptual landmarks, the map now included the contributors, who were positioned in relation to the landmarks and one another.

A grid was superimposed on the map, and the blocks marked horizontally by numbers and vertically by letters, as in a conventional key plan. Each contribution in the book could now be designated according to a set of coordinates. The contributions were placed in the book according to their alphanumerical location on the grid, reading from A1 to J13. The map became a map of contents. Any essay discovered in the map of contents could now be located in the body of the text according to these coordinates.

Apart from revealing the specific location of a particular essay in the main body of the text, the map of contents revealed intensities of interest and common preoccupations through the accumulations of contributions around particular points.

A secondary mapping, the Positions A to Z, was developed as a combination of legend, glossary and guide. This alphabetical listing glosses some of the key concepts and themes of the book through commentary and quotation, and it develops some sequences of readings, pursuing these themes through various contributions. At the end of some of the entries you will find cross-references to other terms in the Positions, or coordinates that will guide you to various works in the book.

The frontmatter of the book consists of three main interconnected sections: a map of contents, a list of contributors and the Positions A to Z. Each of these can be used to locate the essays.

The main body of the text, printed on white paper, contains the essays, arranged alphanumerically according to their position on the map. At the end of each essay you will find directions to essays in a similar area.

The backmatter consists of three sections: endnotes, the sources of the visual material, and an index, supplementary to the Positions A to Z, listing the names of people and buildings, as well as a selection of places and institutions.

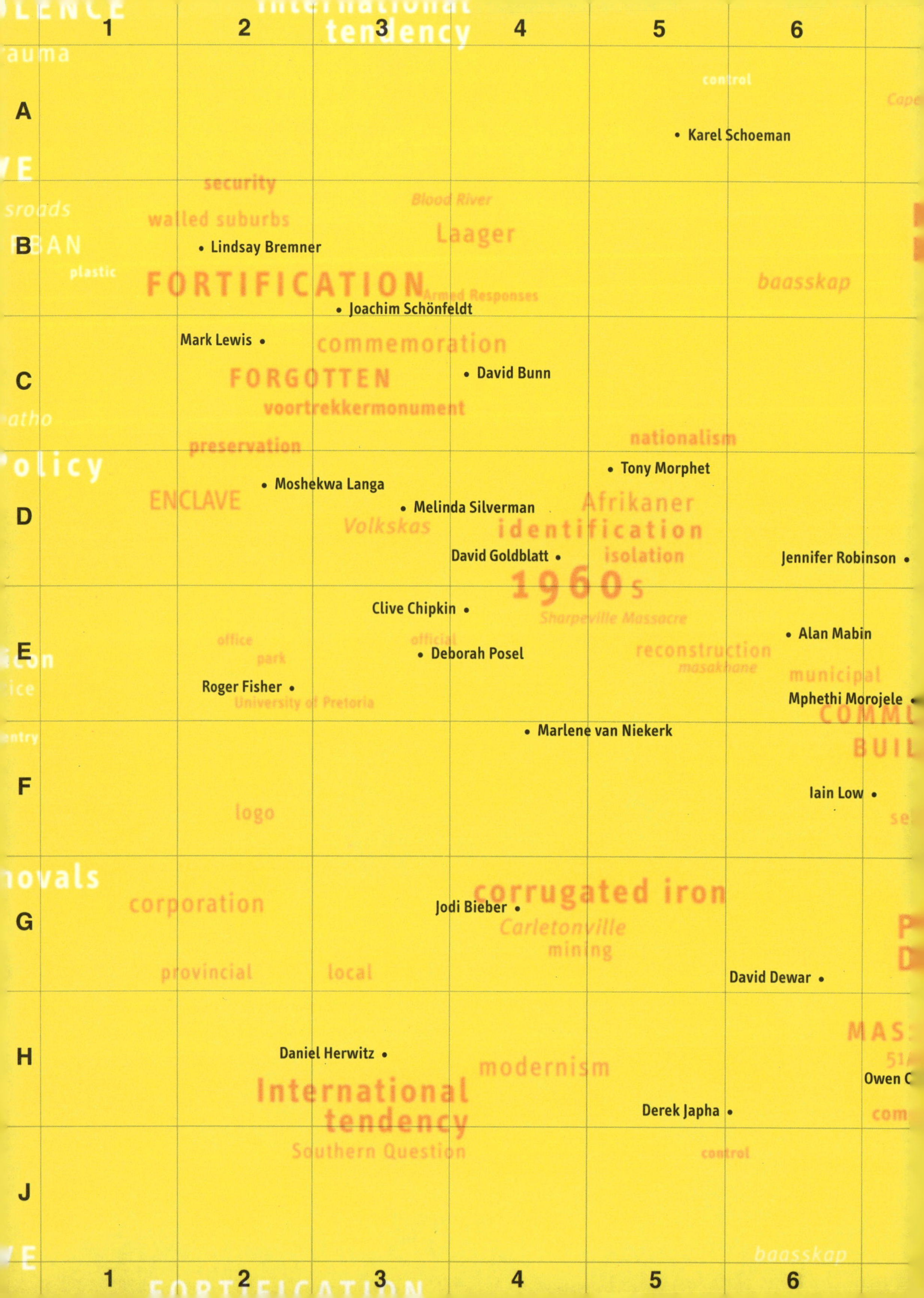

1
2
3
4
5
6
A
B
C
D
E
F
G
H
J
international
tendency
rauma
control
Cape
Karel Schoeman
security
sroads
walled suburbs
Blood River
Laager
BAN
Lindsay Bremner
plastic
FORTIFICATION
Armed Responses
baasskap
Joachim Schönfeldt
Mark Lewis
commemoration
FORGOTTEN
David Bunn
voortrekkermonument
atho
nationalism
preservation
olicy
Tony Morphet
Moshekwa Langa
ENCLAVE
Melinda Silverman
Afrikaner
Volkskas
identification
David Goldblatt
isolation
Jennifer Robinson
1960s
Clive Chipkin
Sharpeville Massacre
Alan Mabin
office
official
park
Deborah Posel
reconstruction
masakhane
municipal
Roger Fisher
University of Pretoria
Mphethi Morojele
COMMU
entry
Marlene van Niekerk
BUIL
Iain Low
logo
movals
corrugated iron
corporation
Jodi Bieber
Carletonville
mining
provincial
local
David Dewar
MAS
Daniel Herwitz
modernism
Owen C
International
tendency
Derek Japha
Southern Question
control
baasskap
FORTIFICATION

8 9 10 11 12 13

VIOLENCE

locations

burn

A

mission stations

thatch

WEAVE

• Chris Ledochowski

heaven

ZCC

OMISED
ND

KTC/Crossroads

RURAL IN URBAN

• Santu Mofokeng

B

burials

Churches

Rayda Becker •

plastic

FOR

dorpe

tradition

SUB-U

NGK

Njabulo Ndebele •

reserves

C

capitals *Mmabatho*

pres

Homelands Policy

African

ENCL

• Gary Minkley

D

AbdouMaliq Simone •

Mdantsane

inner city

frontier

• Lizeka Mda

Themba Hadebe •

INVASIONS

• Ivan Vladislavić

INFORMAL

E

Stephen Hobbs •

house/icon

• Mark Swilling

civics

private practice

TY

• Jo Ractliffe

• Hannah le Roux

NG

breaking and entry

• Achmat Dangor

F

• Angela Buckland

lp

Group Areas Act, No. 41

District Six

• Shamil Jeppie

Forced Removals

segregation

• Rafs Mayet

corporati

ANNED

G

ISIONS

• Zwelethu Mthethwa

Black Spot

provinci

dislocation

OUSING

H

es

Red Sea

aw/Susan Parnell •

d system

VIOLENCE

burn

locations

daily trauma

• Steven Robins

Greg Marinovich •

Tokoza

J

tradition

ssion stations

secu

OMISED

WEAVE

FOR

8 9 10 11 12 13

B11 Homesteads and headrests

Rayda Becker is Senior Curator of the Gertrude Posel Gallery, University of the Witwatersrand. After beginning her career as a teacher in the United Kingdom during the 1960s, she moved to the History of Art and Fine Arts Department at the University of South Africa in 1973 and was promoted to Associate Professor. She is currently completing her Ph.D. at the University of the Witwatersrand on the Tsonga and their headrests. Recent publications are on Southern African topics and include *Ku veleka vukosi ... To bear children is wealth* and *The Arts of the Hlengwe/Tsonga Peoples of Zimbabwe*. She has delivered papers in Bristol and New York and at local conferences, acted as a judge for Vita Craft Now (1997) and is a member of the advisory panel for crafts for the National Arts Council. In her tenure as curator she has organized and coordinated over fifty exhibitions and curated six of her own, including *Convention, Context, Change*; *Planes, Trains and Other Vehicles*; *African Textiles*; and most recently *Clothing and Identity*.

G4 Carletonville

Jodi Bieber In 1991 I completed an intermediate course at the Market Theatre photography workshop while still working as a media planner in an advertising agency. I freelanced for the *Star* for three years leading up to the 1994 elections, which I also covered. Since 1996 I have been freelancing for local and international magazines and have published in *Marie Claire*, *London Independent*, *Geo*, *Süddeutsche Zeitung*, *Reportage*, *Elle*, *De Volkskrant*, the *New York Times* and the *LA Times*. I was chosen to participate in the World Press masterclass held in the Netherlands. I have won two awards in the World Press photographic competition and four in the South African press awards held in 1998. The joint exhibitions I have participated in include the 1995 Johannesburg Biennale, *Colours* at the House of World Cultures in Berlin, *Under the Tropics* at Cardiff University and the recent World Press exhibition. I received a grant from the National Arts Council in 1998 to pursue an independent photographic project.

B2 Crime and the emerging landscape of post-apartheid Johannesburg

Lindsay Bremner is an architect, Professor of Architecture and Head of Department at the University of the Witwatersrand. She holds a B.Arch. from the University of Cape Town and an M.Arch. from the University of the Witwatersrand. She was a member of the Johannesburg Metropolitan Council after the 1994 elections, where she chaired both the Housing and Urbanization Committee and the Planning, Urbanization and Environmental Management Committee. In this capacity, she instigated and was involved in a number of major projects to redress the legacy of apartheid planning in Johannesburg, such as the Baralink project linking Johannesburg and Soweto, and the Constitutional Court competition. She has published extensively on architecture and planning in South Africa, and Johannesburg in particular.

F8 Steinkopf community centre

Angie Buckland was born in Pretoria in 1962 and grew up in various cities in South Africa and Zimbabwe. She began her tertiary education studying Fine Arts at the University of Natal in Pietermaritzburg, majoring in painting, and then studied photography full-time at Natal Technikon, where she obtained a Higher Diploma. She was awarded an overseas scholarship and completed a Masters degree at Birmingham Polytechnic. She worked as an art buyer for an advertising agency in London before settling in Durban. For the past ten years she has been working as a freelance photographer, and is a part-time Lecturer in the Fine Arts Department at the Natal Technikon. She has participated in various photographic exhibitions, and also promotes the culture of photography through the Durban Centre for Photography. A number of her photographs are held in public and private collections.

C4 Whited sepulchres: On the reluctance of monuments

David Bunn is a Professor in the Department of English at the University of the Western Cape. After completing an undergraduate degree at Rhodes University, he was awarded a Fulbright Scholarship to study at Northwestern University, where he received his Masters and Ph.D. Based at the University of the Western Cape since 1984, he has also taught widely in the United States, and has been a Visiting Professor in the English Department at Northwestern and in the Anthropology Department at the University of Chicago. Much of his recent work has focused on contemporary South African cultural studies, with a particular emphasis on the relationship between texts, visual images and landscapes. His published work includes studies of literary modernism, the history of game reserves, landscape studies, and interdisciplinary art historical studies. He also frequently collaborates with his partner Jane Taylor: they were co-editors of the interdisciplinary journal *Social Dynamics*, co-edited the volumes *From South Africa* and *Displacements: South African Works on Paper 1984-1994* (1998), and have co-curated art exhibitions. At present, he is completing a book entitled *Land Acts: Modernity, Representation, and the Making of South African Space*.

E4 The great apartheid building boom: The transformation of Johannesburg in the 1960s

Clive Chipkin was born in Johannesburg in 1929. The University of the Witwatersrand (1954), the old London County Council (1956/7) and CIAM (1956) were important influences, as were the fragrances of India and East Africa. He opened an overworked and underpaid practice at 302 Hollandia House in Johannesburg in 1958. His buildings range from the University Gate flats (1960) to a whole series of industrial and social amenity buildings in Vanderbijlpark (1984-98). He co-authored the Architects Against Apartheid manifesto which disturbed the profession in 1986 and taught in an architectural enrichment programme from 1987 to 1995. Since his first publication in the *South African Architectural*

Record in 1958, he has published some fifty essays and monographs. He is the co-author of *Parktown: 1892-1972* (1972), and the author of the book *Johannesburg Style: Architecture & Society 1880s-1960s* (1993) and the essay 'Preparing for apartheid' in *Architecture of the Transvaal* (forthcoming).

H8 Interpreting the 1994 African township landscape

Owen Crankshaw is a Senior Lecturer in the Sociology Department at the University of Cape Town. Before joining the university, he held research positions at the Human Sciences Research Council and the Centre for Policy Studies. During that time he also taught courses at the University of the Witwatersrand and the London School of Economics. His research interest lies in the relationship between racial and class divisions in South Africa. He recently completed a book *Race, Class and the Changing Division of Labour under Apartheid* (1997). His research has also been published in journals in Britain (*African Affairs*, *Journal of Southern African Studies*, *International Journal of Urban and Regional Research*) and in South Africa (*South African Sociological Review*, *Urban Forum*, *South African Geographical Journal* and *South African Labour Bulletin*).

F10 Apartheid and the death of South African cities

Achmat Dangor was born in Johannesburg in 1948. He lived a nomadic life in the years after completing high school, and sojourns in Cape Town, Port Elizabeth, Grahamstown, Kimberley, Victoria West and a small place called Buurmansdrift greatly influenced his attitude towards life and literature. The small rural towns in particular infused his writing with the 'outsider' theme, as commentators have called it. Politically active from an early age, he was 'banned' for five years (1973-8) by the apartheid government. These were silent but productive years; unable to socialize, attend meetings or indulge in the things writers love to distract themselves with, he wrote endlessly. He has published three novels, *Waiting for Leila* (1982), *The Z-Town Trilogy* (1990), which appeared in Dutch translation, and *Kafka's Curse* (1997), which won the Herman Charles Bosman Award. He has also published three poetry collections, numerous short stories, plays and film scripts. He works as a rural development specialist for a major non-governmental development organization.

G6 Settlements, change and planning in South Africa since 1994

David Dewar was born in Bulawayo in 1945. He studied at the University of Cape Town, where he received a BA Honours, a Masters in Urban and Regional Planning (with distinction) and a Ph.D. He first began teaching at the same university and has subsequently been Director of the School of Architecture and Planning, and Dean of the Faculty of Fine Art and Architecture. He currently holds the BPSA Chair in Urban Planning and is Head of the postgraduate City and Regional Planning programme. He has authored or co-authored seven books, including *South African Cities: A Manifesto for Change* (1991). His publications cover a range of topics, including urban structure, regional development, housing policy and the informal economic sector; a book examining the interrelationship between urban structure and economic development is in press. For the past five years he has served on the statutory South African Council for Town and Regional Planners. He was a member of the Presidential Commission of Inquiry into Delft (1995), the Commission that investigated the powers and duties of the Cape Metropolitan Council (1996), and the Committee of Review into the Vredehoek Flats (1997). He currently serves on the Panel of Assessors to the Land Claims Court, and on the National Development and Planning Commission, which is preparing a Green Paper on the planning system in South Africa.

E2 The native heart: The architecture of the University of Pretoria campus

Roger Fisher is a Senior Lecturer in the School of Architecture at the University of Pretoria. He compiled the book *A Visual Lexicon of the South African Dwelling*, a bilingual guide to the architectural terminology of South African domestic architecture, and co-edited *Die Afrikaanse woning: Herdrukke uit Die Boerevrou* (1989) and *Architecture of the Transvaal* (1998). He received both a Masters and a Ph.D. in architecture from the University of Pretoria, where he now lectures in design, construction and the history of architecture. He has spent the last year developing a core curriculum for architecture and landscape architecture, and revising the professional degrees for both. He writes regularly for the local architectural press, has served on several panels for the Awards of Merit of the Institute of South African Architects, and writes on matters of education and architectural history for local journals. He acts as Advisor to the Northern Gauteng Region of the National Monuments Council.

D4 Offices

David Goldblatt was born in Randfontein in 1930 and became interested in photography while at Krugersdorp High School. He has worked as a photographer since 1962. His professional work for magazines, corporations, and institutions in South Africa and abroad has supported a series of critical explorations of South African society in the medium of photography. These have been exhibited in South Africa, Britain, Germany, the Netherlands, Australia and the United States. They have been published in book form as *On the Mines* (1973), *Some Afrikaners Photographed* (1975), *In Boksburg* (1982), *Lifetimes: Under Apartheid* (1986), *The Transported of KwaNdebele* (1989) and most recently *South Africa: The Structure of Things Then* (1998). In 1989 Goldblatt founded the Market Theatre photography workshop with the object of teaching photographic skills to young people, particularly those disadvantaged by apartheid. Goldblatt's prints are in a number of collections in South Africa, Europe, Australia and the United States. Prints from his most recent book have been shown at the Museum of Modern Art in New York, the Netherlands Architecture Institute in Rotterdam and the South African National Gallery in Cape Town.

D9 Inner City

Themba Hadebe I was born in Soweto in 1969, but my family later moved to Tokoza. When I was in Standard 5 a cousin gave me his camera. There was a demand for pictures at school and I was soon selling them. I bought myself a 35 mm camera and the shooting business became very serious. One afternoon I was on my way home when I came across some guys chasing a cow. I rushed to get my camera and ran back to the scene. The police had been called in to shoot the cow, but they missed and fatally injured a girl. In the trial the police denied having shot at the cow and the girl's father asked me for the pictures as evidence. I had hopes of going to Rhodes University to study photojournalism but because of financial limitations and exam results it wasn't to be. In 1991 I started a course at the Market Theatre photography workshop with the hope of pursuing press photography. It was difficult for me to get home at night because Tokoza had become dangerous, and so I slept at the station until I could catch a five o'clock taxi home. I started working at the workshop and got a permanent post as an administrator. In 1994 I began work at the *Mail & Guardian* as a trainee photographer. The following year I joined the *Star*, where I am now a senior photographer. I have received a number of Fujifilm Press Awards and my work is beginning to be exhibited.

H3 Modernism at the margins

Daniel Herwitz was born in Boston in 1955. He has lived in Durban since 1996, having arrived from Los Angeles, where he taught philosophy and film in various universities. He is Professor and Head of the Department of Philosophy at the University of Natal, Durban. He has published widely in the fields of avant-garde and post-colonial aesthetics and art history. His first book, *Husain* (1987) won a National Book Award in India. His other books are *Making Theory/Constructing Art: On the Authority of the Avant-Garde* and *The Tapestry of Modern Indian Art*, which explores the formation of a lively modern art movement at the margins of global modernity. Herwitz is an associate editor of the *Encyclopaedia of Aesthetics* (forthcoming) and is on the Board of the Cambridge Series in Aesthetics. He has lectured widely in universities and museums throughout the United States, Europe and Latin America. He is currently at work on a collection of essays about art, culture and liberalism, tentatively titled *Inaugurations and Endings: A Philosopher between America and South Africa*.

E10 Erasing roadmarkings, Cnrs. Bezuidenhout and Jeppe Streets

Stephen Hobbs has been the Manager of the Market Theatre Gallery and Rembrandt van Rijn Art Gallery for the past four years. During this time he has curated several projects and is currently working towards a public art project in Rotterdam. His other activities have included part-time teaching at the South African School of Film, Television and Dramatic Art in Johannesburg. He has had two solo exhibitions since graduating with a BA Honours in Fine Art from the University of the Witwatersrand in 1993. He is currently working towards his third solo exhibition scheduled for Cape Town in 1999.

H6 The social programme of the South African Modern Movement

Derek Japha is an architect and Associate Professor in the School of Architecture and Planning at the University of Cape Town, where he is also currently the Dean of the Faculty of Fine Art and Architecture. Research interests include 19th-century vernacular building and settlement at the Cape, the history of mission settlements in South Africa and conservation planning. He is the co-author of *The Landscape and Architecture of Montagu* and *Mission Settlements in South Africa*, and of a number of journal articles and many of the South African entries in the *Encyclopaedia of Vernacular Architecture*. He is on the editorial advisory board of the *Traditional Dwellings and Settlements Review* and is a member of the panel of referees of the *South African Architect*.

G10 Interiors, District Six, c. 1950

Shamil Jeppie teaches in the History Department at the University of Cape Town. He received his doctorate in history from Princeton University in 1996, having worked on the subject of conquest and space in the Sudan in the 19th century. In 1998 he will be based at St. Anthony's College, Oxford, where he will continue and complete his research and writing on the Sudan. He has also written on the history of Cape Town and especially on the city's popular cultures and issues of identity. He is currently working on a project entitled *District Six and Beyond* for Cape Town's District Six Museum, of which he was a founding trustee.

editor

Hilton Judin is an independent curator and partner in Cohen&Judin Architects in Cape Town. He completed his studies in architecture and philosophy at Cornell University, and returned to South Africa in 1991. In 1994 he initiated an extensive research and exhibition project [setting apart], which was produced with the History Workshop of the University of the Witwatersrand and the Newtown Film and Video School in Johannesburg. In 1995 the project was produced with the Mayibuye Centre and District Six Museum in Cape Town. This exhibition of official archive documents and video testimonies examining the segregation of urban spaces continues to be conducted in stages around the country. In addition to making exhibitions the practice is currently working on a number of houses and developing the Living Landscape Project, a group of archaeological information sites located around the town of Clanwilliam.

D2 Falstaff

Moshekwa Langa lives and works in Amsterdam. He attended the Waldorf High School near Pretoria and subsequently took up correspondence studies in botany, landscape architecture and sociology. He has been a contributing producer on *The Works*, a weekly television programme devoted to art and culture, for the South African Broadcasting Corporation. He has participated in discussion and dialogue on various projects, including *the space between my teeth*. His work has been exhibited in numerous exhibitions and several biennales, including the São Paulo and Havana editions. His current projects are *True Confessions: My life as a Disco Queen*, and a publication, *How I lived my life as a spinster*, the true story of a woman in love.

A12 Rural in urban

Chris Ledochowski was born in Pretoria in 1956. After attending school at Waterford Kamhlaba in Swaziland he was enlisted for military service. He then studied at the Michaelis School of Fine Art at the University of Cape Town, majoring in photography. In the early 1980s he joined the

Afrapix photographic collective. Important work during that period included establishing the Film and Video Unit for the Carnegie Inquiry into Poverty and Development and a contribution to the book *The Cordoned Heart*. In 1985 he began recording the formation and development of COSATU and affiliated unions in the Western Cape. He continued to pursue his personal documentation of the Cape Flats townships and squatter camps. The varied cultures and subcultures that emerged led him to embark on a long-term project to document the indigenous art and culture of communities in the Cape Flats. This body of work he intends to publish in the book *Township Details*. He has held solo exhibitions at the Market Theatre Gallery, the Mayibuye Centre, the Bat Centre and MuseumAfrica. He continues to work as a freelance documentary photographer, mainly pursuing self-illustrated projects.

F9 Undisciplined practices: Architecture in the context of freedom

Hannah le Roux graduated as an architect from the University of the Witwatersrand. In 1990 she attended courses at the Instituto Universitario di Architettura di Venezia as an Italian government bursary holder. Since then she has worked as a Lecturer at the University of the Witwatersrand, written on architecture for the *Mail & Guardian*, and practised as an architect in Johannesburg. Her built work includes artists' studios and the upgrading of Bloemenhof Park, a collaborative work with other architects and artists. She convened *Newtown: Informal Sector*, an Internet discussion for the 1997 Johannesburg Biennale. She is currently researching and writing about early modernist architecture in Africa.

C2 Armed responses

Mark Lewis is a photographer living in Cape Town. He began his career as a freelance photographer in 1977 in advertising. In 1983, he moved to London and worked in portraiture and fashion for various magazines in London, Paris and New York. He returned to South Africa in 1993/4 to co-produce *Ndebele: A People and Their Art*. He relocated to South Africa in 1995. Recent projects include documenting the remaining Holocaust survivors in South Africa, works which were exhibited as part of *Fault Lines* in 1997. He contributes monthly to *Marie Claire* and *House and Leisure*. He is now working on a book of portraits of rural communities taken in a mobile studio.

F7 Building and self-reliance

Iain Low is an architect who currently teaches at the University of the Witwatersrand. His practice and teaching are concerned with the possibility of transformation in South Africa, and attempts to work productively within the ideology of reconstruction and development which characterizes the post-apartheid era. He has a B.Arch. from the University of Cape Town and an M.Arch. in urban design from the University of Pennsylvania, where he was Pew Fellow in the Arts in 1993. He teaches abroad regularly, particularly in Rome where he was a Visiting Fellow at the American Academy (1995). Before returning to South Africa, he spent eight years working with various aid agencies in development in the Kingdom of Lesotho, evolving an integrated approach to the design and delivery of rural and urban schools throughout that country.

E6 Reconstruction and the making of urban planning in 20th-century South Africa

Alan Mabin was born in Johannesburg, and has lived in small towns and large cities in South Africa, the United States and Canada. He has travelled and researched widely in Australia, Brazil, Kenya, Malaysia, Namibia and Zimbabwe, among other places. He has held fellowships at Yale University and the Université de Paris. He is the editor of three books, and the author of many articles in the fields of urban planning, economic history and urban geography. Currently he is Associate Professor in Town and Regional Planning and Director of the Centre for Development of the Built Environment, at the University of the Witwatersrand. He is also Deputy Chairperson of the National Development and Planning Commission and chairs the Board of Directors of a non-governmental organization in Johannesburg.

J10 The Dead Zone: The confined space of political conflict, Tokoza township

Greg Marinovich is a news and documentary photographer currently writing a non-fiction novel on the tumultuous period from Mandela's release to his inauguration, through the experiences of four photographers. In 1991 he became the first South African to win a Pulitzer Prize, for photographs showing an execution during the country's political conflict. He covered the political violence intensely, and is extremely familiar with Tokoza's Dead Zone. In 1994, the United Nations gave him an award for Services to Humanity, in recognition of the work he had done in conflict zones from the former Yugoslavia and Chechnya to Rwanda and Somalia. He lives in Johannesburg, some fifty kilometres from where he was born in 1962.

G11 'My porzie, my zla, my koesta'

Rafs Mayet My name is Rafique Mayet, but most people call me 'Rafs'. I was born in 1955 in Durban. I first worked in the shipyards as a welder. I saved enough money to attend the University of the Western Cape, but was unable to complete anything because of the prevailing unrest at the time. In 1983 Omar Badsha offered to teach me the basics of photography and I worked for him as a darkroom assistant. I then got a job working in the darkroom of the East London *Daily Dispatch*. After two years of this, I returned to Durban and started freelancing for local publications. I also joined Afrapix, the first collective photographic agency in the country. I have participated in group exhibitions like the *Staffrider* annual exhibition. Despite being published internationally, I was denied a passport to travel abroad in the 1980s. In 1994 I was one of seven photographers chosen to work for the archives of the Independent Electoral Commission, and some of these pictures were published in a book called *An End to Waiting*. I have since been documenting the area that I grew up in, while continuing along the freelancer's route, as I figure that at the age of 43 I am now pretty much unemployable.

D10 City Quarters: Civic Spine, Faraday Station, KwaMayiMayi and Ponte City

Lizeka Mda has been a journalist since 1984. Much of her experience has been with magazines, but over the years she has written for local and overseas newspapers and produced radio programmes for the British and Canadian Broadcasting Corporations. She is the author of *Stokvel Stories: Sexual Harassment in the Workplace* and co-author of *Rainbow Recipes*. She has worked as a researcher and writer on the Education Information Centre book *The World of Work* and on *The South African Women's Health Book*. She co-edited a collection of children's writings, *Voices From Young Africa*, and currently edits *Women's Health News*, the quarterly newsletter of the Women's Health Project. She has also published short stories. In 1993 she was selected as a World Press Institute Fellow. She received a Mondi Paper Magazine Award in 1994/5 and in 1997 was the recipient of the first Ron Brown Fellowship. She joined the *Mail & Guardian* in 1997 as a senior writer and ran the column *City Limits*. She is the Chairperson of the South African Forum of Black Journalists. Since 1998 she has been an editor at the *Star*.

D11 'Corpses behind screens': Native space in the city

Gary Minkley grew up in the Eastern Cape, studied at the University of Cape Town and has been a historian at the University of the Western Cape since 1987. He is currently a Senior Lecturer and Chairperson of the History Department. He has produced work on a range of topics concerned with the histories of cities in South Africa and particularly in the Eastern Cape, and more recently on questions of public history, landscape and memory, and on place and the politics of identity in South Africa. He is currently working on two monographs for publication, *Border Dialogues: Space and the Industrialization of East London* and *Public History, Memory and Space at the Cape*. He is one of the editors of *Kronos*.

B8 Appropriated spaces

Santu Mofokeng was born in Johannesburg in 1956, and is a documentary photographer at the Institute for Advanced Social Research, University of the Witwatersrand, working primarily on its oral history project. This project seeks to record the lives of ordinary people through photographs and in-depth interviews. He has won numerous awards, including the Third Annual Mother Jones International Photography Award (1992) and the Ernest Cole Scholarship to study at the International Centre of Photography in New York (1990). His most recent project, *Images of Self and Family Histories of Black South Africans: 1890-1950*, aims to create an archive of private images rich with family stories and is concerned with the politics of representation.

E7 Towards an architecture of empowerment

Mphethi Morojele is a practising architect and Lecturer in the Department of Architecture at the University of the Witwatersrand. Born in Lesotho, he completed his undergraduate degree in architecture at the University of Cape Town in 1990, and then studied for an M.Sc.Arch. at the Bartlett Graduate School of Architecture in London. After a period practising and teaching in Cape Town and Lesotho, he moved to Johannesburg, and his practice is currently involved in various urban-renewal and community-based projects in the Greater Johannesburg area. He has also participated in various policy discussions related to the development of the built environment for the new government. He is currently involved in the Duncan Village urban development project, a presidential lead project in East London.

D5 Personal traits: The work of Eaton and Biermann in Durban

Tony Morphet was born in 1940 and grew up on a farm in the East Griqualand district of the Cape Province. After completing school and university in Pietermaritzburg, he spent three years in Britain teaching and taking a further degree in English literature. In 1964 he joined the University of Natal in Durban as a Lecturer in English, and remained in that post until 1976 when he moved into the new field of adult education. After a year's study of the subject in Edinburgh, in 1980 he took up a post at the University of Cape Town, where he is now Associate Professor in the Department of Adult Education and Extra-Mural Studies. His chief academic interest is in the relationship between educational practices and the broader cultural discourses in which they are embedded, and his writing covers a wide range of cultural topics.

G8 Environmental portraits

Zwelethu Mthethwa In 1964 my family was uprooted from St. Xavier Catholic mission station in Durban, where I was born in 1960. We were moved inland to the new township of Umlazi. This was my first taste of segregation. On completion of my high-school education in public schools, I was sent to the University of Zululand to study for a B.Sc. Pre-med, but I dropped out. In 1981 I enrolled at the Michaelis School of Fine Art at the University of Cape Town. There were hassles before I could be fully enrolled, because of the restrictions on black students wishing to study at white institutions. I graduated in 1984 with a distinction in photography and a year later received my Advanced Diploma in Fine Arts. In 1987 I was awarded a Fulbright Scholarship and completed my Master of Fine Arts in Imaging Art at the Rochester Institute of Technology. On my return to South Africa I worked in the commercial industry and in 1994 joined my alma mater as a Lecturer in drawing and photography. My drawings and photographs have been exhibited in major exhibitions such as the 1997 Johannesburg Biennale and La Maison Européenne de la photographie. I have served on the Committee of the Association for Visual Arts for many years, and have been associated with the Friends of the South African National Gallery. In 1997 I was nominated to the National Arts Council's advisory panel for visual arts in South Africa.

C10 Game lodges and leisure colonialists

Njabulo Ndebele grew up in Western Native Township in Johannesburg, and later in Charterston Location. He holds a BA in English and Philosophy from the University of Botswana, Lesotho and Swaziland (1973), an MA from Cambridge (1978) and a Doctorate in Philosophy from the University of Denver (1983). His most recent position was as Vice-Chancellor and Principal at the University of the North. He is the Chairman of the Human Sciences Research Council, member of the Committee of University Principals and serves as Chairman of their Research Committee. He is a Board Member of Southern Life's Future Growth, serves on the

Education Committee of the Urban Foundation and is Convenor of the Historically Disadvantaged Universities and Technikons Forum. He is a past President of the National Arts Coalition and Honorary Life President of the Congress of South African Writers. He is also a prize-winning author, poet and critic. His book *Fools and Other Stories* received the Noma Award for publishing in Africa in 1983. He was awarded a visiting research fellowship to Yale University's Southern African Research Program in 1986. He was a recent recipient of Honorary Doctorates from Soka University, Vrije Universiteit Amsterdam and Chicago State University.

H8 Interpreting the 1994 African township landscape

Susan Parnell is an urban geographer. She has written extensively on the South African city, looking particularly at the history of racial segregation in Johannesburg. Some of that work informed the 1994 exhibition [setting apart] which she co-curated. More recently, her primary academic research focus has been a project on the influence of British Imperial policy on urban Africa. Apart from these historical interests, she has also been concerned with the applied urban issues of contemporary housing provision, gender and the city, and the reconceptualization of local government in the post-apartheid era. She worked for many years at the University of the Witwatersrand, and is now an Associate Professor at the University of Cape Town. She has also taught at the University of London's School of Oriental and African Studies. She serves on the Boards of the Isandla Institute, the Gender Advocacy Programme and the Urban Problems Research Unit.

E3 Does size matter? The apartheid state's powers of penetration

Deborah Posel lives in Johannesburg and teaches in the Department of Sociology at the University of the Witwatersrand. Her primary research interest is in the nature of power, as a theoretical problem and by way of an exploration of the origins, character and fate of the apartheid state. Her publications include two books, *The Making of Apartheid, 1948-1961* (1991) and a co-edited collection *Apartheid's Genesis* (1994). She received her D.Phil. from the University of Oxford, where she was also Prize Research Fellow from 1985 to 1987, and was a Visiting Scholar at Harvard in 1994/5.

E12 House Martienssen

Jo Ractliffe is a practising artist currently living in Johannesburg. She was born in Cape Town and studied Fine Arts at the University of Cape Town (BAFA and MFA). In 1991 she took up a post in the Department of Fine Arts at the University of the Witwatersrand, where she teaches studio practice and art theory. She is also Chairperson of the advisory board of the Market Theatre Galleries, on which she has served since 1993. She has exhibited widely, both in South Africa and abroad, and her work is represented in most public collections in the country. Recent exhibitions include: *Don't Mess with Mister In-between* at the Culturgest in Lisbon (1996), *Guess who loves you* at the Goodman Gallery in Johannesburg (1997), *Aborescence Sud-Africaine: des artists en fin de siècle* at the Nantes Festival (1997), *Alternating Currents* at the 1997 Johannesburg Biennale, and *Art dans le monde: tendences critiques 1998* at the Passage de Retz, Paris (1998). She is currently working towards her fourth solo exhibition, *End of Time*, a series of multiple media site-specific installations in Nieu-Bethesda in the Karoo.

J12 Bodies out of place: Crossroads and the landscapes of exclusion

Steven Robins is a social anthropologist who teaches at the University of the Western Cape. After studying at Columbia University (1986-92), he took up a senior research position at the Kaplan Centre for Jewish Studies. In 1995 he joined the Department of Adult Education at the University of Cape Town, where he worked with the Social Uses of Literacy (SoUL) project. In 1996 he joined the Anthropology Department at the University of the Western Cape. His most recent work examines issues of Holocaust and apartheid memory and history in the urban landscape. In 1996 he worked with an architect on reconceptualizing urban conservation ideas and practices in the cultural landscape of the post-apartheid city. His earlier work includes an analysis of the cultural politics of land-use planning interventions in contemporary rural Zimbabwe, as well as studies on the reclaiming of Nama (Khoi) identity during the course of land struggles in the Namaqualand Reserves of the Northern Cape. He is currently working on questions of land, memory and identity in relation to urban and rural land claims.

D7 (Im)mobilizing space – dreaming of change

Jenny Robinson currently lives in London, where she lectures in the Department of Geography and Environment at the London School of Economics, and is soon to join the Faculty of Social Science at the Open University. She has also taught at the University of Natal in Durban, which is her home and where she did most of her studying, apart from a Ph.D. at Cambridge. She has written on the history of urban segregation in South Africa, both in general and specifically in relation to Port Elizabeth. This work was published as *The Power of Apartheid* (1996). More recent research interests include the spatiality of democracy, transformation and power. She is currently working on aspects of an Empire Exhibition held in Johannesburg in 1936, and planning to write on cities and post-developmentalism. She is a joint editor of *Geoforum*.

A5 'Fort ende Thuijn': The years of Dutch colonization

Karel Schoeman is a major Afrikaans novelist. His fifteen works of fiction published since 1965 have won numerous awards including the Hertzog, the Helgaard Steyn, the CNA, the W. A. Hofmeyr and the Old Mutual Prizes. His novels have been translated into English, Dutch, German and Russian. His works of fiction include *Veldslag* (1965), *By fakkellig* (1966), *'n Lug vol helder wolke* (1967), *Spiraal* (1968), *Op 'n eiland* (1971), *Na die geliefde land* (1972), *Die hemeltuin* (1979), *'n Ander land* (1984), *Afskeid en vertrek* (1990), *Hierdie lewe* (1993), *Die uur van die engel* (1995) and *Verkenning* (1996). Schoeman is also prominent in South African historiography, and his historical works include an illustrated history of Bloemfontein, biographies of Olive Schreiner, a biography of Irma Stern and an illustrated record of the architectural heritage of the Orange Free State. His extensive oeuvre of some sixty published works also includes travel books, translations of dramas and of Gaelic poetry, and adaptations of Gaelic sagas and legends. He was born in 1939 in Trompsburg. He went to school in Paarl, graduated from the University of the Orange Free State, studied at the Catholic Seminary in Pretoria, and completed his noviciate in the Franciscan Order in Ireland. Between 1964 and 1982 he worked in Bloemfontein, at a library in Amsterdam, as a nurse in Glasgow, and again in Bloemfontein, before moving to Cape Town where he is employed by the South African Library.

B3 Silence!

Joachim Schönfeldt was born in Pretoria, but his family moved to Namibia just three weeks later. He completed his schooling in Namibia and initially went to the University of Pretoria to do Fine Arts, but was kicked out after two years. After graduating from the University of the Witwatersrand in the early 1980s, he worked for Meneghelli Holdings as a curator and researcher in old African art, and then became a full-time artist in 1988. In 1989 he worked and lived in Italy before settling in Johannesburg the following year, writing art criticism for a local daily, and curating, but mostly practising art.

D3 'Ons bou vir die Bank': Nationalism, architecture and Volkskas Bank

Melinda Silverman: I am an architect and urban designer, torn between a passion for the architectural past and a preoccupation with Johannesburg's urban future. I have undergraduate degrees in politics and architecture and a Masters in urban design from the University of the Witwatersrand. I co-authored the Provincial Government White Paper on Urban Regeneration for Gauteng in 1997, as well as the Eastern Sector Development Strategy for the Johannesburg Metropolitan Council in 1995. My current work includes a spatial framework for the north-western periphery of Greater Johannesburg, and a project on urban poverty and transport for the World Bank. In addition to teaching Johannesburg's urban history in the Architecture Department at the University of the Witwatersrand, I have written on contemporary architecture and urban design in both popular and academic publications such as the *Mail & Guardian* and *Urban Forum*. I have practised as an architect in Johannesburg and Cape Town for fifteen years, working together with non-governmental organizations on the design and implementation of projects, including a community centre in Cape Town and a crèche in the Northern Province.

D8 Globalization and the identity of African urban practices

AbdouMaliq Simone is an urbanist in the broad sense that his work engages various aspects of the city, with the objective of broadening the understandings and tools of urban development. This engagement has led to university positions with the City University of New York, University of Khartoum, University of Ghana, University of the Western Cape, and presently with the Graduate School of Public and Development Management, University of the Witwatersrand. He has also worked for a wide range of African non-governmental organizations, community associations and municipalities. He has conducted research in the following areas: African urban social economies; notions of 'urban poverty' employed in development policies; the configuration of social identities within highly provisional situations; theoretical reformulations of civil and religious societies and urban social movements; and the interaction of transnational and local dynamics in shaping how livelihoods are produced in African cities. He has published widely in these areas, with the key work being *In Whose Image?: Political Islam and Urban Practices in Sudan* (1994).

E8 Rival futures: Struggle visions, post-apartheid choices

Mark Swilling is co-director of the Spier Leadership Institute, Honorary Professor at the Graduate School of Public and Development Management, University of the Witwatersrand, and Visiting Professor at the Warwick Business School. He was a co-founder of the Graduate School of Public and Development Management and served as its Director. Swilling is currently Chairperson of Planact, an urban development non-governmental organization which he helped to establish in 1985. Swilling is also Secretary of the Executive Committee of the African Research Network for Urban Management, Co-convenor of the South African non-profit sector study linked to Johns Hopkins University, Coordinator of the Southern African chapter of the Global Urban Research Initiative and Acting Chairperson of the Local Governance Learning Network. He has helped to establish non-governmental organizations in various parts of South Africa and is on the editorial board of leading academic journals. He has published books, over fifty academic articles and contributed extensively to public debate in the popular press on issues related to development, democratization, local governance and social movements. His most recent book was *Governing Africa's Cities* (1996). He holds a Ph.D. from the University of Warwick, and obtained his BA and BA Honours through the Department of Political Studies at the University of the Witwatersrand.

F4 'Take your body where it has never been before'

Marlene van Niekerk was born in 1954 in Caledon in the Western Cape. She studied languages and philosophy at the University of Stellenbosch (1973-8) and furthered her studies at the University of Amsterdam (1979-85), specializing in hermeneutic and structuralist approaches to mythology. After her return to South Africa, she taught philosophy at various universities before settling at the University of the Witwatersrand, where she currently lectures in Afrikaans and Dutch literature. She has published two collections of poetry, *Sprokkelster* (1976) and *Groenstaar* (1983), a collection of short stories, *Die vrou wat haar verkyker vergeet het* (1993) and a novel, *Triomf* (1994), which won the Noma Award for publishing in Africa and has recently been translated into English.

editor

E11 Street addresses, Johannesburg

Ivan Vladislavić was born in Pretoria in 1957. He studied at the University of the Witwatersrand, worked as a translator, and later as a fiction and social studies editor at Ravan Press. He was assistant editor of *Staffrider* magazine from 1988 to 1990, and co-edited the commemorative anthology *Ten Years of Staffrider*. He now works as a freelance editor. He has been publishing short fiction since the early 1980s, and his work has appeared in journals and anthologies in South Africa and abroad. His fiction has been translated into French and German, and has won several awards, including the

Olive Schreiner Prize and the CNA Award. He has published a novel, *The Folly* (1993) and two collections of stories, *Missing Persons* (1989) and *Propaganda by Monuments* (1996). He recently completed a novel called *The Restless Supermarket*.

Afrikaans

N.P. van Wyk Louw, Vernuwing in die prosa quoted in 'Prysvraag: Taalmonument te Paarl', South African Architectural Record, May (1966), p. 13. Afrikaans is die taal wat vir Wes-Europa en Afrika verbind; dit suig sy krag uit dié twee bronne; dit vorm 'n brug tussen die groot helder Weste en die magiese Afrika – die soms nog so onhelder Afrika; hulle is albei groot magte, en wat daar groots aan hulle vereniging kan ontspruit – dit is miskien wat vir Afrikaans voorlê om te ontdek ... Maar wat ons nooit moet vergeet nie, is dat hierdie verandering van land en landskap as't ware aan die nuwe wordende taal geslyp, geknee, gebrei het; nuwe woorde, nuwe voorstellings en nuwe beelde laat ontstaan het, ou woorde en voorstellings laat verdwyn het, oor elke riffel en vou van die nuwe wêreldbeeld kon sluit. En so het Afrikaans in staat geword om hierdie nuwe land uit te sê soos geen ander Europese taal nie. – Afrikaans is the language that links Western Europe and Africa; it draws its strength from these two sources; it forms a bridge between the huge bright West and magical Africa – an Africa that is sometimes still so dark; they are both great powers, and the splendid things that could arise from their union – perhaps that is what lies ahead for Afrikaans to discover ... But what we should never forget is that this change of land and landscape honed, kneaded and shaped the new language in the making: gave rise to new words, new conceptions and new images, caused old words and conceptions to disappear, could cover every ridge and fold of the new scheme of things. And so Afrikaans became capable of expressing this new land like no other European language. ►D3 ►E2 ►E3

armed responses

►B2 ►C2 ►E11

bank

►Volkskas ►D3 ►D5 ►E4

Bantustan

'The development of a national community of states' in Homelands/Tuislande (Johannesburg, Van Rensburg Publications, 1975), p. 7. The government of RSA is acutely aware of the unique problems which are caused by a confluence of historical factors which has placed the White nation in the position of guardian to several underdeveloped Black nations ... The government of the RSA is very much aware of interaction between the highly developed White economy – based on the market mechanisms which function in a predominantly urban industrial consumer and free enterprise society – and a backward Black economy with a predominantly subsistence orientated life-style ... Thus the government of RSA was motivated by both socio-economic and political considerations to concentrate the focal points of the development of the Black peoples inside – or as near as possible to – their historical homelands.
►homelands policy ►D11 ►J12

Biermann, B.E.

B.E. Biermann, 'Architecture goes back to the land', Architecture SA, March (1980), p. 6. Of all the curious developments which mark the present state of architecture, surely the most revealing must be our exaggerated concern with the past and the primitive. From our dedicated – almost reverent – conservation of those buildings which were derided a mere generation ago, and the veneration of 'architecture without architects', to our penchant for the expression of crude structure – the tenor of contemporary design seems to reflect a loss of nerve, a crisis of confidence in our traditionally creative endeavours. To the extent that architecture is a mirror of society, this state of affairs should occasion no surprise; but that by itself is an unsatisfactory inference. On the other hand, the day has long passed since the first generation of modern architects imagined that society could be reformed by tampering with its mirror image. ►D5 ►H6

black spot

Even at the height of apartheid, pockets of black South Africans managed somehow to cling to freehold ownership of property outside of the 13 per cent of the country set aside as reserves for the African population. These blemishes in what had been declared 'white' South Africa were known as 'black spots'. ►Natives Land Act of 1913

Blood River

►Voortrekker Monument ►C4

boom

In many ways Johannesburg is the epitome of a boom town. But today the speculators no longer wait for the next building boom to happen. Instead, insurance developers are hard at work creating the circumstances that will produce a real-estate boom. As a result, the malls on what were once the suburban peripheries are now competing centres, which anticipate and encourage the abandonment of the corporate city centre by the old mining and banking élites. From a city of competing towers to a city of competing shopping centres. ►B2 ►E4

bricks

►E2 ►E7 ►E12

Broederbond

►D3 ►D4 ►E3 ►E4

buffer zone

The Native Affairs Department laid down as a general rule that locations were to be separated from areas occupied by other population groups by buffer zones 500 yards wide, and from all other external boundaries by buffer zones 200 yards wide, unless such external boundaries were main roads, in which case the zones were to be 500 yards for a national road and 300 yards for a provincial road. Rows of trees could be planted in buffer zones, but the land could not be developed. ►J12

bureaucracy

►E3 ►E8 ►F7 ►G6

burial

►C4 ►J10 ►J12

Calderwood, D.M.

D.M. Calderwood, Native Housing in South Africa (Johannesburg, University of the Witwatersrand, 1953), p. 41. Psychological aspects are noted here because, in providing housing for Natives, the designer is not altogether aware of what is taking place inside the occupants' minds. The Native may be a newcomer to the urban area or he may have lived there all his life. If he has recently come to the town, he faces a new environment of speed, noise, individualism, and so forth. The designer, in planning a home for this new town-dweller does not really know what he is imposing upon him. Will the home provide help to satisfy him and assist him in overcoming his newfound loneliness, or will its new form disturb him to such an extent that his frustration is even more exaggerated? ►CSIR ►home ►NE 51/9 ►D11 ►H6

Cape Dutch

►preservation ►A5 ►D3 ►D5

Cape Town

►A5 ►A12 ►C4 ►G6 ►G8 ►G10 ►J12

Carletonville

►mining ►G4

church

J. de Ridder, 'Kerkbou – Enkele gedagtes', South African Architectural Record, January (1963), p. 13. Die kerk behoort dus 'n sprekende vertolking van die erediens in konkrete vorm te wees, sodat die gebou feitlik beskryf sou kon word as 'Versteende Liturgie' ... 'n Verdere voorbeeld is die beligting van die kerkgebou. Kan die konsentrasie van lig op die kansel nie ook die belangrikheid daarvan beklemtoon en simbolies die idee vertolk dat die Woord as sodanig ons lig is nie? – The church should therefore be a striking interpretation of the service in concrete form, so that the building could virtually be described as 'liturgy in stone' ... Another example is the lighting of the church building. Could the concentration of light on the pulpit not stress its importance and symbolically interpret the idea that the Word as such is our light? ►B8

civics

During the 1980s and early '90s, there was a vigorous network of urban social movements which mobilized people around issues like transport and rent boycotts. In the democratic period, these civic associations have been taken up in the mainstream, and independent social mobilization has all but ceased. ►D8 ►E6 ►E8 ►F9

civilization

T. Hahn, Report and Proceedings with Appendices of the Government Commission on Native Laws and Customs (Cape of Good Hope, 1883), Appendix C:257. If we mean to civilize the natives we must enforce order and regularity, and naturally the round Kafir hut cannot find place alongside of the square or oblong white man's house. There should be an interdict against the round hut. It certainly breeds vermin. ►round ►B11 ►D11 ►E10

colonization

F. Fanon, The Wretched of the Earth (Harmondsworth, Penguin, 1990), p. 40. A world divided into compartments, a motionless, Manichaeistic world, a world of statues: the statue of the general who carried out the conquest, the statue of the engineer who built the bridge; a world which is sure of itself, which crushes with its stones the backs flayed by whips: this is the colonial world. The native is a being hemmed in; apartheid is simply one form of the division into compartments of the colonial world. The first thing which the native learns is to stay in his place, and not to go beyond certain limits. This is why the dreams of the native are always of muscular prowess; his dreams are of action and of aggression. I dream I am jumping, swimming, running, climbing; I dream that I burst out laughing, that I span a river in one stride, or that I am followed by a flood of motor-cars which never catch up with me. During the period of colonization, the native never stops achieving his freedom from nine in the evening until six in the morning. ►C4 ►C10 ►D7

colour scheme

J. Armour, Your South African Home (Cape Town, Howard Timmins, 1964), p. 52. While some people are naturally colour conscious, a great many more can be said to be colour shy, especially when it comes to anything as lasting as interior decoration. There are many ways in which you can arrive at a successful colour scheme, and none of them very frightening. But first of all, it is as well to know something about colour itself.

commemoration

What past and whose past will it be possible to recover, given the dichotomies of our history? Who are we? How little we are able to imagine a collective past, in the face of the political imperative to construct a single history able to take the place of all the others. These competing pasts are forced into confrontation by the memorials and buildings designed to commemorate a whitened landscape. We begin to imagine how an evolving past must be challenged even as it is constructed. This construction itself is our continuing conflict. ►C4 ►H3

W.H. Coetzer, The murder of Piet Retief and his men, c. 1937.

community

Who exactly is the 'community' in South Africa? Are there not more complex social arrangements as well as conflicting interest groups that must be accounted for? How are these different groups to make up a community? Why is this 'community' always seen to be black and never white? There was a tradition of constructing 'community buildings' in the black areas. These buildings are easy to recognize: they have brightly coloured, curvilinear forms. This style was never pursued in municipal buildings or any other government structures in white areas, where there were, of course, no 'communities' to be accommodated. White public buildings were imagined, designed and built differently, with what must have been other criteria and intentions. ►municipal ►D8 ►E7 ►F4 ►F8

compaction

An Interim Strategic Framework for the Central Witwatersrand (ISF Working Group of the Planning Framework Task Team of the Physical Development Working Group and GAPS Architects and Urban Planners, 1993), p. 25. Within the cells, or interstitial areas, created by the lattice-like structure of the urban system, residential densities can now be encouraged to increase, taking advantage of spare capacity in the infrastructure, making better use of much of the existing social facilities, and providing access to the wider urban system via the comprehensive lattice of movement. How and where residential densities are increased and how the urban poor are integrated into the system, would be the subject of detailed planning within these interstitial cells, taking account of micro issues of character, facilities, costs, infrastructural capacity and special features. While emphasis might initially be on residential densification in these cells, over time non-residential uses compatible with the evolving residential character may offer more diffuse economic opportunities within the overall logic of the urban area's cellular structure. ▶immobilization ▶D7 ▶D8 ▶E6 ▶G6

competition, Klipspruit Town Planning

'The Klipspruit Town Planning Competition', *South African Architectural Record*, September (1931), p. 88. In the winning scheme [by Kallenbach Kennedy and Furner] the whole township has been divided into three main sections, in the centre of each of which a business 'place' has been arranged, a very excellent arrangement in a garden city layout under European conditions, but again somewhat questionable in a native township where the class of trade and trader usually means an untidy, unkept and dusty area. ▶H6

compound

▶hostel

concrete, reinforced

▶C4 ▶E2 ▶E4

conservation

G. Fagan, 'The conservation pyramid', *Architecture SA*, September/October (1988), p. 20.
A language is a living thing and can revive, but this is not so with buildings and artefacts. Victoria has been permanently deposed from her pedestal, and the lesson should be frighteningly clear: when anything is politicized, it will sooner or later be in danger of disappearing together with that political system. ▶Fagan, G.

contact

▶A5 ▶D8 ▶F4

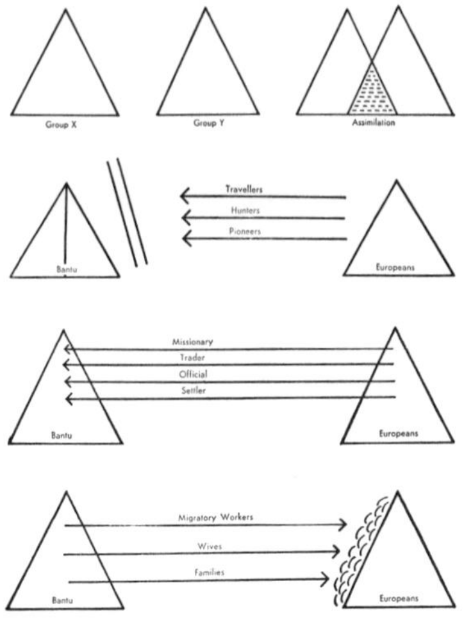

Phases in the process of contact: (1) pre-contact phase, (2) wide contact phase, (3) urbanisation phase and (4) reaction phase.

control

Who exactly wants to control the city and for what purposes? How can control even be exercised in a time of ceaseless flux? Officials, for the most part, go about their work with as little involvement as possible, politicians are left juggling far more constituencies than they can manage, newly-arrived squatters are merely trying to survive, suburbanites are isolated and only appear intermittently as ratepayers, and big business stands helpless as the professionals abandon the city centre, in which the corporations have invested so much. These seldom unified interest groups are less struggling for control of the city, than hedging, hoping and trying to hold onto the wealth and power slipping from their grasp. Meanwhile, territories once buffered from one another continue to collide, and boundaries once set in stone crumble and drift. Where and when will our eventual limits be drawn? ▶B2 ▶D8 ▶E3 ▶E10

corrugated iron

Palace Buildings, Johannesburg, 1889, described in P. Knox and T. Gutsche, *Do You Know Johannesburg?* (Vereeniging, Unie-Volkspers, 1947), p. 15. Materials were hard to obtain but, despite every difficulty, the building emerged as an example of 'French Renaissance'. The fact that the essential features of this distinctive type of architecture were executed in corrugated iron, is in itself, a vivid illustration that lack of materials was not allowed to stand in the way of the architect's aspirations. The steeply-sloping roof, the square tower in Pritchard Street and the corner spire, which came to be known as the 'Eiffel Tower of the Rand' – all are made of corrugated iron skilfully used to serve unwonted needs. ▶E2 ▶G4

crime

The loss of a shared city centre, the fear of the streets, the gradual disappearance of even the suburban neighbourhood, the abandoning of familiar haunts and routes: all represent one side of the landscape emerging from the spread of crime. On the other side there are the precariously secured residential areas, the isolated lifestyles of the old white and new black middle classes, with their privileged access to urban facilities and services, and township neighbourhoods surviving much the same as before. ▶B2 ▶B3 ▶E11 ▶F10

CSIR

Council for Scientific and Industrial Research ◀Calderwood, D.M. ▶NE 51/9 ▶D11 ▶H6

District Six

All that remains to the people who once lived here, in the heart of Cape Town, is remembering, the piecing together of a space and time out of the fragments of memory that serve as the only detailed record. In the world there is very little to remind them: street-signs, broken kerbstones, some strips of tar and a few archival photographs. The spaces of the District's past, surviving as no more than these images and memories, have a tenuous presence, and must be painstakingly recalled and reconstructed, even by former residents. This is the real consequence of the complete and utter destruction of a part of a city. Cape Town can never be a whole city, it can never be put together again. There are, of course, too many examples of the physical annihilation of cities in wars, slum clearances and unbridled commercial developments, but there is no more incomprehensible demonstration of the calm and persistent insanity of bureaucratic planning than the destruction of District Six. ▶G10

dorp

A small country town ▶F8

Durban

▶D5 ▶F9 ▶G8 ▶G11 ▶H3

East London

▶D11

Eaton, N.M.

►C4 ►D5 ►H3

emergency

Under a state of emergency, in the face of coercion, deception and terror, part of the struggle is to remain oneself. In a state of emergence, part of the struggle is to change.

empowerment

►D8 ►E7 ►F7

enclave

►B2 ►C10 ►D8

eviction

Central Archives, Native Affairs Department, NTS 5314 77/313(E), 'Eviction Notice'. I, the undersigned, being an officer duly appointed by the Urban Local Authority for the purpose, HEREBY GIVE YOU NOTICE, in terms of Sub-section (3) of Section 9 of Act No. 25 of 1945, as amended, that I call upon you to take up, within a period of three days from the date of the service of this Notice, your residence in Langa Native Township, in which accommodation is available for you, or in a Native Hostel or in a scheduled native area or released area as defined in the Native Trust and Land Act, 1936, approved of by the Urban Local Authority.

Fagan, G.

◄conservation ►regionalism ►D3

Fort Skanskop

►C2

Freedom Charter

►E6 ►F7

frontier

T.R.H. Davenport, South Africa: A Modern History (London, Macmillan,1977), pp. 113-4. Far more than any other frontier, [the Cape eastern frontier] was one on which policies were thought out and deliberately applied. The blockhouse system and the military village; the buffer strip, the frontier of no outlets and the trading pass; the trade fair, mission station, hospital and school; the spoor law, the treaty system, the government agent, and the magistrate – all these were tried in various combinations, in a bid to maintain order and peaceful coexistence at the meeting point of two disparate but competing cultures.

game park

A photograph from as long ago as August 1960 shows Verwoerd in the Kruger National Park with various Ministers, Administrators, Members of the Parks Board, Members of Parliament and Officials of the Parks Board. The 'bosberaad' – the 'bush council' – became popular thirty years later, during the negotiations towards a democratic order in South Africa, when the leaders of the various parties would withdraw to a farm or game park to confer and plan. This strategy was usually presented as a retreat into a secluded natural environment, conducive to clear thinking and judicious decision-making. But what better meeting place could there be for alliances pursuing new definitions of themselves than one where the landscape itself poses questions about ownership and identity? ►negotiations ►C4 ►C10

garden city

►D5 ►D11 ►H6

golf course

►B2 ►C2

Great Trek

Piet Retief in Grahamstown Journal, 2 February 1837. Numerous reports having been circulated throughout the colony, evidently with the intention of exciting in the minds of our countrymen a feeling of prejudice against those who have resolved to emigrate from a colony where they have experienced, for so many years past, a series of the most vexatious and severe losses: and, as we desire to stand high in the estimation of our brethren and are anxious that they and the world at large should believe us incapable of severing that sacred tie which binds a Christian to his native soil, without the most sufficient reasons, we are induced to record the following summary of our motives for taking so important a step: and also our intentions respecting our proceedings towards the Native Tribes which we may meet with beyond the boundary.

◄commemoration ►laager ►C4

grey area

Group Areas Act of 1951

Central Archives, ARG 9 Act 111/2, Draft Memorandum on the Group Areas Bill, 12 April 1950. The main purpose of the establishment of group areas is two-fold, firstly, to bring persons of the same racial origin for purposes of ownership and occupation together, and so to reduce to a minimum racial points of contact and therefore possible racial friction, and secondly to permit each racial group to develop along its own lines, according to its language, culture and religion, and to give members of the Native and Coloured groups an opportunity under proper guidance ultimately to assume responsibility for their own local government. ►F8 ►F10 ►G10 ►G11

Hallen, H.

H. Hallen, 'Buildings stand still, people move', KZ-NIA Journal, 22:2 (1997), p. 8. BMW had a clear understanding of the symbolic role of buildings for companies such as theirs. They wanted the design of a quality where the image of building and company merged, and that the building and its spaces should be symbolic of its location and setting in South Africa. An enlightened brief! ►C2 ►C4

hawking

roast mealies, herbal remedies, Gucci bags ... ►D8 ►D10 ►F7

Health (and Racquet) Club

The almost familiar space of the suburban gymnasium suddenly spread across the country during the mid-1980s. Partly an international trend and partly the product of a growing franchise, these health clubs must also have filled some sort of spatial vacuum for a particular class of people in South Africa. Could the gym be the primary public (or semi-public) place in our contemporary urban environment? It is one of the few places where bodies converge in close proximity with most of their defences restrained. It is almost the only place where people are exposed to each other. Some might visit the shopping mall, an office park, a friend's housing estate almost daily, but none of these spaces affords the intimacy and oddly distanced familiarity of the suburban gymnasium, where familiar faces reappear and certain interactions are repeated. In other parts of the world, these casual, ongoing relationships are made possible by piazzas and parks; here such urban spaces – even as theme-park environments in malls like Renaissance Square – are all but absent. Concern over a sagging and flabby body seems most marked in a society where there is a daily need to step past wasted and wanting bodies on the way to work and leisure. ►privatization ►F4

heaven

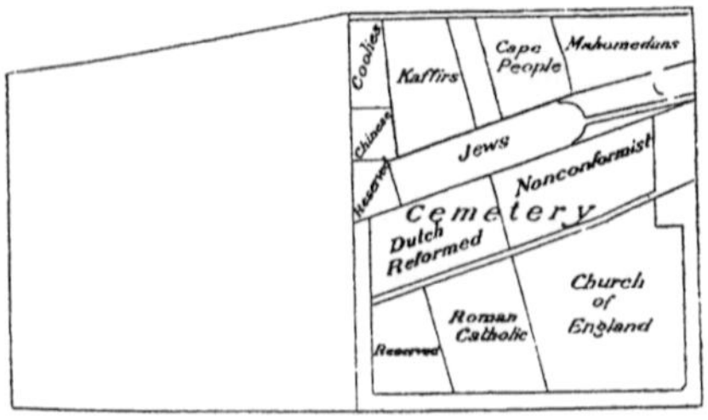

W.H.A. Pritchard, Commercial map of Johannesburg, c. 1896

heritage

Maj. W. Dörning, 'Lessons from the past in dealing with the terrorist threat', Paratus, September (1983) quoted in Maj. W.M. Leonard, Plaasbeveiliging: 'n Handleiding vir die boer (Babelegi, Unibook Publishers, 1988), pp. 1-2. In fact, South Africans should be neither surprised nor unduly alarmed by the recent spate of terrorist attacks ... Forewarned is after all fore-armed. We should not be unduly alarmed, moreover, because our own history and heritage is steeped in examples of 'terrorism' and savage guerilla warfare. We tend to forget that our forefathers – both of Afrikaans and English stock – were brought up in an extremely hostile environment of day-to-day dangers which taught them the virtues of resilience, self-reliance, alertness and fortitude in the face of seemingly hopeless odds. The situation we are faced with today in South Africa is actually nothing new – by inference therefore, it should not be a cause for excessive alarm. Indeed, the more one looks at our past for purposes of comparison with the present, the more one becomes aware of how little has really changed. Many of the problems and dangers facing the early settlers of Dutch and English extraction were almost exactly similar to those confronting us today. Many of the settlers' responses and reactions to these challenges, moreover, bear relevant lessons for all of us as we prepare to confront the terrorist menace. In short, instead of bemoaning our fate, we should set about learning and drawing inspiration from the great tradition and example of our forebears. ◄armed responses ►B11 ►C2

home

house, shelter, fortress, fiction, zero, beginning, ekhaya, sanctuary, temple, archive, landmark, monument, community, comfort, 'slum dwelling', hearth, huis, dwelling, porzie, zla, koesta. ◄Calderwood, D.M. ►homestead ►A5 ►B8 ►B11 ►E11 ►F10 ►G10 ►G11

homelands policy

E.W.N. Mallows, 'Mmabatho – A reply', Architecture SA, August (1981), p. 42. It was at this point that his Excellency, the President, added the instruction that the overall design must reflect the Tswana building traditions, of forming a series of spaces enclosed with encircling walls, and never with straight lines, and still less with a series of rectangular spaces set out on a rectangular grid. These are the gods of the developed First World but they are almost totally irrelevant to the struggling and emerging communities of the Third World. These communities need a totally different philosophy – a philosophy for a cohesive community, for a strong coherent social group determined to make a new way for itself in the world and, as in the great examples of the past, put a permanent stamp on history. ◄Bantustan ►Mmabatho ►tradition

homestead

►A5 ►B11 ►G11

hostel

The apartheid government provided single-sex housing for African migrant workers. Under influx control regulations, Africans were not allowed to remain in urban areas without official permission and were restricted to particular spaces, of which the hostel is the most infamous. Migrants' families were not allowed to accompany them. ◄compound ►G4 ►G8 ►H8 ►J10

hybrid

P. Rich, 'A hybrid architecture takes root', Architecture SA, May/June (1986), p. 34. In identifying with my African roots, my research over the last ten years into the rural dwellings – notably of the Southern Ndebele ('mapogga') and Bantwane – has proved to be an inspiration for my own built work ... The architectural lessons to be learned from the Mapogga are of a universal nature, dealing with spatial and ordering principles which are not far removed from that of Renaissance man. ►surrogation ►H3 ►J12

ideal home

'Report on the Argus Ideal Homes Competition' in the Star, 28 December 1937. From all these influences the South African house is slowly developing; a low light, cool-looking building, with a dark flat-pitched roof, large unobstructed windows sheltered by the deep eaves, and an enclosed yard with the native rooms. This, growing naturally and harmoniously out of its surroundings, may well be the South African style of the future, as the gracious Cape Dutch was that of the past. ►lifestyle ►preservation ►E12

immobilization

Compaction is only one example of the new planning. Why, when there seem to be so many obvious and visible ways of repairing the apartheid city, has there been so little movement? The intransigence of the inherited bureaucracies and the new government's distrust of some of the proposed planning strategies are only partly responsible. While some prototype plans have been attempted in a partial and fragmentary manner, compaction – along with notions of the integrated city, the connected city, the accessible city and the city of corridors – has not been a mobilizing concept around which change can be generated. Instead, the procedures demanded by these plans seem to render the city fixed and unsolvable, producing little more than committees, meetings, reports and requirements, which stifle change as surely as vast national programmes in other spheres. It is clear that simply filling in the gaps, increasing densities, mixing urban land uses or making continuous the previously fragmented elements of the city would only partly correct some of the problems left by apartheid. Nevertheless, given the almost general consensus amongst planners, it is surprising that there is so little to show for their proposals. It may be that in a time of rampant and unrestrained commercial development, the role of planning and planners is negligible. And at the other end of the organizing scale, the myriad individual decisions – informal and spontaneous – that happen outside of government remain the singular force for change in the city. ◄compaction ►D7 ►D8 ►E6 ►E10 ►G6

influx control

E. Kuzwayo, Call Me Woman (Johannesburg, Ravan Press, 1985), p. 31. Many of these women left loved ones behind when they first came to the cities. Some came in search of their husbands, but never found them; some came as a result of the deaths of their husbands in the mines, or because they had become invalids from a mine disease. They were drawn to the cities by the hope of better opportunities and were pushed out of the country by white legislation and control. In the end, they shared whatever profit they made, in cash or kind, with those they left behind. The emotional deprivation of those left behind was compensated for by the material gain brought back from cities by their dear mothers, grannies, aunts or sisters; a contribution which could never be clearly measured in any way but which made a positive impact, no matter how limited, on the lives of those who benefited from it. Most of them have passed on, leaving their followers to improve on their efforts and humble, limited contribution. ►B11

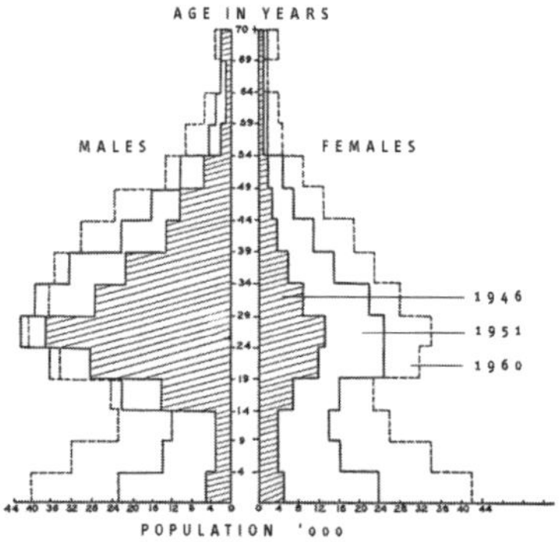

Age and sex structure of bantu population Johannesburg Metropolitan Area.

informal

Instead of simply repeating directions along massively planned pathways, invasions and infiltrations continuously put parts of the city to new uses. Often the very planning elements dictated by the metropolitan government become the structure on which improvisation can take place, marching to a syncopated beat. Zoning and trade restrictions are the impetus for constructing alternative hawking territories. Occupying the leftover, abandoned or previously restricted spaces of the city is more than a survival strategy for isolated individuals. That the city is never so simply solidified is clear from the instant appearance of others to ply their trade in the same area. New connections and commercial arrangements follow the movement of these people into and then all over the city. New parts can be joined together as readily as other linkages are lost. A part of the city that was once strictly white, servicing the suburban, becomes black and tied to the townships and the rest of Africa. Change in the city is no longer being released by plans and ideals, but by chance, crime and consumption patterns. ►D7 ►D8 ►D9 ►E10 ►F9

integration

The extreme inequalities of the starting points for change and the legacy of racism produce an unfortunate psychology: in the areas where it matters most – the changing, integrating parts of the city – almost all white people feel invaded. 'Invasion', with its undertones of war, disease, occupation, becomes the defining experience of integration – and issues in flight, defence, resistance. Small numbers of black professionals and the privileged middle classes find their way into the leafier suburbs, where they essentially assume the existing lifestyle. But in the central city and the inner-city suburbs, where change is palpable, where new urban styles are emerging, whites are largely excluded or exclude themselves. The new spaces are black or 'becoming black'. For most white South Africans, the models of the future city are dirty, decayed, chaotic, rather than colourful, lived in, pleasantly informal, diverse. The future looks like 'what happened in the rest of Africa'. Being unable or unwilling to participate in the creation of the future city, withdrawing into their increasingly remote and impregnable suburban enclaves, whites ensure that the future city will resemble their fears in one respect at least – white faces will be few and far between. Yet there is a flip side to the obsession with degeneration – and that is a fascination with ruined splendour. For some, the tourist destinations of the moment are Zanzibar and Madagascar. Whites would feel better about the future city if its dilapidation could be rendered glamorous. Advertising agencies would do a better job of this than urban planners. ◄enclave ►invasions ►lifestyle ►D7 ►D9 ►E6 ►E11 ►G6

Internal Stability Unit

Under apartheid, control and instability were never opposing terms. On the one hand, the authorities pursued total control over the social environment, constantly introducing more rigid regulations and innovative forms of repression. On the other hand, the authorities – sometimes through the same officials – deliberately created instability. Little propaganda was required to reinforce an order that was the first line of defence against an enemy lurking within or pressing against imagined borders. At the same time, the black population was relentlessly destabilized, denied a permanent place in the city, harassed and intimidated, uprooted and removed, banished to peripheral locations or tribalized territories, allowed to pass through the country only as easily disposable units of labour.

invasions

◄frontier ◄homestead ►squatting ►D9

isolation

◄boom ►E2 ►E4

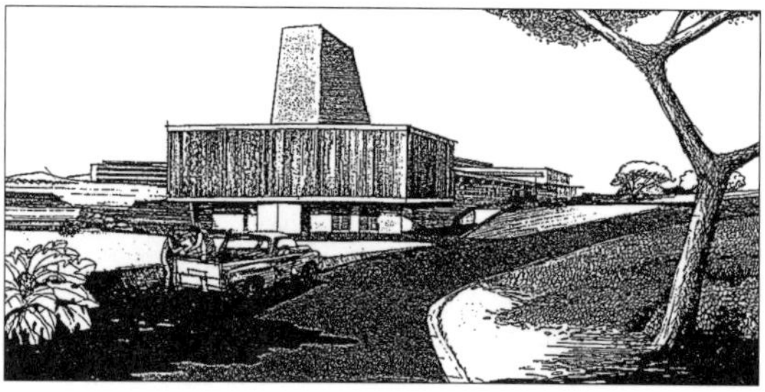
Brian Sandrock, Perspective of Pelindaba Nuclear Research Station, 1963.

Johannesburg

►B2 ►D8 ►D9 ►D10 ►E4 ►E10 ►E11 ►E12 ►F4 ►F10

Karoohuis

G. Viney, Colonial Houses of South Africa (Cape Town, Struik Winchester, 1987), p. 152.

Their aesthetic antecedents stretch all the way back to the eighteenth-century cottage ornée, the verandah, like the gable on a Cape Dutch house, being its most distinctive feature. Though undoubtedly attractive, the verandah was no mere architectural embellishment, for it provided the ideal solution for nineteenth-century Europeans settling in a hot climate – protecting their interiors and furnishings from the strong African sunlight and creating a perfect outdoor living room – shaded in summer and sunny in winter. Massed with ferns and potted plants and furnished with wicker chairs, it fulfilled in the colonies much the same function as the conservatory did in England, for in the African climate glass was not only unnecessary, but also undesirable, violent hailstorms being a not infrequent summer hazard. ►D5 ►H3

KTC/Crossroads

E. Samuel, 'Affidavit' in J. Cole, Crossroads (Johannesburg, Ravan Press, 1987), pp. 142-3.
I saw the yellow Casspir and the van park close to the Zolani Centre ... Then the 'witdoeke' [started] to attack the centre and assault people who were on the grounds ... Women and children who had been [staying there] were running out of it. I then saw the centre begin to burn ... After a while I saw the crowd of 'witdoeke' who had been attacking the centre ... move along the road in the direction of NY5 ... The 'witdoeke' then stopped at the intersection near KTC ... Casspirs in the vicinity [started] shooting teargas at the KTC residents ... At about this time I saw smoke rising from [one] part of KTC ... I then saw 'witdoeke' amongst the KTC houses, which were burning ... Many KTC residents, including myself, then began to move our [possessions] from our [houses] ... Later I returned to KTC and watched the 'witdoeke' ... burning our houses. ►A12 ►J12

laager

◄Great Trek

landmarks

H.A. Sloet, 'Voorwoord' in Afrikanerbakens (Johannesburg, FAK, 1989), p. 7. 'n Volk se geskiedenis word sigbaar deur bakens langs sy ontwikkelingspad uitgebeeld. Dié bakens, wat 'n volk aan sy verlede herinner en vir die toekoms inspireer, is soms groot en indrukwekkend, maar dit kan ook klein en minder sigbaar wees. Tog vertel elkeen 'n gedeelte van die verhaal van die Afrikanervolk sedert volksplanting. – A people's history is rendered visible by landmarks along their path of development. These landmarks, which remind a people of their past and inspire them for the future, are sometimes large and impressive, but can also be small and less visible. Yet each one tells a part of the story of the Afrikaner people since colonization. ►C4

Le Corbusier

►E4 ►H3 ►H6

lifestyle

Cape Weekend Argus (Commercial Feature), 29-30 August 1998. Homes designed exclusively for the Sunset Links residential estate emphasize a relaxed indoor-outdoor lifestyle, making the most of the view and beautiful setting and creating sheltered outdoor areas. The style of architecture is intended to blend harmoniously with the natural surroundings and the contemporary, spacious living areas are light and airy, lending themselves to a sophisticated, yet easy, comfortable lifestyle. Examples of five completed and different homes illustrate the character of the residential estate and may be viewed in the show village. The architects have drawn up building guidelines for the different types of homes, each offering flexibility of floor plan to cater for the individual. Homes with a personal signature may be created within the building line, bulk restrictions applicable to each of the four types of homes found here and architectural guidelines, which emphasize the harmonious nature of the residential estate through elements such as colour, form and texture. ◄ideal home ►F4

location

Areas were set aside for Africans at some distance from white towns and provided with limited housing. ►township ►D11

low-cost housing

►F7 ►F10 ►G6

mall

►C2 ►H3

Martienssen, R.

R. Martienssen, 'The international tendency in contemporary architecture', South African Architectural Record, December (1931), p. 110. The exigencies of economy inevitably produce an intellectual and logical architecture ... As the economic conditions of different countries approach one another, there will be a corresponding approach in architectural style. ►Southern Question ►Transvaal Group ►E12 ►H3 ►H6

masakhane

►RDP

mass housing

'Report of the committee on the costs of building urban bantu houses' in Costs of Urban Bantu Housing (Pretoria, CSIR, 1954), p. 1. Housing of any population starts as a human and health problem. Good housing tends to promote good citizens and hence stable conditions in society. These axioms are frequently written and spoken by persons responsible for housing policies: as principles, the same ideas underlie most housing efforts throughout the world and it is therefore natural that they should also be fundamental considerations in the housing research and housing projects undertaken in South Africa. ►H6 ►H8

matchbox

◄mass housing ►NE 51/9

memorial

How to record historic events in a country where struggle is never isolated but stretches and lies everywhere? Where no place remains untouched and no person unaffected? Forgetting here is inextricably linked with memorialization. We may be sure that the large, heroic events will be commemorated, rather than the routine conflicts and everyday struggles; the massive series of minute events we call 'the force of history' is difficult to make concrete. Fears of offending, discriminating, imposing, stepping on each other's memories, make all but the obvious monumental decisions unlikely. In the meantime, we live in a stormy silence rather than a calm interregnum, in which portrayal and betrayal stand side by side. It is as if one history has been set in stone, which the other can only shatter. ◄commemoration ►C4 ►C2

Minimum Standards of Accommodation for Non-Europeans, 1951

◄CSIR ►NE 51/9

mining

◄Carletonville ◄Johannesburg ►B2 ►G4

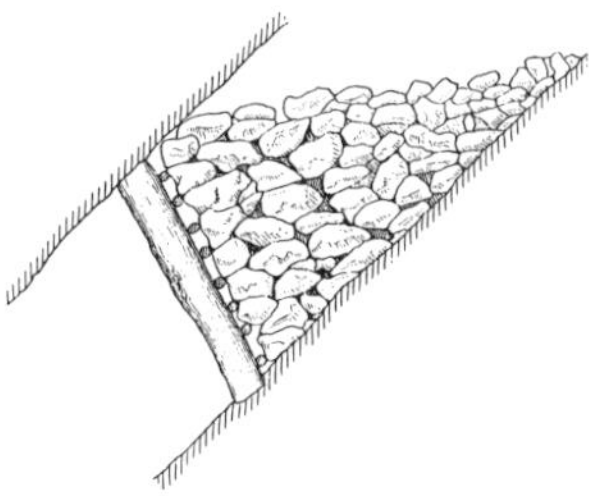

Diagram illustrating the formation of a mining stull.

miscegenation,

G.M. Carter, The Politics of Inequality (London, Thames & Hudson, 1958). Miscegenation out of which the Cape Coloured arose originally, has long been socially unacceptable in South Africa. As far back as 1685, Europeans were forbidden by law to marry freed slaves of full colour, though marriages with half-breeds were allowed ... The difficulty here was not just of colour, or even of shade. Because the Coloured are a very mixed people, no satisfactory definition has been reached by which to differentiate them ... Habitual association with an acceptance as Coloured was subsequently used as a distinguishing feature for the Population Register ... As the parliamentary debate made clear, the Nationalists were not concerned so much with race purity in the biological sense as with strengthening the barriers against increasing infiltration by the Coloured. The special urgency of the problem, they emphasized, arose from the process of industrialization and consequent urbanization which inevitably brought Europeans and non-Europeans into closer contact both in their places of employment and their dwelling areas.

mission stations

►A5 ►B8

Mmabatho

Wilfred Mallows recalls flying over Botswana and photographing the ruins of Tswana settlements. These aerial surveys were then presented to President Lucas Mangope with a series of overlays showing the concentric circles of the proposed homeland capital of Mmabatho. Mallows had a sort of paternal desire for an architecture and capital that would unite the dispersed Tswana nation, provide them with a centre, a focus, an identifiable core. He encouraged the idea of a Tswana architectural arrangement or form – a rounded or bowl-like shape – in order to differentiate the African capital from the European capital with its orthogonal grid. This reversal of the historical enforcement of the square of the European over the round of the Natives is more than ironic. Commercial promotion rather than appropriation of a Native architecture by planners and architects continues. ◄homelands policy ►tradition ►C4

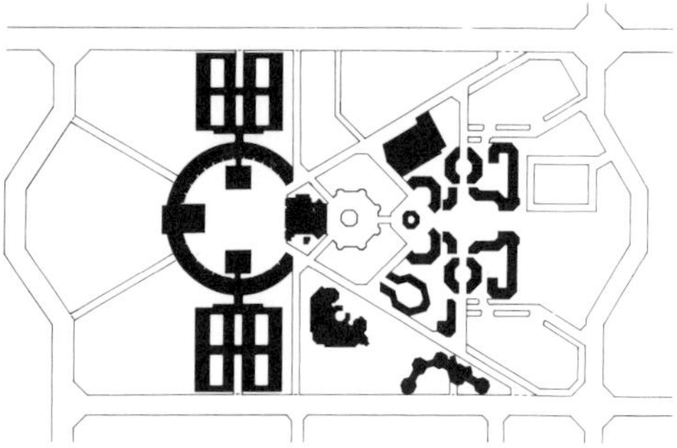

Mallows Louw Hoffe and Partners, plan of Mmabatho government and busuness centre.

modernism

►D5 ►E6 ►E12 ►H3 ►H6

Moerdyk, G.

►Voortrekker Monument **►D3 ►E2**

motorway

It is remarkable how often the spaces under the motorways provide a foothold for the marginal. ►B8 ►D10 ►E4 ►F9

municipal

'Urban Bantu Council Chamber and Offices', Architect and Builder, April (1969), pp. 21-2. The [Urban Bantu] council chamber is overlooked by a public gallery on a higher level with accommodation for Press representatives in the first row. The gallery will seat approximately 50 Europeans and 50 non-Europeans and is provided with a movable barrier so that larger or smaller numbers of either race may be accommodated as desired. The gallery is approached by Europeans from the one side and non-Europeans from the other side by means of separate stairs approached by separate entrances flanking the main entrance. Each stair is separated by glazed walls and doors from the main entrance foyer and first floor lobby to enable the public to have a glimpse of the activities within the building whilst proceeding to the spectators' gallery. On occasion when the public are permitted to approach councillors the stair doors may be opened. When it is desired to clear the gallery of spectators the public retire to the waiting rooms adjoining the public stairs without entering the rest of the building. Public toilets are provided at these points for both races. Europeans who have business with the chairman may gain access to his suite via the European stair no. 2 and waiting room without entering the non-European circulation corridors or the rest of the building. ◄community ►segregation

nationalism

Contradictions in the practice of architecture remain, to be examined in what has been built. Sometimes these can be identified and construed as evidence of a failure to engage: the influence of the surrounding culture is filtered out in abstraction, gestures towards the contemporary are minimal and the awareness of the site is banal. The actual times are abandoned rather than challenged. The actual place, especially in a divided and parochial environment like South Africa, is ignored in the attempt to produce something different. The contradictions and internal flaws of a nationalist project must be acknowledged in equal measure to the modesty and appropriateness of the architect's role. In South Africa today it is tempting to make comparisons between the old and new nationalisms, but the pressures and constraints at work now are so different that we also need to guard against drawing superficial parallels. Even so, the separate and competing professional networks of past and future élites seem to drive attempts at a national architecture towards simplistic symbolic resolutions rather than in fundamentally opposed directions. ►D3 ►D4 ►D5 ►E2 ►E3 ►H3

National Monuments Council

Natives Land Act of 1913

◄black spot ►reserves

Natives (Urban Areas) Act of 1923

►H6 ►H8

Ndebele houses

►B11 ►C4 ►H3

NE 51/9

A series of 'matchbox' houses developed by D. M. Calderwood and a team of architects and planners at the CSIR. ◄Biermann, B.E. ◄Calderwood, D.M. ◄CSIR ►D11 ►H6 ►H8

negotiations

►E8 ►F9

NGK

Nederduitse Gereformeerde Kerk (Dutch Reformed Church). ◄church ►B8 ►G4

offices

▶D4 ▶E3

pondokkie

Cape Archives, 3/CT 26 GV 4/4/6/1, confidential (not for publication) letter from the Medical Officer of Health to the Chairman and Members of the Public Health Committee, 14 April 1949. I have the honour to draw your attention to the fast growing practice of indiscriminate squatting by Natives and Coloured persons on public and private land within the municipal area ... Investigations have revealed that the squatters are scattered over large areas and in groups which are comparatively small. Their 'homes' consist mainly of rough shelters made of sacks, iron or tree branches, or of caves on the slopes of the mountain. Proper water supplies and sanitary facilities are, of course, not available. The squatters are usually careful to avoid obvious accumulations of refuse and filth, and the absence of such evidence makes it almost impossible to obtain prosecutions against them on the grounds of committing nuisances against the public health. ▶squatting ▶A12 ▶D11 ▶G8

preservation

N.M. Eaton, 'Aims and procedures in the preservation and restoration of historic buildings', South African Architectural Record, April (1960), p. 18. My reason for confining myself to this relatively short period of Cape architecture [eighteenth and early nineteenth centuries] is because I believe its buildings have provided far and away the most important category of historic monument in this country from a cultural point of view. It was during this period, after little more than a hundred years of uncertainty, following the arrival of Van Riebeeck in the raw and totally undeveloped land which was then the Cape, that there came into existence for the first time in Southern Africa a complete cultural answer by the European to his needs as a settled and dominant community and we see demonstrated for the first time – and for the last time (as yet) – an agreed national approach to living – (and therefore to building) – which exhibits a consistency and a 'oneness' characteristic of much older countries and much longer periods of civilized development in one place. ◀Cape Dutch ◀Eaton, N.M. ◀ideal home

J.H. Pierneef, House and mountain.

Pretoria

▶D3 ▶E2 ▶E3

privatization

We are undergoing the final loss of the last few shared spaces in the city. The segregated urban environments of apartheid disallowed or severely curtailed interaction in public space; social and political change in the 1990s promised to reopen the borders. But now, as streets, parks, offices and entertainment areas retreat behind walls and security booms, public interaction is set to survive mainly as a marketable concept, one we will have to rely on real-estate developers, franchise operators and full-service attendants to maintain for us. More and more, people are meeting and connecting, moving as they do between the secured zones of housing complexes, office parks and leisure facilities, only within the social spheres they have carefully chosen. Such choices narrow or shut down the routes of confrontation or connection. Are the regional shopping malls and programmed television channels our new arenas of controlled encounter? ▶B2 ▶E11 ▶F4 ▶H3

provincial

The desire to be a part of metropolitan centres, to be continuous with them despite the distances between, more than envy, competition or insecurity in relation to these centres, seems to lie somewhere behind commercial pressures to build towers, malls and housing estates. In the built forms of an international tendency in South Africa, just as in other architectures in provincial settings, we see architects looking to the centres in Europe and the United States, feeling compelled to emulate and impress. There has always been pressure on white architects to mimic the banking blocks of London, the corporate towers of New York, even the state projects of the newly emerging former colonies of Latin America. They have found the sense of being small, insignificant and out of the way hard to overcome. Buildings have generally demonstrated the predictable variation rather than bold and adaptive imitation. The scale of public architecture has often been awkward rather than imposing. Hardly more than an outpost – even in the minds of its own people – South Africa has not produced the grand spaces achieved by some other former colonies. ▶regionalism ▶D5 ▶E2 ▶F7 ▶H3

public health

Central Archives, GNWB285 52/18/72, Public Health Department document, Municipal Council of Johannesburg, 10 March 1925. An area so defined and set apart is precisely what Sect. 1(1)(b) of the Act defines as a 'native village', and it will be observed that its 'defining', 'setting apart' and 'laying out' are essentially the function of the local authority. Moreover, the implication appears to be that any such 'native village' must be owned and controlled by the local authority, because the local authority is empowered under Sect. 1(1)(c)(d) to erect hostels and accommodation for families thereon, and under Sect. 23(3) to regulate very definitely the terms and conditions of residence therein. ◀pondokkie ▶setting apart

racism

Rand Afrikaans University

W. O. Meyer quoted in E. van der Westhuizen, 'W. O. Meyer: Architect and philosopher', Lantern, 42:3 (1993), p. 22. The complex as required by the council of the university was to be a manifestation of the Afrikaners' foothold in the big city. A statement that could only be meaningful when coupled to a particular time and place in the history of the Afrikaner. ▶E4 ▶H3

RDP

African National Congress, The Reconstruction and Development Programme (Johannesburg, Umanyano Publications, 1994), p. 83. (4.3.3.) In general, the RDP recognises the need to break down apartheid geography through land reform, more compact cities, decent public transport, and the development of industries and services that use local resources and/or meet local needs. In this context, the RDP must seek to help people generate economic wealth in their chosen communities. (4.3.4) Macro-economic policies must take into consideration their effect upon the geographic distribution of economic activity. Additional strategies must address the excessive growth of the largest urban centres, the skewed distribution of population within rural areas, the role of small and medium-sized towns, and the future of declining towns and regions, and the apartheid dumping grounds. ◄masakhane ►self-reliance ►E6 ►E7 ►F7 ►F10 ►G6

reconciliation

redoubt

D. Sleigh, The Forts of the Liesbeeck Frontier (Cape Town, Castle Military Museum, 1996), p. 35. The redoubt also played its role in the communications network of the time. If the troops saw the flag on the neighbouring fort Ruijterwacht going up and down as a general alarm for the entire settlement, they had to relay it to the Fort in the Table Valley. When Khoina, Frenchmen and Englishmen approached the redoubt, they had to refuse them entry, lock the door, mount the platform and from there bid them a friendly farewell. The strength of their complement was to be kept a secret. If they were attacked, they had to resist to the utmost of their ability. Furthermore, all persons finding wrecked goods on the beach had to report the find at the redoubt and at the Fort, before they could lay claim to it, according to a placard or proclamation of the Council of Policy in 1658. ►A5

Red Sea

►J12

regionalism

The need for a regional or national style precedes nationalism like the chicken does the egg. The combination of modernism and local materials and cultures seems like an unlikely impetus for any nationalist project. Yet it should not surprise us, perhaps, that the strongest proponents of a regional style in South Africa were the same architects who extended the idea of the modern across the country. Choosing to ignore the fact that a regional style is always readily available to those who make use of the simplest elements at hand, such as local building supplies, building codes and demands, they argued that regionalism is an expression of 'identity'. But if building styles from elsewhere have been imposed and may change with time, and if the social environment has been sterilized in the pursuit of political objectives, what exactly is left to define a particular region? The 'regional' is usually defined in opposition to the 'universal', but the relationship between the two is not that simple. Many cultural traits and historical experiences spill across regional boundaries. The fact that people in different regions may be linked by virtue of shared class positions, religious affiliations or consumption patterns is seldom noted in the architectural formulation of regional identities. The standardization of styles and technologies produced by contemporary capitalism is not easy to counter, especially in an emerging market. For the essential characteristics of its building to be preserved untouched, a region would have to be isolated and autonomous in a way that not even South Africa was under apartheid. In those years, attempts to define or develop a regional architecture often issued in a parochialism that said more about the country's distance from other architectural centres than about some inherent difference. Producing work that was slightly off-centre and out of familiar urban scales, confused by materials imposed on local markets, unsure of their role in dividing the cities, architects in South Africa never quite found a place to call, or build, their own. Regionalism here could only serve to domesticate separation, limiting people to their own areas and reinforcing the myth that each one's place was different. In a land already splintered by apartheid, any further emphasis on regional distinctions was always bound to have a destructive side to it. Creating common cultural artifacts, and demonstrating shared identities and a common humanity, these were the impossible tasks of an architecture that was never to be realized. ◄Fagan, G. ◄provincial ►D3 ►D5 ►E4 ►F8 ►H6

removals

Statement taken from resident of Umbulwane in August 1980 by the Association for Rural Advancement, quoted in L. Platzsky and C. Walker, The Surplus People: Forced Removals in South Africa (Johannesburg, Ravan Press, 1985), p. 271. My six-room house was broken down on the 19th August while I was at work. My wife was out collecting firewood; there was our three-year-old baby inside who was taken outside and ran away. I found my house broken down. All the doorframes and windows were broken, my tools were broken and they left me only one room. They came back later, just to level everything. I did not receive a word of notice. ◄eviction

reserves

◄Bantustans ►C10 ►D11 ►J12

resistance

Restistance forced changes in municipal administration and eventually found a way into the built landscape. Rent and bus boycotts, protest marches and guerrilla warfare all had urban implications, influencing the form of the city, the pressure that was exerted and the parts that broke free under that pressure. Struggle is built into the cities of South Africa as surely as urban planning. ◄civics ►E8

resources

SA Builder, 1960. ... the time is now fast approaching when the resources of the white population will no longer be able to cope without substantial reinforcements. By the same token it is imperative to increase the white population in order that the emphasis on racial discrimination may be suitably relieved.

Robben Island

►B3 ►F9

round

◄Mmabatho ►B11 ►C4 ►D11

SDUs

Self-Defence Units ►B2 ►J10

security

The structural (fences, bars, barbed wire, glass, electric wiring); the symbolic (signage, thresholds, skull and crossbones, dogs, cameras, threats); the serviced (armed responses, guards, booms, satellite tracking devices); and the incremental and desperate processes by which these are acquired (addition, delivery, do-it-yourself, etc.). ►B2 ►C2 ►E11

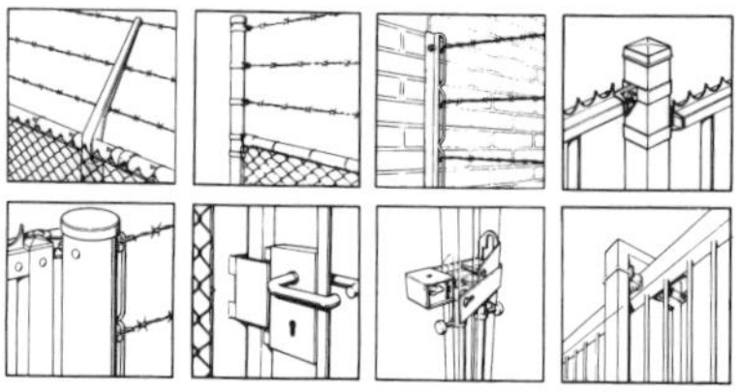

Fencing systems.

segregation

E.A.E. Havemann, 'Planning for residential segregation', paper presented to the South African Bureau for Racial Affairs conference, Pietermaritzburg, January 1952, p. 14. It is possible at this point to sum up the basic characteristics necessary in a residential race zone, Viz.: 1. A residential zone should –

a. have boundaries which will as far as possible constitute barriers of a kind preventing or discouraging contact between races in neighbouring residential zones;

b. have direct access to working areas and to such amenities as are used by all races, so that its residents do not have to traverse the residential areas of another race in large numbers, or do so only by rail or by way of a common highway segregated from the residential areas abutting it;

c. be large enough to develop into an area of full or partial self-government or be substantially contiguous to such an area;

d. provide appropriate land for all economic and social classes which are present in the race group concerned, or may be expected to emerge in the course of time; and for the group institutions, shopping, minor industry and recreation;

e. be so sited that the means of transport most suitable for the group concerned is or can be made available. ►B2 ►E6 ►F10 ►G8 ►G11

self-reliance

►D9 ►F7 ►F9

semi-rural

►B11 ►D11

Separate Amenities Act of 1953

Any person who wilfully enters or uses any public premises or public vehicle or any portion thereof or any counter, bench, seat or other amenity or contrivance which has in terms of sub-section (1) been set apart or reserved for the exclusive use of persons belonging to a particular race or class, being a race or class to which he does not belong, shall be guilty of an offence and liable on conviction to a fine not exceeding fifty pounds or to imprisonment for a period not exceeding three months, or to both such fine and such imprisonment. ►D4 ►F4

setting apart

shack

◄pondokkie ►A12 ►F8 ►G4 ►H8

Sharpeville

21 March 1960 ►D5 ►E4

Southern Question

R. Martienssen in South African Architectural Record, March (1939), p. 82. The southerner whose temperament mirrors the sea and the sky has plastically an enormous advantage over the more active but slightly frozen nordic. He lives close to nature and not in conflict with her. Under the sun his surroundings take on a vividness that demands a counterbalancing repose – a withdrawing from play of form which stimulates and exhausts. His dwelling stands deliberate and separate from the tumultuous pattern of nature. ◄Martienssen, R. ►D5 ►F8

spaza

Few shops were allowed to operate in the townships and not a single supermarket chain opened branches to serve black customers in their neighbourhoods. Squatting settlements were not considered suitable for any kind of commercial enterprise. Spazas, small shops usually run from people's houses, evolved informally to supply packaged goods which would otherwise have had to be purchased kilometres away in the white centres. ◄informal ►G8

squatting

►A12 ►D8 ►D9 ►G4 ►H8

stoep

◄Karoohuis ►F10

stone

►C4 ►D3 ►E2

suburban

►B2 ►F4

surrogation

J.M. Coetzee, White Writing (New Haven, Yale University Press, 1988), p. 7. The landscape remains alien, impenetrable, until a language is found in which to win it, speak it, represent it. It is no oversimplification to say that landscape art and landscape writing in South Africa from the beginning of the nineteenth century to the middle of the twentieth revolve around the question of finding a language to fit Africa, a language that will be authentically African. Of course there exist plenty of authentically African languages, languages indigenous to the subcontinent. But their authenticity is not necessarily the right authenticity. The quest for an authentic language is pursued within a framework in which language, consciousness, and landscape are interrelated. For the European to learn an African language 'from the outside' will therefore not be enough: he must know the language 'from the inside' as well, that is, know it 'like a native,' sharing the mode of consciousness of the people born to it, and to that extent giving up his European identity. So, quite aside from the question of whether it is practical for a European to enter African culture in sufficient depth, quite aside from European doubts about whether the black man anyhow 'appreciates' the landscape into which he was born any better than an animal does, the question has to be rephrased: Is there a language in which people of European identity, or if not European identity then of a highly problematic South African-colonial identity, can speak to Africa and be spoken to by Africa? (This argument pushes the African into an intrinsically double-bound situation: in order to convince the European that he appreciates Africa he must give evidence of a degree of alienation from it; once he is thus alienated he can no longer claim to be by nature at one with it.) ►thatch ►B3 ►C10 ►D8 ►H3

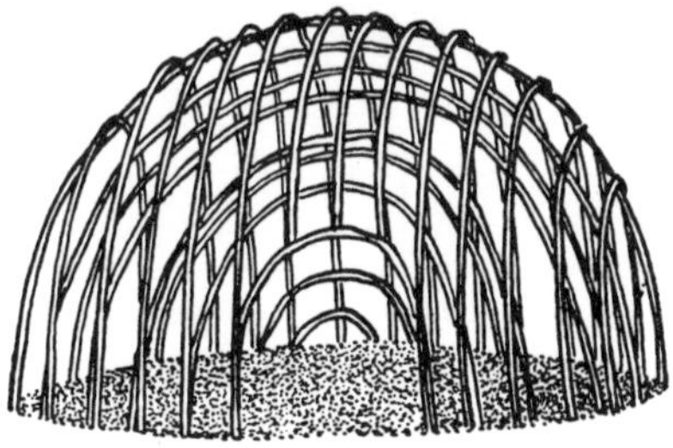

James Walton, drawing of Natal Nguni framework, 1953.

surveillance

Planning under apartheid did not place much emphasis on the structures of surveillance. It was relatively simple, of course, for officials and policemen to spot a black person in a city classified for white habitation. Segregation could be accomplished through the routine bureaucratic mechanisms of physical separation that were manageable without continuous observation. The only strictly panoptic structures were mining compounds and municipal hostels. Control of the population was maintained more through regulation and administration. It is true that bodies needed to be examined to discover contamination and searches conducted to root out surplus labour units. But it was never possible for an official gaze to be everywhere at all times; besides, the spaces set aside for Africans were better left unattended. The impossibility of overseeing an enormous territory, even if it had been fragmented into 'independent' ethnic states, was a factor in the gradual breakdown of control. Even with influx control, forced removal and segregation, Africans were never quite kept out of the white centres or completely contained in their own areas.

thatch

theme parks

►C4 ►C10 ►D2

Tokoza

'Another 12 killed on East Rand', Star, 1990. At least 12 people died in violence in Katlehong and Tokoza yesterday. A police spokesman said a man with an AK-47 was shot dead after he opened fire on a police patrol in Katlehong. Police took possession of the rifle and ammunition found in the gunman's possession. The bodies of two men were found metres from each other in Ntakane Street in Tokoza. They both had multiple gunshot wounds. A woman was shot dead and burnt in Matlala Street in the same township. In Katlehong, a man died after being thrown off a train at Lindela Station. Two men were set alight and burnt to death in the township's Twala and Mnisi sections. A man was shot dead in Letsoho Road in Tokoza and the body of a woman who had been shot dead was found in Nkaki Street. A man burnt to death in Katlehong's Mnisi section. Another man was shot dead and burnt in Everest section in the same township. The body of a man who had been stabbed was found in Khumalo Street in Tokoza. In the township's Dube section, a man wounded a bystander when he fired three shots with an AK-47 at a police patrol. The police were unhurt and the gunman escaped. ►J10

township

◄location ►A12 ►D11 ►G4 ►G8 ►H6 ►H8 ►H6 ►J10

Layout of Alexandra Township, 1975.

tradition

An antithetical discourse maintains the opposition between a developing urban and an undeveloped rural. But the homelands policy and ideas of 'surplus people' should be reason enough for questioning such oppositions. The pressures that apartheid exerted on rural people and the effects of these pressures, visible in a multitude of distorted rituals and relations, invite us to challenge ideas of the natural, the naive and the native that are still tied to the vernacular. Forced removals made impermanence an element of urban dwelling. Materials brought from the city encouraged demands and desires that reconstructed the rural. Tradition now had to account for the concrete block and the plastic bowl. ◄round ◄semi-rural ►B11 ►D8 ►D10 ►D11 ►J12

transition

R. Lewcock, Early Nineteenth Century Architecture in South Africa (Cape Town, A. A.Balkema, 1963), p. 26. Some of the officials under the Dutch were eventually taken into the employ of the British. Louis Michel Thibault had been, at the fall of the Cape, Captain of the Engineers. He therefore felt that decorum restrained him from accepting employment under the new regime, although he had decided to remain at the Cape. During the early years of the British Occupation, however, Thibault allowed the authorities access to his plans; he even toyed with the idea of becoming a building contractor. But when, in 1799, it was suggested that as architect he should take charge and superintend repairs to the military buildings of the garrison, 'Completely ignored for five years by Holland, to the States of which I had rendered most important services, and having suffered considerably by the loss of my profession, I accepted the proposal', Thibault afterwards recalled. He then took the oath of allegiance and endeavoured to serve his new masters as he had served his old. He was given the post of Surveyor of Buildings, a purely civil position, but it was understood that he would furnish advice to the Barrack Master when requested. Certain of the officers in the Royal Engineers studied fortification under him, although General Dundas was of the opinion that 'As an engineer officer his capabilities are mediocre, but he can be usefully employed in architecture, which has been his principal study and in which he has given proof of much taste.' ◄emergency ►E6 ►E8 ►G6

Transvaal Group

►E2 ►E12 ►H3 ►H6

Union Buildings

►D5 ►E3 ►F9

urbanization

Report of the Committee for the Constitutional Affairs of the President's Council on an Urbanization Strategy for the Republic of South Africa (Pretoria, Government Printers, 1985). ... neither the present system nor any other form of 'negative' influx control should be retained. There is, however, a need for a positive approach to urbanization that would allow the orderliness of the process to be promoted. It is necessary for influx control to be replaced by a positive urbanization strategy that, by making use of market forces, subsidies and development, among other things, will encourage people to settle in certain suitable areas rather than forbidding them to move to certain areas. ►D9 ►E6 ►E8 ►E10 ►G6 ►H8

Verwoerd, H.F.

Speech by H.F. Verwoerd, 3 September 1948, in E. H. Brookes, Apartheid (London, Routledge and Kegan Paul, 1968), pp. 7-8. Nobody has ever contended that the policy of apartheid should be identified with 'total segregation'. The apartheid policy has been described as what one can do in the direction of what you regard as ideal. Nobody will deny that for the Native as well as for the European complete separation would have been ideal if it had developed that way historically. If we had here a white South Africa in the sense in which you have a white England and a white Holland and a white France, and if there had been a Native state somewhere for the Natives, and if this white state could have developed to a self-supporting condition as those European states have developed by themselves, then we should certainly not have had the friction and difficulties which we have today. Surely it would have been an ideal state of affairs for him. And if that is the case, then surely it cannot do any harm to see it and to state it; it can only do good. If you appreciate that you are saddled with a complicated situation, a highly complicated situation, you must have the direction in which you wish to move to solve your problems clearly in mind. In every field of life one has to fix one's eyes on the stars, to see how close one can come to achieving the very best, to achieving perfection. For that reason I say this: keep in view what promises to be best for your country and try to approach it within the realm of what is practical. ◄segregation ►D5 ►E4

VOC

Vereenigde Oostindische Compagnie/Dutch East India Company. ►A5 ►B3

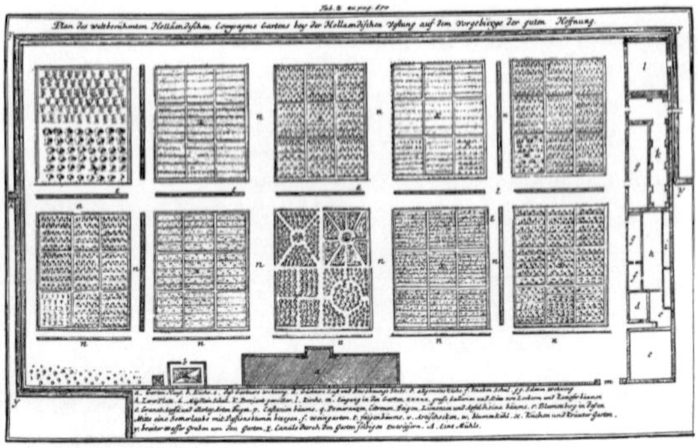

Plan of the Company's Garden.

Volkskas

◄bank ◄Fagan, G. ►D3

Voortrekker Monument

G. Moerdyk, 'Die wording van die Voortrekker Monument', 1949, original manuscript in University of Pretoria Library Archives. Die monument moet dien om ons 'n eiendomsreg aan hierdie land te gee. Indien 'n stuk grond gekoop word, dan kry u 'n dokument daarvoor en daarop staan geskrywe: Hierdie grond behoort aan so en so en die prys daarvoor betaal is dit of dat en die prys wat daarvoor betaal is maak die grond die eiendom van dié sekere persoon. Indien 'n vreemdeling in ons land aan die Afrikaner vra: 'Aan wie behoort hierdie land? Julle het dit tog maar van die kaffirs geneem en die Engelse het dit van julle geneem en indien die Russe more kom en die land neem, behoort dit dan aan hulle?' As antwoord sal die Afrikaner aan die vreemdeling sê: 'Kom saam na die Voortrekker Monument. Kyk die prys wat vir hierdie land betaal is; 'n wrede prys in bloed en trane! Dit is my land! Ek is erfgenaam in gees of liggaam van die Voortrekkers wat daardie prys betaal het, en ieder een wat 'n derglyke prys betaal het, het ook dieselfde reg daarop!' – The Voortrekker Monument must serve to give us ownership rights to this country. If a piece of land is bought, you get a document for it on which is written: This land belongs to so-and-so and the price paid for it was such-and-such, and the price paid for it makes the land the property of this particular person. If a stranger to our country asks the Afrikaner: 'Who does this land belong to? After all, you just took it from the Kaffirs and the English took it from you, and if the Russians come tomorrow and take it, won't it then belong to them?' In answer the Afrikaner will say to the stranger: 'Come with me to the Voortrekker Monument. Behold the price that was paid for this country: a cruel price in blood and tears! This is my land! I am heir in spirit or body to the Voortrekkers who paid that price, and anyone who has paid a similar price, has the same rights to it!' ◄commemoration ◄Moerdyk, G. ►E2 ►H3

vulnerable

A city torn apart, divided, fragmented, exposed and abandoned becomes a ready landscape for victims of crime. The implications of vulnerability are felt in each and every brutalized body and violated space. The various everyday crimes are diminished in the statistical summaries on the inside pages of the newspapers, even as the lexicon of criminality expands: not just mugging, violent assault, breaking and entry, rape, but serious economic offences, car-jacking, cash-in-transit heists, taxi violence, farm murders. ◄crime ►B2 ►D9 ►F4

ZCC

Local congregations of the Zion Christian Church and other separatist churches conduct their services in open lots, suburban parks, under motorways, in the leftover spaces of the city. These congregations establish their own cosmological centres: a rock on the beach, a mountain top, a tree. Their distinctive uniforms reinforce the identity of their members and make their passage to and from gatherings an extended part of a dispersed but centripetal ritual. A line on the ground is often the only edge between sacred space and the city. ►A12 ►B8

'Fort ende Thuijn': The years of Dutch colonization

Karel Schoeman

A

J. Schumacher, The farm Winterhoek, 1776-7.

In 1649 two officials of the Dutch East India Company drew up a report recommending the establishment of a 'Fort ende Thuijn' at the Cape of Good Hope for the benefit of the Company's shipping between the Netherlands and Batavia.

The 'fort ofte redoute', as they described it elsewhere, was to accommodate a garrison of sixty to seventy men, and was obviously needed for protection: apart from the Company's many commercial enemies, the Netherlands were at war with Portugal at the time and the First Anglo-Dutch War would break out only three years later, while the indigenous Khoikhoi or 'Hottentots' were also not trusted.

As far as the proposed 'thuijn' of the memorandum is concerned, this may be translated conventionally as a garden, the vegetable plots and orchards which were in fact laid out here, referred to more precisely elsewhere in the document as a 'hof ofte thuijn'. In this particular context and period, however, the word might also mean a fence or palisade, an enclosure rather than the area so enclosed. Jan van Riebeeck, subsequently Commander of the Dutch settlement established at the Cape, suggested enclosing the fields and meadows of the colonists with a dense hawthorn hedge, an idea which he carried out in part, and it is in this sense that I would prefer to interpret 'thuijn' for my present purpose.

Shelter, enclosure, keeping together, shutting out, protecting, defending, establishing a presence and ensuring its survival – the 'Fort ende Thuijn' envisaged by the Company seem potent images, encapsulating much of what was to be attempted in South Africa by white settlers over the following three centuries and more.

Van Riebeeck and his small group of colonists landed at the Cape in 1652, and the proposed settlement with its fort, gardens, orchards and water furrows came into being slowly and painfully, and not without resistance from the Khoikhoi, who saw themselves being dispossessed of their pastures. In 1657 the Company abandoned its initial attempt to keep the colony under its own control, and granted land to free burghers in a fertile and well-watered area close to the fort, which up to now had regularly been visited by the nomadic Khoi pastoralists. Inexorably, however, the settlers moved deeper into the country, occupying the valleys and crossing the mountain ranges onto the plateaus of the interior, driving out the Khoikhoi or incorporating them into their own economy as labourers. The newcomers met with furious opposition from the Bushmen, who seemed at times able to hold their own against white men with guns and horses, but it wasn't until they came up against the numerous Bantu-speaking tribes of the north-east at the end of the eighteenth century that their progress was checked.

At the Cape, where the original fort was superseded by a Castle and a hamlet developed which would grow into the city of Cape Town, the Company, with its cumbersome apparatus of officials, soldiers and slaves administered the refreshment post with an eye mainly to profit. The Company made only sporadic and half-hearted attempts to control the burgher population moving steadily further beyond its reach, establishing a few villages as centres of government – Stellenbosch, Roodezand (Tulbagh), Swellendam and Graaff-Reinet – appointing ministers and authorizing the building of churches, and carrying out such duties as were forced on it by circumstances, reluctantly and without interest. In 1795, during the Revolutionary Wars in Europe, the Cape was occupied as a temporary measure by the British. The Company, unwieldy, corrupt and bankrupt, was dissolved, and in 1803 the Cape was handed over to its legal successor, the Batavian Republic. In 1806, however, during the course of the Napoleonic Wars, it was reoccupied by Great Britain, and in 1814 British occupation was confirmed.

This essay offers a brief survey of the 154 years during which South Africa was in effect a Dutch colony, and may perhaps be described as a meditation or even an improvisation on a number of broad themes: on shelter, enclosure, keeping together, shutting out, protecting, defending, establishing a presence and ensuring its survival; on the Fort ende Thuijn of the early memorialists; on space and structure.

Thomas and William Daniell,
Cape of Good Hope.

A

Space first of all, the small wooden ships on the open sea, bounded by the horizon. Three ships brought the first party of colonists to the Cape, with 86 men on board the first, 75 on the second and 20 on the third, besides a small number of women and children, all cooped up for much of the voyage in constricted cabins or between decks. Peasants, farming people and townspeople from the Low Countries, North Germany or Scandinavia, largely illiterate; some of them had seen service abroad as soldiers, sailors or Company officials, but many had now left Europe for the first time and had never been at sea. Their passage was quick, however, and on the afternoon of 5 April 1652 the first mate of the commander's ship sighted, 'God be praised, the land of Cabo de Boa Esperance, namely the Table Mountain, E and E of S at a distance of about 15 or 16 miles'. How many of them had ever seen a mountain? Three puny vessels, their masts, sails and bright pennants dwarfed by the granite mass of mountains before them, the sea stretching out behind, the sky above: Europe encountering Africa, the colonists arriving in the land to which they were laying claim.

Space first; then structure. The soil was cleared, gardens laid out, enclosures made, trees and hedges planted; the fort was built as planned, and small houses were erected by the farmers, in imitation, most likely, of those they had known at home, using the materials to hand. The fort and houses provided shelters at night and during the long, wet Cape winters, protection from the wild animals still roaming the Cape Peninsula, lions visible from the fort on the bare slopes of the neighbouring mountains, and leopards, lions and jackals attacking the sheep and fowls at night, even in the shadow of its bastions.

The colonists waited anxiously for the unpredictable arrival of cattle-owning Khoikhoi from the North with whom they might barter, and one night the darkness beyond the fort was suddenly lit by the innumerable fires of Khoi encampments spread out over the plain between the Salt River and Tygerberg. They watched impatiently for ships from the fatherland or from Batavia, to bring them news of the outer world from which they were cut off completely, and reminders of the life they had once known. Infrequently and irregularly, groups of sails would become visible on the far horizon. Between the shore and the land they established themselves precariously, dwarfed by the mountain massif, reaching out with one hand to the unfamiliar continent where they had to survive, reaching back with the other to the distant countries they had left, most of them for ever.

Turning from the sea to the interior and exploring the country, they discovered streams, hills, mountain ranges and thickly wooded ravines to which they gave Dutch names – Liesbeek, Bosheuvel, Houtbaai, Tygerberg, Bergrivier – ignoring and obliterating the Khoi names by which these landmarks were already known. Gradually, with patience and persistence, they established themselves, planting wheat and laying out vineyards in the fertile valleys of the area around Cape Town that would become known as the Boland, and developing, by the intensive use of slave labour, a way of life that was stable, prosperous and reasonably comfortable. That life is embodied in the thatched and gabled 'Cape Dutch' manor houses which were built during the eighteenth century and have proved so profitable to the tourist industry of the twentieth. With their solid, whitewashed walls, sash windows, inner shutters, floors of flagstones or broad yellowwood planks and exposed beams they preserve memories of the seventeenth-century Netherlands, and in many ways resemble buildings erected in Batavia and elsewhere in the Dutch trading empire, but at the same time they contain other elements as well, built as they were by slave labour – masons, plasterers, carpenters and thatchers – drawn mainly from the East. Primarily these houses were meant for shelter too, of course, but by this time the need for protection or defence had diminished and the farmers and landowners for whom they were built intended them largely for display, setting off their furniture, silverware and porcelain, and the lavish, wasteful way of life made possible by slavery. The slaves themselves were herded together in barracks somewhere among the outbuildings, the jongenshuizen and meidenhuizen which are not usually on display for tourists, even when they have survived in a recognizable form.

Samuel Daniell, Passing a kloof.

But the Boland is not South Africa. This is a report on the era of the Dutch East India Company, but it is not a company report: an improvisation rather, as has been said, or a meditation, and highly subjective in its nature. The Cape and the Boland, then, are not South Africa: South Africa begins beyond the folded mountain ranges, on the plains of the interior, a harsher and sterner landscape of ironstone and scrub and semi-desert, of stony hills and sheer granite mountains, of empty river beds and violent thunderstorms, of floods and droughts, parched summers and bitter winters white with frost, bleak and empty by day to the eye which has not yet learned to look and discern, and splendid only briefly in its sunsets and the clarity of its night skies blazing with stars. A landscape of the imagination, admittedly, generalized, idealized, romanticized; but as basis for a meditation or an improvisation it will do.

A single, armed man on horseback, a few white men with their Khoi servants, a single man on foot, stumbling over the rocks, a fugitive slave or criminal: uncertainly they explore the valleys, probe the ravines and turn back where no further passage is possible to try elsewhere, make their way laboriously up the slopes, stones slipping under the horses' hooves, and mount to the ridge, not knowing what they will find on the other side, constantly expecting danger and uncertain when or in what form it will come, exploring and discovering the unknown country which in the course of generations they will finally, in a manner of speaking, make their own. An itinerant farmer with his wife and children, two or three Khoi drivers or shepherds, or perhaps a slave or two, a horse, some mongrel dogs, a gun, a wagon and a flock of sheep, moving up the slopes, hauling up the wagon, driving up the sheep, making a road where there is none, searching for water or for pasture, entrusting their future to a gamble, reaching at last the crest of the hill or the summit of the mountain to discover beyond a sea of rolling hills stretching away in the smoke-grey haze, or a great plain dappled with the shadows of passing clouds where herds of zebras or buck are grazing.

A single family, a few servants of dubious loyalty, a few guns, a wagon, moving boldly into the unknown, over those dappled plains where the grazing buck look up as they pass in the distance, then start, and wheel away in a cloud of dust. At night a fire is made and the wagon chest lifted down to serve as a table or a seat; the family sleep on stretchers in the wagon under coverings of sheepskin, their servants on the ground below in the space between the wheels. This is all there is, the wagon with its fragile canvas tent and the shade it provides in the heat of the day beneath a near vertical sun; lumbering over stones, shrubs and anthills as the oxen drag it along, the tent swaying and shuddering, a white dot like a sail on the sea, marking the passage of the little party over the plains, through that almost infinite space, under the vastness of the sky. They find water at the infrequent fountains, they shoot game, they make a fire and crawl into the wagon or under it for the night. It is enough.

They learn to live here like the Khoikhoi and the Bushmen before them, adapting what they know or remember from the life they have left behind or of the traditions transported from Europe by earlier generations, discarding, changing or combining pragmatically as circumstance demands: survival is the most important consideration, and after that bare subsistence. They do not ask or expect a great deal. They learn the uses of plants and the habits of animals, they learn to interpret the weather and to read the landscape, they give names to the infrequent streams and the hills. Their language loses its structure to become a dialect with a vocabulary and an idiom of its own. Their clothes and shoes are made of skins they have dressed themselves.

Where they stop for longer, shelters are erected with the scanty materials available, a framework of branches covered with scrub or reeds or woven mats; where they decide to remain, however, memories of the distant European past emerge, and they construct as best they can, in the absence of suitable timber for beams, simple rectangular buildings of stone or clay with thatched roofs. These are mere shelters for the night, and inadequate even as such, leaking in thunderstorms and bitterly cold in winter, but in a sense they may be seen also as beacons, defining the line of the colonists' advance into the country and the boundary of the area implicitly claimed by them. One may imagine the family gathered there at night by fire- or candlelight to listen to a reading from the seventeenth-century Dutch translation of the Bible, clinging to guidance and consolation in a language which has already become strange to them, and singing the metrical Dutch psalms composed a hundred years earlier, their voices dying away and finally lost in the silence and darkness around them.

A low, thatched, clay-floored house of one or two rooms, an outdoor cooking area behind a screen of branches, a freestone sheepfold and an outspanned wagon, a little complex scarcely visible at a distance where it blends with the stone, shrub and grass of the surrounding landscape. An outpost of white advance, in a sense, and beacon of what, with its bibles, wagons and guns was at that time known as 'civilization'; but the occupation it indicated was by no means seen as permanent yet. The farmers lived like the nomadic Bushman hunters they were supplanting, trekking after water or grazing and abandoning their houses for a time, piling up stones in the doorway to prevent wild animals from entering in their absence, or perhaps not returning at all, leaving the clay of the walls to crumble and the stones to be scattered. Sometimes they were forced to abandon what they held onto so precariously and flee before the attacks of the Bushmen who contested the fountains and veld of which they were slowly and surely being dispossessed, in a guerrilla war stretching over generations; but the colonists were stronger, and eventually they returned to the house, the sheepfold, the candlelight, the fire in the dark. It was a world of isolation and silence, of hospitality and suspicion, of piety and callousness and a sudden, casual violence that was to become part of life in this country, woven into its pattern. A white family, Khoi servants little better than serfs, slaves owned as chattels, and Bushman women and children captured after some skirmish in which the men had all been killed. How could there be trust, confidence or security in these scattered little communities, linked uneasily together by brute force, powerlessness and mutual dependence? The house as shelter, shutters closed against the night, the candlelight and the voices at prayer. The house as fortress, the gun constantly to hand, and danger always lurking in the surrounding darkness just beyond the threshold, announced by the barking of dogs or the terrified whinnying of a horse; sudden ambush or attack, disappearance or death, betrayal, treachery or revenge, unreported and unquestioned, in a region beyond the reach of law.

In 1785 the Dutch East India Company, in a final attempt to assert its authority over people who had long outgrown its control, founded the village of Graaff-Reinet, the most northerly outpost of white administration; it became the seat of a landdrost or magistrate, and a church and parsonage were built in the colonial style, shaped from memories of Europe and the East as adapted to local conditions and materials, white walls and gables blinding in the sunlight reflected on the stony hills. Big gardens and water furrows were laid out behind the houses and orange trees planted along the streets. It was not until the early years of the nineteenth century that the outpost took on a more definite shape, but the building of the drostdy, the magistrate's residence, and parsonage, which have survived, may be seen as the final achievements of the Dutch period in South Africa, its culmination and completion. After that everything changed, slowly, almost imperceptibly at first, but inevitably, and Dutch South Africa increasingly became a memory, a single strand among many others.

The house as shelter, the house as fortress. To the north of the fledgling village the Bushmen held on among the mountains and in the ravines, but they were driven back steadily, exterminated or expelled. To the east, successive wars with the Xhosa erupted along the frontier and proved more difficult to resolve, sometimes menacing the village itself, but eventually they were resolved as well, after a fashion, at any rate, and for the time being. The colonists were in control; after a fashion, and for the time being.

The house as fortress, the house as shelter. On the very borders of colonized territory, many days' journey from the centre of government at Cape Town, the village held out almost as in a state of siege against the country in which it was situated, beleaguered by the reality of Africa surrounding it: the constant threat of war or attack, the leopards in the neighbouring hills, the droughts and floods, the silence and desolation, preserving as well as it could and in the face of almost insurmountable difficulties the amenities of Europe, the amenities of 'civilization' as these people understood it – the bright tricolour flag with the Company's monogram, the authority of Government, however tenuous its hold over the people it governed, the authority of the Word of God, though it was preached in a formal, foreign language and for long periods the congregation did not even have a minister. A fortress still, and a shelter, beating back, shutting out, defending, guarding and preserving.

During the early decades of the nineteenth century, as mission stations came to be established deeper still in the interior, missionaries from Europe would land at Algoa Bay and travel inland by ox-wagon. They would break the long journey at Graaff-Reinet, where they were welcomed by Andrew Murray, the Scottish-born minister of the Dutch Church, and his South African wife, and be sent on their way with seeds, seedlings and slips for planting in mission gardens beyond the Orange River. The sojourn at Graaff-Reinet is described in many missionary autobiographies, letters and journals, and one may easily imagine it, the long, slow, uncomfortable journey in the heat and the dust of a strange country, living mostly on black coffee and the meat of whatever could be bought, slaughtered or shot along the way, sleeping on stretchers or on the ground, unable to wash or do laundry, often held up by damage to axles or wheels or injuries to oxen, by rivers in flood or droughts, day after day and frequently enough week after week. And one can also imagine the arrival, the cool, darkened house where the shutters have been closed against the heat of the day, the bare feet of slaves over the floorboards, water being brought, the sound of water being poured, the sound of running water, towels being brought, clean linen, the table laid with a white cloth in the candlelight, the voices around it, the coffee, the bread, the fruit, the bed with its feather pillows and bolsters, briefly before the journey was resumed, northwards to labour and loneliness, preaching the Word of God to tribes who had not asked for it and would not listen, forcing literacy, Bible tracts, calico dresses, shirts and rectangular houses on people who had no need for any of these things and could see no use for them either; planting the seeds, the seedlings, the slips, nursing them through the droughts and the hailstorms, and in a good season finally picking the flowers or the fruit.

Vergelegen in 1709.

Driving from Cradock to Graaff-Reinet by car, a distance of some 150 kilometres, a journey lasting little more than an hour, the harsh, bare, red, unshadowed landscape of sand and rock reflects the glare of the sunlight. The old drostdy has become an hotel, and one can sit in the deep shade of the pergola in the inner court and order cold drinks which are brought by a young coloured waiter, a local man most likely; he says 'meneer' – 'sir' – for the term 'baas' or 'master' is no longer used. Facing the hotel at the other end of Parsonage Street, the old Dutch parsonage is now a museum, its high-ceilinged rooms cool in the heat of the day; a long, open terrace runs along its width at the back and a curving double flight of steps leads down into what remains of the garden. Fortress and shelter, keeping out, holding in, defending and protecting. From the cool rooms, from the shadow of the garden, one looks out at whitewashed walls, blinding in the sun, the brightness of a new flag on public buildings, the stony rampart of the surrounding hills.
Fort ende Thuijn. What is being shut out and held at bay and what preserved and guarded? We no longer know.

Rural in urban
Chris Ledochowski

1 Double-storey dwelling, Site B, Khayelitsha.

2 Brewing mqombothi (traditional beer), Umkhonto Square, Nyanga East.

3 Farm workers being offloaded, Nyanga Junction, Nyanga.

4 Free Zion Church, KTC informal settlement.

5 Philippi.

6 Meat market, Kwakiki Hostel, Guguletu.

FREE ZION

A

Fairway no. 17
Fairway no. 3
Fairway no. 5
Fairway no. 2
Fairway no. 1
Fairway no. 18
Fairway no. 9
EPPING DRIVE
NORTH
STAPLEFORD AVENUE
ENFIELD STREET
HATFIELD STREET
SOUTH
WALTHAM AVENUE
HEMPTON AVENUE
Practice Area
Jukskei River
Clubhouse

Crime and the emerging landscape of post-apartheid Johannesburg

Lindsay Bremner

B

> A woman shrieks, blood pumping wildly from her stomach, her life flowing into a municipal drain. A young man walks away with her handbag, rummaging: R20 spending money for the rest of the evening. Johannesburg 1997. A motor car, a television set, a microwave, a bracelet, a pair of sunglasses ... these things have more value than a human being.[1]

A city shaped by segregation

The city of Johannesburg was founded upon the discovery of gold in 1886. In little more than a hundred years it has grown from a mining camp into a teeming metropolis of between 3.8 and 4.5 million people. Over the years successive governments, driven by the imperative to extract the enormous wealth beneath the city's surface, took steps to stabilize its rapidly urbanizing population. The practice of racial segregation was the primary strategy adopted – whites and blacks were separated from one another, the white working classes separated from the black, and the labouring classes from the dangerous.[2] The concepts of physical order, health, social stability and control which lay behind segregation brought together the discursive networks of government, urban planning, public health and urban administration.[3]

As Johannesburg grew, the working classes living close to the city centre were gradually relocated in large slum clearance programmes, justified by notions of unsanitary conditions, overcrowding and immorality. The first of these removals took place in 1906, when members of the Washerman's Guild were moved thirty kilometres south-west of the city to Klipspruit (where the Freedom Charter would be signed some fifty years later). The Urban Areas Act of 1924 formalized this process and compelled local authorities to set aside land for African occupation. A systematic programme began, under which black people were evacuated from the centre to subsidized housing south of the city, in the area that became known in the 1960s as Soweto. By the 1990s, this sprawling dormitory suburb, banally named after its location in relation to Johannesburg (south western township),

Site plan of Hertford Village, Dainfern.

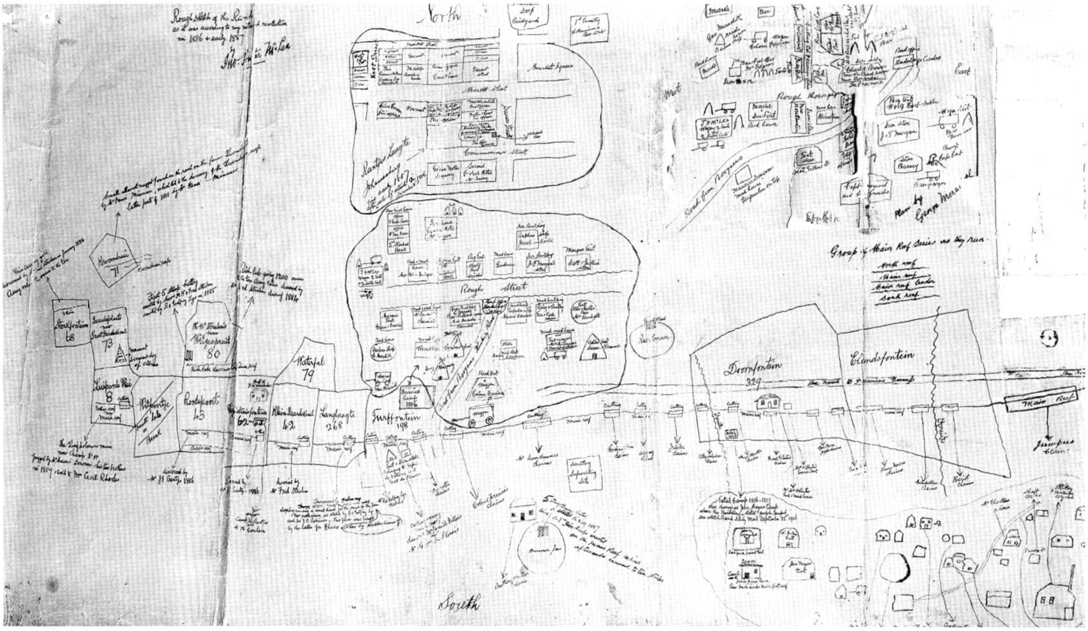

was home to approximately 2.5 million people. White suburbs, characterized by large plots and single-storied, free-standing houses were developed to the north of the city centre. By 1933 the whole of Johannesburg had been proclaimed white, and by 1938 the bulk of the black population had been moved south.[4] The only black spot in the white landscape to the north was the freehold township of Alexandra about twenty kilometres north of the city centre. It had been proclaimed in 1905 as a white working-class suburb, but was settled from 1912 onwards by black people after attempts to attract white buyers failed. By the 1990s, Alexandra had become a severely overcrowded black working-class ghetto, comprised of single-sex hostels, state-built apartment blocks and makeshift structures in backyards, along pavement verges or on the banks of the Jukskei River. Around it lay the neat suburban mansions of the white bourgeoisie.

Racial segregation became the fulcrum of the national and urban political vision of the apartheid state. Under apartheid, racial segregation, practised by previous governments to promote physical order and social control, became an instrument for the political and social exclusion of African people and their restriction to certain areas of economic life. A host of governmental, administrative and professional discourses, such as urban planning, public administration and criminal justice were built around and contributed to this vision. Modern town planning principles and scientific surveys of housing needs and production processes were the basic technologies of township development; racially differentiated local authorities administered urban areas; racially based legislation controlled every aspect of urban life; the movement of people was strictly controlled and policed.

These successive strategies to exert control over the population, overlaid on the geography of the region, where the dominant features are the east-west mining belt, layers of parallel ridges, and an arc of unstable dolomitic land, have resulted in a fragmented, spatially discontinuous city. Areas are buffered from each other, either by natural features or vacant land, on the basis of land-use zoning, income group or race. Like most South African cities, Johannesburg was characterized by a central core, where employment opportunities were located, and peripheral dormitory suburbs until the 1960s, when capital began to relocate to suburban business nodes north of the city – Rosebank, Sandton and Randburg. These remained mainly retail and commercial centres serving the white middle-class residential areas around them. Their development was not

J. Hunter McLea, rough sketch of the Rand as it was in 1886 and early 1887.

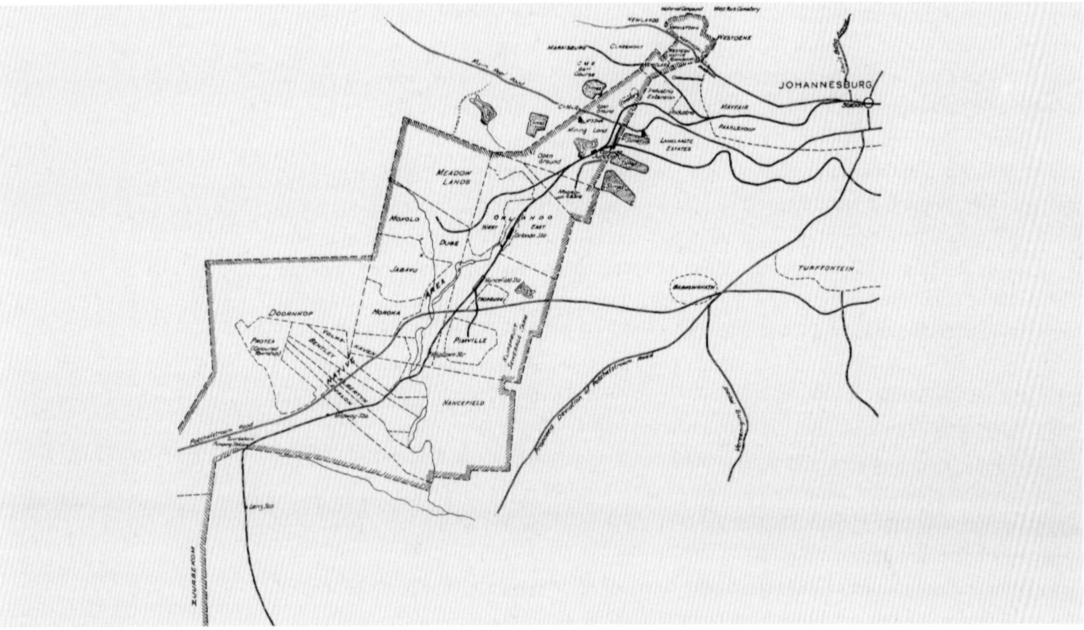

accompanied initially by new working-class housing or industrial areas (although Sandton and Randburg began to develop limited industrial bases from the 1980s onwards). Apart from Alexandra, the black working class continued to live in the south and commute to the city.

Political liberalization and space

Since 1994 there have been far-reaching changes in the urban areas of South Africa, and they have surely been felt most intensely in the large metropolitan areas – Johannesburg, Cape Town and Durban. Johannesburg, lacking the natural beauty of Cape Town or the regional specificity of Durban, has become a field of violent contestation between extreme wealth and extreme poverty, between luxury and subsistence, idyll and inferno, excess and need. Many who were confined by apartheid to townships and rural bantustans, or to the countries beyond our borders, have converged on the streets of Johannesburg to claim its promise of a better life. Public space is being occupied in new ways. Previously uncluttered, sanitized urban parks and open spaces are now dotted with braziers and campfires, and used for storing goods overnight or conducting commercial transactions; pavements have become crowded with hawkers, tailors and hairdressers; streets are congested with taxis. People jostle anarchically for turf; white capital flees ever northwards in an attempt to preserve the illusion that money is clean and safe. The spaces it vacates, whether commercial, retail or residential, are boarded or bricked up, 'mothballed' against occupation by the poor, the destitute or the organized homeless for whom sparse and inappropriate shelter is better than exposure on the street.

Urban governance in this period has undergone internal restructuring. Thirteen formerly racially-defined local authorities have been amalgamated under one metropolitan authority and four local ones. Boundaries have been redrawn, administrations redeployed, and powers and functions redistributed. New local authority politicians and officials, thrown with no experience or role models into the task of managing and servicing the city – maintaining and developing infrastructure, confronting the rising tide of urbanization or directing an aggressive property development industry – have responded reactively.

Johannesburg municipal locations, 1953.

In early 1996 there were two major land invasions involving thousands of homeless people. One targeted a large vacant tract of agricultural land known as Moffat Park in the white working-class southern suburbs of Johannesburg; the other took place on land overlooking Alexandra, in an area earmarked for development and known as the Far East Bank. The former was mobilized from a nerve centre in the white southern suburbs by leaders who promised people houses if they occupied the land; the latter involved existing residents of Alexandra, frustrated with the slow pace of the government housing programme, mobilized by a fly-by-night leadership. Both invasions drew violent reactions from surrounding areas: Moffat Park was witness to violent hostility between squatters and white working-class residents; the Far East Bank invasion, mushrooming in a period of about three weeks into a settlement of three thousand shacks, drew a violent response from the remaining residents of Alexandra who felt cheated of their land. The local authority reacted with force. Private security was hired, fencing erected, and people forcibly relocated to designated areas on the urban periphery. This was achieved at great cost (R3 million in the case of the Far East Bank) and by means reminiscent for many of the forced removals of the apartheid years. The effect has been to eradicate land invasions or demonstrations of popular power on this scale and of this visibility. Instead, the homeless are finding shelter invisibly in the already overcrowded townships, the inner city or private smallholdings on the urban periphery, where 'shack farming' has become a viable economic enterprise.

The metropolitan authority's efforts to redistribute resources in line with the injunctions of new local government legislation, the Local Government Transition Act of 1994, have also given rise to tensions. Under apartheid, white and black local authorities were administered differently and supported by different economic bases. White areas were governed by elected councils, which collected rates and service taxes from properties under their jurisdiction; black areas, where the administration boards of the early years gave way to nominally elected but widely discredited community councils, were financed by the central state. All properties in these areas were state assets, and businesses were prohibited. Since 1994, in addition to 'normalizing' local government administrations, there has also been a need to redistribute their resources. Residents and businesses in some white areas have reacted by appropriating the tactics used by township residents against apartheid: they have boycotted the payment of rates and service taxes, and have almost succeeded, despite negative legal rulings, in bringing the local authority to its knees.

The transformation of local government has produced, among other things, enormous lacunae in the bureaucratic procedures of planning – policies, frameworks, town planning procedures, zoning and building regulations, and so on. To start with, such procedures used to apply to only half the city; now they have also been held in abeyance by new legislation, with no new procedures yet in place. The result has been uncontrolled speculation across the city. From the hasty conversion of garages on suburban streets into shops or dry-cleaners, to the reuse of retail space in the inner city for housing or manufacturing, to the explosion of new suburban office parks, control of development is no longer in the hands of the city's officials. Instead it is in the hands of the entrepreneur – the hawker eking out a survival selling tomatoes and bananas, the Senegalese trader making cross-border deals from Johannesburg's east end, the casino developer pouring billions into rapacious theme parks. Everywhere development is taking up the slack, working through invisible networks of associations in the spaces between what was and what is still to be defined.

The few proposals that have been put forward for confronting the spatial separations of apartheid have met with resistance and been abandoned. For instance, the metropolitan authority's Rapid Land Development Programme, an innovative proposal to house 5,000 people from the city's most hazardously located communities on four pieces of land within the existing urban area, met with fierce resistance from surrounding residents. They organized protest meetings and marches, and blockaded streets to show their disapproval of the introduction of 'crime and poverty' into their areas. In all but one case local councils pulled back, swayed by the argument that poor people reduce property values and increase crime. In Lombardy East, adjacent to Alexandra, agreement was reached to proceed, and a small, pilot housing neighbourhood has been built.

To date, the only discourse that has tried to provide a logic for reconceptualizing urban development in apartheid's wake has been that of 'participative governance'. This underpins a number of discursive and institutional practices, such as community policing, land development objectives and public-private partnerships. These involve statutory joint decision-making, monitoring and implementation processes between the state, local authorities and citizens on every aspect of urban life, from safety and security to service provision, road-making, and health and leisure. While these processes remain new and need time to develop, one wonders to what extent they will exacerbate apartheid's divisions. Based as they are on the neo-liberal model of 'community' as a grouping of empowered individuals who voice their opinions, offer their expertise and take responsibility for their actions,[5] the citizens participating are those who already have the skills to do so. The poor, the marginalized, the uneducated, the 'illegal' are further excluded and resources channelled towards those with the voices to claim them.

Into this situation, a new discourse and set of practices have emerged – those of crime. Crime – petty, organized, invisible, brutal, commercial – is working on and through the surfaces of the city to produce a new landscape whose properties lie deep within and yet far beyond the spatial and social economies of the past. New urban spaces, new divisions of power, new urban cultures, whose primary properties are segregation, privatization, militarization and fortification, are emerging.

B

Crime in Johannesburg

> Petty crimes. Burglaries. Armed robberies. Assaults. Muggings. Attacks. Hijackings. Rapes. Murders. These things happen to our friends and colleagues. Our brothers and sisters. Our mothers and fathers. Our wives and husbands. Our children. Ordinary people. Ordinary life. Johannesburg is the near-death experience. Johannesburg is not, of course, the only city in the history of mankind to have gone to the edge and looked over ... It's just that in Johannesburg we don't get short sharp glimpses. We are rubbed raw, face to face with something most humans would prefer to avoid.[6]

During the apartheid years, crime in Johannesburg, and indeed in most of South Africa, was confined largely to black townships. White South Africa was immunized against crime by the state security system, whose strategies and tactics were designed to protect it. Ironically this has now positioned whites as uniformly privileged, racialized targets, as 'the enemy' in relation to those for whom state security meant oppression, exploitation and denial. In the past the criminal justice system was directed almost exclusively towards the policing of apartheid. The state security apparatus defended white rule through 'fire-force', incident-driven policing; the route to promotion for policemen and women was through the infamous state security branch.[7] Criminality, from the breaking of pass laws to the political violence of the 1980s and '90s, was defined almost exclusively as a negative relation to apartheid. A multitude of petty offences were criminalized through racially discriminatory laws. Conversely, extreme forms of violence were justified as weapons of struggle, both within the formal institutions of the state and beyond them, and not considered criminal by their perpetrators.[8]

New houses in Alexandra River Park Development Project, 1998.

During the 1980s, when the apartheid state faced its strongest challenge, crime increased significantly. This was the period when the townships burned – when politically inspired violence, state repression, state-sponsored vigilantism and third force killings were at their height; and when whites were most defended against knowing what was really going on, through the state security apparatus, state-controlled media and Christian National Education. According to police figures, over this period serious offences rose by 22 per cent, less serious ones by 17 per cent, murder by 32 per cent, rape by 24 per cent and burglary by 31 per cent.[9] Ignorance, silence, refusal, guilt, distance and apartheid's network of complicity lay between white South Africa and this inhuman reality.

The rate of increase in levels of crime peaked in 1990, the year in which political transition began, and then showed absolute increases over the following four years, with increases in the recorded levels of all crimes except murder (because of declining levels of political violence). While the murder rate declined by 7 per cent to 14,920 in 1994, assault increased by 18 per cent, rape by 42 per cent, robbery by 40 per cent, vehicle theft by 34 per cent and burglary by 20 per cent.[10] No accurate figures exist, but it is certain that commercial crime, concentrated in Johannesburg, Durban and Cape Town, also increased.

The political and social transformation has affected the country profoundly and on every level. As the old has been dismantled or displaced and the new set up, an inadequate and corrupt order has been exposed. Certainties have been expelled, and uncertainty prevails; deprivation has turned into entitlement, guilt into resentment, hope into fear; old attitudes have hardened, and old resistances have been entrenched; new alliances between old enemies have violated all principle; 'the other' has been redefined.

As in other countries undergoing transition, new areas for lawlessness and criminality have opened up as society and its instruments of control are reshaped. There has been a dramatic growth in organized crime – it is said that 481 criminal syndicates are now operating in the country, engaged in activities ranging from drug and weapon dealing to vehicle smuggling. In the first six months of 1996, the murder rate – 30 people killed per 100,000 head of population – was nearly four times that in the United States.[11] The criminal justice system has been unable to adjust to these new realities.

The state has placed great emphasis since 1994 on community policing as a tool for transforming the police service. However, the service remains underskilled in conventional policing functions, and the areas of detection, prosecution and incarceration are seriously flawed. In 1995, for instance, only 25 per cent of robberies, 20 per cent of housebreakings, 10 per cent of vehicle thefts and 50 per cent of murders were solved.[12]

The South African Police Services Act of 1995 established community police forums as a means of improving relations and establishing partnerships between communities and the police. Transforming the police force into a community-sensitive service and enhancing its accountability and transparency were additional objectives. The principle of community policing has created the potential to broaden the response to crime beyond mere law enforcement to include strategies like prevention and visible policing. A new style of policing has emerged, fostering personal contact between communities and police, cooperation between street committees and the police in combating crime, the participation of citizens in running and resourcing police stations, and so on.

In certain parts of Johannesburg, such as Yeoville, Norwood and the peri-urban areas of the north, these methods are proving effective. In these areas, citizens and business interests generally come from a liberal bourgeois tradition and have the resources of time and money to supplement public sector policing. But the notion of 'community' is extremely tenuous in poor areas, which are fragile, unstable, constantly shifting and divided.[13] Here people have far fewer resources than their middle-class counterparts to devote to engaging proactively in joint policing initiatives. Their response to crime is often simply to move.[14] Community policing initiatives in such areas have not proved successful.

The space between things falling apart and things being put together is this highly charged, criminalized one. Having its roots in the old social economy of apartheid, it is an intense network of violations, attacks, counter-attacks, incisions and manoeuvres. New divisions between victim and criminal, fear and bravado, vulnerability and immunity are criss-crossing the old ones of race, class and gender in the creation of Johannesburg's new economic, social and spatial order.

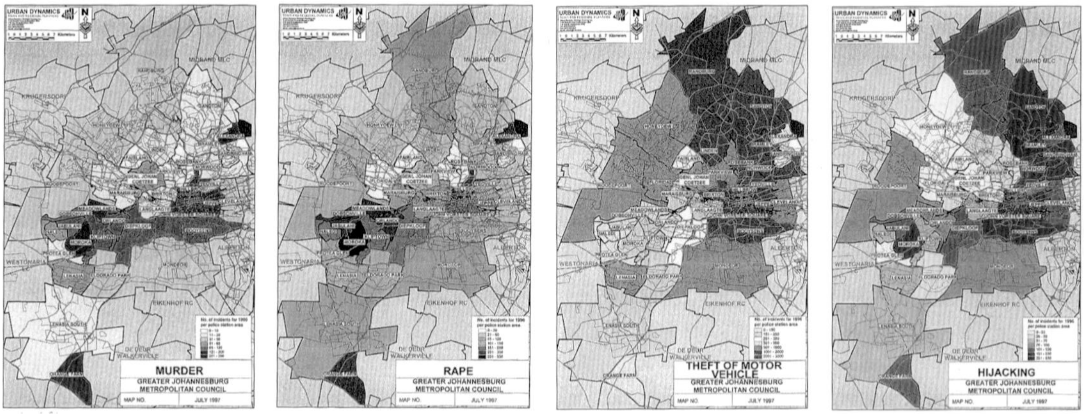

Crime discriminates

> That afternoon in Rosebank I felt I was walking among The Living. I had come within a hair's breadth, a whim, of being killed. And now I was back. That's how it felt: I was back. I was walking around. I looked the same as everyone. But I was walking among The Living ... Six months later: I still have no idea what actually happens deep inside when you find yourself standing a metre from your own death.[15]

The geography of crime is a geography of vulnerability. In Greater Johannesburg, it is drawing to the surface new dimensions of apartheid's mapping of the city and adding further dimensions to its social and spatial divisions.

A recent mapping of the city's crime indicates that the areas most disadvantaged or least protected under apartheid are now most vulnerable to murder, armed robbery, rape and violent assault – Soweto, Alexandra and Orange Farm.[16] These areas were characterized by the most extreme forms of political disempowerment and economic hardship. They are fragmented, disjointed, demeaning places, designed as warehousing for migrant labour. They exhibit high levels of domestic violence, violence against women, rape and murder. The mining land, disembowelled and abandoned, that separates Soweto from the inner city is particularly susceptible to these violent crimes against the body. Rapes, murders and serial killings frequently occur on this polluted and infertile waste ground.

By contrast the inner city, where levels of serious crime are also high, is cluttered, intensely overcrowded and unkempt. It is owned by no one. Abandoned gradually from the mid-1980s onwards by property owners fleeing its foreseen demise, its economic and social base is now substantially outside the law. People simply take over buildings; foreign nationals produce and sell goods for export markets; health and safety standards are widely infringed; buildings are dilapidated and overcrowded. People cram streets and pavements with makeshift structures, cheap commodities and litter; taxis line pavements and fill open spaces. Crime is fast, armed, anonymous, unexpected and invisible.

Roodepoort, a middle-class urban node to the west of the city, previously a separate town supplying urban services to the mines and related industries, has seen massive capital flight in recent years. Its streets and shops have been deserted as mines have closed and suburban shopping centres have attracted business to more secure retail environments. The development of business activity in the nearby township of Dobsonville has further contributed to its decline. Johannesburg Metropolitan Council statistics indicate that this vacancy has been filled by high incidences of drug-related crime. It provides a blanket of cover for the lucrative drug trade.

Spatial maps of crime in the Greater Johannesburg Metropolitan Area.

The traditionally white residential suburbs are most vulnerable to so-called less serious crime (motor vehicle theft and theft from residential and business properties), the incidence of which is very low in the former townships – due at least in part to a lack of reporting, and possibly to small stands and busy streets. Increasingly, however, these less serious crimes have become associated with extreme brutality – the taking of hostages, murder, rape, violent assault. Gangs cruise suburban streets after dark, armed with laser-sighted pistols, Uzi semi-automatic weapons and military issue R5 rifles, and employ terror tactics to intimidate and overpower families.[17] Victims are shuffled from room to room and continually threatened and assaulted while burglaries are taking place, or are held captive and guarded while rooms are methodically stripped and valuables removed. Car hijackings are similarly accompanied by brutal attack and threat to life.[18] These crimes are committed under conditions which render the body extremely vulnerable – spacious homes, abandoned during the day, sprawling lawns, thick shrubberies, high walls, empty suburban streets, long driveways, anonymous freeways. What were signs of privilege have become conditions of extreme vulnerability as apartheid's barriers are torn down.

Segregation

> It is a Wednesday evening and the winter chill is setting in. The usually bustling streets of Pimville are deserted, and not a barking dog can be heard. Nombuyiselo Ntolo stands in front of her house, her feet covered in the dew from the long grass of her small garden. The small gate is wide open and her little red Uno is parked around the corner of the house, almost against the wall, next to the bedroom window ... Does she feel unsafe? Well, she says, looking across the road, 'that house over there belongs to a policeman, the four guys who stay opposite me are criminals – that car parked over there must be their fiftieth – and they have guns. If they hear a noise they'll come out with their guns. I am also installing burglar bars. What more do I need?'[19]

Differing levels and types of crime are reflected in different perceptions of the problem and the strategies used to combat it in the different areas, the outcome of which is to reinforce the patterns of apartheid segregation.[20]

Residents of the traditionally white middle-class suburbs and property owners in the inner city regard crime as the prime threat to confidence in the new South Africa. It is seen as a breakdown of policing standards and a sign of the weakness of the new state. The black poor are automatically identified as the perpetrators (black people whose socio-economic status has improved tend to share this view).[21] Middle-class people respond to crime either by leaving the country or by doing everything possible to insulate themselves from it.

Householders install ever more sophisticated physical security measures. They raise their low, picturesque garden walls by two, three or sometimes four metres, and top them with spikes or glass chips; they unfurl razor wire (a particularly cruel form of barbed wire developed in South Africa for counter-insurgency purposes) along their perimeters; they add electric fencing, designed to shock when touched; they install automated driveway gates and intercom systems. Entry into houses and even passage through them is barred by burglar-proofing of prison-like dimensions and layer upon layer of metal security gates, which divide various sections into secure zones – to pass from sleeping to living to kitchen areas may involve unlocking three security gates. Security consultants abound, offering advice on the most effective security ('If I were you, ma'am, I'd skip the palisades and go straight to the electric fencing'). People spend substantial amounts of their disposable income ensuring that their homes are secured. If one house on a street installs an electric fence, the others feel pressured to follow suit, afraid of becoming the most vulnerable property on the block. Security has become a way of life.[22]

It has also become big business. Since 1980, security has been the fastest-growing sector in the

South African economy, with an annual growth rate of 18 per cent. Private security personnel now outnumber the police by two to one.[23] Names like Standby, Fearless, Stallion, Sentry, Peaceforce and Armed Response hint at the services offered by different companies. Some portray themselves as bobbies on the beat: Sentry Security, Your Friendly Security. Others aspire to the image of the Los Angeles Police Department: For Real Security, Call in The Force – Peaceforce Security. Yet others promote their mercenary past: A New Deal ... A Young, Dynamic, Efficient Guard Force ... Star Security: In Israel We Fought for Freedom! In Rhodesia We Fought Terrorism! In South Africa We Fight Crime! Many in the private security industry are disgruntled policemen, laid-off counter-insurgency operatives of the former South African Defence Force or cadres of the liberation armies.

These companies provide minimal levels of proactive patrolling, and electronic guarding and armed response functions. Some conduct the fight against crime as a paramilitary force, offering sophisticated weaponry and armoured vehicles as part of the service. They have contributed significantly to the militarization of space and society in recent years. The distribution which developed during the apartheid era – 'while private security firms policed the suburbs, the former South African Police concentrated on policing apartheid'[24] – still operates.

In the townships south of the city, where people have been living with high levels of violence for decades, crime is not seen as a threat to democracy but rather as a symptom of social and economic inequality, a sign that political democracy has not yet been consolidated in the social and economic spheres, and that its institutions need strengthening.[25] Here the protection of the working class and the poor remains in the hands of the police, who are short of resources (and often distrusted). The devices used in middle-class areas, such as burglar-proofing and alarm systems, are rarely found, partly because people cannot afford them, partly because houses in the townships still belong to the state, and partly because they would be useless anyway, as the perpetrators of crime are most often not from outside the walls but from within the household circle.[26] Township residents simply keep their doors locked.

The inner city areas of Johannesburg, 'greying' since the early 1980s, exhibit the symptoms of

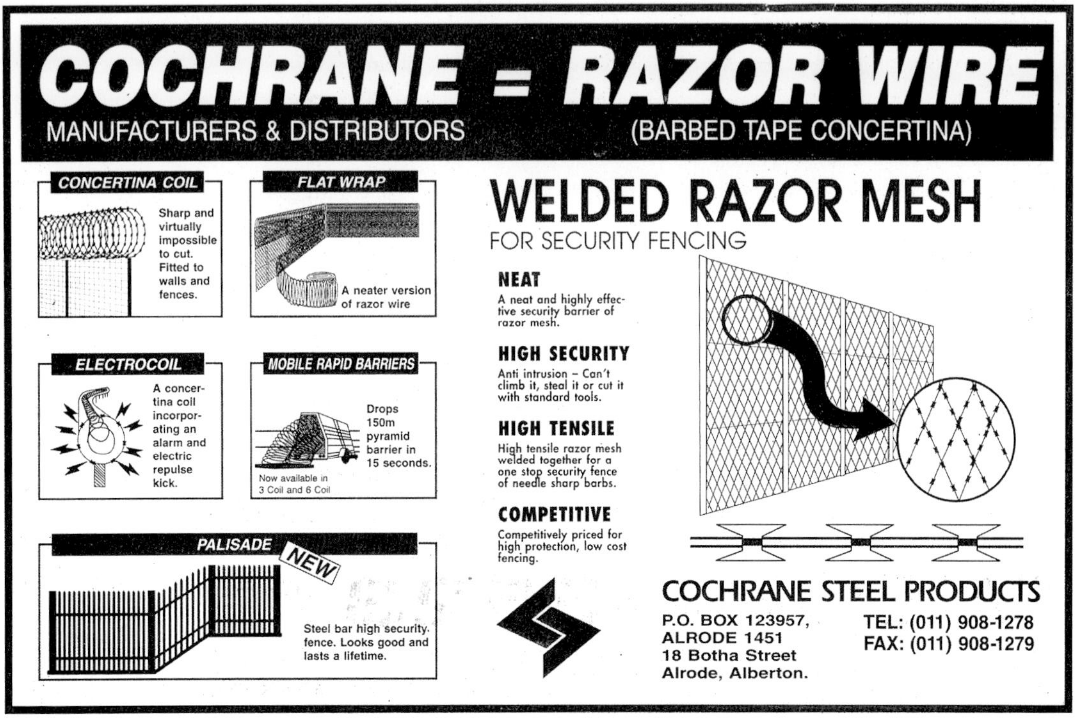

political, social and economic liberalization most visibly. Property here is still largely in the hands of the old white monopolies – pension and provident funds, mining houses, banks and the like. Streets and public spaces are in the hands of the people – street vendors, taxi drivers, the unemployed, and black consumers, for whom the inner city remains the most convenient place to shop. Between these two groups lies a gulf, filled to a large extent by ignorance, fear, paranoia, entitlement, resentment and socio-economic inequality. The major institutions, seeing their investments eroded by capital flight and demographic shifts, have pointed a finger at the new government and its inability to deal with crime or manage the public environment. This argument has been adopted by those in public office – who are now based in the city centre – and they have launched many fire-fighting initiatives to combat crime, including police blitzes, the training of traffic officers in policing, partnerships between police and street traders, and between police and the business sector, the creation of 'Business Improvement Districts', and the installation of closed-circuit television cameras. All in an attempt to protect and preserve the image of middle-class prosperity in the face of increasing socio-economic diversity, a certain amount of decay and the absence of law and order.

These dynamics are producing an increasingly disparate, separated city. The gaps between the worlds of the township, the inner city and the suburb are widening. The chances that the people of this city will develop a sense of shared space, of shared destiny grow slimmer by the day.

Privatization

> 'If the council allows this to continue it's a case of total anarchy and vigilantism,' says Adv Kraut, whose front gate is presided over by no less than four 'Beware of the dog' signs, with one canine dripping blood from menacing bared fangs. 'If we take this to its logical but absurd conclusion, my fear is that when residents become aware that they can close off roads with impunity ... most of the roads in Gauteng will soon be privatized and closed off. So in order to travel anywhere we'll be like rats in a maze.'[27]

One consequence of the growing economy of crime has been an increasing privatization of the public realm. New legislation gives precincts of private property the right to decide about and provide their own services, over and above those of the local authority; cleansing, security, licensing of street trading, gatekeeping of urban parks all now potentially lie in the hands of the private sector. New rules of exclusion based on private property rights are beginning to shape public space and its use. In the inner city a number of 'Business Improvement Districts', proclaiming their presence on colourful banners and flags, and featuring hanging baskets of petunias and cheerful, bib-clad parking attendants, are trying to attract desirable tenants and consumers back from the commercial enclaves of the north. Driven by the imperatives of private capital rather than social need, they reveal the uneven distribution of wealth and the collision of different values in the inner city. Pockets of privilege and ghettos of shame, businessmen clutching briefcases and taxi-industry hit men bearing AK-47s exist side by side in this extraordinary conflation of space, time, powers and cultures.

In the suburbs, walls, booms and security personnel are transforming streets, parks, offices, shops, suburbs and entertainment areas into security enclaves with controlled access points; those living within the walls are sometimes even offered private schooling for their children. Residents clash frequently with local authority officials and the police in attempts to close off roads without permission. As citizens close streets, wall off suburbs, install security gates and employ the services of private security companies, anything from a street to an entire suburb is excised from the public network.[28] For those living inside these barriers, there is a new sense of security and communality. They can leave their gates open, children can play in the streets and move freely between each other's homes again, and crime levels fall.[29] But the cost paid for this new communality is that freedom of movement is restricted, chance contact is eradicated and public interaction limited to that between self-defined, homogeneous groups. And the result is that separation deepens and a sense of shared space is lost.

Militarization

> It is clear there is military training involved in these heists. It is so obvious, as in the Bronkhorstspruit robbery when, within seconds, two people fell victim to precision shooting, with tracer bullets going right through their heads.[30]

The militarization of South Africa is not new: in the 1980s it was virtually a military state. The apartheid authorities mapped space along military lines according to the ideology of 'total onslaught'. They destabilized surrounding countries, trained covert paramilitary units, and developed counterinsurgency practices, the full extent and barbarism of which have only started to emerge at the Truth and Reconciliation Commission.

On its side, the African National Congress adopted strategies to infiltrate the country, to build up internal underground structures and to render the townships ungovernable. In 1976 a turning point was reached in the militarization of the struggle against apartheid. After the Soweto uprising there was an exodus of young people from South Africa for military training in the camps of the ANC and other liberation movements, and this continued throughout the 1980s. These cadres were the élite of the struggle. Politically educated and trained not only in the strategies and tactics of guerrilla warfare, but also in organization, propaganda, intelligence and counter-intelligence, they formed the backbone of the war against apartheid. After 1990, the ANC continued to recruit, arm and train internal underground structures known as Self-Defence Units, primarily to counter pre-election violence in KwaZulu-Natal and Gauteng.

Some of these cadres regard the suspension of the armed struggle by their national leaders to make way for negotiations as a betrayal of everything they gave their lives for. The transition has drastically reduced, if not obliterated, the significance of the military for the liberation struggle. The politics and machineries of war and insurrection have been displaced by those of social and economic development, fiscal restraint and globalization. War has given way to politics. Despite assurances that they would be integrated into the new South African Defence Force,[31] many have been demobilized, while others have deserted military camps, apparently disillusioned with conventional military life.

Since the first democratic election, the state has revised its entire security network and the national security strategy upon which it was based, moving beyond counter-insurgency and the administration of total war to emphasize socio-economic, developmental, psychological and regional dynamics.[32] Many of the old security policemen, schooled in the ideology and methods of total onslaught, have not been able to adjust. Ample evidence has emerged, through the Truth and Reconciliation Commission and other avenues, that some of those previously central to the security apparatus in its most sinister guises – such as the Civil Cooperation Bureau and the Vlakplaas Unit – feel betrayed and have established links with the criminal underworld.

Demilitarization has thus left many feeling betrayed and placeless: operators of the old security apparatus disowned by their political leaders; cadres of the struggle, demobilized and disillusioned. United in their sense of having been discarded by the new political order, these elements have come together and established new strategic alliances.

During apartheid, both sides amassed weapons of war, inside and outside the country. The peaceful transition to democracy has released vast numbers of these, which the state has not found the means to monopolize.[33] Instead, they have been circulating on illegal routes and arming increasingly violent and militarized crime.

These three consequences of the transition – the sense of betrayal by former freedom fighters, the disaffection of former security policemen, and the ready availability of illegal weapons – have created explosive configurations that are particularly susceptible to alliances with international crime syndicates. Elements of the Russian mafia, involved in smuggling diamonds and weapons, Chinese triads, who specialize in the trade in endangered species, and Nigerian drug rings have moved into the gaps.[34]

The most visible of these militarized crimes involve vehicles – car theft, vehicle hijacking and, more recently, a series of military-style cash heists on the highways of Johannesburg and surrounding areas. The transport routes of the city have become high-risk zones, where motorists suddenly confront shoot-outs reminiscent of scenes in movies like *Heat*. Masterminded by a former Self-Defence Unit member, who has brazenly appeared at official government functions, these heists have orchestrated the actions of employees in cash-in-transit companies (who supply details of vehicle movements), underpaid policemen and paramilitary operatives in precisely planned swoops on the armoured vehicles of private security companies.[35] Security personnel are ruthlessly gunned down, usually on busy public freeways, and vast amounts of cash stolen. In recent months some bank and supermarket robberies and vehicle hijackings have taken on these military qualities too.[36] It is no longer surprising to see men armed with automatic rifles outside the local grocery, standing at taxi ranks or riding shotgun on delivery vans.

In short, any citizen now entering the public and semi-public spaces of the city – streets, highways, shopping centres, parks – might well witness or be caught in the crossfire of increasingly violent crime. Crime has been militarized, the civilian spaces of the city ravaged by its brutal manoeuvres. The state's response has been to call in the military: in 1997, for instance, the Defence Force was called in to patrol the streets of Hillbrow, an inner-city suburb, when crime on its streets spiralled out of control. All kinds of crimes, from bank robberies to domestic burglaries, are now carried out with weapons of war and planned with the precision of those trained in warfare. Ordinary civilians are defenceless against this kind of crime, except by arming themselves – and so continuing the cycle.

Fortification

> To enter you pass through two security gates, each with its own intercom. The first lets you into a courtyard, the second into the house. Despite the vigorous security measures, on January 13th this year, the resident drove into his garage and from his car window, found himself staring up the barrel of an AK47.[37]

The middle-class is fortifying itself. People surround their homes and businesses with walls, razor wire, electrified fencing, security gates, intercoms, cameras and armed human shields to blank out the criminal reality of the public realm. Neighbourliness has been replaced by isolation as a laager mentality reasserts itself. The white suburbs, with their tree-lined streets, grassed verges, snug suburban homes and good neighbourliness are being reconstructed according to the logic of fortification. New barriers are erected and new definitions of the urban enacted. And yet security remains precarious. Residents of my own street, unable to introduce effective access control because the street is a thoroughfare, rely on the somewhat quaint practice of blowing whistles to alert neighbours in moments of distress.

The new city is being constructed on the same logic. Speculators combine nostalgia for lost suburbia with the need to fortify against or blank out the grim reality. Gone are the old rationalities of urban management, town planning or public health in the shaping of the environment. Gone are the technologies of race. In their place are the new technologies of security, image and style:

> Dainfern: Invest in your future! Country-style living in a secure natural environment. Perimeter walls topped by electric fences, radio and telephone links to security control centres, 24hr perimeter and entry control guards. Life is for living ... at Dainfern. Crestwood Hill: In your drive to the top you've discovered the power to shape destiny ... Now you've found the address that reflects your success ... Designed and styled for the aware – guardhouse, electric fencing and intercoms,

Security personnel at a suburban barricade, 1996.

walled stands, lockable 'Hollywood' garage. Tanglewood Theme Village: tucked away in a secret forest setting ... you'll find a very special place called Tanglewood. Unique upmarket theme village, real country lifestyle, three eco-sensitive architectural styles – Italian Tuscany/Traditional Highveld/Environmentally Aware. High Meadow Grove: Gather beneath the trees and the great blue sky – take a walk, ride a bike, play squash, swim, or simply enjoy a lazy day with friends in the village estate. Security centre, controlled single access, perimeter wall, electric fence top. Brentwood Estate: We undo crime so you can do life. No more worrying about strange sounds outside your home at night because at Parkor, we put security first – secure home, secure investment, secure future. Needwood: Paradise regained – a totally secure environment, tranquil country living, completely self-contained.

Words conjure up images and create aspirations for lifestyles divorced entirely from reality – Victorian, Tudor, Mediterranean, Medieval, Modern. Style becomes a vehicle for denying the violent context of the city and creating the image of a preferred lifestyle; if you can't emigrate, you can at least dig in, with style. The city is becoming a giant theme park, an assemblage of fortified and styled enclaves, residential, commercial, retail or leisure, to which access is guarded and selectively granted. Gaining entry is difficult – much more so than in the 1980s, when security guards, backed up by images of limpet mines and hand grenades, searched bags at shopping centres. Now impregnable perimeter walls and access points set up rules of exclusion and inclusion for most aspects of urban life. Guards record entry and exit times, personal details and motives. No photographs are allowed. To be inside is to be safe and someone; to be outside is to be unknown and feared; and to be in between is to be nowhere.

These so-called 'Planned Community Projects' or 'Security Parks', sprawling over the slopes of northern Johannesburg, are obliterating public space from the urban realm. Spaces between are simply movement channels along which the body must pass in moving from one insulated enclave to another. The city is further fragmented, dispersed and divided.

One city or many?

One of the most devastating and ineradicable traces of apartheid will be its planning of the city. The marks apartheid left on human lives will fade in the course of time. But its spatial logic will continue to affect people's daily lives for generations to come. Because of apartheid, people live great distances from where they work; standards of urban infrastructure vary enormously; parts of the city are devoid of shops, businesses, entertainment venues and schools, while others are saturated with them; chasms separate one citizen from another, so much so that people feel like tourists in each other's worlds. Since 1994, these divisions have not been blurred through the efficacies of principled, moral urban administration or planning as might have been expected, but rather through new, less normative logics – those of necessity, speculation and crime. A new city is emerging, in which certain of apartheid's social and spatial divisions are being deepened, at the same time as other, largely illicit ways of controlling, managing and using urban space challenge its rules.

Necessity has driven the urban poor to reinvent the city in ways that challenge the utopianism of modernist planning. People live in the cracks, cook on the streets, bed down on the pavements; shops appear on street corners; warehouses shelter families; office blocks become factories; houses turn into shops; chickens, goats, mealies appear on inner city kerbs; Taiwanese watches are displayed next to Nigerian bags, next to local tomatoes. The old oppositions between urban and rural, public and private, residential and business, black and white merge in indistinguishable new combinations; boundaries are porous; peoples merge; the city is vitally, colourfully grey. The normalization of this spontaneity, in the interests of good governance, is no longer possible – the scale of the intervention required and the management of its consequences lie beyond the scope of the democratic, neo-liberal state; and even if it were possible, it would bring to the surface hosts of networks, upon whose invisibility the fragile economic survival of the city's poor depends.

This city of necessity is traversed by the city of crime and of speculation. Crime creates new centres of power and locales of weakness. It weaves through the soft underside of the emerging landscape – the inner city suburbs, the townships, the mining land. It makes incisive forays into the vulnerable white suburbs, where signs of privilege become indicators for attack. Smart cars, high walls, stylishly designed homes, expensive jewellery, electronic devices, empty buildings – all these signs of luxury, wealth or status become their inverse, indications of a lucrative haul. Protection involves ever more sophisticated technologies and defensive lifestyles. A new security aesthetic dominates: walls, wire, barbs, locks, gates, intercoms, fortifications ... fading into fantasy and pastiche. Combine this with the signs of poverty, with squalor, irregularity, clutter, leaking sewer pipes, leering corrugated walls, broken windows, and you have the image of the emerging South African city.

Not just crime, but the elaborate defence against it – the car-tracking device, the walled suburb, the insurance policy – is becoming the base of the new social economy of the city, with huge interests vested in keeping it that way. Public discourse is dominated by crime; after-dinner talk, braaivleis (barbecue) chatter, newspaper columns, political rhetoric turn with predictable repetition around crime, its victims, its culprits, its consequences. Public interaction is marked by caution and suspicion. Social divisions are deepening, social circles narrowing.

While national political rhetoric stresses the importance of commonly held values and communally held goals, the lives of ordinary South Africans are increasingly marked by division and self-interest. Society is fractured into a myriad of exclusive, hostile, intersecting or conflated circles. Some see this as symptomatic of a society in transition, waiting for visionary leaders to instil new public values to which all can aspire and so overcome the divisions of the past.[38] Others see the new forces at work on the city and its economy transforming them irreversibly into a conglomeration of different and often (but not necessarily) hostile worlds, developing along different lines, yet held together in structural interdependence by speculation, scarcity and, if not crime, at least an underground economy. It remains to be seen which of these views more accurately describes the emerging landscape, but the experience in other countries over the last decade suggests that we are more likely to move relentlessly towards a multiplicity of worlds in a divided city.

Research assistance by Thorsten Deckler and Shiuan-Wen Chu.

Entrance gates to security suburbs: Brentwood Estate, Bushwillow and Beverley Hills.

►B3 ►**C2** ►C4 ►E11

low to vote in the loc… elections

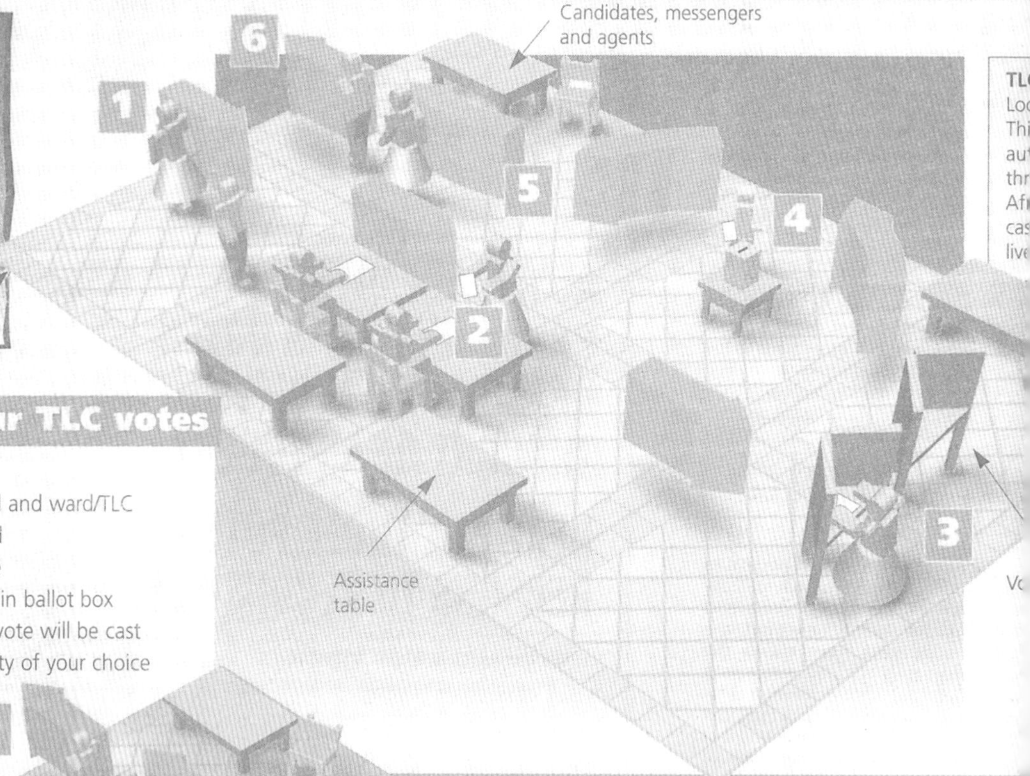

TL…
Loc…
Thi…
au…
thr…
Af…
cas…
live…

asting your TLC votes

ID book checked
Voter's roll checked and ward/TLC
ballot papers issued
Cast ward/TLC vote
Place ballot papers in ballot box
An additional 2nd vote will be cast
for the political party of your choice
Exit

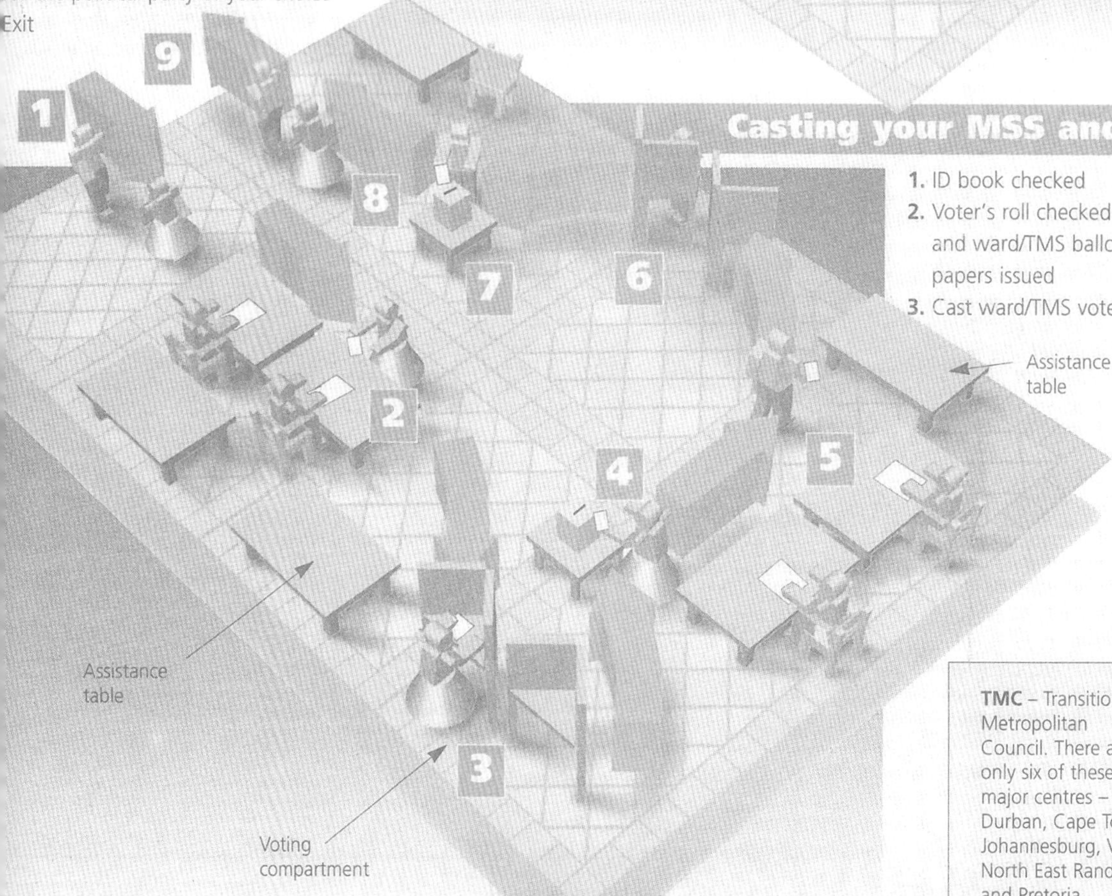

Casting your MSS and TM…

1. ID book checked
2. Voter's roll checked and ward/TMS ballot papers issued
3. Cast ward/TMS vote
4. Pla… in… bo…
5. Vo… an… pa…
6. Ca…
7. Pl… ba…
8. Ar… vo… th… yo…
9. Ex…

TMC – Transitional Metropolitan Council. There are only six of these in major centres – Durban, Cape Town, Johannesburg, Vaal, North East Rand and Pretoria.

M… S… L… a… o… m… w… re… T…

RAPHIC: FRANCOIS SMIT

Silence!

Joachim Schönfeldt

B

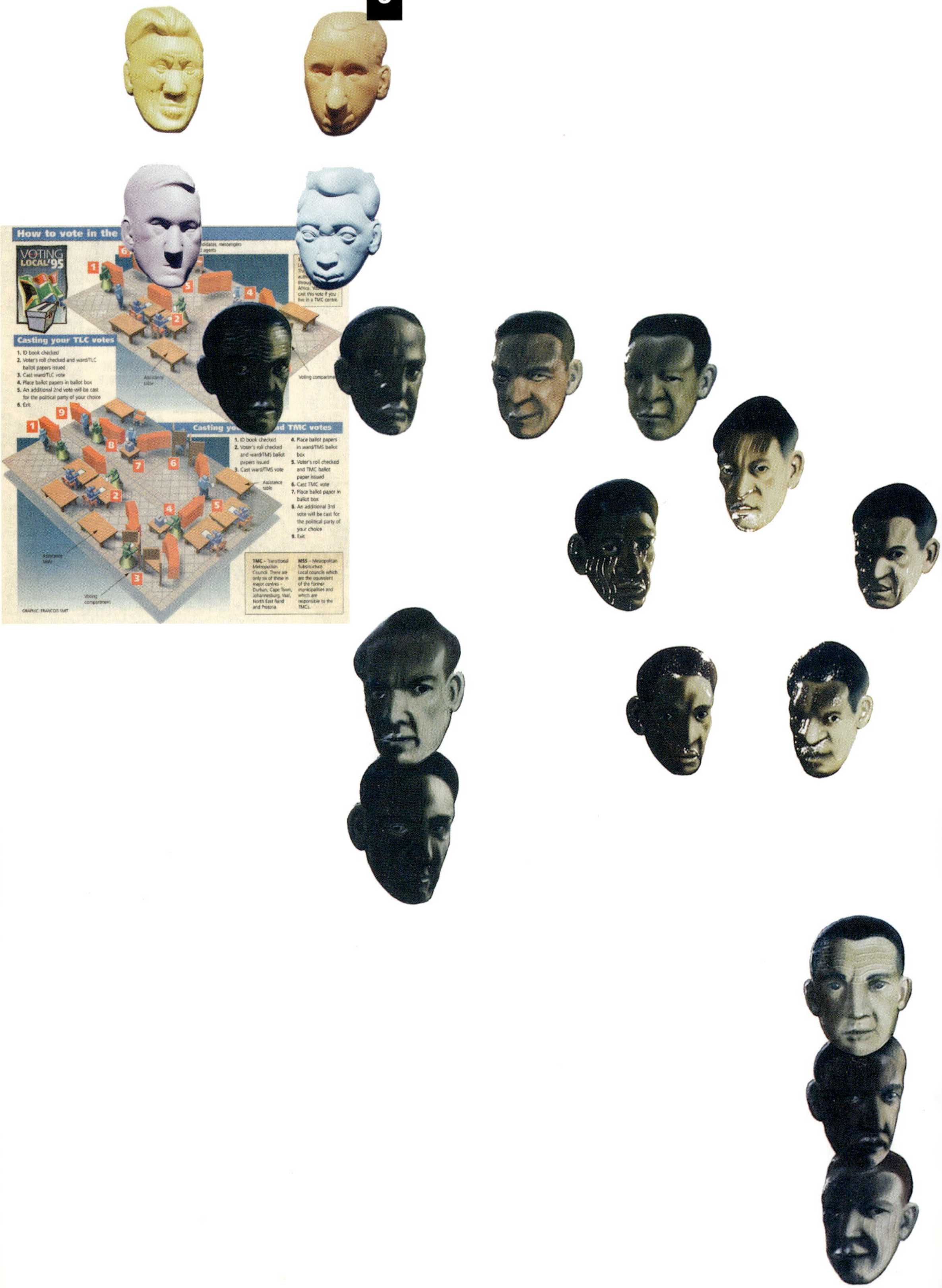
How to vote in the
VOTING LOCAL'95
ndidates, messengers
agents
cast this vote if you
live in a TMC centre
Casting your TLC votes
1. ID book checked
2. Voter's roll checked and ward/TLC ballot papers issued
3. Cast ward/TLC vote
4. Place ballot papers in ballot box
5. An additional 2nd vote will be cast for the political party of your choice
6. Exit
Assistance table
Voting compartme
Casting yo
nd TMC votes
1. ID book checked
2. Voter's roll checked and ward/TMS ballot papers issued
3. Cast ward/TMS vote
4. Place ballot papers in ward/TMS ballot box
5. Voter's roll checked and TMC ballot paper issued
6. Cast TMC vote
7. Place ballot paper in ballot box
8. An additional 3rd vote will be cast for the political party of your choice
9. Exit
Assistance table
Assistance table
Voting compartment
TMC – Transitional Metropolitan Council. There are only six of these in major centres – Durban, Cape Town, Johannesburg, Vaal, North East Rand and Pretoria.
MSS – Metropolitan Substructure. Local councils which are the equivalent of the former municipalities and which are responsible to the TMCs.
GRAPHIC: FRANCOIS SMIT

prison island.
Leaders of the African National Congress, the Pan Africanist Congress, Black Consciousness
Movement … other groups were jailed there.
housed there. Cr
Island. The last o
prisoner transfer
B
Tidal pool used
by female lepers
Three 9" guns
for defence during
World War II
The light house
built in 1863
1
– the highest
the island
Landing strip
for aircraft
Stone
Van Riebeeck's
quarry
Staff
graveyard
The Anglican
Church
built
Lime quarry
6
The prison
8
graveyard
The island
school
4
The old male
leper church,
1895
Site of former
7
The old leper morgue,
now a bank
Administration
buildings
Medium
security prison
Correctional
services facility
The Kramat
former
female
leper colony
Quarry
Main penguin
nesting area
Dias
0
0.25
0.5
0.75
ESCAPE:
some who
tried
1659: Autshumato esca
1690: A convict, Jan Ry
Robben Island.
1820: The Xhosa prophe
ter, tried to escap
man and Trompe
the consparacy, S
is still sometimes
OW
ttlement was built at the
and to accommodate a
g the early 1840s a
dence and personage
on Minto's Hill in 1864.
ivity took place on the
KGROUND AN
d is a low lying lozenge of rock and sand, gua
able Bay. The early Dutch called the Island "R
Eiland" - "Robbe" being the Dutch word for seals. There w
RDP
1
2
3
4
5
6
7
8
RATES OFFICE

Appropriated spaces
Santu Mofokeng

Home is an appropriated space; it does not exist objectively in reality. The notion of 'home' is a fiction we create out of a need to belong.

Home is a place most people have never been to. Home serves a similar function to zero in mathematics. It provides us with a beginning or a basis from which to evaluate other spaces: how they fulfil functional and aesthetic needs as we relate to or move through them in the business of living.

Here is another kind of appropriation of space. A look at how people appropriate space in order to invest spiritual meaning in it. This is a phenomenon which is not necessarily peculiar to South Africa, although it does seem peculiarly pervasive here.

Nation-building in this country in the 1920s was informed by a need to remove black people from places designated white and urban, and to dispatch them to the ethnic ghettos of the countryside. Such space as there is in the cities does not adequately fulfil the needs – or is deemed inappropriate for the ritual and spiritual needs – of the majority of black people. As for the other places of prayer, they frequently find them alienating.

1 'New Jerusalem' of Jackson Hlungwani, Mbhokota, Northern Province.

2 Clarens, Free State.

3 Nederduits Gereformeerde Kerk, Ladysmith.

4 Botshabelo Mission, Free State.

5 Doornfontein, Johannesburg.

6 Doornfontein, Johannesburg.

7 Delta Park, Johannesburg.

8 Salt River, Wakkerstroom.

INTERIOR DESIGNS

Homesteads and headrests

Rayda Becker

A linocut print by Sandile Goje entitled *Meeting of Two Cultures* (1993) sets the scene for this short essay. It literally illustrates an aspect of the discourse on rural architecture in South Africa and shows how other kinds of objects can serve as catalysts in the interpretation of architecture.

The bodies of the figures in the *Meeting of Two Cultures* have been transformed into houses. On the left, the torso and head have been replaced by a cone-on-cylinder dwelling (known colloquially as a *rondavel*) with an arched doorway, thatched roof and finger-painted walls; on the right, the body-surrogate is a rectangular building of bricks and mortar with four recessed windows, which seem to be lit from within. The limbs sustain the dialectic: one pair of legs is black and barefooted, while the other is clothed and shod. The hands, which are black and white, register and reinforce the persistent South African preoccupation with race and colour. Together these imaginative constructs make visible the two cultures of the work's title and give form to an oppositional discourse. On the left, the traditional, indigenous and rural; on the right, the modern, imported and urban. Other binaries are present too, for instance, in the method of building (the handmade as opposed to the manufactured) and the degree of complexity (one room as opposed to many).

The people-as-houses are shaking hands, that Western sign of male greeting, fellowship and reconciliation. The surrounding landscape is desolate, and in the light of the title we may be tempted to interpret it as a place and a past ravaged by the differences the work is meant to symbolize. But the encounter between the figures overrides that reading, and ultimately the work is optimistic, reflecting the time in which it was produced, that euphoric moment between the unbanning of the political organizations and the birth of the promised 'New South Africa'. The work is witty, charming, comical, and the artist has made visible the discourse around rural and urban homesteads; but in his thinking about difference, he has also simplified the dialogue and reinforced stereotypes. In reality, the situation in Southern Africa is not that clear-cut. Square houses and stone buildings are also traditional, to mention one example, as are large towns. Although the question prompted by this last observation cannot be answered here, it is worth asking: Would these large towns built

Woman lying on her headrest, Manjacaze, Mozambique, c. 1938.
Photograph by Reverend E. Kaltenrider.

B

Sandile Goje, *Meeting of Two Cultures*, 1993.

for sizeable populations, the ruins of which now lie scattered in the rural areas of the subcontinent, be considered urban? Or is that term reserved for modern cities built on foreign lines?

In the 19th century, before the advent of mechanized transport, and in a time of change from subsistence to a cash economy, men would walk from the countryside to the cities, and mainly to the mines, in search of employment. Walking severely limited what they could carry with them to town. Shangaan workers from Mozambique carried 'blankets, clothing, pots, knobkerries, a sleeping mat and rolls of tobacco for exchange purposes'.[1] Headrests, though they were small and easy to carry, were not brought to the cities, which is surprising given their highly personal and significant content, and they play no role in the formation of mine culture.[2] These wooden 'pillows' were originally designed to protect the elaborate hairstyles of their users, but through use, ownership and personal history there accrued to them a greater value, which transcended their utilitarian function.

In another time (before the 1940s) and another place (the rural areas) headrests were very much a part of daily life. They were common, individually owned and used every night, but they were also cherished. Like certain other personal objects, headrests were intimately associated with the body. Sieber put it this way: 'Objects constantly handled ... are believed to be imbued with a physiological exuviae as well as with the mystical quintessence of his individuality, creating a powerful psychic bond between owner and object.'[3]

A headrest could be used by no one except the owner while he was alive.[4] As the object became stained with sweat and was decorated with personal materials it became more individualized. Indeed, it became so much a part of the owner that, upon his death, the headrest, together with other personal items, was usually buried, burnt or placed on the grave. On the other hand, because of this highly personal, accumulated content, the headrest might also be preserved for ancestor evocation and rituals associated with the dead. The use and meaning of the headrest changed during the owner's lifetime, and could change again after his death. Some headrests thus gained value with the passage of time.

Only two of the 350 headrests listed in the MuseumAfrica collections in Johannesburg were found in mine compounds.[5] One of these is South African and is classified Zulu, while the other is Chinese.[6] Obviously, then, the majority of extant headrests were found in rural areas. Since headrests were used by married people, their absence in the cities would suggest that only unmarried men worked on the mines. While this was true initially, the situation changed for a number of reasons, primarily the introduction of cash and the influence this had on the payment of the bride price.[7] It was a change appreciated by mine management, who preferred to employ slightly older married men. Marital status alone does not explain why headrests were left at home, and there may be a more compelling reason which sheds some light on attitudes towards the rural homestead.

As a marriage item, the headrest provided a bond to the owner's wife; it also represented a connection to his kin, his ancestors and his ekhaya. Although 'ekhaya' can be translated simply as 'home', its connotations are much richer, suggesting a place of tradition and custom (a sanctuary), of family and value (a temple), and of history and memory (an archive). The headrest was a deeply significant home item, and as such could not be taken to the bleak, communal compounds where labourers were lodged in cities like Kimberley and Johannesburg. Apart from explaining the absence of headrests in the city, this view reminds us that the idea of 'home' carries more profound associations than an outsider can begin to grasp, and that the dual identities constructed by the urban and the rural are accordingly more complex.

Names are a revealing index of this. Black people tend to have many names, one of which is kept for city use.[8] Like so much else in the city, such names deny or conceal a sense of home and African identity. Dual lives become a way of being. Anyone who has taken a road out of the city on a Friday evening, or has travelled back from the countryside on a Sunday night, will know that for many who live and work in the city it can never be 'home'. The road is animated by lines of lights, a living thread, a vital contact between city and country.

Headrest (xikhigelo) from Bushbuckridge, Mpumalanga.

Headrests have not survived as items of everyday use. Their demise was brought about by the disruption of the social structures in which they were used (hastened, no doubt, by the availability of softer options). A few continue to be found in circumstances where a ritual connection between the object and an ancestor is retained, and this means that traditional healers are now the major users of headrests. It is an interesting fact that a very large majority of black South Africans continue to consult traditional healers, and so the headrest, which once represented home, is now bound up with notions of healing and continuity of tradition. It is also striking that headrests continue to be found mainly in the rural areas and are still not brought into the cities. In September 1996, a traditional healer commented in an interview that she kept her headrest at home in the small town of Tzaneen, although she owned a house in Chiawelo, Soweto, as well. In my experience, no headrests are found in the urban markets catering for traditionalists in Johannesburg, such as Mai-Mai or in the Diagonal Street area, although sticks, drums, beadwork and medicines are found in abundance.[9]

Rural homes have always been more than places of shelter. Significance was built into their very substance, a fact which should make us question the notion of impermanence as a limitation. Mud and other materials were chosen not just because they were available but because they could be integrated into ritual and social strategies. After a man died, for instance, his house, which was part of his essence, was destroyed (along with his other worldly possessions, as we've seen). Then again, the building systems and materials were so flexible that new houses could be erected quickly when people had to move. When asked why they paint the walls of their houses, Ndebele women often provide a general explanation in terms of ethnic identity: to show the outsider that 'Ndebele live here'. Then again, the designs they paint – street lights, double-storey houses, staircases, sweet papers – are often drawn from visits to the city and poignantly express personal longings: 'I paint electric lights on my wall because my house does not have lights.'[10]

While rural homes are rich in meaning, their surroundings are usually unambiguously poor. The status of rural women has declined steadily, and their areas have become more and more impoverished. Now 'rural' and 'poor' are practically synonymous. But you would not think so to judge by the books that deal with South Africa's wall art.[11] The images are often breathtaking, the sunshine bright, the landscapes untroubled. The poverty, the sparse interiors, the lack of facilities, the rural slums are never shown. Like Goje's cheerful linocut, these beautiful images simplify and camouflage difference.

B

◄A12 ►D11

Armed responses

Mark Lewis

1 Van Deitz and Werner, Fort Skanskop, Pretoria.

2 Anton van Wouw (sculptor), Vrouemonument, Bloemfontein.

3 Sunset Beach, Cape Town.

4 Hallen and Dibb, Voortrekker Monument, Winburg.

5 Stauch Vorster and Partners, Sanlamsentrum, Parow, Cape Town.

6 Meyer Pienaar, Reserve Bank Building, Johannesburg.

7 Westlake Golf Club, Cape Town.

C

MARITZ
UYS

Edgars
JET
SK
STER-KINEKOR
CLICKS
TRUWORTHS
Open
YOUR ACCOUNT
TODAY !!!
ULTRA SERVICE

C

2

C

4

Whited sepulchres: On the reluctance of monuments

David Bunn

When her lover, Denys Finch-Hatton, died in a fiery Kenyan plane crash, Karen Blixen decided to bury him in the Ngong Hills. On a rainy day in 1931, the flag-covered coffin of the white hunter was lowered to its final resting place. At that precise moment, according to Blixen, a startling transformation took place:

> As [the coffin] was placed in the grave, the country changed and became the setting for it ... the hills stood up gravely, they knew and understood what we were doing in them; after a little while they themselves took charge of the ceremony ...[1]

The African earth, in this instant, experiences a change of state: it welcomes the unfamiliar white body into its embrace and then apparently learns, like local native authority, to govern such ceremonies independently. Yet despite this consoling hallucination, Blixen worried for the rest of her life about the fate of Finch-Hatton's grave. Unable to see it from her coffee farm in the valley below, she marked the site with three white poles between which a white cloth was stretched, and then later added an edging of whitewashed stones. Still later, the dead hunter's brother erected an obelisk on the site, and his old schoolmates in England built a little monumental stone bridge in his memory across a stream between two fields at Eton. The rusticated causeway had the following inscription on its balustrade: 'Famous in these fields and by his many friends much beloved.'[2]

This story contains a parable about colonial monuments generally. In Africa, as much as in other colonial contexts, monumental architecture bears the burden of several racially specific contradictions. Imagined as a white tradition, it is thought to surpass the ethical understanding of native communities, for which it is an obscure promise of future independence; at the same time, white monuments run the risk of becoming invisible or being neglected, because they rely on the memorial practices of an embattled minority group of settlers and their children. This paradox has general implications for the symbolic functioning of all monuments. All architectural memorials

Site of proposed Kruger Monument in the Kruger National Park, 1969.

try to naturalize themselves as 'geological outcroppings in a national landscape'.[3] However, South African monuments, to put it bluntly, find it almost impossible to be the bearers of collective meaning; instead, they are inhabited by contradiction, because of their reluctance to imagine the idea of citizenship outside the boundaries of race.

I Force and care

Despite a rich record of indigenous memorialization practices, 19th-century monumental architecture in Africa imagines itself to be a lone, literate tradition in a wasteland of illiteracy. To establish itself, it tries to adapt to local conditions an imported British landscape-architecture paradigm, in which the memorial is a meditative stopping point in a landscape circuit. At the same time, however, it will only allow certain racialized subjects to be invoked as full citizens in the monument's discriminating shade. Thus a compromise becomes necessary: monuments are forced to behave as though the earth itself, or Nature, joins the small group of local whites to form a responsive audience; alternatively, once the dedication of settler loyalists has been exhausted, the fetishistic devotion of African servants will suffice. Not surprisingly, after Karen Blixen left Kenya for ever, she was comforted by reports of Finch-Hatton's grave being tended by other pilgrims. Ali bin Salim, she is told, would 'go out and lie on the grave and weep, in the Arab way', and eventually a pair of lions established themselves at the site, lying prostrate on the grave at times. 'It was fit and decorous', says Blixen, that these noble creatures 'should come to Denys's grave and make him an African monument'.[4]

How does one make an African monument? Many 19th- and early 20th-century colonial monu-

Donkin Memorial, Port Elizabeth, 1820.

ments have a dual reference: to the unfamiliar local landscape, and to the bearers of national memory in far-flung metropolitan centres. The earliest memorials are like fortified watchtowers, signalling to distant pockets of white citizenry, while defending themselves at the base against local attack. In fact, the first white settler monuments in the Eastern Cape do not even concern themselves with the problem of an unreceptive context. They are, in effect, forerunners of a later imperial process for which, at present, there is no local audience. The Donkin Memorial in Port Elizabeth is one such structure. Like many Georgian estate follies in England, it is in the Egyptian style, and was erected in 1820 on rising ground above the bay to the memory of Elizabeth Donkin, Governor Rufane Donkin's young wife who died 'at Meerut in the Upper Hindustan of a fever'. Commissioned by a husband whose soul was 'still wrung by undiminished grief', it is but one element of a wider inscriptional project: Elizabeth's name was also bestowed upon the emerging settlement below, and her heart was buried at St Pancras's churchyard in London. The pyramid stands within a zone of legally sequestered space known as the 'Donkin Reserve'. Significantly, the term 'reserve' is usually associated with early settler forts and watchtowers, many of which had a perimeter zone or rayon of sequestered military space where no civilian building could take place.

C

So the Donkin Memorial does not try to resolve the problematic relationship between monument and site. Instead of appealing to a community of mourners, it simply secures a defensive zone, projects its meaning on to the town below, and beckons to the distant metropolitan centre. Thus a memorial in the idiom of Chatsworth's garden follies is left stranded on the imperial periphery. It calls out to the imperial traffic passing between Britain and the Far East, and its main audience when it was built would have been those temporarily alighting from ships rather than settler citizens. Quite appropriately, the monument shares its defended space with a lighthouse.

Some of the most famous and elaborate attempts to resolve the colonial problem of site and contested local memory are those of the imperialist architect Herbert Baker. It used to be claimed that in Herbert Baker the great story of South African architecture was begun. I shall argue, rather, that Baker's grand corpus of imperial buildings epitomizes the collaboration between ideas of force and charity. His importation of the Arts and Crafts movement style, and its reformulation in terms of an invented Cape vernacular tradition, is a tale obsessively retold by an older generation of art historians.[5] More recently, though, a different narrative has started to emerge. Peter Merrington, for instance, has revealed how Baker's building was part of a conscious attempt to forge a locally distinct form of Cape Edwardian aesthetics, one with strong allegiances not only to Ruskin but also to the Masonic symbolism that was a pervasive presence in much imperial discourse of the time.[6] Baker was closely associated with the group of clever young Oxford-trained administrators appointed by Alfred, Lord Milner, British High Commissioner for South Africa. Jokingly referred to as 'Milner's kindergarten', together they played a major role in inventing a newly appropriate aesthetics of Union.

I wish to resurrect the question of Baker's monumental use of stone. Structures crafted from roughly dressed stone, as he put it, are proof of the fact that 'good architecture must be indigenous [and] must take its origins from the natural resources of the country'.[7] Such statements lead architects to say that Baker was the first to imagine a locally appropriate form of building. Put slightly differently, stone, for Baker, enables a metonymic association between settler identity and natural landscape; it suggests that a new national presence is being built out of the local, and the stone itself is evidence of the necessarily rough care with which that identity is forced to fashion its new traditions. Baker's renowned houses on Parktown ridge, and his Cape Town churches, use hammer-dressed koppie stone, sometimes without pointing, with 'the mortar joints ... kept back slightly from the edges of the stone, [to make] their various sizes and shapes show to the best advantage'.[8] Both house and church therefore appear to be intrinsically related to the landscape; it is as though an expression of settled European identity is coaxed out of the rock, with rough tutelage, or through a return to pre-industrial craft processes. It is as though, in some reversal of temporal sequence, the marks of settlement had somehow always been present in the native rock.

What we see in Baker's use of roughly dressed stone is a fascination with indigenous materials that yield readily to the educated industrial understanding of the imperial settler, now choosing to work in a picturesque, pre-industrial style. In fact, African stone is that archaic material that requires only rough shaping by craftsmen to make it reveal an underlying will-to-order. This is the essence of the imperialist vision: the idea of bringing territories under the control of the metropolitan paternal authority is closely associated with the idea of following older precedents, such as the Roman, Babylonian or Phoenician empires, with whom there is sympathetic identification. Thus in the idiom of stone we find expressed a search for an older language of rough rule that has already traced itself in classical and medieval ruins. This, in turn, produces an interesting confusion of descriptive categories in much empire writing. The boundaries between geological forms and ruins, between the marks of weathering and the signs of prior force, are elided, because novelists have an obsessional desire to find evidence of older, European-inspired builders. Marks that appear to show evidence of earlier forms of rule, particularly when they are inscriptions on stone, are of deep fascination to the typical colonial romance. In Rider Haggard's *She*, for instance, the expedition inland is encouraged by the discovery of ancient stone masonry: 'Is that not stonework?' says one character, pointing to a swampy verge where the earth has been eroded. Quatermain, the explorer protagonist, is quickly persuaded: 'I only whistled. For there, bared by the removal of the earth, was an undoubted facing of solid stone laid in large blocks, bound together with brown cement so hard I could make no impression on it.'[9]

Stone, in Herbert Baker, is thus not simply a reflection of the pre-Raphaelite nostalgia of the Arts and Crafts movement. Indeed, it has a different history to the use of stone in the Victorian Gothic, and it expresses something unique about settler identity and imperial time. To get closer to what this is, we must examine Baker's complicated relationship with the ruthlessly imperialist diamond millionaire, and later Prime Minister of the Cape, Cecil John Rhodes.

South African architectural history enthusiastically remembers the story of Rhodes's patronage of Baker, something that involved the re-education of the young architect in the grandiose styles and influences dear to his patron. Rhodes was a fierce proponent of the thesis that the Cape was a 'Mediterranean' environment, and in 1900 he packed Baker off to Europe on an all-expenses-paid grand tour to see Athens, Delphi, Olympia, Palermo, Agrigentum and Paestum, amongst others, stopping in Cairo on the way.[10] But both patron and architect believed that raising African civilization to a higher order also required the retraining of local craftsmen in pre-industrial guild skills. Baker's drawings are frequently crowded with marginal notes about vanishing skills, such as the production of wrought-iron embellishments, and the need to teach locals 'to hammer in iron and cast in brass and bronze, as in the golden days of the crafts before the hostile influences of machinery'.[11] That is to say, in South Africa, the pre-capitalist relations of production offered opportunities for a fantastical return to the feudal order of benevolent master and skilled peasant that had long since passed in Britain. The elaborate bars and decorations of the Lion House, which Baker designed for Rhodes's Groote Schuur estate, express this nostalgia perfectly. Colonnaded like the cloisters and quads of Baker's Parktown ridge schools, the Lion House is a metaphoric extension of Rhodes's own powerful, restless presence. It is a projection of his spirit into the world: as the collector of lions, and as a restless, pacing imperial force trapped by the dull, unadventurous sensibility of London bureaucrats, he appears to be a cross between Caesar and P. T. Barnum. He is a man whose building *in the present* is already of monumental proportions.

This extension of the power of his clients into the South African wilderness through the idiom of stone is one of Baker's most striking achievements. In stone houses on ridges, where their new money allowed them to imitate the old prospect-devouring architecture of Whig estates, and in statues on plinths of Table Mountain sandstone, the Kimberley and Witwatersrand mine bosses

Herbert Baker and F. E. Masey with Henry Pegram (sculptor), Cecil John Rhodes statue, Cape Town, 1908.

C

became larger than life. Both the houses and the statues celebrated the alliance of local business and imperialism. 'Your hinterland lies yonder,' proclaims the motto on the statue of Rhodes in Cape Town's Gardens. With that possessive pronoun, the voice of the statue challenges passers-by to defy the Liberal laggards urging caution in London. The future of Empire, it says, rests on a return to unmediated mastery. It is a vision of heroic boldness and manorial authority, closely associated with feudal nostalgia for a time before class, and made possible by the violent context of the colonies.

Rider Haggard's novels are also founded on the idea that big, benevolent tyrants find their proper sphere for action in Africa. In King Solomon's Mines, Ignosi, the rightful king of the Kukuanas, gives the three white adventurers coats of mail, which feature the 'most wonderful chain work' they have ever seen. 'These steel shirts,' says the narrator, 'which evidently had been made for men of a very large stature ... fitted [Sir Henry's] magnificent frame like a glove.'[12] Haggard's epic account of 'Kukuana' warfare was inspired by his South African tour of duty with Sir Theophilus Shepstone, the Secretary for Native Affairs in Natal, and his admiration for Zulu regimental tactics. Colonial South Africa, in this version, is a fantastically primitive environment, where the strictures of dull metropolitan life are cast off and white administrators become like medieval lords, attended by fiercely loyal subjects, their expansive gestures unquestioned. As if in a dream, ancient weapons from the time of giants fit themselves to modern hands.

Because of this fantastical element in colonial representation, South African monuments diverge from metropolitan building traditions. When Baker services Rhodes's fantasy, he combines elements of medieval guild production with references to Pharaonic architecture. Imperial power

Herbert Baker, Rhodes Memorial, Cape Town, 1905-8.

is dramatized in an almost erotic desire to carve a place for the white body out of the very rock of Africa. In Groote Schuur, for instance, the Prime Minister's massive granite bath anticipates his later grandiose entombment in the rock of the Matopos.

So grandly is Rhodes's restless spirit embodied in the Gardens statue, that the whole of Cape Town seems to become a theatrical backdrop for his pacing. In fact, Baker originally intended to realign the entire city centre on an axis with the Rhodes statue. Standing at the intersection of Wale and Adderley streets, with shops swept aside to make way for the line of sight, the statue would direct the attention of citizens to the great, uncompleted romance of continental domination. Even though the city did not oblige, the great figure – hat in hand, with an informal attitude that speaks of the male pragmatism of the colonial project – still returns your gaze and directs it northwards.

By far the most famous of Baker's monumental works is the Rhodes Memorial, on the slopes of Table Mountain. Like much of his domestic architecture, this monument commands a spectacular view: in the metaphor of an older, English landscape tradition, class privilege is expressed in the excursive eye looking benevolently down upon a picturesque scene. On the colonial periphery, however, new contradictions emerge, and it is as though a single vantage point can no longer be maintained. Instead, the colonnaded monument includes two meditative stopping points. Near the crest of the hill, a pillared atrium forms a proscenium arch for a bust of Rhodes, with the famous epitaph declaring that the spirit of the great man will 'quicken' the emerging civilization below. Further down the slope, at the end of a series of huge granite steps, this visionary intent seems to be literalized, catapulted outwards, in G. F. Watt's equestrian statue of 'Physical Energy', with its naked rider gazing out to the horizon. In the entire monument, in other words, a solution to the colonial problem of monument and site is found by splitting the metaphoric vantage point in two, producing one point associated with meditative brooding and another with the masculine energy of the scanning eye.

For generations, the children of Cape Town have adored the polished bronze backs of the lions at Rhodes Memorial. What they could not have sensed, however, is the economical way in which Baker's site dramatizes the combination of force and care that underlies all notions of imperialist rule. Rhodes's bust broods meditatively and protectively over Cape Town; but the sexualized rider, a synecdoche for his restless spirit, is also evidence of the force required to disseminate this vision. The same combination of force and paternal authority underlies most Lugardian forms of indirect rule in Africa, which British administrators believed to be the most suitable means of administering the backward, native social relations in the colonies. In truth, though, the administration of force under the guise of care is also one of the characteristic forms of modern government generally. This is what the philosopher Michel Foucault referred to as pastoral power: 'If the state is the political form of a centralized and centralizing power, let us call pastorship the individualizing power.'[13]

Baker's projects for Rhodes reveal that white imperial monumentality is stylistically and politically regressive, always longing for an older mode of administration in which paternal authority is invested with wide, unmediated political powers. What may not be immediately obvious, though, is that race is the absent signifier upon which this nostalgic vision is built. Victorian colonial monuments are able to make the connection between force and paternal care because of the special conditions they imagine are required for 'native' administration. In turn, this makes it possible to avoid problems of racism in the metropole itself. Racist violence at home, as Homi Bhabha and others have shown, was frequently described as a temporary aberration, an irruption of archaic forms of brutality more common in the colonies and not intrinsic to the evolution of metropolitan modernity.[14] Colonies, in other words, are a kind of screen onto which contradictions intrinsic to late 19th-century Liberal government are projected and played out without damage to the system as a whole.

Again and again, colonial architects return to the monument as a sort of stone tower or viewing platform with a defended base. One of the most bizarre examples of this is Baker's monument to the siege of Kimberley during the South African War, when Boer forces trapped the despised Rhodes in the very diamond-rich city where his fortune had been made. One version of the original design for this monument was based on the classical model of the Tomb of Aruns. The built version is a tower designed to broadcast the meaning of the siege of Kimberley to succeeding generations. However, when the structure is approached, it ceases to function as a signal tower and becomes instead a plinth for the display of another symbolic object: the heavy gun 'Long Cecil', which was made at Rhodes's De Beers Consolidated Mines during the siege. Kipling's epitaph on the plinth makes the association of care and necessary force explicit:

> This for a charge to our children, in sign of the price we paid: the price that we paid for freedom, that comes unsoiled to your hand. Read, revere, and uncover. Here are the victors laid: they that died for the city, being sons of the land.

A price is paid for freedom. That price entails the use of force, in this instance an alliance of mining capital and imperial power embodied in the locally manufactured gun itself – 'Long Cecil', another monumental manifestation of the spirit of Rhodes. The reward, though, is not just 'freedom' – a vague enough concept anyway given the racial exclusiveness of South African civil society – but an achieved relationship between landscape and genealogy: the dead are 'sons of the land'. Force, in the form of the artillery piece at the base of the monument, combines with vision, embodied by the tower, to unify the monument and its landscape context.

Thus far I have been dealing with white monuments in South Africa. This is inevitable, because African memorial practices – memorial performances, burial sites and ancestral presences, sacred groves and the ubiquitous stone cairns known as isivivane, the memorial division of gendered space in cattle-byre burials – are largely ignored by the architectural tradition. However, this lack is acknowledged at another level. The absence of any engagement with questions of black citizenship means that no monument can claim to represent 'nationhood' fully. As we shall see, even the most dogmatic, racist memorials are truly whited sepulchres, in that they are inhabited by a sense of absence and lack which does not even have the substance of haunting.

Those monuments I have been examining tend to broadcast their meaning over the heads of surrounding African communities. Some, like the memorial to missionary James Stuart in the Eastern Cape, literally overlooked busy Xhosa communities, yet instead of addressing these local audiences, they preferred to speak in abstract, racist generalizations about the war between darkness and light. This is not to argue that imperial pastoral power ignored the memorialization of Africans altogether. On the contrary, administrative discourses of the time were quite amenable to celebrating the memory of colourful or compliant chiefs. Consider the model established by Shepstone, the controversial administrator whom we met above. The 'Shepstone System' in Natal involved the segregation of African communities into controlled reserves or locations, and the co-optation of Zulu chiefs.[15] Central to the success of this quite complex scheme was the understanding that native administration should be based on customary law; in Natal, this involved reference to what British administrators imagined to be the ruthlessly efficient rule of King Shaka in the early 19th century. This precedent justified the implementation of a 'customary' forced labour system 'painfully at odds with notions of governance current in Britain'.[16]

Shepstone's thirty-year rule in Natal was punctuated by elaborate public rituals in which local African leaders were encouraged to recognize white administrators as 'higher chiefs' in the mould of earlier rulers like Shaka. The Zulu state under Shaka was highly militarized, being organized on the amaButho age-regiment system. This masculine, regimental authority was at once feared and admired by the British, who paid tribute to the Zulu warrior in a thousand monumental friezes on buildings in South Africa and abroad. However, the legendary authority of Shaka was also crucial to the making of modern Zulu nationalism. When Africans themselves took the initiative to build

Sytze Wierda, Paardekraal Monument, Krugersdorp, 1890.
Photograph by David Goldblatt.

C

monuments, the colonial authorities reacted angrily. In 1930, for instance, the Zulu nationalist Inkatha movement tried to shore up internal cleavages by raising funds for a Shaka memorial.[17] After controversies around the misappropriation of funds, and serious squabbling, a sentimental, highly decorative monument was unveiled. Seven years later, the South African Historical Monuments Commission was still refusing to grant it official recognition.

II Lig van bô

Discourses of conquest often imagine themselves to be reiterative. Typically, Rhodes's monumental pretensions were described by admirers as a return of classical order to Africa. Early 20th-century Afrikaner memorial traditions were very different. Setting themselves against rival African kingdoms and against the forces of British imperialism that were changing the landscape with fortifications and barbed wire, they had little interest in the language of pastoral power. Instead, the entire focus was on the idea of originary inscription. Moreover, this inscriptional force became associated with a single founding narrative – the Great Trek (as it later came to be known). In 1838, closely knit bands of farmers, the Voortrekkers, reacted against oppressive British rule and the emancipation of the slaves by moving out of the Cape in search of new land and political autonomy. Leaders like Retief, Trichardt and Potgieter led these ox-wagon migrations into territories already unsettled by the rise of the Zulu state and internecine warfare. The trekkers quickly came into conflict with independent African societies and some hideous battles

Centenary celebration of the Great Trek, Volksrust, 8 November 1938. Photograph by David Goldblatt.

took place, including the massacre of Piet Retief's party by Dingane and the subsequent battle of Blood River, where the trekkers exacted a terrible revenge on the Zulu. It was prior to this battle that the Boer leader Andries Pretorius was said to have made a covenant with God, swearing that if He gave them victory the date of the battle would always be honoured.

These historical events in the life of the volk were seen in allegorical terms by later generations. Recent historians have argued that the Great Trek was not a consolidated, self-conscious process, and have shown that Voortrekker parties were riven by dissent. Furthermore, while it is clear that the early trekkers did identify with biblical narratives such as the exodus from Egypt, at the time there was little overall sense of religious predestination or a defined mission.[18] In the work of later interpreters, however, events were given a strongly Calvinist colouring, so that the trekkers became a chosen people, through the imagined descent of the Word to certain leaders. In narratives of the late 19th century, the Word was said to have been manifest in the very journey itself, as the wagon wheels cut their meaning into the receptive earth.

The idea of meditative wandering, so frequently alluded to in the British monumental tradition, and the Afrikaner understanding of trekking might seem to resemble one another, but they are in fact very different. Late 19th- and early 20th-century Calvinist histories described the Voortrekker leaders as subject to directed restlessness. Itching with the sense of an imminent future, these leaders are depicted as having an entirely focused, linear desire to move to new pastures, to found a new nation, and to set up memorial beacons on the way. Not for them or their later chroniclers the thoughtful wandering of British imperial representations.

In fact, in many Afrikaner monuments height is not associated with prospect or contemplation, but with a goal to be reached or an obstacle to be overcome. The crest of a ridge overlooking a valley is not a place of meditative pause. Rather, it is associated with inscriptional force, with the breaching of a barrier and the sighting of a promised land. The ruts the wagon wheels score in rock both mark a claim and anticipate that future moment when the plough will break the first furrow in the fertile earth.

This attachment to marking and breaching, and to monuments as a sign of the vertical descent of the Word to earth, was a central ideological element in early Afrikaner nationalism. It was also deeply disturbing to the British authorities. During the South African War, British troops went out of their way to deface memorials such as the Taalmonument – the monument to the Afrikaans language – in Burgersdorp.[19] But more than any other, it was the Paardekraal Monument they hated. Paardekraal began as a cairn of rocks erected spontaneously by a Boer crowd incensed at the memory of Britain's annexation of the Transvaal. Later, a stone obelisk was built, which enclosed the original cairn while keeping it visible through an iron grille at the base. In the course of the South African War, the British wrenched out the original stones and tipped them from railway trucks into the Vaal River.

Why should so much effort have been expended on destroying the Paardekraal obelisk? Perhaps the British understood something about the relationship between monuments, ideology and national memory that remains opaque to us. To grasp this relationship, let us regard architectural monuments not singly, but as emerging systems or points of organization that may come into conflict with others. Thus it might be said that Burgersdorp and Paardekraal mark the beginnings of a nationalist monumental project, a means of organizing symbolic resistance against the visibly imperialist forms of the built environment.[20] Each new monument, and the performances associated with it, sets up an increasingly systematic relationship, a visible syntax linked to the collective historical memory of an identifiable group. At the same time, however, this presents a problem. The meaning of the individual monument is no longer in and for itself, but dependent on a system of differences across the total field. This unsettlingly conditional meaning is threatened even further by the prospect of generational amnesia.

In response to this threat, the architects of national memory try to turn the monument into an icon rather than a sign, by incorporating into the body of the building some part of the event to which the memorial refers. Stones cemented into the base, the mark of blood, signatures on walls, wagon ruts in rock, all of these may lend the monument iconic status and provide an anchoring point for the total system. Then, in a moment of transformation, it is as though the obelisk or tower ceases to reach into the heavens, but instead strikes downwards into the earth like a dagger, pinning down temporarily what is essentially an unstable field. Psychoanalyst Jacques Lacan provided an account of such symbolic anchoring points, referring to them as points de capiton. Slavoj Žižek has interpreted him as follows: 'The multitude of "floating signifiers" ... is structured into a unified field through the intervention of a certain "nodal point" ... which "quilts" them, stops their sliding and fixes their meaning.'[21]

Some monumental architecture seems obsessed with the loss of fixed meaning or a potential break in the transmission of the historical narrative. Monuments such as Paardekraal cannot abide the idea of the passing viewer. Unlike the Rhodes Memorial, which relies on horizontal movement, casual visiting and projective vision, many Afrikaner monuments are essentially rigid, upright forms, which collect and focus power vertically. They are like pulpits, rather than memorials; often their steeple-like structures emphasize the fact that these are places in which to congregate and worship. Central to this tradition is the idea of lig van bô (light from above), of benediction descending in a stream of light which is the Word made visible, forging a reciprocal relationship between racialized national subjects and the Divinity.

The purest expression of this benedictory principle may be found, of course, in South Africa's most notorious memorial, the Voortrekker Monument outside Pretoria. Unlike scores of other nationalist monuments to battles or massacres, this edifice is squat and stolid, like an art deco pepper pot. At the same time, it is less like a building than a machine for reproducing forms of affect associated with the central fiction of Afrikaner nationalism: the founding exodus of the Great Trek. As we have already noted, the allegorical interpretation of this event is a later adaptation. It arose particularly in connection with nationalist sentiment around the time of the 1938 centenary celebrations of the Trek. In that year, nine replica wagons from all corners of the country converged on the site of the future monument at Pretoria. Huge crowds orchestrated by the newly established Broederbond – an intensely secretive organization that sought to infiltrate every social sphere in order to further Afrikaner interests – gathered to greet the wagons, and scenes of mass hysteria accompanied their passage. Most towns organized greeting committees, suitably garbed in period costume, and in many the wagons were driven through specially poured concrete slabs to immortalize the wheel ruts.[22] The great significance of the 1938 trek was that 'it invented white nationalist traditions and celebrated unity where none had existed before, creating the illusion of a collective identity through the political staging of vicarious spectacle'.[23] Historians generally agree that the Eeufees – the centenary celebrations – marked the beginning of a new phase in the consolidation of white Afrikaner racial identity, a movement that 'reached its zenith with the inauguration of the Voortrekker Monument in 1949'[24] and was designed to separate out white working-class Afrikaners and prevent them from being absorbed into the horror of racial mixing.

With its laager of 64 encircling concrete wagons and its great protective dome, the Voortrekker Monument is a gigantic tomb containing the symbolic sarcophagus of the martyred trekker leader Piet Retief. Every year on 16 December, the day of the Boer victory at Blood River, a dagger of light falls directly from an aperture in the dome onto the sarcophagus. The ceremonial celebration of this moment is part of the same architectural language found at Paardekraal, in which the monument itself renews its historical referent by allowing those present to reiterate the original vow.

Such monuments are essentially devices for keeping selective memory alive. Past traumas – Blood River, the Bloukrans massacre in which five hundred trekkers and their servants died, betrayals – are contained and recirculated for each new generation of white children. But the monuments cannot avoid the problem of racial conflict entirely, and so they try to manage it by creating

an outer frame of reference to black bodies. In the marble frieze that surrounds the Voortrekker Monument, as Liz Delmont points out, there is an almost eroticized depiction of muscled African figures. The architect Moerdyk conceded this when he remarked that 'natives ... are always represented as worthy opponents, very well developed as far as their physical characteristics are concerned'.[25] This kind of reversal is characteristic of many forms of racist discourse.

Because they fear the disseminating capacity of the sign, such structures are also defensive. With the advance of modernity, and the spatial impress of apartheid after 1948, they abandon completely the old notion that memorials should also address wanderers and random visitors. Their sole function is to keep traumatic memory flickering on down the Afrikaner generations, until it can flare up again in occasional official ceremonies. The Danie Theron monument, for instance, like a giant candle with a stylized copper flame, addresses passing traffic on the main road between Johannesburg and Potchefstroom rather than the surrounding countryside. Built in the period of high apartheid to memorialize the exploits of a legendary Boer scout killed in 1900, this monument alludes to the device of the eternal flame or unknown soldier; ironically, however, it cannot afford the democratic gesture of a lit wick guttering in an open public space, and so it raises its rigid flame high into the air on a defensive concrete tower.

There is evidence to suggest that the entire project of nationalist memorialization entered a crisis in the 1960s. This is somewhat surprising. After all, this was the period of the new republic, of large-scale public building, grand apartheid, and an economic growth rate of 8 per cent per annum.[26] Yet in their memorial architecture, as much as in other aspects of social and economic life, Afrikaners felt a new pressure to modernize. The focus of the older monumental tradition, on the tower that

Hallen Theron and Partners, BMW Head Office, Midrand, 1984.

contains its own referent and re-enacts an originary inscription, on the monument as pulpit or steeple, was ill-suited to the ideological task of modernization. It is precisely in this period that the intervention of architects becomes crucial.

The Voortrekker Monument at Winburg in the Orange Free State is an important statement by Hans Hallen, one of South Africa's most influential architects. The firm of Hallen Theron and Partners has been prominent in the country's corporate architecture. In fact, Hallen's 1984 head office building for BMW provides insights into what he was trying to achieve in the much earlier Winburg monument. One of the first buildings in the new industrial area of Midrand, between Johannesburg and Pretoria, the BMW building is placed ostentatiously on a flat site. Intriguingly, Hallen's notes about the project suggest a monumental intent, referring in detail to structures like St Peter's and Great Zimbabwe.[27] But seen in its panoramic context, the work is also strongly reminiscent of Boullée. With its striking, aluminium-clad reflective surfaces, and its processional approach axes reminiscent of Great Zimbabwe, the building combines elements of the iconic with a monumental theatricality. More than many of the other Jahn-inspired office buildings, with their reflective glass curtain walls, the BMW building creates a corporate landscape presence for a new generation. It was not simply designed for an avenue approach; it also displays to passing freeway traffic the fact that it is a literal embodiment of the BMW bonnet emblem. It is a temple of the logo, rather than the Logos.

Hallen and Maurice Dibb were joint winners of the design competition for the Winburg Voortrekker Monument in 1965, and there are detailed records of their submission. The competition was administered by the Federasie van Afrikaanse Kultuurverenigings (FAK), an umbrella body representing hundreds of Afrikaner cultural associations. This was, of course, the second great Voortrekker Monument in the country, and there was an immediate and inevitable relationship between the Pretoria edifice and this one. To make matters more complicated, Winburg was understood to be the symbolic heartland of the Great Trek: according to the FAK, this was the area where the leaders had been most united in their political and religious aims.[28] Rietfontein farm, the site of the monument, was the birthplace of President Steyn, another leader associated with Afrikaner unity.

Hallen's design reconciled older symbols, such as the bowed ox-wagon tent and the yoke, with more expressive references to yearning and forward movement. Responding to the uneven slope, the monument consists of five towering, reinforced-concrete wings or sails of unequal height, arranged around a circular space. The sails represent the reconciled but uneven influences of trekker patriarchs: Trichardt, Potgieter, Maritz, Retief and Uys. Like many other Afrikaner monuments, it combines a sense of restlessly directed nationalism with an inward defensiveness, especially in the dramatic contrast between the vast, fluted towers and the projecting gutters at the base – like cannons protruding between the wagons in a laager – which deliver water into ornamental storage dams.

At the time, the adjudicators of the competition saw Hallen's design as a generational step forward in the attempt to solve the symbolic contradictions of the Trek: 'Die sprong na sodanige selfstandige vorme vanaf die onvermydelike betonossewas en die marmerosse in 'n staties onbeweeglike laer,' says the FAK commentary, 'is groot en dien as onderskeidingsteken.' ['The leap from the inevitable concrete ox-wagons and marble oxen in a static, immovable laager to such autonomous forms is huge and serves as a mark of distinction.'] That is, the memorialization of the Trek has been modernized, in a new symbolic dialectic of restless forward movement and protective enclosure. As the judges realized, Hallen had also managed brilliantly to modernize the older concept of benedictory light descending upon a chosen few, for whom the land is divinely reserved. From the fortified central enclosure, the view out is not so much prospective as defensive. But perhaps the most inspired conception of all was Hallen's solution to the problem of realizing a relationship between building and landscape at the height of apartheid's aggressive dispossession of the majority of the country's citizens. In this monument, the metaphor of a limited

Hallen and Dibb, Model of Voortrekker Monument, Winburg, 1968.

C

exchange between subject and landscape is perfected. Overall, the monument celebrates the phallic authority of the patriarch. The tall concrete wings enclose a protected central zone, which the judges associated with intimacy and the role of women in the Trek.[29] The passage of light downwards into this dark interior then becomes associated with an inseminating masculine authority. The same symbolic language allows for a further, limited metaphoric exchange with the outer landscape: five fountains – the seminal presence of the five leaders – spill water outwards into five dams. The latter in turn represent ''n invloed of gees wat verskillende landstreke deurvloei het' ['an influence or spiritual current which flowed through various regions'].

At face value, the Winburg monument seems to employ the same dialectic of care and force we saw in earlier architectures. Significantly, though, the logic is entirely gendered, and the question of race is elided. By emphasizing authority, and the limitation and containment of symbolic fluids, the building speaks directly to the modernization of apartheid, with its legislation against the mixing of blood and genes and for the separation of populations into their 'own areas'. Bizarrely, Hallen's monument becomes a sort of imaginary means by which the Afrikaner nation can imagine itself into a limited yet righteous relationship with the land. This idea of the land itself conspiring to produce a segregated flow of influence was especially pleasing to the judges. They noted, for instance, that rainwater would be recycled through the catchment dams, swelling the stream of life-giving fluids and dramatizing the unity of the Voortrekker movement.[30]

Of course, the problem of modernization was not confined to monumental architecture. Afrikaner capital was also trying to make inroads into areas like banking and manufacturing, efforts which were significantly enhanced by the rise of the Broederbond. In the 1930s, the Broederbond was instrumental in the founding of Volkskas, the first Afrikaner bank, and Sanlam, the life insurance company, both of which helped to consolidate white power across classes by dealing with Afrikaner poverty. In the following decades, these companies and others like them tried to establish a modern public image. Corporate architecture was a crucial part of this, and nowhere was it more evident than in the parastatal buildings, municipal offices and new Afrikaner corporations crowded on to the reclaimed Foreshore in Cape Town. In 1962, the Sanlam Centre, Southern Africa's tallest building, was completed, making use of reinforced-concrete technologies to withstand wind velocities of 190 kilometres per hour. It was designed 'as one of the two tall verticals to contrast the monotony of the 120-foot height of surrounding buildings dictated by the 1947 Foreshore plan',[31] and it also broke Table Mountain's picturesque horizon line for the first time. Such buildings were intended as a rebuke to the great English civil and corporate engineering projects after the time of Union, projects which themselves triumphally proclaimed the virtues of large-scale building in reinforced concrete. One of the main reasons the adjudicating committee accepted Hallen's design for the Winburg monument was because it outshone the civil engineering evident in the neighbouring Rietfontein Dam.

The essential ingredient in Hallen's design was its 'modernity' – a quality closely associated with reinforced concrete. Shell-shaped, reinforced-concrete forms, the judges declared, are the very stuff of high 20th-century building and of 'ons vernaamste monumentale strukture' ['our foremost monumental structures'].[32] By way of example, they referred to great Southern African civil engineering projects like Kariba Dam, where some 6,000 cubic yards of concrete were poured a day during construction, and the Athlone power station, with its cooling towers made of vast sheets of reinforced concrete. Even more evident in the surrounding Free State landscape, of course, would have been those monuments to large-scale agriculture, the grain elevators.

Concrete had another appeal. By breaking with the by-now oppressive chilliness of marble and bronze, the national narrative itself could be made attractive to the rising generation of Afrikaners, the new pioneers. Hallen used bright white concrete poured in rough wooden formwork sections. This made for a lively, textured surface combining large spans, impressive verticality, curved tensile strength and apparent lightness. The monument is a metaphor for the adaptive identity strategies of contemporary Afrikaners, conscious of the old but alert to the challenge of the new. It is also

less dependent on periodic ceremonies to re-establish the currency of the past. Instead, it enters into a syntactic relationship with surrounding examples of new capital investment, and is designed to appeal to a newly mobile population of holidaymakers, passing on the nearby freeway.

III Monumental mistakes

Monumental architecture in South Africa, I have been arguing, was at times split between two contradictory traditions: the one, prospective and imperial, achieves its landscape context through an association between vision and care; the other, evoking vertical authority and autochthonous origins, focuses on connections between the spirit of the nation and natural processes such as the movement of light and water. In the Voortrekker Monument at Winburg, the building itself stages an allegorical set of associations relating Afrikaner historical trauma to the rightful segregation of the land. However, while the building follows a highly gendered logic, with its 'feminine' interior spaces and 'masculine' fluids, it cannot represent the whole body of the nation. The problems of unequal citizenship under apartheid reveal such white monuments for what they are: partial, disjointed, dismembered.

Monuments would like us to believe that they are haunted by the spirit of the past, that they are chambers echoing with the voices of the heroic dead. In time, however, most South African monuments have come to be haunted by what was repressed to achieve their exclusiveness, and then their meaning has appeared to desert them. I will examine two examples of this representational failure – a monument which was proposed but never built, and one which was built but has now fallen into ruins.

Orange River Scheme, Hendrik Verwoerd Dam, Orange Free State. Minister of Water Affairs Fanie Botha inspects the dam, 19 November 1971.

By 1968, the Kruger National Park had thrown off the vestiges of its old colonial administration and become an arm of the fully realized, racially exclusive state.[33] Part of its transformation into an apartheid institution involved the erection of memorial plaques and tablets along the routes the trekkers were likely to have taken through the area, thus displacing the memory of the old order of imperial custodianship exemplified by Colonel James Stevenson-Hamilton, the park's legendary first Warden. Stevenson-Hamilton's historical role was written everywhere in the park, but nowhere more visibly than at the cluster of gigantic boulders on Shirimantanga Hill known today as 'Stevenson-Hamilton Rocks'. Here, high on a hilltop overlooking an endless vista of conserved bushveld, the Warden, like Rhodes before him, had blasted a tomb in the rock. In the end, he was not buried in it. His ashes and those of his wife Hilda were simply scattered into the open hole and a bronze memorial plaque set up. Stevenson-Hamilton had picked out the site himself. It was a perfect location, he said, because of the commanding view:

> The underlying idea is thus that the local natives being still very superstitious, the fact of my being so to speak 'in situ' would probably act as a deterrent to native poachers in the vicinity, and as the said kopje is the highest point in the southern areas, and can be seen for miles around, they would feel 'Skukuza' [his Shangaan nickname] was watching them.[34]

The Warden – the ghost of an eye on a hill – would watch over the estate long after his death, his pastoral power registered in the fetishistic responses of the natives.

Mock-up of the proposed Kruger Monument at the Kruger National Park, 1969.

Later Afrikaner cultural historians had this British landscape tradition in mind when they began to lobby for a permanent monument to President Paul Kruger. It was not enough that the entire park was named after Kruger; distrusting the semiological drift of names and naming, they wanted an unambiguous, vertically anchored embodiment of the President himself. In 1968, the National Parks Board accepted a proposal from the sculptor Coert Steynberg to carve a huge bust of Kruger into the granite of a koppie in the reserve.

A fierce controversy erupted around this R100,000 commission, and the Parks Board was bombarded with letters of protest from a wide variety of organizations, including the National Monuments Commission, the South African Association of Arts, the Wild Life Protection Society, the National Council of Women, and the Cape and Transvaal Institute of Architects. To the horror of Kruger's own descendants, Steynberg announced that he would create a diminutive Mount Rushmore, with the unsmiling head of the Boer patriarch glowering down upon his bushveld preserve. At the height of the controversy, the sculptor sent a montage rendition of the planned monument to one of the national newspapers. Liberal art aficionados were appalled. One member of the Association of Arts described the work as a 'tragedy in granite'. While prominent artists like Walter Battiss railed against the autocratic insensitivity of the Parks Board, Afrikaans newspaper cartoonists parodied the idea of this monumental 'baboon castle'. Some older liberal conservationists cunningly appealed to the iconoclastic tendencies in Calvinism: Charles Astley-Maberley argued that 'every one of these natural features – including the boulders of koppies – are the work of the Supreme Artist and should be left to be enjoyed as such by mankind'.[35]

The Parks Board remained obdurate. In a sense, they claimed to be simply making visible what was already there. The head, once revealed, would stand for the historical impress of the founding patriarch in the landscape. It would also make apparent the idea of the park as a sort of body governed by the consciousness of the supervising fathers. However, the controversy also pointed to something that remained unsaid in the wider debate about monuments: in the end, memorial discourse in South Africa often had as much to do with the management of Africans as with the preservation of memory. If there was competition between the Ozymandian bust of Kruger and the lingering ghost of Stevenson-Hamilton, it was about the administration of 'unconscious' citizens by rational ones, in a protected environment of archaic labour relations, where Africans were scarcely more than bodies – eyes, ears, muscles. It is a division that persists today, in the form of a mainly white senior management and an army of black trackers and field rangers.

The white public hated the idea of the Kruger bust. For many Afrikaners, it suggested a return to the pre-modern, to the hard-eyed rule of the forefathers, and scores of letters to the press spoke of the need for an end to the age of monuments. As one correspondent put it: 'Ek vrees die standbeelde is stom, en ons geslag, en die wat kom, sal nie hul taal verstaan nie'[36] ['I'm afraid the statues are dumb, and our generation and those to come will not understand their language'].

Eventually the Parks Board compromised, and a huge, free-standing bust of Kruger was placed on a plinth near the entrance gate that bears his name. Right up until the moment of dedication, some organizations continued to press for a memorial in the tradition of British landscape. The National Council of Women suggested that a toposcope be erected, continuing the British association between the unseen, surveying eye of the landowner and class privilege. In the same year, in fact, a toposcope memorial to the British 1820 settlers was erected on a hill overlooking the Eastern Cape village of Bathurst. This stone-walled viewing platform marks out the compass-point references of all the white settler farms in the district, and in some ways is even more autocratic than the Kruger head. But with the battle lost, the Kruger head was literally severed from its national park body; in the end it was perhaps too literal a sign of direct administrative authority to find a place in the park's apparently laissez-faire landscape management system.

So much for the monument that never was. For a monument that existed but ceased to serve its original purpose, we will turn to Ciskei, an impoverished section of the rural Eastern Cape. It was

one of ten homelands established under grand apartheid, and the second of two 'independent' states for Xhosa-speakers.[37]

In the late 1970s, Chief Lent Maqoma, a lineal descendant of Maqoma, a great Xhosa resistance fighter of the 19th century, met a prophetess who claimed she had had a vision of his ancestor's grave on Robben Island and would help him to bring the bones back to the Ciskei for reburial. When the story came to the attention of the South African state, they seized upon it as a propaganda windfall. The Departments of Prisons and Defence helped to transport the bones back from the Island, and on 13 August 1978 a crowd of 15,000 people gathered on the hill known as Ntaba ka Ndoda to see them reinterred.[38]

Lennox Sebe, Chief Minister in the homeland government, seems to have fixed on the idea of transforming Ntaba ka Ndoda into a national shrine shortly after a visit to Israel in 1977, and the reburial was the first step in that direction; he apparently imagined the hill as a type of Masada, where the spirit of Xhosa heroes who had fought against colonialism could be invoked. In 1981, when the Ciskei became 'independent', Sebe's Ciskei National Independence Party won the elections and he was installed as President. The following year, the Sebe government had a massive concrete monument built on the hilltop, something between a triumphal arch and a pair of bull's horns; aligned along a north-south axis, the monument appeared to address and draw its strength from Maqoma's grave. East London architects, Chris Swales and Willem Marais, were responsible for the original design, which is reminiscent of the reinforced-concrete towers and spires of Dutch Reformed churches of the 1970s, or even the Taalmonument in Paarl (designed by Jan van Wijk). At the formal dedication, Sebe announced that in future, 'successful students, professional men, soldiers, policemen and politicians would receive their honours, certificates and credentials at the shrine':[39] here an emergent generation of middle-class government employees could be theatrically interpellated into Ciskeian identity.

In 1988, new plans were announced for expanding the monument at an estimated cost of R90 million, following designs by John Rushmere, one of the most prominent architects of the Eastern Cape. Rushmere was faced with the task of transforming a monumental landscape that had been discredited by its links with apartheid. The great concrete amphitheatre was singled out because of its association with 'political propaganda', and Rushmere planned to redecorate its bleak, totalitarian surfaces 'with traditional designs by Xhosa artists using coloured tiles set in an earth-coloured pigmented cement plaster'. He also wanted to offset the north-south alignment of the central spine with a series of symmetrically placed buildings, creating a proud new acropolis for the Xhosa nation. There would be a cultural museum, with four pavilions centred on a 'Mother Hut': 'Cultural symbol and spiritual symbol,' he said, 'will in this way be tied together to form the single heritage of the Xhosa people.'[40]

The violent, layered history of Ntaba ka Ndoda speaks eloquently of the compromising relationship between architecture and the state in the late apartheid period. What architecture offered, par excellence, was a way of stitching together ethnic particularism and ideas about the deep past in monumental forms that were seen to be indigenous. When Rushmere came up with his rescue plan for Ntaba ka Ndoda, he spoke of how 'Afrikaner culture is represented in the Voortrekker and Taal Monuments and the English culture is celebrated by the 1820 Settler Monument outside Grahamstown'. 'The Xhosa culture,' he added, 'needs to be likewise celebrated and anchored in a physical symbol of equivalent stature.'[41] Mercifully, after a few stone walls and a symbolic homestead had been built, Rushmere's plans were abandoned, as Ciskei plunged into a new, catastrophic phase of its history. Following the coup by Brigadier Oupa Gqozo, Ntaba ka Ndoda was taken over as a military base by the Ciskeian Defence Force.

In its last years, under the guise of a sacred purpose, Ntaba ka Ndoda did no more than act as a huge resonating chamber for Sebe's voice. The grey perimeter wall, originally meant to focus attention on Maqoma's grave, ultimately enclosed a different object: a statue of the dictator himself on a plinth. Interposed between the grave and the podium from which Sebe would address

C

ZAI Architects, Chris Swales and Willem Marais, Ntaba ka Ndoda, Eastern Cape, 1979.

his hired crowds, the monumental figure thus became the dictator's real audience, in a massive ideological tautology. Today, however, it is in ruins.

One way of understanding the fate of Ntaba ka Ndoda is to say, drawing on Žižek, that Ciskei was purely and simply a zone of uneven development for the Big Other, apartheid capitalism.[42] To live in Ciskei was to live a nullity, and the monument represented the impossibility of 'Ciskei' stabilizing itself as a nation in the face of the traumatic truth that such an entity did not exist, could not exist, because it was subject to the forces of uneven development that had their origins elsewhere. After the collapse of apartheid, the local people, who saw this 'shrine of the nation' for the empty gesture it was, helped themselves to whatever they could carry away.

IV Roundness is all

What do I mean by the 'reluctance' of monuments? First and foremost, I mean the inability of memorial architecture in South Africa to go beyond servicing certain narrowly defined notions of racialized citizenship and reach a more democratic understanding of memorial representation. But it is also important to consider the general relation between the South African architectural project and modernism.

Throughout European and North American modernism, whether in Gauguin, Picasso or Braque, in Lawrence's Mexico novels, in Huxley's utopias or in MoMA exhibitions of African art, there is a deep nostalgia for the forms of symbolic community destroyed by the global advance of market economies. In all modernisms, this produces an elegiac neo-primitivism which is monumental in effect: it mourns the loss of what it conceives as primitive, organic cultures, while at the same time wistfully acknowledging the primary role of capitalist culture in this decline. Many buildings of the 1930s and '40s express this contradictory impulse. In the façade of the Johannesburg railway station, for instance, entry into the modern world of rapid transit is framed by two emblems of the archaic: trumpeting bull elephants and, on the outer edges, Zulu warriors with shields and assegais.

Global discourses of modernity are therefore monumental in a general sense: they are deeply conscious of the loss attendant on the advance of civilization and of the need to memorialize pre-capitalist communities – and if necessary to invent them. As the century advances, and globalization along with it, this need intensifies and accelerates, until the very hotels and casinos built on the ancestral graves of local communities come to include fantastical representations of lost worlds.

Commodity capitalism in the late 20th century produces the intersection of corporate and monumental architectures. In itself, this monumentalizing style might be seen as the final stage of pastoral power, the power of disciplinary administration that defined imperialist cultures and inaugurated modernity, while at the same time appearing to mourn the passing of conquered cultures. In late apartheid South Africa, as part of the same global continuum, there is a nostalgia for imagined forms of lost African identity. This manifests itself in the fantasy that architects are building for Africans who have lost touch with their past, and it typically entails reference to the idea of 'roundness'. The simple dialectic between square houses and round huts has been fundamental to the political debate in South Africa since the 18th century. As scholars like Clifton Crais and John and Jean Comaroff have shown in relation to mission stations, there was widespread resistance by African peoples to the imposition of rectilinear design.[43] But this is a long way from the vague equation of African identity and 'roundness'. The use of rounded forms is often justified on the grounds that they are natural to the African body or compensate for apartheid's grid-like impositions. In truth, 'roundness' marks a peculiarly modernist nostalgia for primitive essences, as well as a confused recognition that life in a racist society lacks fullness and wholeness.

South African modernism is too complex to explore in detail here, but the strong sense of neo-primitivist nostalgia in the writing of architects like Norman Eaton is intriguing. For Eaton, as for many Lawrentian modernists, the white body has lost touch with its instinctual relations and primitive affect. This has ethical consequences. White urban development, he believes, is conceited and arrogant, spreading 'like ugly cancerous growths over the fair face of the land',[44] while white domestic architecture has lost touch with the ethics of the organic community, especially as symbolized in the kraals and communal living areas of the Transvaal Ndebele. Ndebele architecture, for Eaton and for a host of other South African modernists, is a 'revelation in the art of living', a perfect expression of the collective in harmony with landscape. Their kraals, he says, 'combined in themselves all the essentials of simple human living', and they have a transcendental purity like 'simple music and the motions of animals'.[45]

Much of South Africa's modernist domestic architecture, including Eaton's own, mourns the passing of organic community and the sensory acuity he imagined was still visible in certain African village forms. Eaton sought to draw the African monumental past into his designs. His brick paving, reminiscent of Iron Age wall patterns, is one aspect of this urge. But the memorializing tendency is perhaps most visible in the complex surrounds and exterior landscapes of his domestic architecture in Pretoria.

Pretoria was a special kind of city. It was the administrative capital of apartheid and mainly Afrikaans-speaking; it was also where the 'real' African bushveld began. How were élite whites to figure themselves in this landscape? Several of Eaton's houses allude to the passing of instinctual experience beyond the reach of whites. At the centre of his sites there is usually a conventional, rectilinear modernist dwelling – but the edges fall away into roundness. Outdoor recreational areas are shaped like kraals; swimming pools look like gourds; and the whole is surrounded by walls of random stone quarried on site. At the edges of the domestic world, there is a reminder of another kind of sensory experience.

This monumental referencing to village life and lost civilizations reaches a bizarre conclusion in Eaton's Greenwood House. Here, random stone walls form the usual Africanized outer perimeter; but there are also servants' quarters in the shape of thatched stone rondavels and a central structure like a kraal around a tree. Conical stone towers, like Iron Age grain silos, conceal water cylinders, and these, together with the round huts and a ceremonial stone gateway, give the impression of a miniature Great Zimbabwe. As in Steynberg's desire for a diminutive, Africanized Mount Rushmore, there is a hint here of the tourist's interest in souvenir architectures.

Greenwood House is a paradoxical response to the same problems faced by the earlier monumental tradition. The solution it proposes is a sort of therapeutic monumentalizing, in which exploitative labour relations are concealed by an architectural fantasy about vanishing tribal identity and the past. The unequal exchanges between the master's house and the servants' 'village' are theatricalized as a relationship between modernity and African tradition. Servants are like defenceless villagers huddled up against the protective enclosure of a benevolent chiefly power.

A great deal of notable South African architecture has drawn on this tradition – most recently, the houses of Peter Rich with their Ndebele references and ethnicized servants' quarters. But very similar ethnic references were deployed in the design of apartheid buildings in the 1970s – in the homeland capital of Mmabatho, for instance. Mallows Louw Hoffe and Partners were responsible for the project, but they were constrained by the direct intervention of the homeland dictator, Lucas Mangope, who 'issued a directive indicating that the plan of the capital should reflect local Tswana customs and traditions'.[46] 'By combining aspects of formal baroque planning with ethnic Tswana architectural forms,' said the architects, 'a modern government centre is being developed that will reflect the strength, tradition and essential humanism of the Bophuthatswana nation.'[47] What was offered, in the end, was a mise en scène of democracy: the Mangope dictatorship was able to stage its operations in buildings around Government Square, a circular space 'reminiscent of a Kgotla, the central meeting space of the traditional Tswana village'.[48]

Even in these homeland structures, the question of racial exclusiveness is elided. References to the architecture of European democracy – the agora, the acropolis, the town square – are spliced together with simple-minded versions of the relationship between space and civil society in Southern African societies.[49] Such exercises in monumental folly are essentially ethnographic theatre; but they are also the end point of earlier imperial fantasies about pastoral care, and at times they bear an uncanny resemblance to the imaginary architectures of colonial romance novels. It is interesting that Mallows had trained in aerial survey during the Second World War, and that his initial ideas for Mmabatho were triggered by a flight over the ruins of Tswana settlements in Botswana. In fact, Mangope was persuaded to accept the design after being shown large-scale aerial photographs of Serowe. Town planning on this scale, in the service of apartheid's ethnic particularism, was heavily reliant on disciplines like ethnography to provide stable, readily identifiable categories of ethnic affiliation. That is not to say that there was a one-way traffic of ideas or that architects simply imposed a language of tribal difference on reluctant participants. Indeed, one of the most powerful influences on architecture and development planning today is the alliance between certain forms of archaeology and ethnography in the service of African communities who see the need to define themselves – or advertise themselves – as distinct 'tribes' with fixed boundaries, traditions and ancient ruins.

One could argue that similar imaginary connections govern the faux monumentality of hyperreal tourist environments like The Lost City (by Wimberly Allison Tong and Goo) or certain upmarket game lodges. Glass-fibre reinforced concrete, with its lightness, tensile strength and variability of finish, is the ideal material for white dreams of a time of empires and indigenous monuments more accommodating than the present. The link between colonial romance and The Lost City has been wittily analysed by Martin Hall – himself a leading archaeologist – who warns that the recent academic interpretations of medieval Shona history offer 'immense possibilities for hotels, casinos and Hollywood special effects, all designed with sensitivity to the cultural heritage of the host community'.[50] For the purposes of our interpretation, the imperial narrative that used the language of rough-hewn stone to signal a relationship between pastoral power and indigenous cultures here reaches a new conclusion. Glass-fibre reinforced concrete must inevitably replace actual stone in such buildings, simply because of their scale and the speed with which they must be erected. The global tourist economy has massively accelerated the rate at which marketable indigenous cultures are transformed into Hollywood versions of themselves. Under these conditions, it is hardly surprising that it is now not always easy to distinguish between monument and tourist destination.

In memoriam

We have arrived at a transitional moment in the language of monuments. There are few grand plans for memorial buildings in post-apartheid South Africa, and the dust of absurdity has begun to settle over some of the more venerable historical edifices. But for many, including the millions displaced from their homes under apartheid, and the relatives of those who died at the hands of the security police, there is a complete disjunction between personal suffering and public memory. Apartheid's worst torturers relied absolutely on the fact that it was possible to kill, maim and massacre without any record of their actions passing into the public domain, let alone into the monumental tradition. When policemen like Gideon Niewoudt burnt the bodies of Siphiwe Mtimkulu and Topsy Madaka, wrapped the ash and bone fragments in rubbish bags and dumped them into the Fish River, they expected the waters to obliterate all trace of their victims. We do not know why they chose this place for their grisly disposal, but there is a certain historical irony in the choice. In the colonial period, the Fish River was the symbolic edge of the colony. Even today, the early 19th-century signal towers and posts dotted along its banks are preserved as national monuments. Many of these sites later became police stations, retaining their original colonial names like 'Kaffir's Drift'; their graveyards, crammed with British colonial dead, are tended by the Imperial War Graves Commission. Some months ago, the widows and children of the men murdered by Gideon Niewoudt finally learned, in confessions before the Truth and Reconciliation Commission, what became of those who were thought erased from the historical record. Some time after the hearing, a simple ceremony was held at the approximate site where the bone ash was thrown into the river. Those who had gathered to remember, tossed wreaths into the water and watched them carried away towards the sea.

C

◄B3 ◄C2 ►C10

20
21
22
23
24
RTA
de Africa
Esperanze Sino al
erio Monamotapo
a, Scoperto dell'
Commandante
se Pisani
BRIQUAS of BINAS of DAMARAQUAS NATI
Aqua Calda
No 1
SIERAQUES
Nation Barbara
Lake
REGNO de Grand No 3
NAMAQUAS
BOSMANIE NATION
de
GGEVELD of HANTOM
A flat plain Coutry the Inha
Una Terra Piana Habitata de i Ba

Game lodges and leisure colonialists

Njabulo Ndebele

In July of 1997, while holidaying on the north coast of KwaZulu-Natal, I struck up a friendship with a family of American tourists. As we exchanged experiences of life in a game lodge, one of my new friends commented: 'Now I understand what it meant to be a colonialist.' I was intrigued by this comment because it seemed to ring true of my own experience of game-lodge living. Doesn't the game lodge represent the ultimate 'leisuring' of colonial history? Honed to a commercial fine art even more dramatically in post-apartheid South Africa, the game lodge resonates with an aspect of our history which has remained relatively untouched in the discourse of freedom. In essence, the game lodge impedes the emergence of an image of Africa and its diverse cultures as transforming historical phenomena.

But how did it feel to be a colonialist? There I was, having secured my own space through an advance booking in a game lodge that promised relief from the accumulated stresses of professional life. It promised isolation, unobtrusive personalized care, camp-fire camaraderie and pre-dinner drinks with a small number of fellow guests in the evenings, a dinner presided over by the managers, and late-night or early-morning game drives. Much of the lodge was built on stilts so that it would be environmentally friendly. This, I thought, was a slight departure from the usual style, where you felt that you were entering a precious cleared space in the middle of a frightening, threatening forest. To make up for the loss of that sensation, this particular lodge, raised up on its wooden posts, allowed you to enjoy the illusion of being lifted protectively above all the 'creeping things' of the earth. But wouldn't those things still come creeping up the stilts? Soon I learned to put this niggling anxiety aside and got down to enjoying myself.

There are some interesting features common to game lodges. There is the clearing in the middle of the bush, signifying civilization. This clearing will have neat green lawns, which contrast with the dense, chaotic bush just beyond their trimmed edges. That clean-cut edge is crucial. It indicates the perimeter of civilization. In the precious clearing you 'unexpectedly' yet gratefully find all the modern conveniences. Although they were promised in the promotional brochure, it is most reassuring to confirm the presence of comfortable, elegantly decorated bedrooms, each with its own bathroom containing toilet, shower and bathtub, hot and cold water. The towels and toilet paper, the rugs, the bedside reading lamps never fail to convey a sense of hospitality warmly offered, 'far from home'. Thank God there is no television set! Its pervasive absence enhances the general silence. Especially at night, when you finally lock the door and turn off the light to sleep, vaguely grateful that there is a key.

The pleasure of the game lodge lies in its ability to provide personal conveniences and luxuries far from home. These conveniences are an essential link to the home base. Signifying the success of conquest, they are the concrete manifestation of the movement of the dominant culture across time and space, and its ability to replicate itself far away. Of course, in the case of the contemporary game lodge, the violent and bitter history of conquest is long over. So you visit the lodge, the secured space in the bush, not to administer the threatening wilderness that presses in on all sides, but to participate in the continuing enjoyment of the fruits of conquest. There is nothing 'out there' to subdue and control. Whatever it is, out there, it is guaranteed to stay at bay.

The contemporary tour of duty in a game lodge is of a special kind. It is to reaffirm and celebrate a particular kind of cultural power: the enjoyment of colonial leisure. For isn't it true that relaxation comes from the uncontested simulation of hardship in the bush, enduring the chill and the bumpy tracks on night drives, sweating through walking trails, living by the light of the campfire rather than the television screen? The sense of simulation is enhanced by the ease with which escape is possible. In case of trouble, or in a bout of weakness, the telephone at the bedside is within arm's reach. Keeping the hand away from that phone is the measure of the leisure colonialist's discipline and determination to be isolated successfully. After all, you could simply drive away. Moreover, finding in the morning that your car had been miraculously cleaned, and every trace of the bush removed, you could drive away feeling overwhelmed by the greatness of small gestures, thinking: how thoughtful they can be! So, whether you succeed or fail in your simulated enterprise, you will be rewarded with care. Colonial leisure is the pleasure of risk without danger, or risk with the guarantee of safety.

Guaranteed safety? Not quite. If there is any guaranteed safety it is safety from the past. But if the past is gone, there can be no safety from the future. For the game lodge has become a leisure sanctuary where moneyed white South Africans can take refuge from the stresses of living in a black-run country. Once the game lodge was an extension of their power; now it is a place where those who have lost power go to regain a sense of its possession. Everything there is still in place: the measured conveniences, of course, but also the faceless black workers, behaving rather meekly, who clean the rooms, wash the dishes, make the fire, babysit the children, and make sure that in the morning the leisure refugees find their cars clean. Living somewhere 'out there', beyond the neatly clipped frontier, the black workers come into the clearing to serve. And then they disappear again. In their comings and goings, they are as inscrutable as the dense bush from which they emerge and to which they return. This coming and going of 'servants' triggers off among the leisure refugees a low-intensity anxiety. Who knows what the potential of these 'servants' is for transforming into the unknowable nightmare, so frequently reported in newspapers, in which a white farmer and his family are brutally murdered by killers, most probably black, who appear out of nowhere and vanish back into it again? After all, they have political power on their side these days, they can join trade unions, and come and go as they please.

Into this situation enters the black tourist. Until very recently, one of the distinguishing features of the game lodge was the marked absence of black tourists, but now they are beginning to show up in steadily increasing numbers. Being there, they experience the most damning ambiguities. They see the faceless black workers and instinctively see a reflection of themselves. They may be wealthy or politically powerful, but at that moment they are made aware of their special kind of powerlessness: they lack the backing of cultural power. They experience cultural domination in a most intimate way. Especially when they go game viewing. It is difficult not to feel that, in the total scheme of things, perhaps they should be out there with the animals, being viewed. Caught in a conversation with their white fellow refugees, brought together with them by an increasingly similar, stressful lifestyle, they can engage in discussions which bring out both the artificiality and the reality of their similarity.

The black tourist is conditioned to find the political sociology of the game lodge ontologically disturbing. It can be so offensive as to be obscene. He is a leisure colonialist torn up by excruciating ambiguities. He pays to be the viewer who has to be viewed. He is expected to engage in conversations around the campfire, about bush stories and lion kills, and hunting jokes which hold no interest for him. He is expected to be knowledgeable about 'white things', at the same time as he is transformed into an informant about 'black things', which are then analysed and interpreted by his campfire companions. Whenever he is asked his opinions about these interpretations, he is irritated by a tone of questioning which suggests that he ought to confirm their correctness. The more generous ones treat him with studious respect, wondering if they are not in the presence of a member of the new black élite, someone who may have useful connections. Desperately wanting to forget momentarily where he comes from, he is held up for display in the structure and content of the pleasure laid on for him as a paying customer. He finds no peace here. He can only experience himself as a caricature of a tourist. Seeking peace, and sensing that he may only succeed in adding colour to the white leisure colonialists' pleasant memories of the game lodge, he pays for being pushed into a stressful state of simmering revolt. The entire world of contemporary tourism carries no intuitive familiarity for him.

But his travail does not end there. The relationship between the black leisure colonialist and the black worker at the game lodge is full of pitfalls. For a moment, the black worker is not sure how he should respond to the black leisure colonialist who is caught up in the structure of 'white things'. Should he enter into a conspiracy of familiarity? Or should he play the game in which one of his kind is to be treated as if he were in fact 'the other'? If he chooses this last course, he puts the black leisure colonialist in a terribly invidious position. For the black leisure colonialist it is difficult to distinguish between being treated like a pampered guest or like a black guest who is doing 'white things'. The comfortable status of the privileged guest is only possible where there is a shared culture of leisure between the worker and the tourist, a culture which flourishes and finds legitimacy within a hegemonic political, social and economic dispensation.

On the other hand, if the black worker enters into a 'conspiracy of familiarity' with the black leisure colonialist, familiarity may breed contempt. Given that the black worker may regard the black leisure colonialist as an admired 'representative' in the white world, if the conversation between them becomes an exchange of gossip about 'white things', as it well might, the black leisure colonialist is in danger of losing his dignity. How can he, from his position of 'power', complain with the powerless about the powerful? This ludicrous position clearly confirms him as a caricature. Surely this conspiracy is impotent! After that, the professionalism which the black leisure colonialist, as a paying customer in search of peace and relaxation, expects from the black worker is compromised. Having been exposed as lacking an integral identity, the guest is left with a terrible choice: either to treat the workers with masterful aloofness or to engage them in harmless pleasantries. Either way, he gets to keep his dignity; but he keeps it at the cost of avoidance and self-deception. Both the structure and the content of leisure offer no escape.

But there is a possible escape route. It is to engage the white leisure colonialist and the owners of the game lodge in a cultural contest, in which the cultural history of the game lodge is deconstructed and a new structure and content of leisure are brought into being as expressions in a new society. The liberation of leisure is an essential aspect of the new experience of freedom. To begin that liberation we need to pose some questions:

How can the game lodge evolve forms of leisure that are rooted in contemporary South African experience, catering for a new leisure clientele and guaranteeing profitability? How can the game lodge participate in the general liberation of leisure? How can the game lodge become more than an outmoded colonial outpost routinely (yet probably unintentionally) tolerated by black governments? A new black government will surely be concerned about being seen to guarantee the survival of negative, outmoded anthropologies by allowing culturally entrenched forms of white privilege to continue to exist unchallenged!

This leads me to what is perhaps the most frightening aspect of culture in post-apartheid South Africa, something that speaks to the nature of evolving forms of national consciousness. Is it possible that South Africa is one big game lodge where all its black citizens are struggling to make sense of their lives, like people who awake in an enormous vacation house which is now supposed to be theirs but which they do not quite recognize? Do they strive to be just like their fellow citizens who have mastered the economics of the game lodge, and who may seek to consolidate a cultural condition in keeping with their strategies of survival by marketing an image of South Africa as a haven of safety and success in a dark, violent and threatening continent? Doesn't it pay to belong to South Africa, to be free from the 'chaos in the north', to keep the north at bay at all costs? Doesn't it pay to be the onlooker, gazing out at 'the rest of the continent' from the window of a vacation house that offers comfort and security? What does it take to keep things this way?

Are we evolving a split personality which may generate its own forms of creativity? What does it mean to use the vacation house as a vantage point from which to look down on others, when we have yet to prove that the house belongs to us and that we are its rightful owners, when we still live in an environment in which we are the ones being viewed? As I write, the landscape of apartheid is reproducing itself with a vengeance. Townships are bursting with informal settlements, reinforcing old dichotomies in the landscape. The psychology of apartheid, the culture of the game lodge, would teach us to regard informal settlements as a potential threat to civilization, menacing the Europe in our midst. While defending this European residue may allow us to keep the vacation house intact, it may also prevent the emergence of the recognition that what is going on in the townships carries the defining characteristics of our new society. The informal settlements and all the problems they present – are they not a vital context in which we can define, plan and build for ourselves, not merely maintaining the vacation house but constructing a new home? Could the game lodge itself be transformed in the service of rural development?

The ambiguities and choices are difficult, even painful. Now we want to throw off the psychological burden of our painful past; now we want to hold on to it. We know that death may be a very real consequence of throwing off the burden altogether in one big heave. Surely who we are and who we finally become is bound up with all these questions and contradictions! Surely we are an inseparable part of Africa, our home! Yet our history intricately binds us to the rest of the world, and such ties cannot be broken without a serious threat to our survival. And again: we are very much ourselves, we have many demons to exorcize, and yet much has been achieved that we can build on. We remain complex and we have a responsibility to confront that fact. Our survival will depend on our ability to develop successful skills in carving coherent and sustainable meanings out of this definitive field of complexity.

And so, as we leave the game lodge, we notice the electrified fence that surrounds the whole reserve (we remember the electrified fences on our northern borders). The fence reminds us that the game lodge, that inner core of cleared space, is not carved out of an unbroken wilderness but out of another contained space, sealed off from the country at large. It is a world of make-believe whose charm depends on the brief enjoyment it gives us to be a colonialist. On the edge of the real world, we stop the car, as the black gatekeeper opens the gate with an expectant smile. If we are white leisure colonialists, we will wave with a smile or give a generous tip. Either gesture will be appreciated. If we are black, we wonder if we should tip at all? How will it be interpreted? If it is too little, the gatekeeper will think we are insulting him. If we don't give anything, we will fit the stereotype of the stingy rich blacks. If we give too much, perhaps he will think we are ostentatiously displaying our wealth. In the end, we rationalize. We give what we think is generous under the guise of 'spreading wealth'. It seems to be appreciated. Then we drive away, a bundle of mixed emotions and troubled thoughts. How is it that a simple quest for peace and restoration turned into an unexpectedly painful journey into the self? We think: there is no peace for those caught in the process of becoming.

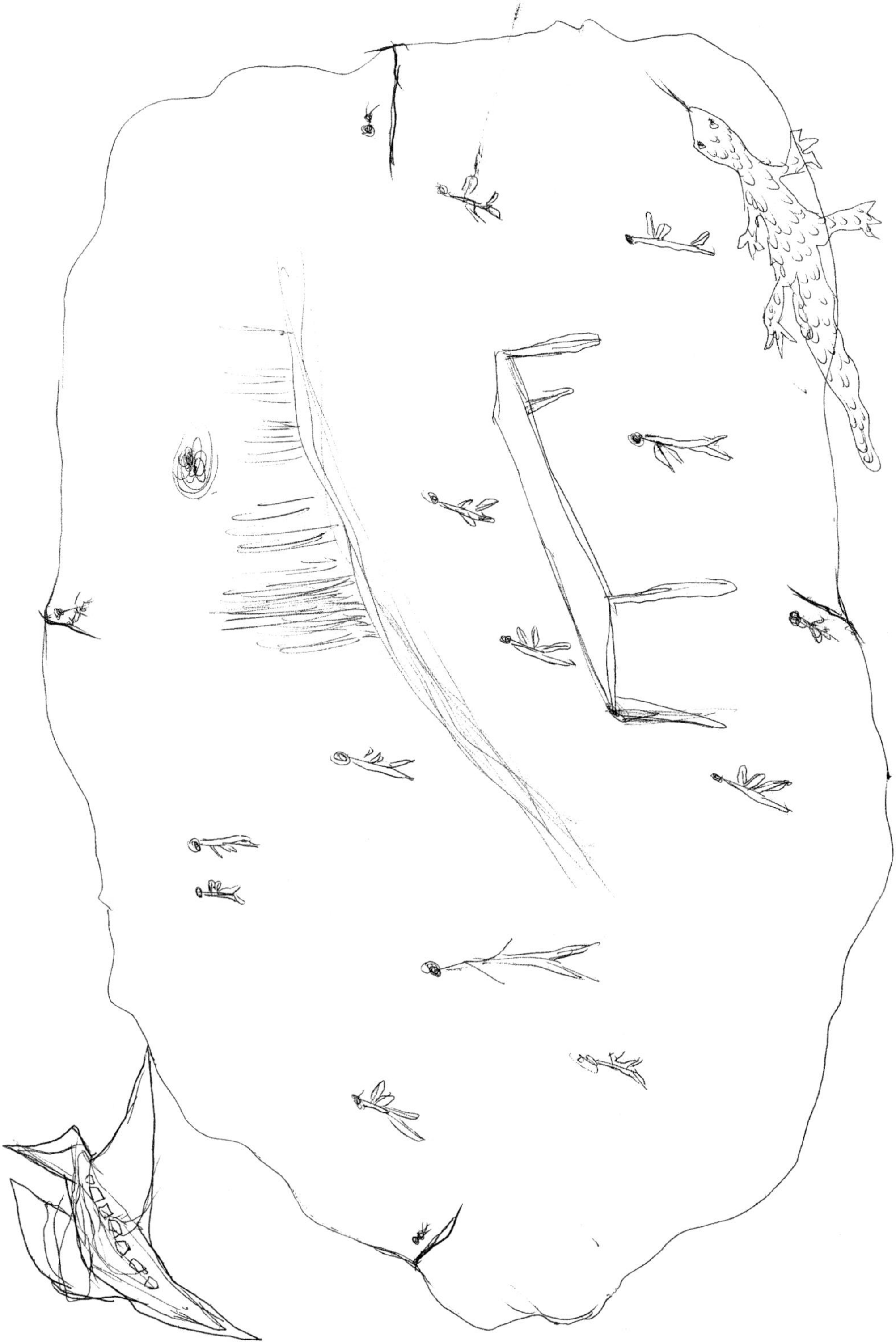

Falstaff
Moshekwa Langa

The initial foundation had been laid by the riverside. One had to take a boat to get there. (I thought it an inconvenient exercise.) The area was temperate. There was one outlook point. The place looked within. This was the observation tower of that place. I was glad to leave within a short time.

D

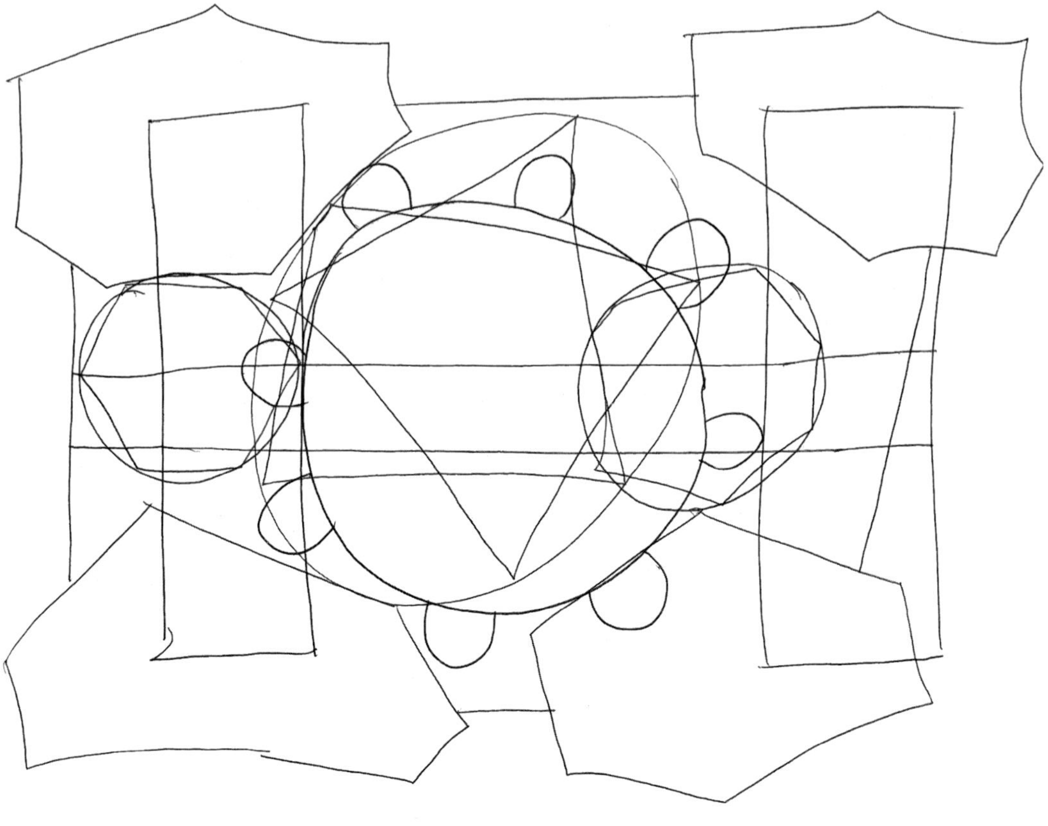

Falstaff after Xavier, a schematic of one of the buildings seen from above.

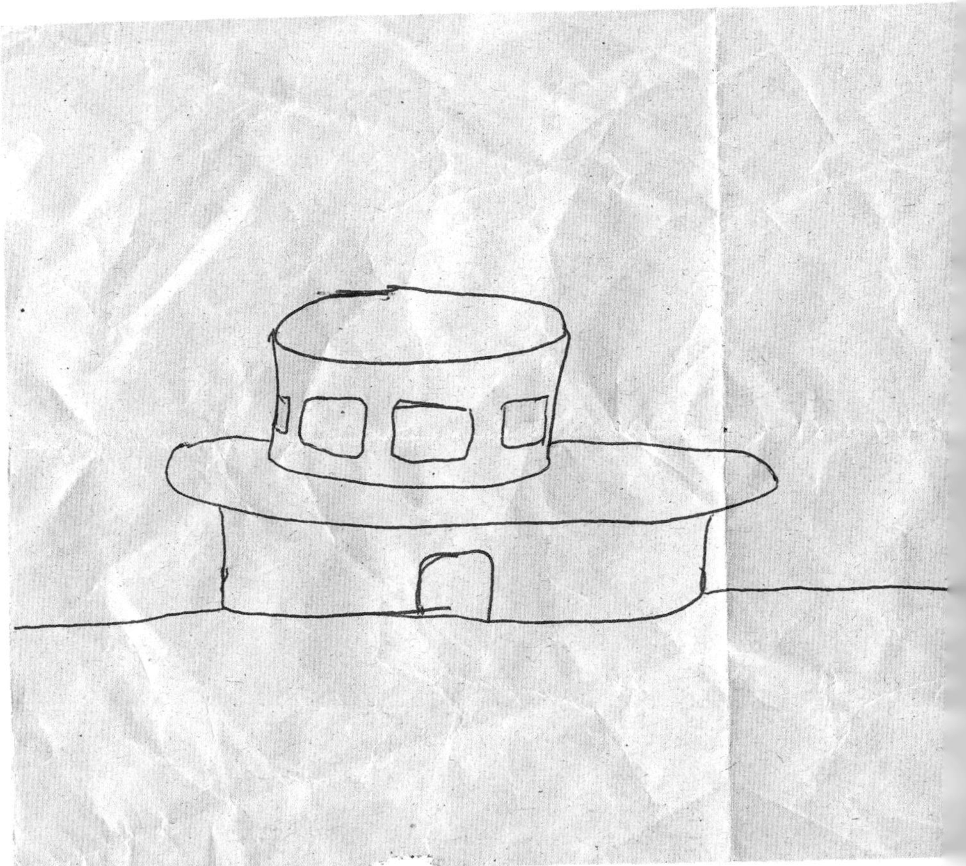

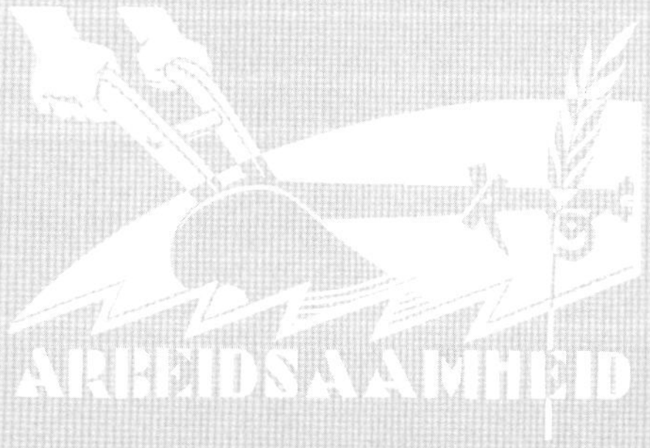
ARBEIDSAAMHEID

'Ons bou vir die Bank': Nationalism, architecture and Volkskas Bank[1]

Melinda Silverman

The top floor of the Volkskas Bank headquarters in Pretoria affords a panoramic view of the city and its surrounding koppies. Dominating these koppies are significant icons of Afrikaner nationalism. Fort Klapperkop is a defensive icon from a century ago, a modest 19th-century redoubt intended to protect the Transvaal Boers from hostile Uitlanders. The Voortrekker Monument, a squat fifty-year-old icon of aspiration, was designed by Gerard Moerdyk to commemorate the centenary of the Great Trek, and is a symbol of Afrikaner claims to South Africa's land.[2]

The third, more modern manifestation of Afrikaner nationalism is the Volkskas building itself, which on completion in May 1978 was Pretoria's highest edifice. Designed by Samuel Pauw, it speaks of nationalism triumphant and economic dominance. It is the city's rebuttal to Johannesburg's skyscrapers.

These three buildings share a common heritage, each representative of a particular phase in the evolution of Afrikaner nationalism. Shifts in nationalist ideology have generated corresponding stylistic responses in the architecture of Volkskas's own buildings, beginning with a sentimental evocation of an idealized rural past, particularly in the work of Gerard Moerdyk and Wynand Louw; followed by the modernist – and modest – projects of Gawie Fagan as Afrikaner capitalism matured; followed by Pauw's monumental skyscraper; and followed finally by the abandonment of custom-commissioned buildings in favour of rented accommodation in office parks.

Volkskapitalisme: Gerard Moerdyk and Wynand Louw

The Volkskas Bank was a project of Afrikaner nationalist ideologues, established after the First World War to allow the *volk* to create its own wealth outside institutions of British imperialism. It was a bank inspired by such ideas as nation-building and economic empowerment, and it gave deliberate expression to these ideas in an ambitious building programme that stretched from small rural towns to the major cities. Indeed, the bank's own two-volume history – *Die Bank van Oom Bossie* and *Van Akker tot Eik*[3] – devotes substantial attention to these building projects. A cynic might note that the history was written by the man who ran the Volkskas building projects

Volkskas logo.

for four decades, Carl Engelbrecht, but that would be missing the point. From its very inception, Volkskas was projected as nothing less than the embodiment of the volk, and its buildings were seen as manifestations of this ideological fervour. 'Volkskas,' said J.J. Bosman, the first manager of the bank, 'is 'n hoogstaande instelling van die Afrikanervolk. Die Afrikanervolk is 'n hoogstaande Volk en daarom verlang Volkskas hoogstaande geboue wat 'n waardige indruk maak.'[4] ['Volkskas is a distinguished institution of the Afrikaner Nation. The Afrikaner Nation is a distinguished one, and Volkskas therefore wishes to have distinguished buildings that make a dignified impression.']

L.J. du Plessis, a leading ideologue of Afrikaner development in the years after the First World War, first suggested the idea of an Afrikaner bank in 1924. As one historian of Afrikaner nationalism, Dan O'Meara, writes: '... the structure of the South African economy offered few opportunities to those whose home language was Afrikaans. The economy was dominated by "imperialist" interests.'[5] The fear among Afrikaner thinkers, in the context of the Fusion government's attempts to encourage a broader South Africanism based on cooperation between English-speakers and Afrikaners, was that the latter would eventually be enslaved. In 1933 Du Plessis wrote of the dangers of imperialism in the guise of economic collaboration: 'Our monetary system, our commercial and banking policy, our industrial sector will remain Imperialist orientated and grow increasingly so. In place of the old political subjugation we now enter a period of economic dependence. And the golden chains so forged are much stronger and more dangerous than the old [political] chains because they are more difficult to recognize, and once forged, are not easily discarded.'[6]

Economic mobilization was placed high on the agenda of the Afrikaner Broederbond, the secret society devoted to the strategic advancement of Afrikaner nationalism. Casting this new economic movement as the 'Tweede Trek' – the Second Trek – the ideologues articulated their longing for the idealized unity of the Great Trek that had taken place a century before. In terms of this mythology 'all were farmers united against external enemies, class divisions were seen as the product of "imperialism" and its alter ego, "foreign" capitalism'.[7] Instead of foreign capitalism, the concept of 'volkskapitalisme' – an indigenous amalgam of cooperative and capitalist economic relations – was advanced by the various commissions of inquiry into economic affairs conducted within the Broederbond under chairman L.J. du Plessis or treasurer J.J. Bosman. Volkskapitalisme was intended to help Afrikaners improve their position in the industrial economy and ultimately take control of South African capitalism itself. While the Carnegie Commission of 1932 had characterized 25 per cent of Afrikaners as 'poor white', there was also an acknowledgement that 'three-quarters of the people still had the capacity to help themselves',[8] and that there was untapped potential in mobilizing Afrikaner capital within exclusively Afrikaans institutions. Volkskas – literally 'the People's Treasury' – was conceptualized by J.J. Bosman as one such institution. The bank was formally established in Pretoria in April 1934 by sixty Broederbond members, with L.J. du Plessis as the first chairman and Bosman (the 'Oom Bossie' ['Uncle Bossie'] of the corporate history) as the first manager.

The ideological foundations of the bank included notions of industriousness and self-help, a growing sense of national identity and pride, and a nostalgic affirmation of a shared rural history – aptly symbolized by the plough in the bank's first logo. This was coincident with the romantic nationalism – and in some instances nationalist socialism – sweeping through both Europe and South Africa.

The position of Volkskas contrasted sharply with that of its rivals: Standard and Barclays were colonial offshoots of substantial imperial banks based in England, while the Netherlands Bank was an extension of a Dutch financial institution. Volkskas was home-grown, anti-imperialist, born out of economic need and initially premised on volkskapitalisme. This hybrid economic form was echoed in the financial structure of Volkskas, which started out as a 'cooperative bank' for the Afrikaner masses. Six years later, in 1940, it became a conventional commercial bank. Although it was 'not announced at the time', the bank later acknowledged that it had always intended to abandon this cooperative form. Responding to charges that the Board had misled the public, it argued that the initial adoption of the cooperative form was necessary 'to gain the co-operation of the Afrikaner masses'.[9] When Volkskas changed its status, it immediately faced great hostility both from the big commercial banks and from the existing *volk*'s banks. The former refused clearing facilities and tried to get Volkskas prosecuted under the Usury Act, whilst the latter bitterly attacked it within Afrikaner ranks as a 'capitalist institution'.[10]

For the first six years of its existence, when ideological reservations about capital accumulation were still strong and there was little capital to spare, the bank relied on rented accommodation. It was only in 1940 that it ventured into property for the first time and employed an architect to work on sketch plans for the Pretoria office. Gerard Moerdyk, the key Afrikaner ideologue on the subject of what constituted a genuine South African architecture in the context of the Afrikaner's 'cultural struggle',[11] was an obvious choice as the bank's first architect.

The Pretoria building, which has since been demolished, was a restrained art deco structure, with nothing to indicate that it had aspirations to be a nationalist icon. The building had neither the ideological nor the monumental qualities that were to become evident in Moerdyk's later work for the *volk* – in the form of the Voortrekker Monument – or for the bank.

There can be no doubt that Moerdyk's perception of nationalism was broadly shared by the bank. Both were in search of exclusively Afrikaner vehicles. In 1932, in a newspaper article on the development of a specifically South African style of architecture, Moerdyk argued for the Cape Dutch style as '*'n suiwere Afrikaanse produk*' ['a pure Afrikaans product'] and blamed British colonialism for its demise.[12] The following year he wrote: '*Die Kaaps-Hollandse boustyl is op dieselfde manier*

D

Gerard Moerdyk, Volkskas Building, Central Street, Pretoria, c. 1935.

3

H. Vermooten, Bethlehem Bank, c. 1949.

'n Afrikaanse produk as die Afrikaanse taal, die Afrikanerbees en, per slot van rekening, die Afrikaner self.'[13] ['The Cape Dutch style is an Afrikaans product in the same way as the Afrikaans language, the Afrikander cow and, in the end, the Afrikaner himself.'] The argument, however, was disingenuous. Cape Dutch, as the name itself suggests, was an import from the Netherlands and often used to signal the presence of European culture in an otherwise alien and hostile landscape.

Debates about architecture within the corporate structure of Volkskas itself largely echoed Moerdyk's position, but were articulated for the first time in 1946 during a professional tiff about the design of the Somerset East branch. Here, the appointed architect, J. A. Smith, saw fit to express reservations about the appropriateness of the Cape Dutch style.[14] At the recommendation of Wynand Louw, the bank's consulting architect, Smith was dismissed and the more pliable H. Vermooten appointed in his place. By 1949 Vermooten had produced a classical reworking of the Cape Dutch style adorned with fluted pilasters that gained the approval of Wynand Louw and the bank's directors. Similar arguments beset the design for the Bethlehem branch in 1949, when Vermooten once again took over the work, this time from Philip Nel. The Bethlehem branch is a neo-classical reordering of the desired Cape Dutch style.

Moerdyk's most significant design for Volkskas was conceptualized during a brief period that he spent in the offices of Louw and Louw, to whom the building is often ascribed. The design was for the giant Market Street branch of Volkskas in the very heart of Uitlander territory – Johannesburg – situated not far from the rival Standard Bank. The importance of this bank in Volkskas's eyes was demonstrated in company advertisements when it finally opened in 1949. 'Another Monument,' they announced with reference to Moerdyk's newly unveiled Voortrekker Monument. 'Nog 'n monument het verrys in die daeraad van 'n volk se ekonomiese bewuswording. 'n Monument deur 'n volk self opgerig wat in die annale van sy geskiedenis aangeteken sal staan as die eerste suiwer nasionale handelsbank, gevestig op die eie bodem wat hom steeds sy groeikrag gee.'[15] ['Another monument has risen in the dawn of a people's economic awakening. A monument erected by the nation itself, which will go down in the annals of its history as the first pure national commercial bank, founded on the native soil that still invigorates it.'] The intention was to announce the arrival of Afrikaner capital in the centre of imperial economic power and the home of 'Hoggenheimer'.[16] The nearby Standard Bank, in classical and somewhat overwrought imperial style, was all dressed stone, Doric columns and cupolas.

Moerdyk, by contrast, took his standard Cape Dutch vernacular and reinterpreted it to suit an entirely different building typology – that of the urban, commercial office block. Cape Dutch architecture is invariably low-rise, rarely more than two or three storeys high. Its rural domestic incarnation places strong emphasis on steeply pitched roofs and tall, ornate gables. These plastered and whitewashed homesteads, approached from afar along axial driveways, are often dwarfed by mountainous rural landscapes. Even in its urban incarnation, traditional Cape Dutch differs significantly in form and content from what Moerdyk set out to achieve in Johannesburg: the traditional version is still plastered and whitewashed and, most significantly, set back from the street edge by means of a stoep or small flight of stairs so as to allow proper appreciation of a symmetrical façade. Here, by contrast, was a high-rise commercial building in an urban context, with the roof-line so high as to be invisible from the street below, built hard up against the street edge and rendered in dark granite.

The tensions of transporting the Cape Dutch style without reference to programme or context are evident. Some elements of the Cape Dutch which are maintained are quite obviously out of place: 'Cape residential-style windows in hardwood',[17] for example, are ill-suited to a large-scale commercial building or the harsh weathering of the Johannesburg climate. But where other elements of the Cape Dutch have been abandoned, important spatial qualities have been lost. The set-back from the street edge afforded by the stoep in urban prototypes of the Cape Dutch has been omitted, with the result that there is inadequate space to view the essential symmetry of the street elevation. Another more successful departure was a tentative attempt to express on the exterior the spatial complexity of the interior, particularly the double-volume banking hall. This required altering the proportion of the windows and deviating from the standard pattern where each row of windows expressed each floor. Whitewashed plaster has been replaced with dark-brown granite

Gerard Moerdyk (completed by Wynand Louw), Market Street Bank, Johannesburg, 1949.

at ground-floor level and dark face brick above, more appropriate in the harsh highveld light.

If the architectural hybrid is awkward and anachronistic both in time and place, the iconography of the artworks that decorate the building more eloquently expresses a version of nationalism based on a new-found alliance between a rural past and an urban future. The building is adorned with an ox-wagon frieze and other rural motifs; but also visible at pavement level is the work of sculptor Willem Hendrikz, whose bronze door panels and marble engravings 'depict a people of both skilled workers and businessmen, an alliance of agriculture and industry, of working and professional classes ...'[18]

Modernization: Gawie Fagan

The Nationalist victory in the election of 1948 came as a surprise to most people, including the Afrikaner nationalists themselves. Political power was tentative at first, with the National Party only a hair's breadth ahead of the opposition. But the enormous expansion of Afrikaner enterprise and the post-war industrial boom gave the state an increasing sense of confidence. The new government embarked on a comprehensive programme of modernization, including expansion of the state itself.

Deborah Posel has shown how this expansion echoed ideas about statecraft in other parts of the world at the time, such as Roosevelt's New Deal, the British post-war reconstruction programme, and the Nazi programme for Aryan supremacy, each of which were 'particular instances of a wider consensus about the prospects for large-scale social transformation, and a confidence in a suitably modern state's capacities to bring it about'.[19] Apartheid, according to Posel, became part of this modernizing project, which during its first phase 'was a commitment to coupling white supremacy and economic prosperity by way of a more systematic, thoroughgoing racist order, with Afrikaners at the political helm – recognizing the 'realities' of the market and therefore the impracticality of total segregation'.[20]

Afrikaner nationalism had in the past been defined by its marginality and underdog status, by notions of struggle and recourse to a shared rural past. By contrast, the new ascendant Afrikaner nationalism needed a new self-conception within a culture of modernity. The 1959 Commission of Inquiry into European Occupancy of the Rural Areas, for example, argued that a sentimental attachment to the small white rural family was dangerous to Afrikanerdom's long-term survival.[21] As one Department of Agriculture official put it: 'We will not succeed in luring the youth to the platteland by idealizing farm life or by romanticizing unrealistically the farm and outdoor life ... We must develop the idea of farming as a profession rather than indulging in sickly romanticism about mother earth, land and the boereplaas [farm].'[22] Professionalism, modernization and progress entered the rhetoric of Afrikaner nationalism.

Corresponding modernization was taking place within Volkskas Bank. This included initiating trade in foreign currency (1946), listing on the Johannesburg Stock Exchange (1952) and appointing a new general manager, Dr. J.A. Hurter (1945), who emphasized the need to look beyond a parochial Afrikaner nationalism to the broader South African economy. His intention was to expand the bank's clientele to incorporate both English economic interests[23] and a potential black constituency. By 1958 the bank had opened its first branch in a black township.[24] Rural blacks were to become an increasingly important client base, as Volkskas was often the only bank in the area.

Volkskas grew in tandem with the economy. But while industry, which was generally located in the cities, accounted for the bulk of economic development, Afrikaner capital, which was tied to agriculture, was still located firmly in rural areas. What was needed was a project to market the concept of a modern capitalism and associated industrial investment in small rural towns, the dorpies. Volkskas was therefore obliged to embark on an ambitious building programme, quite different from the programmes of the large 'English' banks. The English banks were dominant in the cities, and so they undertook large-scale building in a small number of places. Volkskas, by contrast, had to be present throughout the platteland, which required large numbers of branches, each catering to a small number of clients.[25] Since this spread the bank's resources thin, the branches were of necessity modest structures. There were also legal constraints – only 25 per cent of a bank's capital could be tied up in property;[26] and time constraints – the bank had to move immediately to capture the tide of Afrikaner nationalist fervour. Finally, there were stylistic constraints – a sentimental attachment to Cape Dutch would prove inappropriate in a context emphasizing a broader South Africanism, progress and modernity.[27]

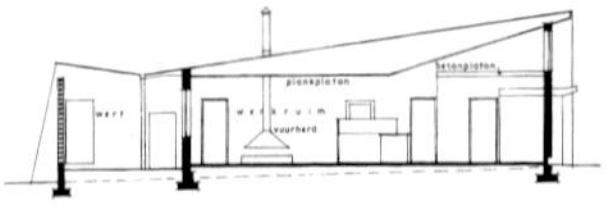

The need for many buildings to be constructed over a wide area as cheaply as possible created a number of cost-saving imperatives. This required a comprehensive and radical restructuring of the bank's architectural project. In 1952 the bank's property manager, Carl Engelbrecht, created an in-house architectural office and stopped employing high-profile private practitioners. Engelbrecht hired a young architect named Gabriel (Gawie) Fagan from a patrician Afrikaner family (son of a judge, and nephew of H. A. Fagan, chairman of the pragmatic Native Laws Commission under the Smuts government), a man whose ten years as the official bank architect created a new style.

Fagan was a graduate of the newly established School of Architecture at the University of Pretoria, which produced its first qualified architects soon after the National Party victory. According to architectural historian Roger Fisher, 'ideological fervour superseded the academic rigour of these young graduates, and ... this was fundamental in allowing an empirical and intuitive response ... [There were] funds for State commissions, materials of local manufacture, a patronage sympathetic to the aesthetic of the Modern, a rich diversity of indigenous building materials and a will to achieve a distinct cultural identity in all its manifestations.'[28]

The Pretoria School was an early champion of European-style modernism, and became a seminal influence on Fagan and other architects who passed through it. The key figures at the School were prominent architects: Gordon McIntosh, a member of the 'zerohour' group which propagated the work of Le Corbusier; and Helmut Stauch, a German immigrant who brought the ideas of Walter Gropius and Mies van der Rohe to South Africa.

While the functionalist programme of modernist town planning, with its connotations of social transformation, resonated with the rather different social-engineering programmes of the National Party government,[29] the formal elements of European modernist architecture found an equally receptive audience. Much like the Cape Dutch, the International Style was another European import,

Gawie Fagan, Belfast Bank, 1954.

but in this instance could be used to express both the notion of progress and a more inclusive, cosmopolitan South African identity. Even if the International Style failed to speak of here, it most eloquently spoke of now. The Pretoria architects, however, unlike their Johannesburg counterparts, reworked the modernist idiom to South African conditions. According to Gilbert Herbert, in his history of the Modern Movement in South African architecture, '[In] Pretoria the tendency is away from the purity of style, its doctrinaire aspect is softened and freely adapted to the specifically local demands of time and place. In its use of materials, in its relationship to irregular sites, in its adaptation to climatic needs, there would appear to be more flexibility, more versatility, in Pretoria than in Johannesburg.'[30]

Fagan's early works for Volkskas demonstrate a distinctive and thoroughgoing modernism. In his design for the branch in Belfast, a small town on the eastern edge of the highveld, which he started two years after being employed by the bank, Fagan immediately deviated from the traditional symmetry associated with bank buildings. Applying a system of proportioning based on the Fibonacci series as evolved by Hambidge, which was taught at the Pretoria School, the entrance portico is shifted off to the left and the remaining expanse of wall on the right punctuated by a small window serving the manager's office. Another characteristic modernist element – the horizontal strip window – runs the full length of the façade and illuminates the raked ceiling inside. This ceiling, which affords a volumetric complexity to the interior, is achieved by the simple but innovative inversion of a conventional truss.

The Belfast building is both tentative and modest. A few years later, in more accomplished works, Fagan demonstrates a more confident modernist aesthetic. Large expanses of glass curtain walling characterize the branch in Hartswater (1959), where the influences of Mies and Gropius are evident. Here, behind the double-volume glass curtain wall, the stairway connecting two floors is visible. Fagan positioned this stairway far from the offices it serves, thus necessitating a walkway that wraps around and enlivens the space of the banking hall: a utilitarian element becomes sculptural. This device was repeated far more dramatically in the Roodepoort branch (1959), where a glazed spiral stair occupies the acutely-angled street corner. Comparisons can be drawn with the glazed spiral stairs articulating Gropius's Model Factory and Office Building in Cologne, described by Giedion as 'movement seized and immobilized in space'.[31]

Gawie Fagan, Hartswater Bank, 1959.

This passion for modernism was not exclusive to Volkskas. It was enthusiastically embraced by the Nationalist government in the construction of its large public buildings. In Pretoria, the Wachthuis – headquarters of the South African Police designed by Norman Eaton – and the Receiver of Revenue building designed by Moerdyk and Watson together with Meiring and Naudé, both demonstrated a thorough modernist aesthetic. And the private sector was equally enthusiastic, as evidenced by the rash of skyscrapers in Johannesburg. But what distinguished the Volkskas projects was the pioneering use of modernism in small, conservative towns in the South African countryside. Stylistically, these buildings were revolutionary, unlike any other buildings in such dorpies, self-conscious architectural statements of modernist intent.

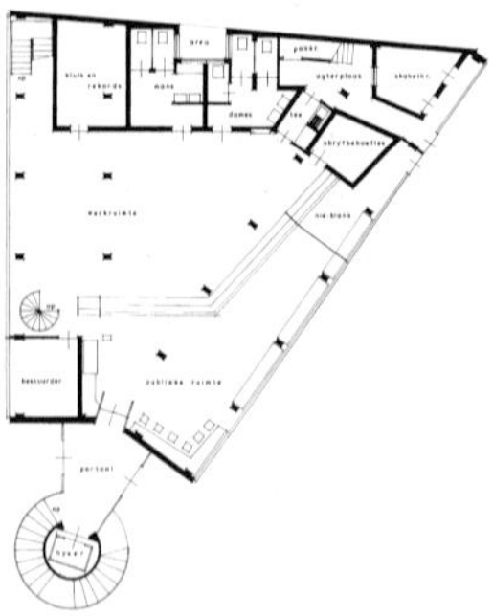

Despite this, the banks designed by Fagan were sensitive to their surroundings. An aspect of this was their modest scale: in the small towns the banks were single- or double-storey buildings of about 300 square metres, often including a shop that could be rented out to help subsidize building costs. Fagan argued that this modesty emerged from a respect for local context. 'In urban situations, good neighbourliness is ... important, and I think the many commercial buildings designed for Volkskas bank during the 1950s bear testimony to my attempts to make quiet buildings that would not shout unduly for attention, and sit comfortably between their neighbours ...'[32] His boss, Carl Engelbrecht, made the same point even more pithily: Fagan's buildings were ones that said, 'Ekskuus, laat ek hier moet staan.'[33] ['Excuse me for standing here.']

Roger Fisher argues that this contextual sensitivity arose out of the need for economic efficiency: 'Fagan persuaded the directorate that the cheapest and quickest way was to provide buildings suited to the local circumstances, that is, regional designs, rather than to follow the route of corporate identity.'[34] Building costs for the banks were unusually low, averaging R50 per square metre in the early 1960s. One reason for this was the use of inexpensive local materials of the kind readily available in small towns. In some instances this was face brick (as in Belfast); in others, plastered stock brick, with Fagan deferring to local custom. Roofs were generally of corrugated iron.

In his design for the branch in Ladybrand, in the Orange Free State near the Lesotho border, Fagan argued that he had no option other than to use the local stone, that this affirmation of local context and natural landscape was the inevitable response of an environmentally sensitive architect: 'Toe die nuwe Volkskas-gebou in Ladybrand egter beplan is op 'n terrein wat aan 'n ou klipgebou

Gawie Fagan, Roodepoort Bank, 1959.

grens en van waar ek dieselfde klippe kon sien in die rante wat 'n perdeskoen om die dorpie vorm, moes ek van die klip gebruik maak.'[35] ['However, when the new Volkskas building in Ladybrand was planned for a site which bordered on an old stone building and from which I could see the same stone in the ridges that form a horseshoe around the town, I had to make use of the stone.']

The main body of the Ladybrand building, including the public and working areas, is a double-volume space projecting outwards and upwards, distinguished from ancillary spaces on either side, which are single storey and set back. The ancillary spaces contain the manager's office and safe on the one side; and the 'non-white' entrance on the other. The main volume is articulated by large piers built out of local dressed stone and projecting on both the outside and the inside of the glazed building envelope. The ancillary elements are plastered brickwork.

If the use of stone was merely the instinctive response of a sensitive architect, the branch manager discovered deeper layers of nationalist symbolism in the building. In his speech at the opening ceremony, he said that the stone pillars symbolized the strength and reliability of Volkskas. The use of glass demonstrated the bank's commitment to transparency and pride in its Afrikaner workforce: Volkskas was proud to show 'dat dit volbloed jong Afrikaners is wat hy in diens het, en dat hy niks het om oor skaam of bang te wees as dit gesien word nie' ['that it had full-blooded young Afrikaners in service, and that it had nothing to be ashamed of or afraid of by showing it']. Another feature of the building noted in the speech was a small recess in the plaster at the front of the manager's office. Although it might have been put there simply to break the flat surface, the manager said, he saw it as a symbol of 'die oop plek vir goedgesindes wat nog nie die moed gehad het om Suid-Afrika ook op ekonomiese gebied eerste te stel nie'[36] ['the place kept open for sympathizers who had not yet had the courage to put South Africa first in the economic sphere as well']. Failure to bank with Volkskas was clearly a failure of nationalist commitment.

The metaphor of stone – stone extracted from the land and transformed through hard labour into the building blocks of nationalist icons – must surely have resonated with an institution whose corporate logo was the plough. In fact, the use of stone in the Ladybrand branch proved so successful that Fagan started using the material elsewhere during a very brief period of experimentation with a uniform corporate style. Branches in geographical locations as far afield as Warrenton and

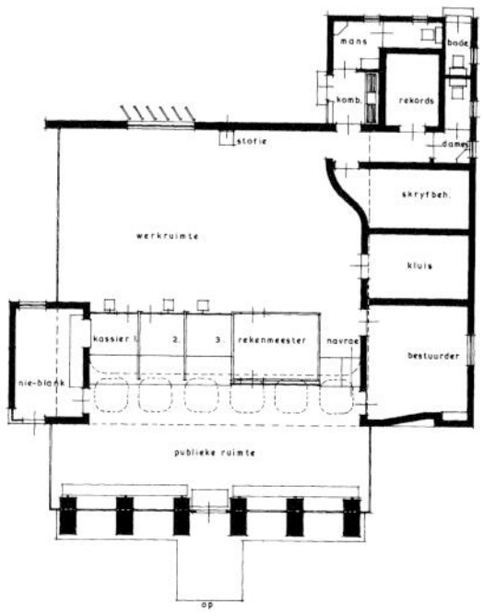

Gawie Fagan, Ladybrand Bank, 1958.

Warden in Natal (1959 and 1960 respectively), Brandfort in the Karoo (1960) and Bonnievale in the Western Cape (1962) have similar plans and elevations with panels of stone masonry on either side of the entrance door.

Technical issues and building materials should not distract from what Fagan believed to be the primary element influencing built form: 'But climate, available materials and technology, are far from being the only or even the prime determinants of built forms. Rather form is the result of a whole range of socio-cultural factors with climate, materials and technology seen as modifying only.'[37] In his Western Cape buildings, this theme manifested once again in references to the Cape Dutch. Fagan, like his predecessor Moerdyk, was respectful of Cape Dutch architecture – some of his best-known work, much later in his career, would deal with the conservation of early Cape Dutch buildings. But unlike Moerdyk, he never attempted to recycle the style into modern contexts. He wrote approvingly of the Japanese architect, Kenzo Tange, who opposed the superficial regurgitation of the traditional: 'Now regionalism, by its very definition, as it presupposes a thorough understanding and appreciation of local architecture, should avoid the easy clichés, and at the same time be socio-culturally orientated ... [Tange] sees the role of tradition rather as that of a catalyst which furthers a chemical reaction but is no longer detectable in the end result.'[38]

Before the advent of Tange, another Pretoria modernist, Norman Eaton, had written much the same about the Cape Dutch vernacular: 'A real appreciation of the underlying principles embodied in this early work – rather than only a superficial knowledge of its purely visual charm – will ... point the way to a revival of a truly great indigenous architecture in this country, different in function and outward appearance though the result must undoubtedly be.'[39]

Fagan's 1959 bank in Montagu in the Western Cape is an interesting example of how he incorporates aspects of the Cape Dutch style without simplistically applying its dictates. The Montagu building has a double-volume banking hall with subsidiary spaces wrapped around it on both sides. The volumes are rectilinear, defined by the crisp lines of the glazed envelope. These contrast with a gentle curve in plan directing movement into the entrance, and the tapering of the monumental brick piers that articulate the front façade. Rendered in plaster and whitewash, the masonry echoes what Fagan identifies as 'probably the most beautiful and certainly the most unifying characteristic of our Cape Dutch architecture ... the plastic quality of the softly plastered lime washed walls'.[40]

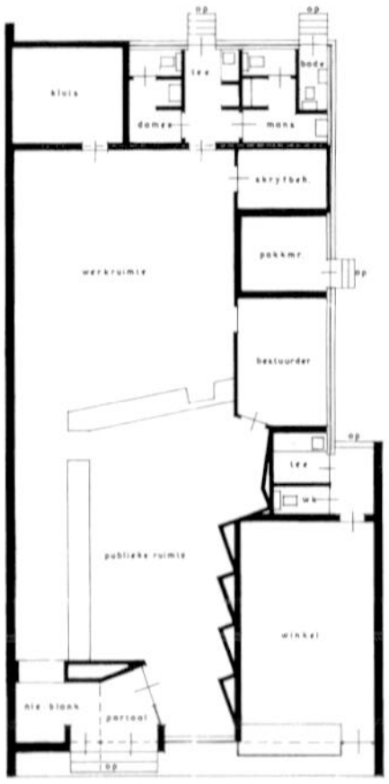

Gawie Fagan, Warrenton Bank, 1959.

The Montagu building is not a copy of the Cape Dutch, nor an appropriation of its particular 'visual charm', but the abstraction of essential stylistic elements in order to create an architecture that speaks poetically of both here and now.

In the 1960s, apartheid's heyday, an architecture of here and now was also an architecture where considerable design energy was devoted to solving the technical problems of racial separation. This was not a new issue. By the turn of the century, the historical precedent for dealing with segregation had already been formalized by the Public Works Department with regard to public buildings such as post offices and police stations.[41] Here, the 'white' entrance was given prominence on the front façade, whereas the smaller 'non-white' entrance was located around the side. But commercial buildings often did not provide separate entrances. Most of the 'English' banks did not bother to segregate their public areas, at least not until the 1960s, when local managers in conservative towns began to demand it under pressure from their clients.[42] But Volkskas, as the bank of nationalism, pioneered separate entrances in banks. From 1950 onwards their architects were required to find ways of duplicating resources for white and non-white customers without multiplying expenses. Ironically, one reason for the difference in approach between Volkskas and the English banks was that for a long time the latter had very few black clients, while Volkskas, as mentioned earlier, had many.

Initially Fagan followed the convention that had been established by the Public Works Department: in both the Belfast and Ladybrand buildings, for example, whites and 'non-whites' entered through separate doors, but were served by the same clerks 'om die hoek', around the corner, behind a wraparound counter. It soon became evident, however, that in small buildings, with front façades often no more than 16 metres wide, there was little room for two doors without seriously compromising the compositional gravitas of an elevation befitting a bank. It was Fagan who came up with the most ingenious solution to the problem, using a single large door, hinged on a central pivot. The door could be swung open to create two unequally sized entrances, each barricaded from the other by the massive expanse of the door itself, while the same bank clerks moved back and forth between the two sides. With appropriate modernist tools, even the problems of 'petty apartheid' could be solved in new and inventive ways. Branches in Warrenton, Warden, Brandfort, Bonnievale, Leeudoringstad, Steynsrus and Warmbaths were all equipped with pivot doors.

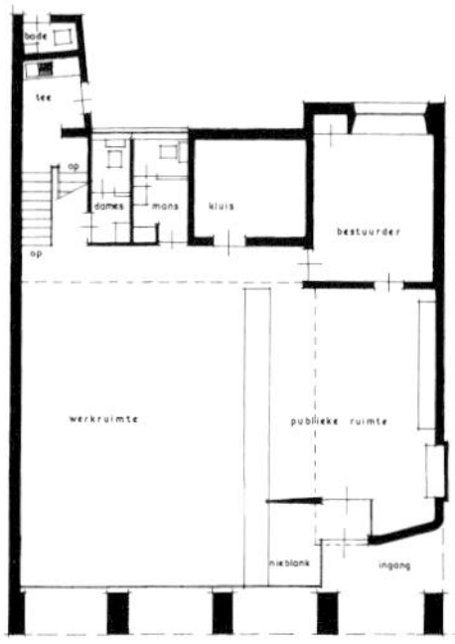

Gawie Fagan, Montagu Bank, 1959.

In 1963, Engelbrecht drew up a survey to gauge the responses of bank managers to building issues in which he devoted considerable space to this matter of spatial segregation. No comment was received about the door specifically, but the feedback indicated that the 'om die hoek' solution was not working. Having to share counters annoyed white customers, who did not like the idea of bank clerks dividing their attentions with an unseen queue of blacks on the far side of the barricade. At the same time, white corporate clients wanted improved service at the 'black' end because they sent their black messengers to the bank daily and wanted them dealt with swiftly and efficiently. Management advised tact and patience until a better solution could be found.[43]

Domination: Samuel Pauw

By the mid-1960s, the 'Tweede Trek' to forge a class of Afrikaner financial, industrial and commercial capitalists had achieved its aim. With the emergence of this class, Afrikaner nationalist ideology was transformed once again. Modest and tentative efforts gave way to an overwhelming sense of economic, social and political domination. Insurance giants Sanlam and Santam, tobacco corporation Rembrandt, industrial investment vehicle Federale Volksbelegging, financial institutions such as Trust Bank and Volkskas, and various parastatals enjoying government protection, like the iron and steel manufacturer Iscor, ensured significant Afrikaner control of the economy. The result was that 'these twentieth-century Trekkers ... learned to express themselves in the language of the stock exchange and boardroom ... "Hoggenheimer" was no longer the oppressor of the Afrikaner volk, but a trusted and valued partner in the joint quest for profit.'[44]

The new spirit of the era was best captured by the Volkskas headquarters designed by Samuel Pauw, a building which had the bank's public relations department reaching once again for an iconic phraseology: ''n Afrikanermonument om saam met die ander hoës van die twintigste eeu die hoogte in te skiet'[45] ['An Afrikaner monument soaring to lofty heights beside the other greats of the twentieth century']. For the second time, Volkskas put their faith in a young, avant-garde graduate of the Pretoria School. This new building, however, marked a departure from the previous Volkskas policy of building with restraint: from the moment of its conception, there was nothing modest about it.

The project was born when the Pretoria City Council decided to transform the city's historic market square, once the dusty gathering place of subsistence boere from the surrounding farms, into a granite-paved plane commemorating J. G. Strijdom, the leader of the National Party who became Prime Minister in the 1950s. The new square, abutting the recently proposed opera house, would accommodate a large fountain and a monument to Strijdom, an enormous bronze head – the work of Coert Steynberg – under a halo-like concrete shell. This plan required a large building to serve as a backdrop for the monument, so large that the Pretoria town-planning regulations were amended to allow for a fivefold increase in the permitted building bulk. An anecdote proudly related in the Volkskas company history tells that the bank's general manager, J.A. Hurter, was so determined to win the tender for the site that he spent all day watching over the tender box, with three separate tenders in hand, waiting to see who his rivals would be. At the end of the day, he submitted the highest of his offers, half a million rand higher than his second alternative. He won, and this victory underlined a change in bank policy: from now on prestige was more important than pragmatism.

Nor did Hurter's ambitions stop there. Throughout the period of construction he repeatedly lobbied the city council to allow him to increase the height of the building. Pretoria's city council, acutely conscious of reigning over the national capital, had decreed that no commercial building could be higher than a state building. State buildings could reach 122 metres, commercial buildings only 92 metres. But Hurter's persistent lobbying won him the right to reach 133 metres, so far in excess of any other building in Pretoria at the time that, in a city filled with monuments, Volkskas become the dominant landmark.

In some ways the new headquarters, rising up on Strijdom Square, represented a continuity with prior bank buildings; in other ways a radical departure. Whereas the Standard Bank employed the

German architect Helmut Hentrich to design their new headquarters, and Anglo-American commissioned New York's Skidmore, Owings and Merrill to design the gigantic Carlton Centre in Johannesburg, Volkskas still insisted on using local talent, and in 1969 appointed architects Pauw and Botha. Their first task was not to design, but to travel. They visited 140 bank buildings in various Western countries to study the latest trends and find what their client required – 'die beste en die jongste'[46] ['the best and the latest']. Once again the emphasis was on modernism, but the final product was very much a monument, and a Pretoria-style monument at that. Entirely without the elegance associated with tall buildings of the time, there was a brutalist quality to its concrete forms. In many respects it was identical in its granite-like solidity to Moerdyk's Voortrekker Monument, just shorn of the decorations and stretching 38 floors above the ground.

Partly this reflected a deliberate rejection of the pervasive aesthetic of the 1960s, of the 'gladde eenvoudige anonieme glas- en staalgordynmuur-geboue wat 'n kenmerk is van die sogenaamde "form follows function"'[47] ['smooth simple anonymous glass and steel curtain-wall buildings of the so-called "form follows function"']. Reinforced concrete was used with excessive zeal, typically for the horizontal but, unconventionally, also for all the vertical elements. The lifts and air-conditioning ducts, usually the central core of a building, were shifted to the exterior, in order to articulate the façades and break up the symmetry. The windows were so deeply recessed, in response to South Africa's harsh sunshine according to the architects, that the solid reinforced-concrete elements predominated. The architects described the result as a more plastic and sculptural sort of architecture, especially suited to the sharp sunlight and deep shadows of the local climate.[48] The entire structure was tiled in mosaics – indeed, the building's small claim to a place in history is that it used a world-record number of mosaic tiles.[49] The only modulated curtain-wall elements were used right at the top, for the penthouse offices reserved for the most senior management.

The building took ten arduous years to complete, the construction site itself becoming a central talking point in the city, with progress regularly covered in the capital's newspapers. It was to become a monument in several senses, most of them unintended. It marked the transformation of the market square, where subsistence Afrikaner farmers had eked out their living, into a symbol of Afrikaner capital accumulation. It was also to become the backdrop for one of the apartheid era's most chilling massacres, when the right-winger Barend Strydom fired at random on black pedestrians here in 1988, killing seven people. And it marked both the high-point and the end-point of the Volkskas building project.

Postmodernism

By 1991, Volkskas itself was no more. A series of mergers in the financial sector drew Volkskas along with three other banks into the new Amalgamated Banks of South Africa. The once-proud Afrikaner identity of the bank was subsumed. At present, the bank's headquarters are being relocated from Pretoria, once the home of the Nationalist civil service, to Johannesburg, the centre of international capital – a move which represents more than a geographical shift. Custom-built branches are no longer being designed, and the bank, like its competitors, relies increasingly on leased property in decentralized office parks. A bland global architecture which makes no reference to place epitomizes Volkskas's current corporate style.

From the top floor of the Volkskas headquarters another icon is visible: Herbert Baker's Union Buildings, British colonial down to its foundations, but also the backdrop for Nelson Mandela's inauguration as President. On that day, Afrikaans poets shared the stage with African gumboot dancers while apartheid-era military jets swooped past overhead, sketching out on the clear blue sky the new colours of the post-apartheid national flag. It was year zero in the creation of a new South African nationalism.

Soon after the inauguration, Pretoria's city council, then still under the control of the National Party, suggested that Strijdom Square be renamed Mandela Square as an act of reconciliation. This

Samuel Pauw, Volkskas building on Strijdom Square, 1978.

suggestion has not been followed up by the African National Congress city council that came to power in 1997. In the meantime, it is possible to have your portrait taken alongside a cardboard cut-out of the new President by the black street-photographers who now ply their trade in the square under the stern gaze of the old Prime Minister, J. G. Strijdom. When not in use, the life-sized cardboard cut-outs of Nelson Mandela lean against the pedestal of the oversized bronze bust.

D

►E2 ►E3

— POSKANTOOR —
SENDERWOOD
— POST OFFICE —
BLANKES
WHITES
NIE-BLANKES
NON-WHITES

SENDERWOOD
— POST OFFICE —

Offices
David Goldblatt

Senderwood Post Office, Johannesburg, 1974.

Senderwood Post Office, Johannesburg, 1988.

►E2 Brian Sandrock, Administration Building, University of Pretoria, 1968.

►E3 George Wilsenach for Richter Wilsenach Bloem Architects, The Accident Provident Fund Building, Pretoria, 1978.

►E4 Skidmore Owings and Merrill with Rhodes-Harrison Hoffe and Partners, Carlton Centre, under construction, Johannesburg, 1968.

►E4 Carlton Centre, Johannesburg, 1973.

►E4 Taljaard Carter and Partners, Die Eike, Johannesburg, 1974.

Personal traits: The work of Eaton and Biermann in Durban

Tony Morphet

This essay explores one small corner of the drama of space in South Africa. The control and the use of space have been at the heart of an historical conflict that predates even the arrival of whites at the southern tip of the continent, and remain a focus of dispute to this day. The essay will restrict its attention to what may at first seem very much a side issue in this long contest. However, in the course of the discussion I hope to show the lines of the larger drama being played out here with unusual intensity. The central themes of the action – the pressures of power and the necessities of resistance – are in themselves nothing new, but in this account they take an unexpected form.

My immediate subject is two beautiful buildings. Both are the masterworks of their respective designers and builders. One is the Netherlands Bank building in Smith Street, Durban; the other is House Biermann on the Durban Berea. Norman Eaton was the architect of the bank, and Barrie Biermann designed and built the house at 38 Glenwood Drive for himself. There are many grounds for considering them together, but the first and the most obvious is that they are buildings from the same period. Both were designed and built in the early years of the 1960s, and I will argue that their significance, both individually and together, derives chiefly from the context in which they were created. It goes without saying that their meaning is not confined by that context and that they retain their resonance and expressiveness into the present, but it is in reading them first as forms of response to their time that we can make contact with the larger drama which has shaped the country and the buildings themselves.

In 1960 the National Party government had been in power for twelve years. A minority of the white minority brought it into office in 1948 and its immediate hold on power was not strong, but by the end of the 1950s it had won two more elections and gained firmer control of the state and the country. Its relentless march through the legislative programme to institute the apartheid plan meant that by 1960 it had already set in place the main body of required law. In 1961, when Dr. Verwoerd led the country out of the British Commonwealth and into a republic, the project of Afrikaner dominance was close to fulfilment. All that remained was for the volk to reap the benefits of the suppression of blacks, accumulate wealth and outstrip their erstwhile English overlords in all fields.

From colonial times, resistance had never been far below the surface of ordinary life, but the rising power of the Afrikaners gave it a new urgency and meaning in the 1950s. In 1955 the Congress of the People produced the Freedom Charter, the document that set out the political constitution of the ANC alliance and would act as a guide to political resistance over the next forty years. However, between 1960 and 1963 the opposition movement suffered a series of defeats which broke its power and left it demoralized and leaderless. The massacre at Sharpeville in March 1960 had been the first signal that the state was prepared to use maximum force to suppress any challenge to its authority, and the ensuing State of Emergency showed that law would provide no defence against the power of the state. The arrest, trial and conviction of the leadership of the ANC in 1963 (the so-called Rivonia Trial) completed the action and gave the government undisputed capacity to do whatever it wished. The same sequence of events signalled the end of constitutional government and the effective beginning of a civil war. The decade of apparent peace which followed concealed from no one the fact that both sides were preparing for a struggle to the end. It became difficult to imagine a future beyond the vision that it would be bloody and destructive.

No one now questions the pathological nature of the apartheid state, but the inner configuration of the pathology remains an issue of conjecture and debate. The public face of the state expressed the driving energy of a confident modernism, yet not far beneath it lurked a profoundly anxious, pre-modern, theocratic spirit which asserted that the locus of authority lay beyond reach in God himself. In the vast social plan, the instrumental rationality of modernity was put to work to shape and enforce an Old Testament order of being. An army of bureaucrats managed the machinery of universal control, but the sources of authority remained beyond question in the realm of the revealed truth granted to a chosen people.

The demarcation of space was at the centre of the social plan. Boer trekkers making their way into the interior had dreamed of an empty landscape, and when they found people in their path they were beset by genocidal fantasies.[1] The vision of the vlakte, the open plains, runs all the way through Afrikaner literature and painting: endless spaces humanly marked only by remote Boer farmsteads and villages. The new message which came with the access to power was that the promised land, recovered at last from the imperial thieves, would be returned – free, whole and entire – to the chosen people for them to use as they thought fit. But the planners at least could see that people would have to be moved for the promise to be made good. The modern face masking the primitive desire spoke blandly of separate spaces and 'separate development'; everyone 'along their own lines' as the phrase went. That the lines of division were unequal was beside the point – every person would know where they belonged and where they dare not trespass. And so the land would be recovered. Each colour-coded and classified body would find its space assigned in the grid-like order of the system.

The reconstitution of the modern space of the country could only be achieved by building on a massive scale. Every hamlet, village, dorp, town and city was brought under the dictate of the law of division and separation: each was obliged to carry the design through into the physical structures of housing and of work. It was at this conjunction that architecture as a profession began its long and ambiguous relation with the dominant power. In the post-war boom, the hundreds of thousands of black people moving to the cities produced a crisis which had to be solved, and it fell to the planners and designers to come up with the solution.[2]

As an organized profession, architecture does not have a long history in South Africa. The major works of the past were all products of specialist metropolitan architects who found their way into the colonial milieu by one route or another.[3] It was only in the 1920s that local universities established schools of architecture and the profession began to gain some degree of independent identity. The tradition of commissioning buildings from foreign metropolitan architects continues into the present, but it is now more than balanced by professionals who have been locally trained.

It was perhaps the shallowness of the tradition that made it possible for the new South African schools to take a leading role in the development of the modernist style of Le Corbusier and Gropius outside Europe and the United States. The key figure in the local development of the International Style was the young professor at the University of the Witwatersrand, Rex Martienssen, who first joined the staff of the School of Architecture in 1931.[4] The group of modernist enthusiasts who gathered round Martienssen, known as the Transvaal Group, successfully overthrew the British-derived late colonial style of the Baker school which had dominated the early years of the century after the British victory over the Boers in 1902. Sir Herbert Baker's most famous creation is the Union Buildings in Pretoria, which is both a significant symbol of the British victory and a celebration of the terms of white accommodation reached in the founding of the Union. Its most recent international appearance was in the televised record of the inauguration of President Nelson Mandela in May 1994 – yet another accommodation which the impressive building seemed able to stage all too easily.

The international modernist movement had its own form of commitment to social planning. In Le Corbusier's formulations it was the application of scientific principles of planning and design that would provide the basis of freedom for the working masses of the great European cities, and it was the responsibility of the architectural profession to pursue its purpose regardless of the political authority under which it was to operate. There is evidence enough to show that modernism was prepared to make its peace with regimes of either left or right in order to gain sufficient support and resources to carry out its designs. Architecture was to bring about the social revolution of the 20th century.

There are many overlaps between the modernist manifestos and the thinking of the National Party ideologues, but none is more telling than the view, expounded by Le Corbusier himself, that the housing planned for workers should be understood as the provision of temporary, space-occupying labour units.

> We must never, in our studies, lose sight of the perfect human 'cell', the cell which corresponds most perfectly to our physiological and sentimental needs. We must arrive at a 'house-machine',

which must be both practical and emotionally satisfying, and designed for a succession of tenants. The idea of the 'old home' has disappeared and, with it, local architecture, etc... For labour will shift about as needed, and must be ready to move, bag and baggage.[5]

Though it comes from a different angle, this theorization follows the same lines as the view taken of 'the Bantu' and their place in the South African urban areas. In government eyes they were to be 'temporary sojourners', present in the city for the requirements and purposes of labour only, and due to return to the rural homelands where their true identity was secure, and where the 'old home' and the local culture would be maintained through customary law. However, the South African modern movement was by no means uniform and unanimous in its endorsement of Le Corbusier's vision of urban transformation through planning. In the late 1930s and early 1940s there were intense debates within the movement on whether architecture alone was sufficient to bring about the revolution in consciousness or whether architecture should subordinate its interests to a wider, more embracing political vision of the role of the working class in transforming the social basis of production.[6] The debate was left unresolved because, even by the end of the 1940s, architectural modernism had lost its capacity to inspire passionate support and unconditional commitment. But modernism was to continue its ambivalent connection with the powers of the state.

Mumford's influential critique of the modernist programme[7] also became ambivalent and ambiguous in the South African context. His attempt to reconcile local and regional cultures with a scientific approach, in order to produce an 'organic' plan, was reshaped by the logic underpinning white power into the principles for the design of the black urban township. Thus the idea of the local and organically conceived 'region', conceptualized as a whole and kept apart from the city, was reinterpreted to mean the legally defined, closed, uniform and racialized world of the 'Bantu township'. On the drawing board, the township was made to look like the 'garden city' designs of Europe, but in the minds of the labour bureaucrats it was understood as the labour dormitory of the temporary working class, an ambiguity that was easily sustained in the social planning vocabulary of the National Party government.

If the modernist ambition of bringing freedom through planning found itself subverted in the field of mass public housing, its fate in the construction of the large public and corporate buildings in the centre of the white parts of the cities was no less severe. In both contexts, the simple truth of the situation was that the basic design and its stylistic accoutrements were made subject to the cultural logic of power. Such logic works itself out through the discourses which silently configure forms of identity within and through the structures and practices of a milieu. The identity message of the township house and the location landscape was one of humiliation and abuse in the face of defeat, while the counter-message of the cityscape conveyed the arrogant stare of power. The modernist scale and the brutal undecorated surfaces of concrete, steel and glass confirmed, for the new holders of power, for their bureaucrats and professionals and their industrial and commercial captains, that their plan was secure and their domination of the complex modern systems of the society complete.

The same architectural language informed the new constructions of the rising Afrikaner social élite, as the huge cultural complexes of opera houses and state theatres, hospitals and universities were built to cement and celebrate their rise to ascendancy and control. These public buildings were, explicitly and by law, for whites only, and they were intended to represent the triumph of 'the European' in Africa. The style reached an apotheosis, appropriately enough, in the H. F. Verwoerd Building in Plein Street, Cape Town. With its huge geometric form towering over the neo-classical parliamentary complex, and its exact symmetrical ribbons of blind, bronze-glazed windows set in forbidding concrete, it begged comparison with the centres of authoritarian power in Nazi Germany and the Soviet Union.

As the 1960s progressed, the spatial plan was elaborated to include separate 'ethnic homelands' through which the logic of the central power was extended into the far corners of the country. The determination to make the policy work led to the further duplication of putative 'capital' towns in the designated territories, each with its legislature and administrative block, together with the inevitable 'independence' stadium to organize the necessary popular support. Quarantined outside the urban zones, ethnic universities carried the message of division, separation and subordination to the rising generation. The architecture of such places sustained a complex synthesis of the modern Western and the pre-modern tribal ethos. The style was obliged to communicate a dependent form of power: a derivative of the real centre of authority in the white state, but comfortable and assured in its 'own situation'. The results are some of the strangest constructions in the country: aggressive and servile at the same time; full of fake pomp and ersatz luxury; sufficient to cow and seduce the uninitiated, but repulsive to the undaunted.

Thus far I have sketched a background against which the works of Biermann and Eaton can begin to take on some of their contextual significance. As will be readily evident, my account of the historical discourses of South African architecture in the early years of National Party rule owes less to the record of the buildings built than it does to a reading of the complementary and conflicting cultural logics shaping the profession and the practice of architecture in the new Afrikaner state. I have taken this route because my wish is to show that what distinguishes both of the artists is their capacity to construct an alternative architectural discourse. In the next part of the essay I will try to show how they encountered the conditions of pressure in their different personal ways, and how they embarked on conceptual and imaginative projects in order to reclaim the independent authority and creative power of the discipline and the practice – and the price they had to pay to do so.

Eaton and Biermann did not work together; neither did they owe a common allegiance to any expressed programme. Each worked in isolation and in different spheres, Eaton as a professional architect in Pretoria, Biermann as an academic teacher in Durban. Eaton was older than Biermann by more than twenty years, and his professional experience spanned the period of change from the later years of the Baker school to the modernism of Martienssen and beyond. Biermann, by contrast, finished his doctoral studies in 1952 – the year which he later identified as the effective end of modernism. Yet there were deeply structured similarities in the cultural positions of the two men. Both had family roots in Afrikaner culture and felt themselves to be natural inheritors of the legacy of Cape Dutch architecture. Both had been educated in English schools and universities, which had given them a critical distance from the main line of nationalist thought and commitment, and both had shown from early on a desire to broaden their perspectives on both architecture and culture. In 1929 Eaton won the Baker scholarship, which took him to Rome for a year's study. Biermann, in his fourth (practical) year at the University of Cape Town, in 1946, worked his passage to Brazil on a sailing ship and there conducted a detailed study of Portuguese colonial architecture. Portugal, as he saw in Brazil, provided the critical connection between the classical forms of the Cape Dutch styles and the architecture of Rome itself. In his small, now classic book, Boukuns in Suid-Afrika,[8] he argues the case that the Dutch officials and craftsmen brought with them the influences of both the colonial and metropolitan Portuguese architecture, which carried within itself the forms of the original Roman models. The classicism of both men had been stimulated by Martienssen's studies in Greek architecture, which had set a standard for any well-informed young professional, but they went further than Martienssen, whose early death in 1942 robbed the profession of a crucial influence.

A critical factor that distinguished both Eaton and Biermann from their contemporaries was their interest in the vernacular architectures and cultures of Africa. Biermann wrote an early essay on the use of mud as a building material, tracing its use back from the flat-roofed houses of the Free State to the houses of Egypt and the Middle East. Part of his argument was that mud could provide the technical answer to the African housing problem. Both men gave close attention to the richly decorated flat-roofed housing clusters of the Ndebele, and both wrote about the grace that characterized the style. Biermann, based in Natal, studied the domed, grass hut of the Zulu and

House Biermann, Durban, c. 1962.

took pleasure in pointing out to the visiting Buckminster Fuller that his geodesic dome was nothing new.[9] Their interest in Africa, moreover, went well beyond the borders of South Africa. Eaton in particular travelled widely in East and Central Africa, somewhat in the manner of the artist, Irma Stern, searching out the forms and artefacts that carried what he saw as 'the unique African feel'. The impression made on Biermann by Great Zimbabwe found its expression in the tower form which he incorporated into his house in Durban.

For both architects, Africa also provided the most potent and expressive forms of the natural world. The painter, Alexis Preller, gave this description of Eaton:

> He loved being in Africa and of Africa. His concept and spaces and proportion and materials were derived from and concerned Africa: light and shade and vast areas of empty space, natural forces of rock and stone and desert and plants and trees, a fusion of the elements of a continent and its creative traditions.[10]

Peter Melvin saw Biermann in similar terms:

> It was in this remote environment [the upland Free State] of mountains, bright blue skies, rocks, water erosion, mud and desert that Barrie came alive. He was a master of the wilderness and deftly enhanced each simple act or event with some aspect of his knowledge in an appropriate way.[11]

The connections with Africa, the common interest in classicism, both in the original and in its derivations in Cape Dutch architecture, and the desire to gain the broadest perspectives set both men apart from the main lines of the profession still largely shaped by commitments to modernism and to functioning within the order of power. But the disassociation had deeper and more personal roots as well. These can be glimpsed in the strong connections which both had with the world of art and artists. Eaton's lifelong friendship with Alexis Preller is well documented; so too are his close relationship with Anton Hendricks and his connections with Pierneef and Walter Battiss, Anna Vorster, and Cecil Skotnes. In Biermann's case the connection was primarily with Andrew Verster, Aidan Walsh, and the group of painters, sculptors and other artists who came together in Durban from the mid-1960s. It might be appropriate to describe both Eaton and Biermann as artists first and architects second.

The similarities between the two men extend to their personalities. Nearly all of the descriptions make reference to their reclusiveness. Both lived alone and defended their privacy, and the biographical texts repeatedly state that both were 'intensely private' people. In fact it has only recently become possible to break the code of the 'intensely private life' and say, quite simply, that both men were homosexual. This is easier to say with reference to Biermann since, in the more tolerant and expressive climate of the present, it has become possible for his friends to speak openly about him in this way. Eaton's life remains shrouded in secrecy and ambiguity, but the inferences are clear and strong enough to support the view.[12] It is an important fact which opens a new perspective on the work of the two men. In the discussion of the two buildings which follows, I will try to suggest that the expressiveness of the works is linked to the marginality imposed on homosexual identity in the 1960s. For the moment, however, I want to make the simpler and more obvious point that their personal orientation placed both of them well outside the dominant culture of their profession, and compelled them to work alone towards realizing their personal and private vision in public forms.

To be homosexual in South Africa in the 1960s was to be under constant threat. Inevitably homosexual practice was against the law and, with the police able to raid any premises at any time without a warrant, there was a direct risk to any form of homosexual relationship. Prosecutions were in fact rare, but the danger of public exposure and vigilante hounding was palpable and permanent. The risk to the interior life was perhaps even more intense, since to many denial, refusal and repression came to seem the only way of achieving even a degree of normal protected personal and social life. To pursue any kind of expressive public life required not only heroic internal discipline but a wariness and skill that would be able to deceive and inform at the same time. The cultured and the clever could use irony and wit to sustain and defend themselves; for many others their lives were split apart and lived in separate places and ways.

Eaton and Biermann chose discipline and expression, the 'intensely private life' and the complex public creation; both held together with all the resources of the cultures of the world that they had mastered. The essence of their work, as I hope to show, lies in the way in which they were able to bring dense layers of alternative meanings into unifying forms.

There is no dispute about the masterworks of the two architects. Eaton's Netherlands Bank in Smith Street, Durban is recognized by all as his finest achievement. Lord Holford expressed the consensus in the following way: 'Eaton's most complete, most perfect design, is in Durban. It is one of the most charming modern buildings in the world.'[13] Biermann's private house in Glenwood Drive, Durban has been saluted in similar terms as the most significant architectural achievement of his life. Jack Barnett, writing in 1992, said that 'it is literally a tract in brick, pavings, plants, garden walls, space, detail infused with humour, slightly cynical at times and full of intellectual vigour'. And he summed up his view with the comment that the house provided 'an important yard-stick of the community's aesthetic maturity'.[14]

The central strategy of both buildings is to recontextualize urban modernism within the natural and built conditions of the Natal coast. I think Peter Melvin got it the wrong way round when he described the Biermann house as 'the rich cultural dichotomy of Durban ordered by the rigour of European modernism'[15] – it is Durban which does the ordering. The same recontextualizing strategy gains a longer and wider reach from the way the Natal location is made to resonate with a range of other cultural contexts. Some are local to South Africa, especially the classicism of the Cape Dutch style apparent in both of the buildings; more precisely, in the Biermann house, the humble Karoo-huis, with its corrugated-iron roof and shady stoep. Wider references come from the native vernaculars of the Ndebele and Great Zimbabwe. From the still more distant ranges come Japanese and Brazilian influences, ultimately leading back to Roman and Greek classicism.

At the time, Natal itself was an extraordinary mix of peoples and cultures. To some degree it escaped the full flattening pressure of the apartheid state, since it was at the edge of the main drive coming from the central power. The province was under opposition-party control and there was constant talk of secession from the Republic. The local powers that could be sustained against the pressure of the central government were jealously guarded and used largely for the protection of the weak and faded British traditions of the whites. Black citizens suffered much the same fate as their counterparts in the other provinces, although the Zulu refusal to accept the terms of integration into the homeland system provided them with some room for negotiation and defence. Afrikaner penetration of the province was limited to small local areas in the north and pockets along the coast. Durban, then and now the busiest port in Africa, was well on its way to becoming a large conurbation incorporating a remarkable mix of ethnic cultures. It had the largest population of Indian people in the country, and the massive black townships on the northern and southern edges of the city brought a large, black working class into direct contact with the old, white colonial precincts set around the bay and along the ridges running parallel to the coast.

In topographical and climatic terms the city has more in common with port cities to the north – Maputo, Zanzibar, Mombasa – than it does with highveld Johannesburg or the Mediterranean Cape. The subtropical climate gives the region a unique light and air – pale, dense and humid in the summer, clear and mild in the winter, and without a noticeable spring or autumn season. The winds come in off the sea throughout the year, with a fresh warm northeaster off the Mozambique current setting the prevailing airflow and the occasional cold southwester following the movement of a cold front up the coast. Very infrequently the city finds itself at the edge of hurricane winds on the Indian

House Biermann, Durban, c. 1962.

Ocean. The region was originally covered in dense coastal bush, though even in the 1960s only small protected pieces of it remained – some, happily, even within the city boundary. The present vegetation of the city is more controlled, and shaped by the suburban styles of the population, but it does not contradict the feeling of lush abundance that must have characterized the area in the past.

Biermann made the Natal coast his region. His house speaks with its own eloquence about his engagement with the climate and the vegetation, but it was the cultural mix of the city and the region which he found exceptional and stimulating. He once astounded the eminent art and architecture critic, Nikolaus Pevsner, by offering to show him 'the world of Alexander the Great fossilized behind the shop windows of Grey Street' – the Indian shopping area.[16] He saw that Alexander's Greece had been brought to Africa by the indentured Indian labourers of the sugar fields of Natal. He argued that the Hindu temples along the Umbilo River, decked in flowers and filled with noise and the smoke of incense, showed what the original Attic temples had been like. He compared the Drakensberg cave paintings of the Khoisan to Altamira and Lascaux, and the city itself to Venice. He made the Venice comparison in a silent 'lecture' given at the Durban Art Gallery, where he simply showed parallel sequences of slides: one set of Venice, the other of Durban. He thought the city should gather the will 'to drop the image of a lower middle class English bathing town and really get some touch of international style', adding, 'We have everything going for us.'

Eaton's region was Pretoria. Educated in the Cape and at the University of the Witwatersrand, he returned from his scholarship year in Rome to settle in Pretoria in 1932. His practice was in the city and he remained there until his death in 1966. Most of his early work was on private houses in the area, but in the war years he began to produce public buildings – in particular a sequence of buildings for the Land Bank in different country towns.[17] However, his largest public commission, for a proposed building to house the Ministry of Transport in Pretoria, fell foul of political and administrative infighting during the period leading up to the fateful election of 1948, and his design was never realized. The later work produced further private houses in the Pretoria area, an office block for the South African Police (the Wachthuis) and the most important of all of his works, the two buildings for the Netherlands Bank – one in Pretoria and the classic building in Durban.

Throughout his career he was an ardent public campaigner for the proper development of his home city. He founded the Pretoria Architectural Society and used it as the place to set out his broad vision of the city as a 'verdurous and humanised Pretoria', in which he imagined Church Square as a 'great enclosed central park filled with fine trees and shrubs and all manner of bird life such as in the botanical garden in the heart of Cape Town'. But he also used the Society as the vantage point from which he could launch his criticisms of the direction the city had taken, attacking what he saw as the

> ... fatalistic laissez-faire attitude [which] seems to explain our silent acceptance of the near-level heighted, careless, architectural mixture that characterises too much of our city building, showing as pompous or non-descript façades that flatly line the dull vistas of its streets. These are more dull for being subject to the monotonous grid-iron pattern which calculating land surveyors imposed upon the natural and better logic of the old radiating foot and wagon paths, connecting poort to poort [ford to ford], through the embryo town in its earliest days.[18]

It is useful and relatively easy to see Eaton as a Pretoria Regionalist, but harder to see that, like Biermann, he articulates through his regionalism layers of cultural and historical awareness that locate him simultaneously in quite other places and other times. The Durban building shows both a regional and a universal awareness which owe nothing directly to Pretoria.

Eaton's Durban site came to him with the commission from the Netherlands Bank. The location of the bank is itself not without cultural and political interest, since it was part of the deliberate policy of the local and European boards of the bank to search for a middle position between the rival banking services of the English capital bloc and the newer competitive Afrikaner bloc. With

Barclays and the Standard Bank on one side, and Volkskas and the Trust Bank on the other, the Netherlands Bank sought a prestige segment of the market in the corporate business and foreign exchange sectors. The bank wanted to be recognized as distinctly European but fully engaged in South African life, without being tied to any political group.[19] In its buildings it was in search of prestige and a distinctive presence rather than size and commanding grandeur. Eaton had designed the headquarters building in Pretoria and he was the obvious choice for Durban.

Smith and West streets run parallel from east to west along the full length of the central business district of the city. Despite the fact that the open sea and the bay are only short distances away, the streets are topographically undistinguished, without views or prospects and with almost no open spaces or trees. The section of the city marked out along these streets was the obvious site for post-war development, as the older, rambling two- and three-storey hotels and business houses were replaced with the characteristic high-rise geometric forms of the modern style. At the time that Eaton came to work on the Smith Street site, the southern side was bounded by the Durban Club, one of the early, low-rise, richly decorated colonial buildings fronting on to the bay and surrounded by the palms and lush shrubs typical of the vegetation. On the north side was the degraded modernist face of Smith Street, and to the east and west, dull shopfronts and offices.

Eaton turned the undistinguished site into a significant opportunity by refusing the dominant logic of the street. His initial design for a fifteen-storey building fell foul of both the city regulations and an economy drive at the bank, but he was able to secure agreement to a second plan to have a four-storey cube, set back from the street front. The realized building demonstrates his success in finally defining the terms of the commission.

A short flight of steps leads up off the macadamized pavement to a marble podium roughly a metre above ground level and some five metres wide. It runs across the full face of the building along the street, and it is sculpted to include gardens of palms, bush trees and flowers, as well as four decorative ceramic fountains. Amidst the full heat and crush of the city street, the pedestrian suddenly finds a water garden set in marble, just below eye level. The transformation of the rhythms, perspectives and sense impressions releases a set of feelings that the modern city has inevitably come to exclude – feelings of pleasure at the exchange between aesthetic and natural forms, and a sense of generous abundance that such pleasures should be available to anyone walking down the street. The last time I saw the podium there was a man on the pavement scooping water to drink from one of the fountains, while at another a child was playing with the streams that flow down from the raised bowl into the reservoir at the base.

Biermann described going into the banking hall as like going to do business in a tree, and Rodney Harber speaks of being in the building as like being in the coastal bush. These comments pick out the most distinctive feature of the banking hall: its sunscreen of green glazed bricks falling more than three-quarters of the way down the three outer glass walls.[20] The hollow bricks, made to a special measurement and individually glazed to a colour determined – after much experimentation – by Eaton himself, are threaded vertically onto steel rods, and the whole construction, held firm by horizontals at even brick-length intervals, is suspended from the flat roof. The filter effect of the screen is most dramatic when passing through the recessed doors at the front of the building. The greening of the light as the reflections from the spaces pass into the large open room, and the dappling of the floors, create just the effects that Harber and Biermann speak of. The design made provision for a roof garden which would hold indigenous trees on the same scale as those on the podium, so completing the interchange between the natural and created effects of the coastal world. The trees in the roof garden flourished briefly, but are no longer there.

The imaging of nature within the hall produces one form of harmonization of the senses, but it is accompanied by other diverging impressions. The whole of the banking hall, including the full floor, the tellers' counter, the side desks with their seats, and the standing tables where clients complete their forms and calculations, even down to the waste-paper bins and ashtrays, is furnished in travertine marble. A cool creamy-white colour, it is streaked and veined with the marks of the

House Biermann, Durban, c. 1962.

water which formed it and is polished to a smooth permanent natural shine. The marble order of the room sets the visitor in the world of classical Rome; but it is a Rome which looks out across the dappled floor and through the green-tinged light into the trees of Natal. Rome in the Natal bush is a remarkable thing to discover – as much for the daily user as it must have been for the creator.

The further one explores the building, the richer the resonances and the interior complexities. Detail speaks to detail across the varying forms and functions that are necessary in a building dedicated to use: the aquamarine mosaic on the pillars and across the back wall of the hall echoes in miniature form the pattern of the screen; the curved line of the marble skirting that tracks down the edges of the stairwell repeats a curve in the external podium edge where it rises to secure the glass sheets which form the outer wall.

The most startling feature of the experience of the building, and the one that leaves the most lasting impression, is the realization that it has a consciousness of its own. This is not an easy thing to pin down and analyse since it lies in the secret relations between the parts and the whole. Detail is in conversation with detail; space with structure, line with volume, surfaces with masses; aesthetics with functions. Yet there is nothing solemn and portentous in the exchanges. In essence it is a form of serene play that is going on within the building and, whether one chooses to notice it or not, the consciousness lives. The presence of the genius loci is palpable.

The wonderful creative flow that the building lives in, and reproduces in the visitor, comes of course from the architect – at least in its origins – though the craftsmen who made the building must have their share of the credit. Like a painting or a poem, the materials of the created object are so saturated with the consciousness of the artist, and so ordered in their relations by the same consciousness, that they take on and hold within themselves their own expressive life. The source of the viewer's engagement is here.

Biermann's appreciation of Eaton's building registers the presence of the personality in the building itself:

> One recognises Norman's personal traits in his buildings not so much by the eccentricity of the forms themselves, as by the way in which they reflect their author's character: his fastidiousness, his eclecticism, his detachment from the common herd ... Although these set him apart from the fat and greasy citizenry, such characteristics did not cut him off from the common run of humanity, nor make his buildings in any way 'precious'.[21]

Eaton's building reminds us that space can be made to carry different forms of meaning. Structured space holds the power to constitute and shape identity, and buildings work within and reproduce the broader cultural logics of which they are a part. The buildings of the black township and their counterparts in the white centres of power, were intent on setting strict definitions and limits on the identity of their users. As buildings they offered only one restricted language, and the secret purpose in their design was to lower and restrict the awareness of the user against any wider range of possibilities and meanings. Their work was to slip the users silently into their appointed place without them even noticing the imposed limits. Eaton, by contrast, takes us into a self-conscious space, a space in which there are many dialects and voices and references, and which, as a result, opens up an encounter between the user and the building. This is the secret within the experience of enlargement and illumination that one finds in the building. Eaton is famous for his apparently technical declaration that all sides of a building carried the same importance – he would not countenance any idea of the 'back side' where the pipes and lifts would be located. The prescription, however, is much more than technical. The building has to be complete to itself; it cannot afford to have a hidden or an open side through which its meanings can be controlled, or where they can leak away. The prescription is essential to the creation of the self-consciousness of the building; it must declare itself in full and hold its meanings within itself.

These points are not trivial. What is at stake is the difference between a world that is humanized through the history of creative labour and a totalitarian order in which the human dimensions are lost in the circuits of power.

Biermann's house is more radical in every sense than Eaton's bank. He was building for himself and his lover alone,[22] and he was free to make the full range of his imagination and his learning visible and real. The only direct limits that he had to recognize came through the site and the available finance. The site was a sloping piece of ground on the west-facing side of the Berea, just over the crown of the ridge. It had been part of a larger homestead and, when he bought it, had a small run-down cottage on it. To the north it was overlooked by the Entabeni Hospital, and the original landowner's house was close by to the south. There were two access streets, one above and one below.

At the time, the western slope of the Berea was regarded as unattractive and unpromising, and the land was doubtless cheap. The reason for the low valuation, though partly simply fashion, was basically climatic and topographical. On the east side of the ridge there are spectacular views of the bay and the open sea, and this is the side which gains the advantage of the sea breezes by day and by night. The west side, by contrast, looks inland, faces directly into the afternoon sun and fails to catch the cooling air off the water. In a climate as hot and humid as Durban's these can be severe drawbacks. For Biermann, however, apart from the low cost, there were two critical advantages to the west face. It had not been suburbanized and it offered seclusion.

The plans for the house were submitted in 1959, and building was begun immediately, although it was in the nature of Biermann's work that the house's form continued to evolve over several years. Students who at different times lived in the apartment were drawn into the design and construction of the building phase by phase. In the rush of details that claim attention in this extraordinary house, perhaps the first is the use of the sloping site. In contrast to virtually every other house in the same position, no levelling was done. Instead, the slope of the ground was used to layer the house. The upper living area is set above the lower apartment, which keeps them separate and gives the upper level a view to the west over the top of the lower roof. The roof-lines of the whole structure follow the line of the landscape as it falls from the crest toward the valley below. It is perhaps worth noting, in terms of influences, that this design comes directly from the Cape Dutch rural villages of the Karoo. In fact, the whole design owes much to the Karoohuis, although the compact form of the original style is broken open to make an inner courtyard within the three sides of the U. One might say that this represents a local disciplining of modernism.

The house took its first bearings from the cottage which had been demolished. Its foundations provided the base for the upper-level structure, but from there on the creation was all Biermann's own. It is a secret, hermetic house when viewed from without. There are two external doors, one in the upper house and the other into the lower apartment. Besides these two there is no other entrance – neither window nor door – and even when the main doors are opened it is not possible to see in from the outside. Screening walls block the line of sight. The house gives the sense of having been designed and constructed to make the private life safe and secure against the outside world. Screened by the dense foliage of both the huge trees and luxuriant shrubs and creepers, it is more or less invisible from either the upper or the lower street and it neither invites attention nor offers display – the exact reverse of the prevailing suburban forms.

Once through the upper door, the transformation is total. Where Eaton worked to dissolve the boundaries of his building, Biermann sets the tightest definitions to the outside and the inside. The public world stays on the outside and the interior gives full scope to the private life. The sense of secured freedom is the dominant feeling produced by the living spaces on the upper level. The living room and its adjoining kitchen stretch across the full width of the house and they look out through glass-panel sliding doors across the rolling hills to the west. The lower apartment has the same view, but it is seen through a cast-iron screen made of found sections from a demolished colonial hotel. The house makes full use of modernist innovations: flat roofs with skylights; displaced walls to create specialized spaces like the interior courtyard garden; glass and aluminium sliding doors and louvre windows, and built-in benches and tables. But the drama of the structure arises out of the way the modernist style is worked against the other local and global influences. The walls are all bagged brick, and Biermann was assiduous in limewashing them every year with a special lime mix made with washing blue to absorb shades of light. The white purity of the walls gives a monastic austerity to the building as a whole, a sense crystallized most forcefully in the tiny cell-like bedroom which Biermann himself used. At the same time, both visually and texturally, they recall the humble form of the Cape Dutch tradition, a point wittily underlined by a strange, enclosed dovecote set into the sweeping garden wall. In the context of these impressions, the house becomes the home of the *vita contemplativa*.

But it has another side which expresses something like a Mediterranean sensuality. This comes partly from the light which enters the building in a variety of colours through all sorts of unexpected apertures in the roof and the walls, partly from the lush vegetation of the *monstera deliciosa* plants in the courtyard garden, but also from the careful placing of marble tables and benches and the air of relaxed variety that permeates the whole structure. The sweeping, angled curves of the garden wall and its wavy topline play out the sensuality against the austerity of the monastic side. The feeling evoked by these references is one of deep leisure and a sophisticated enjoyment of the senses. Biermann's book, *Red Wine*,[23] gives an eloquent account of the education of the senses through the experience of culture, and its closing page carries a photograph of the dining area of the house set for dinner with a bottle of wine on the table.

Biermann noted that Eaton's buildings 'reflect their author's character', and so too does his. The 'intensely private' legend is carried by the exterior; the rich and varied interior reveals a delight in the senses and the pleasures of cultivated sociability.

Eaton and Biermann worked across both place and time. Greece and Rome were as present to them as the most recent of the modernist developments. As Andrew Verster put it, 'When he [Biermann] talked of "the modern world" it wasn't the time since the war, or even this century, but the period from the Greeks onwards.'[24] Lord Holford made a similar remark about Eaton. 'After Rome, Norman Eaton gave all his heart and mind to South Africa.'[25] The depth not merely of their learning but of their imaginative life provided the crucial resources for their creations. Like the Netherlands Bank, the Biermann house has its own complex consciousness. The conversations that go on inside the walls are different, both more austere and demanding as well as looser and more privately expressive. But there is also a common language which both buildings share. It is not a language that has been widely shared or even known in South Africa. I say this because neither man has had the successors that one might have expected. In his later years, Eaton suffered deep disillusion and depression and, as Harrop-Allin expresses it, 'Though he was constantly hailed as the doyen of South African architects, his diaries repeatedly contain the entry: "No work in sight."'[26] Biermann too, though he preferred to teach than to build, found that the commissions which he did undertake ended in acrimony and dispute. In both cases it was the artistic construction of the role that people found difficult to accept. They wanted clever builders who would speak a familiar language and look after the job in hand, and what they got were individuals preoccupied with the languages of time, space and form.

There are signs that it will be through Biermann's teaching that his legacy to his region and the country will be fulfilled. Working in Durban are several young architects who trained under him and whose work shows the strength of his intellectual influence. One might mention Cindy Walters and Michelle Cohen, who designed the NSA building in Bulwer Park; and Janina Masojada and Andrew Makin, who won the competition for the Constitutional Court building. Still to emerge fully are the black and Indian architects of the region for whom university study has only recently become possible. It will be of special interest to see what they do with the cultural mix which Biermann so loved in Durban.

My focus has been narrow, but the implications of the two buildings in their context are large. They are critical instances in which the lines of force in the larger drama of space and power can be seen with special clarity.

The wider context was characterized in the preceding discussion in terms of movements of ideas and practices: nationalism, modernism, regionalism and, in a different register, resistance. What can be seen in the progress of these movements across time is their inevitable transvaluation. Each begins with the promise of some form of liberation. All end with their hopes defeated and their meanings turned. The avant-garde positions which they initially represent find themselves translated into power, which is then turned back to defend limited positions of privilege.

Nationalism was founded in the urgency of the Afrikaner need to break free from the domination of the British, but, in the hands of those who clung to it, it turned into the means for inflicting an even greater oppression on black South Africans.

Modernism was the last great intellectual avant-garde of the European enlightenment. It dedicated itself to freeing the mass of the ordinary people by transforming the conditions in which they lived, but eventually found itself the instrument of political and economic power, as it provided the fastest way to make private money and the cheapest way to house and control mass populations.

Regionalism began with a vision of the importance of the local and the meaningful. It set itself against the flattening effects of the universalizing drive of modernism, but in South Africa especially it turned in the hands of its advocates into crass provincialism on the one hand, and an instrument of domestication on the other. In a sense, South African architecture under the pressure of apartheid lost the positive meanings of both modernism and regionalism. Instead it got the worst of both movements. The designs and techniques of the International Style were put to work to fragment the population into culturally insulated locations and 'homes' from which they could not escape.

Activist resistance took root in the determination to defend the lives of the poor and the marginal against the drive of power. Solidarity and defence were its first goals, but power turned out to be its second. Obliged to organize the struggle, it found itself enmeshed in power which took it to the same place it had set out against.

Under the stress of these terrible torsions, which apparently turn the best into the worst with the inevitability of the seasons, the fate of two buildings and their creators will seem of little interest until it becomes clearer that, though themselves products of the same pressures, they were also able to gain a foothold on firmer ground.

Both architects were participants in the movements and the practices that have been described. Nationalists they were – of a sort; neither held any brief for the colonial British hegemony and both gave their full commitment to the country. They were modernists as well, both fully trained in the modernist vision and in its techniques which they used freely and with supreme confidence. Their regionalist credentials are undisputed – Eaton of Pretoria and Biermann of Durban – and both of South Africa. Activists of a political stamp they were not, but both gave their energies in writing and speaking to try to educate their listeners into an awareness of what was going on around them.

The crucial point, however, is that they were also always alive to other places, other times and other practices, and they pursued their thought with such energy and diligence that they were able to secure a vantage point that was outside the limits of the definitions which dominated others. Putting the point in the language of the essay, one might say that they were regionalists who never lost touch with the universal spirit of modernism – or, vice versa, that they were modernists who were able to let the local speak through its forms.

It is this vantage point which the essay has worked to describe, and it rests in the most basic of issues. Most simply I think it can be described as the refusal to yield their individual perception and judgement to anyone else. The difficult part in understanding such a position is to find the sources of its security and resolution. It is relatively easy to see that both men were immune to professional and political power. In part, this was because their defences were so personal and so deeply constructed that they were deaf to the voices which promised advancement in return for consideration and support: Eaton's rage at the cheap architects who would stoop to anything for a commission and at the sloppy bureaucrats who would sell anything and everything at the cheapest

Netherlands Bank, Durban, 1965.

price, and Biermann's fury at the clients who thought that they could turn him into a builder are, in the end, parts of the same thing. They could see what power could do, but they could not understand how a person could do it.

I suspect a fuller answer lies in a paradox which has been working itself out through the argument of this essay: they were able to be so secure and so definitive in their work in South Africa because their attachment to the immediate available definitions of the space was so slight and so ironic. They needed and were able to appropriate for themselves the cultures of the world because there was no place at home where they felt comfortable. A sentence in a paper on critical regionalism by Alexander Tzonis and Liane Lefaivre catches exactly one side of this paradox. They refer to Proust as the human type of the modern world.

> The hero represented in the thirteen-volume A la recherche du temps perdu is not only Proust, a regionally, ethnically, sexually, culturally ambivalent intellectual whose life is irrevocably stolen by time. He is us, any contemporary individual deprived of community and place.[27]

What they do not go on to do is show how Proust recovered his 'place' in the world by redeeming time. This is the second part of the paradox, and it is made plain and specific in the two buildings on which this discussion has focused. The buildings are the most sophisticated metaphors for the real battle of the two architects with the world. Both are brilliant and brave creations which model the way humans, given their history and their technical capacities, their vulnerabilities and their desires, ought to be able to live. One speaks to the civic, the other to the private life. The metaphors work through the silent materials and forms which recover the space of the human, not merely from the distortions and corruptions of their South African present, but from all time.

The buildings carry a simple and critical legacy. They are spaces which invite and await the appearance of the human out of the flow of time. The form of the asking is new and it addresses a new form of the human identity. It is at this point that their artistic and personal lives reach fulfilment. The legacy was won in the hardest of times and required intense dedication to the intuitions of what the human could mean in that present. The struggle to sustain the insights and to give them lasting form in their work measures the extent of the resistance with which the two men confronted the destruction that was taking place around them.

A recognition of the significance of these artists and their works leads towards a revaluation of the meanings of modernism and regionalism in South Africa, and of the idea of cultural resistance itself.

Netherlands Bank, Durban, 1965.

(Im)mobilizing space – dreaming of change
Jennifer Robinson

1 Imagining

The transition from apartheid urban space to – something else – draws our attention from the fixing moments of these historically divided cities to experiences of mobility, interaction and the dynamism of spaces. The enthusiasm for change which is symbolized by the end of apartheid not only sets out a new way of relating to space now; it also suggests that we look again at experiences of apartheid spaces. Were those spaces so fixed, so divisive, so certain in their form? Our imaginations have lived for so long with the lines of apartheid city space, with the blank spaces in between, the deadening images of power drawn on the ground. We have uncovered many reasons for the emergence of these dividing lines: sanitation, health, planning, government, administration, policing, racism, disgust, employment, class, development strategies, industrialization, political order ... Can we begin to shift our experiences and our visions to capture and understand the world of always-moving spaces? What do the spaces of change and dynamism look like? In what sense was even the apartheid city – a city of division – a place of movement, of change, of crossings?

Here is one story of a changing space:

> In the afternoon Toloki walks to the taxi rank, which is on the other side of the downtown area, or what is called the central business district. The streets are empty, as all the stores are closed. He struts like a king, for today the whole city belongs to him. He owns the wide tarmac roads, the skyscrapers, the traffic lights, and the flowers on the sidewalks. That is what he loves most about this city. It is a garden city, with flowers and well-tended shrubs and bushes growing at every conceivable place. In all seasons, blossoms fill the site.[1]

Toloki, the central character in Zakes Mda's novel, Ways of Dying, has fallen on hard times and invented a new kind of job for himself – he's a professional mourner. The funerals he amusingly graces with his moaning and crying are a harsh reminder of the violence and death which accompanied apartheid and the years of its demise. In this extract, he is making his way from the shelter near the sea where he sleeps, to see an old friend from his village whom he met at a funeral, and he passes through the city. Mda has Toloki 'strut like a king' through the empty streets. Today, the rhythms of urban life have left the city centre deserted, the taxi rank quiet, the pavements devoid of shoppers and workers.

Not only has the space of the city centre been changed by schedules and routines; it is changed by Toloki himself as he walks along, imagining himself a king ... He imagines he owns the whole city – the skyscrapers, lights, roads. The modern city is part of the things he loves, the things and places and feelings which are part of himself. He loves the flowers, the great ships passing into the harbour, the green and flourishing shrubbery, the trees. All this belongs to him, and he makes himself, his sense of who he is, through his experience of it. So he goes on, crossing the spaces of the city, moving from town to township, harbour entrance to taxi rank.

People always passed across the lines of the apartheid city, across its cruel divides. Meeting in places of work, sharing the streets, looking up at the same buildings rising behind makeshift builders' walls. Moving across the spaces of the apartheid city evidently had different qualities and meanings for different people: the domestic worker in a white home, for example, whose crossing of the divide meant she was cruelly separated from her children; the family who visited the old neighbourhood they had been forced to leave; the nurse working in a suburban rest home;

the man visiting his lover late at night; night workers waiting in the inner city for the first bus home; men waiting on street corners for casual work; the soldier riding on top of the armoured vehicle watching for stone-throwers; the madam taking her domestic worker (almost) to her home with her extra baggage; the rent collector walking from house to house, catching up on family news and picking up the rent; the township manager fetching his son after cricket practice at school, driving back to his house on the edge of the black city ...

Just as the spaces of the apartheid city divided, they also generated crossings and interactions: crossings as people moved and lived and worked in different places; crossings as the memories and meanings of different places were carried with them; crossings as people imagined what those other places were like, places they'd never seen except on the TV or in magazines. The networks of advertisers' images, for example, slipped easily across the borders (even in a time when the fathers of apartheid tried to control what sort of adverts could be seen where). Further on in Ways of Dying we find Toloki helping his friend rebuild her shack, which has burnt down. He visits a furniture store in town:

> Back in the city, he goes to furniture stores and gets as many catalogues as he can carry. He tells the salespeople that there are some customers from his village who would like to buy furniture. They would like to see the furniture first before they come to the stores to buy furniture. Of course, the salespeople don't believe him. But they don't see any harm in giving him the catalogues, which are free in any case. Then he goes to a newspaper stall and negotiates with the owner to buy ten back issues of Home and Garden magazine. He buys them at only ten percent of the cover price.[2]

Toloki takes the magazines to his friend – to decorate her walls. After attending a funeral, they spend the late afternoon and early evening walking among the splendid furniture, lazing on the soft bed, frolicking in the garden ... She thanks Toloki: 'Today you taught me how to walk in the garden. I want to walk in that garden with you every day.'[3] The tiny space of the shack moves in the imaginations of the two friends, they dream of the opulence of ovens which switch off automatically, the luxury of lace covers, the inexhaustible attractions of endless gardens – as Toloki says, 'There is much more to it than we explored today. Many corners we have not seen yet.'[4]

The magical realism of the novel does not undo the spaces of poverty – but it refuses to treat experiences of these spaces as one-dimensional. Shack settlements may be spaces of exclusion, of poverty and neglect on the part of the authorities. But they are still part of the city, part of the creative potential of modern urban life. They are places where people build everyday lives, imagine and reimagine themselves, and make homes from which they set out to negotiate – and change – city spaces.

Arturo Escobar and Sonia Alvarez make this point in their discussion of urban movements in South America.[5] Rather than seeing these movements of the poor as being simply about material resources and needs, they suggest that collective organization and everyday life in poor areas of cities are also about reimagining identities, about using creative cultural capacities to remake the meaning of places and communities. Escobar calls for a 'cultural theory of social movements',[6] in which we pay attention to the wide variety of everyday practices of ordinary people, rather than reading their experiences through the dominant categories of social science. He cites Ruth Behar to suggest that 'there are possibilities for seeing Latin American women in terms different from those already fixed in much academic and political discourse (mothers, wives, activists, "beasts of burden" and so forth). "It suggests that, if looked at from a cultural perspective, Latin American women can emerge as thinkers, cosmologists, creators of worlds."'[7]

Just as 'third-world cities' have been seen through the lens of 'developmentalism', South Africa's cities have been seen through the lens of 'apartheid' – as sites of domination through spatial segregation and racism. Writers on cities in poor and post-colonial countries are increasingly drawn to consider the creative urbanity of these places and the people who live in them.[8] South African cities would surely provide a rich field for this approach. As AbdouMaliq Simone notes, 'Even though it is difficult for a man, woman, or child to imagine, reflect, conceive, or create on an empty stomach, empty stomachs do not terminate the existence of the imagination. The question will continue to be how these endeavours of the imagination can be incorporated into national and institutional life as aspects of a coherent cultural project.'[9]

It is these cultural resources and creative enterprises which transform city space, as much as – or perhaps even more than – political struggle and institutional reform. The imagination, then, is a crucial part of (re)making city spaces. Does this have theoretical purchase? What does it mean for (re)planning cities?

2 Dreaming

South African cities are born, as perhaps no other urban spaces are, of the kinds of spatialities Lefebvre refers to as 'abstract space', or 'representations of space'.[10] This signifies a geometric and homogeneous space of separation and power, built upon a dominance of the visual, of formal relations amongst objects organized on the basis of technical knowledge. Abstract space has come to dominate the form of the modern city. It is exemplified by the homogenization and division involved in the capitalist commodification of land and the construction of alienating environments in which the possibilities for alternative spatialities are repressed.

And yet Lefebvre is not pessimistic about the possibilities of changing such spaces. One source of change which he identifies should feel familiar to scholars of South African urban spaces. He identifies in the 'contradictory' nature of abstract space the material inconsistencies of the ways in which cities are organized through the regimes of abstract space – the contradictions of the space which its (not only) capitalist form has produced.[11] The dialectic of centrality, for example, he sees not simply as a contradiction in space but as a contradiction of space. In many different historical contexts, he suggests, the centre 'concentrates wealth, means of action, knowledge, information and "culture". In short, everything.'[12] The relation with the periphery, created through the assertion of dominance by the centre, is potentially explosive, potentially driven by a dialectical conflict, or potentially burst asunder as a consequence of pure opposition. Similarly, dynamic contradictions are embodied in the parcelling out and fragmentation of homogenized space – which is nonetheless unified and made part of a whole by the space of the city.

The other potential source of change, though, is less familiar, and ensues from Lefebvre's critical consideration of the possibility of a 'psychoanalysis of space'.[13] One route into this is through his concept of 'representational space'. Alongside spatial practice (how space is produced and used in particular societies) and representations of space (conceived space, the space of scientists, planners, urbanists and so on), he describes representational space, which is 'space as directly lived through its associated images and symbols, and hence the space of "inhabitants" and "users", but also of some artists and perhaps of those, such as a few writers and philosophers, who describe and aspire to do no more than describe. This is the dominated – and hence passively experienced – space which the imagination seeks to change and appropriate.'[14]

In representational space we find a spatiality which draws on cultural and historical resources, the possibility and memory of ways of living in spaces other than those dictated by the dominant order, designated as representations of space. Lefebvre's ambivalent attitude to this space as a source of change is indicated by his dismissal of writers, artists and so on as simply describing – an ambivalence which runs through his rather testy engagement with psychoanalysis and semiotics.[15]

But as he seeks to determine the source of potentially new spatialities, the body and the unconscious come into view to signify the possibility of spaces beyond the dominant, abstract space. The body is drawn on because it is a lived, sensual realm beyond and potentially disruptive of the visually based orderings which underpin abstract, or conceived, space. The unconscious also signifies this possible other space because it is a space of 'affectivity' which cannot be reduced to the rationality of abstract space, even though it is produced, like the individual unconscious, through the denials of domination (by the ego; by rational space): 'Affectivity ... along with the sensory/sensual realm, cannot accede to abstract space and so informs no symbolism, is referred to by a term that denotes both a subject and that subject's denial by the absurd rationality of space: that term is "the unconscious".'[16]

The unconscious represents (an element of) the subject which is at the same time present and denied; and the realm of affectivity, Lefebvre suggests, stands in a similar relation to abstract space. The unconscious supposedly consists of material which cannot be symbolized, which we cannot put into words, formally excluded from the conscious world of language. Similarly, abstract space, which is founded upon rationality and symbolism, cannot make sense of the realm of affect, which it excludes from and subordinates to the ordering regimes of the visual, the geometric, the planned. It is to these excluded, subordinated, repressed realms of emotions, affect and physical sensuality that Lefebvre looks for the possibility of new spaces. As he writes,

> Social space ... contains potentialities – of works and of reappropriation – existing to begin with in the artistic sphere but responding above all to the demands of a body 'transported' outside itself in space, a body which by putting up resistance inaugurates the project of a different space (either the space of a counter-culture, or a counter-space in the sense of an initially utopian alternative to actually existing 'real' space).[17]

The subject moves in space, experiencing and remaking the meaning of spaces initially constituted to speak of power. In their everyday activities, subjects are witness to the possibility of other forms of spatiality through their bodies and their movements, as well as in their imaginations, in the dynamism of their inner worlds which are both made through, and themselves remake, the 'external' spaces of the environment.[18] The body, the unconscious and our inner worlds clearly play an important role in the production of the meaning of space, and in its potential transformation.

What about the dream? Lefebvre himself mentions the dream as one aspect of representational space, which he characterizes as 'alive: it speaks', and as 'essentially qualitative, fluid and dynamic'.[19] In further exploring his use of the space of the unconscious as an image of the dynamic potential present in representational spaces, dreams are a helpful point of access. It is in dreams that we have regular contact with the space of the unconscious, a space generally lacking in symbolization, existing largely beyond language (as Lefebvre points out). Dreaming, although it is not the only way in which we find the unconscious present in our waking memories, gives us some way of speaking about this space.

Yet the dream as an image of the possibility of transformation is a seriously compromised one. This despite the fact that it has served as one of the most persuasive metaphors of political change, from Martin Luther King's 'I have a dream' speech, to current feminist writings where dreaming of the new (or dancing ...) sometimes seems to be all that is possible![20] The more practical forms of political dreaming – political programmes, policy platforms, and even legislation – bring the figure of the dream in from the realm of the visionary, the ecstatic or the sublime, to the contested world of conscious politics. And this appropriation in itself might prompt us to consider that the dream, like the unconscious, is not such an 'other' place.

Freud, it seems, had definitely come to think of the dream as less than completely other, yet it was to dreams that he turned to learn of the unconscious, and it was the analysis of dreams in The Interpretation of Dreams that led him to produce his first major account of psychoanalysis. In his 'rambles through the problems of dream-life',[21] Freud postulates the existence of different agencies or systems within the 'mental apparatus' as a means of explaining the nature of dreaming. He seems unwilling to invest too much in the model which he develops of the workings of this apparatus, suggesting that 'we have been obliged to build our way in the dark'.[22] In this story, the components of dreams are made up of elements of unconscious memories which a 'critical agency' generally prevents from surfacing during waking hours. At night, he supposes, the censorship imposed by resistance is lowered and the memories obtain access to consciousness in the form of dreams. He ascribes to these unconscious memories a desire to be known, an energy which motivates their movement to the space of consciousness. In the dream, these repressed memories join together with elements of the 'day's residue' – more recent memories – to create pictorial narratives, which we call dreams.

Although he fails to account for the pictorial and sensational form of dreams, Freud suggests that their visual form is crucial. The forms of representation chosen by the dream are limited by the need to present feelings and memories visually (words play a minor part). But the specific form of the dream is also produced by the battle between the unconscious and the repressive 'critical agency'. So the difference between the 'latent dream-thought' (lurking in the unconscious) and the manifest 'dream-content'[23] (revealed in the dream) lies partly in the problems of representing complex ideas mainly in pictures; and partly in the need of the dream-content to evade the censorship of the repressive agency, and to be sufficiently hidden not to startle the dreamer into a waking state. The process of translation between these 'two versions of the same subject-matter in two different languages', Freud terms the 'dream-work'. Retranslating a dream, moving from pictures to words or memories, based on the numerous conscious associations which the dream-images provoke, was Freud's astonishing contribution to dream interpretation.

D

The now familiar-sounding processes of condensation (many different associations coalescing around one representation) and displacement (the energy of one unconscious thought displaced to another one with less intensity) are, for Freud, the two key factors which are responsible for the (pictorial and somewhat cryptic) 'form assumed by dreams'.[24] And, most importantly for what I am interested in here, the distortions of the dream-thoughts which these processes instigate are not only about enabling pictorial representation of complex memories: they are also a result of censorship. As Freud comments, 'those elements of the dream-thoughts which make their way into the dream ... must escape the censorship imposed by resistance'.[25] This partly explains why he says that dreams are usually the guardians of sleep: they are structured in such a way as not to alert our conscious selves to the dangerous thoughts, emotions and memories in the unconscious which have now been worked into dream form.

In Freud's account the dream is thus an accommodation between the energy and challenges of unconscious memories and the watchfulness of a repressive agency on behalf of the sensitivities of our conscious selves. It is also an unpredictable space of unusual and innovative juxtapositions or overlays, strange associations and disturbing images.[26] The dream then may well be a good image to use in seeking to understand the emergence of new kinds of spatialities. But as an 'accommodation', as a vastly compromised negotiation between our unconscious and conscious selves, the dream also seems like a peculiar choice for inspiring our hopes of transforming society and its spaces. Or perhaps not.

The term 'unconscious', for Lefebvre, signified the possibility of other ways of creating spaces, of other spatialities beyond the rational ones of planners, architects and capitalists. The parallel was between the unconscious and the potential embodied in affectivity and sensuality, as subjects moved through, imagined and used abstract spaces. Now, if dreaming captures something of the ways in which unconscious memories surface, the dynamic ways in which the repressed 'returns', then the sort of transformation or invention associated with the unconscious might involve a rather compromised movement from one sort of spatiality to another. Somewhat more compromised, perhaps, than the change envisaged by many formal visionary plans or utopian revolutionary projects. Perhaps the simplicity and certainty, the (merely different) geometry of alternative or even oppositional utopian visions of the city are once again repressing the dynamic potential of other spatialities, foreclosing on the possibility of something new emerging?

Everyday dreams and nightmares

The image of the dream suggests that there is potential for new spaces to emerge beyond abstract space. But in exploring the idea of the unconscious through the figure of the dream it seems that these other spaces might appear in a rather compromised and mediated relation to more familiar ones. There have been great expectations in South Africa that the spaces of apartheid might be overcome. If we follow this 'dream analysis', we would not be surprised to find a more complicated outcome; in fact, we might expect that the transformation of city spaces will be slow, halting and unpredictable.

Lefebvre's notion of representational space invites a fairly promising tale about how we might imagine spaces changing. Every time we move around in the city we potentially use spaces differently, imagine them differently. Walking down the street, differently. Walking past another person, next to me, then far away. Walking past and not seeing. Walking past and seeing. Walking past and hiding inside. Walking past and smiling. Stopping in the street. Not walking. Driving. Hair streaming out the window. Driving. Windows up. Walking along, touching. Walking along. Dreaming.[27] Different people in the city have different resources to draw upon in their imaginative reuse and remaking of the city – different histories, different positions. The creative potential embodied in the diverse populations of South Africa's cities would appear to be vast. Surely there is a real possibility of imagining and shaping new kinds of space, of finding spaces transformed, moved, shifted into strangeness, as if in a dream ... But what if the dream is a nightmare?

Certainly, there are many forces at work (some of which might be determined to repress the potentially dynamic space of everyday experiences, sensuality and affect) blocking or compromising transformative efforts. Indeed, insofar as the unconscious is a place where we hide horrifying experiences and feelings, where we lock up our secrets, it is potentially as much a source of immobility as of mobility. There are some memories we never dream of or cannot recognize in the guises they have adopted to save us from their horror. Are there doors before which we stand immobilized? Places we cannot bear to enter or even know about? And who are 'we'? Whose fears and anxieties will immobilize the city? Whose dreams will reshape it?

Jane Jacobs tells of the 'uncanny' return of the Aboriginal past, repressed by the history of settler society in Australia.[28] She traces examples of urban development conflicts in which Aboriginal claims forced settlers to confront this past. The haunting of the present by this undisclosable past penetrates to the heart of settlers' fears, anxieties and uncertainties, just as it challenges the imposition of rational, capitalist and white plans for the future. The potential 'other' spaces which arise do not evoke some untainted and primordial Aboriginal spatiality; rather, they are compromised, modern, hybrid – and potentially different.

But this is not the only possible outcome. White South Africans have enormous resources of repression at their disposal. These are no longer the armoured vehicles, administrative sanctions and legal exclusions of apartheid. Rather they are the private security arrangements around every home, the constant search for exclusive, safe, white neighbourhoods, the retreat to the shopping mall with its security guards and sanitized aisles, the rising fear of driving around town, the no-go areas (downtown, townships, 'white' areas that have become 'black', roads past new shack settlements, certain freeways at certain times of day or night, the street outside after dark), the reluctance to walk anywhere at all, the anxious looking around as they get out of their cars. Keeping (black) danger out has become an obsession, and spaces are made and used in ways which reflect these fears. Long traditions of maintaining separateness in situations of intimacy (such as sharing a home with a domestic servant) inform these spatial practices. White urban dreams are nightmares of anxiety, of danger and loss of self – if they emerge at all, that is, from beneath the everyday rituals of security, shopping, television, sport, travel. The city is the scene of nightmares, and changing spatial practices work to repress anxiety. Defensive, immobilizing and horrifying, these practices find their counterpart in the waking decisions of capital, whose expanding spheres of operation try to impose their (abstract) logic on the shape of cities. Where in all this is the potential for change, for mobilizing space? Do these nightmares matter?

Planning (im)mobility

The type of space which Lefebvre looks forward to as an alternative to abstract space is 'differential space' – a heterogeneous space of difference and diversity. In order to make a new society, he suggests, a new space is necessary: 'Thus, despite – or rather because of – its negativity, abstract space carries within itself the seeds of a new kind of space. I shall call that new space "differential space", because, inasmuch as abstract space tends towards the elimination of existing differences or peculiarities, a new space cannot be born (produced) unless it accentuates differences.'[29] And again: 'A revolution that does not produce a new space has not realized its full potential; indeed it has failed in that it has not changed life itself, but has merely changed ideological superstructures, institutions or political apparatuses. A social transformation, to be truly revolutionary in character, must manifest a creative capacity in its effects on daily life, on language and on space.'[30]

The resonances with South Africa's segregated cities and their potential transformations are deep. For the rationality of capitalist homogenization and fragmentation which Lefebvre discusses has been supplemented here by a political ordering of space, drawing on the logics of planning. Zoning, which Lefebvre describes as 'responsible – precisely – for fragmentation, break-up and separation under the umbrella of bureaucratically decreed unity',[31] laid the foundations for the segregations of apartheid on the basis of a calculation of racial difference. Planners worked for decades to eliminate difference and diversity from the country's urban spaces, to create single-use and single-race neighbourhoods, to keep apart rather than bring together, to separate out the colourful mix that more cosmopolitan urban traditions celebrate and advocate.

Is the new post-apartheid society producing new spaces? Are these fragmented and singular city spaces being reused, reimagined? What sorts of dreams and plans have begun to reshape the cities? Are they still partly shaped by elements of abstract apartheid spatiality? To what extent are the visions for remaking apartheid space productive of difference? To what extent has Lefebvre's 'representational space' been a source of new types of spaces?

Planners wanting to reshape these cities have devised (or appropriated) the visions of the Compact City, the Integrated City, the Sustainable City. These are formally opposed to the divisive planning principles common to South African and many other cities, principles which have contributed to urban sprawl, poor accessibility and a fragmented environment, problems that were compounded under apartheid by the location of segregated residential areas for the poorest groups on the peripheries of cities. David Dewar, for instance, summarizes some of the spatial strategies which should be adopted to develop compact cities, characterized by connection, interaction and integration, rather than disconnection and separation: densification and infill projects, the mixing of land uses and activities, the use of linear geometries in planning, especially those suggested by the dominant transport routes, and so on.[32]

Some find it hard to imagine that the cities will change too quickly; Mabin, for instance, writes pessimistically of the persistence of long journeys to poorly paid jobs for the majority of South Africans living in isolated townships.[33] Bringing poorer people closer to the city centres seems important. Unfortunately, problems of land availability and costs, and the privatized neo-liberal nature of housing provision itself, have meant that new housing for the poor is still being developed on the fringes, usually close to existing townships. Slow bureaucratic procedures, funding crises and political conflicts have also helped to ensure that apartheid spaces persist. We may try to redraw the lines of the apartheid city in our planning dreams, but changing them in reality could be a very long and difficult task. As John Western notes: 'To actively dismantle the apartheid city which is so evidently and intendedly reflective and indeed constitutive of [racial] inequality would cost a great deal. The money it would take to pursue social engineering significant enough to somehow rescramble the racial and/or ethnic groups (as formerly defined) seems to make such a prospect utterly remote.'[34]

Certainly some elements of the segregated apartheid city are unlikely to disappear, and we may want to ask whether it really is important to imagine rearranging the spaces in question. Perhaps the more important thing is to encourage the connections and flows which may improve the quality of life and opportunities of those living in segregated areas. Instead of trying to change the spaces of the city, we could try to influence the spatial relations and networks through which they are connected. Dewar mentions the importance of creating 'extroverted' spaces, spaces that look outwards to the opportunities of the wider city instead of inwards to local areas. Rather than the fixations of conceived or rational spaces, concerned with the location of physical things and the visible arrangements of space, the mobility and dynamism of city spaces could be brought into view. Here we would consider the changing and restless flows of people, of resources, of ideas, which constantly reshape – or mobilize – city spaces.[35]

Mobilizing spaces

It is not just the flows and connections within cities that reflect and generate their dynamism, and might change their spatiality, but the way they are connected through a wide variety of different linkages to other cities, other places, other times.[36] Different parts of the city are connected differently: the linkages in and out of inner-city, high-rise Hillbrow and suburban Sandton have always been different. Today, however, Hillbrow is not only connected to townships in Johannesburg and other cities, rather than to white suburbs and the white city centre as before, but the routes of many of its residents stretch the length of Africa.

These dynamic and changing flows have not only transformed the social and economic character of the city; they have also produced a new differentiation of urban space. Fragmentation in the city does not end when planners stop trying to impose it. While the dynamic connectedness of cities contributes to reshaping their internal forms, this could just as well lead to separation as to integration. Newly-arrived immigrant communities, for example, make their own spaces in the city. Nonetheless, the diversity and unpredictability of city economies and the variety of networks which constitute urban spaces mean that the potential for new opportunities and new spaces is always being generated. It was so even under apartheid.

So while planners and government officials try to find ways to rearrange the city, or to encourage reconnection and integration, ordinary people are reusing and remaking urban space at a rapid rate. Faced with a restricted local market in poor townships, many informal sellers have relocated to the city centres. The streets of downtown Johannesburg, now primarily a retail and service centre for outlying Soweto, are covered with stalls set out in the shadows of the skyscrapers, selling everything from fruit to handbags, cosmetics and clothes, providing haircuts, shoe repairs, photographic services, telephone calls! The major retail stores continue to trade behind the ranks of hawkers. Through the symbolic spaces of the dominant class, its power expressed in sheer verticality, all kinds of people are walking along, thousands of people like Mda's Toloki, using the pavements of the modern city, making it, experiencing it and imagining it different(ly). Some traders find it necessary to stay on the streets with their goods overnight and a few street settlements have sprung up. There are also a number of more central areas where squatters have seized the opportunity to build more permanent shelters in a well-located area, rather than on the more abundant but more remote land on the edges of the city where most newcomers and homeless people are forced to seek shelter. The lines of the city are crossed, redrawn, reimagined; outside the conceiving spaces of planning visions. The city of everyday experience and imagination is already a different space, it is already a space of difference.

Planners do well to try and keep up with people's energetic redrafting of city space: providing concentrations of sellers with stalls and facilities, arranging transport services in response to new needs, offering services and subsidies in the wake of land occupations; learning from the creative reuse of space rather than trying to reassert formal and rational ideas about the proper use of certain kinds of spaces. In any case, post-apartheid city plans are overturned by government decisions – to locate housing on the fringes of the city, for instance – as much as by ordinary people's activities. In some spheres a new de facto relation seems to have emerged between the planning visions of a dominant abstract spatiality and the representational spaces of everyday life, in which the meanings and inventions of everyday life are dominant. Is it possible to claim that a new form of spatiality has already emerged?

Here the dream offers us another useful metaphor: in dreams, symbolization is only ever partial. Locked into the form of the picture, muted by the 'repressive agency' and working in the terrain of the unspeakable, the dream is never an uncompromised 'other' space. In the same way, we make new spaces in the city that are guarded and muted by the spaces of the old order, and in the face of fierce opposition from those to whom our dreams seem like nightmares. Even our dreams of new spaces may be unable to leave behind elements of the past; in the spaces we dream of creating, the restricting voice of past times may always echo. Our planning dreams, for example, speak in the only language they know: a physicalist, ordering and visual perspective on the internal relations of the city. But there is always the possibility of re-viewing those spaces, seeing them differently, trying not to bring them into the sharp focus which has always enabled dominant orderings of spaces. We could stretch our imaginations to draw in those other everyday, affective and sensual experiences which are constantly remaking urban space. Perhaps, if we face up to our fears, if we lay to rest the haunting ghosts of the unconscious, we might start to dream differently. The dream of a non-racial, diverse and dynamic city is not yet dead.

►D8 ►E6 ►G6

8

Globalization and the identity of African urban practices

AbdouMaliq Simone

D

Every year, one of Senegal's major figures, a man prominent in the religious, the political and the commercial worlds, puts together a lavish spread and a wholesome evening's entertainment for a cross-section of Dakar's élite. At these gatherings, the intricacies of politicking and the niceties of sizing up changes in intraclass relations are frequently punctuated by religious blessings and invocations. During a particularly prolonged gathering held recently, the estate was overrun by hundreds of youths wielding knives and clubs, who not only grabbed what they could from necks, pockets and tables, but stripped naked several of the most honoured guests and humiliated them in foreign tongues, whose origins no one could make out at the time or cared to remember afterwards. Despite the presence of security guards, police and chauffeurs, the youths had mounted a sneak attack, after which most of them escaped into the nooks and crannies of surrounding shanty towns. Those who were captured were all definitely Senegalese, which prompted an outcry from many citizens: what about the 'foreign tongues'? They were also all wearing 'bowl' haircuts with short dreadlocks on top. Within two months, no self-respecting young man would be caught in public without this cut, and neither would the cosmopolitan Dakaroise in places like Rome and Paris.

The house next door to where this raid took place is the nerve centre of a collection of disparate associations loosely united by a common Soninke identity. This is the identity which prevails in the villages scattered along that piece of the border of Senegal, Mauritania and Mali marked by the Senegal River. The task of the centre is to diffuse information relayed by Soninke entrepreneurs through the various Soninke networks operating in most major African, European, North American and Asian cities, so that realities and opportunities experienced by Soninke in any one location can be assessed and cross-referenced in relation to experiences in others. In this way, prices, custom regulations, markets, support networks, the nuances of micro-politics and the proliferating spaces between the official and the unofficial can all be appropriated and deployed as a potential resource. The task of the centre is also to make sure that remittances earmarked by migrants for the development of their villages get the best value for their money, and so the centre facilitates negotiations for infrastructure and other development inputs. In the reception area at the centre is a long cast-iron couch with mud-cloth cushions. It is a prototype of those being produced for the homes of the new black political class in South Africa, in workshops established somewhat clandestinely in the eastern parts of central Johannesburg. The flight of light manufacturing from these parts has left many vacant properties, which are increasingly filled by such informal workshops. Saddam Hussein, a Congolese trader based in Johannesburg, recently found himself sleeping on one of these locally manufactured couches at the apartment of a Senegalese fellow merchant, El Haj Sy. This was after Saddam had been kicked out of his bunker behind a boxing club in Melville, because a South African cameraman, busy making a documentary about the lives of francophone merchants in Johannesburg, dared to tell the white owners that an African renaissance was in the making. Saddam was so excited about the workmanship in his friend's couch that he called his brother in Brussels, who had his nightclub order three; and since Saddam had his special contacts in customs, the couches were on their way in no time.

Between inside and outside

The changing shape of the urban everywhere is one of the predominant features of the changes in economic, cultural and political space referred to as 'globalization'. This changing shape emerges from the capacity of firms and economic networks to disperse and yet integrate increasingly complex components of productive activity throughout the world, breathe new life into city centres, grow exurban zones marked by residential exclusivity and segregation, set up back offices, and hollow out vast spaces of marginality.[1] The reach and penetration of contemporary forces of production and apparatuses of control and management also produce spaces which, because they offer little to global economies, start to fall apart and become factories of poverty no outsider would dare to enter.[2] A geography of control and inequality increasingly shapes zones of relative order and influence set against other zones of unruliness and structural violence.[3]

The impenetrability of these 'neglected' spaces, combining the extremes of poverty, infrastructural decline, economic emptiness and social danger, tends to ward off the outside world. But these spaces are often also 'communities', characterized by an intricate interweaving of social organization, economic practice and governance generally seen as informal or provisional. Such informalities can create the impression that everyday life in these places never changes, and that communities here are removed from the ways and means of doing things that might provide broader access to the world. Or these informalities can institutionalize a constant state of flux, often spawning networks and circuits of movement that reach far and wide.[4]

But to what extent is the appearance of a never-ending sameness also a kind of mirage? To what extent do fluid networks, always reaching out to more distant places, also help bring about a sense of stability at home? How do communities improvise on the ways in which survival and social cohesion are attained?[5] In even the most depleted spaces, popular ways of organizing social life intersect with the operations of formal institutions to make visible specific social subjects and processes.[6] It is through such localized popular processes that specific identities, aspirations and understandings of citizenship and place come to the fore, and establish a framework for what is considered possible. Based on such understandings, localities develop specific reactions to the outside, attempt to regulate what is visible to that outside, and assess just what activities are worth investing in and how.

How a locality actively situates itself in relationship to the larger world is thus neither a manifestation of an intrinsic urban culture nor a total subjection to external power, but a search for capacities and a platform on which to build viable political action, whether that action aims to put bread on the table or change the current regime. No matter how isolated, communities are rarely completely removed from larger spheres of action; and no matter how dispersed local populations may be, they are never far from home. Furthermore, making it seem as if nothing changes can mask the existence of great fluidity and activities stretching across great distances and sectoral divides, while the impression of incessant change can mask the persistence of particular social practices and points of view. In this sense impenetrability becomes a strategy for keeping a community's head above water by making ambiguous just what is going on. This may be an intentional tactic, as much as an implicit description or summary of the interaction of diverse social, political and economic processes which converge from the inside and outside of localities.

I am going to review some aspects of this complex phenomenon of impenetrability in African cities and show how ghettoization and translocal networking operate in specific inner-city neighbourhoods of Dakar and Johannesburg.

Africity today

It is not an exaggeration to say that African cities live precariously along a cusp where things can happen very quickly or seem not to happen at all. At times, this sense that nothing changes in Africa is a product of the sheer speed with which information can be relayed and a workable sense of social alliance and consensus put together to accomplish a particular task. At other times, the stasis is simply an accepted 'norm', which allows almost any attempt to try and change things to appear either persuasive or inappropriate. In the African city it is increasingly difficult to ascertain just what a meaningful response to the development aspirations of its citizens would be. Similarly, the rapidity with which impressions can be fixed in the popular imagination and unanticipated resourcefulness organized often rules out certainty about the ingredients or processes involved.[7]

Yet, in many important ways, the city fails to exist in Africa. National authorities, external observers and interveners, and even local populations, tend to approach African cities not as failed versions of urbanization, but as densely localized conglomerations of ethnicity, histories of settlement, and estates colliding with one another or coexisting in an uneasy truce. Of course, the fact is that it is primarily in African cities that things change – behaviours, languages, economies and social configurations. Yet the prevailing and institutionalized attitude towards urban space, the refusal to acknowledge and approach the whole city as a particular kind of African organism, severely curtails the effect those actual changes may have on the structures of governance, social life and economic production.

In most African cities, some degree of breakdown or transition in formal metropolitan governance and sheer population growth are combining to make life highly unsafe for residents. In both poor and wealthy neighbourhoods this is narrowing down what people do and where they do it, and making their interests more parochial.[8] Residents concentrate on protecting their compounds, blocks or immediate neighbourhoods, and develop increasingly singular strategies to consolidate social ties and the opportunities these may hold. Their strategies often clash with those of other blocks or neighbourhoods, or are difficult to connect with them at least, even among physically contiguous quarters. In places like Kinshasa and Lagos, new churches, associations and entrepreneurial groupings crop up all the time, but without significant connections between them. Rather than linking groups and households, these associations act like households themselves, providing a sense of stability that fragmented families and extended families have lost.

The profound fissuring tendencies in Africa may reflect a dissolution of conventional solidarity and integration, but do not lessen the need for groups to find ways of acting in concert in the larger world. The difficulty in reading the urban social field is that the very real social disintegration taking place, and the rise of ethnonationalism and parochial conflicts, also mask practices which connect communities to a wide network of interdependencies and groups. The visible 'wholeness' or 'intactness' of neighbourhoods, ethnic and religious groups is simply a point of reference, a means of establishing nodal points in larger networks.[9]

These larger networks or cross-community ties do not imply any essential stability, as networks are fluid and changeable. Even as they seek to connect themselves to different 'stories' and to larger networks of production and exchange, urban communities increase their exposure to being buffeted and fragmented by competing demands and influences. At the same time, they must constantly be piecing together provisional mechanisms for maintaining a coherent sense of who they are and stabilizing the interactions of local residents, workers and affiliates, who collectively participate in thousands of different connections.

For the individual, making the wrong moves or decisions may be disastrous. Downfall and marginalization await those who do not act according to the prevailing norms – even though these are often the product of a short-lived consensus.[10] When one has to improvise incessantly, it is difficult to predict the implications of one's own actions, and life becomes a gamble in which the stakes for guessing both 'right' and 'wrong' are high.

These politics affect the use of urban knowledge in several ways. There is a hedging of bets in which the uses of various types of knowledge coincide and none takes precedence – so that sorcery, religious beliefs, personal memories, family and kinship narratives, ethnic myths, academic structures and bureaucratic procedures are all played like cards, whose values change depending on one's playing partners and audience.[11] Stating clearly that one is committed to a particular point of view or identity might restrict the flexibility required to keep one's options open, to find ways of operating in the growing number of different spaces and experiences making up the city. It then often becomes difficult to distinguish between aspirations and compensations, cynicism and strongly held values, corruption and moral integrity.[12]

As economic liberalization opens borders and frees up economic activity, the very instruments and arrangements deployed by local urban populations to generate more extensive transactions face greater difficulties. These difficulties may revolve around stretching limited capacities to cover more territory, to go farther afield; or, conversely, around narrowing the scope of the activities or the range of persons involved in particular transactions.

Although conventional firms and entrepreneurship, both local and foreign, are burgeoning in African cities, informal sector activities remain the core of their economies. But increasing their absorptive capacities now often demands a simultaneous narrowing of social fields and a wider dispersion of economic processes over larger territories.[13] Membership in social networks and neighbourhoods may therefore become more tightly drawn – sometimes along religious, ethnic or cultural lines.

At the same time, economic necessity forces many from their homes. The African neighbourhood often becomes a stage the actors are desperate to leave, and the leaving itself becomes increasingly complicated. The nature of the economic crisis, the increased demand for emigration and the scope which small and medium-scale trade of all varieties must now assume in order to be successful, make access to work opportunities in Europe or the United States, for instance, and the movements of bodies and goods dependent upon intricate social arrangements, increasingly transnational in nature and ruthless in operation.

The expansion of informal economies has various effects on social organization. In reaction against the uncertainties of the formal financial system – and this was especially evident during the recent period of structural reform – growing surpluses are not put into liquid assets but into land, housing, goods. Accumulation based on such holdings may curtail the mobility and independent actions of those household and associational members who own or are dependent on them.[14] This constraint on mobility reinforces the need to invest time and attention in the politics of social connection. Access to liquid capital remains highly dependent on one's position in a known social network. The amounts available are usually small and go towards financing a single purchase or deal, rather than establishing the borrower in a position of greater financial independence in the long run.

New entrepreneurial groups are formed as the costs of both travel and distributive trade increase. Individual traders may form small, short-term consortiums to make bulk purchases, share transportation and import costs. As these arrangements become more common, the traditional marketing networks become more fluid as well. Where once the disposition of goods was largely tied to a steady network of retailers and hawkers, the growth of distributive and cross-border trade – which has increased as markets liberalize – means that traders are not assured of buyers for their goods.

The delinking of marketing practices is a new source of conflict in neighbourhoods. The tolerant notion that 'what goes around, comes around' used to allow individuals and groups to ply the same trade, to sell the same goods to the same customers, even to share orders; now a more laissez-faire, sometimes renegade approach to entrepreneurship introduces new tensions along with new opportunities.

This combination – the narrowing of scope and social composition, and a broader diffusion of activities over larger territories – has its correlates elsewhere. The most obvious are the constraints on movement brought about by increased levels of insecurity and crime, and by political clientelism, which has broadened its territorial claims to the extent that certain quarters in some cities are no-go areas for anyone not affiliated with a particular political party or grouping. It must be said at the outset that high levels of everyday insecurity, which are in fact of relatively recent origin in many African cities, are not peculiar to Africa, and neither are the responses of residents.

In both Lagos and Kinshasa, moving around the city has become a cat-and-mouse game, with the élite varying their routes from enclave to office in order to avoid the shakedowns and attacks organized by criminal gangs on the roads. In Johannesburg, where a car is hijacked every thirty minutes, security companies offer satellite tracking systems for vehicles. In protected estates, such as Maryland or Anthony in Lagos, access is strictly controlled even for residents, and yet gangs still find a way in, and let it be known that they will be back for money within a day or two.

Well-organized neighbourhood patrols, with residents posted all night at every intersection, are the norm in thousands of localities across the continent. At the same time, a general disillusionment with the authorities' ability to control escalating crime often leads to instant justice. The mere claim that someone has stolen or raped may result in a summary beating or killing. In many cities, someone bringing a suspect to the police will be expected to pay the costs of maintaining the accused in prison until the case is heard. In some cities, the prisons are so overwhelmed that all the institutions of justice prefer to see 'local solutions'. Though neighbourhoods may feel they have little choice but to take matters into their own hands, their actions often undermine justice entirely and exacerbate the problems they are trying to solve. Where people feel that no element in the society has the ability or legitimacy to exert control, both rich and poor find their freedom of movement and use of the city severely curtailed.

In the attempt to deal with some vulnerabilities others may be created. For example, the tolerance of sex work in African cities is placing new strains on the social fabric, as energies must be spent absorbing intense contradictions. In some quarters of Khartoum, where overt support for the Islamic movement has been very strong, young girls order shopkeepers on certain streets to close their gates at a certain hour of the night because the streets now belong to them and their business. Sometimes an emphasis on a woman's right to control her own body is simply there to obscure the fact that a household depends on the use of that body for its income.

Fear tends to feed on itself. Defensive enclosures and divisions are signals of vulnerability, which those with little are quick to exploit (although it is usually a case of the poor preying on the poor). The vulnerable seek to create greater social divides in order to control the risks; but many poor communities cannot sustain such divides, or can do so only by taking actions that directly contradict the symbolic integrity of the group.

In the last decade, for instance, there has been an apparent hardening of ethnic and religious identities in Khartoum, and a tightening of the 'borders' between enclaves and quarters that at times could hardly be distinguished along ethnic lines. Nevertheless, certain psychological stratifications have arisen. The ascendancy of political Islam, the enormous growth of the city and the persistence of civil war have complicated everyday relationships in the public spaces which different groups have to cross. Equally significant, although it has remained covert, are the scores of ways in which apparent antagonists have continued to collaborate. Based on the relative advantages of their respective positions, and their differential access to various networks, inputs or opportunities, sworn enemies go on working together.[15] While none can acknowledge these collaborations, and they would probably not work if they were brought into the open, new or reinvigorated forms of urban sociality are emerging where one least expects to find them. That they may be occasioned by intense, unarticulated feelings of collective vulnerability, and may exist as highly vulnerable social instruments themselves, does not change the fact that a small glimmer of the cosmopolitan is being generated by the parochial.

In trying to understand the African city, we must go beyond rudimentary divisions of formal and informal, cosmopolitan and parochial. We need to look at the interweaving of potentials and constraints that activate and delimit the specific initiatives of local communities to maintain a sense of social cohesion; and at how these potentials and constraints exceed this cohesion at any given time, giving rise to unforeseen opportunities and mitigating the negative effects of acting as opportunistically as possible.

Soirée in Soumbedioune

Soumbedioune is a former Lebu fishing village now incorporated as an extension of the Greater Medina in Dakar. Although this densely populated quarter is still home to scores of fisherman and an important fish market, its proximity to the central city has drawn to it a very diverse set of residents and economic activities. People live in conventional compounds, which include self-constructed wooden barracks, privately capitalized apartment buildings for both low- and middle-income earners, one of the first public low-cost housing schemes in the city, and student dormitories. There are also several large residences occupied by politicians. The quarter's coastal location and the presence of woodworking and other craft shops have brought a modest infusion of tourist money. Over the years, its location and the diversity of residential opportunities have also attracted large numbers of 'foreign' residents, mainly from other francophone countries, especially Congo, Cameroon, Guinea and Mali.

Apart from activities linked to the fish market, the local economy centres on small businesses and stalls, many of which line the length of one of the city's main sewage canals – artisans' workshops and telecentres, tailoring, furniture-making, vulcanizing, car repairing, hawking and the selling of used clothing. Many residents also work in the public bureaucracy and central city businesses. A multiplicity of guild organizations operate, and the area is an important site of political contestation in the ongoing struggle for influence waged primarily between the ruling Socialist Party and the Democratic Socialist Party. While community forums concerned with specific issues have allowed for representation from various ethnic, guild, gender, age and religious organizations, both the major political parties have impeded the effective establishment of more open-ended community associations.

The political, economic and social lives of most Dakaroise neighbourhoods have one important factor in common – the turuq. These Islamic brotherhoods with their roots in Sufism are a linchpin in the cohesion of Senegalese national identity. Perhaps the most important of these groupings is the Mouriddiyah, which forms the focal point for the elaboration of an urban popular culture that blends Islam, home-grown Rastafarianism, self-help, political resistance and multinational corporatism. Dakar has become increasingly rife with a certain volatility stemming from and yet also held in check by this reinvented sense of cultural heritage.

The Mouriddiyah commits itself to the possibility of salvation through diligent work. Its moral ethos combines the rigours of Islamic discipline with an almost Messianic vision of individuals transcending their material and social conditions. The city of Touba, the brotherhood's centre, is a sovereign state unto itself. No Senegalese state authorities are allowed access without permission. The deceased spiritual leader, Shayk Amidou Bamba, acts as the guarantor of Senegalese identity and his picture is found in every Dakar neighbourhood. Some of their tenets, such as the suspension of prayer and the encouragement of forbidden activities for a 'warrior class', have distanced the Mourides from the conventional Islamic world. Yet the Mouriddiyah has parlayed its traditional organization of groundnut production into a worldwide network of traders who sell watches, Gucci bags and brass ornaments in every large city of the world. Income derived from these activities has been invested in large real-estate acquisitions in New York, Paris, Dakar and, more recently, south-east Asia.

The state has tried to reduce the power of the Mourides several times to no avail. Even when state marketing boards offered significantly higher prices to groundnut farmers, they continued to place their harvests in traditional marketing systems controlled by Mouride networks. The Mouriddiyah presently controls large swaths of commerce in the central city and has made major inroads into traditional Lebanese domination of this sector. Loyalty is cultivated in part by using the religious context to provide individuals with business opportunities and to institutionalize the sharing of resources.

Senegal is also the centre of the Tejanniyah – the largest Sufi organization in Africa – which has used its very extensive networks to control much of the mercantile sector of the Sahel and, more recently, the highly lucrative trade in consumables and electronics from Asia. While the organization and personnel of the country's dominant party have been highly secular (Léopold Senghor, the first president, was a Christian in a country that is ninety per cent Muslim) each election victory has been secured by courting the rural base controlled by the religious leaders of these two turuq, Mouriddiyah and Tejanniyah. Their positions have been strengthened by their domination of the transport sector and a growing hold on petty commerce and large-scale entrepreneurship, through which they are able to provide employment while the public sector is generally shrinking. In addition, a largely Lebu and urban-based Islamic reform movement, popularly known as 'The Lion', is on the ascendancy and draws more and more support from residents in Soumbedioune.

All the forms of social, political and religious organization command strong loyalties. As individuals are likely to have multiple memberships across different organizations, there is a continuous process of contestation and amalgamation. At times, sectoral groupings such as tailors will coalesce around specific issues: sometimes this might result in specific affiliations to certain political parties or turuq being institutionalized; at other times alliances will be more fleeting. Then again, there may be a hedging of bets, with various social organizations engineering an implicit division of labour, so that different members sustain affiliations to different organizations. The outcome is a complex topography of intersecting social networks, which simultaneously dissolve into each other and maintain often rigid operational hierarchies, norms and criteria for participation. On top of these institutional affiliations there will be strong personal networks, established on the street and in face-to-face encounters, which are important in very dense residential areas.

Given the past opportunities offered to Senegalese to educate themselves abroad, the opportunities to travel organized by Mouride and Tejani networks and the growth of expatriate communities in places like Paris, Rome and New York, the dynamics of local organizations are increasingly influenced by understandings, social practices and money derived from outside the city. Investments in local residential and commercial structures come primarily from repatriated earnings. Popular urban styles in thinking, attitude and appearance are also heavily influenced from the outside. The intersection of competing identifications and practices, dissatisfaction with some of the anachronisms of the old social and religious organizations, and external influences combine to elaborate new styles of affiliation and coordination.

It is increasingly important now to be thiof. The concept, derived from the name of the fish which is a staple of the daily diet, refers to a proliferating set of unwritten rules for what an individual must do to become successful – or at least appear to be so. While most of these 'rules' specify the elements of a lifestyle, they also deal with how to behave or talk and, importantly, how to get others to do your bidding and circumvent the wide range of restrictions imposed by local cultural norms, social organizations and politics. Increasingly 'thiofness' is incorporated into various aspects of public life. For those who fail in their 'thiofness', 'traditional' family and religious ties are reinforced and reinvigorated.

There are thus residues of ambiguity everywhere in Soumbedioune, and this renders the quarter impenetrable. It is impossible to get a firm sense of what makes the place tick. Yet the ambiguities in the organization of social life enhance the speed and mobility of transactions, resources and alliances; for if no clear roles and channels of exchange are institutionalized, if opportunism is a way of life and almost everyone is prepared to do something out of the ordinary, things can happen very quickly, if not necessarily efficiently. This keeps communities on their toes, but it also makes them vulnerable to implosive disruptions, and solidarity, coherence and functionality must be pieced together again almost every day.

In Soumbedioune, who one goes to see to straighten out small disputes with neighbours, or to discuss matters of cleanliness on the streets, or to organize social events, varies continually, depending on which of one's neighbours has acquired newly important connections, on whether elections or religious events are imminent and on what kinds of deals have been made between particular people and networks at any given time. In fact, there seems to be an incessant precipitation of problems, in excess of those usually associated with such living conditions, so that one simply is forced to find out who has what status and opportunities at any point, and to reaffirm the fluidity in how local power is organized and deployed. Because this process can be tedious, many people end up doing as they please, while others seldom do anything different at all.

A recent example will illustrate these dynamics. A project to manage the completion of a large housing estate was being tendered by one of Dakar's top companies. The company was obliged to tender, even though it clearly had every intention of keeping the entire project 'in house'. An architectural firm was to be hired, as well as a general contractor to secure materials and labour. In a cursory gesture, simply to abide by the rules, it was announced one Thursday evening to a nearly empty conference centre that tenders would close at seven the next morning. The timing was significant: on Thursday evenings many people participate in special worship in the mosques.

Nevertheless, the night after the announcement saw a flurry of visits among architects, engineers, labourers, politicians, deal-makers, marabouts, members of soccer clubs, youth organizations, artisans' guilds, and scores of their relatives, all discovering pathways of influence to the person who would award the contract. Although this official no longer resided in Soumbedioune, his sister occupied the family compound. While she received many visitors, most of the activity was in the surrounding area, as neighbours, friends and purported social connections sought one another out and held discussions. Hundreds of thousands of francs changed hands, scores of sexual scenarios were played out, prayers were offered, family injunctions invoked, pleas made, obligations reiterated, 'chance' encounters arranged. A broad array of rhetorical strategies, memories of past infractions and promises, personal knowledge, cultural etiquette, political procedure, technical know-how, sorcery – all were circulating in various constellations, marking gaps and hybrid conjunctures.

While professional firms unofficially joined the fray, there were also people looking for any opportunity to connect with the project. Even if they themselves could not design or build or supply materials, they knew others who could, and so they hoped for 'finder's fees' in kind or the possibility of parlaying information into other opportunities.

By morning, no official tenders had been submitted – but it became clear to the company that there were hundreds of options to choose from; theoretically, hundreds of different housing estates might have arisen from these nocturnal deliberations. Dakar has roughly one hundred architects and a smaller number of contracting firms capable of handling a project this size. The political and religious loyalties of these players are common knowledge. But with a flurry of activity crossing boundaries of all kinds and producing strings of possible alliances, workforce compositions, inputs and cash flows, it was not clear what the implications of any choice might be. People known to be unwilling to work together were now expressing their willingness; best friends had parted company for the moment to broaden their chances. There was an opportunism and a knack for cutting across social divides, networks and alliances that could not be absorbed by any formal representation. The company asked for more time to weigh a decision that had probably already been made a long time before.

In such circumstances, a neighbourhood can demonstrate enormous resilience, as its members mobilize the symbolic, material and social resources at their disposal to enhance their overall advantage, and act on the conviction that it is always possible to make something happen. Trying to separate the religious from the political, the political from the entrepreneurial, the familial from the public, in an effort to establish effective urban governance and regulatory environments, may weaken the very mechanisms through which African urban neighbourhoods maintain a foothold in a rapidly changing global economy. On the other hand, the proximity of these 'ways of life' may not allow enough space for changes within particular domains to take hold, and so generate new forms of independent action and innovation that could be brought into the public sphere. The interdependencies between religion, government, politics, family life and business make it difficult to shift the internal dynamics of any one sector because the stakes are so high. Though it may be possible to draw on the influences and resources of other sectors in resolving a difficulty in any one of them, independent action is also constrained.

Outside in the Johannesburg inner city

Johannesburg has long been Africa's most developed city. This is a status it attained through an oppressive political system, which severely regulated access to urban space and services and enforced two distinct development trajectories – a city with all the Western amenities for whites, and impoverished peri-urban labour reserves for blacks. The racial zoning of urban residential communities that was enforced under apartheid kept blacks from the inner city for several decades. Then, in the mid-1980s, although their presence in the white city would remain illegal until 1991, blacks began moving into what became known as 'grey areas'.[16]

Initially, to keep things from spilling over, from leading to a crackdown by the local state or to social conflict, an uneasy peace was maintained. Blacks did not want to lose the provisional foothold which gave them easy access to business districts and work. Whites did not want to antagonize their new black neighbours out of fear that they would 'gang up' on them.[17] But as the 'greying' proceeded, the white exodus to the suburban areas accelerated and this, coupled with intensifying economic recession, pushed up vacancy rates in the neighbourhoods of Hillbrow, Bertrams, Joubert Park, Berea and Yeoville. The apparent devolution of the inner city quickly followed.

As most housing construction and shelter opportunities moved further to the peripheries, large numbers of black households and individuals amassed in the inner-city vacuum created by the transition. Psychologically, this sense of vacuum was particularly severe for a society accustomed to the imposition of administrative order on settlement patterns and social movement in general. The greying of the city was not only a matter of racial mixing; the customary relationships that had existed among different social sectors and activities, also segregated by apartheid, were placed in close proximity to each other and produced a volatile mix whose properties were almost impossible to predict.

Today the mix of people and projects remains volatile. Visible moves to consolidate territory or establish dominance, and even structured local community initiatives are risky undertakings. Guns are everywhere, and people are not slow to use them. The inner city is becoming an increasingly desperate place, overcrowded and insecure, and lacking a strong cohesive core. Because nearly all the black South African residents are recent arrivals in Greater Johannesburg, there is a sense that conditions are wide open for the intersection of many groupings. The absence in the city of stable black institutions, long displaced to the peripheries, contributes to this perception.

Despite a general demand for accommodation, there has been almost no housing development in the inner city for the past two decades, with bank financing being expended almost exclusively on new suburban developments. This has contributed to overcrowding and the deterioration of the available housing stock. The limitation in secondary markets has led many small investors to make no improvements or even to abandon properties altogether. Many abandoned spaces are occupied by growing numbers of homeless people, and this adds to the perception of insecurity in the inner city. While some of these people are unemployed, most have simply been forced into provisional housing strategies in order to be close to their sources of income.

There are problems built into the way housing acquisition is conceived, as several recent initiatives have shown. A trust concerned with the upgrading of inner-city housing was established in 1993 and tried to find ways of collateralizing loans made by banks for the purchase of units. But the requirements for ownership and the continued red-lining of the inner city by most financial institutions made the programme ineffective. Even revised arrangements, which allow for different forms of ownership or rental, have been unable to unlock finance for the rehabilitation of existing housing. The provincial government has made a subsidy available, but this covers only about a fifth of the average cost of a fully refurbished unit in the inner city.

The rapid turnover of populations has itself provided a feasible cover, if not necessarily a major motivation, for the immigration of foreign Africans to Johannesburg. This migration, in turn, has substantially shaped inner-city life and commerce, opening them up further to internationalization. The inner city is one of the most circumscribed and densely populated urban spaces on the continent, with neighbourhoods such as Hillbrow made up of row after row of high-rise apartment blocks, and so this sociocultural reconfiguration has taken place more or less invisibly.

What is perhaps most significant about the transformation of the inner city is not so much its character but the speed with which it has come about. Indeed, demographic and economic change – the transition in racial composition, the depreciation of infrastructure, shifts in institutional life – have happened so quickly that the conventional ways of monitoring and assessing social change prove largely inadequate. This in turn permits a kind of arbitrary growth: because it is not clear where the inner city is going, it is difficult to make reasonable cost-benefit assessments of what is required, in capital outlays and other more diffuse social expenditures, to maintain various stakes in the city – property ownership, commercial ventures, preferred lifestyles. The uncertainty leads to sudden and substantial divestitures of all types, which further impede monitoring by adding a large volume of transactions to the flux. Insecurity intensifies, and so does the practice of getting rid of property and position at a cheap price.

The inner-city economy outside of the central business district is increasingly based on transience and the attempt to manage transience. This is reflected in the nature of businesses and emerging institutional orientations to land use, property development and investment. The forty or so hotels located in the inner city are used more and more for protracted short-term stays rather than overnight visits. These open-ended arrangements have encouraged illicit activities and some hotels have become havens, especially for young people. Several of them are quasi-dormitories, with large groups of teenagers sharing rooms, along with single mothers and their children. The various 'household forms' that emerge are not readily compatible with the frameworks applied by conventional institutions, landlords or public agencies.

Often loosely structured bands of South African youth, usually sent to the city for schooling, become attached to particular groups of foreign migrants, who subsidize the youngsters and use them to gain entry into various local networks. Names and school registrations are frequently appropriated. The young people in turn use their positions – almost as local agents who speak the language and know the ropes – to consolidate some sense of stability amongst themselves.

Some hotels have cultivated an international clientele and become centres of a burgeoning trade in narcotics. Others maintain an orderly environment for foreign Africans who either have steady jobs or are likely to find them. These hotels set reasonable tariffs to ensure high occupancy rates, and mandate the length of each stay. On the other hand, a rapid turnover of occupants in apartment blocks allows rents to be raised incrementally, and some landlords therefore prefer to let to migrants whose stays may be shorter. These migrants, who are often without proper documentation, may also be charged special 'service fees'.

The internationalization of the inner city has given rise to a large measure of xenophobia, and foreign Africans are blamed for an overcrowded informal trading sector, the growth of the narcotics trade and the general physical deterioration. Many South African residents believe that this foreign presence discourages government authorities and the private sector from investing in upgrading or providing services.

Although migrant labour from throughout the subcontinent has been indispensable in the South African economy for more than a century, the nature of migration changed radically once conduits of transport were opened up along with opportunities for individual entrepreneurs. While most migrants still come from southern Africa, the inner city has become a staging area for individuals from the francophone countries, Ethiopia, Somalia, Nigeria, Ghana and Kenya.

Much of the initial African migration corresponded to shifts in the stance of the South African state. Political favours offered by African countries, and their cooperation in circumventing sanctions and creating trade opportunities and havens for capital, were often rewarded with relaxed entry and stay requirements. At different times, visas were waived for Congolese, Ivorians, Malians and Senegalese. Changing circumstances for migrants in other countries also contributed to the move south. Most of the early Malian arrivals came from diamond smuggling syndicates in Zambia, which faced crackdowns during the early days of the Chiluba regime. And the long-term cooperation between South African multinationals and the Congolese ruling hierarchy produced an almost wholesale transfer of Zaïre's ruling élite to South Africa when the political crisis there began.

Economic survival in much of the continent depends on the constant search for new opportunities and markets, and so practically every conversation will include an exchange of information about the relative advantages of particular places. South Africa's relatively well-developed infrastructure, and its substantial ignorance of how migration-based economies work, quickly made Johannesburg a desirable destination. Both large and small merchants in the franc zone, sensing the imminence of devaluation and the possibilities for later profit-taking, rushed to take advantage of highly disparate currency values to buy large amounts of non-perishable commodities.

Any businessperson knows that making financial transfers and receiving payment for commodities in Africa can become a nightmare. But, while large-scale conventional trade hobbles along, there is an almost excessive abundance of trade at lower levels, as an economy less dependent on money and credit, and especially on hard currency transactions, proliferates through various barter arrangements. A wide range of alternative methods for acquiring and distributing goods has been developed. As these arrangements circumvent bank guarantees, prepayments and letters of credit, other ways must be found to ensure that transactions are trustworthy. These often involve family and kinship ties, with family members placed in different locations to acquire and transfer goods. Such family arrangements are often linked to syndicates of merchants, fellow nationals, ethnic or political associates.

Consider an example of how this works. A bureaucrat in the Ministry of Public Works in Dar es Salaam over-invoices for an order of spark plugs from Taiwan meant for government vehicles. The bulk of the shipment is diverted to associates on the private market. The plugs could be sold locally, or they could become part of a counter-trade agreement, say for a shipment of canned goods from South Africa, acquired in turn with a collateral of gemstones smuggled into the country from Congo. The merchant group informs a Tanzanian colleague in Johannesburg when the spark plugs have been shipped from Dar bound for Durban, and the shipment of canned goods is timed to coincide with the incoming one. When 'steerers' in Dar and Johannesburg confirm the arrival of shipments, the collateral is withdrawn and applied to other transactions. Usually the collateral consists of manageable commodities of high value – diamonds, gold, gems, and a cash reserve that is moved from deal to deal.

There are many variations on these arrangements, and different levels of complexity and complicity among public officials, large and small entrepreneurs. But they almost always require a tightly coordinated group of associates, who opportunistically cultivate contacts in various locations, and assiduously compare regulations, prices, procedures, and so on.

Since a great deal of entrepreneurship in Africa is based on socially-intensive labour – the ability to mobilize and manipulate different social networks – many entrepreneurs choose to live and work in dense inner cities.[18] This allows them to stay close to the ground, to observe the ebb and flow of transactions and position themselves in a nexus of information exchange. Patronage is the key to success: the entrepreneur must command the loyalty of a group of individuals, many of them engaged in petty tasks the entrepreneur could easily perform himself, which adds to a general impression of success and importance.[19]

Consider those Congolese professionals employed in the South African multinationals that dominate mineral production in the Democratic Republic of Congo. Their high salaries would allow them to live in the wealthy northern suburbs of Johannesburg, and some may even acquire property there. Yet they continue to live in dense inner-city apartment blocks such as Ponte, the largest residential complex in Africa, where they stay close to their less privileged compatriots and cultivate a following among them. Young men will be given various assignments, from arranging sexual favours to delivering goods to the professional's relatives back home.

On the other hand, many small traders with limited resources actively create the impression of success by presenting the conventional signs of it – things like expensive clothes and designer accessories, the badges of the up-and-coming entrepreneur. A rampant ambiguity is produced around people's real capabilities and connections. Although this may undermine the creation of reliable partnerships, many entrepreneurs use this ambiguous front to force potential customers and suppliers to reveal more about their own abilities, knowledge and styles – the better to manipulate them. At the same time, if everyone is aware of the game, an investment must also be made in more intricate means of defending against such manipulation: the actors in this drama try to balance opportunism and necessary collaboration.

In the information economy of inner-city Johannesburg, information about new acquisitions and opportunities is closely guarded. Such information may become the primary instrument in a parasitism in which social ties to neighbours, co-workers, affiliates and even family members are manipulated in order to cultivate vulnerability, and therefore to take advantage.

Although they are increasingly susceptible to parasitism, immigrant communities continue to share information as a resource for expanding the capacities of the group. But such sharing has its protocols. No matter how close social, national, family or religious ties might be, one rarely enquires into the precise nature of someone else's activities. People must be given the space to carry out the procedures necessary to function in a climate of great uncertainty. Overly intrusive scrutiny or even curiosity constrains the possibility of working jointly with others on any given activity. While immigrants may feel obliged to support one another, this obligation can only be acted upon if it works in ways that are somewhat distinct from the mores at home. One of the main reasons for emigration is to find the space necessary to accrue some savings outside of the tightly knit family networks which can quickly eat up earnings at home, and so individuals must insist upon flexibility in how they manage their work, social lives and movements. The common-sense view is that people can only support each other if they have the freedom to pursue various alliances, contacts and activities – so long as they do not render their associates unduly vulnerable in the process.

Such flexibility adds a comparative advantage in that it allows for new and unconventional combinations. Opportunities are expanded by putting together disparate activities within a framework of trust and solidarity. For example, Soninke entrepreneurs from Mali and Senegal, who were among the 'pioneers' in the inner city, have linked a range of distinct specializations built up over years. By virtue of their long presence in Brazzaville and their participation in networks linked to various Angolan political factions – which have served to connect anglophone West Africa and

Angola – the Soninke were able to dominate a highly lucrative trade in supplying Angola with consumables from South Africa. Those Soninke traders originally based in Dakar and Conakry have also cultivated a wide range of activities in south-east Asia, particularly in textiles, clothing and electronics. Having now built up contacts in Cape Town's port, they are able to circumvent customs controls by simulating repackaging deals, in which containers are supposedly destined elsewhere, especially Luanda. By converging these formerly distinct networks, they have created a great deal of functional ambiguity, which allows them to manipulate the loading and offloading of various goods depending on relative prices and market opportunities.

Although the fluidity of the inner city provides an opportunity to put in motion or improvise upon many of the now standard practices of African entrepreneurship, conflicts between South African small entrepreneurs and foreign Africans have bubbled to the surface. Because South Africans have not participated much in the circuits of movement and exchange that dominate the rest of the continent, they know little about other African cultures and practices. Local people often conclude that the success of foreign hawkers and well-heeled businessmen is at their expense. Foreign Africans, accustomed to the relative safety of public space, have been easy targets for muggers and conmen. Frequent assaults, and many cultural misunderstandings and disputes about space and access, have made diffuse foreign African communities more defensive.

Foreign Africans of different nationalities seldom align themselves collectively against local Africans. Locals do try to provoke disputes among distinct groups of foreigners. Given the rapidity of social and demographic change, the absence of entrenched black institutions and the prolonged search for appropriate local political forms, opposition to foreigners can easily become a rallying cry. At times, South Africans attribute an almost monolithic solidity to certain groups of foreigners – 'the Nigerians', 'the Senegalese' – as if to encourage newcomers to the city, isolated like themselves, to join forces against a threat. Just as Mozambicans, for example, may have their special haunts, some South Africans claim buildings, streets or bars as 'their places', trying to introduce consistency and tradition into their own social affiliations and movements. You will frequently hear South Africans saying that French-speaking foreigners never deal with English-speaking ones, that Cameroonians never deal with Nigerians ... so why should locals deal with any of them?

On their side, some foreign Africans are trying to overturn these assumptions by 'Africanizing' their associations and building their personal networks from many different national communities. While ethnic and national affiliations are maintained, many traders, hawkers and business people are beginning to establish collaborations across these divides, from the joint acquisition of buildings to the merging of hawking and service groups, to cross-border trade. Ethiopians, Congolese, Mozambicans and Zambians are increasingly consolidating their individual plans and networks to give themselves greater scope and flexibility. Thus local efforts to 'ghettoize' and constrict the operations of foreign migrants are prompting forms of organization that enable them to reach beyond the confines of the inner city.

Going forth into the world

As Mbembe and Roitman show, the process of putting together something new is a difficult one in African cities experiencing prolonged political and economic crisis.[20] The incessant need to come up with some new scheme or way of getting by, while dealing with the absurdity created by the constantly shifting parameters of what is effective and what is not, usually serves both to reinvigorate and to diminish the existing institutional categories. In what Mbembe and Roitman call 'do it yourself bureaucracy', the consumers of public service largely provide the service themselves, while the contents of that service, its formalities and objects, remain the property of public power. The apparatuses of administration neither go away nor exert an order, but rather constitute a site of 'undetermined interpretation'. Here there are no institutionalized sets of pragmatics, guidelines or interpretations which enable people to confidently predict the outcomes of their interactions with a so-called 'public power'. What will happen in the space between what is supposed to happen and a constantly changing reality can only be determined through often lengthy processes of bargaining, in which having to pay for not receiving anything – services, justice, predictability, security, goods – has become routine.

But the questions being posed here are not really about viability or sustainability. It is not clear what will happen to cities such as Kinshasa or Lagos if their inability to establish adequate forms of governance persists. It may be important to speculate, taking into account the lives of those condemned to remain in cities that are unable to provide them with discernible and predictable benefits, such as employment, legality and shelter. Yet the urban continues to offer the possibility of circumventing such considerations altogether. On the one hand, the trappings of a 'normal' life are not guaranteed by these capacities for survival and plenitude, by what is provided, sustained or developed, or by whatever democracies and administrations are put in place; on the other, volatile, subversive and proliferate dimensions of the urban are at work – at times messy and violent, at other times capable of consolidating vast stretches of disparity, conflict and contradiction into functional spurts of change and growth.

A critical area of research would be to follow these dynamics as they intersect with the functioning and reach of specific institutions, politics and economic activities. If urban life is characterized by intensifying segregation and fragmentation, it may be important to chart the flows of complicity, cooperation, interpenetration and affiliation which come and go across the city and its neighbourhoods. In what ways are segregation, disjunction and fragmentation also something else – punctuation in the operations of networks that deploy coherent effects but may not appear continuous or traceable.

The methods for such research would be far from easy. But it is important that we take seriously what is accomplished, even in the most deprived neighbourhoods or cities, by those who spend their entire working lives in one place – the tea-seller, the newspaper vendor – or those who are always on the move, delivering things to different offices and homes each day. Especially in the poorest neighbourhoods, cities or families, being stationary is an intense position – waiting for things to come to you, finding ways of exerting control over a specific place, extracting income from that control. Being in constant motion is a powerful position too. There are young people in Johannesburg who spend twelve and more hours a day simply passing through different neighbourhoods, different parts of the city, seeing what can be taken easily, but also running into others like themselves, who pass along information and impressions, sometimes teaming up to do 'jobs', sometimes steering each other in the wrong direction. In neighbourhoods such as Nima in Accra, Medina in Dakar, Obalende in Lagos, Adjame in Abidjan, between a fifth and a quarter of local residents are 'travelling' outside the city at any given time.[21] Between these extremes which are not extremes, between those who never move and those who never stand still, lies the entire gamut of transactions. There are people who set off for work each day, walking six, eight or ten miles because they cannot afford transport or because they live in settlements far removed from roads. What do they see, who do they share the journey with, what do they talk about, what stories and events must they pass through in this necessary daily ritual?

The approach to cities I am emphasizing does not stay within neighbourhoods, sectors or institutions. It finds ways to traverse the networks, pathways and routes along which a wide range of the city's productive capacities and potentials are made. Of course, these movements and crossings have their spatial correlates and frameworks. Perhaps our grasp of them could begin in a very basic and obvious way: by recovering the original functions of the majority of African cities – as points and organizers of entry and exit, as ports, railheads and crossroads. How are the dynamics of ports organized, of gare routiers, train stations, airports, taxi ranks? These are the real places of people and goods moving back and forth. Who operates there, when, and under what circumstances? What are the links between these places, how do they interact, both within and between cities?

In a fundamental way, the question of where African cities are going could be answered by a consideration of where African urban residents are going, pursuing their own objectives, within their own time frames. While it is true that urban poverty is growing worse, and that African urban life is increasingly ghettoized, urban residents are not standing still. There is something going on, people are trying to come up with new ways of earning a living, of helping others out, of making interesting cities. How unfortunate it is that this inspiring sense of responsibility found in Africa today meets with such an irresponsible reaction in the rest of the world.

◄D7 ►D9 ►D10

Inner City
Themba Hadebe

1 1 July 1998, North Street, Johannesburg.

2 3 July 1998, roof, Pretoria Street, Hillbrow, Johannesburg.

3 23 June 1998, Nugget Street, Johannesburg.

4 1 July 1998, Bree Street, Johannesburg.

5 1 July 1998, former Witwatersrand Command Military Headquarters, Johannesburg.

6 8 June 1998, former Turbine Hall, Newtown, Johannesburg.

7 8 June 1998, West Street, Johannesburg.

JUMBO LIQUOR MARKET
CASTLE
LAGER
t's stood the test of time
The t
LIQUIDATION

KwaMayiMayi

Civic Spine

City Quarters: Civic Spine, Faraday Station, KwaMayiMayi and Ponte City

Lizeka Mda

1 Civic Spine

What on earth were they thinking? The city council spent more than R10 million revamping the Library Gardens to create what it called Johannesburg's 'Civic Spine'. And the result is a monstrosity that just makes you shudder!

In 1990 the council in its wisdom bestowed on us these structures along President and Market streets made of brick and green-painted steel like unfinished zoo cages. Nicknamed 'Eddy's Folly', after town-planning chief Eddy Magid whose brainchild the project was, the Civic Spine was supposed to provide relaxation for weary city dwellers. Instead, the eerie green cages and face-brick enclosures that look like Zozo huts are a vagrant's paradise, as lumps of blankets and other tatty possessions testify.

It's got so bad that all but one of the staircases leading down into the parking garage underneath the Gardens have been closed. The other dark entrances provided a perfect cover for muggings and other antisocial behaviour. Now the city would like to give the impression that it won't tolerate any of that nonsense. A guard has been stationed at the only remaining entrance to the garage on the corner of Harrison and President streets.

He is responsible for the handwritten sign on the landing of the stairs that reads, in Zulu: 'Ayikho itoilet apha. Umasikutholile sizokushaya. Ungakhali. Siyabonga.' Roughly translated it means: 'This is not a toilet. If we catch you, we'll beat you up. Don't say you haven't been warned. Thank you.'

There is very little evidence that Johannesburg's growth was planned at all, to judge by the shapeless jumble we have inherited. Yet the township of Johannesburg was pre-planned, albeit in a hurry. The natural centre of the town was a traditional Market Square, bordered by Rissik Street to the east, President Street to the north, Sauer Street to the west and Market Street to the south.

A series of changes starting in the second decade of this century have choked up this open space and incrementally diminished the liveliness of the square. First the market was moved to Newtown. Then the City Hall was built, taking up almost half the eastern part of the square. Hot on its foundations came the Public Library, which took the whole of the western end. Finally the manicured gardens between the City Hall and the library were divided by two very busy streets, Harrison and Simmonds.

What's left? It isn't Market Square any more – the fresh-produce market can be found in City Deep these days. This space is now called the Library Gardens, even though there is very little that is garden-like about it.

The City Engineer wrote in the 'City Centre Report' in 1975 that '... one can view a city itself as entertainment or culture. Its sculpture and statuary fountains, architecture and parks can provide an education as well as mystique and beauty. In this respect Johannesburg fails. There are few imaginative public spaces ... Little care has been taken to preserve worthy features of its past. There is not enough space for walking, sitting and relaxing, too little shade and too much paving. The city lacks "punctuation" and character.'

At the Simmonds Street end of the Library Gardens there is a monument, a nondescript structure similar to those that grace most of the Voortrekker Roads of the country's platteland towns. This one was erected in memory of the men of Johannesburg who laid down their lives in 'The Great War 1914-1918'. Even the significance of wars is relative, I suppose.

At the other end, right in front of the steps that lead up into the library, is a sculpture of a couple of indeterminate age, but definite Caucasian features, holding a child aloft between them. This was a present to the people of Johannesburg from the *Star* newspaper. It's the kind of present that, had it been a jersey, you would have exchanged it the very next day. The sculpture is quite ugly. We citizens of Johannesburg haven't done too well in the public statuary department.

And the paving! At the Market Street end the pavement is coming apart. Oozing out between the jagged bricks is a watery sludge whose stench and colour do not invite close scrutiny.

The serviceable brick terraces could never be mistaken for the Spanish Steps. However, they do serve as seats in this garden where there are just four trees, one at each corner. Here and there is a green, iron park bench. The men who sit here do not look as if they are simply pausing on their way somewhere: they have the look of people who have arrived at their destination. Their daily existence is here on this square. They show very little interest in the young men who play chess on a giant board in front of the library. Once in a while the layabouts are displaced by public protesters – supporters of the Inkatha Freedom Party protesting their innocence, municipal workers demanding higher wages, citizens anxious to see the death penalty reinstated. This week it was the turn of the hawkers.

The few shops in the square are so downmarket they would be completely at home on Phomolong Station or any other suburban stop on the Metro lines. Once there were plans for restaurants, bookshops, an information centre, even an art gallery. But nothing came of it.

The buildings around the square are not much to look at, except perhaps for the First National Bank building on the corner of Simmonds and Market. The City Hall, built in the neoclassical style of the British Empire, with its back to the square, has become the Gauteng legislature. The façade on Rissik Street is closed to entry and has all the appeal of a cowshed. The Gauteng legislators have handed it over to vagrants and pigeons.

Across the street is the distinctive red-and-whitebrick Rissik Street Post Office, built at the turn of the century but now abandoned. On the dial in the clocktower the time is stuck at twenty past one.

The Gauteng legislature has an understated entrance on the corner of Loveday and President streets. The City Hall noticeboards are still out, though there is no news from the Gauteng government. Instead some A4 leaflets have been stuck on the boards by the Greater Johannesburg Hawkers Planning Committee, inviting hawkers to a

'Unity Day: 22 April' at the Library Gardens. 'Only SA citizens will trade in the pavements of our cities. No selling, no going to market. Foreigners must go.'

Talk about holding up a sponge mattress against a raging tide. Perhaps if the hawkers put as much effort into learning the basics of running a business as they do into harassing foreign traders they might eke out a decent living from their labours. Five different people selling identical plates of bananas on the same stretch of pavement does not seem like the way to go about it.

The exciting aspect of change on the square comes from the Public Library, which has been transformed into a real place of learning. Every day, hundreds of students with school bags on their backs stream into the library. Many go to the reference section which also acts as a study area reserved for the exclusive use of high-school pupils. The rest – students from technikons, universities and colleges – have to wait in long queues to get into this quiet room, with its high, pressed-steel ceilings, ancient shelves and reassuringly solid reading tables. The sounds in here are muffled as if an exam is in progress, but the tone of the notices on the computer terminals is scolding: 'This terminal is available for enquiries about authors, titles and subjects. It is not a PC. It does not have computer games.'

There is no doubt that Johannesburg's soul, if it still exists, has sought refuge in the Public Library.

2 Faraday Station

Where Eloff Street Extension begins, right under the M2 motorway and above Faraday train station, there is a corner of KwaZulu-Natal in Johannesburg.

Sadly this insular little community on the southern fringe of the city centre is a legacy of political violence. Widowed in the ongoing conflict in their home province during the eighties, many poor and uneducated women found themselves with no means of supporting their families. Dozens left their destroyed homes in places like Mbumbulu, Mhlabuyalingana, Nongoma, Mahlabatini, Mtwaluba, Mkomazi, and armed only with their knowledge of muti, the medicinal uses of herbs and roots, came to Johannesburg. Many of them set up shop here on a traffic island directly beneath the motorway.

MaMkhize Ngcobo, who came from Mbumbulu in 1991, says a man was knocked down by a car just this morning. But she hardly pays any attention to the cars speeding past this open-air hyperpharmacy. Not far from this death trap, MaMkhize's seven-month-old granddaughter Sthabile and her mother Dumazile are lounging inside one of the metal cupboards which the municipality rents to the herbalists.

MaMkhize is busy sorting out different kinds of bark. This one, she says, is called intelezi and you can drink it or wash with it to counter the evil spirits of those who do not like you. She has a bark for every ailment: mlahleni, sehlulamani, inyazangoma, maphipha, nukani. And she has roots that look like turnips and others that look like black coral. There is even a beetroot with dreadlocks, which she calls labatheka, and which is apparently very useful for bone disease.

'Even whites come here for it,' she says.

It's amazing how a harmless root begins to look ominous when it comes in the guise of muti. You're even afraid to touch it. But then again the fear is probably understandable when the onion-like root in question, nguduza MaMkhize calls it, is not destined for the gravy-pot but the male private parts.

On this tiny patch of pavement there are about twenty herbalists, and beyond them dozens and dozens more, all selling the same roots and barks. Even MaMkhize does not know the total number of people who do business at the muti market. Anyone can set up. But she says she has her own customers, who trust and believe in her because they have a long-established relationship. It can't be too profitable, but from her point of view it's still better business than if she had gone to Durban, for instance. 'There are very few people left in Natal,' she says. 'The war finished them.'

The main market where all the herbalists stock up is in Durban. You can see that MaMkhize's neighbour on the left has very fresh and plentiful stock. But MaMkhize herself will only make the journey to the coast in a week's time. Sometimes when she wants a specific root or bark that she cannot get at the usual market, she travels to Pondoland, where she has some relatives.

Across the street some Indian men are selling loaves of bread and shoes, alongside two brothers, Mzikayifani and Gilani Mthembu, who are skinning a rock rabbit. It's fresh from KwaZulu-Natal, they say; it arrived this morning by taxi. Apparently women who are struggling to become pregnant find its intestines useful. Hanging from the fence behind the brothers are the carcasses of a small animal called isambane and the skins of various snakes.

This is not a place that encourages lingering, or so you would think, infested as it is with fat flies and an intolerable stench. Yet in the midst of it all there is a boy selling sweets, women selling fruit, people chatting.

At the end of the day the vendors just cover their wares with sailcloth. There are security guards who will look after the whole area until morning. Taxis from the nearby rank take many of the women back to Jeppestown, where they live. A few go towards the Putco buses, and others go down the stairs to Faraday Station, on to the windblown and dilapidated platform, to wait for the train to Soweto.

3 KwaMayiMayi

It seems like a lifetime since Ntombeyiningi 'Ningi' Zondi, escaping the violence in KwaZulu-Natal, arrived in Johannesburg not knowing anyone here except her mother and an uncle. She remembers how she would cry herself to sleep at night. That was 1994.

Zwangobani, Ningi's mother, had a meat-grilling kiosk in Anderson Street, and Ningi began to help her with that. Two years later they were so comfortable that Zwangobani was able to go home to Msinga, where she opened a *spaza* shop, while Ningi carried on the business in town. Just six months later, in May 1997, Zwangobani was killed by robbers, and Ningi, who was then nineteen, had to take over the financial responsibility of providing for her siblings. It was just as well that she had a successful business to run.

Every morning, six days a week, she leans a table against a cement pillar under the Anderson Street off-ramp from the M2 motorway and sets out her wares: kidneys, liver, brisket, heart, *wors* and *binnegoed*. Customers who go for this à la carte arrangement pick their favourite meat and Ningi grills it over the open fire, where two pots of maize porridge are also cooking, one of crumbly *phutu* and one of stiff *pap*. The cooked meat is served on a chopping board with tomatoes, chillies (should a customer require) and a plate of *phutu* or *pap*.

Zwangobani, Ningi's late mother, started grilling meat on this spot thirteen years ago. It's a well-placed location, just outside KwaMayi-Mayi men's hostel. The surrounding shops and offices include a drycleaner, a fast-food outlet, some *sangomas*' consulting rooms, a fruit and vegetable stall, a grocery store and the offices of the Johannesburg City Engineer. Grilling meat turned out to be not just a way for a woman alone, and with children to feed in the countryside, to survive in a hostile city, but a way to make a very decent living.

Unfortunately, in the manner we've grown used to in Jo'burg, when one person makes a success of a business someone else will come rushing to try and duplicate the feat a few metres away, and so there are now five grill kiosks under the bridge.

By far the busiest one is Nelisiwe Maphumulo's, no more than a dozen paces away from Ningi's. Nelisiwe is a generation older than Ningi. She has two assistants, and all three of them bustle about, resplendent in traditional Zulu regalia.

It is not immediately clear what makes customers choose one grill over the other because they all seem to offer the same meals. However, Ningi operates in a semi-hygienic way, covering her meat with a white lace cloth which is lifted only for customers to make their selection. Hers is service with sass and swinging hips, and there is a lot of talking and flirting with the customers, many of them taxi drivers. Nelisiwe and her assistants, on the other hand, serve quietly, one could even say with servility.

Each kiosk has its own special clientele, and these regulars, rather than the passing trade, keep the businesses going. They come from the farthest ends of the city, but they come. It depends a lot on which part of KwaZulu-Natal you come from, Ningi says. People from the Msinga district, where she was born, provide her with business, just as Nelisiwe's 'homeboys' from Ladysmith support her exclusively.

'I find the atmosphere very pleasant,' says Bhekisisa Nkosi, a journalist who drives from Braamfontein at least twice a week to eat at Ningi's. 'When you think that back where these people come from their villages are probably at war with each other, and yet here everyone minds his own business, it's a very liberated place.'

The motorway criss-crosses above; the tomato-box splinters that are used as firewood lie around among the garbage heaps waiting for the municipal cleaners; the braziers smoke. From across the street, Zulu music blasts through very powerful speakers placed at the door of a music store. Here on the eastern edge of Johannesburg refugees from strife-torn KwaZulu-Natal have found a home.

4 Ponte City

'Sometimes,' observes Marco Polo in Italo Calvino's *Invisible Cities*, 'different cities follow one another on the same site and under the same name, born and dying without knowing one another, without communication among themselves.'

That's as true for Johannesburg as it is for Ponte City, one of its most recognizable buildings.

Ponte was completed in 1976. It must have been a dream commission for the architectural firm Manfred Hermer and Grosskopff – to create a self-sufficient city, where residents home from work in the evenings need not venture outside for anything. The architects created a cylindrical tower with 54 floors of apartments perched on seven levels of parking bays. Its location on a hill made the building look even taller than it really was.

What grandiose plans were laid with the foundations! And how grandly it all worked in the beginning. Who needed the Botanical Gardens beyond the ridge when the courtyard of the entrance from Lily Avenue provided gazebos and park benches? Who needed the shops down the road when the commercial level of the tower was a shopping centre all on its own? Residents could do all their shopping here, their laundry, even their banking. There were recreational activities too – a coffee shop, a bowling alley.

Today it is all changed. The gazebos look like broken clothes lines. Only a few grimy panes stubbornly cling to the window frames of the glassed-in enclosure. Many of the shops inside the building have long been abandoned, lending the commercial level a dingy and scary atmosphere. Only the supermarket is still operating. What was once the recreation hall is now the Missionary Centre Church, started by French-speaking immigrants mainly from the former Zaïre. The hairdressing salon is run and frequented by Ethiopians, who have supplanted Zaïrians as the majority tenants in the flats. They too, like the waves of residents past, represent the essence of Johannesburg, a city of immigrants.

Getting into a prison would be easier than getting into Ponte. At the security turnstiles non-residents are required to hand over identity documents or passports before they are allowed in. To spend the night, you have to obtain a letter of permission. Even so, many of the so-called visitors, according to the building manager, Steven Adams, are really squatters who contribute to the overcrowding in the flats. As a result, signs have been posted at the entrance: 'Too many visitors. No more letters will be issued.'

For over two decades Ponte has welcomed its fair share of Johannesburg's immigrants. In the beginning these were whites, of course, and those deemed 'honorary whites'. But then the neighbourhood took on grey overtones, as Indians, then coloureds, and eventually Africans moved in.

After the release of Nelson Mandela in 1990, South Africa opened up to the rest of the continent, and immigrants streamed in from Gabon, Angola, Ivory Coast, Central African Republic, Ghana, Togo, Nigeria, Zaïre and lately Ethiopia. They all came to Ponte. At one stage the nightclub on the premises was the place to hear the Zaïrian pop sound kwasa kwasa. In the manner of inner-city people everywhere, most residents of Ponte are just passing through. Its attraction lies in its furnished flats. Once people are established they move onward and upward.

With Hillbrow and Berea losing the appeal they once had, as buildings run down and criminals move in, Ponte has been struggling to attract the right kind of tenants – families looking for tranquil surroundings to raise their children, hard-working young professionals, people who will be house-proud for the duration of their stay. Instead, the building has become a dormitory for immigrants whose funds are so limited that they sometimes live ten to a one-bedroom flat, and students from the Witwatersrand Technikon down the hill; you can't get more transient than that.

Three years ago the current owners, Vincemus Investments, got wind that the Department of Correctional Services was in need of space to accommodate 4,500 awaiting-trial inmates in the Johannesburg area alone. So they turned to the architects Osmond Lange Mosienyane and Associates for plans to transform Ponte City into a prison.

The firm came up with proposals that incorporate space for 5,000 inmates, a police station on site, a courthouse, ample parking and a shuttle service for people who need to get to the magistrate's court. This safe parking is important: it will solve the problem of witnesses who show up late in court or don't show up at all because they cannot find parking in the street outside.

The proposals also include a computerized system involving fingerprinting and identification bracelets, allowing the authorities to track every person – inmate or warder. 'The foundation of modern correctional architecture is unit management, security and direct supervision,' says Paul Silver, the American architect behind the plans. Silver describes himself as an expert on correctional architecture, and claims to have designed two hundred correctional facilities on five continents. 'I have had more influence on this business type than anyone else alive. Not just as a practitioner but as an innovator.'

But what's the attraction of Ponte?

'Those apartments are just awful,' he says, 'but they would make a good prison. Fundamentally the building is in good condition. The engineering was conservative, which makes it a solid structure for a tall slender tower on top of a hill.'

Sensory deprivation, which has always been an integral part of traditional correction, is inhumane, says Silver. The windows will stay, but with some added security features. Prisoners need sunlight for health. And it's been proven that having a view makes inmates calmer. Instead of causing trouble, all they want to do is to sit in their cells and sup up the view.

What they won't be supping is Coca-Cola. For the last two years, Ponte City has been crowned by a five-storey-high illuminated Coca-Cola sign. The sign has had a fantastic response, according to the company. 'Consumers associate the sign with the landmarking of Johannesburg, much like Times Square in New York,' says S'bu Mngadi, the divisional director of communications for Coca-Cola Southern Africa. 'It puts Johannesburg on the world map. It symbolizes our belief that South Africa is a good place for global companies to invest, and that Coca-Cola has a long-term future in South Africa.'

Should the tower become a prison, however, Coca-Cola's ten-year contract with Natanya Signs, which amounts to R2 million a year in management fees and electricity, would have to be reviewed. 'It's not an association we would want to foster,' says Mngadi. 'Government buildings do not carry advertising anyway.'

When word went out that Minister of Correctional Services, Sipho Mzimela, had given the Ponte Prison project his blessing, questions were raised about such a decision being taken without the proper tendering process. So the department backtracked.

'Specifications still need to be drawn up,' says Major Bert Slabbert, the Department's media liaison officer, 'by Correctional Services, Public Works, Justice, and Safety and Security.'

Silver is very confident. 'At the moment, 40,000 cases are processed through the Hillbrow police station each year,' he says. 'There are only six holding cells. Sometimes there are as many as 22 people in one room. It is inhumane what's happening. We cannot solve the crime problem without facilities to make correctional programmes work.

'My only concern is whether Ponte can be efficiently transformed into a correctional facility in a way that would look after the constitutional rights of inmates. Is there a design? Yes. Does the government like it? Yes again.'

Photographs by Ruth Motau.

◄D9 ►E4 ►E11

Postcard of East Bank Location,
East London, c. 1910.

11

'Corpses behind screens': Native space in the city

Gary Minkley

'One City working together.' This is the vision of East London contained in the new city framework plan of 1998. The plan, coordinated through Meld (the Mdantsane-East London Development Corridor), is designed to deal with 'the lack of facilities, housing, transport, services and development and work opportunities in the Mdantsane area' and to create integrated and empowered communities in a unified new city. In this planning and development vision, the East London of the future will no longer be a divided city, a white and a black city, but an interconnected unit that will 'overcome the unequal distribution of resources ... due to past racial laws'. The black spaces of the city – Duncan Village location and Mdantsane township – will be 'incorporated' into white East London, not just formally but in meaningful ways. The result will be a city that is neither black nor white. One City.

Daily Dispatch, 20 February 1998, p. 1.

Daily Dispatch, 13 November 1997, p. 1; 14 January 1998, p. 2.

In the same moment, the African National Congress and the South African National Civic Organization in East London call for the 'immediate end to the erection of illegal shacks in the East London, Mdantsane and surrounding areas ... People must stop erecting squatter camps in informal settlements ... the invasion of land must come to an end because the land belongs to the government and the local authority.' Community leaders are asked to help the government put an end to squatting, so that the housing programme can be implemented effectively. 'We recognize that everybody must have a roof on top of their head, but this must be controlled ... there was no control over the proliferation of shacks ... Now the situation must change.' As such calls are made for the control, removal and 'flattening' of 'squatter settlements' in and around the emerging 'One City', their inhabitants, the 'shack dwellers', are increasingly represented as illegal outsiders who threaten the ideal of an integrated East London.

Daily Dispatch, 22 November 1997, p. 2.

Daily Dispatch, 5 December 1997, p. 1; 14 January 1998, p. 2; 9 March 1998, p. 1.[1]

Township. Location. Squatter settlement. The unequal, separate black spaces of the South African city now requiring integration (a form of removal). Not so long ago, these urban native spaces required separation (and forced removal). What does it mean to think of East London, or of the South African city in general, as two cities? As one?

1 'A blot on the landscape': The pondokkie and urban native space

If you had stopped off in East London in 1910 and wanted to send someone a postcard depicting your visit, you might have chosen one of the East Bank Location.[2] Native space in the city would have appeared to you orderly, spacious, filled with promise. The visible dominance of the 'round hut'[3] would not have escaped your attention, and neither would a growing number of houses built of 'galvanized iron'.

But you would have been unaware – unless you had friends on the city council to enlighten you – that native space in the city was unsettled white space. As such it had to be controlled. It had to be demarcated and defined, 'located' if you like, as temporary space of specific dimensions. Ownership of the structures erected upon it had to be determined by a 'regular will to work' and those structures themselves routinely crammed back into the boundaries of 'wattle and daub' which they repeatedly overspilled.[4] And you would have been unaware too of increasing parsimony and neglect on the part of the council, the gathering crisis of inadequate accommodation and miserable services in the location beneath a 'semblance of cleanliness', and the growing numbers of 'ramshackle tin shanties' and 'miserable huts for which rents are extorted'.

Izwi Labantu, 19 May 1908, p. 1.

However, the 'round hut' and the 'tin shanty' increasingly signified a set of opposed meanings related to the presence of the tribal native in the city. In 1917 this was elaborated by Charles Lloyd, East London's Location Superintendent for the first three decades of the century: 'When [East Bank Location] was first established it was designed for Round Huts and spaces of 40' by 40' were allotted. Whilst this may have been right for Round Huts it is not sufficient for square places, and when the Native mind replaces Round Huts and puts up Square Houses that portion of the Location becomes congested.' Initially, the Square House, if it was a 'better type of house', was made of 'poor quality galvanized iron'; but as time went by it was made more often of 'tin-lining i.e. the lining taken from packing cases' and of 'any other material to hand: wood, branches, cloth, scraps, mud'. This shift reflected the nature and potential of houses 'built by the Natives themselves'. 'Things generally are going backwards out there, the majority of the houses are unfit for [use], are not desirable dwelling places, but this is what the Native builds for himself, any tumble down sort of a place where there is no room to get among the houses, it is his want when he can no longer have a Round Hut.' In short, Lloyd concluded – and the council agreed – that 'the Native is a tribal being ... he is not able to think or to build in the same way as the European. As long as he is left to himself in the Location the Square House he replaces [the hut] with will be undesirable.'

CA, 3/ELN, 6, Evidence of C. Lloyd to Committee re Nursing and Medical Treatment of Natives at the Locations, 20 November 1917.

CA, 3/ELN, 6, Reports of Location Superintendent and Medical Officer of Health (MOH).[5]

CA, 3/ELN, 6, Lloyd to Committee 'A', 21 September 1917.

CA, 3/ELN, 6, Lloyd to Committee 'A', 21 September 1917.

The answer for the council was 'some system whereby the Municipality should put up a certain number of houses yearly and allow the Natives to rent the ground and take over model dwellings'. By the 1940s, such a system had been implemented to some extent, but most of the people in East Bank Location still lived in housing they had built themselves. Although these residents were never officially designated as 'squatters' (because their houses were built on rented and demarcated municipal sites within the official boundaries of the location), the notions of site-holding, lodging and overcrowding in the self-built housing effectively fell within the same discursive formation as squatting.[7] The place was variously described as the slumyards, the shackyard, the wood-and-iron section or the packing-case location; the houses themselves were referred to as shacks, hovels, warrens or pondokkies. Here, in the eyes of the authorities, a form of overcrowded squatting had been 'forced underground – instead of adding-on, rooms were added-in through sub-division ... [the natives] cramming themselves into already unsanitary and second hand houses with no regard to moral and human dignity'. The Thornton Commission of the late 1930s said that East Bank was perhaps the worst location in the Union, and that it was 'a blot on our civilization that such a place exists'.

CA, 3/ELN, 6, Lloyd to Committee 'A', 21 September 1917.[6]

CA, 3/ELN, 918, Reports on Social Health and Economic Conditions, Councillor Taylor, 11 May 1949.

CA, 3/ELN, 6, Correspondence: Edward Thornton, 1937, p. 2.

Many of the descriptions of the 'tin town slum' mapped out a particular meaning and future for the pondokkie as an independent native space in the city. 'Some houses contained as many as 10 rooms and more leading off a single passage, ventilated only by a door at each end, and each of these rooms contained a household. Cooking, eating and sleeping all took place in the same room which might contain 4 or 5 adults, and 4 or 5 children.' This description, and countless others like it, evoked the 'round hut' not just by implication but quite explicitly, in references to the 'customary fireplace in the centre of the Hut', or to a 'single room as in a Native Rondavel', or to the multiple uses of domestic space as 'would be done in their huts in the reserves'. The threat to the orderly white city had a named past and identifiable presence as primitive, traditional and tribal.

BCI, Box 25, File W1, MOH Report, July 1947.

CA, 3/ELN, 6, ELM, File 80, MOH Reports, 1943-47.

In the 1940s, East London was not alone in facing what became known as the 'pondokkie threat'. Throughout the Cape and indeed South Africa these second cities and towns were building themselves (as it seemed to alarmed white residents), springing up, becoming 'swollen overnight'. The white cities found themselves confronted by a 'mass of unsightly pondokkie settlements'. Social chaos, dislocation and menacing poverty were suddenly everywhere, in the eyes of officials and the public, as shanty dwellers and pondokkies became visible in 'aggregations' or 'clottings' of 'black spots'.

See, for example, the Britten Commission of Enquiry and Report, UG 18, Cape Town, 1942/3; the Welsh Commission of Enquiry into Location Conditions, East London, 1947.

Commissions of enquiry, official reports and public bodies formalized and further inscribed these 'blots on our landscape' as a new extension of the 'native problem' in the city. Social scientists, planners and administrators variously identified what was lived and perceived with what was conceived.[8] In the very language of these investigations and reports, the 'advance of irregular

It is the pondokkie which stands out consistently as the symbol of the end-result of uncontrolled [native] migration. To thousands the pondokkie is 'home', a tangible retreat from the rigours of competitive living; to the casual observer it is an 'eyesore', a 'blot on the landscape'; to the scientist it is the natural excrescence of a diseased economy ... The word pondokkie is doubtless a diminutive form of the Afrikaans word 'pondok', meaning a hut or hovel. That is a fair definition but let it be admitted frankly without further elaboration that the structure that has left its image so deeply impressed on the mind of the committee is capable of pictorial definition only. The pondokkie of the Cape Flats, in its design, owes nought to any school of architecture, European or Asiatic, ancient or modern. Its conception is determined entirely by the scraps of material that go into its structure, pieces of corrugated iron, old tins and drums, rough boughs, sacking. Anything which can possibly offer protection against the weather. Piece by piece, scrap material is bought, begged, or filched and added to make room for a growing family. There are no windows, ceilings, and very often no door. Sanitation is non-existent. Many of these hovels would do a disservice to animals. The pondokkie is the lowest standard of human habitation, and the term is not used to describe houses, which, though producing similar insanitary conditions, at least conform to elementary standards of architectural design ... There are a number of pondokkie 'black spots' on the Cape Flats. These communities can at the most be called pondokkie aggregations ... clottings of pondokkies. Here abide a dissolute and lawless conglomeration of Coloured and Native persons, some of whose habitations are primitive in the extreme ... They are of the lowest cultural category ... little more than corpses behind screens.

Britten Commission of Enquiry, Cape Town, 1942

Britten CommissionReport, p. 14.

urbanization' and the 'fungus of haphazard planning, insanitary housing, disease and crime' were associated with the increasingly dominant urban form of the 'pondokkie slum'. Defined into these representations of space, in fact the congested point around which they all cohered, was a body and an identity 'intimately acquainted with this wilderness', this 'evil', this shapeless 'fungal growth': 'The chief offenders are Natives.' Bodies became spatial maps of meaning, identity and power.

Britten Commission Report, p. 4.

The official archive illustrates graphically how the urban crisis of the 'Hungry Forties' in East London and in the Cape more broadly – primarily a crisis of intensified movement to the city, poverty, employment, wages, housing – became a 'native crisis'.[9] The shanty dweller and the pondokkie embodied the notion of a permanent urban native outside of official boundaries and therefore beyond control. As the people in these settlements touched, tasted, crept, leapt, imagined, desired, talked, and listened their ways through the city, whiteness fixed a different spatial imprint on the meaning of the 'pondokkie black spot' in the social and political landscape.[10] It became a malevolent, invasive, forbidden space that must be hemmed in or rooted out.

Once it had been quantified, mapped out and named into space through 'lists of localities', health reports, the declarations of location superintendents, the investigations of the mounted police and the social surveys, the pondokkie problem could then be related to the 'phenomenal spread of slums' throughout the Cape. New thresholds of fear (figured as shame, embarrassment and disgust) and of desire produced new metaphors for the pondokkie slum and its influence. And yet every written description tended to reproduce certain characteristics, as the representations of pondokkie space congregated around a range of related and mutually reinforcing spectacles.[11]

First there was the spectacle of filth. The visible 'mess and filth' of the pondokkie slum offended the senses. This filth was sufficient to render the concept of 'home' itself ambiguous: the slums 'create a home for the native, a home formerly built of wattle and daub, but to-day of wood off-cuts, poles, drums, newspapers, and malthoid; in fact of any material'; yet such a place cannot be fully a home, for here 'homeless persons are now living in filth and indescribable squalor'. The focus on filth led to an obsession with cleanliness and the need to 'clean up' the city.

CA, 3/ELN, 938, Ref 1575, LAB 16 September 1947; 1240, MOH Report on Welsh Commission, 18 January 1950.

Then there was the spectacle of disease.[12] Pondokkies were linked to dirt, dirt to excrement, excrement to disease, and disease to the moral degradation of the inhabitants: 'You cannot walk in the streets without getting your boots fouled by human detritus. This is not an abnormal circumstance ... it is a normal condition. The children of the location play on these streets: they have no proper playgrounds ... A good deal of washing and laundry goes out to the location to be washed in foul, utterly disgusting water.' To make matters worse, these primitive creatures were responsible for 'their own evil environment ... cramming themselves into these packing cases without moral and human dignity'. They confirmed their moral degradation by contaminating their own surroundings, producing a slum described as the 'worst in the Union'. 'For vile indeed are the conditions under which the human [native] population ... exists ... they are simply the devil's slaves engaged in the degradation of themselves and their fellows.'

Daily Dispatch, 9 August 1949, p. 14.

CA, 3/ELN, 918, Reports on Social Health and Economic Conditions, 1943-49, 11 May 1949 and attached correspondence.[13]

Daily Dispatch, 24 July 1952, p. 1.

The related spectacle of invasion, as the city became encircled by alien architectures and evil conditions, inscribed race onto the reasoning of the landscape. The 'native spaces' of East London were perceived and conceived through the fracturing trauma of invasion and siege. These spaces were the outcome of 'deficiencies inherent in the [pondokkie] dweller himself, in his distinctive social group and in the relationship his group bears to other more powerful social groups in a class – and racially – stratified society'.[14] In this light, new racialized spatial distinctions were elaborated and used to redraw the map of the city.

In native spaces, according to this new mapping, all that was 'low' and degraded was commonplace, extensive and habitual. Here, white people were told repeatedly, crime, drinking, promiscuity and 'verkaffering'[15] were visible and routine, were endemic to such 'inaccessible areas'; but these vices were also attractive to the primitive 'native mind' and that was why the areas were 'penetrated to the degree that can be seen to-day'. Ordinary surveillance and policing would no longer suffice to contain the threat of contamination. White East London was warned: 'The women of the location nurse European children ... the people who live in slums like this come into your homes as servants everyday.' Dirty bodies and dirty spaces could not be confined to the slum: they moved through the city and would continue to do so until native space had been more tightly defined and circumscribed.

CA, Welsh Report, pp. 4-7, and see also Britten Commission Report, p. 6.

ELN, File 80/20, MOH Annual Reports, 1943-47; CA, Welsh Report and correspondence; Daily Dispatch, 24 July 1952, pp. 13-14.

Official and public discourse was thus simultaneously about constructing new spaces in the city and about fixing new racial identities and boundaries. Municipal records and the press are full of photographs which show what this mapping entailed. On the one side are those photographs labelled 'Municipal Housing'; on the other, those labelled 'Private Housing: Shack rooms'.[16] The picture theory of the former is pleasant and desirable – an image of neatness, order and control; that of the latter is threatening and objectionable – an image of congestion, disorder and chaos. These images are reflected time and again, both visually and verbally, in all kinds of official and public constructions.

The pondokkies, with all their negative associations, are described as 'Private Housing', implying that they are expressions of individual choice. They also carry labels such as 'natives in town' and 'native living conditions', forcefully constructing these ramshackle structures as common, 'natural', almost 'traditional'. By this point, and by an odd inversion, the pondokkie, the 'Square House' made of wood and iron has in some senses become the authentic native shelter, the urban synonym of the 'Round Hut' made of wattle and daub. As such it is also a remainder and symbolic reminder of tribal lands beyond the boundaries of the city.

While much of the visible arena of dispute in the representations of space in East London in the 1940s appeared to be about the causes of these urban conditions – poverty versus influx – it was also about contesting the definitions of 'native space'. Focusing on poverty implied an acceptance that black people had a certain permanence in the city and that their needs would have to be dealt with there; focusing on influx implied that the 'problem' was transitory and that it might be repatriated to the rural areas. Poverty required a model of incorporation for new permanent and healthy subjects; influx required a model of control centred on the reception depot, the location superintendent and the pass. Both would require new model townships, if for different reasons.

2 In-between spaces and 'dismal places': The location

If the pondokkie slum was cast as a threatening native space in the city, one which needed to be removed in favour of the 'double articulation'[17] of the model township, the 'location' was equally important as a related but different urban native space, sections of which had a peculiar 'in-between' status.

Duncan Village, which grew out of East Bank Location in East London, was marked by particular spatial practices and representations that were characteristic of many other South African locations in the 1940s. Duncan Village was roughly and unevenly divided between the 'municipal sections', where the housing had been constructed by the state and was rented out, and 'shackyards', where the housing had been built by the residents themselves. In fairly typical patterns of continued neglect and disgust, the 'temporary' status attached to black bodies was mapped on to both areas. This meant that the routes, networks, buildings and enjoyments of the residents, in the municipal sections as much as the shackyards, were also 'temporary', and therefore had to be continually named, watched and policed. Both parts of Duncan Village represented the 'space of the kraal' in the city, but the municipal sections had a more complicated intermediate status too.

CA, 3/ELN, 880, Report on Native Housing, August 1945.

At the time, various official and internal categories of distinction held a spatial tension between the reserves and the 'tribal native' on the one hand; and the cities and the 'detribalized native' on the other. These categories included temporary as opposed to permanent residence; the supposed cultural differences between the 'red blanket native' as opposed to the 'dressed native', and the shackyards as opposed to the municipal sections. Thus, while the entire location was 'temporary' from one white perspective, from another the municipal sections occupied a position in between the primitive and the modern. In some ways the municipal sections replicated 'European' styles; in other ways they continued to transgress the standards of 'modern and civilized' white urban space. Behind the veneer, behind the mimicry – as it was expressed – a permanent tribal difference remained. Duncan Village was seen to contain internally differentiated tribal spaces, with the municipal sections reflecting an 'in-between' status most clearly.[18] The furnishings and bodies contained in the municipal houses were then also 'in-between' – a sense which Monica Hunter captures so acutely.[19]

D

However, it was the shackyards, the 'dismal places', that formed the focus of regulatory discourse and intervention in Duncan Village. Although internal differentiation was acknowledged, the location as a whole was closer to the spaces of the temporary, the illegal and the poor. Under a 'regime of false economy', most locations had become places of impoverishment, oppressive homogeneity and essentialized difference by the 1940s. Location bodies and spaces were unitized and aggregated to the beat of police and patrol, as they were administered and legitimized 'out of sight'. The spatiality of the locations enabled this separation and difference, but so too did the materiality of space within them. In the 'vast slum of the Location with the passage of years, the inhabitants [became] habituated and hardened to a demoralizing way of life'.

CA, 3/ELN, Box 1240, 6 July 1949.[20]

What was regular was the 5 a.m. raid and the steam disinfector station, the registration office, the police cell, the court, the pick-up van, the spot fine, the location permit and countless other forms of surveillance. In the pre-dawn raids, policemen 'inspected the petticoats of women and on finding a louse, the entire household would be conveyed to the dipping tank', where heads were shaved, bodies sprayed and clothing boiled. The 'key office' of the location administration increasingly dominated everyday life. As this administration became more callous and bureaucratic, it also increasingly conflated the conditions in the locations with the character of the inhabitants. 'Left to their own devices this is what will result' ran the administrative refrain. The location, 'by reason of its being inarticulate', had to be administered from without.

CA, 3/ELN, Box 877, Ref 1960:80, Minutes of Public Health and Native Affairs Meetings, 1942-3.

CA, 3/ELN, 1240, Welsh Commission Report and Evidence, 1949/50.[21]

By the 1940s the location could be represented as naturally and 'factually' racially distinct: an urban space made and used by natives when in the city in order to work. Practically every aspect of space and its use, from house, street and communal lavatory to journey, emotion and encounter, from hunger to sexuality, from the 'washroom' to the 'recreation hall', was overlaid in official representation by the accretions of the slum – filth, infection, illegitimacy. The location was also represented as a space of difference – tribal, backward, primitive, inferior – an urban expression of the reserve. So, in the 1950s, the location could be described as a 'slum with a rural overtone ... as fowls peck around the unpaved streets; streams run in wet weather. People are often outside in the sun. The bush and the green hills are not far away.'[22] In the contrast between the location and the 'white space' of the city, the 'fact that races differ so greatly from one another' could be perceived and then reconceived in the dominant official representations.

CA, 3/ELN, 1150, Letter from 'resident' to Joint Council, 15 June 1953. [23]

As in the case of the 'pondokkie slum', spectacles of filth, contamination and invasion proliferated around Duncan Village (and other locations) in the 1940s, until a moment of crisis was reached. In the face of administrative shambles, growing neglect of the location and the fear of 'widespread dissatisfaction', representations of the location as a tribal, temporary space began to fragment. We could say (following Jenny Robinson) that the new positions cohered around two poles in the professional technologies of urban power.[24] Around the pole of native administration gathered the Manager of Native Administration, the conservative 'ostrich City Council' (as someone dubbed it at the time) and various 'commercial men and land speculators'. Around the other medico-administrative pole were to be found the Medical Officer of Health, the Public Health and Native Affairs Committees of the City Council, and a series of welfare and 'interested lay organizations'.

For East London the consequences were far-reaching. A series of investigations and commissions of enquiry were undertaken which supported the need to remove the 'tin town slum areas' of Duncan Village and to rebuild on what was called 'an urban basis'. What followed was nearly two decades of conflict, disagreement, planning and replanning, revision, implementation, delays, removals, and finally, in the 1960s, the development of the new Bantustan township of Mdantsane.[26]

CA, 3/ELN, 870, 877, 1240, 1241 and 1150-56 contain much of the correspondence and reports on these issues. [25]

Initially the plan was that building would start on the outskirts of 'tin town': residents would be moved progressively into the new municipal housing, their empty shacks demolished behind them and new houses along 'urban lines' built on the sites, until all the wood-and-iron houses had been replaced. In this way the council would kill two birds with one stone: they would demolish a vast and threatening slum (which was represented as polluting both the city and Duncan Village Location), and they would provide a 'model township with minimum cost' and with only 'minimum extensions of existing boundaries'.

CA, 3/ELN, 1150-56, 1351, 1400-03; and see Minkley, 'Border dialogues', pp. 310-31. [27]

During the 1940s and '50s this rebuilding happened in fits and starts. New model township 'suburbs' were built – with names like Duncan Bowl and Duncanville. At the same time, the shackyards

Second hand furniture is bought at sales, and in the house of a well-to-do tradesman or teacher one finds the horsehair sofa, plush tablecloth, lace curtains, and elaborate frilled bed hangings of Victorian England. Only the aspidistra is lacking. It is often replaced by artificial flowers. In these surroundings a gramophone is a bizarre modern note. Only goatskins on the linoleum-covered floor remind one that the owner's father was a herdsman. Often the walls are papered with sheets of old magazines as the only available substitute for wall-paper, the photographs of members of the family or of school teams, and crude prints, usually representing Biblical scenes, are hung up. The crudity and ugliness often make one shiver, but the shabby European furniture is treasured, and most women take a housewife's pride in their rooms. Outside many of the better houses are borders of flowers or rows of pot-plants, or sometimes a small patch of vegetables ... Contrasted with these Europeanized houses of the better-off people are the ramshackle warrens of rooms occupied by the poor in 'Gomorra' [a section of the Location]. Lacking both the pots, mats and other utensils of the peasant, and the furniture of the Europeanized – dank, and dark, and small – the room of the poor is a dismal place.

Monica Hunter, *Reaction to Conquest*, 1936 [28]

were prohibited and then demolished in smaller sections, starting with Gomorra.[29] As the vectors of local power veered between the 'native administration' and 'medico-administrative' poles, Duncan Village was remodelled and rebuilt, at least in part, even as 'forced consensus' increasingly shifted towards the idea of removal and a new township on a new site. The parameters for a remodelled Duncan Village and then for the Bantustan township of Mdantsane were being mapped out. In both instances, the existing racialized meanings and materialities of location spaces, as well as representations of the 'model township', were taken up and refashioned.

3 'Natural development in proper conditions': The new model township

Two versions of the 'new model township' were visible through the 1940s and '50s: the township reconstructed within a location (which is what actually happened in East London over these decades), and the township built from scratch on a new site (which is what became accepted from the late '50s onwards).

Support for a new township within the city, and then increasingly for one beyond its borders, came from the local native administration nexus. From their perspective, the dangerous spaces of the location needed to be removed: these 'glaringly insanitary honeycombed shacks' were 'unlivable, ill-ventilated' and 'crammed with sewerage, syphilis and sedition'.[30] Such spaces needed to be replaced by planned grids of urban life which were regular, clean, visible and open to surveillance. It would be even better if the native were relocated outside the city on a 'more tightly controlled and populated basis', which would 'regulate contact between European and native' and allow for their 'natural development in proper conditions'.

CA, 3/ELN, 1165, and 1074, Correspondence 12 February 1943 – March 1953 between R.C. Cook, the Location Manager, and the Council over the state of the locations and their future.

Support for a new model township also emerged out of the intersecting concerns of liberal and medico-administrative discourses about poverty, moral degradation, the breakdown of family life, illegitimacy and the generally 'undesirable state of affairs' in relation to housing, amenities, sanitation, education and recreation. In such surroundings, it was agreed, the location inhabitants could not escape social, moral and individual 'relapse' or 'return to their former conditions'. The curative journeys upwards and outwards could only be made permanent with 'rehousing, improved living conditions and the raising of general environmental standards' to create a 'healthy Location' – essentially a 'new model township'.

CA, 3/ELN, 877, 1240, Joint Public Health and Native Affairs Committee, Welsh Commission and MOH Reports for the 1940s and early '50s.

CA, 3/ELN, 877, 1240, Joint Public Health, Welsh Commission and MOH Reports, 1941-52.[31]

In order to realize the vision of the township built on the ruins of the location, and so meet the needs and desires of the native and provide a new, healthy form of 'community' life, there would have to be thorough investigation and planning. This would necessarily include 'roads planned on the contour, curbed and guttered', 'sewerage, water supply to each house, taps over concrete washing areas, electric lighting of streets and adequate dwellings, fences and gardens'. This model of the township intersected with national developments in urban planning and housing frameworks. The 51/ series and particularly the 51/9 house provided the blueprint in the 1950s.

CA, 3/ELN, Box 877, Ref 1960/2, Report of City Engineer, 11 May 1943, Native Affairs Committee, 1 March 1945, City Engineer Reports, 1949-52.

See CA, 3/ELN, 1150, Joint Council Minutes and Reports, 1948-61.

The visible grid of plot, block and street would allow the authorities to control access to and movement within the remodelled township. This would 'result in much better control of the residents ... throw out a lot of people who should not be there [and] balance movement between location and reserve areas'. But the inventors of this new modern space had more ambitious aims. By developing new townships and new forms of housing they hoped to redefine urban native space and produce new citizens, new families and new communities that were stable, urban and responsible. The 'conscious and determined policy to urbanize the Non-European population on a family basis' thus involved the construction of houses that would meet 'the modern conception of a workman's cottage'. The rebuilt townships – and especially the new 51/ houses – would provide not only for the residents' material needs but also for their 'mental needs'. They would provide for 'new people'.

Daily Dispatch, 15 July 1949, p. 12.

Daily Dispatch, 15 July 1949, p. 12.

CA, 3/ELN, 1240, MOH Report, 18 January 1950, reflecting on the Welsh Report; and also 1150 and 1151 for Council discussion and agreement, Minutes of Meetings, 1950-53.

CA, 3/ELN, 877, Ref 1960, MOH to City Engineer, 15 June 1953.

These developments around 'model townships' marked a new archaeological moment for planning in South Africa. New model townships, 'whether conceptual or physical, [were] tropes in the sense of instruments built to be engaged, inhabited, lived ...'[32] Combining elements of what Paul Rabinow has called 'middling modernism' with a particular rereading and silencing of the histories, cultures and politics of a racially stratified society, an administrative-planning complex sought to model and develop 'new non-European men' in relation to 'healthy township spaces and forms'.[33] This moment increasingly anticipated the breaking apart of sedimented practices, particularly those related to the racialized customs of 'wattle and daub' and the pondokkie. The older race and type understandings were giving way to a stratification and distinction grid. This began to displace the race-based disciplinary tactics of hygiene, as well as the obvious associations made between 'slum' occupation and identity.[34]

The planning of these 'non-European residential areas' was a highly complex matter. Alan Mabin and others have persuasively highlighted the political, material and bureaucratic processes that led to what Mabin calls 'reconstructionist thinking' and planning.[35] Tying the problems of 'native administration' to the lack of housing, Mabin outlines how a new planning and housing model emerged. The Department of Native Affairs, the National Housing and Planning Commission, the Department of Commerce, the National Building Research Institute (NBRI), the Council for Scientific and Industrial Research (CSIR), prominent architects and particular model sites all influenced the emergence and shaping of housing and planning programmes that laid down 'minimum standards', drew on relatively high 'scientific measures' and achieved a tremendous degree of standardization.

It is around these 'scientific approaches' to housing and township design that we need to delve a little deeper. The social-technical environment arrived at from the 'long process of defining standards' meant that non-European residential areas, as they were named, and the housing schemes they entailed were redefined as abstract questions of technical spaces and scientifically established needs rather than as specific questions of discipline or control.[36] At the same time, these technical standards were linked to various Western norms for the occupation and use of space. These norms were based on the 'family unit' and on the 'conventional single storey, detached, semi-detached and row houses with their own private residential gardens'. The planned stable and rational resident, household, plot and area would allow houses and families to be classified according to four standards: 'Superior ... of high class with good finishes and amenities; Good ... affordable; Austerity ... partly subsidized; and Minimum ... described as that minimum shelter which will just provide for the minimum requirements of health, family life and decency.' The minimum standard centred on 'the family: defined as husband, wife and children'. Future state interventions would try to create and stabilize this family structure.

D.M. Calderwood, 'The planning of non-European residential areas in South Africa', *National Building Research Institute Bulletin*, 7 (December 1951), pp. 1-24.[37]

CSIR, *Costs of Urban Bantu Housing*, 'Report of the Committee on the Costs of Building Urban Bantu Houses', p. 3.

Successful administration required more comprehensive and sophisticated knowledge of the population – hence the flurry of local and national social-science investigations into subjects ranging from poverty to labour migrancy. It also required more planning. The 'plan' – from site-selection tables to studies of plot size, from space-requirement percentages to density and area graphs – became the metaphoric link between social organization and the individual. Thus the township plan – 'a housing scheme is an area in which persons are housed in surroundings which create an environment conducive to a full life' – also became a life plan. The township and its residents would be formed and normed literally at the will of the 'steering mechanisms' of the residential area and the house, and according to the delivery of public services like water, sanitation, roads, health and education. Rabinow's argument applies: 'The priority was no longer the isolation and rectification of islands of pathology; rather, the new program amounted to a blueprint for the scientific administration of modern life as a whole.'[38]

CSIR, *Costs of Urban Bantu Housing*; Calderwood, 'The planning of non-European residential areas', p. 1.

The degree to which this technocratic modernism guided the planning of townships and housing is startling. The key planning manuals – *A Guide to the Planning of Non-European Townships* and *Minimum Standards of Accommodation for Non-Europeans*, and the later *Costs of Urban Bantu Housing* – all emphasize the shift in thinking. They are guided by the notion that 'there appears to be no doubt that, amongst the urban Natives, the family unit is replacing the tribal unit as the

An envelope of catastrophe

But what about the uncanny reality and inescapable presence of race, the historical pathology of body and soul – and of space – that so fractures the pondokkie and the location. That inheritance haunts the science of the township; it is an 'envelope of catastrophe' for the pictures and plans. 'Every description is more than a fixation, it is a culturally creative act, with distributive power and performative force – which, when brought together, founds spaces.'[39] What did it mean to plan and build on the borderline of a 'slum' and to the dictates of a 'non-European standard of space'? Consider these extracts from the 'Report of the Sub-Committee on the Technical Elements in Urban Bantu Houses', prepared in 1954 and used extensively by apartheid officials in East London.

CSIR, Costs of Urban Bantu Housing. The extracts are from pp. 28; 34-5; 98; 113; 116, b5; 24; b9; b14; b7; b13.

... taking into account the fact that many of the persons to be housed in urban Bantu houses have been living in shacks or traditional Bantu dwellings, many of which are known to leak severely during rain, it is reasonable in the lowest-cost housing to accept that occasional dampness in buildings is tolerable, providing no structural weakness in the building result from such damp conditions ... these observations lead one to believe that the effects of occasional dampness on healthy persons are more psychological than physical and ... is more cause for irritation than actual physical illness.

Consequently for minimum construction, as must apply for Bantu housing, it must be expected that there will be an even greater number of days on which the comfort range [in the thermal environment] is not achieved ... It is admitted that under these limiting conditions the buildings might at times become rather uncomfortable, but comfort cannot be afforded in houses which are subsidized.

Rimlocks are not well favoured because the small number of differs makes burglary easy: they are more difficult to fix to concrete door frames and the local authority faces difficulty with the loss of keys. The preferred types are those for which the occupant provides his own padlock.

A tap should not be provided in the kitchen as this will require further cost for a sink and drainage for the sink, and in the Sub-committee's view it is not imposing too much hardship in the lowest-cost housing to expect the water to be carried from a tap just outside the building.

Pail Latrines. These are the most commonly encountered systems in low-cost housing. There is no limitation to the size of a township that can be served in this way ... these need not be accompanied by undesirable smells so long as they are situated at least 15 ft from any dwelling. This factor gives rise to inconvenience in bad weather ... however this is Non-European custom and the most practical.

... the minimum standards of accommodation for non-Europeans concern the human requirements in buildings, namely the minimum requirements for the health, decency and family life of the occupants of the dwellings ... in the 51/9 house these requirements are already very close to the minimum requirements of the Slums Act.

The South African standards are far from luxurious but, for the promotion of health and decency, they are being formed along correct lines.

Standards are dependent upon the persons for whom they are prepared.

In South Africa, the non-European standard of space is about half that allowed in highly civilized countries.

... the accepted minimum standards of housing accommodation for non-Europeans in South Africa are at a minimum ...

basic cultural unit. While it may be desirable and possible to retard this process, and perhaps to a degree even to restore tribal influence and cohesion, it seems necessary in urban communities to ensure, as far as possible, the building up of stable family life. A stable family is the foundation for a stable community ...'

F.R. Rodseth, F. van Heerden and J.E. Jennings, 'Native housing research in South Africa', National Building Research Institute Bulletin, 6 (June 1951), pp. 7-15. [40]

To build a house was to build a family, was to build a community, was to build stability and normality. Minimum standards, scientific planning, technical expertise, the figure, graph, diagram and table, the model and the test, knowledge and experimentation, standards for foundations and floors, superstructures, doors and windows, roofs, painting and glazing, fittings, plumbing, sanitation, structural stability, rain resistance, indoor thermal environments, durability, technical requirements, material requirements, time studies – such things would provide the basis for stable and normal communities.

CSIR, Costs of Urban Bantu Housing, Reports and papers on bantu housing, pp. 1-287.

The technical plan of the new township house also defined the normal use of such a shelter, making this a condition of occupation. The functions of rooms were specified – 'bedroom, kitchen-dine., living-sleeping, bath rm, passage'; and the proper furnishings for the interiors sketched in – 'bed, table, chairs ...' The 'spatial requirements' were also specified according to 'type and size of dwelling' and 'average occupancy rate', based of course on the 'average family size of 5 persons'. A residential plot must also 'house the dwelling and provide space for (I) privacy (II) laundry and clothes drying (III) children's play (IV) cultivation (V) sufficient overall area to allow for fresh air and uninterrupted light'. These 'scientifically cautioned conditions of habitation established the means of the extension of the normalization process'.[42] They implied a regular wage, a regular family structure, and regular habits for a stable community.

CSIR, Costs of Urban Bantu Housing; D.M. Calderwood and P.H. Connell, 'Minimum standards of accommodation for the housing of non-Europeans in South Africa', National Building Research Institute Bulletin, 8 (June 1952), pp. 1-23; and D.M. Calderwood, 'Site selection in non-European housing estate layouts', National Building Research Institute Bulletin, 7 (December 1951), pp. 25-32. [41]

4 'A thousand alien tongues': A decade of documents[43]

Through the 1950s, the planned rebuilding of Duncan Village Location into new township space was undercut by Group Areas planning interventions and disputes, by central and local government disagreements over the growing role of the Native (and later Bantu) Affairs Department in the administration of the location, and by the evolution of the Bantustan policies.

In all this the official designations of white space were always central, defining the green buffer zones, parks, natural valleys and open spaces that would 'divide the different types of development from each other', and determining the internal development of Duncan Village and its ultimate relocation to Mdantsane. At the same time, the silences about the location and the nature of the native spaces within it grew more profound, as the authorities were caught between the options of extension and removal. White Group Areas – Amalinda and North End – significantly determined the fate of their black neighbours – or, as it was expressed in a memo to the Town Clerk, 'those inhabitants numerically more than all other "groups" together, but occupying 1/18th of the area in which we live'.

CA, 3/ELN, 1341-5, Town Clerk Correspondence, 18 September 1952.

The selection of documents presented here provides a glimpse of some of the agents who shaped this particular 'native space': councillors, administrators, residents, town planners, health officials and, not to be forgotten, the Architect-in-Chief. It also suggests how they achieved their ends. Let us imagine the proposals, recommendations, interjections, principles, approvals, permissions, proclamations, opinions, examinations and resolutions piling up in Lloyds Building (the home of the location manager), in council chambers and Native Affairs Department offices.

City Council Urban Reform Plan, 15 October 1949

CA, 3/ELN, Box 877, Ref 1960, Urban Reform Plan, 15 October 1949, p. 2.

The ward and headman system will provide for the general supervision of the behaviour of his people, to warn and later to report persons guilty of continued drunkenness, to see the houses, pavements, gardens, etc are kept neat and tidy, to carry out any orders given him by the Manager of Native Administration, to make known to his people and explain the implication of any regulations, and to keep the manager generally informed of what is transpiring in his ward.

Bowling and Floyd, Town Planners and Consultants, Report, March 1950

CA, 3/ELN, Box 1343, Ref 50/665/3/2, Bowling and Floyd Report, March 1950.

It is no longer sufficient to relegate the location to any odd area of land for which no other use can be found ...

If the Wilsonia-Amalinda Commonage A land is developed for industries as we suggest the farm portions of Amalinda will be wedged between the present location of Duncanville and the industrial areas, and will not be eminently desirable for European residential purposes. On the other hand this land is suitable for the extension of Duncanville and we recommend the use of this land for such purpose.

The new layout of the Duncanville location will provide for a further 1,000 natives over the above figure of 25,000. To arrive at this figure the following requirements would need to be met:

- the separation of 5,000 coloured inhabitants into their own location
- the disposal of 16,000 unemployed hangers-on or hanger-ons in the location
- the enforcement of 6,000 native male and female domestic servants to reside in the provided premises of Europeans.

We suggest that the new location – the extension of Duncanville – be laid out on the lines of a garden city approach. The use of road-bays economizes road construction and services and gives a pleasant grouping of dwellings. It assists the use of the headman system of administration and provides numerous small open areas where natives may gather and chat or children may play.

D

East London City Council, Minutes, 29 August 1950

CA, 3/ELN, Box 1370 and 1371, The Group Areas Act, Council Minutes and Reports, 29 August 1950.

That the Council adopt in principle, the recommendations of the Town Planning Consultants in regard to the extension of the East Bank Location boundaries to include the land shown bordered red on Plan No. TP 201 ... The plan is professional, comprehensive and scientific.

The Divisional Council and the NAD oppose extension into the Amalinda area. The Council however, approves a block-by-block rehabilitation scheme, and the erection of 400 sub-economic houses within the existing precinct of the East Bank Location.

Secretary for Native Affairs, Letter to Town Clerk, 18 September 1952

CA, 3/ELN, Box 1345, 25/3/3.N, Letter from Secretary for Native Affairs, 18 September 1952.

The Department gives limited and restricted permission for the Amalinda extension of the EB Location for a 1,500 site-and-service scheme. However an immediate search ... for a suitable site elsewhere which will absorb any further increase of the native population must be undertaken.

Land Tenure Advisory Board, Proclamation of Group Areas in East London in Terms of the Group Areas Act, 1950 (Act No 41 of 1950), 16 February 1953

Daily Dispatch, 16 February 1953, p. 1.

It is hereby notified that the Minister of the Interior outlines the following Group Areas for ownership and occupation by members of the White Group; Chinese Group; Coloured Group; Indian Group and Malay Group.

City Council, Alternative Group Areas Proposal, 5 May 1953

CA, 3/ELN, Box 1370 and 1371, The Group Areas Act, Council Minutes, 5 May 1953.

That the Council was of the opinion that the racial position locally did not present any real problem and was in fact opposed to the implementation of the Group Areas Act in East London, but ... it had no option in the matter; and that the Council's own proposals were considered to be the most lenient and most satisfactory, having regard to all the circumstances, but the Council was prepared to consider any counter proposals.

Bowling Richardson and Floyd, Town Planning Consultants, Johannesburg – Letter from Mr Floyd, 4 July 1953

CA, 3/ELN, Box 1343, 50/665/3/2, Letter from Bowling Richardson and Floyd, 4 July 1953.

From the examination of the proposed group areas as suggested by the City Council and those suggested by the Planning Committee of the Land Tenure Board we conclude that there is no conflict as regards the principle of establishing group areas. There appears also to be no difference of opinion as to the general area or direction in which the areas for non-White races should be located. Finally we strongly recommend that the first scheme goes forward.

Meeting of White Residents, 20 August 1953

Daily Dispatch, 20 August 1953, p. 1.

We in the Eastern Province have practised an apartheid ever since we settled in the Eastern Cape. That is we have kept ourselves separate, be it native, be it Asiatic or otherwise ... I am proud Amalinda has made a protest against setting up in its area something which, in time, must become objectionable ... Stands there a man in this hall who can say he is not colour conscious, and becoming more so? But in our colour consciousness we do not want to lose sight of the fact that whatever the colour might be, we want to be fair to him, we want to give him the best opportunity we can for his progress and uplift. But it must not be at the expense of the European.

Greenfields Residents, Memo to City Council, 14 September 1953

CA, 3/ELN, Box 1156, Memo of Greenfields Residents to City Council, 14 September 1953.

The proposed extension to the location will fall directly across the river, within our field of vision and become a source of squeal and squall arising from the location. No one likes to have a Native location on their doorstep, or to have the peaceful serenity of rural surroundings shattered by the babel of a thousand alien tongues.

Department of Native Affairs, Minutes, 10 April 1956

ELM, Minutes of Native Affairs Committee, 10 April 1956.

The Department wished to give the native his right place in the sun. The native wished to enjoy the benefits of civilization to the same extent as the European did, and therefore the Department's opinion was that he be given every opportunity to develop to the fullest extent in those areas of South Africa which had from time immemorial been his homelands ... If the native residential area was placed adjacent to such a reserve, the residents were immediately in contact with their own people in their own reserve. There they had an outlet for all their ambitions ... they could establish themselves in the native reserves and also still retain employment in the City.

H.F. Verwoerd, Minister of Native Affairs, 7 December 1957

CA, 3/ELN, Box 1402, Report of Meeting, 7 December 1957.

Wake up! East London must come into line! I am tired of this 'wait and see council'. I will only accept the complete and ultimate removal of the Bantu locations from the City.

Minister of Bantu Administration and Development, 20 February 1962

CA, 3/ELN, Box 1351, Memo from Bantu Affairs Department, 20 February 1962.

The proposed new location for East London will not be a municipal project but the government will assume all responsibility for the creation of a black city in the Ciskei. This would be sited at Umdanzani and the City Council 'resolved that it would subscribe to an agreement to undertake to develop it [the new township]'.

Department of Education, Arts and Science, Linguistic Authorities on Bantu Languages, 12 March 1963

CA, 3/ELN, Box 1403, Letter from Department of Education, Arts and Science, 12 March 1963.

Not Umdanzani, the correct spelling is Mdantsane.

5 'Loneliness was all around us': The homeland township of Mdantsane

New model township (1963); homeland township (1966); largest urban centre of an 'independent country' (1981). Also a commuter town and a dormitory township – a shadow of a city. Alternatively, a 'fully fledged town', a 'model town with all the amenities of comfortable living'. Although it was located on the border of the Ciskei Bantustan and later incorporated within it, constructed around forced removals and relocations and subsequently administered and ruled under the whip of an

Surplus Peoples Project (SPP) Report, *Forced Removals in South Africa*, vol. 2, *The Eastern Cape* (Cape Town, University of Cape Town, 1983).[44]

imagined nationality and ethnicity, Mdantsane was one of the major townships built in the 1960s and '70s. By the end of the 1970s it was the second largest black township in South Africa after Soweto.

Daily Dispatch, 14 September 1979, p. 1; SPP Report, The Eastern Cape, p. 182.

The Ciskei in the Eastern Cape was a product of the apartheid state's Bantustan policy. The Bantu Self-Governing Act of 1959 and subsequent legislation aimed to define and consolidate ethnic and tribal identities as Bantustan nationalities and to displace South African citizens into scattered 'homelands'. In 1972 the Ciskei was proclaimed a self-governing black territory under the National States Constitution Act, and in 1982 it became a 'national state'. All the accounts of the history of this Bantustan are bleak, full of poverty, repression, corruption and violence. Mdantsane was the Ciskei's largest 'city' by a considerable margin.[45]

Discussion between the East London City Council and the Department of Bantu Administration in the early 1960s suggested that because Mdantsane was a 'homeland township' it should ultimately be developed 'along the same lines and to the same standards as a European Township ... with the same services, facilities and conveniences'.[46] However, 'all usages could not be immediately envisaged'. Modern town-planning concepts based on Howard's 'garden city' were applied in what can only be described as a self-congratulatory style by the Council and the City Engineer. The basic plan included a centrally sited 'high order civic and business centre' and a number of 'neighbourhoods' or, more accurately, administrative zones of residential units arranged in linear patterns around the centre. The familiar township grid was replaced by 'curves, loops and triangles'. Plot sizes were larger, freehold title would be granted to 'Ciskeians', and greater involvement in local government was envisaged. The fact that the township was forcibly sited on a 'dissected rolling landscape not commonly utilized for low cost housing' meant that there was also a 'greater percentage of open space than usual'.[47]

D

Other features could not be so easily extolled as corresponding to a 'European' or 'international' model, supposedly 'in keeping with modern planning principles the world over'.[48] The 'view sites' occupied by zone administrators and the 'dominating hilltop site' for the civic and business centre and sports stadium gave the authorities an imposing, all-seeing presence. Residential plots were not allowed to back onto undeveloped land, officially for 'health reasons' (such land was seen as a channel for uncontrolled contamination from the tribal reserves). No cul-de-sac streets were permitted, and the entire township was 'encompassed by a perimeter road, [with] ... access to the settlement ... by means of one road only, which crosses the whole built up area ...' It was not hard to envisage, even before it happened in the 1970s and '80s: the roadblocks, the armoured vehicles, the troops. These were separate-development roads, state-security streets, pathways of fear, white spines in non-European space. When, in 1982, Mdantsane disappeared from South Africa as if by white magic, into a twilight zone somewhere between Nicosia and Taipei, no 'European' models were required.[49]

ELM, City Engineers Department, Mdantsane Files, 1963-76.

As in all the townships planned in this period, space was differentiated in Mdantsane. However, only 1 per cent of the land was allocated as 'owner-build areas' where 'those residents with the financial means to do so may have houses erected to their own design'. For the rest it was 'single-storey, free-standing constructions'; originally type 51/6 and later 51/9. Four rooms, no ceilings, floors of uncovered concrete, walls of unplastered, painted concrete blocks, outside sanitation in the 51/6.[50] The houses were allocated randomly, and people qualified for occupation on the basis of their present place of residence and inscribed Ciskeian nationality.

Not everyone who moved to Mdantsane was forced: by the 1980s more than half the residents had moved by choice. For people trapped in the location dramas of Duncan Village and nourished on public narratives (by the Bantu Administration and the City Council in particular) and visions of European housing developments in Mdantsane, needs and desires had their effect. Paradise was just fifteen kilometres away – or at least 'a paradise of a homeland in an urbanized form', 'a wonderful model township for our freedom'. One resident put it simply: 'We wanted at least a four-roomed house, not that one-roomed house of ours.'

SPP Report, The Eastern Cape, pp. 181-2, Interviews with residents.

Initially the new township and the new house gave a taste of freedom: 'It is like four houses in one. I have got a garden and everything to myself ... I have my lavatory.' Home ownership was

At first it seemed very raw, that place, because they were new houses. There were rough pieces of cement lying in our way, and the earth was all dug up, and the grass around the house was all overgrown. I felt very heartsore because the place was strange and I knew nobody. I felt, really, I'm now quite thrown away. There I was just put in a new house with my children, but there was nothing there, no people in the houses next door, no doors inside, only a front door at the front and a back door at the back. But the house was clean, there were cement floors and panes in the windows, but no ceilings, you had to put them in yourself. There was a water pipe in the kitchen but you had to buy the tap and fix it. The house stood on a slope; there were three steps inside. Yet it felt very hard when I walked round the house and saw there was no other person living near us. We had been put in a desolate place. Loneliness was all around us.

I was thinking why had they put me in a house on the dirt road. There were three empty houses on the tarred road, but they had to give me one on the dirt road. So I decided I wasn't taking that house. I wrote down the numbers of two other houses, 3351 and 3353 ... After a week they started filling the place up. They brought in people any old how. If the houses stayed empty the skollies messed them up, and took out the panes to sell. Many people came from Duncan Village which was a slum and being broken down and Punzana location, others from Mossel Bay, and Beaufort West and Noupoort. Cape Town was only given three houses a month.

Elsa Joubert, *The Long Journey of Poppie Nongena*, 1981[51]

The Sisa Dukashe stadium has banked concrete seats around three sides of the soccer field. On the fourth side is a grandstand. Around the stadium is a high brick wall. The wall was manned by vigilantes with shot-guns and pellet guns. Underneath the grandstand there were numerous change rooms estimated to be approximately 7-8 metres square. The vigilantes took up accommodation in all but two of these change rooms. In the remaining two, captives would be kept. There was often no sexual division, neither food nor water was provided to those detained. At times there were to be up to 80 persons locked into one change room. There is no running water. Accordingly the detainees were forced to defecate on the floor. The floor was at some stages littered with piles of faeces ... It was general practice to sjambok persons who were brought there. No blankets were provided ... no medical attention was given ...

Nicholas Haysom, *Ruling with the Whip*, 1983[52]

appealing in itself: 'We came to purchase a house in Mdantsane.' Physical space and 'independence' all moved people: 'Here I have four rooms which belong to me. The house is airy and light, compared to the stinking shacks we lived in at Duncan Village ... Altogether it is a pleasant place to live' ... 'We are no longer crowded and all on top of one another. The nearby gutters are not full of rotten food and human droppings.' The plans for schools, shops, clinics and services were also attractive.

SPP Report, *The Eastern Cape*, p. 192, Interviews with residents.

Illusions shatter, dreams are broken ... by regulation, by racial modernism, by the 'internal engineering' of houses, Primus-stove meals, separation and loneliness, by 'non-European standards of space'. Cold, hot, leaking and damp, broken taps and window panes, doors that require padlocks... the administrative keeper of keys ... Dreams are broken by administrative neglect and surveillance from the hilltop, gardens full of rubble, the 'Igati' and the 'Spine', the Gate and the Highway, by exhausting walks – like 'worn-out corpses' – to the screens of distant identity for money, food, medicine, permission ... Increasingly, a repertoire of complaints patterned the response to the township: 'Houses should be built for lodgers ... Bigger and better houses should be built ... When I wake up early in the morning, I do not have tea because of starvation ... We have no money here, work is scarce ... we are still unemployed here ... rents are high ... we pay expensive buses ... here we are sitting helpless ... Mdantsane is a place where a cow misses its calf ... the people I stayed with live far from me now.'

SPP Report, *The Eastern Cape*, pp. 177-96, Interviews with residents.

As the more spacious Mdantsane house replaced the confined single room of Duncan Village, as the relatively open space of the plan replaced the closed labyrinth of the shackyard, the internal networks of contact, support and identification produced by the location were eroded by a different set of representations of urban form and imagination. The township became a place marked by uniformity and separation, by loneliness and hardship, by starvation and unemployment and distance.

Location space was by definition native, tribal, backward, temporary; it was rural space out of place. The spatial stories of the location were about journeys to 'permanence' in the face of losing or preserving rural connection; about patron and client networks, about class, kin and status, about being 'red' or 'school'; about internal differentiations and identities, and the impermanence and inadequacy of these within the 'white spaces of representation'. The room, the site, the washroom, the shebeen, the street, the particular locality, the sports field, the hall and the meeting ground all anchored spatial practices that built and maintained wider social and material practices and capacities of survival, assimilation, difference, opportunity and assertion. Mdantsane, however, took on different meanings, generated new spatial stories amidst the old. As a place of fixed permanency, as a new tribalized urban space, it became the paradise lost of a Bantustan in urban form. The urban became identified as a hollow category, and was represented as a place of loss and desolation, hardship and loneliness, not only in relation to older rural spaces but also to the locations.[53]

Where stories are disappearing, being reduced to museographical objects and removed memories, there is a loss of space. 'Deprived of narrations the group and individual regress towards the disquieting, fatalistic experience of a formless, indistinct and nocturnal totality,' suggests De Certeau.[54] New journeys, maps and (dis)placements in the township entailed the founding of new spaces of meaning and habitation – but these too were curtailed and enclosed, at least in part, by 'non-European space' and the dichotomies of community and resistance.

'Monday morning I went to the small office at the gate they call Igati ... and they asked where I had worked before and wrote it down and gave me a stamp to take to the big office in East London.'[55] Movement also confronted the topographies of 'non-European space' within the township and across its frontiers. 'Buses do not enter the area and you have to travel to reach the bus stop' ... 'We have to pay expensive buses to carry us to town.' Daily journeys, to the madams and masters, the factories and administration offices, and the shops and clinics, took away time and money, but also a sense of place. The township, littered by night with the fragments of yet another day spent crossing and entering the white spaces of East London, simply reinforced these 'intimate relationships' between 'the white man's town – East London' and Mdantsane.[56] Buses seemed to do no more than carry people out, away, towards East London, and then back again to a central point. Everything ran according to East London time – routes, stops, the schedules of the 'expensive buses'; for most people, movement in Mdantsane was a regime of walking and waiting outside the bus terminus, East London's daily space in the township.[57]

SPP Report, The Eastern Cape, p. 193, Interviews with residents.

In 1983 these frontiers were contested through a prolonged and particularly violent bus boycott. Organizers were detained, tortured and killed, commuters were searched, harassed and whipped at roadblocks, especially at the entrance to Mdantsane, private cars were impounded, and curfews imposed by a combined force of South African police, Ciskeian police and soldiers, and vigilantes – the 'green berets'.[58] Assaults, shootings, body and document inspections, detentions and disappearances became routine for the inhabitants of Mdantsane. The sports stadium – Sisa Dukashe – came to symbolize not just this moment, but the space of the township in the 1980s.

The space of terror extended to the street and the house. The curfew provided that no one should be on the streets between 10.30 p.m. and 4 a.m., and not more than four people should walk together on the street or be in anyone's house during the day. Houses were searched, people were assaulted, many disappeared. Township space, already represented as desolate and lonely, as hollow, now filled up with fear, threat and denial. The violence of living the everyday according to a 'non-European standard of space', zoned by an increasingly rigid bureaucracy, was dramatically intensified by the invasions of the sjambok – the whip.[59]

Terror erased the line between public space and private home. Systems of terror, as one resident put it, 'have got us where we live', and no place was safe any more.[60] A corrosive and contagious violence was unleashed that blurred all physical, moral and judicial frameworks. Scenes of political violence were not limited to prisons and torture chambers but were played out on public streets, in private houses, on human bodies. The invasion of the house, signifying the Ciskei 'nation' (in its largest, most urban and most modern surroundings), the family home and the body's protective shell, indicated that the three spaces – social, familial and individual – increasingly collapsed into one.[61] At the same time, white spaces imposed by power and black counterspaces posited by resistance, all regulated by paper, inhabited by design or by sanction and decree, invaded by terror and silenced by fear, grew more and more separate. There was no prospect of integration as a defining 'thirdspace'.[62]

6 A non-European standard of space: Here, now

The townships were built out of the 'tribal' extensionality of the locations of East London and other towns and cities, and of the reserves and rural areas. Loss was more acutely felt in these new places, whose dimensions now included the racial modernism of a 'non-European standard of space'. Loneliness, isolation, unemployment, poverty, restriction – these stories were increasingly lived in the interiors of the 51/9 house and in the landscape of the zone, the perimeter fence, Spine Road and Parade Boulevard, the bus terminus. The Urban Foundation shopping mall and the garden beautification contest dramatized at two extremes the possibilities of a different urban form in a space which was everywhere filled with administrative intrusion and neglect.

The directions spatial stories took from these 'magnitudes' resolved into 'odd functions' of the coordinates. Different generations of inhabitants drew on nostalgia or rebellion to tell of community, identity and place. Narratives of tradition constructed an African sense of space outside of history, the 'white man' and the city, while narratives of resistance sought to remake the township through a sense of 'community'. In between these two poles, spatial stories told of victimization and nurturing, of desperation and survival, of loss and gain in the teeth of the passbook and the 'Umgqkomo lorry'.[63]

The place of the township was fractured by the equivocations of these stories. The house was not a home, the street was not a public road, the zone was not a neighbourhood. The administration was alien, the police were feared and the plan of 'tired feet' was despised. However, it was through the 'semiotics of [this non-European] space that activists elaborated the terms of their opposition', or that residents narrated their affinities for home, family and community 'within the categories officialdom had delivered to them'.[64] The deeper grammars that structured the township as a space of whiteness remained largely unremarked.

In the embrace of a much more visible normality – this is the lived space, the existing and current model for black people in the city – whiteness was rendered normative and invisible. In the struggle over housing, rents, transport, forms of governance – the whole gamut of neglect in the township – the politics of survival and resistance contested the workings of this model, but not the spatial imprint of the model itself. In fact, the spatial imprint and distinctive spatial dichotomies of race were also unintentionally fixed by this oppositional politics, and they remain so in the here, now. A rigid civic language and hermetic set of narratives developed out of the ways space was and continues to be segregated.[65] And despite the 'One City' vision now propounded for East London and other cities, the segregated spaces themselves continue to map out the development frameworks and public discourses and be mapped out in them in turn.

In this way the township and the squatter camp continue to be defined as the black spaces of the city. What were previously the apparently distinctive 'non-white' spaces of exclusion and opposition are now the key sites for reconstruction and development. Fundamentally and actively transforming the lived spaces of the city is necessary, desirable, fundamental. However, '... segregation has become the spatial imprint of our cities and the deep structure of our imaginations and memories'.[66]

If we fail to recognize this, we will surely fail to unpick the locks of 'the fabulous keeper of keys' or restore the souls to the 'corpses behind screens'.[67]

The history of urban spaces for Africans – pondokkie slums, locations, model townships, homeland townships, 'One City' – is marked by absence and continuity. What is absent is any actual progression in the making of such spaces; what is continuous is the making of a variation on 'tribal' space in the city. In the historical meeting of modern town planning with apartheid, and in the contemporary meeting of its spatial imprint with the 'incorporationist' model of the unified city, these continuities need to be acknowledged. They are most visible now in the calls to 'flatten' and remove the squatter threat, even as camp after camp springs up, apparently overnight (in the familiar language), apparently spreading like a 'fungus' or a 'disease'.

The various attempts to recompose these spaces, to verify, collate and displace their frontiers, cannot easily escape the fact that it is the accumulated white partitioning of space that structures the township and the squatter camp from within as 'native', as 'non-European', as 'black'; that these categories are lived and imagined from within the frontiers and fracturing traumas of race as much as in opposition to them. As De Certeau says, 'There is no spatiality that is not organized by the determination of frontiers, from the subject and its exteriority, to that which localizes objects, from the home, constituted on the basis of the wall to the journey, constituted on the basis of a geographical elsewhere, or cosmological beyond.'[68] Race creates its own looking-glass world, concrete here, even if it does not appear – even if it is 'blank' – on city maps now.

D

◄B11 ►J12

2

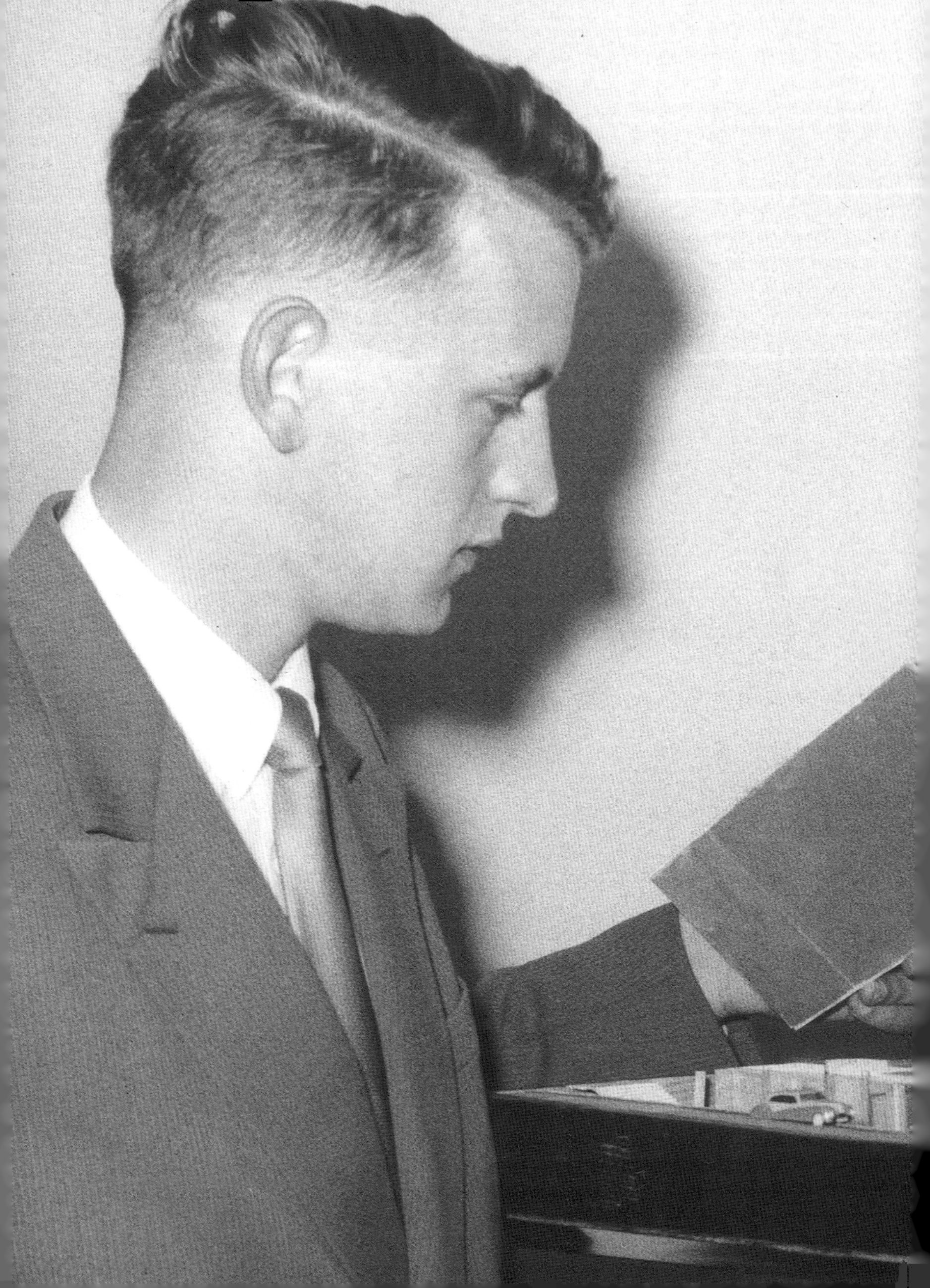

The native heart: The architecture of the University of Pretoria campus

Roger Fisher

Karel Jooste at Philip Nel Architects, model of The Aula, c. 1952.

The Hill of the Jackal

Mapungubwe, the Place of the Jackal, lies on a hilltop near the confluence of the Limpopo and the Shashi rivers, where the Republic of South Africa, Zimbabwe and Botswana meet. The rediscovery of this ancient citadel is a tale worth retelling.

In 1927 a farmer of the area, a certain E.S.J. van Graan, came to hear about a man called Lottering, who lived the hermit's life on the banks of the Limpopo. Apparently this Lottering had brought down a clay pot off a nearby granite outcrop, a koppie, of a style unlike that of any contemporary local earthenware. In 1932 Van Graan, his son and three friends located the koppie. The son of a local chief named Mowena revealed the secret path to the summit and there, amongst the potsherds, copper bangles and glass trade beads, the men found a trove of artefacts, including the famed golden rhinoceros. They shared the bounty five ways between them, just like Rhodes' agents when they discovered Great Zimbabwe. But here the story has a happier ending. The Van Graan lad, a student at the University of Pretoria, realizing that the finds were of scientific importance, brought them to the attention of one of the professors of archaeology there. As a result the land was secured by the government, the bounty retrieved by the university's Department of Archaeology, and excavations commenced.

The people who occupied Mapungubwe between AD 950 and 1250, like their successors in Great Zimbabwe, belonged to the Zinzho tradition. Then the Limpopo River was not a political divide, as it is today, but the natural element around which cultures flourished and declined. At its height there were some twenty thousand souls in Mapungubwe. Beads and seashells attest to their status as traders, and gold and other metal artefacts to their skill as smelters and workers of ore.

At the time that excavations began at Mapungubwe, the architect Gerard Moerdyk was serving on the council of the University of Pretoria, having been elected to that body in 1930. The Mapungubwe finds deepened in Moerdyk an interest in African culture, first aroused by a tour to Egypt and the Levant, and from then on he was to pursue the Africanization of his architecture, not only by using indigenous materials, but by employing motifs and symbols with an African origin or association. At this time, when the African origins of Great Zimbabwe were being contested, Moerdyk was adamant, although he did not much admire the workmanship, that it was indeed the product of an indigenous culture.

Moerdyk's first involvement with a project which required a degree of symbolic interpretation was the Merensky Library on the campus of the University of Pretoria. Like the symbolism of the later Voortrekker Monument, which Moerdyk would make widely known through his writings in both the English and the Afrikaans press, the symbolism of the Merensky Library was overt and explicit. The granite was of the African soil and symbolized the great age and immensity of the continent, attributes he associated with Great Zimbabwe. The zigzag stonework band was also derived from and linked the building to Africa. The zigzag is an archetypal symbol of water and fertility found in indigenous African culture, and part of its potency stems from the scarcity of water in the subcontinent. For Moerdyk it was also associated with the Voortrekkers as a chosen people whom God had watched over in the African wilderness.

Many of the symbols in bas-relief on the Library walls Moerdyk himself traced to Zimbabwean influences. The architraves of the entrance depict the crocodile and Zimbabwe bird. The crocodile, as spirit of the water, once again suggests a powerful, fertile culture, while the bird, as spirit of the skies, refers to the spiritual inspiration of the creative writers of Afrikaans (and perhaps of the architect as author of the building). The baboons trooping across the lintel of the door remain symbolically obscure. Perhaps it is no more than an architect's humour – after all, he has sheep in the same position on the Reserve Bank he designed in Bloemfontein.

The curving of the walls to the entrance represents the open book, knowledge revealed, especially biblical knowledge. An open Bible was a feature of old Boer homes, and a Bible opened at a particular verse is always placed on a lectern in Afrikaner churches. If we pursue Moerdyk's symbolism to its conclusion, the verse here must be from the Old Testament, God speaking to His People.

Gerard Moerdyk, Merensky Library, 1933-6, bas-relief of main door architrave.

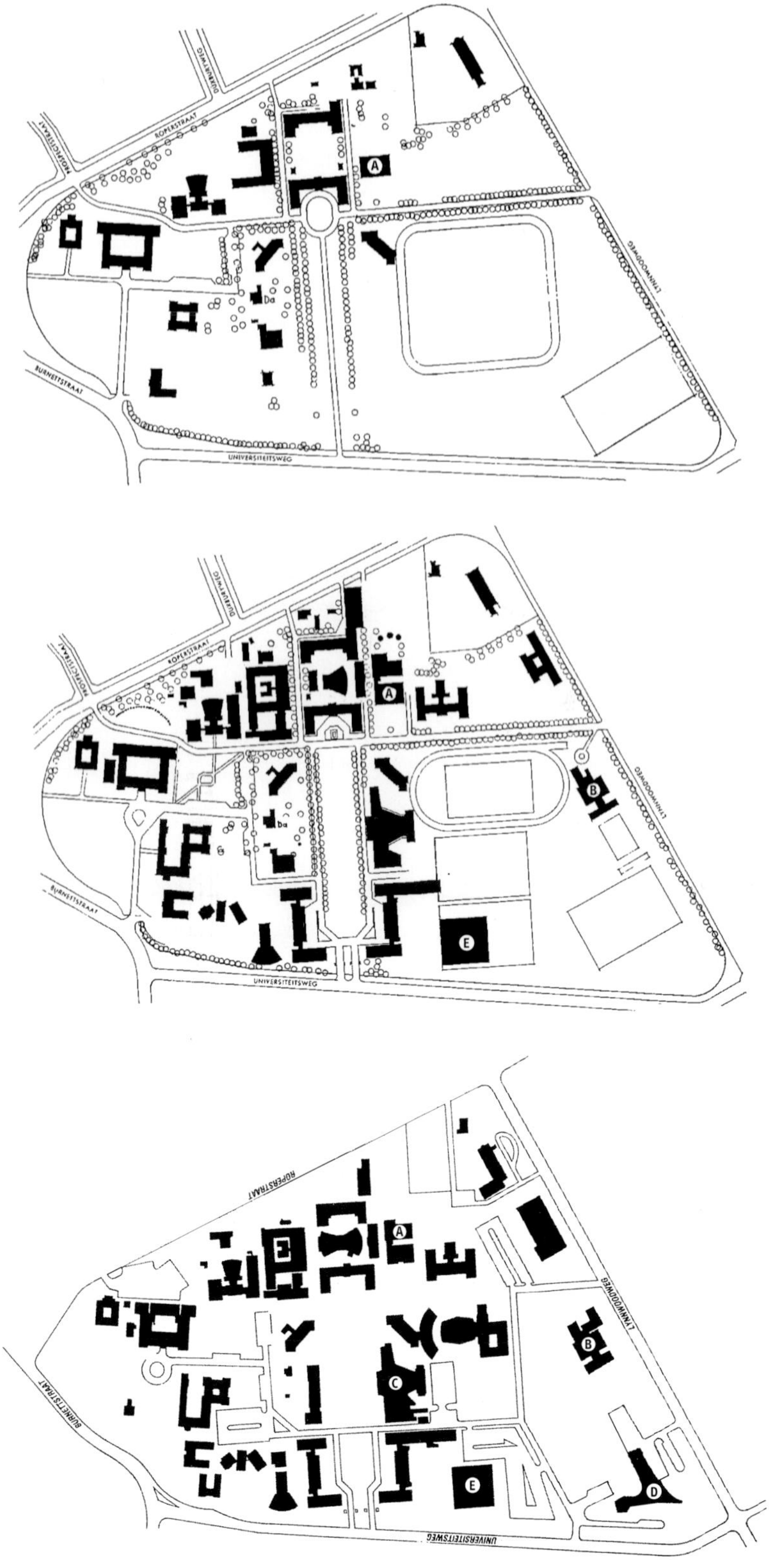

University of Pretoria, 1943, 1960, 1970.

A Merensky Library

B Physical Education Building

C The Aula

D Administration Building

E Heavy Machinery Building

1 The inheritance[1]

Late in 1880, after war with Britain, the Boers of the Transvaal won their independence from the colonial authority and proclaimed the Republic of South Africa once again. It was around this time that Frans Lion Cachet, the Dutch clergyman who became embroiled in the church politics of the Boer Republics, made the observation that Pretoria was so full of foreigners one could barely conceive of its status as capital of an independent territory.[2] But, by the following year the independence of the South African Republic had been affirmed and the Boers were masters of their own destinies, for the time being at least.

The first Act of Parliament in the restored Republic dealt with higher education and recommended the erection of a *normaalschool* or college in Pretoria in order to bring '*eene behoorlijke wetenschaplijke opleiding binnen het bereik van het blanke bevolking der Zuid-Afrikaansche Republiek*' [a proper scientific education within reach of the white population of the South African Republic]. The envisaged teaching fields included Pedagogy, Law, Commerce and State Administration, alongside Military Science and Agricultural Science, while Theology was purposely omitted as church affiliations were in flux at the time. However, this grand idea was stillborn, because of the difficulty of finding staff who would not taint the '*zuivere Afrikaansche geest*' [pure Afrikaans spirit]. The only suitably qualified teachers would of necessity be Dutch, and there was a suspicion that they would bring their language prejudices with them to Africa.

In the 1890s, the gold rush and the rise of the Uitlander population brought a new threat. On the eve of the Anglo-Boer War, *De Express*, a newspaper based in the Orange Free State, made an appeal for the two Boer Republics to establish a '*zuiver Hollands-Afrikaansche*' university to counter the '*zuiver Britische scholen van de Ekstein's, Beit's en hun bewonderaars aan de Rand*' [pure British schools of the Eksteins, the Beits and their admirers on the Rand]. The Anglo-Boer War put paid to that scheme for a while, but we can discern in it all the components that would characterize the University of Pretoria – a city-based, white, Afrikaans tertiary institution serving the needs of a farming community.

It was Jan Smuts who decreed in 1907 that a Pretoria campus separate from the Transvaal University College in Johannesburg be established and that the Arts be moved there. His rationale was that Arts subjects in Johannesburg were not drawing students, because the rural students who generally accounted for most of this enrolment did not find the city appealing. Pretoria would be a better setting for the teaching of these subjects.

By this time the Transvaal had become a Crown Colony under Britain, and the Pretoria campus therefore fell under the educational programme of the newly arrived British colonial masters. The architects who came to work in the colony's Department of Public Works followed Herbert Baker so closely that their architectural idiom became known as the 'Baker school'. Among these young architects was Piercy Eagle, who designed the Faculty of Arts building (1910), the first on the new campus.

Only in 1930, after agitation from staff and students, and under a council which included Gerard Moerdyk, did the University of Pretoria become an Afrikaans-language institution. From then onwards the new buildings on campus would be authored by Afrikaner architects, all concerned in one way or another with Afrikaner culture and identity. The architecture on the campus thus presents, in a fascinatingly concentrated and representative form, elements of a *volkskultuur* produced in relationship to broader international trends. This has much to tell us about the production of architecture in a provincial setting and about aspects of the style of architecture that has been termed 'Pretoria Regionalism'.

Volk is a word that does not translate easily into English. Neither 'folk' nor 'people' has the connotational depth of the Afrikaans. As a result, the compounds that are so much a part of the language and the culture it expresses – *volkskultuur*, *volksgeskiedenis*, *volksmond*, *volksvreemd* – become obscure in translation and help to keep the Afrikaner psyche a mystery to English-speakers. Perhaps the language of architecture, spoken by champions of Afrikaner culture in an Afrikaans environment,

Gerard Moerdyk, Merensky Library, south-east elevation.

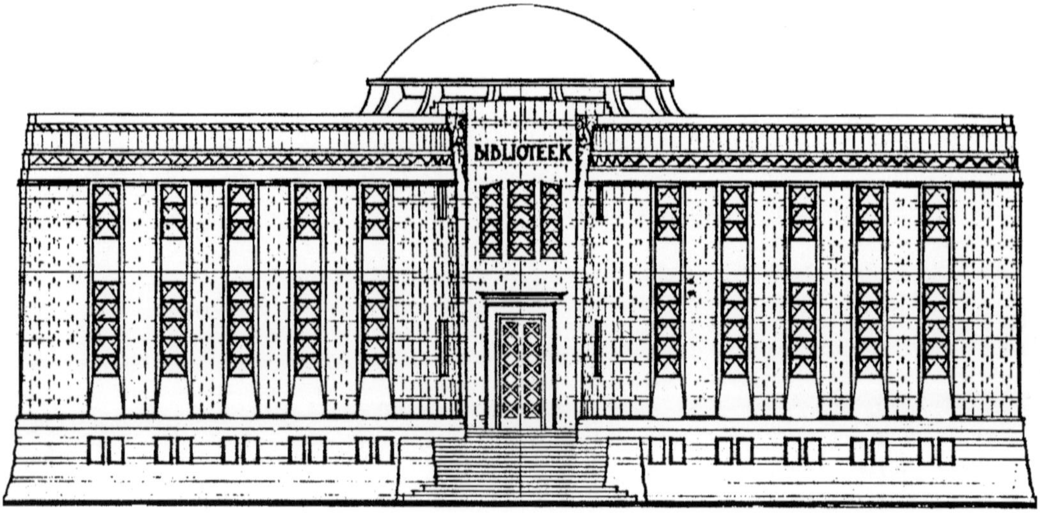

will be more immediately revealing about the people. Of course, even the term 'Afrikaner' is contentious, but in the setting of the University of Pretoria's early days we will take it to mean those who used Afrikaans as their language of preference and identified themselves with the cause of group identity and Afrikaner advancement in the institutions of state, church and academia.

E

2 Early nationalism

The idea for a Voortrekker monument on campus housing a library dedicated to Afrikaans literature had already been mooted in 1920, but lost momentum. The project was revived in 1934, and Moerdyk, who was probably instrumental in this, was given the commission. The Library was built by public subscription, and the main subscriber, the mining and forestry magnate Hans Merensky, lent it his name. The second-biggest donor was Pretoria's Jewish community, a fact Moerdyk acknowledged in the Star-of-David screens around the gallery. Ironically, Moerdyk's brother-in-law, Oswald Pirow, who served as Minister of Defence in the 1930s, was a staunch Nazi supporter and once proposed to buy bombers for the South African Air Force from Hitler.

The Library building foreshadows the Voortrekker Monument in many ways, both in form and materials. The grey granite exterior presents a very stolid appearance. The building is set back from the transverse axis of the campus, allowing for a view of its shallow saucer dome and for a gathering area in a forecourt. The battered walls create an illusion of greater height and lend a remarkable monumentality to a relatively small structure.

The entrance portico is pinched, more like the stoep of a traditional Boer house, but the interior is one of Moerdyk's more successful secular spaces, bilaterally symmetrical with ancillary rooms off a central domed area. A gallery at first-floor level is concealed behind screens, which fill the windows in the arches beneath the dome. Originally the ground floor had a central circular cut-out to the basement, and a Foucault pendulum swung from the dome and inscribed its path beneath. Like the oculus of the Voortrekker Monument, this gave the local a universal, even cosmic dimension. Unfortunately the pendulum has now been removed and the floor closed over. The invented Corinthian capitals of maize leaves and cobs provide a particularly local flavour. In spirit and motif the

Merensky Library, west elevation.

building relates more to the beaux-arts of art deco than to the modernist buildings then rising in the suburb of Brooklyn just down the road.

Moerdyk had received his first private commission in 1917 to design the Dutch Reformed Church in Bothaville, Orange Free State. More than eighty such commissions would follow, ranging from the Cape to Rhodesia (now Zimbabwe), and from South West Africa (now Namibia) to the Eastern Transvaal (now Mpumalanga). This gave Moerdyk the opportunity to foster an ecclesiastical style for the Afrikaans churches, an ambition reflected as early as 1919 in his privately published booklet on church design, *Kerkbou vir Suid-Afrika*. Interestingly, he eschewed overt symbolism in his churches, whereas his secular shrines to the volk and its accomplishments – the Merensky Library, the Voortrekker Monument, the Reserve Bank in Bloemfontein – are symbolically laden.

Moerdyk has been spurned by South African architectural history, a trend which started even before his death. His obituary in the *South African Architectural Record* was two lines long.[3]

3 Building in brick

The brick aesthetic has come to characterize the buildings of Pretoria and manifests in all its stylistic variants, from early Public Works Department projects of the South African Republic, through the prevalent modernist work, which shows the expressionist influences of the Amsterdam School, to the current polychromatic postmodern revivals.

For the Boer pioneers, fired-brick dwellings lay at the end of a long progression – from tented wagons and reed *scherms* (mere screens in the veld copied from indigenous example), to wattle and daub and stone masonry. Brick houses finally proclaimed that the newcomers were permanently settled and in possession of the land.

The Public Works Department originated the brick tradition in Pretoria. The Dutch architects imported by Kruger were well versed in brick architecture, as is demonstrated by such buildings as the Nederlandsche Bank on Church Square by Sytze Wopkes Wierda. Looking further back, the tradition and the institution of public works itself owe much to the Prussian state, and specifically to the architect Karl Friedrich Schinkel.

In 1826 Schinkel visited Britain, where the novel construction of industrial buildings astonished him, especially the use of brick on a monumental scale. Industrialization had seemed to him to threaten the very existence of architecture as the art of building within society. He had dreamed of founding a new modern architecture, and now saw that brick was more than a mere aid to regions poor in building-stone. He came to see that, on both aesthetic and structural grounds, it could fulfil the demands of the architecture of the time better than any other building material. By turning to brick, Schinkel showed the way to a modern architecture developed from the direct use of materials, and made brick for public commissions respectable.

John Kirkness, a Scottish immigrant, established himself in Pretoria in 1887 and started his brick-works on the southern side of Muckleneuk Hill. At any one time, the works had a million bricks and half a million decorative elements in production. Buildings as far south as Groote Schuur Hospital in Cape Town and as far north as the Post Office in Harare (then Salisbury) were built of Kirkness bricks and the name was once synonymous with the product. The diversity of bricks produced encouraged the use of prefabricated elements for embellishment and decorative innovation, and contributed greatly to the evolution of the tradition.

Without being fanciful, we might speculate that the material fitted comfortably within a Protestant ethos. It is plain material and it makes for honest expression. It is inexpensive and easy to come by, and its inherent geometry resonates with a severe, unfussy functionalism. In times of frugality it has served the regionalist practitioner well. In the years after the Second World War, over-fired and malformed bricks, which would otherwise have been discarded as useless, were taken up by cash-strapped builders looking to cut costs and the rough-brick, 'clinker' aesthetic even became fashionable.

The full stylistic range of Pretoria's brick architecture is represented on campus: the Agriculture Faculty building of the 1920s is a Cape Dutch revival by James Bowman Dey, a Baker school architect of the Public Works Department; the Weather Bureau building of the 1930s is a Public Works variant of modernism in red-brick by the Bauhaus-trained émigré, W. H. Fleischmann; Moerdyk's Chemistry and Botany buildings of the late 1940s and early '50s were inspired by Dudok and probably influenced by his employment of Dutch draughtsmen after the Second World War; the Theology Faculty of the early 1950s, the first deliberately retrospective styling of a building on campus, is by Burg and Lodge; and the Economic Sciences Faculty building is a postmodern block by Samuel Pauw.

E

The Department of Physical Education was established in 1946, when post-war shortages were still imposing restrictions on materials. The architects of the Physical Education building were Meiring and Naudé with Burg Lodge and Burg – the number of consulting architects was indicative of the shortage of commissions at the time – and the designer was Basil South.

Initially the brief included a swimming pool and changing-rooms, but these were omitted from the final contract. What was built was a simple, clearly articulated brown-yellow face-brick shed with an iron roof. Corrugated iron was in short supply because of the war, and its use attests to the prestige of the project. Although it has been insensitively altered, the core of the building is still there in all its simplicity: a monopitch roof cantilevered over high northern lighting, easily articulated junctions, standard steel windows. This architecture was almost idiomatic in the Pretoria of the 1950s and '60s, in domestic, commercial and retail structures. It created on an exaggerated scale a homogeneous place of brick-and-iron buildings with rural temperaments, alas now fast disappearing.

South, who studied with the leading lights of the Transvaal Group, became a studio master and teacher at the Pretoria School of Architecture. He did not have his own practice and worked in association with colleagues. The Hillcrest High School, done under the auspices of Vivian Rees-Poole's office, can be attributed to him. He designed stage sets for local repertory companies, and this made him particularly sensitive to the effects of light in architecture. This can be seen in his articulation of façades, modelled for sun control in emulation of South American architects like Niemeyer. Forms, shapes and groupings were handled in accordance with Hambidge's 'Dynamic Symmetry'.[4] South impressed these principles upon receptive students such as Karel Jooste and Gawie Fagan.

Basil South for Meiring and Naudé with Burg Lodge and Burg, Old Physical Education Block, 1948, north elevation and detail of north-east corner.

2

Karel Jooste at Philip Nel Architects, The Aula, south elevation under construction, c. 1957

4 Monumental modernism

In 1929, after it had been decided that the education of architects would in future be entrusted to the universities rather than the technical colleges, courses in Architecture and Quantity Surveying were introduced at the Transvaal University College in Pretoria, with H. Bell-John as head of department. Soon afterwards it was mutually agreed that the Transvaal University College would award qualifications in Quantity Surveying and the University of the Witwatersrand those in Architecture, although the courses were offered on both campuses.

This arrangement was terminated in 1943 with the establishment of the Pretoria School of Architecture at the University of Pretoria. The School's first graduates qualified in 1948, the year the National Party came to power. Wynand Smit was one of the first graduates to become a part-time studio master at the School. Another early graduate who subsequently taught was Karel Jooste, and he was followed by two of his partners, Carl (Gus) Gerneke and Anton du Toit. Other noteworthy early tutors were Gordon McIntosh, Norman Eaton, Helmut Stauch and Robert Cole Bowen. McIntosh was prominent in the Transvaal Group and one of the original protagonists of the Modern Movement with Rex Martienssen and Bernard Cooke.[5]

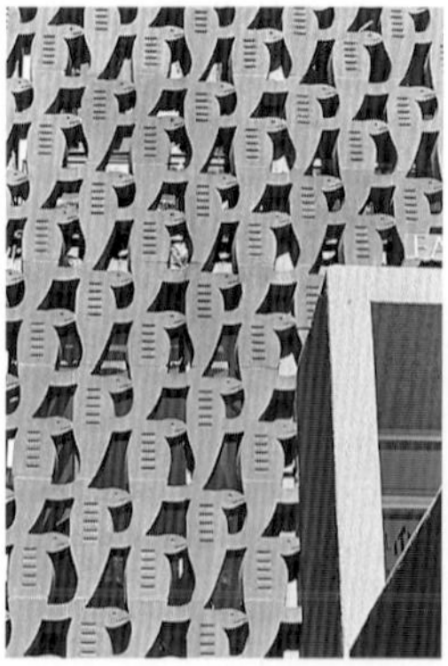

Meiring and Naudé, Heavy Machinery Building, 1959.

Under the tuition of a largely English-speaking teaching corps the Pretoria School developed a strong, pragmatic identity. Two common factors seem to have characterized the teachers: they were all South Africans born and bred, with strong rural ties; and many had felt the formative influence of the Public Works Department.

Cole Bowen, for instance, a functionalist but creative designer who worked with a clear and simple rationale, had been employed in the Department, designing a good Dudok-influenced building for the Krugersdorp Post Office. He introduced an adventurous and somewhat less academic strain of thought into the School.[6] He taught the design of an economical courtyard house, for instance, using excellent examples from his own work, and advocated accuracy based on detailed anthropometric data – sizes for furniture and sanitary fittings, the sizes of folded sheets for linen cupboards, the minimum height required to hang a long evening dress.

E

In the year the Pretoria School was founded, the Museum of Modern Art in New York staged the 'Brazil Builds' exhibition. This exhibition moved modern architecture out of the preserve of the privileged and into the public realm and established it as an expression of newly independent statehood, exemplified in Brasilia and Chandigarh. The book *Brazil Builds* was to post-war students in Pretoria what *Vers une Architecture* had been to Martienssen's generation in Johannesburg, and in the years to come its influence left an enduring mark on the architecture of Pretoria. Nikolaus Pevsner later called Johannesburg 'a little Brazil',[7] but the description may have suited Pretoria even better.

The transatlantic influence was soon felt on the campus. The shortage of sheet-iron during the war years had encouraged experimentation with roofs of formed concrete, and this developed a confidence in the use of the material.[8] The skills of engineers and builders were tested to the limit by daring concrete inventions – ribbon stairs, pioneered by the Roberto brothers in Rio's Santos Dumont Airport (and tried out on penguins in London), along with hyperbolic, folded or saddle-curved canopies and roofs. The first free-standing ribbon stair in South Africa (now demolished) was tacked on to the outside of the Aula on the University of Pretoria campus.

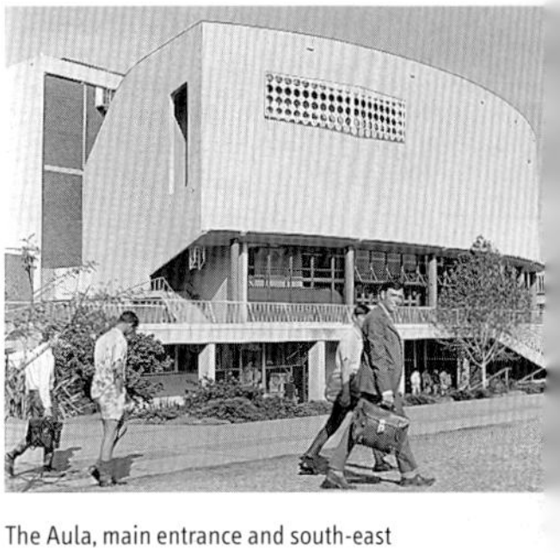

The Aula, main entrance and south-east elevation.

The idea of building a hall to celebrate the 1938 centenary of the Great Trek, like the idea for the Merensky Library, was first mooted in 1920. The '*gedenksaal*', or memorial hall, was back on the agenda in 1929, and there was talk of a 'Hall of One Thousand' on the campus in 1935, but the Library was the only project that came to fruition. However, a Voortrekker Hall designed by Eaton's mentor Gordon Leith was built in the city. It is appropriate that Karel Jooste, who continued the Leith-Eaton lineage, should have designed the Aula.

Although the project was initiated in 1951, the hall was finally built between 1956 and 1958. Had it been built immediately, the Aula might well have been the first monumental modernist building in the country, ahead of Stauch's Meat Board Building. The university authorities certainly succeeded in creating a prestigious cultural centre, and the Aula remained the major venue in the city until the State Theatre was completed in the early 1980s.

The auditorium remains the type of the Moderns, adhering to the 'form follows function' injunction and yet showing great structural daring, with the precarious balancing of large masses on slender pilotis. The huge mass of the Aula hovers above the Rautenbach Student Hall below, an effect emphasized by the transparency of large sliding glass doors on the western and eastern walls.

The concrete is béton brut, and its use in the main foyer was novel and adventurous for its time. Finish and structure are articulated as distinct, with the waved ceilings floating between exposed concrete ribs. Stairs are cut free of the supporting floors to emphasize their structural independence. In the Student Hall the young architect took his greatest liberties – the sculpted free-form cut-out concrete screen, the concrete lectern, the wedge-shaped ancillary screen to the dais. The sliding doors are part of the repertoire which distinguished the Pretoria School – an innovative exploitation of ordinary off-the-shelf industrial materials. In a remote corner is the most offbeat device, Georgian wire glass set directly into the jagged edge of a random-rubble wall.

The Aula is a building in the round, showing its structural muscle, clearly identifying its functional spaces. It has weathered both the elements and the vagaries of architectural taste well; its worst enemy has been the university itself with insensitive demolitions and additions.

Jooste was one of the early students of the Pretoria School, obtaining his diploma in 1947 and his degree in 1953. He undertook various study tours to Europe and briefly met Le Corbusier in the year before his death. As a student Jooste worked in the office of his mentor Norman Eaton, and this relationship made him the natural heir to that strain of architecture that could be termed Pretoria Regionalism, whose major proponent was Eaton.

Jooste established a practice in Pretoria in 1957, and his associates and partners included Gus Gerneke, Willem Steyn, Francois Viljoen, Anton du Toit, George Wilsenach and Johan Malherbe. His oeuvre comprises private houses, hospitals, banks and public buildings, but much of it remains relatively unknown because of its remoteness – some of his largest commissions were rural hospitals – and because the firm eschewed publication of their work or the use of architect's board, believing that good architecture is its own advertisement. The Aula was his earliest work, produced under the auspices of the architectural firm Philip Nel even before he graduated, and remains his crowning achievement.

5 New Brutalism

While the Smithsons and Paul Rudolph visited South Africa and left their mark on its architecture, New Brutalism arrived at the University of Pretoria through Brian Sandrock. Sandrock had been active on the campus since 1956, when he added a wing to the second Mathematics and Sciences building, using face brick in a reserved Dutch Modern style. Eventually he would dominate the campus, just as he dominated the southern gateway to the city with his building for the University of South Africa, with projects that were ever larger and more stolid, culminating in the New Humanities tower block of 1973, which bestrides Roper Street between the old and new campuses.

As chief architect to the university, Sandrock's idiom prevailed even when other firms were commissioned, for instance, the New Merensky Library on the old campus and the Faculty of Law on the new campus, west and east of Sandrock's tower block, which are both by Tectura, the heirs to Norman Eaton's practice. Sandrock's involvement in the Atomic Energy Board complex at Pelindaba seems to have nurtured a fascination with the plasticity of concrete and a confidence about its engineering, which he explored on the campus even when it was not a functional requirement. His buildings are daringly engineered: the concrete façade of the Administration Building is suspended on rubber hangers, the floors of the Engineering tower are suspended from central service towers on cables, the New Humanities building rises off an enormous concrete bridge podium. Yet the planning is uninspired and often bad, and spatial qualities are ignored – except in the Administration Building.

Brian Sandrock, Administration Building, 1968, main entrance and rectorate with cantilevered pergola.

It was Sandrock who recommended that the new Administration Building be located in the far south-western corner of the campus, in an area known to students as 'Die Gat' ('The Hole'). It was thought at first that the Loftus Versveld rugby stadium would be relocated and the campus expanded to the west, which would have placed the new building at the centre of the enlarged campus, but later it became clear that expansion would happen to the east instead. Nevertheless, the site was retained, on the grounds that it would make the building readily accessible to the public.

The site elicited a delta-form plan, with a windowless 'prow' projecting out towards the junctions of Lynnwood and University Roads. Through the heart of the delta a double-volume hall rises, where students conduct their administrative affairs. This is light, with finely-detailed counters and fittings, and rough-hewn quartzite floor tiling – one of Sandrock's more successful spatial inventions (and possibly a tribute to Alwyn Burger, then head of the School of Architecture, who was project architect). A spiral stair coils up at the prow, grandly conceived but lost in the tight space, leading up into the remote and sombre halls of the rectorate. The whole speaks of another time and another order.

The office accommodation soon proved inadequate as the bureaucracy burgeoned, and the office wing was extended to the east, compounding the labyrinthine extent of passages. The northern façade shows the concern with sun penetration, which is a trade mark of Pretoria architecture: deep-set windows with brise-soleil devices, in this case a set of suspended horizontal louvres. In the south the banded windows are flush with the façade and take the corner to emphasize the structural daring of suspended concrete spandrel bands.

As with most buildings in this climate conducive to lush growth, the starkness of the block has been softened by trees, shrubs and creepers. But it still declares its status, announcing that design and control have captured even a remote corner of the campus that was once little more than a dumping site.

Sandrock was a pragmatic man not given to symbolism, as his bas-relief in the Administration Building demonstrates. Although a competition had already been arranged to find an artist for this work, the architect eventually designed a decorative device himself. The story goes that he arrived at the design late one night while trying to retrieve an insect from the plaster-of-Paris presentation model. The massive concrete wall on the western side, structurally suspended on rubber brackets, forms an acoustic shield for noise from the railway line across the road: functionality on a monumental scale.

Brian Sandrock, Administration Building,
University of Pretoria, 1968.
Photograph by David Goldblatt.

Despite Sandrock's distinct lack of iconographic intent, his buildings attract nicknames. The Administration Building is 'Die Skip' because of its distinctive ship-like prow. The New Humanities tower is 'Die Konsertina' and the student hostels are 'Die Kaasraspers' ('The Cheese-graters'). The University of South Africa building, dramatically cantilevered from Muckleneuk ridge on a single foot, is called 'The Singer Sewing Machine'.

Sandrock was a large, shy man. He worked as a part-time lecturer in his younger days, when the School was still in the city centre, and some recall that he would cross the street if he saw a student approaching. Yet he inspired confidence in his clients, especially those relatively anonymous corporate bodies of universities and boards, with his efficient management of projects and budgets. The obituaries described him as enigmatic, and the reason why he received so many enormous commissions remains obscure. We do know how he first came to work with the Pretoria University authorities: Samuel Pauw, a young architectural student in his office, whose father was then rector of the University of South Africa, made the introductions.

6 Postmodernism and the Romanesque revival

What was the first postmodern project in Pretoria? Was it Bannie Britz's Sterland cinema complex? Louis Peens's De Bruyn's Park? Perhaps that garish roadhouse by the Frame brothers called The Crack? The question is still open to debate. But there is no doubt that postmodernism was given official sanction by the new headquarters building of the Human Sciences Research Council in Schoeman Street in central Pretoria. The project architect was Samuel Pauw, who had earlier designed the innovative Volkskas headquarters tower. It was Pauw, and young associates like Piet de Beer, freshly returned from postgraduate studies in New York, who brought postmodernism to the University of Pretoria campus in the late 1980s.

In those years the university approached Pauw to design a new building for the Faculty of Economic Sciences, then the fastest-growing and largest faculty on campus. The brief was simple: give us another assertive humanities building in the Sandrock mould. Style and size had been predetermined, all that was needed was some fine-tuning on the specifics.

It took Pauw three months to persuade the faculty, and another nine the university, that what was needed was a building that would create a feeling of unity and campus life. By scaling down an imposing tower to a three-storey office block, placed along the walkway that traverses the eastern campus, Pauw created a background building with three courts, each belonging to one of the divisions of the faculty.

The building reverts to the brick tradition, although the bricks are of cement rather than clay and are used polychromatically; the windows are standard steel sections regularly arranged, the only peculiarity being the staggered square configuration taken through the inner corners of the forecourts. In true postmodern style, elements are exaggerated and mannered – the squat, round-arched arcade on the ground floor seems sunken beneath the weight of the architecture. The scale – the human, the elements to the whole, the whole to its surroundings – is excellently judged. The building has created an atmosphere of campus life on a once isolated extension. It has even managed to enliven the dead space between the new Humanities building and the Law Faculty.

In the lecture hall concrete is used more prominently, while the conference facility, planned as a baptistry with a monastic loggia, is a light-hearted indulgence.

Pauw graduated from the Pretoria School in 1961. His Masters thesis was a critical reappraisal of Le Corbusier. Pauw approaches the postmodern as a liberation from modernist functionalism and an opportunity to recover the humanizing aspects of style, especially those manifest in eclectic pre-modern buildings. His design for the Economic Sciences Complex was a chance to concretize these thoughts on postmodernism. He turned a blind eye to the New Brutalism which dominates the campus and, instead, sought inspiration in those buildings where aspects of a Romanesque revival find a precedent – the old Arts building, Moerdyk's club building on the central campus, and the monastery which adjoins the site and now belongs to the university.

Ancient echoes

In his writings on church style, Moerdyk argued against the neo-Gothic as an appropriate style for the Afrikaans church. He associated this style with the cold northern countries, and found the architecture of southern Europe more suitable to South Africa's climate. He thus made a case for a Romanesque revival to suit the requirements of Afrikaner Calvinism. Something in the Afrikaner psyche seems drawn to early Christian culture. While Romanesque architecture may appear remote from the African present, strangely even more removed from us than the time of classical Rome, it is contemporary with the culture of Mapungubwe, which too seems more ancient than it really is. For some, perhaps, an association with distant times and ancient traditions holds out the promise of permanence.

◄D3 ◄D4 ►E3

Samuel Pauw, Economic and Management Sciences Building, 1988.

3

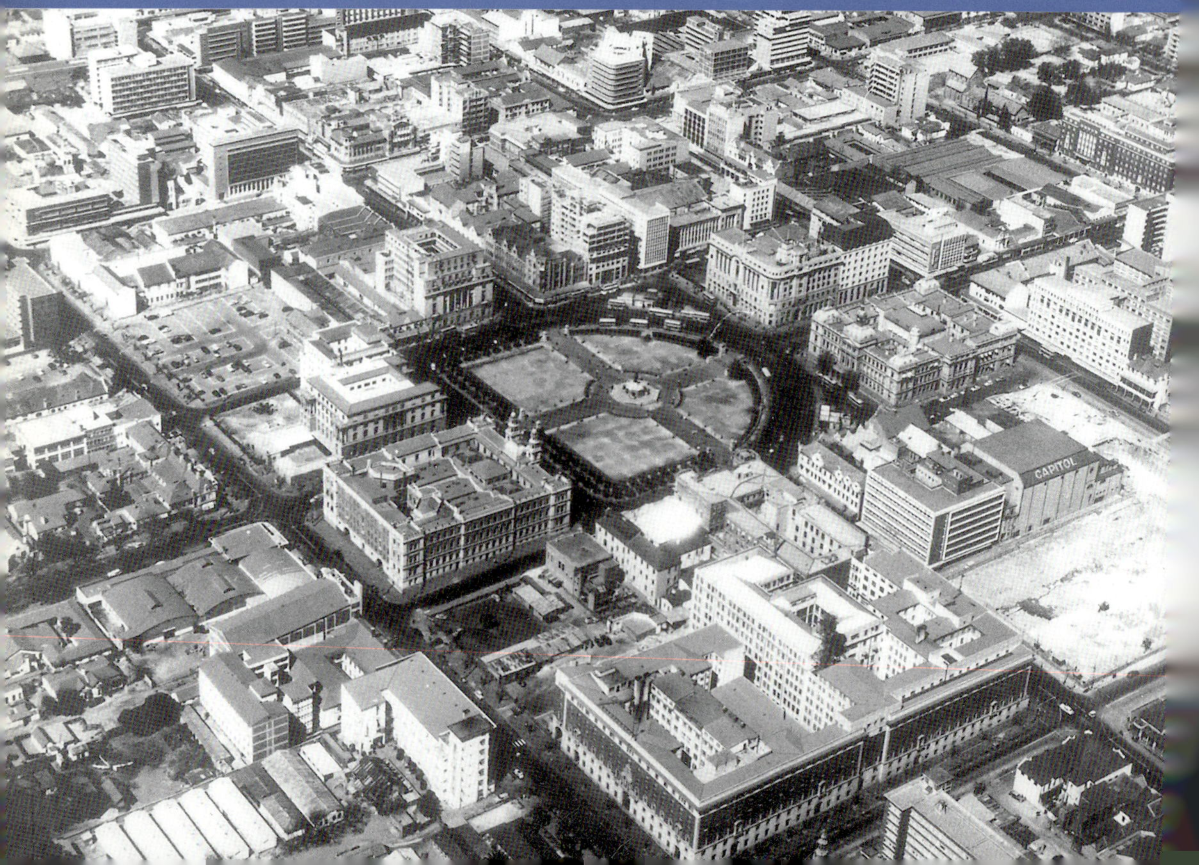

Does size matter? The apartheid state's powers of penetration
Deborah Posel

At the time of Union in 1910, the entire South African (central) state fitted into the Union Buildings in Pretoria. By 1970, the business of governing from the centre had expanded and diversified to the extent that it had taken over scores of buildings, many of them huge, sprawling structures. A glance at a map of the Pretoria city centre in the mid-1970s suggests that more than a third of the buildings were occupied by state departments. The physical expansion of central government predated the National Party's accession to power in 1948, but the architects of apartheid developed their own distinctive enthusiasm for the process. New architectural conventions and aspirations in building the offices of government were closely related to new imaginings of the powers and scope of the apartheid state. 'Imbued with the ethos of modernity and renewal',[1] the graduates of Pretoria University's School of Architecture enjoyed 'enormous commissions for enormous complexes',[2] as the construction of new offices of government both facilitated and signified the rapidly expanding orbit of an increasingly ambitious new state. But visions of power, especially when overblown, seldom coincide with the more complex realities of its exercise. During the apartheid years, the state got bigger – much bigger – yet there is no simple correspondence between its size and its powers of penetration in the wider society. This essay looks at the changing character of the central civil service after 1948, focusing on the paradoxical relationship between overreaching aspirations to power and declining bureaucratic competence within the apartheid state.

E

The transition to apartheid: New versions of modern statecraft

South Africa's first nationally unified state was created in 1910 with the Act of Union. No sooner was this state established than it started to grow. Between 1910 and 1920, the number of state departments ballooned by 75 per cent, from 12 to 21. By 1940 it had increased further to 24.[3] This process of bureaucratic expansion was closely bound up with changing notions of statecraft – the modes of political reasoning about the responsibilities, powers and entitlements properly claimed by the state. Early political traditions which favoured a strong degree of the decentralization of power to local authorities (both urban and rural) were challenged by visions of a more unified, integrated national state, making for more effective central planning and coordination in the exercise of political power. These ideas were not unique to South Africa. Since the Depression of 1929-32, with Keynesian arguments about the need to use political measures to correct market failures having gained in popularity and influence, many Western states had taken to the idea of national economic and social planning as a major responsibility and prerogative of the central state. These new versions of state power underpinned a variety of different political regimes, from the Nazi Third Reich to the liberal welfare state in Britain and other European countries. What they shared was a confidence in the capacities of a suitably empowered, rationally effective state to solve all manner of social problems. It was a bold and ambitious version of the state, as the engine of modernity in bringing grand, visionary social change to fruition.[4]

By the 1940s, South Africa's (white) polity was also growing increasingly enthusiastic about the idea of a larger, more interventionist central state as the key to social and economic progress.

The most systematic and detailed exposition of this position was developed in the early 1940s by the government-appointed Social and Economic Planning Council, which devoted one of its reports to the state and its bureaucratic apparatuses. Reflecting on the developmental trajectory

Union Buildings, Pretoria, 1910.
Church Square, Pretoria, 1955.

of modern states, the Council declared that 'in the general interest the State is in growing measure impelled to assist, to guide, to regulate and to initiate'.[5] This in turn necessitated a larger, bureaucratically more effective and efficient state, with 'wider responsibilities ... and greater powers'.[6]

Little ensued from the Council's report, but by the 1948 election, calls for bold reforms to the central state echoed across the (white) political spectrum. Both major contenders in that election – the United Party and the Herenigde Nasionale Party (which became the National Party) – promised a new order of central social and economic planning, particularly in response to 'the native problem'. It is possible, therefore, that South Africa would have seen a larger, more assertive and ambitious state, with a bigger, more powerful civil service, whatever the outcome of the 1948 election. But the National Party, which emerged victorious, gave its own twist to the process, resulting in an expansion of the size and powers of the state on a much greater scale than in many other developing and developed states in the West. Once installed in government, leading Nationalist policy-makers harnessed broadly Keynesian notions of statecraft for their own particular and distinctive project of 'modernizing' racial domination. What differentiated and distinguished apartheid statecraft, in my view, was the opportunity to link a modernist confidence in the powers of the central state as an agent of large-scale social transformation with a more aggressive, thoroughgoing commitment to white supremacy, in a form compatible with the renewal of white economic prosperity. By re-imagining the capacities, scope and entitlements of the state along more 'modern' lines, it became possible in turn to imagine a society in which constructs of race became the all-embracing, ubiquitous basis of the social order fashioned by that state. The apartheid version of a modern state was one which was sufficiently large, powerful and centrally coordinated to keep every race in its 'proper' place, economically, politically, socially and culturally.

In this version of the proper role of the state, the discourse of planning developed a new-found prominence. Clearly, it behoved the state to represent its policy-making as the result of rational, systematic planning, with a comprehensive, integrated vision of how to solve the problems confronting the country. These representations of power attributed a greater degree of visionary control to the process of apartheid governance than was ever evident in practice. The routines of politics in apartheid South Africa always revealed a shifting combination of foresight and myopia, control and confusion. Still, the discursive repetition of the need for 'orderly planning' underscored the ambitions and confidence of a state which saw itself as the key to 'the new South Africa' (as the National Party called it in 1948). There was no 'problem' which could not be solved by a suitably big, powerful, well-informed state.

If the development of apartheid depended fundamentally on this rethinking and restructuring of the state, the ambitions of apartheid ideologues were also profoundly limited by their new state's capabilities. The expansion of the size and scope of the central state went hand in hand with the deteriorating capacities and skills of its bureaucratic personnel. Widening powers and responsibilities were being allocated to an increasingly less qualified or competent civil service. This is not to suggest that what emerged was a weak or wholly ineffectual state; apartheid was driven by a state which thrust itself increasingly into every sphere of life in the country. My point is rather that we need to think of power qualitatively as much as quantitatively, in order to recognize the spasms and lapses which coexisted with the harder, more sustained lunges. A full exploration of this unevenness would require a much longer study. This essay exposes some of it by tracking a few of the institutional, bureaucratic developments born of apartheid statecraft and then reflecting on their consequences for the exercise of power. (In the interests of brevity, the discussion focuses only on the central government departments; it excludes, along with provincial and local government, the governance of the Bantustans and self-governing homelands, which constituted another arm of the apartheid state. If these bureaucracies had been taken into account, the contradictions of power identified here would have been magnified.)

Bureaucratic bulk

Apartheid produced a stupendously long list of procedures and prohibitions, all of which required official surveillance. Unsurprisingly then, the most obvious feature of the state's development during the apartheid era was the unremitting proliferation of bureaucracy, or what the National Party proudly referred to as 'an abnormal growth under this Government in every sphere'.[7] The number of government departments increased, as did the size of their establishments. The Department of Native Affairs took the lead, rapidly transforming itself from a small, under-resourced department into the vanguard of apartheid policy-making; by the mid-1950s an increase in the size and number of state bureaucracies was evident across the board. There seem to be no reliable measures of this expansion within the civil service in particular,[8] but statistics for the growth of the public service[9] more generally give an indication of a trend which was mirrored (if not in identical proportions) in the civil service more narrowly. According to data compiled by the Public Services Commission, in 1939 the public service had employed a total of 57,000 people of all races in permanent positions. This number rose to 110,000 by 1950, and then to 139,000 by the end of 1958: an increase of 144 per cent in twenty years.[10] This expansion surged ahead throughout the 1960s and '70s, albeit at proportionately lower rates. By 1967, the number of permanent appointees in the public service had grown to 212,788[11], a substantial increase of 53 per cent over the 1958 figure.[12]

Many thousands of people working in state departments, however, were temporary appointees. Taking their numbers into account produces a picture of even greater bureaucratic obesity. Again I have not been able to find appropriate breakdowns of the statistics for the civil service (those staffing central government departments) alone, but figures for the public service as a whole give a good indication of the relevant trends. According to one set of measures,[13] a total staff establishment of 140,042 in 1930 had doubled by 1950, swelling by a further 62 per cent to 454,692 in 1960 and then rising again by 21 per cent to 549,865 in 1970.[14]

At the same time, the number of government departments steadily increased. On the eve of the National Party's political takeover, there were 26 government departments; by 1970, this figure had risen to 41.[15]

Afrikanerization

The transformation of the state under apartheid included a commitment to colonizing the state for the Afrikaner volk, in ways which seriously undermined the modernist logic of bureaucratic rationality. With the energetic help of the Afrikaner Broederbond (a secret think-tank at the heart of the Afrikaner nationalist movement), the National Party introduced what amounted to a tacit policy of affirmative action for white Afrikaners. Afrikaners were actively recruited for positions of influence in as many social, political and economic organizations as possible. The colonization of the state was perhaps the most important part of this strategy. English-speakers who were already civil servants, and especially those in powerful or prominent positions, were discouraged or more forcibly prevented from holding office. And Afrikaans-speakers formed a growing proportion of new appointees.[16]

Once again the Department of Native Affairs was the trailblazer, replacing officials considered 'liberal' with more pliable, loyal Afrikaner nationalists.[17] But this trend soon became a very conspicuous and controversial feature of the state as a whole. By 1959, 'Afrikanerization' had advanced to such an extent that out of more than forty government departments and sub-departments, only six had English-speaking heads. The 'last bastion' of English-speakers was then alleged to be the financial specialist departments: Treasury, Inland Revenue, Customs and Excise. Yet even here, there were moves to evict English-speakers. The experience of a Mr Paige, Collector of Customs and Excise in Durban, who was forced to take premature retirement at the age of 55, was not uncommon. No official reasons were given to him, other than that his retirement was in the interests of 'organizational reforms', commonly understood as a euphemism for the Afrikanerization programme.[18] By 1974, English-speakers accounted for only 20 per cent of senior staff in government departments,[19] and the proportion had fallen even lower by 1976, when only 7 of these 146 posts were held by people with English surnames.[20]

Shrinking capacity

One of the more bizarre features of the apartheid state was that it continued to expand the size of its bureaucratic establishment in the midst of serious shortages of personnel. It was not altogether a problem of apartheid's making: staff shortages were inherited from the previous regime. In 1944, the President of the Public Servants Association (the principal staff association representing white public servants generally, including civil servants) had 'issued a serious warning that things are going from bad to worse in the Public Service and the number of resignations is increasing ... Public servants are leaving the Service.' As a result, he went on, 'the supply of labour for other than purely routine work is not equal to the demand'.[21] However, it seems that the National Party's ambitious plans for expanding the state had been launched without any thought being given to this problem of poor bureaucratic capacity. And the strategy of Afrikanerization exacerbated the problem profoundly, as the available labour supply fell far short of the escalating demand.

The problem of staff shortages, which had been discussed within the civil service itself since the 1940s, became a regular item in the English-speaking press from at least the late 1950s, with reports of increasingly serious shortcomings in the state's capacity to function effectively. By 1961, staff shortages in the Department of Inland Revenue and the Auditor-General's office were already considered 'critical'[22] by the incumbents themselves. In 1962, the annual Conference of (government) Department Heads devoted itself exclusively to discussing the 'serious shortage of qualified personnel'.[23] By 1965, staff shortages were reportedly 'crippling' across the board.[24] Many government departments complained of further deterioriation since 1963, when one out of every five permanent state posts had been unfilled.[25]

But still the state continued to swell, as the ambitions of apartheid's policy-makers reached new heights. In 1966 alone, 11,000 new posts were added to the establishment, despite the fact that only 6,305 people joined the service in that year and 5,557 resigned.[26] By 1968, the situation was so bad that the Public Servants Association issued one of many public warnings about the 'total dislocation and disintegration of the service' due to disastrous staff shortages. Some departments were now understaffed by up to 60 per cent.[27] And attempts to investigate the full extent of the problem were themselves 'held up by staff shortages'![28]

The Public Servants Association was especially concerned about shortages in more senior positions, the minimum requirement for which was a matriculation exemption, that is, a pass in the final year of secondary schooling qualifying a student to enter university. 'The present trickle of matric recruits, let alone graduates',[29] they said, made for 'alarming' gaps in the higher ranks of the bureaucracy, while also inhibiting the prospects for officials appointed at lower levels, without the requisite educational qualifications, to rise up through the ranks to fill these positions.

If all of this was already old news in some bureaucratic circles, the full import of the disclosures did not yet sink in. With the Public Services Commission (the body responsible for staff recruitment in the state) defensively inclined to underplay the seriousness of the problem, it was only in the late 1960s that parliament suddenly woke up to the fact that there was a staffing crisis. In 1968, the opposition United Party called for an immediate probe into conditions in the civil service, noting the serious staff shortages and a 'virtual collapse of administration in many spheres'.[30] The following year, a parliamentary Select Committee produced 'shattering revelations of staff shortages' in many important branches of the civil service. The Financial Institutional Division of the Treasury (controlling all financial institutions, such as banks, building societies and insurance companies) was reported to be on the verge of collapse because 'there are simply no people to do the work'.[31] A similar situation was reported in the Department of Inland Revenues, Agriculture and Labour.[32]

There were several reasons for this staffing crisis. A matriculation was the minimum requirement for permanent graded posts in the civil service. But the matriculation rate amongst Afrikaners was still relatively low. English-speakers, on the other hand, were increasingly unlikely to consider a career in the civil service, having been alienated by the National Party's Afrikanerization programme. Also, the 1960s was a period of unprecedented economic expansion for the country. Given that job reservation policies were still largely in place, white people with any hint of talent or experience were bound to find far more lucrative jobs in the private sector than in the civil service. As one personnel manager in the motor industry put it, 'Any genuine white worker who presented himself at your gate and ... hadn't been to prison for six or seven months in the last two years, you said, "Okay, give him a try. He's white." So that you didn't actively kick whites out.'[33]

With the private sector draining most of the white labour pool, the 1960s saw uncomfortably high rates of resignation from the public service generally and the civil service in particular. By 1964, the attrition rate from the public service was measured at 3,158 resignations for the year, which amounted to 8.8 per cent of the establishment.[34] Between 1956 and 1964, a total of 22,106 public servants resigned.[35] In 1967, almost as many people resigned as were hired, an overall resignation rate of 10.3 per cent of the establishment.[36]

In 1968, Prime Minister B. J. Vorster made a rather feeble effort to deter what he called an 'alarming number of resignations' from public service, by appointing a special committee of inquiry[37], but it had little effect. In 1970 civil servants tried to galvanize the government into confronting the personnel shortages head-on by calling for a 'scientific investigation to be instituted as early as possible' to assess the full extent of the problem and suggest appropriate solutions[38], also with little success. Shortages persisted and resignations continued to accelerate, rising to 14 per cent by 1970.[39] In 1975, more people left the public service than joined, despite the fact that the size of the establishment grew by up to 20 per cent in some of its divisions.[40]

'Factory rejects'

The combination of a bloated state, increasingly ambitious in its efforts at social engineering, and worsening staff shortages had devastating effects on overall levels of competence and efficiency in central state departments. Once again this was a problem with a much longer historical trajectory. During the early 1940s, the Public Servants Association was already anxious about 'mediocrity' in the public service.[41] But inefficiency and low productivity plunged to new depths after 1948, and particularly after 1960, as the Afrikanerization drive grew more aggressive.

All South Africans are familiar with the local genre of jokes about 'Van der Merwe', a stereotypically boorish, incompetent, ill-educated, intolerant, crudely racist white Afrikaner whose sensibilities are out of tune with a modern urban way of life. But few are aware that these jokes originated as a caricature of the new breed of apartheid official.[42] This idea of Van der Merwe as the bureaucratic buffoon already had wide currency by the mid-1960s, the perception of an incompetent civil service having impressed itself vividly on white social consciousness.[43] By 1964, bureaucrats themselves were speaking openly about 'the rot in the personnel structure' of the civil service, and calling on the government to face the problem directly.[44] But, true to form, nothing was done and the situation continued to deteriorate. In 1967, with opposition politicians clamouring for an official inquiry into incompetence in the civil service, the characteristically defensive Nationalist government conceded 'it is true that there [are] lazy and inefficient public servants'.[45] However, politicians were also keenly aware that tackling the problem might undercut the strategies of political patronage behind the Afrikanerization drive. For example, in 1967, Secretary for Transport, Mr. Danie Joubert, admitted that there were many in civil service posts for which they were wholly unqualified, including in his own department. But incompetence was a small price to pay for political loyalty and racial pride, he declared:

> What would happen if you gave them their walking tickets? They would be thrust out in a hard commercial world with which they would not be able to cope. These officials invariably have wives and children, where at present they had their self-respect and the children can thrust back

E

Marais Viljoen - Gebou /

George Wilsenach for Richter Wilsenach Bloem Architects, The Accident Provident Fund Building, Pretoria, 1978. Photograph by David Goldblatt.

their shoulders at school because their father is employed. Maybe the salary paid to the father is higher than his service warrants, but at least it is helping to bring up children who may one day be good South Africans.[46]

The full extent of the incompetence problem emerged publicly two years later, after an internal government investigation in 1969, which found that about 50 per cent of officials in the public service had held four or more jobs outside the service before entering it. As the author of the report put it, 'In view of the more advantageous working conditions that apply in the private sector, the question inevitably arises whether many of these people, figuratively speaking, are not "factory rejects" who were not competent to make a living in the more competitive labour field outside the public service.'[47] The Auditor-General made a similar point: 'In the past, the public service only accepted the better matriculants; but today we grab anyone, no matter what his attainments are.'[48]

The lack of adequate expertise and training reached farcical proportions in the civil service's legal posts. Repeated complaints had surfaced during the 1960s about a dearth of suitably qualified legal staff. A worsening problem given the rapid rate at which the apartheid state sought to proliferate legislation and regulations during this period. This led to the appointment of people to legal positions without the appropriate skills, on the understanding that they would register full-time for a B.Juris-degree (an undergraduate training in law, offered at Afrikaans universities), drawing full salaries while studying. Yet by 1976, only 153 out of 653 posts for legal assistants were filled by officials with anything resembling the desired qualifications. It seems that in this year alone, 250 out of the 675 officials doing the B.Juris- were withdrawn from the degree because of 'unsatisfactory progress'. Nevertheless, being full-time appointees of the civil service, they kept their jobs as legal officials![49]

The effects of job reservation on the staffing crisis were highly ironic. Intent on protecting privileged spheres of employment for whites, the apartheid state had created its own labour shortage problem. On the one hand, whites were streaming into better-paid jobs in the private sector with little competition from blacks; on the other hand, the very same job reservation policies prevented the state from training black people in sufficiently large numbers for the civil service positions which the available white labour supply was too small to fill.

Staff shortages were so severe that efforts to keep the civil service white could not fully succeed, and blacks made substantial inroads into the civil service during the 1960s. White women also came to feature more prominently in the bureaucracy.[50] But there were very definite limits on the work prospects of both blacks and white women in the civil service, which continued to see itself as a bastion for white males. So, when the Secretary for the Interior told the annual conference of departmental heads that the civil service was 'losing its backbone', what he had in mind was the mounting absence of 'promising, productive men in the middle grades'.[51] Or, as a Mr. Van der Merwe of the Transvaal Provincial Administration put it, 'Where are the people going to come from to fill the senior posts in future if the civil service cannot appoint and keep young men?'[52] It went without saying that such men would be white.

As the economic boom faded and a recession set in, the many problems facing the civil service did not ease. In fact, in many respects they continued to worsen. As a senior bureaucrat remarked, 'All the time the service is responsible for providing more and more services as the country expands, but the loss of staff is constantly getting worse'.[53] By 1976, the public service reported a turnover of more than 50 per cent of its staff in only three years.[54]

Although a sense of crisis was expressed in some bureaucratic circles as early as 1961, very little was done to face the problem before the late 1970s,[55] when P. W. Botha took office as Prime Minister. The organized business community had begun wielding its political muscle by the mid-1970s, which included posing a series of embarrassingly public and probing questions about the ailing, bloated state bureaucracy. P. W. Botha tried in some ways to take the problem in hand, producing a plan for the 'rationalization' of the public service. Alwyn Schlebusch, newly appointed Minister of the Interior, announced the need for a 'thorough-going reorganization' of the civil service in particular, which had proved itself 'incapable' of providing the necessary 'manpower requirements under present conditions'.[56] The number of government departments was progressively reduced, from 39 to 22. Botha also saw to the creation of the rank of Director-General, a new 'super-managerial' position to replace that of Departmental Secretary, with salary and perks designed to compete favourably with the private sector, although the salary scales and benefits were never made public.[57] In keeping with Botha's new-found infatuation with the business community, the position of Director-General was intended to woo new talent into the civil service from the private sector.

Botha's interventions revealed occasional flashes of insight into the need for a complete overhaul of the civil service, including new modes of management. But he failed to grapple with the root of the problem, which went well beyond the realm of senior management. Indeed, Botha's strategy can be read as more of a political manoeuvre to marginalize right-wing opposition within the civil service than a comprehensive programme of rationalization and restructuring. The civil service had become one of the strongholds of Afrikaner reactionaries resistant to the reformist agenda. The enormousness of the apartheid bureaucracy gave senior officials potentially lethal powers to block the reformists' plans. By the late 1970s, after decades of being indulged by the National Party's patronage, the rump of the civil service was simply too big and comfortably entrenched for Botha to have undertaken major bureaucratic reforms without running the risk of alienating a large chunk of electoral support among civil servants. However, his 'rationalization' drive did create an opportunity to reconfigure power relations in the top echelons of the civil service[58] – a more limited intervention but with less political fallout. Some senior bureaucrats considered obstructionist thus found their authority superseded by newly appointed Directors-General drawn from outside the civil service, while compliant Secretaries could be rewarded with internal promotions to the same position. Moreover, in the name of 'rationalization', the scope of the Prime Minister's own office was greatly enlarged. All 'planning functions' were now reallocated there, giving Botha autocratic powers within both state bureaucracies and the Cabinet.[59]

E

Apartheid's bureaucratic absurdities ensured that the civil service continued to grow, all in the name of 'rationalization'.[60] Indeed, the Public Services Commission, in rather cryptic vein, reassured civil servants that their numbers would continue to increase: 'This is inevitable in any increasingly industrialising country ... But the rationalisation process will definitely lead to a smaller increase in the long run.'[61] With 'the long run' a long way off, the problem of staff shortages also still loomed large. In 1980, even the Public Services Commission, traditionally cautious and defensive about admitting to problems in its sphere, conceded that 'the already grave personnel situation in ... the civil service [had] deteriorated even further'.[62] By 1981, civil servants were speaking openly about 'the near collapse of the civil service',[63] which was facing the most severe staff shortage in its history.

Cabinet Minister Dr. Piet Koornhof offended civil servants deeply when he compared the civil service to a tortoise: if you leave it alone, he said, it will proceed at its own pace but if you push it, it will stop dead.[64] But in the reptilian scheme of things, the more profound description of the apartheid civil service came from United Party MP Marais Steyn in 1968, when he likened it to 'a dinosaur with a massive body and small brain'.[65]

The question of power

So: does size matter? How do we make sense of the powers of a state which grew inordinately large and ambitious, despite being populated by vast numbers of what insiders themselves called 'factory rejects'? How do we make sense of a state which reached what some see as the zenith of its powers in the late 1960s, in the midst of a widely perceived crisis in the competence and productivity of its bureaucracy, especially at senior levels, a crisis which in fact never abated until the final collapse?

The size of the apartheid state was simultaneously a source of immense strength and the root of serious weaknesses. The sheer bulk of apartheid bureaucracies enabled the state to penetrate far more deeply and powerfully into the lives of its citizens than had ever been possible before. The apartheid years saw the proliferation of a wide range of bureaucratically routinized modes of surveillance directed at an increasing number of people and spheres of life. This was the state which classified almost the entire population according to a set of officially designated racial categories, and then infiltrated every other aspect of people's encounters with the state, and indeed their social interactions more broadly. This was the state which could raid townships across the country in the early hours of the morning to snatch any 'illegals' into waiting police vans; which could forcibly remove nearly three and a half million people to officially demarcated tracts of barren land; which could create networks of informers to infiltrate any vaguely suspect political or community organization; which could expose and humiliate men and women engaged in sex 'across the colour bar'; which could create a countrywide labyrinth of labour bureaux in a bid to 'canalize' African labour from areas of 'surplus' to areas of 'shortage'; which could compile voluminous statistics on the numbers of 'registered work-seekers' compared to the number of service contracts signed in any one month.

And yet in other respects, the growth of the state paradoxically undermined its aspirations to power. The grandiosity of these ambitions led directly to the dilution of the state's bureaucratic capacity, spreading diminishing expertise increasingly thinly. As the scope and scale of state regulation expanded, so the chances of ever being able to police all of these prohibitions decreased. As a result, all of the surveillance was at best spasmodic. The number of 'illegals' ensnared by the state was always a fraction of the numbers of people who flouted the law. Also, labour markets never yielded to politically configured models of economic rationality. Although the state achieved the power to smash organized resistance movements, 'informal resistance' to apartheid laws never abated and contributed to the eventual crumbling of some of the pillars of the system.[66] With large, if unknown, numbers of people in breach of the law evading detection and arrest, the quest for the sort of comprehensive knowledge required to exert the grandiose control imagined by the architects of apartheid was also flawed. Heaps of statistics copiously compiled by a range of bureaucratic divisions and subdivisions were widely known to be perpetually incomplete and unreliable.

There were significant lapses of surveillance within the state too. For example, the Auditor-General's office, responsible for ensuring the authorized expenditure of state funds, was one of the first departments to experience serious staff shortages. The Afrikanerization drive caused a dramatic haemorrhage of expertise from the early 1960s onwards, creating anxieties that the department could not fulfil its functions effectively, and things only got worse during the course of the decade. By 1969, the Auditor-General felt compelled to write of his 'growing concern that the spending of money voted by Parliament and the control over stores and equipment are not being efficiently handled to an increasing extent'.[67] The problem of corruption in the apartheid state requires a study in its own right, but it is easy to see how the problem could have flourished as a direct consequence of limited bureaucratic capacity.

If the way in which the apartheid bureaucracy grew tended to undermine the capacity for internal scrutiny, it offered its leading bureaucrats and politicians powers of internal discipline by other means, which may in turn have nurtured the possibility of corruption. The National Party's efforts to reconstitute the civil service as a site of sheltered employment for white Afrikaners were born of a politics of patronage. Masterminded by the Broederbond, whose members infiltrated most if not all of the top positions in the political and administrative arms of government, this strategy allowed the National Party to reconfigure the civil service as a stronghold of party political support. In respect of these motives, the problems of inefficiency and incompetence within the bureaucracy offered compensatory political rewards. If the civil service employed people whose job prospects in the private sector were minimal, then their loyalty and obedience to their patrons were likely to be more secure as a consequence. And if such compliance was not spontaneously forthcoming, then the Broederbond's networks in the civil service made for more intimidating disciplinary techniques. These powers of clientelism became somewhat more tenuous from the late 1970s onwards, once a new cadre of National Party leaders tried to change direction against the political grain of much of the bureaucracy. But the tradition of patronage had long since robbed civil servants of the organizational or ideological wherewithal to rebel.[68]

In short, the rapacious expansionism of the apartheid state was shot through with contradictions. While this state was typically modern in many of its aspirations, there were significant lapses and breaches in its capacities to function along these lines. With dwindling bureaucratic expertise, particularly in the senior echelons of the civil service, the capacities for 'rational, orderly planning' were at best fractured and uneven. The lapses in rationality and foresight were compounded as the state got bigger: the greater the number of parts, the more patchy the expertise, and the more difficult it was to coordinate an effectively functioning whole.

◄D3 ◄D4 ◄E2

4

The great apartheid building boom: The transformation of Johannesburg in the 1960s

Clive Chipkin

E

Monty Sack: plan for Johannesburg Central Business District, c. 1971.

Johannesburg's architecture, like its political economy, has always responded directly to cycles in the world market.[1]

The Share Boom of 1895 transformed what had been a mining camp on a remote and treeless plateau into a sprawling urban conglomeration complete with man-made woodlands – the 'stronghold of capitalism', as Colquhoun characterized it in 1906.[2]

In the 1930s another period of intensified growth occurred as a result of the dramatic rise in the price of gold in the midst of a world depression. This wave of prosperity converted Johannesburg into a little New York with corridor streets of art deco buildings and, by 1938, five real skyscrapers, the highest modern buildings on the African continent. The most prestigious of these, Escom House at 21 storeys and Anstey's building at 17, established the benchmark for the city's verticality until well into the 1960s.

There was growth again after the Second World War. This building expansion, more an upsurge interrupted by shortages than a continuous boom, produced the facile modernity of Hillbrow, the so-called Hillbrow vernacular much admired by the architectural historian Nikolaus Pevsner during his 1952 visit.

These are major precedents for the great apartheid building boom of 1962 to 1972, which once again transformed Johannesburg out of all recognition and left the uncritical talking of 'a golden age of prosperity'.

Sharpeville and the 'economic miracle'

On 21 March 1960, in a little-known black location 75 kilometres south of Johannesburg, the police fired on a peaceful crowd protesting against the carrying of passes. By South African standards the Sharpeville massacre was hardly an unusual event. Over the years, successive governments had crushed rebellion, protests and strikes, on occasion employing tanks, artillery and even aircraft. But the shots that rang out at Sharpeville were heard around the world.

For several days afterwards the authorities appeared to be in a state of shock. Then, as one observer noted, it slowly dawned on them 'that they really had nothing serious to fear, that with determination all opposition outside Parliament might be crushed absolutely, perhaps for all time'.[3] Or so it seemed then. Sharpeville ushered in a period of triumphalism on the one hand and political quietism on the other that was to last until the next serious challenge to government authority erupted in 1976.

For the country at large, the economic consequence of Sharpeville was a major crisis in business and investment confidence that led to massive outflows of capital and a critical fall in the gold reserves. The government responded with draconian measures, imposing exchange control and pushing ahead with its Bantustan policy. By 1962 the economic situation had been dramatically reversed, resulting in vast inflows of overseas capital and a spectacular real growth rate, which reached 9 per cent per annum in 1963.[4] The South African 'economic miracle', which was to last for a decade, was under way.

At the end of 1966, *Fortune* magazine quoted an American businessman in his Johannesburg office: 'This is the only real industrial complex south of Milan.'[5] In the following year the London *Financial Times* noted 'the country's confidence and near invulnerability'. Despite South Africa's isolation, this report noted, 'the Government has thrown itself into the task of building up a self-sufficiency which can defy the world'.[6] The flood of foreign capital sustained the investment surge from 1963 into the early 1970s, when cheap fossil fuels were still in plentiful supply at under $3 a barrel. The result was a 'fast money' economy that culminated in the heady days of the apartheid share boom, which lasted from around January 1968 to December 1970. During this period the morning newspapers contained a rash of advertisements, extending over several full pages, detailing share portfolios and directors' addresses in the northern suburbs for new listings on the Johannesburg Stock Exchange.

Street placards proclaimed: 'FRENZY IN JSE' ... 'NOG MILJOENE KOM BEURS TOE' – 'MILLIONS MORE FOR THE EXCHANGE' ... alongside 'NEW BREAD SHOCKS' and 'PUTCO BUS FARES RISE'. On a Sunday in 1969 Beeld's headline read: 'NET ONGELOOFLIK' – 'JUST UNBELIEVABLE'.

City of towers

New listings, new acquisitions, new mergers indicated large-scale structural changes taking place in the South African economy and an increasing concentration of economic power in the hands of giant financial conglomerates, now inspired by a new breed of decisive managers, including the first sprinkling of graduates from the Harvard Business School. A new generation filled with American taste, youthful gusto and a sense of modernity, as well as an infatuation with sheer size. All these qualities were waiting to find architectural expression. It is not surprising, therefore, that some in this new generation were easily persuaded to look overseas for their architects, turning not, as the older generation had done, to major London practices like Burnet Tait and Lorne, but to the up-to-date technical wizardry of Skidmore Owings and Merrill of New York, Helmut Hentrich of Düsseldorf and Marco Zanuso of Milan.

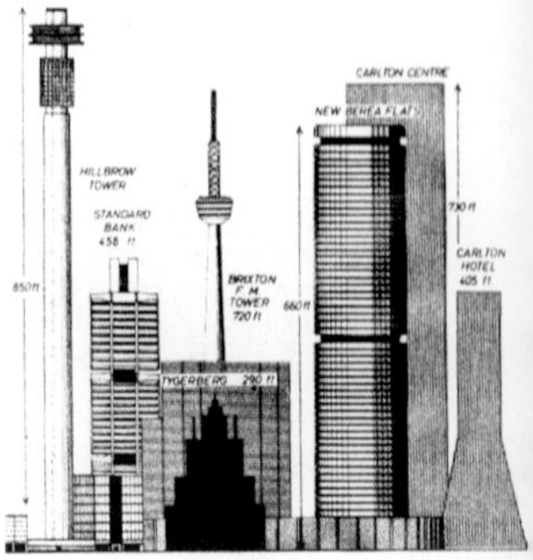

Johannesburg city towers, 1968.

A new sense of bigness in the economy was soon reflected in the new scale of the architecture: new tower blocks in the central business district, massive residential buildings, a new radio tower in Hillbrow, the new Johannesburg Hospital on the Parktown ridge and vast enterprises, including a new campus for the Rand Afrikaans University on Johannesburg's western periphery.

From 1966 onwards the South African architectural press carried amazing photo-montages of proposed new tower blocks superimposed on the existing townscape, images portending a quantum leap in building size as financial institutions, awash with cash, invested in city-centre building. J. G. Ward, a perceptive observer of the time, said in 1972: 'There is no doubt that the rash of Stock Exchange flotations between 1968 and 1969 gave rise to an epidemic of new buildings. With a high fever and loaded with money, the developers lowered their heads and charged straight into the building of new offices on an unprecedented scale.'[7]

The Johannesburg Central Business District (CBD) was dislocated by this vast rebuilding programme. As the city rebuilt, massive Edwardian buildings came down, revealing for the last time their skeletal steel frames with mill-imprints from Dorman Long's works at Middlesborough or, in the case of the old Carlton Hotel, from the Bürbacker Hütte Werke, Saarbrücken.

Visitors looking for old landmarks could not recognize downtown with the ubiquitous tower cranes amongst the debris and dust of frenzied construction, the tearing up of streets for new sewers and water reticulation and electrical cables, or the crescendo of roaring compressors and pounding pneumatic drills and the percussion of Kanga hammers and concrete vibrators. The shudder of blasting at the larger developments caused teacups to rattle on their trays three or four blocks away. At night the floodlights of the night shifts at the Carlton Centre site were visible high above the old rooftops, while interminable eddies of cement dust from sandblasting of concrete surfaces settled like beach sand on distant pavements.

Under the new town-planning codes, as the foremost town planner of the day Professor Wilfred Mallows explained, building bulk, the permitted size of a building, could now be expressed vertically. This is the origin of Johannesburg of the 1970s as a city of competing towers, a growth that swamped the visual predominance of the 1930s skyscrapers, which had once been the highest buildings in Africa and were now reduced to insignificance.

Carlton Centre

In a single decade, sixty tower blocks rose above the 1938 benchmark. The Carlton Centre, at more than 200 metres in height, established clear predominance, the highest reinforced-concrete building in the world. To the west of the Carlton Centre cluster was the spectacular and elegant Standard

Skidmore Owings and Merrill with Rhodes-Harrison Hoffe and Partners, Carlton Centre, Johannesburg, 1968 and 1973.
Photographs by David Goldblatt.

E

Bank Centre point block. Mallows wrote approvingly: 'Now at last it was possible to build in Johannesburg on the scale appropriate to a metropolis ... There for all to see, Johannesburg had finally broken the constraints of the diggers' camp and achieved a new image: the image of a city of a million people.'[8]

The physical dimensions of the Carlton Centre speak for themselves. There are five principal elements on a site covering four city blocks, with the intermediate cross streets closed to create pedestrian space. In descending order of scale, these elements are the office tower rising fifty floors above the piazza; the 31-storey, 600-room hotel; a detached lower cube accommodating a major department store; an underground shopping arcade; and a parkade with exhibition space. The building components are located around open civic space, the so-called 'plaza' of American inner-city precedent, a term used in several of Johannesburg's developments, although it never took root.

The architects were Skidmore Owings and Merrill of New York working in conjunction with Rhodes-Harrison Hoffe and Partners of Johannesburg. By the end of the 1950s, SOM had come to be regarded as the most sophisticated, most technically proficient architects of their era. Gordon Bunshaft, the design partner in the 1950s and '60s, had in his formative years come under the influence of Le Corbusier's *Vers une Architecture*. But the younger partners had inherited modern architecture in a less didactic way, 'as sculptural form without knowing it as an agency of social reform'.[9]

By 1962, SOM had completed Chase Manhattan Bank – sixty floors straight up, flat-topped, ribbed with external columns faced in Vermont marble – a single giant cube that helped create the imagery of corporate America with its complex spatial needs for labyrinthine committees and vast specialist staff. SOM's architecture, based on detailing that attained a 'standard of near perfection', produced buildings that exuded confidence and what has been called 'opulent simplicity'.

The firm's design for the Carlton Centre represented a major transfer of technology and culture from New York to Johannesburg. Robin Fee was working on large projects in SOM's New York office when the Carlton Centre was on the boards.[10] He returned to Johannesburg in 1967 to become project architect on the centre, joining Rhodes-Harrison Hoffe and Partners. In 1991, Fee described the Carlton Centre as 'a breakthrough of momentous proportions'. He was still captivated by the 'romantic heroics – of which tall buildings can be the epitome'.[11]

The question arises: Why New York? Why SOM? Why did the Anglo-American Corporation, one of the principals of the Carlton Centre, make the major shift from the London office of Burnet Tait and Lorne – the firm that designed the corporation's headquarters at 44 and 45 Main Street in the 1930s and '40s respectively – to the New York office of SOM? When I asked this question of Harry Oppenheimer, former chairman of Anglo-American, he replied that skyscrapers were the architectural fashion of the time. Anglo-American looked to the 'leading architects in the Western world... we felt the best experience was in America'.[12] In this casual way the cultural hegemony of the United States was acknowledged.

Wilfred Mallows was no more forthcoming. Mallows, with his Cambridge tripos behind him and his Architectural Association background, together with his younger colleague Julian Beinart, the leading planning theorist of the 1960s, was responsible for re-zoning inner-city terrain in preparation for a giant leap forward that would take the breath away. Yet Mallows seems to have shown very little interest in the form of the buildings. Harry Gottlieb, he said, engineered the project. In fact, Mallows the Town Planner never moved without Gottlieb the Land Developer.[13] Apparently the design team was chosen from a list of architects of world standing. SOM were appointed for the Carlton Centre and Hentrich of Düsseldorf for the Standard Bank Centre.

Such answers only go some way towards explaining the sociology behind these bids for modernity. Nor do they reveal what the rulers of the *ancien régime* and the dictators of the 20th century alike discovered; that power is expressed not so much by single buildings and monuments as by giant ensembles.[14]

Commercial architects and real-estate developers do not generally see themselves as the 'ideologists of society'[15], but simply as men and women making a living by implementing practical proposals. But even they must admit they have prototypes in mind for their buildings; models with which to buttress their own proposals. The models the Johannesburg developers drew on were recently completed New York buildings, specifically Chase Manhattan and the Seagram Building. These were elegant steel skeletal forms. Gordon Bunshaft had commented on their structure in this way: 'In contrast to the foreign use of reinforced concrete we employ steel framing as a basic structural system for most urban buildings.'[16]

Here lies a paradox. Why look to trabeated steel-framed buildings as your model when the native tradition in Johannesburg was reinforced concrete, and had been at least since the 1920s and '30s? In the Edwardian period, Johannesburg had used imported steel skeletal construction, but from the 1920s onwards this fell into disuse as the country embarked upon import-substitution, using local materials wherever possible. Of all Johannesburg's new high-rise buildings only one, the Trust Bank, a 33-storey Miesian replication on its own plaza, was built with structural steelwork, and even here the core was in reinforced concrete which had to be disguised by the enveloping window wall.[17]

Concrete plasticity on the scale of the Carlton Centre is a very different matter to steel precision. This change in material brought out the latent Corbusian elements in SOM's design philosophy and recreated in Johannesburg a transmuted vision of Le Corbusier's Ville Radieuse, in tune, perhaps, with the city's own Le Corbusier tradition made resident through Rex Martienssen's contacts with 35 rue de Sèvres in the 1930s. In place of Miesian steelwork we therefore have Corbusian béton brut, raw concrete poured in situ and sandblasted to expose the rough, coarse aggregate, creating cliff faces of reconstructed stone.

At the Carlton Centre, the dramatic play of prismatic forms is given unity by the overwhelming presence of raw concrete. Office block, hotel, department store; vertical tower, slab block, cube; all flat-topped with secondary shapes; piazza with oculus to make the lower levels visible; exhibition space backdrop with interweaving helical parking ramps.

Le Corbusier's ideas come to mind continually; from Algiers, from the Unité d'Habitation blocks; from the art gallery planned for Tokyo as recently as 1957, but based on long-standing ideas; even memories of Plan Voisin de Paris (1922) or of Saint-Dié (1945). This is SOM's version of the Ville Contemporaine, divorced from social theory and adapted for commercial use. From the city as a collectivity to the city of private real estate. The Ville Radieuse reinterpreted for the market economy.

Standard Bank Centre

Strategically situated in the financial district, the Standard Bank Centre is a single, dramatic tower block on its own piazza in a largely Edwardian and post-Edwardian context. This is the work of Helmut Hentrich, with Stucke Harrison Ritchie and Partners of Johannesburg responsible for coordination and administration. Work commenced in 1967 and was completed in 1970. The brief requested a prestige headquarters building of national and international status. The solution was a tower block 137 metres tall and occupying only a quarter of the site.

Four central service cores built with sliding formwork and clad in white marble; massive haunched cantilever brackets which project nearly fourteen metres from the cores; structural hangers suspended from the brackets to support the individual floor slabs with perimeter beams, an assembly of pre-stressed components raised and anchored to in situ work in order to transmit the highly complex building loads to the foundations. This, and a minimum of finishes, is the architectural language of this elegant tower, where engineering, bridge-building technology and architectural expression are integrated into a single architectural statement.

The clients wanted a special building; like the developers of the Carlton Centre they went overseas for the latest ideas, and what they got was a technological wonder to put Johannesburg in 1970 on the world map. But it must be noted that the next time Standard Bank built on a large scale in

Johannesburg, it was not a high-rise point block with perimeter office space only, but three vast low-rise, deep-space, low-energy superblocks at the south end of the CBD.

Sanlamsentrum

Sanlamsentrum, situated four blocks north of the Carlton cluster, is another product of the high-rise era of the 1960s and '70s. It marks the entry of what Dan O'Meara has called volkskapitalisme – the mobilization of capital in the interests of Afrikaner advancement and unity – into a commanding position in the CBD.[18] Sanlam, a life assurance giant, emerged in 1917 from the era of 'poor whites' and sought to advance Afrikaner interests initially in agriculture and later in commerce. The company's expressive motto was 'Uit die volk gebore om die volk te dien' – 'Born of the people to

Standard Bank Centre under construction, 1968.

serve the people'. Even at the time of Sharpeville, Sanlam was so self-confident that it 'was one of the few buyers of equities then'.[19] By the 1960s the company was a financial powerhouse.

The building is a single massive tower block set back from the Jeppe Street frontage on its own windswept piazza, another dubious gift of space to the city made possible by the adoption of New York planning standards. A sunken garden introduces greenery to the site. White marble-clad verticals, separated by black anodized window strips, rise straight up without interruption. A commanding presence to challenge the financial clout of the Carlton and Standard Bank centres.

The architecture is part of an alternative modern skyscraper tradition derived from New York's Daily News Building (1929) and Rockefeller Center (1931). This tradition was brought to Johannesburg in the 1930s, and persists in the Escom Centre (1954) and the Sanlamsentrum (1978). The architects are Rinaldi MacDonald and Crosby, the same practice that had earlier designed the headquarters for Escom, the electricity parastatal, in Braamfontein.

Motorways and the 'potential of the periphery'

The elevated freeway that sweeps around central Johannesburg on its western, southern and eastern perimeters was conceived in the mid-1950s by American consultants in order to exploit the 'potential of the periphery' (to use the subtitle of a paper written some ten years later by Mallows and Beinart).[20] As Mallows foresaw, the creation of a southern gateway to the central city would augment the northern street filters and have the exquisite effect of inverting the existing traffic flow from the wealthy northern suburbs.

The basic geometric constraints were the work of the City Engineers' Department, while detailed structural designs were carried out by teams of civil consultants. Construction began in the 1960s on the Braamfontein overpass sections of the M1, as it was designated, continued southwards, juxtaposed against mine-dumps, and culminated over undermined ground and urban clutter in the south-east with the magnificent sweep of the steel viaduct labelled 'Bridge 6' on the Heidelberg interchange. It is this great flexible overpass, designed to cope with random ground movements, that Shirley Zar has characterized as 'a giant adjustable meccano set'.[21]

An unexpected problem arose in the use of terminology. W. Pryce-Rosser, the Deputy City Engineer and an English purist, objected to the American term 'freeway', and on his insistence it was replaced by the more pedestrian 'motorway': 'The tracers had the unenviable task of painstakingly erasing the word freeway wherever it occurred on the dozens of drawings churned out by the design teams.'[22]

The advent of the motorways resulted in new growth points and 'changed totally work-home-shopping relationships'.[23] Far-flung hypermarkets and gigantic shopping malls like Eastgate and Sandton City were the progeny of the motorways. In addition, the southern entry into the CBD produced new growth points in the city itself, 'opening up the undeveloped southern tract of defunct mining land' and resulting in a southern ring of office tower blocks such as Penmore Towers (1974) and, later, Nedbank corporate headquarters (1987).

The motorways also enabled the corporate headquarters of public companies to begin the migration to the urban peripheries. This process began in 1973 when the Edgars retail clothing chain commissioned Marco Zanuso of Milan to design Edgardale, their new national headquarters, at a site in Crown Mines, now made accessible by the new M2 West. In 1976 Barlow Rand began work on the company's new corporate headquarters at Barlow Park, designed by Rinaldi MacDonald for a semi-rural site in Sandton made accessible by the new M1 North.

In *The Home of Man* Le Corbusier had envisaged city ground given over to the pedestrian while cars rolled along on elevated routes five metres above.[24] In *La Ville Radieuse*, his 1933 projection of a machine-age civilization, there is a principal high-rise edifice 150 metres tall alongside secondary low-rise cubes. By 1972, bits and pieces of this vision had materialized in Johannesburg: a high-rise tower of more than 200 metres on a site given over to the pedestrian; an elevated freeway around the city's perimeter; office parks on the urban periphery. But, unexpectedly, these were not components of a utopian 'radiant city', but of a new social phenomenon: the Apartheid City.

Broederbond wedge

Since before the turn of the century and continuing well into the 1930s, Johannesburg's western urban periphery was a refuge for the rural poor moving in from the platteland, now held together in their urban dorpies by grievances and small parish churches.[25] The spires of these churches, often perched on rocky koppies like relics of medieval townscapes, are still visible by the dozen in areas like Paarlshoop, Mayfair West, Brixton, Vrededorp, Cottesloe and Melville.

The extension of this cultural preserve into Auckland Park, a mainly residential suburb served by Kingsway, with its monarchal English ring, and scattered with Thames-side street names from

Opening of the Brixton Tower, 14 September 1962.

Henley to Cookham, seems a logical development. Certainly it must have appeared so to the Broederbond, who in the 1960s picked a 32-acre site on Henley Road to create a major cultural presence in the country's largely anglophone financial centre.

South African Broadcasting Corporation

The South African Broadcasting Corporation (SABC) complex was the first of the major architectural statements of Broederbond provenance. The architects were Brandt Snyman Spruyt and Crafford of Pretoria, a practice relatively unknown in Johannesburg. Planning began in 1966 and by 1968 reports were appearing about the proposed new tower block for the SABC in Auckland Park.[26] The building work took place between 1968 and 1975, the heyday of state triumphalism. There is a podiumgebou consisting of parking and promenade, a studio building for radio (the advisability of television was then still a point of debate in government circles) and an administration building, a huge folded slab with 36 levels above ground and three below. The latter seems to be influenced by European models like the Phönix-Rheinrohr building (1960) by Hentrich, whose name was already well known in South Africa, and perhaps also by the dominating presence of the Pirelli tower in Milan (1960), which is of a similar scale and prominence.

The architects have described their building in functional terms, explaining how it met the broadcaster's various requirements. Nevertheless, it makes an unavoidable political statement, rising up in splendid isolation. The details, the external tiling and aluminium fins, emphasize verticality. The glazed split tiles on the blank end faces have deeply recessed joints to emphasize their vertical thrust. Visible on Brixton ridge above is the pinnacle of the Hertzog FM radio tower (1961), once the tallest structure in South Africa. Together, these two towers, like the news bulletins and propaganda commentaries masquerading as 'current affairs' reports beamed out daily from this site, proclaim the message of government political and cultural hegemony in the age of apartheid.

E

Die Eike

In 1968, the year the SABC's administration tower was under construction, H.J. Klopper, in a celebratory speech on the fiftieth anniversary of the Broederbond, reminded his listeners that the organization had given the country its governments and every one of its prime ministers since 1948.

> Do you realise what a powerful force is gathered here tonight between these four walls? Show me a greater power on the whole continent of Africa! Show me a greater power anywhere, even in your so-called civilised countries ... We are part of the State, we are part of the Church, we are part of every big movement that has been born of the nation. And we make our contribution unseen; we carried them through to the point that our nation has reached today.[27]

The point reached in Johannesburg was a series of projects in Auckland Park and its environs to house institutions dominated by the Broederbond. Besides the SABC there was the Rand Afrikaans University (RAU), Goudstad Onderwyserskollege (teachers training college) and the J.G. Strijdom teaching hospital. Nearby lay the headquarters of Perskor, the great newspaper empire, and the building known as 'Die Eike', if not the nerve centre then the major administrative facility for the Broederbond. In time, the overspill from these institutions would create the lively café society of Melville with its distinctive Afrikaans linguistic milieu.

Die Eike is situated opposite the SABC complex in the neighbouring suburb of Richmond. An office building, it is strategically placed near the entrance to the Johannesburg Country Club, that archetypal English institution, and was designed specifically to house the administration of the Broederbond and other affiliated bodies, including the national student association and an umbrella body representing more than two thousand cultural organizations. The architects were H. Taljaard Carter and Partners and the commission came from the Christiaan de Wet Fonds. The design dates from 1974.

E

Taljaard Carter and Partners, Die Eike,
Johannesburg, 1974.
Photograph by David Goldblatt.

This ideological centre is lost amongst the foliage of the adjacent country club and the older jacarandas and younger white stinkwood trees on the site. It is an inconspicuous administration block reflecting a partial béton brut brutalism of the 1960s, particularly in the street front of the Council Chamber, which is in skoonsigbeton – fairface concrete – seemingly able to withstand a rocket attack.[28]

The Christiaan de Wet Fonds was a powerful reserve fund initiated and controlled by the Broederbond. In 1977 total funds exceeded R2 million, including an amount of R655,000 shown in the balance sheet and designated 'office block, Die Eike (administrative headquarters)'.[29] In that same year the Broederbond was able to inform its members in a circular: 'Our office is now in the new building Die Eike, 1 Cedar Avenue, Auckland Park.'

Many senior figures in the Broederbond came to head key institutions. Dr. Pieter Meyer, chairman of the Broederbond, became chairman of the SABC. He was known as a man who liked to do things on a 'grandiose scale'. The scale of the SABC building programme, we presume, owed much to this impulse, as did the furnishing of the offices with South African paintings and antique pieces to create the appropriate cultural ambience.

Rand Afrikaans University

Professor Gerrit Viljoen, chairman of the Broederbond, was given the enviable task of planning and overseeing the building of a new Afrikaans university.

RAU was the most spectacular of the grand apartheid projects, built to a scale and with a self-confidence that reflects the unique conditions and opportunities in South Africa during the 1960s. Like the nearby SABC complex it was 'to be a manifestation of the Afrikaner's foothold in the big city'.[30] To lesser mortals, the budget seemed to be limitless. In reality, the cost of building a new campus from scratch was R500 million.[31] During the 'frenetic building operations served by 19 cranes', weekly certificates of around R3,5 million were issued over a three-year period.[32] The built area of the main buildings was 100,000 square metres, and of the student housing 30,000 square metres. The entire project was conceived and completed within five years.

The principal architect was Wilhelm Olaf Meyer. He was scarcely into his thirties, and working from a makeshift office in Parktown, when the phone rang one day in 1967 and a voice said: 'We are thinking of a new university in Johannesburg and it would most likely be in Auckland Park.'[33] This was the prelude to a three-hour meeting which ended with Meyer and the Pretoria architect, Jan van Wijk, receiving the appointment.

One imagines Meyer's ability to impress, to entrance his listeners with the semi-mystical, partly obscure, partly lucid manner of his mentor Louis Kahn and, at the same time produce rough, compact sketches to capture fleeting ideas. To speak of the 'highest aspirations' and of 'compelling visions in the impossible'. It is not surprising that in the profile of the practice for the period 1967 to 1978 there appears this fulsome dedication: 'An immeasurable debt, intermingled with an emotion of reverence, is also recorded towards our teacher, Louis Kahn.'[34]

What must Viljoen, the classical scholar with a political agenda, a member of the inner circle of the Broederbond, have thought of this young, unconventional visionary? Born in Pretoria in 1935, Meyer belonged to a new generation of Afrikaner intellectuals, groomed for big things. He came from a distinguished Afrikaner family: his father was Frederik Meyer, chairman of Iscor and a technocrat reputedly uninterested in the petty politics for which South Africa is renowned. The son was distinctly not a member of the Broederbond, nor even of the triumphant National Party; indeed, his political loyalty was in doubt, as there were rumours in the secret world of South African politics that he and his English-speaking wife were supporters of the opposition Progressive Party.

Meyer had been a brilliant student at the English-speaking University of the Witwatersrand before going on, via scholarships, to the Master Class of the University of Pennsylvania at Philadelphia under Kahn. One might have anticipated that one day Meyer would stand beside his mentor in that pantheon of 20th-century architects that contemporary razzmatazz has created ... if only South African

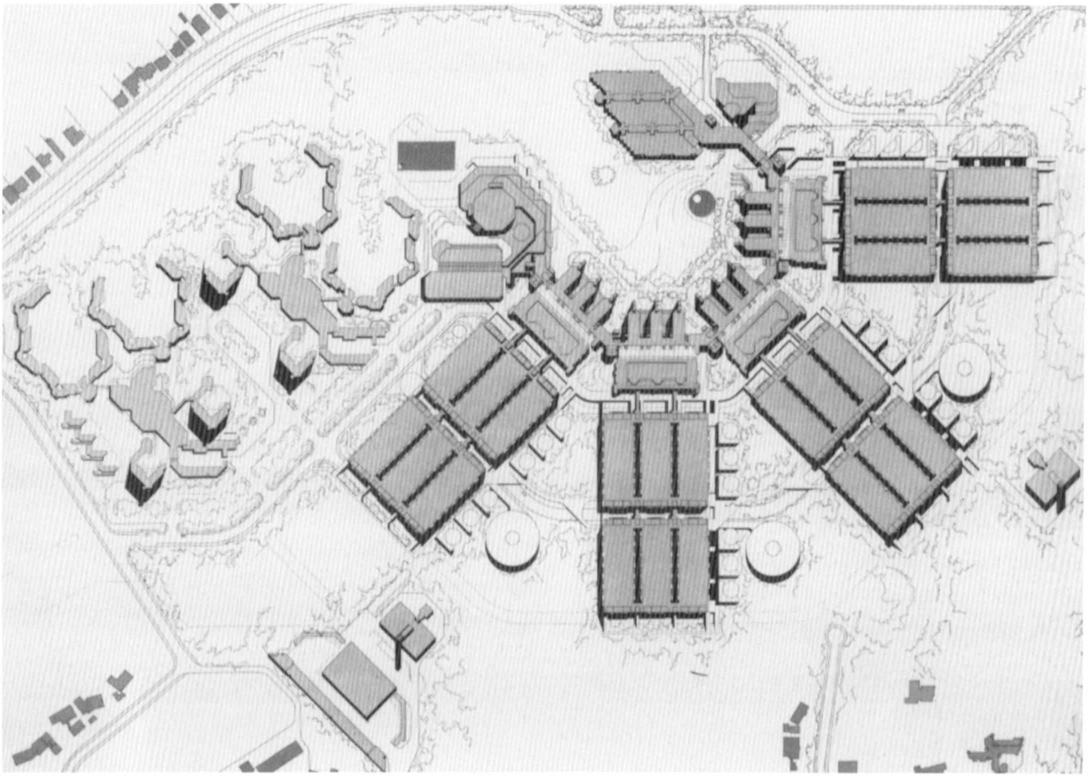

E

architecture had not become entrapped in the apartheid ghetto.

In any event, Meyer had secured the largest, most prestigious post-war commission available: to design an entire Cité Universitaire. The following year he was sent to inspect 35 new universities abroad.[35] Evidently the Afrikaner's 'foothold in the big city' had to equal, or surpass, the best in the world.

The university that resulted from this strange confluence is built around a startling inner landscape, a contoured hillside slope the size of Church Square in Pretoria, we are told.[36] This space is partly enclosed by radial faculty buildings with attached lecture theatres and laboratories behind. A multilevel pedestrian spine, conceived as a central movement gallery and designed with nooks and crannies to create interactive space, connects the separate faculty buildings, establishing a relatively compact pedestrian campus. The grandeur and public scale of the campus is a product of the monumental pylons; of the bare off-shutter concrete, where the post-tension cable studs provide decoration like triglyphs on classical architecture; and the spatial amplifications of the pedestrian galleries. The giant pylons and columns are, in fact, hollow service ducts or cores. Everything has a place and purpose in a brilliant intellectual synthesis.

In contrast to the public scale of the working campus, the adjacent student housing complex was 'conceived as a village' and built to a red-brick, domestic scale. The entire ensemble orchestrates a host of ideas to produce a Cité Universitaire of historic significance.

In retrospect, Meyer's words convey too little. A foothold, yes; a cultural bridgehead, definitely; but in the eyes of government ideologues more than that – a wedge driven into the urban defences of the anglophone stronghold of capitalism. The Rand Afrikaans University, the adjacent enclave in Auckland Park, the new Johannesburg Hospital dominating Parktown ridge, the towers in the city centre, the police barracks and interrogation centre at John Vorster Square, all these taken together could be valued not only for their utility but for their 'power to signify'.[37]

Willie Meyer with Jan van Wijk, Rand Afrikaans University, 1976.

Johannesburg Hospital

When the Johannesburg Hospital and the adjacent College of Education, both second-tier government projects, were built in Parktown, many of the large, historic houses of the old anglophone mining élite had to be demolished. The hospital itself was built on the site of Hohenheim, the first great house on the Parktown ridge, which by 1970 had been allowed to fall into disrepair.

The new academic hospital complex is a city within a city: there are five 400-bed hospitals, a medical school with science facilities, living quarters in three 17-storey blocks and two lower blocks, parking for 2,000 cars, and communal facilities including a bank, post office, library, dispensary, crèche, occupational therapy unit, and so on. A vast linear building 370 metres long, in two parallel blocks separated by an internal 'Hospital Street', it was implanted on the high ground above the northern suburbs, completely ignoring the pristine topography, leaving a huge, rectangular container beached on one of Johannesburg's principal ridges.

The architects were Colyn and Meiring in collaboration with Cowin De Bruyn and Cook. The building was a product mainly of the 1970s: planned in its essentials by 1971, it was under construction from 1972 to 1978 but only officially opened by the State President in 1983.

John Vorster Square

John Vorster Square, police headquarters in Johannesburg, was a product of the 1960s. It was named after Verwoerd's Minister of Justice, a man who had the credentials to succeed Verwoerd as Prime Minister, but lacked his mentor's sense of divine mission.

The building was designed by Harris Fels Jankes and Nussbaum, a prominent commercial practice, who produced what is essentially a commercial office complex, based on standardized modular windows with appropriate blue spandrels and situated abruptly against the new elevated M1 motorway. This proximity proved problematic for a building with a grim, hidden history, and in 1986 the open façade was enveloped in a louvred aluminium screen to afford the secrecy required by the apartheid state in its final stages. The secret history of this building has yet to be written.

Colyn and Meiring with Cowin De Bruyn and Cook, Johannesburg Hospital, 1978.

Johannesburg, apartheid city

No single feature can be said to define Johannesburg's metamorphosis from a colonial centre of capital into an apartheid city, a special form of urbanization marked by a characteristic spatial system, manifested not only in separation and division at the micro level but in decentralization at the macro level.[38] The transformation was a complex one. It is revealed most obviously, most visibly in the vast marginalized townships that make up Soweto. Here, mass housing provided by the state was used as a means to coerce and subjugate an impoverished population, quarantined behind buffer zones from the main areas of urban wealth creation.

Yet this peculiar form of urbanization, filled as it was with contradictions and distortions, reveals itself equally in the city of towers that grew up on the back of the great economic surge of the 1960s and the great share boom at the end of the decade, when white hegemony still seemed invulnerable. The CBD then was the unchallenged home of finance capital in South Africa and an area of massive property speculation as well. Meanwhile, on the western urban periphery around Auckland Park, a series of projects was asserting another aspect of the dominant ideology.

Linked to the city of towers by the new elevated motorways, which neatly bypassed the townships of the black proletariat, was the zone of affluence in the northern suburbs. From the 1970s onwards, vast air-conditioned shopping malls and hypermarket warehouses packed with consumer goods arose to service these mainly white and wealthy areas. Sandton City on the north-eastern periphery, built in 1972 and extended in 1982, would grow to 100,000 square metres of decentralized shopping space and 50,000 square metres of office space, while Eastgate on the eastern urban periphery, built in 1979 and extended in 1991, would bring almost 100,000 square metres of shopping space onto the market. (Both schemes were by Gluckman De Beer and Margoles.)

At a broader level, Johannesburg's areas of advanced development and sophistication cannot be separated from the areas of chronic rural underdevelopment created by a century of discriminatory legislation. The apartheid state tried to excise these poor areas from 'white South Africa' by drawing dotted lines around them on maps and passing laws that declared them 'independent states' with political institutions of their own. Then instant capital cities had to be built on the bare veld 'to house the new parliaments and the quarters of the new bureaucracies'. These too must be seen as part of the context of Johannesburg, Apartheid City.

E

Convergence and contradiction

The historian, A.J.P. Taylor, describing industrial capitalism in Germany after 1871, observed:

> Industrial capitalists, it is commonly held, are in politics liberal, but this view is an abbreviation of the real course of events. Industrial capitalists, like all businessmen, judge everything by the standard of success. A good businessman is one who succeeds, a bad businessman is one who 'fails'. When industrial capitalists enter politics they apply the same standard and adopt as their own the party and outlook which prevails.[39]

The parallel with South Africa, where there has been a complex symbiotic relationship between state and capital since 1924, is unavoidable. In the 1960s, both internal and external capital found the environment of the apartheid state, with what Martin Legassick has called its 'labour coercive economy', congenial for rapid business expansion. Prime Minister Vorster's speeches of the late 1960s are peppered with references to 'the calm, peace and prosperity we have in South Africa'. In 1969, after-tax returns on foreign investments ranged from 10.5 to 16.8 per cent,[40] and during this period 'returns for American investors, both direct and indirect, were twice as high as anywhere else in the world'.[41] No wonder there was a comfortable convergence of interests, not to say open support, in many quarters.

But there was a growing divergence too as the internal contradictions of the apartheid settlement began to appear. As early as 1964, there were reports of chronic labour shortages as a result of the boom in the manufacturing sector of the Witwatersrand.[42] Despite job reservation laws, the inflow of African workers was pushing white operatives into supervisory positions. The rise of this new class of white 'bosses' would lead to the massive growth of what were later recognized as newly emergent blue-collar communities which accompanied the spread of endless suburbia, for example along the Ontdekkers Road spine on the West Rand during the P. W. Botha era.

By the mid-1970s some capitalists, the principal economic beneficiaries of apartheid, were bemoaning 'an economy which could not move forward', as Harry Oppenheimer later put it,[43]

Harris Fels Jankes and Nussbaum, John Vorster Square, August 1968.

because core apartheid policies like the Group Areas Act and the rigmarole of restrictions prevented effective industrial and urban management, and could 'dictate where and how factories might operate, whom they might employ and in what number ... The determination to control every aspect of social life led, in time, to a strangling network of economic restrictions, subsidies, penalties, charges, prohibitions and taxes.'[44] Apartheid, it seemed clear, 'was no ideology for a state that wishes to be part of the emerging world industrial economy'.[45] Thus we observe the essential non-coherence of the apartheid state.

Epilogue

In 1970, when headlines still announced 'LACK OF OFFICE SPACE ON RAND', the Carlton Centre presented a bold image of the modern capitalist city.

But after more than a decade, the frenetic expansion that had produced the Carlton was running out of steam. In 1974 the oil price quadrupled to $10 a barrel and the era of cheap imported fuels was over. In that same year, the voice of General Spínola, crackling over the air direct from Lisbon, heralded the collapse of the ramshackle Portuguese Empire in Africa. This was followed by the Soweto uprising of 1976, like a sudden spark to dry tinder. Soon afterwards the great apartheid building boom ground to a halt. In 1978 a solitary construction crane was visible in downtown Johannesburg. The property pages told a new story: '600,000 SQUARE METRES OFFICE SPACE VACANT.' Placards were seen on every block: 'TO LET' ... 'CORNER SHOP TO LET' ... 'PRESTIGE OFFICES TO LET' ... 'LIQUIDATION SALE' ... 'ALL STOCK TO BE CLEARED.'

The expansion was over, for the time being. Johannesburg, inevitably, was waiting for the next boom.

◄D4 ◄D10

Reconstruction and the making of urban planning in 20th-century South Africa
Alan Mabin

Most people would support the view that urban planning has crippled the ability of South Africa's cities to offer a decent urban life to the majority of their citizens. The spatial planning which characterized apartheid has seen to that. Yet the intricacies of urban history are such that, as moves are made to overcome the legacy of the apartheid years, urban planning again finds advocates who value its promise of a new 'city tomorrow'.

There have been several periods of extreme stress and turmoil in South Africa over the past century. During each of these periods, the idea of reconstruction after the damage caused by war, depression or internal conflict has been an attractive theme.[1] Each epoch of reconstruction has led many people to think in modernist terms of urban planning as a primary tool for reconstructing society. As less turbulent times returned, governments tried to reshape the society, and more particularly the cities, by developing new institutions, laws, visions, systems, personnel and plans. In most cases, however, such programmes went not with a bang but a whimper, as the complexities of governing overwhelmed initially exciting but idealistic visions. In the other cases, the vision of reconstruction was overtaken as new regimes acceded to power and co-opted institutions, systems and plans into their own programmes.

Before apartheid, there were four main periods in which reconstruction planning emerged and then receded again: after the South African War; after the First World War; after the depression of the 1930s; and during and after the Second World War. The last of these periods saw a much more explicit and optimistic reconstruction movement, which arose in 1943 and evolved into the apartheid era.

Once apartheid came under sustained assault there were new crises in urban South Africa, and new responses – always involving some form of urban planning. Further phases of reconstruction thus began after the Soweto uprising of 1976; and in the period of 'late apartheid' after 1985.

Following the turmoil and recession of the later 1980s, South African society has passed through a period of democratization in which reconstruction has again been on the lips of many. Once again, urban planning has been reformulated as a primary instrument for reconstructing South Africa after apartheid, much as it was reformulated several times before under very different political conditions.

Planning in the context of global modernism

The South African experience of reconstruction and the uses of urban planning has its own special, sometimes intriguing, and often nasty features. But it is hardly unique. Indeed, at almost every stage in South Africa's urban past, it is precisely from foreign models that the outlines of reconstruction have been drawn. Pictures from British housing manuals of the forties show model estates not wildly different from the 'townships' of the 1950s. Peter Wilkinson, in his essay on the Social and Economic Planning Council, has shown how a discourse of modernist planning appropriated from abroad inspired South African planners at the close of the Second World War.[2]

It might be argued that physical reconstruction after massive bombing raids or even nuclear holocaust is quite different to reconstruction in a country where no major physical destruction has occurred; perhaps, as some French scholars have suggested, one should not use the term 'reconstruction' here at all. But, of course, the discourse of urban planning in South Africa has explicitly used the term in that physical sense, and has drawn on the international experience of physical reconstruction several times in recent generations.

If the European literature is replete with cases of reconstruction and the use of urban planning

Perspective of the Grand Boulevard, Cape Town Foreshore Scheme, 1940.

E

to accomplish it after war, and if the American literature is similarly replete with examples of reconstruction to overcome economic disaster, it should not surprise us that these images have predominated in South African treatments of urban reconstruction. In a world where English holds sway, South African cities are usually described, analysed and planned in similar rhetorics. The key themes are those of modernism – modernization, and the management of urbanization and urban space.

Consider these post-war examples: the new company towns of Vanderbijlpark (Iscor steel), Welkom (Anglo-American gold) and Sasolburg (the Sasol oil-from-coal plant) were planned in the image of new towns in Britain and America; the plans for the Cape Town foreshore replicate features drawn directly from the reconstruction of bombed cities like Plymouth.[3] Apartheid itself borrowed extensively from the modernist rhetoric of urban planning, as it strove to create new (segregated) neighbourhood units and to encourage urban renewal in (mixed) inner-city areas. Apartheid used the images of modernism to enormous effect. The apartheid government employed the planning institutions created by the modernist reconstructionists of the forties to achieve its extraordinary reshaping of urban space in the 1950s and '60s.

The challenge to apartheid and urban reform

Although apartheid appeared to be a stable and successful urban regime in the 1960s, the centre could not hold against the contradictions. In the 1970s things began to fall apart, and as they did so a reformist regime came to power, dedicated to reconstruction where the previous system had failed. In 1978, in the wake of the Soweto uprising and the subsequent turmoil across the country, the ruling National Party elected P. W. Botha as its leader. His government embarked on a centralization of power precisely in order to accomplish 'reform',[4] one major element of which concerned urban policy and planning. In the process, government adopted new thinking propagated by business organizations. So significant was this aspect of the Botha reform programme that, for a time, the national office which sought to oversee urban planning was moved from the Department of Planning into the enlarged Office of the Prime Minister. Although the 'physical planning' function later moved through a succession of departments, for a time it remained within the central strategic offices, such as the Department of Constitutional Development and Planning. Urban policy now incorporated ideas which had been anathema to previous National Party leaders, such as home ownership for all and the transfer of rented state housing to the tenants, as part of the retreat of the state from township life. However, elements of orderliness and control drawn from the particular strain of modernism which apartheid had made its own still persisted.

Botha's constitutional reforms introduced three racially divided Houses of Parliament, each with responsibility for the planning and housing concerns of their particular constituencies. The administrations associated with the coloured and Indian Houses as well as the Bantustan governments not only engaged in substantial planning, but also hired significant numbers of black planners to undertake it. Rejected as illegitimate products of apartheid, these administrations nevertheless disposed of considerable resources. Some of their planners were graduates of those few planning schools which had begun to admit black students in the late 1970s; others had studied abroad, and a few came from other African countries such as Ghana. For the first time the planning profession began to include blacks.

At local level, Botha's government tried to create 'black local authorities' in 1983. Some urban planning functions were entrusted to such authorities. However, the townships over which the black local authorities had jurisdiction supported few substantial commercial or industrial activities, and their tax base was entirely inadequate. By 1984 the urban reconstruction which had been initiated in response to township revolt had thus had a number of effects, both in general and for planning in particular. But this neo-apartheid mode of reconstruction, based on the same exclusions as the old form, could not last.

Urban planning in the late apartheid years

The introduction of the tricameral parliament and the black local authorities provoked an enormous and angry political response. Corruption in these authorities and their insistence on raising rents on public housing (inevitable given their lack of any substantial tax base) led to revolt, beginning with the 'Third Day of September' in Sebokeng, south of Johannesburg. The scale of the 1984-5 rebellion, and the level of military intervention required to put it down, may be gauged from the 25,000 troops deployed in the townships in 1985 and the 26,000 people detained without trial over a period of a year beginning in mid-1986.[5] This was a civil war by any definition – and the government's victory a pyrrhic one for, although a semblance of order was restored by 1987, the political initiative had passed to the broad opposition to apartheid. Nevertheless, in the aftermath of the war the government, like some others before it, tried to amend its urban policy in order to reshape urban society in the later 1980s. This time reconstruction was pursued by the same regime that had led the country into destruction.

The state embarked on a programme to 'win the hearts and minds' of the urban populace, largely by making material improvements in the townships. Particularly troublesome areas, or 'oil spots', were targeted for physical upgrading – sometimes carried out under the protection of the military. At the same time, the system of 'joint management committees' at all levels of government meant that almost every public service office included a representative involved in the security network, and this had a profound effect on the workings of many of these offices. As far as planning was concerned, the implications for public sector planners who stepped out of line were potentially devastating, and what little creativity there had been dwindled away.

Through the late 1970s and early '80s the pace of urbanization continued to accelerate. The population of Durban, for example, is said to have doubled in these years. Increasingly bitter conflicts developed between the state and the residents of unauthorized shack settlements which burgeoned around many of South Africa's cities. In 1986 the government released one of its most significant urban policy documents for decades – the White Paper on Urbanization. This document effectively reversed years of policy aimed at discouraging urbanization. Instead a 'positive' urbanization strategy was embraced 'which recognised that urbanisation was inevitable and could be used positively to enhance the quality of life of all South Africans'. In this new vision of the cities, the creation of new politically and economically autonomous satellite towns around the major metropoles and at some distance from the core cities would allow continued urbanization on the one hand, and ensure the security of whites on the other.[6] Enormous semi-formal settlements, where residents were provided with a site and basic services, resulted at Orange Farm south of Johannesburg, Khayelitsha east of Cape Town, and Motherwell north of Port Elizabeth, amongst other places. Meanwhile, the planning system in the core areas went on trying to manage detailed land use, sheltered both from the violent reality of the townships and from developments in planning abroad.

Small numbers of middle- and upper-income black people would be absorbed into existing white residential areas through gradual reform of the Group Areas Act. But partly as a result of the shift from 'class compression' to 'class differentiation' among the African population, hundreds of thousands of people moved into these new orderly informal settlements, mostly from existing townships. At the same time, others moved into new, privately built township extensions, and some into 'white' inner cities – thus greatly altering the social map of the urban areas.[7]

Despite these changes, as the 1980s drew to a close, South Africa found itself trapped between a concerted security clampdown and an increasingly disruptive and organized rebellion. Far from reflecting urban reconstruction, the media coverage of the period presented a picture of destruction. The attempt at privatized and segregated urban reconstruction had changed the cities, but failed to produce political stability. As the attempted reforms continued, so their failings stimulated popular revolt from below, which left a lasting mark on the trajectory of urban planning and reconstruction. Particularly important in this regard was the rise of civic organizations across the country in the late 1970s and through the following decade. These 'civics' were urban social movements

6

MEADOWLANDS
AGRICULTURAL
HOLDINGS
MEADOWLANDS
ORLANDO
WEST
MOFOLO NORTH
ZONDI
JABULANI
DUBE
MOFOLO
ORLANDO WEST
EXTENSION
CIVIC CENTRE
JABAVU
MOLAPO
MOROKA
EMERGENCY CAMP
MAPETLA

E

which mobilized mainly around rent and transport issues. By the mid-1980s there were civic organizations in all the townships and some other areas.

In their struggles with the state, civic organizations often needed some form of technical support and so they began to interact with urban planning students, academics and practitioners. In the mid-1980s such planners founded several non-governmental organizations (Built Environment Support Group, Planact, Development Action Group) to assist civics and the progressive trade union movement. For the first time in South Africa's history, a significant body of urban planners tried actively to assist the most disadvantaged segments of the society. What had previously been a rather conservative and sedate profession was suddenly subject to internal tensions brought about by these new relationships. As one community activist told practitioners, 'We say, with respect, that planners in South Africa have an important choice ahead of them. The choice is one of either willingly being the functionaries of the apartheid system and all those unjust policies that go with it, or on the other hand, becoming participants in actively formulating a future approach.'[8]

Among progressive planners, and the organizations with which they worked, there arose a halting new vision of urban South Africa, a vision of the country that would be reconstructed after the fall of apartheid, elaborated in meetings with the then-banned ANC in Zimbabwe and elsewhere in the late 1980s.

Amidst the rising tide of neo-liberal analysis and policy in the 1980s – the era of Reagan and Thatcher – there were hints from some quarters that urban disaster in South Africa was not merely the doing of the apartheid state, but the logical consequence of *all* government action in the urban terrain. Thus tensions were set up which propelled the vision of the urban future and how best to realize it between two poles – the World Bank image of 'improving performance through markets' and the left-modernist idea of the state as an instrument for reconstruction. These tensions were resolved through proposals to 'level the playing field' and bring the private sector into housing production – while at the same time reducing the state's role to one of providing the subsidies that would get the profit-making private sector on to the scene and into the black.

Reconstruction and urban planning after 1990

Massive social problems and political paralysis underlay the forced retirement of P. W. Botha and the rise of F. W. de Klerk in the palace coup of 1989. Almost immediately, significant changes began to occur in urban politics, and space opened up for the expression of new visions of a (reconstructed) post-apartheid urban future – a future which planning would help to accomplish.

With the release of political prisoners and the unbanning of opposition organizations, began an era of negotiations at all levels. Reconstruction formed a frequent leitmotif of *local* negotiation. Thus the Greater Soweto Accord of September 1990 called explicitly for investigations which would lead a thoroughgoing exercise in urban reconstruction. In 1990 and 1991 the Urban Foundation, an organ of business, released several policy documents in a series quaintly titled *Policies for a New Urban Future*. The World Bank, returning to the country after many years' absence, argued that South African cities were among the most inefficient in the world and called for restructuring to achieve higher densities and more compact urban development. The National Housing Forum sponsored investigations into the 'restructuring of the built environment'. Various academic authors called for reintegration and a focus on urban reconstruction; some even connected their ideas explicitly to the reconstruction movement of the forties.[9] The influential *Labour Bulletin* wrote of the shift 'from resistance to reconstruction', while the urban NGOs produced a new supplement for the monthly magazine *Work in Progress* (subsequently for the newspaper the *Mail & Guardian*, and now for the *Sunday Independent*) which is titled – inevitably? – *Reconstruct*.

Most prominently, the ANC-led alliance produced a manifesto for the historic 1994 elections titled the *Reconstruction and Development Programme*. The subsequent Government of National Unity, led by the ANC, turned this programme into policy as a series of White Papers, as a powerful agency in the Office of the President, and as a discourse to which almost every actor in the urban planning environment claimed to subscribe. Presidential Lead Projects in several areas, funded from the national RDP budget, sought to remake urban space in a variety of ways after the destruction wrought by apartheid: to rebuild houses and community facilities destroyed during violence in townships such as Katlehong, south-east of Johannesburg; or to redevelop, for people of lower incomes, large areas like Cato Manor in Durban, from which thousands had been forcibly removed in the 1950s and '60s.

Much of the work which informed negotiations and policy documents employed a rhetoric based on that of modernism, right down to the Modern Movement's well-known calls for compact cities in the 1930s. However, the discourses framed in these terms were often turned to political rather than material purpose in South Africa: they were used to establish dominance in local negotiations, for example, rather than to promote a plan for accomplishing physical change.

Whilst many of the calls for urban reconstruction stressed the need to shape the future of South African cities through higher densities and infill, consensus on the direction of this reconstruction should not be assumed. Although some actors (the Urban Foundation, the World Bank) called for functionally efficient and compact cities, their emphasis on shallow subsidies to boost the housing supply pointed in the opposite direction, towards a sea of site-and-service schemes on the urban periphery. Others argued for an emphasis on urban quality.

Since April 1994, planning itself has entered a phase of reconstruction. The unification of local authorities that were separated under apartheid and the creation of nine new provinces have demanded the construction of new planning departments, in which concerns long divided – planning for housing, land use, towns and townships, cities and Bantustans – are to some extent being integrated. Policies of restitution are trying to make up for some of the damage caused by forced removals. Proponents of a turn to reconstruction have moved from civics and NGOs into government. In 1995 the national government passed the first major piece of planning legislation of the post-apartheid era, the Development Facilitation Act (generated by the RDP Office), which allows old planning mechanisms to be bypassed, calls for the setting of Land Development Objectives by all authorities, and provides for a Commission to lead further change in planning.

E

Post-colonial reconstruction and planning

Another source of imagery, and one which has become increasingly forceful since the ANC acceded to power, is the post-colonial experience of planning. The term 'reconstruction' has perhaps been less heavily worked in post-colonial planning discourses than in some Northern and Western ones, but a related and sometimes similar set of ideas has shaped post-colonial policy. Both during struggles for independence and after they had achieved success, the notion of recasting society to correct the distortions of colonialism obviously loomed large. Planning came to the fore as a means to this end.

However, the political, intellectual and professional classes involved were small initially, and so the notion of planning was concentrated at national level. At this level of planning, examples could also readily be found in other parts of the world: the first independence celebrations after the Second World War, those of India, Pakistan and Indonesia, saw national planning committees preparing national plans, and trying to focus the role of the state on the development of the national economy and the transformation of society. The five-year plan became a necessity of most post-independence governments. This conception of planning spread to Africa in the 1950s and '60s, where even the least 'socialist' of governments, like Botswana's, adopted it after independence. The idea that planning, planners and the plan could provide the solutions to post-colonial ills became deeply rooted; it could be discerned in the South African democratic movement during the years of grand apartheid, and was expressed in many documents from the Freedom Charter onwards.

Urban planning in post-independence Africa was slow to move away from its colonial origins, however. In cities fairly comparable with those of South Africa, such as Nairobi, master-plans for the physical development of the city prepared a decade after independence still took the same general approach as those which much earlier planners (some of them based in South Africa) had proposed in the colonial era. But the accumulation of problems, fiscal crisis and, in some cases, breakdown in what came to be called 'urban management' in the 1980s led to quite different notions of the role of planning in the 1990s, when South Africa's 'negotiated revolution' was consummated.

At the same time, the large and relatively well-resourced leadership of the South African democratic movement penetrated into municipal government with a sense of urgency about remaking urban space after apartheid – a task often seen as similar to the remaking of opportunity and power in post-colonial circumstances. However, the ideas which local leaders brought back from their many foreign expeditions in the early years of post-apartheid rule were often more vivid when they came from Europe and North America (especially ideas on urban regeneration and local economic development), or at least from Latin America, and less dramatic when they stemmed from more recently post-colonial Africa and Asia.

Yet in the reshaping of opportunity, South Africans could draw profoundly on the example of post-independence India, and even more directly on that of Malaysia under its New Economic Policy. This policy was intended to help bumiputras – those of original Malay descent – to gain much greater access to economic power, while promoting rapid economic growth. Such goals very closely parallel those of present government policy in South Africa. But to what extent do the ideals of remaking urban space in the ways emphasized by discourses of reconstruction contribute to similar ends? Complementarity and contradiction are both possible, and are beginning to be tested.

In post-colonial societies, planning is a form of modernism which does not necessarily engage successfully with the material and political contexts. Urban management has therefore come to the fore as an alternative discourse and (sometimes) set of practices. The appeal of urban planning as a means not only of effecting physical change after apartheid, but of contributing to social transformation, may be fading in South Africa under the developing political prerogatives of the society. Thus debate and dispute continue, in an urban environment which demonstrates many features of large project development, deregulation, and a growing concern with local economic development familiar to planners in cities elsewhere. But in South Africa, different images of fundamental social transformation are also in contention – something which is beginning to affect and perhaps to fragment planning and its once vaunted role in post-apartheid reconstruction.

(Post-)modernism and reconstruction

In closing it is worth reflecting briefly on the prospects for real and progressive urban reconstruction. The South African experience of reconstruction in the 20th century illustrates the catalysing role that war and social upheaval may play for planning initiatives. During each period of extreme stress and turmoil, it has been assumed on all sides that urban planning may be a primary tool for reconstructing society. On all previous occasions in South African history when the fervour for reconstruction ran high, the follow-through into actual urban reconstruction was disappointing to the enthusiasts, with the single and major exception of apartheid's racial reconstruction of the cities.

Like others before them, those who implemented apartheid found that the complexities of government and the configurations of interest at local levels threatened to subvert their vision. They stuck to the task with exceptional commitment. But to do so they had to resort to increasingly authoritarian measures (reflected in the tendency throughout the period to centralize decision-making). Moreover, the single-minded pursuit of the apartheid vision necessitated profligate spending. This was possible in the halcyon days of economic growth in the 1950s and '60s but, after revolts in the following decades, the implementers of a reformed urban vision had to pursue their modified apartheid in the context of economic stagnation. In the 1990s, growing income inequality and a fiscal policy aimed at reducing the deficit have made reconstruction still more hazardous.

Urban reconstruction in post-apartheid South Africa is an exciting prospect, with new visions, far wider participation and a developmental perspective lacking in previous planning. But as planners embark on their first attempt to reconstruct the cities in the image of a brave new democracy, warning bells are ringing. The course of urban development in the late 20th century presents significant problems for the modernist notion of reconstruction. The modernist ideals of the ANC, as embodied in the Freedom Charter of 1955, for example, confronted quite different, 'postmodern' urban conditions in 1994.[10] The Reconstruction and Development Programme (RDP) is viewed by some as an exciting and programmatic approach to reconstruction after the ravages of apartheid.[11] Others might be more inclined to treat it as a political discourse, relatively loosely related to the limited capacities of a haltingly modernist state to effect 'development'. The evidence suggests that this view has some credence. The national RDP Office was closed early in 1996. The slow pace of change led to a realization that making any positive impact on the cities may be a lot more difficult than was first thought. In place of grand schemes at national and local levels for remaking space after apartheid, the local-government section of the Department of Constitutional Development – which is what remains of the RDP Office – now urges municipalities to enter into public-private partnerships as a step towards 'developmental local government'.[12] But it also requires 'integrated development planning', a rational and comprehensive approach at root which potentially contradicts some of the less modernist thrusts of local government.

Others have cautioned against simple optimism about the ability of urban planning to accomplish miracles in South Africa's future. Jennifer Robinson, for instance, points out that 'the durability of parts of the old order ... especially that fixed in the built environment and embodied in professional knowledge and language' is likely to ensure that 'the struggle for liberation' will not be over soon.[13] To the persistence of older social and physical forms might be added the argument that past programmes of urban reconstruction have tended to be overtaken by the realities of power and its limits, which have often perverted the idealism and vision of reconstruction to less attractive ends.

◄D7 ►E7

OPLE SHALL HAVE SKIL
PLE S HAVE JOB

Towards an architecture of empowerment
Mphethi Morojele

After the African National Congress came to power in South Africa's first democratic elections of April 1994, it introduced the Reconstruction and Development Programme (RDP). The RDP, which was to be implemented by all public sector departments, was aimed specifically at alleviating poverty and furthering development among the historically disadvantaged black communities.

A central element of this initiative was a national public works programme, using public sector building and infrastructure projects to create jobs, develop human resources and empower previously disenfranchised communities and local authorities. This programme was required to pursue labour-based construction techniques and to promote technologies appropriate to the capacities and skills of emerging contractors. Projects had to be designed in such a way that they allowed for technical and administrative training, thereby enhancing the ability of local communities to plan, implement and maintain development projects.

Since 1995, these projects have been implemented through the various provincial Departments of Public Works under the Community-Based Public Works Programme (CBPWP). The CBPWP recognizes that building and infrastructure projects need to be controlled by the communities for which they are intended, right from the identification and initiation phases through to implementation, operation and maintenance. Funds for such projects are given directly to the community through properly negotiated structures.

The Lakeside Community Crèche and Pre-School, built mainly in 1996 and completed in April 1997, falls under the CBPWP. Mphethi Morojele Architects were responsible for the design. The experience at Lakeside presents an opportunity to explore, in practical terms, a few of the theoretical issues that confront architects in the context of 'development'.

Lakeside, a housing development of about 1,000 houses, was established in 1989 by white private-sector developers, who acquired the land from Evaton Town Council for the nominal cost of one rand. It was one of the few black housing estates then being developed in the Vaal region, a highly industrialized and heavily populated area south of Johannesburg, and it offered a fortunate minority a way out of cramped backyard shacks and four-roomed houses in the established townships. Most of those who moved into the free-standing dwellings of about 48 square metres were in fact municipal and government employees with privileged access to mortgages.

Like most townships before it, Lakeside was some distance from the nearest town, which in this case was Vereeniging, more than twenty kilometres away. The new development was bordered by the established townships of Evaton and Sebokeng on one side, and the squatter camps of Thina Selahliwe ('We have been dumped') and Tonosa on the other. No community facilities were provided; there were no schools, no clinics, no recreation centres. Lakeside was conceived simply as an extension of the dormitory townships surrounding it.

Given the centrality of spatial and architectural planning in the enforcement of racial segregation under apartheid, it is not surprising that strong community-based resistance movements should have formed around housing and other civic issues. After the democratization of South Africa in the early nineties, these movements formed the basis for new civic organizations. One of these – the Lakeside branch of the South African National Civic Organization (SANCO) – was the client for the childcare facility discussed here.

The need for local community participation in development is particularly strong among black South Africans, no doubt because of their political history. Projects that do not follow the consultative process have often been rejected by the people they were intended to serve. Professionals who

Lakeside Crèche launch, September 1996.

have blundered in this regard, wittingly or unwittingly, have many stories to tell about projects being delayed and personnel being thrown off sites – or even held hostage – until community involvement is assured. Of course, the definition of 'community' in this context is no easier than anywhere else, and this only adds to the difficulties.

In 1995, SANCO Lakeside approached the CBPWP for assistance with its development needs. The CBPWP facilitated the drawing up of a business plan, in consultation with the community, in which a 'childhood development centre' was identified as a priority. Lakeside being a relatively new area with a young population, it was hoped that a project concerned with the care and education of children would bring the community together. The centre would have a crèche providing day-care facilities for thirty children from the age of three months, and a pre-school catering for up to ninety children.

The drawing up of business plans under the CBPWP requires a mix of social and technical consultancy. Professionals from the building environment – architects, quantity surveyors, planners, engineers – are usually appointed as project managers to guide this often difficult process. The appointment normally includes managing the implementation of the project.

The business plan sets out the framework under which the development will take place: the ownership arrangements; the structure and management of community participation in planning and implementing the project; the plans for training and building capacity (whether technical, administrative or operational); the management of the actual construction process (the technical team, labour, tools, materials); and the solicitation of support from other private, public and community bodies in the area (the municipality, government departments, construction firms, suppliers, transport companies, and so on).

As a public works institution, the CBPWP naturally limits the range of possible developments to those involving the construction, extension or maintenance of community buildings or physical infrastructure. However, it falls beyond the scope of the Public Works Department to equip, staff or operate such facilities, and these projects therefore require support from other government departments, local authorities, and sometimes the private sector. Project management, especially during the implementation phase, is therefore a crucial function, requiring not only the coordination of the design and construction teams, but a sensitive handling of the more social aspects of development.

The architects were appointed after a selection process conducted by the project committee and facilitated by the project manager, who had drawn up the initial business plan and was then retained for the implementation stage.

Our main architectural concerns at Lakeside were tectonic, born directly out of the requirements of the CBPWP. We were required to develop a design strategy that allowed for community participation at all levels; and to employ labour-intensive construction technologies which would be within the capabilities of locally trained contractors and artisans, while also extending their experience and developing their skills. We were to learn about the structural limitations imposed by the conventional nature of practice in such a context.

The choice of design and, more particularly, of construction technology was predicated on the 'Domino Theory'. Here the architect's role extends to orchestrating the activities of others, by setting up a framework which allows the various participants to make the appropriate design decisions.

Initially, we were provided with a sketch of the proposed facility, which the committee had arrived at when the business plan was being drawn up. This included classrooms of the kind found in a conventional school. To facilitate discussion about the advisability of avoiding this, we organized a tour of other established crèches. Unfortunately only the most senior members of the committee, who were all male, attended the tour; the real users, the women identified in the community as teachers and childcare assistants, therefore did not benefit from viewing other possible layouts.

After the tour, the weekly consultation meetings revolved around the choice between having compartmentalized or open-plan play areas; compartments are usually favoured where resources allow for a large supervisory staff, while an open plan is better where the anticipated child/staff ratios are high. Eventually a compromise was reached, whereby the play areas would be partitioned at the child's level but open above, so that one or two assistants could monitor all the play groups simultaneously. While this arrangement was successful in those terms, it does not do much to keep noise levels down.

Apart from the play areas, staff offices, kitchen and toilets, the people of Lakeside also wanted a hall or gathering space incorporated into the crèche. There was no such facility in the area and, in the course of developing this project, with the community participation it entailed, the crèche had evolved into the main meeting place. As the original business plan did not allow for this addition, it was decided instead to combine two of the play areas into one larger space and to provide ample storage, so that the resulting space could double as a hall.

The application of the council by-laws led to animated discussion. Under apartheid, the townships were governed by different space standards and regulations (when these were enforced at all). It was clear that the by-laws now being applied had been developed with the previously 'white' areas in mind. For instance, one of the regulations stipulated that staff be provided with showers. The committee found it ludicrous to think that a black woman – especially one with an expensive hairdo! – might get under the shower at work. Predictably, the showers have never been used and have been turned into storage space.

Designers confront some interesting challenges in a context where cynical deprivation has imbued certain forms and materials with political meanings. People tend to be unreceptive to materials and finishes they think of as 'inferior', such as rendered external surfaces (as opposed to fairface brickwork) or exposed timber trusses and raised ceilings. Raised ceilings especially remind people of apartheid housing, where ceilings were often omitted to save costs. In the Lakeside crèche, the need to let sunlight into the interior spaces of a building with a deep plan led the architects to propose raised ceilings, something that did not immediately find favour with the community. A compromise solution was negotiated, which was to provide dropped ceilings in some of the play areas and not in others. With hindsight, this has actually made for a more effective and differentiated design: the dropped ceilings delineate calmer areas where quieter activities can take place.

E

As far as the management of the construction process was concerned, there was a choice between a contractor who would supply materials and labour and one who would supply labour only, with the community itself taking responsibility for procuring materials and safeguarding them on site. The committee opted for the second option on the grounds that it would foster a sense of community ownership, and this was borne out by the absence of theft or vandalism (which persists even now, long after the building was completed). The second procurement method was also designed to suit small contractors, who often have cash-flow problems and cannot raise bridging finance.

Attempts were made to involve the artisans in design decisions. For instance, the chief bricklayer was given bricks of two different tones and asked to design the patterning of the exterior walls, within certain parameters. Similarly, when the framing allowed for various types of glazing the choice was left to the artisan. On the internal walls, a decoration schedule was produced for only one block of the crèche and the painters were asked to apply their own mixes to the other block, using the given palette. The only rule was a practical one – that cold colours, which are more resistant to sunlight, be used on continuously exposed surfaces. Most of the decorators were women, who usually proved to be better at this work than men, perhaps because women in rural settings are traditionally involved in similar activities. Nevertheless, the use of less skilled builders on such projects means that detailing has to be 'forgiving': where a detail has not been properly handled, a strategy must be devised to cover it up – in the manner of the artist who sees a mistake on the canvas as an opportunity.

The 'domino' approach to design is time-consuming and difficult to pursue given the time constraints on most building projects, as well as the 'standard' levels of involvement and disbursement prescribed for the architect in statutes and letters of appointment. There is a great need for architects to become more involved in this potentially rich process, which would help to reduce the gap between design and construction. This gap is often cited as a general structural inefficiency in the construction industry, and especially in development projects. As we discovered at Lakeside, artisans are seldom trained in the design aspects of their trades.

The ready availability of industrial processes in the cities has created resistance to labour-intensive construction methods. For instance, there was a distinct lack of enthusiasm for mixing concrete and manufacturing timber trusses on site, although this was always done until quite recently, and indeed still is in remote localities. The manufacture of materials like blocks, pavers and tiles on site would increase the proportion of funds going to labour, but this could only happen if everyone involved, including professionals, accepted lengthier processes. The project cycle itself would then have to be redefined. Perhaps the methods required to develop skills and create jobs are better suited to ongoing programmes, running parallel to sets of similar projects in a specified area, rather than to individual projects.

In redefining the project cycle and the relationship between professional and client, it must be made possible for architects to spend more time on fewer projects. In some countries, the architect is even required to live in the project area for a specified period.

Contractual arrangements can lead to bitter conflict, and emerging contractors or subcontractors require managerial support and training in this area.

In Lakeside there were disputes when subcontractors, who had been outpriced in an open tender, claimed to be more 'local' than the competition and expected to be awarded the contract at the lower price. These disputes were mediated by the committee and the project manager. Often the only solution was to split the contract between the two parties, which left the technical team with a more difficult monitoring task.

The goal was to see that women and youth made up at least 40 per cent of the workforce. However, some contractors argued against employing women on the grounds that their generous proportions would prevent them from climbing the scaffolding!

Our experience indicated that development projects would run more smoothly if there was closer collaboration between architects and construction managers on site. Crucial decisions, often about matters that could not have been anticipated during the planning stages, have to be made on site all the time. For instance, when it came to the counters and cupboards in the crèche, joiners who lived in the community were contracted to do the labour, in direct partnership with the large manufacturer who supplied the materials. The established firm involved had little enthusiasm for this unaccustomed arrangement, with the result that the local joiners did not receive the support they would have enjoyed as direct employees. Had we anticipated the problem, we would have designed finishes and detailing that required little machining.

Giving preference to the 'local' community in development projects also has its pitfalls. The very act of defining the catchment area for labourers, contractors and suppliers is often highly political. In Lakeside, a local resident who enjoyed the trust of the committee, and had been employed to work on the site himself, was also tasked with ensuring that all the other workers were really from the 'local' community. Without proper checks and balances this position can be abused by unscrupulous individuals, resulting in 'élite capture' as it is termed, and reinforcing the existing power structures in the community.

In South Africa, 'community participation' occurs almost exclusively in public sector projects in previously disadvantaged black areas. In fact, the term 'community' itself has acquired colour and class dimensions, and is seldom applied to the wealthier, traditionally white areas. However, the consultation process quickly dispels the assumption that black 'communities' are homogeneous and harmonious. It is also clear that the merits of the process are being recognized more and more in the private sector and in more affluent suburbs.

Community participation requires a serious commitment of time and energy. Some of the older people of Lakeside especially grew tired of the drawn-out processes involved. 'We've waited so many years for this facility,' they said, 'and now we have to put up with all these meetings. Why don't you just get on with it?' People drafted onto the management committees sacrificed their time and work, and were not remunerated despite being entrusted with the project's funds. Committee members were also not allowed to be employed on site.

In Lakeside, the committees arranged a string of ceremonies to celebrate the project's various milestones – from the turning of the first sod to the final launch – inviting local and national politicians and other important people to view their good work. Some might argue that the monies spent in this way would be put to better use equipping the facility, but such ceremonies offer the only opportunity for committee members to gain recognition and political benefit, and may be very worthwhile in these terms. The question of remuneration for committee members on community projects is always sensitive, and deserves to be given more serious attention. Remuneration of some kind may help to avoid the problems found on certain projects, such as the misappropriation of funds or materials, or the extraction of 'finding' fees from suppliers and labourers.

When it comes to public works projects, one of the most important measures of success is whether the facility can be sustained as a fully-fledged business in the long term. How does the Lakeside Community Crèche and Pre-School measure up?

The building was completed within budget and some savings were made. The facility is well used by the community. School fees cover staff salaries and operational costs, but generate no excess. The crèche has not yet been fully equipped, and the project committee still has to raise funds for this from the private sector. It is a positive sign in itself that the committee continues to function. They have already approached the architects to produce sketch proposals for a community centre with sports facilities. They are developing the business plans for this proposal themselves and have identified possible sponsors.

More broadly, our experience with the CBPWP highlights several issues of importance to the practice of architecture in South Africa now.

Empowerment means very different things in different situations. The contractual arrangements and technical solutions in different projects must accordingly be much more flexible. Architects should find ways to revise their documentation and contractual obligations to suit this variety.

Design and construction teams are temporary groupings, and the lessons learnt are therefore not easily transferred from one project to another. The time limitations imposed by project cycles also make it difficult to achieve the programme's ideals, especially with regard to training. Contractors are not encouraged to invest in plant, materials and methods suited to community development.

If a new architecture of empowerment is to emerge, architects will have to be much more closely involved in development projects. Only then will they be able to seize the opportunities offered by technical and contractual exigencies. Our identity as practitioners is not forged through a self-conscious, autonomous process of design, but through an ongoing struggle to better the quality of life of particular people in particular places. When we have acknowledged this fact, our building will begin to reflect our society.

◄E6 ►F7

THIS IS A JOINT DEVELOPMENT
BY THE BENONI TOWN COUNCIL
AND THE
WATTVILLE
CONCERNED RESIDENTS COMMITTEE

8

Rival futures: Struggle visions, post-apartheid choices

Mark Swilling

It was late afternoon, and the usual frantic buzz in the inner-city offices of the service organization had only just begun to subside. The administrative staff were packing up, fieldworkers were trickling in to gather themselves and check their correspondence, those who had spent the day in committee meetings were drifting back to their offices to start the work they were supposed to have done that morning. But the day was not going to end like other days – not that there were too many usual endings in organizations like this in the late 1980s ...

'The comrades have arrived, something's up.' The word quickly spread through the corridors. Some closed their doors, hoping to avoid being assigned another task, or sat behind their desks, too exhausted to investigate; others gravitated towards the hubbub, which confirmed that something important had happened.

Eventually, a room was found and a meeting convened – young activists and weary professionals around a table. The usual drawn-out formalities had to be gone through first – greetings, introductions, choosing a spokesperson. Always an afterthought: who will take the minutes? And then, inevitably, the latecomer – he'd been talking on the telephone somewhere: in the days before the cellphone, that was often the main reason for visiting the offices of a service organization – and the latecomer always turned out to be the most important person, so everything had to be gone through again. And then the meeting could start.

The minutes of this particular meeting read: 'The comrades from Invasionville reported that a land invasion had taken place the previous night. About 100 shacks have been erected, and more are going up. The police are all around, but negotiations have begun with the Council. If bulldozing starts, there could be violence. Many youths are getting ready to defend the community. Their request is as follows: they want us to attend the negotiations with the Council that are taking place tomorrow morning at 9; tomorrow night they must report back to a community meeting on how Invasionville is going to be upgraded.'

The minutes did not record whether a decision had been made. That was always assumed. No one thought to ask whether this particular service organization had the know-how to assist in this matter. That was also assumed. And no one dared suggest that something else planned for the next morning might actually be more important than what was happening at Invasionville.

Then the comrades had to go, because 'the transport' was waiting – meaning the poor guy whose car had been commandeered to bring them to town – and the staff members who were left behind gathered to assign tasks. The comrades were known to some people in the organization, so their bona fides were not a problem. But their request raised some tricky political questions. 'How can we just go to the negotiations when we don't know what the real needs are on the ground? We've never worked with that community!' 'What happens if we're forced into negotiating on behalf of the community around technical issues which the leadership doesn't understand?' 'What if the leaders reach agreements with the Council based on our advice and then the community rejects them?' Gone were the days when there was time to discuss the finer points of political and professional conduct. 'There's no choice, we'll just have to go and report back afterwards. We'll see how things go as the process unfolds.'

Invasionville was in an area that already had a 'Project Manager' in the service organization, so obviously that person had to be at 'the negotiations'. And a technical person should go along to deal with technical issues. Whatever information could be dug up in the offices – maps, aerial photographs, planning documents – was dumped on the Project Manager's desk. 'Home time' suddenly seemed a long way off.

Tamboville, 1992, Abie Nyalunga (right), Chairperson of the Wattville Concerned Residents Committee.

'The negotiations' the next day embodied the classic paradoxes. On one side, community leaders who needed to win concessions from the authorities in order to ensure the survival of the newly constructed Invasionville community, but who belonged at the same time to a movement that believed it could bring about the collapse of the state through the coalescence of local struggles. On the other side, stony-faced officials who had rules to apply and political dictates to follow, but who also needed to reach some kind of agreement in order to lower the levels of conflict in their areas and shift the focus of embarrassing international attention.

Not surprisingly, the role of the service organization at the negotiating table was ambiguous, to say the least. Simply by being there and speaking a technical language, rather than the political language of conflict, the organization's representatives allowed a discussion about compromise to take place. Eventually, the simultaneous presence of these two languages produced a split in 'the negotiations': in the more general forum, political positions were stated for purposes largely unrelated to the local context; while in the 'technical committee' local solutions were hammered out in an emerging techno-developmental language. While the short-term consequences of this split were vaguely apprehended at the time, no one anticipated the longer-term consequences for how urban dynamics would be defined and contested in the future.

Over the following two years, 'the negotiations' became the focal point for all decisions about the fate of Invasionville: here it was agreed that it would not be bulldozed, that emergency services would be installed, that the area should be 'upgraded'; here the long and complicated participatory planning process and the actual construction started; and here, every step of the way, the habitual crisis had to be dealt with, inevitably involving some form of direct or threatened violence by one party or the other.

But in the end, in this particular case, any real progress was destroyed by a combination of violence, bad faith, and the sheer determination of those who depended on hidden abodes for their survival to keep things as they were. By then, 'the negotiations' had become a euphemism for a type of interim local governance that no one wanted to recognize, no theory could contain, and everyone was part of.

This history is still with us in the present.

On telling untold stories

This essay tells the story of South Africa's 'urban service organizations' (or simply 'service organizations', as I'll call them here for the sake of brevity). Today, most of these organizations, commonly referred to as 'NGOs' now that the country has been reincorporated into the mainstream development world, belong to a national coordinating body known as the Urban Sector Network. But I am interested in the period from about 1985 to 1994. This period began with the founding of various organizations by small groups of people, mainly with a professional training, who had decided to use their knowledge and skills to support community-based organizations engaged in 'urban struggles'. By the time of South Africa's first democratic elections in 1994, these organizations had evolved into large and complex structures that were articulating significant post-apartheid conceptions of urban change. These conceptions were rooted in the development projects undertaken by community-based organizations, in the local-level negotiations concerned with the transformation of local government, and in attempts to formulate policy to support the positions of the democratic movement during the transition period. After the elections, the service organizations provided the newly elected government with some of its most capable technical staff and officials at national, provincial and local levels.

Six organizations were founded during this ten-year period: the Built Environment Support Group in Durban, Planact in Johannesburg, the Development Action Group and the Foundation for Contemporary Research in Cape Town, CORPLAN in East London, and the Urban Services Group in Port Elizabeth. By 1994, these six organizations together employed more than 150 people and had a combined budget of nearly R100 million. Along with COPE in Johannesburg, UMZAMO in

Cape Town and the Centre for Community and Labour Studies in Durban, they now form the core of the Urban Sector Network.

Why were these organizations established? What did they do during the decade that led up to the founding of the democratic state? What were their visions of the future of the South African city? Why have these visions not been realized more fully? What are their possible future roles?

In trying to answer these questions, I hope to tell a story that has not been told before. But I openly admit that I am telling it with the present in mind and as a direct participant in the formation and development of these institutions.[1] My fear is that by not telling this story we have allowed ourselves to forget about practices that were aimed exclusively at enabling oppressed and exploited urban communities to understand their conditions, formulate alternatives, and engage in collective struggles to achieve their demands. This is not just an exercise in historical reconstruction, therefore, but an attempt to restore our memory about a way of doing things that grows more and more imperative in the new South Africa, if we are seriously committed to development and democracy.

The founding intentions

The service organizations that emerged around 1985 were founded mainly (but not exclusively) by white professionals who were already politically engaged in some way, but wanted to use their knowledge and skills outside the conventional environments of consultancy, in the private or public sectors, and academia. The founding group in each case involved some combination of academics, professionals in private practice, activists working with support organizations linked to the democratic movement, employees of businesses or business-linked organizations, and (in Cape Town only) professionals employed by local government. Invariably, the founding group initially constituted a voluntary association, with themselves as the executive committee. After working on a voluntary basis at first, they were soon forced to raise funds to employ people, and so began the long journey of building an institution.

The members of the founding groups had a mixed set of motives. Those with a technical training in disciplines such as architecture, planning and engineering wanted to establish an alternative form of professional practice, in much the same way that human rights lawyers, for instance, set up the legal resource centres. Those with a background in the human or social sciences, like their colleagues in the professions, often had a political commitment to providing community-based organizations and social movements with the knowledge they needed to engage in urban struggles more effectively. Both groups drew their theoretical inspiration from an eclectic mix of Marxist urban sociology, welfarist community development theory, technocratic participatory-planning ideas – 'if people are involved, resources are used efficiently' – and anti-apartheid discourse. There was also a small group of liberals, trying to improve social conditions but not necessarily committed to radical social transformation.

The context must be recalled. The 1985-6 State of Emergency was in force, and except for a brief interlude in the second quarter of 1986, severe Emergency rule would continue until 1989. Social movements were a familiar feature of everyday community and political life across the country. Countless local struggles had already generated a set of martyrs, leaders and organizational models. One could mention, for instance, the housing battles in 1979 that produced the Port Elizabeth Black Civic Organization (PEBCO) and the Soweto Committee of 10 (later the Soweto Civic Association), or the schools boycott in Cape Town in 1980 that produced the first civic associations at neighbourhood level. There was the rent struggle in Durban in 1982 (associated with the Joint Rent Action Committee), the bus boycott in East London in 1983, the Vaal Uprising in 1984, the stay-aways in Port Elizabeth and Uitenhage which led to the Langa massacre in March 1985. National formations like the United Democratic Front (UDF) and the National Forum were voicing general political demands common to most local struggles while, in the workplace, national trade union federations were making economic, and certain political, demands.

In virtually all the local struggles, community-based organizations of various kinds managed to mobilize local communities around demands for better services, land and housing, and around opposition to the racially exclusive local government structures that were created in 1982 as part of the state's 'Total Strategy'. These local struggles challenged two strategies. The first was the state's reform policies, which were aimed at creating a category of 'urban insiders' strictly segmented from the 'rural outsiders'. The second was a concerted effort by organized business to invest in development projects for middle-class and upwardly mobile urban wage-earners and to support attempts to change urban policy, with a view to deracializing the urban system in accordance with the principles of economic liberalism. The Urban Foundation was responsible for managing this latter strategy, which was later adopted by the apartheid state during its 'repressive reform' period in the late 1980s.

Inspired by the left-wing critique of these strategies as an attempt to preserve white rule and maintain racial capitalism, local community leaders and progressive professionals started to link up with one another in workshops and discussions aimed at formulating an alternative approach. They shared the assumption that the 'struggle for the city' was the locus of the struggle to define a post-apartheid future. Not surprisingly, the central issue in the strategic debate during 1985 and 1986 was whether or not to engage the state around immediately realizable demands. For some, this confounded the general principle of non-participation in state structures. They argued that the real issue was state power, and that local struggles were only important to the extent that they built up a national democratic movement which, at some point in the future, would detonate the collapse of the state. Others took their cue from the trade union movement, which had successfully married bargaining with employers around economic demands and mobilizing against the state around political demands. An analogous approach to community struggles, it was argued, involved negotiating locally around 'collective consumption' or 'social wage' demands, while contributing to mass mobilization nationally by participating in bodies like the UDF.

Although this debate remained unresolved – and there were those who preferred to suppress it altogether – the proponents of the second position faced a theoretical problem, the solution of which contributed significantly to what has become a robust urban sociological tradition. The theoretical problem was this: the democratic movement had a theory and a strategy that applied to the relationship between the 'oppressed people' and the 'white state' (the 'people-power bloc relation') and to the relationship between employers and workers (the 'capital-labour relation'); but there was no framework for making sense of the phenomenon and specificity of urban communities. All this changed with the publication of Doug Hindson's work on the 'urban proletariat'. Here, for the first time, was an empirically substantiated theory that made it possible to go beyond the 'cheap labour power thesis' and see the formation of townships, and therefore the nature of the apartheid city, in a different light. Hindson's theory, the work of the social historians associated with the History Workshop at the University of the Witwatersrand, and the new planning framework developed in the writings of Jeff McCarthy and Dan Smit at the University of Natal, all contributed to the eventual acceptance that urban struggles were distinct from national political struggles or struggles in the workplace – something that made South Africa unique in African anti-colonial theory and strategy. In the language used then, the struggle was not only for political citizenship through democracy, and industrial citizenship through a democratic labour relations framework, but also for urban citizenship through the democratization of our cities, which meant the establishment of 'non-racial municipalities' and a single tax base (the slogan 'One city, one tax base' captured the feelings about redistribution). As I wrote at the time, 'city politics came of age'.

Although the specificity of urban struggles was never fully accepted in the democratic movement, the idea created strategic space for certain local community leaders, who were facing a problem that had never been anticipated by the national leadership of the UDF or ANC. As popular mobilization escalated around 1985, many local leaders found themselves for the first time with a mass base, organized at the level of the community, the neighbourhood and the street. Leaders began to come under severe pressure from this organized following to resolve immediate problems related to things like urban services and infrastructure – something they could only hope to do by engaging the authorities responsible for providing these services. Local leaders were on the horns of a dilemma: they could sustain their mass base by engaging with the state to win concessions, and in the process compromise the national political principle of non-participation; or they could remain loyal to the national political line, and risk losing their mass base by failing to resolve day-to-day problems. Leaders probably chose the one option as much as the other. However, there is no doubt that those local leaders who had been most successful in organizing their communities were also those who faced the greatest pressure to engage with the state. (Strict non-participation might have been pursued if all parts of the country were equally well organized and if there was a viable national body to orchestrate a single mass action and topple the regime. This, of course, would have been the revolution that many talked about, but few really believed was possible.)

The combination of an emerging urban sociology and the dynamics of engagement with the state in the better-organized communities opened up the strategic space in which the service organizations were founded and developed.

This is not to imply that all the founding members understood this context. Rather, most of the founders of the first service organizations were probably responding to demands from community leaders, who needed very practical, immediate advice on how to deal with the new conditions of struggle that had emerged at different times and in different places. It was only later that this initially reactive technical advice generated a knowledge base for more complex project implementation and policy work.

It is worth noting that all the first service organizations sought funding from international donors. Planact was started in 1986 with a R10,000 cheque which Beyers Naudé wrote out in the name of the author, after a five-minute briefing about plans to support the people of Langa (Uitenhage) in their struggle to resist removal. He never asked us to account for the money, and none of us would have betrayed his trust in our intentions by misusing it.

Going with the flow

Towards the end of the 1980s, the budgets and staff complements of the service organizations grew rapidly, a trend that peaked in 1993-4 before many left to take up government positions. By then, most had substantial office infrastructures, organized policy statements, relatively stable funding bases and secure strategic positions in their respective operational environments. However, 1989 was the real turning point – a year that has received remarkably little attention in journalistic and academic accounts of the transition.

In the political realm, F. W. de Klerk rose to power, and it was he who made the key decisions to release the hunger strikers, allow the defiance campaign to take place, ease the State of Emergency and reign in the securocrats, and eventually prepare for the unbannings and the release of political prisoners a year later.

Organized business tried to set the development agenda by convincing the government to allocate R2 billion to what became the Independent Development Trust (IDT). The Trust was to finance large numbers of urban upgrading projects around the country, on terms defined by the logic of economic liberalism, legitimated by a politically correct Board and justified by a conservative 'basic needs' approach to development.

The largest single land redistribution action in South African history took place in mid-1989, when communities around the country took up the UDF's call to invade land. Although these invasions have never been analysed systematically, there is enough anecdotal evidence to suggest that they broke crucial barriers to the occupation of urban land that were keeping the poor on the margins of the urban space economies.

The rent boycotts escalated everywhere, forcing the local government system into a terminal crisis. By 1989, arrears owing to local governments exceeded R1 billion. It was this fiscal crisis that drove the state to accept the need for negotiations across the country (but mainly in the Transvaal) at local level with civic associations and related structures.

The civic movement reached its height as a loosely associated network of local organizations with strong support bases and capable leaders. But when the South African National Civic Organization (SANCO) was constituted as a unitary body in 1990, the local accountability and creative responsiveness of local civic leaders were betrayed. This betrayal was redoubled in 1997, when newly elected local councillors reneged on their previous undertakings to resign from leadership positions in civic associations if they were elected to local government – a principled position that had been adopted in the name of an 'independent civil society'.

And finally, there were the velvet revolutions in Eastern Europe, which brought an end to the Cold War and established a new balance of global power that no longer worked in favour of the apartheid regime. Ironically, the rise of a global order dominated by the United States and structured according to a multiplicity of economic nodes massively strengthened the hand of the 'negotiators' on both sides of the South African conflict.

The service organizations found themselves having to respond to large numbers of communities caught up in various processes. Firstly, there were service and housing projects that had emerged out of land invasions or had been initiated by the IDT (and some land invasions which had become IDT projects), alongside projects initiated by local or provincial government, NGOs or private sector developers. Secondly, there were local government negotiations, arising out of the establishment of local forums that brought together town councils, civics, service utilities such as Eskom, business, and other interests. These negotiations were eventually formalized through the local forums established in every town and city under the Local Government Transition Act of 1993. Thirdly, there were education and awareness programmes aimed at informing people about the changes and strengthening their capacity to handle new conditions.

In addition, the trade unions, continuing a trend that arose during the Emergency years, had become major players in the field of urban development, both in relation to policy and to internal company projects. National formations such as the Congress of South African Trade Unions (COSATU) and the UDF needed policy assistance, as did the ANC after it was unbanned.

As the service organizations grew in response to these conditions, they underwent significant internal restructuring. In the early years there had been a generalist approach, where small, tightly networked groups cooperated closely in a non-hierarchical, non-specialized way on all aspects of the work. Even administrative responsibilities, like financial control and office administration, fell to people whose main functions were project or policy work. Now, with the help of consultants in most cases, the service organizations (increasingly referred to as the 'urban sector NGOs') were restructured. A full-time administrative staff of financial controllers, office administrators, receptionists and even secretaries was established. Separate 'departments' (or 'units' or 'programmes') were created, each with a specialist focus. Invariably, there was a group to manage 'implementation projects' – usually the upgrading of informal settlements – and another to coordinate support for local government negotiations. Another increasingly prevalent group managed the various capacity-building programmes aimed at developing skills and creating awareness of key policy issues. Some of the larger organizations established dedicated research units to coordinate the growing amount of incoming information and produce succinct briefings on emerging issues. (Later these units would feed policy proposals directly into local and national negotiations.) More and more black staff members were employed, including graduates and skilled community or union organizers wishing to develop their technical abilities and build longer-term careers. This generation eventually took over the leadership of the service organizations in the 1990s.

The most remarkable feature of the service organizations during that 24-month period starting in early 1989 was the massive concentration of knowledge that resulted from what was being learnt about towns and cities across the country. As exhausted project workers returned from local government negotiations and meetings with urban upgrading projects, they brought with them stories, experiences and information that drastically expanded the collective knowledge base of the organizations. Working under extremely pressured and stressful conditions, catapulted from one meeting to the next, they had no choice but to depend on one another and to learn quickly. A remarkably capable and talented group of people emerged, who found ways of developing skilful negotiating tactics, enough technical knowledge to understand what was going on most of the time, and a reasonably shrewd political judgement.

The main problem, however, was that the external demands were so great that there was insufficient time to invest in building up sustainable and supportive internal organizational environments. Instead, internal change was provoked by crises of various kinds. And the mistake was to rely too heavily on private sector consultants to resolve these crises. They were quick to introduce control hierarchies and neatly structured visions and missions into organizations whose energy flowed from intuition and the dynamics of the relationships between the people involved, rather than from a clear-sighted understanding of strategic positioning or mutually exclusive, rationally conceived 'objectives'. But it was the international donors who did most to arrest the great flow of creativity with the dead hand of high rationalism by introducing 'Logframe' into the South African transition. This instrument for project design and management has done more to dilute the high energy of the early 1990s than anything else (excepting, perhaps, the formation of SANCO).

The making of a conversational revolution

Traditional revolutionary theory assumed that those who have political power do not voluntarily relinquish it. Armed or unarmed action was necessary to 'seize power'. For Lenin, the road from 'barbarism to civilization' lay through the territory of armed revolution. But in various parts of the world in recent times – southern Europe in the 1970s, Latin America in the 1970s and '80s, Eastern Europe in the late 1980s, Africa in the 1990s – a new form of 'regime transition' has appeared that defies the traditional logic. As O'Donnell et al. observe, these 'non-revolutionary regime transitions' occur when powerful economic élites realize that they can democratize political power without putting the basic structure of economic power at risk and opponents of the regime conclude that they have more to gain from negotiating than from holding out for revolution and risking complete failure.[2]

Little attention has been paid to the fact that this shift in the nature of regime transition took place in societies characterized by relatively high levels of urbanization and multi-nodal rather than uni-nodal urban hierarchies. For revolutionaries who 'seized power' by storming the Bastille or the Winter Palace, it was possible to take a country by taking a city (often from a rural base); at the end of the 20th century, taking the key city in a complex society is no longer synonymous with seizing power. Power is now contested over a dispersed urban terrain, as indicated by the fact that the parties to negotiated transitions are often social movements with a mainly urban base.

South Africa's negotiated settlement cannot be called a traditional revolution, nor a traditional decolonization, nor even a 'non-revolutionary regime transition' as defined by O'Donnell et al. As Johannes Rantete has argued, it was a bit of all of these. It was both a decolonization of a 'special type', and a 'non-revolutionary regime transition' that was not brought about by the usual primary causes of social change in the 20th century, namely state implosion, armed insurrection, external invasion, war or classical decolonization.[3] Rather, as in so many similar transitions over the past 25 years, it came about largely because the society – and the cities in particular – became increasingly ungovernable for the regime and provided the power bases for their opponents.

But how was this achieved in practice? What were the 100,000 or so hard-core activists who built the union, student and community movements doing on a daily basis during the 1980s and early '90s? What was their main way of achieving highly cohesive organization in opposition to the regime? The answer, to put it bluntly, is that they talked. They had no guns, few media resources, no access to institutional power, and few friends in the establishment. All they could do was get people talking and singing, so that when the call came to strike, to march, to boycott, a critical mass of grass-roots supporters knew what it was all about. And this was not achieved mainly through mass rallies, but through countless meetings of smaller groups in homes, churches, fields, factories, mines, schoolyards, cemeteries, streets. All the studies of local struggles show that social movements were built through countless conversations among poor and largely urban people, which gradually produced an oppositional consensus that the mass media could not counter. In short, apartheid was talked out of existence.

What did the service organizations actually do to support this process of conversational organizing? Clearly they broke away from the primary duty of most professionals in most societies, which is to provide organized information and specialist analysis to those with the resources to finance 'knowledge production', and to answer questions posed by those who govern society or manage economic institutions. Instead, the service organizations sought to answer questions that arose in community or workplace struggles around the social wage and the spatial distribution of resources. In the language of the time, they wanted to use their skills to empower communities, by providing them, rather than the state or business, with information and specialist analysis. They did this in three main ways.

Firstly, they provided organizers with the information they needed to counter the definitions of problems and proposals for solutions presented by government or business. To be credible within their own constituencies, organizers needed to demonstrate why the dominant knowledge should be rejected, and do so in terms not too dissimilar to those used by 'the enemy'. A good example is the report entitled the Soweto Rent Boycott, which was commissioned by Frank Chikane on behalf of the Soweto People's Delegation and compiled by Planact. The state's definition of the problem, which was broadly accepted by business, was that agitators were intimidating people into withholding rents; the Planact report redefined the problem as one of deep structural imbalances. These imbalances made it more expensive to live in Soweto than in Houghton, because the white suburbs were subsidized by rates levied on business whereas the townships were not. This report gave rise to the 'One city, one tax base' slogan, which escalated the rent boycotts and reconstituted the national policy discussion about urban reform and non-racial local government. There are countless examples of such connections between knowledge and collective action in the 1980s and early '90s, where the knowledge embedded in collective action was extracted through a participatory research process, making explicit what had been implicit, sharpening the contradictions, and reinforcing the articulation of alternative solutions. The problem, of course, was that the unorganized were left out of this loop.

Secondly, the service organizations supported the negotiation processes. As early as 1985-6, when Mkhuseli Jack led negotiations with the Port Elizabeth Chamber of Commerce to end the consumer boycotts, he turned to academics and NGOs aligned with the UDF to create a knowledge and information base to support his positions, so that he would not have to rely on the 'other side'. Later in the '80s, when social movements organized around rent boycotts and land invasions, local organizers explicitly demanded and helped to ensure that the emerging service organizations were properly funded, so that they could provide free support during often long and complex negotiations to resolve local problems. The negotiation processes, which we could see as having institutionalized the conversations that changed the nature of local governance in South Africa, may not have occurred if local leaders did not have access to independent sources of information and knowledge.

Thirdly, from the late 1980s onwards the service organizations provided information and analysis to support policy formulation. With the sudden shift from opposition to 'preparing to govern', enormous demands were made on the service organizations to write up policy documents on a wide range of issues, and to second personnel to various structures. However, in many ways, formulating policy to support the national transition process was not all that different to what service organizations had already been doing for some time in local negotiations (the main difference being the particular language and format required).[4]

It would be a serious mistake to assume that these three activities coexisted happily in the service organizations. While they all eventually performed all three activities in one way or another, they all felt the consequences of trying to hold together activities with divergent strategic objectives and motives. Packaging information that will be used at the grass roots to build a movement and sustain collective action is radically different from packaging information for negotiation forums or policy formulation processes. The detailed practical problem-solving required in local negotiations was also vastly different from the more abstract exercise of writing policy: negotiations were rooted in tangible realities, whereas policy formulation was often about finding the linguistic generalities needed to ease through nationally negotiated agreements (the original Reconstruction and Development Programme is the best example of the style).

More importantly, the shift from supporting mass action to supporting negotiations and policy formulation fundamentally altered the nature of the service organizations, without them being fully aware of what was happening. In essence, questions that arose in grass-roots struggles were no longer at the heart of analysis. Rather than focusing on the distinct positions of particular parties, the focus now fell on the need for agreement among many parties on general policy positions. In the past, even when mass action had been directly linked to negotiations, as in the rent boycotts, the service organizations were still pursuing their founding purpose of providing information and analysis for a particular set of movements and interests. However, once mass action was uncoupled from the negotiation of local solutions, the skills and knowledge of the service organizations were redeployed to support policy changes bound up with national agreements. The service organizations now required a new methodological validation to establish the credibility of their policy arguments. Previously they had derived validation from their daily experience in local struggles and from whether or not the knowledge produced served the communities involved. Policy analysis, on the other hand, depended on an abstract, positivist methodological validation rooted in traditional epistemology, including the 'objectivity' of the analyst. These strictures, and the need to derive all policy from founding principles (the Constitution, the RDP, and so on), made it impossible to practise the guerrilla sociology of the 1980s and early '90s, which had been so exuberantly subversive of established power.

Unsurprisingly, the policy discussions held in the many regional and national forums, covering virtually every major issue, involved 'experts' drawn from three main interests – government, business and the democratic movement, with the service organizations supporting the latter. Where 'leaders' were brought into these processes, they were either denied access to independent sources of information and analysis; or, like many of the 'experts' representing the democratic movement, they willingly – but often unwittingly – participated in discussions designed to suppress demands for radical urban change. Some slowly realized the trap they had been caught in. The new, generalized consensus required, by definition, the suppression of discourses that reflected unmet needs and demands. What better means to achieve this than the depoliticized language of policy analysis or strategic planning – often drafted by the very same people who in the past exposed these needs and demands?

This is not to imply that people acted in bad faith. On the contrary, they often did their best to win progressive positions, but the framework was against them. The technocratic language used to build the consensus was formulated by an army of experts drawn from local business, the public service and international aid agencies. These experts shared the unimaginative assumptions of mainstream development theory, which were generally far more utopian than the seemingly 'radical' arguments of those who had come out of the service organizations and social movements. Often it was simply easier to go along with the 'respectable middle road' than to hold out for what came to be branded as the 'impractical radical' positions, especially when the making of new careers depended on being 'mainstreamed' rather than 'marginalized'.

Visionary alternatives or alternative visions?

To understand the full complexity of current debates about urban policy, it is essential to have some insight into the debates that took place within the service organizations in the late 1980s and early

'90s. In particular, the current division between housing policy (managed by the Department of Housing) and local government policy (managed by the Department of Constitutional Development) reflects the way many service organizations divided their support and policy work in that earlier period: invariably, there was a team that included planners and engineers, who dealt with housing projects, and another that included people with social science and legal skills, who supported the local government negotiation processes. As a result – and the effects are still being felt today – there was no coherent and authentic post-colonial sense of the city, of the kind that should be reflected in an integrated urban development policy. What masquerades as urban development policy today is largely an extension into the present of the technocratic, environmentally destructive, market-driven developmentalism that was originally articulated by the Urban Foundation in the 1980s to legitimize a largely European and North American conception of urban modernity as the norm.[5] But the notion of the 'compact city', which was so central to this ideology, is fundamentally contradicted by current urban development processes and policies: housing subsidies are granted for building projects on cheap land on the urban peripheries; the new multiracial middle class resists densification and low-income developments in the suburbs; designs continue to replicate the stand-alone household in a fragmented community; and there is a frankly bizarre commitment to conventional, standardized engineering services (using purified water to flush toilets, water-borne sewerage over long distances, conventional energy sources), when even richer developed countries are installing cheaper, ecologically responsible systems.

At the moment, the only effective alternative to such policies is the counter-vision implicit in the land-invasion movements, most of which lack the kinds of support once provided by service organizations. Not surprisingly, this makes them vulnerable to populist elements in opposition parties and self-aggrandizing patronage movements, which are more interested in using these new local struggles for their own gain than in their potential as bearers of post-colonial urban forms and functions.

But what were the debates in the service organizations that help to explain where we are now? Starting in the mid-1980s, service organizations found themselves supporting community-based organizations and trade unions on a wide range of issues connected with housing: the upgrading of informal settlements, the planning and development of new housing projects, the costs of services and infrastructure, the quality and cost of new privately owned houses, the transfer of rented housing, opposition to removals, upgrading of hostels, company housing strategies for employees, and so on. As I have already argued, support for these struggles was unproblematic at first, because the progressive outcome was seen as a function of having empowered organized formations in poor communities. In other words, the relationship between immediate actions and ultimate goals was resolved through faith in the inevitable demise of apartheid, which would be brought about by the collective actions of the oppressed and exploited majority. However, when the emphasis shifted from supporting local struggles to supporting the policy formulation process, this connection was broken, and the scene was set for an unresolved debate between two main positions.

The first was focused on the formulation of pragmatic national policies for determining what sort of housing the state could provide, taking into account the existing 'resource constraints'. The focus was therefore on specifying in detail what the state should do, how much it should spend, and how this should be organized. There was a split within this position between those who accepted the extremely conservative, neo-liberal definition of the constraints agreed upon in the National Housing Forum, which allowed for no more than a starter unit in the form of a serviced site with a bit of top structure, and those who were branded as 'radicals' because they called for much higher expenditure on housing to meet all the needs.

The second position was more interested in how communities could continue to be empowered to control the resources for meeting their own needs. This position was sceptical of state delivery options, no matter how much was allocated for this purpose. The constraints here were not how much the state could 'afford', but what capacity there was 'on the ground', in communities and local governments, to manage increased financial flows into housing and infrastructure. The devastating consequences of violent conflict within communities over the distribution of development resources brutally highlighted the problems.

The second position was clearly the minority one, with proponents in only some of the service organizations, sectors of SANCO, some trade unions and, most prominently, an independent formation called People's Dialogue. As the national policy dialogue in the National Housing Forum and subsequently in the Department of Housing reached its final stages in 1994-5, it was the conservative version of the first position that won out. The key person in this process was Billy Cobbett, a former Director of Planact, who had been seconded to the ANC's Housing Department and was then appointed as the Department of Housing's first Director-General after the election.

It was largely up to Cobbett to decide which elements of the democratic movement participated in the formulation of the national housing policy. When questioned about why he largely kept the service organizations out of the process, he said that his political bosses wanted the emphasis to fall on direct representation by political and civic leaders, rather than on 'experts' from the service organizations. This contrasted markedly with the strategy of organized business – in particular, the banking institutions – which seconded large numbers of experts, and in so doing directly influenced policy in a way that would be impossible today (and would have been so even under apartheid). The democratic movement's overcommitted political and civic leaders were not equipped to deal with this army of technical experts entrusted with broad negotiating mandates. The consequences of this strategic miscalculation will be felt for many years.[6]

Policy on local government had a different history. For a brief moment in 1991-2, the ANC advocated an integrated national forum for all development policy, including housing and local government, but this was soon relinquished as business, protecting vested interests in housing, secured agreements that housing and infrastructure policies would be formulated separately. In the meantime, the deepening crisis in local government forced the National Party and the ANC into national negotiations, which eventually resulted in the Local Government Transition Act of 1993. The Act had a purely institutional focus, and provided the framework for a three-stage transition to democratic, non-racial local government: a non-elected 'pre-interim' phase, which would emerge out of local negotiation forums; an elected interim phase; and a final elected phase, after the adoption of a new Constitution and related legislation for local government. Andrew Boraine, another leading figure in Planact, was the key person in these negotiations, and subsequently managed the implementation of the new framework as Deputy Director-General for Local Government in the Department of Constitutional Development and Planning. Boraine was more open to drawing people from the service organizations into these processes than Cobbett was with respect to housing policy.

In 1992, Planact published Towards Democratic Non-Racial Local Government in South Africa, the first formal policy document on local government to come out of the democratic movement. This document provided a framework for thinking about redistributive and democratic processes, drawing quite heavily on proposals then emanating from the Central Witwatersrand Metropolitan Chamber (which we will return to later). In particular, it envisaged a two-tier system of government for metropolitan areas, with a strong metropolitan level to effect redistribution, and a large number of small, locally accountable councils at primary level to facilitate democracy. This suited both the Soweto Civic Association and the Johannesburg City Council: both believed that a larger metropolitan tax base was needed to cross-subsidize the development of the poorer areas. It did not suit the Alexandra Civic Association and the Randburg Town Council, both of which feared a massive redistribution of resources from the northern part of the metropolitan area to Soweto in the south. The Alexandra Civic Association correctly believed that this would not favour residents in their township, who represented a small pocket of need compared to Soweto; the Randburg Council wanted to prevent the mainly white, middle-class residents in its area from footing the bill for post-apartheid redress.

The problem for Planact was that it numbered both the Soweto Civic Association and the Alexandra Civic Association among its clients, with Billy Cobbett and the author serving as project managers to the former, and Andrew Boraine to the latter. Naturally, the different governance models for metropolitan areas, including the associated tax bases and planning systems, were the subject of heated and ultimately unresolved debates within the organization. The legacy of these debates is still being felt today, with Johannesburg and Cape Town pursuing diametrically opposed courses on metropolitan governance. Boraine, as it happens, is now Cape Town's City Manager.

It needs to be reiterated that whatever direction policy on housing and local government took for reasons specific to the dynamics of each arena of conflict, neither were really rooted in a coherent, shared conception of the post-apartheid city, including new forms and functions. Although isolated attempts were made by certain people in the service organizations to develop this meta-synthesis, time and pressure intervened. This is a pity, because much of today's failure to manage our cities as dynamic, organic systems of complex conversations stems from the absence of an authentic sense of the viable, post-colonial African city. It was only in the Central Witwatersrand Metropolitan Chamber that the outlines of such a conception began to emerge. However, the ANC's Gauteng leadership closed the CWMC down before it could bring this conception to fruition.

The rise and fall of the conversational city

The CWMC was established in 1990 as a result of the Soweto Accord the previous year. The Soweto Accord was a tripartite agreement between the three Soweto Councils, the Transvaal Provincial Administration and the Soweto People's Delegation (led by Cyril Ramaphosa, with technical support from Planact). It brought an end to a three-year rent boycott by meeting four core demands – the scrapping of all arrears, the transfer of state-owned houses to residents, the upgrading of services, and the establishment of a single, non-racial tax base for Greater Johannesburg (Randburg, Sandton, Alexandra, Johannesburg, Roodepoort and Soweto).

Over three years, the CWMC evolved into a widely representative forum. There were 53 member organizations (local authorities, civic associations, ratepayers' and residents' associations, and political parties), 32 official observer organizations (trade unions, parastatals, business associations), and six working groups covering different spheres of development (constitutional, institutional, financial, economic, social, and physical). The Chamber functioned as a mechanism for managing crisis and resolving conflict and as a forum for developing urban policy, trying to grapple with complex problems in an integrated and participatory way.

Between 1990 and 1994, the CWMC undertook what remains the most comprehensive and integrated urban policy review ever attempted in a major South African city. On average, the six working groups each had six committees dealing with various policy issues. The working groups integrated the reports presented by their committees into work-in-progress reports on each sphere of development. These reports in turn were tabled at the Chamber's monthly plenary sessions. By 1993-4, the process of integrating the working groups' sectoral reports was just starting and, if the Chamber had not been disbanded, would have issued in South Africa's first integrated development plan.[7] The spatial foundation of this integrated development plan was completed in 1993 and was called the Interim Strategic Framework. When the renowned urban sociologist, Peter Marcuse, reviewed the post-apartheid urban plans of South African cities in 1995, he found that the Interim Strategic Framework was the only one that took poverty and class as its points of departure, rather than race and Group Area boundaries.

Planact staff members were involved in all the working groups and in most of the fifty or so committees, providing technical support to the civic associations, in particular the Soweto Civic Association and the umbrella body called the Civic Associations of Johannesburg.

Although the intellectual and policy achievement of the CWMC was impressive, this work was suppressed immediately by the ANC leadership that came to power during the pre-interim and interim phases of the local government transition. No rationale has ever been provided for this, but it is clear that the Chamber's recommendations for a strong metropolitan government and a large number of weaker primary councils contradicted the electoral analysis of the new ANC leaders at local and provincial levels. Despite warnings from all the major actors in the Chamber, the ANC leadership opted for four very strong 'metropolitan sub-structures' grouped under a weak metropolitan government. Now that this has been recognized as the disaster its critics predicted, the work of the CWMC is being dusted off and brought back into discussions about a more democratic and developmental alternative.

The Chamber's great significance lay in the participatory processes it pioneered and consolidated. A large number of governmental, business and civil bodies were involved. The monthly plenary was a grand affair, with the council chamber packed from the inner horseshoe to the benches at the back of the gallery. The atmosphere buzzed, the debating format was simple so that everyone could have their say, and the documentation was impressively detailed. Similarly, all members could send representatives to the working groups and their committees. The policy-making process was thus completely open, and issues could be inserted into the discussion at any point, from a plenary session down to a committee meeting. Most importantly, the entire structure operated outside any legal or regulatory framework. The CWMC set its own goals, defined its own procedures, decided on its own membership, and constantly adjusted the way it operated to suit the prevailing conditions.

Why did it work? It worked because it was well administered and simply designed, and provided a supportive environment in which wide-ranging conversations about immensely complex issues could take place. And it did so by creating an open system which allowed anyone to participate at any level. The scope of the conversations and the composition of the participants were largely unconstrained. At first glance, this seems like a recipe for disorder, but in reality it was remarkably stable, despite being very far from a state of equilibrium. The results were neither predictable nor controllable. The creativity of the results lay in what complexity science refers to as 'emergence' – a multiplicity of seemingly random transactions gradually coalesce into a self-organized pattern, generating results that could not have been planned at the outset. This depended on a growing level of trust between the core participants, namely the civic associations (excluding the Alexandra Civic), the Johannesburg City Council and the Transvaal Provincial Administration. Without the gradual formation of networks that cut across formal positioning, emergence would have been impossible.

In short, the CWMC was a glorious experiment in participatory governance. It demonstrated in practice the enormously creative power of a conversational approach, based on a deep faith in process. But then a leadership came in which feared what could not be predicted and distrusted what could not be controlled. The false promises of certainty rose up again, and the conversation broke down. It is only now, some five years later, that this certainty is being recognized for the folly it is. Whether an authentic conversational culture can re-emerge from the echoing hallways of conventional governance is a moot point. Perhaps that extraordinary moment will never come again.

Future roles: Doing by learning?

Early in 1998, at a meeting of the Planact Board, I asked for an analysis of how the current projects had been initiated. To my surprise, I learnt that only a small percentage had arisen in response to requests from community-based formations. Most of the requests had come from government or development agencies, while some projects had been initiated by the organization itself with the support of funders. By contrast, around 1989 the vast majority of projects in Planact, and indeed in all the service organizations, were initiated by requests from community organizations or trade unions.

Today, service organizations tend to be involved in the following kinds of activities: facilitating the implementation of projects; developing policy, mainly for government; doing research to support general awareness and education; consulting on strategic planning; building capacity and providing training; organizing events to facilitate discussion, education and networking. These roles are debated passionately, but with a pragmatic awareness of the realities of financial survival. I would like to argue that it has become increasingly imperative also to focus on the service organization's traditional role, that of supporting the organizational empowerment of the urban poor, as residents in their communities and workers in their workplaces. But can the 'urban sector NGOs' in fact return to their traditional role, given that the two conditions which made it possible – the existence of urban social movements and the ready availability of large-scale, generalized funding support for work in civil society – are now virtually absent?

This question has a major bearing on the future of the South African city. There is ample evidence from around the world to show that it is increasingly difficult to govern cities in the traditional way. The old-style, bureaucratic administration of uniformly designed and delivered urban services is no longer possible: it is too expensive and unresponsive. The past two decades have seen the rise and gradual decline of the neo-liberal experiment to replace the bureaucratic model with a public-choice one, which brings the market, the contract and individual choice directly into the provision of services, while the private sector replaces government as the central actor. It is now accepted that though this approach may (at best) deliver better-quality services to those who can afford them, it also deepens problems associated with poverty, crime and the environment. Cities everywhere are searching for a model of governance that is based on collaboration across the spectrum rather than on public-private partnerships only; that truly empowers civil society rather than merely maximizing individual choice; that combats poverty rather than merely providing access to the market; that uses resources in a sustainable, ecological way rather than merely conserving the environment; and that produces accountability and transparency in all decision-making about the city's future, whether by banks, developers or NGOs, rather than in government decision-making only. Wherever this model of governance has been implemented, the key factor in its success has turned out to be the quality and depth of the conversations that take place throughout the city about its vision, forms and functions. Conversations release the creative energies that make the complex processes of democratic governance possible.

South Africa is ideally suited to this model of governance: it has been primed by a recent history of organization and mobilization in civil society, negotiations, participatory decision-making, and a culture of networks and discussions. The rapid disintegration of a great city like Johannesburg is largely due to the failure of an absurd mixture of authoritarian, bureaucratic political styles and neo-liberal management strategies. The city can only be salvaged if there is a return to the kind of conversational democracy that the Metropolitan Chamber made possible in the early 1990s. This, in turn, will only be possible if independent urban social movements re-emerge. Without such movements, business and government will be allowed to establish comfort zones of bland, technocratic consensus. Complex uncertainties and creatively subversive values and demands can only be articulated by movements that emanate from the heart of civil society, with all its eccentricities. Diversity is the lifeblood of creativity, and creativity is the energy of dynamic development and a robust and lively democracy.

This brings us to the crucial question all South African cities must face: How can the urban social movements be revived? If we look to the 1980s and early '90s for lessons in this regard, then we must take into account two conditions that made it possible to build locally accountable social movements during that period. Firstly, the most effective organizers came from three sources: localized self-help bodies like burial societies and stokvels (mutual aid and savings syndicates), the student movement, and the trade union movement. The organizational disciplines of trained shop stewards, in particular, had the greatest influence on the way the social movements operated. Secondly, as I have been at pains to explain, these movements had access to the service organizations that provided them with independent sources of information and analysis, thus allowing them to deconstruct what they were opposed to and formulate coherent and informed alternatives. Without this capacity, the knowledge systems and the 'experts' who administer them in government and business will simply ignore oppositional voices expressing things about the city that systematized knowledge has not yet codified.

Two strategic conclusions flow from this analysis of the past. Firstly, the trade union movement should encourage shop stewards to go out into the communities, as they did in the early 1980s, to organize broadly based, independent social movements committed to representing marginalized interests. Trade unions have an interest in this, because a narrow base in the workplace will weaken their capacity to influence macroeconomic policy and urban development strategies. Secondly, the urban sector NGOs should build up a funding and skills base that will enable them to support this organizational drive with knowledge and information.

Certain changes in our society should favour these strategies. We now have thousands of democratically elected councillors looking for a role in local government. Unfortunately, some councillors have styled themselves as political managers, along the lines of cabinet ministers, and so they have failed to make the distinctive contribution of the local government politician as an organizer and representative of civil society. If shop stewards, councillors and urban sector NGOs could find a way of cooperating, so that communities can be reorganized in ways that lead to empowerment, without partisanship, around local demands and projects, we may be able to rebuild the urban social movements. But this will only happen if organizers listen more than they talk, and build cooperation across divisions rather than competition and conflict. We need to foster strong relations of trust and reciprocity in communities, so that they can find their own inner resources to counter the violence, crime and poverty that are rapidly destroying them.

The demise of SANCO as a political force nationally and an organizational force locally, clears the way for a return to loosely connected networks of local associations, rather than a hierarchical, centrally controlled structure. This opportunity should be seized with zeal, and the fact that some NGOs have already taken policy decisions not to work for SANCO is a promising sign. The rise of independent formations like People's Dialogue, the non-aligned squatter movements, the anti-crime movements, and community-based environmental groups are also indications that a new and diverse civil society is emerging.

The challenge we face now is to complete the task of building an authentic, post-colonial sense of the future of South Africa's cities. I say no more than a 'sense', because we do not need another codified vision in another unread policy document. We need a sense of place that emerges from continuous practice as we re-engage our cities in a new set of conversations about their identities, structures, forms, functions, conflicts, poverties and potentials. We will have to replace the certainties of policy and strategy with the uncertainties of dialogue and interaction. We will need a new kind of leadership, which derives security not by intensifying control but by maximizing participation in decision-making and policy formulation. We will have to accept that our cities are ungovernable by conventional means, but that they can find ways of governing themselves. In the absence of active urban social movements, the future of our cities will belong not to an increasingly empowered majority but to a new non-racial minority. The urban sector NGOs should therefore support the re-emergence of urban social movements and help to rebuild them, so that they are able to participate effectively in the new conversations that are bound to arise as the crisis in all our cities deepens.

1
2
5
6
9
10
13
14

Erasing roadmarkings, Cnrs. Bezuidenhout and Jeppe Streets
Stephen Hobbs

It is interesting to note that in a city such as Johannesburg signs of order and regulation – stop signs, no-parking zones, yellow lines, red lines, and broad yellow grids painted onto the roads and pavements – appear to function purely as decoration.

Regarding the erasure of ALL of the road markings and road signs, please 'fill in' or 'paint' over the sign or marking with as close an equivalent as possible to the colour and/or texture that exists 'behind' the marking or sign.

1 Apart from the obvious markings on the road, i.e. the yellow and white arrows, and the white lines around the traffic islands, please note the diagonal parking grid in the lower left-hand corner and erase that too.

2 Same as above. Note the red and white one-way arrow sign tucked behind the lamp-post, the stop sign with its back to us, and the black and white chevron markings on the pavement opposite it.

3 Not much in this block except for the odd white marking in the parking lot.

4 Nothing to erase here.

5 Traffic light, red and white one-way arrow and its post, black and white pavement chevron, the rest of the diagonal parking grid from block 1, white lane lines, and the paved red-brick pedestrian walkway.

6 Remaining pedestrian walkway, red and white one-way arrow, top of the traffic light from 10, additional traffic light, faded black and white chevron on the pavement, white lane lines, and yellow arrow.

7 Remaining pedestrian walkway, traffic lights x 3, red and white one-way arrow, and the faded black and white chevron on pavement. (NB) Behind the billboard there is the white-lined parking bay and the grid of the parking lot. You could also white out this billboard.

8 Remaining pedestrian crossing paving, two traffic lights, faded white lane lines, and black and white pavement chevron.

9 White lane lines and the remaining pedestrian paving.

10 Traffic light and the pedestrian paving.

11 Pedestrian paving, cut-off yellow arrows, white lane lines, traffic light, and the black and white chevron markings on the traffic island.

12 Pedestrian paving, white lane lines and arrows, bottom part of traffic light from 8, and the faded black and white chevron on the pavement.

13 Nothing.

14 Nothing.

15 One white lane line.

16 White lane lines and front end of white arrow in the top right-hand corner!

10
NEWTOWN CULTURAL PRECINCT
THE DANCE FACTORY
MEGA MUSIC WAREHOUSE
ENTRANCE
JEPPE ST
GOCH ST
BEZUIDENHOUT ST
E

HOUGHTON ESTATE
THE WILDS
The Pines
Johannesburg Hospital/-hospitaal
Medical School
Hoërskool Die Kruin
Roedean Girls' School
St. John's Boys' College
St. John's Preparatory School
King Edward VII Boys School
King Edward VII Preparatory
OBSERVATORY
Sacred Heart
Torath Emeth College
BELLEVUE
Observatory Girls' Primary School
CARSE O'GOWRIE
ST. ANDREW
Johannesburg College of Education
ST ANDREWS
LOUIS BOTHA
Randjeslaagte Beacon
MITCHELL PARK
Beth Jacobs Girls' High School
RALEIGH
YEOVILLE SQUARE
YEOVILLE
Holy Family Convent
Yeoville Boys' Primary School
Sha'arei Primary School
HUNTER
ROCKEY
BELLEVUE EAST
VICTORIA
PIETER ROOS PARK
Park Lane Clinic/-kliniek
Brenthurst Clinic/-kliniek
JHB. BOWLING CLUB
J.Z. DE VILLIERS PARK
Johannesburg Girls' Prep. School
Johannesburg Girls' High School
Yad Vashem Memorial Hall
Happy Autumn Nursing Home
Clayton Nursing Home
MACKIE NIVEN PARK
RAND VIEW
Union Observatory
Unie-sterrewag
Yukon
EMPIRE
Roseneath Primary School
Rand Clinic/-kliniek
ALEC GORSHEL PARK
BEREA
HILLBROW
J.G. Strijdom Tower/-toring
Child Health Institute/ Gedenkinstituut vir Kindergesondheid
DONALD MACKAY PARK
HIGHLANDS
NORTH
Harley Nursing Home/-verpleeginrigting
JUDITH'S PAARL
Bertrams Primary School
PRETORIA
KOTZE
Fort
Florence Nightingale Nursing Home
PULLINGER KOP
CHARLTON TERR.
BEREA
GORDON
LORENTZVILLE
BERTRAMS
Civic Centre
Burgersentrum
Miners Memorial
Hillbrow Hospital/-hospitaal
Lady Dudley Nursing Home
Hotel School
Windybrow
Friedenskirche
Joubert Park Laerskool
SARATOGA
Witwatersrand Technikon
DOORNFONTEIN
(ELLISPARK)
FULLER PARK
ELLIS PARK
SMIT
WOLMARANS
Leyds Technikon
JOUBERT PARK
Art Gallery/Kunssaal
I.H. Harris Primary School
M.B.S. Hospital/-hospitaal
Johannesburg
Railway Museum/-spoorwegmuseum
NZASM Locomotive/-lokomotief
Witwatersrand Technikon
UNION GROUND
Doornfontein
Ellis Park
NEW DOORNFONTEIN
ELLIS PARK
Standard Bank Arena
TROYEVILLE
KITCHENER
APPOLONIA
OP DIE BERGEN
COMMISSIONER
MALVERN
Jeppe High Prep School
Builders College
Fireman's Tower
Fairview Junior School
FAIRVIEW
JOHANNESBURG
Chris Lessing Boxing Museum
Connex Travel Bureau
Supreme Court
City Hall/ Stadsaal
Cuthberts Building
Rissik St
First National Bank Museum
Geological Museum
Carlton Centre/-sentrum
Jewish Museum
MARSHALLSTOWN
Poswohl Synagogue
Randjeslaagte Beacon
CITY & SUBURBAN
CITY & SUBURBAN INDUSTRIAL
Jeppe
JEPPESTOWN
NORTH DOORNFONTEIN
Edith Hinds Special School
John Mitchell Primary School
MURRAY PARK
JEPPESTOWN SOUTH
WOLHUTER
DROSTE PARK EXT
MAIN REEF
DROSTE PARK
SALISBURY CLAIMS
Faraday
WEMMER
NEW CENTRE
PARK CENTRAL
Village Main
PROLECON
Kaserne West
R 55
R 24
R 22
R 29

Street addresses, Johannesburg
Ivan Vladislavić

How bad a man was Scrooge, that model of solitary mean-spiritedness?

'Nobody ever stopped him in the street to say, with gladsome looks, "My dear Scrooge, how are you? When will you come to see me?" No beggars implored him to bestow a trifle, no children asked him what it was o'clock, no man or woman ever once in all his life inquired the way to such and such a place, of Scrooge.'[1]

The unequal exchange of directions is one of the most touching relations possible between people in the city, and so it is the most shocking measure of Scrooge's inhumanity that he was never once, in all his life, engaged in it. In asking for directions, city people, who set great store by their independence and hard-won knowledge of the streets, who like to think that they 'know their way around', declare their vulnerability; in giving directions, they demonstrate a capacity for dealing kindly and responsibly with a life entrusted into their hands by fate.

In the countryside, it is different. Strangers and locals stand in a simpler relationship to one another. Strangers are few and far between, and they are therefore less threatening rather than more so, as one might suppose. Locals know the world around them like the backs of their hands, as the saying goes, and landmarks are more conspicuous and easier to describe. In any event, a country person (if he did not have the whim to send you on a wild-goose chase) might think nothing of walking along with you, or driving ahead, to show you the way.

The busy city person must rely on words and gestures to guide the stranger through a landscape cluttered with irrelevant detail, with dead ends and false turns on every side, some of which might prove disastrous to the unwary. Giving directions is therefore a singular skill, and doing it well a reliable measure of character. We need not be judgemental: the way we live in cities today, it is possible to lead a useful, happy life without learning the names of the streets in the next block. It is also true that the complexity of cities, the flows of traffic across ever-changing grids, coupled with the peculiarities of physical addresses, occupations, interests and needs, produces for each one of us a particular pattern of familiar or habitual movement over the skin of the earth which, if we could see it from a vantage point in the sky, would appear as unique as a fingerprint. It is literally impossible for certain of these paths to cross, which is why acquaintances may live in the same city, meeting by appointment as often as they choose, without ever running into one another in the daily round. But this is all the more reason why the crossing of paths, the places where they touch like wires in a circuit, for no better reason than chance, should be taken seriously ...

When I was a child, my father, a city man through and through, a lover of both walking and driving, profoundly attuned to change in the world around him and therefore able to give directions with creativity and precision, taught me that it never harmed anyone to have a map in hand. No lost soul was ever turned away from our door without a set of directions that would take him to his exact destination. We lived in a new suburb then, carved out of the veld on the outskirts of Pretoria; the world belonged to us, we were masters of all we surveyed. These were the days of the garden-variety wire fence, long before the advent of the candy-striped boom and the two-metre wall, when some stranger who had lost his way might hail a man mowing his lawn or tinkering with the engine of a car in the driveway. More often than not my father would recognize the place at once and be able to give directions off the cuff. But even when he knew the way himself, he liked to send me or my brother Branko to fetch his map of the area, a detailed one acquired specially from the municipality, and spread it out on the bonnet of the stranger's car, to point out the route. Perhaps the whole exercise was an excuse to have the stranger get out from behind the wheel and pass the time of day.

Since then, experience has taught me – and a host of writers, as unalike as Robert Louis Stevenson and Walter Benjamin, have confirmed – that getting lost is not always a bad thing. One might even consider misdirecting a stranger for his own good.

1 The alarmed house

When a house has been alarmed, my good friend Marilyn says, it becomes explosive. It must be armed and disarmed several times a day. When it is armed, by the touching of keys upon a pad, it emits a whine that sends the occupants rushing out, banging the door behind them. There are no leisurely departures: there is no time for second thoughts, for taking a scarf from the hook behind the door, for checking that the answering machine is on, for a final look in the mirror on the way through the hallway. There are no savoured homecomings either: you do not unwind into such a house, kicking off your shoes, breathing the familiar air. Every departure is precipitate, every arrival is a scraping-in.

In an alarmed house, you awake in the small hours to find the room unnaturally light. The keys on the touchpad are aglow with an uncanny, luminous green, like a night-light for a child who's afraid of the dark.

2 New lives

I live just around the corner from the Marymount Nursing Home. In fact, I often use it as a landmark when giving people directions to my door. In the winter months, when you can see through the naked branches of the oaks in the dead end of Blenheim Street, the building announces itself in large white letters on orange brick. In summer it all but disappears behind the foliage.

Several times over the years, it has happened that a guest in my home, leaning on the parapet of the stoep with a cup of tea, and looking out over the treetops into the valley, has suddenly recognized the building jutting out on the ridge, and exclaimed: Is that the Marymount? I was born there! A silence always falls after this unexpectedly intimate revelation, as if the spirit of place still had the power to cast a spell over our rootless hearts. But it only lasts a moment: there is something about the marmalade-brick building, with its white plaster and corrugated-iron roof, that prevents us from thinking too deeply about our origins.

I used to consider it a remarkable coincidence that so many in my circle should have had their beginnings within a stone's throw of my house. But Branko, who is more of a realist than I am, boiled it down to statistical probabilities. In the fifty years of the Marymount's operation, more than two hundred thousand babies came into the world within its walls. Ten or eleven babies a week, on average, with peaks around September. You can hardly turn a corner in Johannesburg without bumping into a Marymount baby.

Branko also took the mystery out of why I was always being called upon to direct the anxious parents-to-be towards the nursing home, a service I performed five or six times in as many years. It stands to reason, he said, that anyone following the sign from Kitchener Avenue will lose their way on the corner of Blenheim and Argyle. It's the first point at which they have to make a decision for themselves. And seeing that your house is right there, and that you must go in and out through the front gate every day, someone casting about for directions is bound to seize upon you from time to time. It's the law of averages.

Although I cannot claim to have chosen my house on the strength of its proximity to the Marymount, like some peasant eager to live in the shadow of the church or within walking distance of the well, its presence was always reassuring (I would never admit this to my brother): every day, a squad of new human souls came into the world on my doorstep. And so it is a pity that the home has closed down. The last baby was born there in June 1997. The number of births had been tapering off for years, as more and more white doctors moved further and further north, taking their patients with them.[2] People in the northern suburbs can no longer believe that a decent person would want to be born on this side of town.

It was a year before posters went up in the neighbourhood advertising the public auction of the property on 9 July. Two groups with very different plans for the place made bids for ownership: a consortium of midwives and doctors intended to revive it as a nursing home; a consortium of businessmen proposed to transform it into low-cost housing or a park for light industry. Dry-cleaners and panel-beaters. New lives of a different sort. But neither group has been able to raise the finance.

3 The Gandhi House

A few days after the auction, the cobbler who has set up shop on the corner of Nourse and Hillier streets was putting one of the posters to good use by spreading his tools out on it. The neighbourhood's first street-corner hawker. He has chosen an auspicious location, opposite the neighbourhood's national monument: the house where

Mahatma Gandhi lived in the first decades of the century. You can see the little plaque from the National Monuments Council on the west-facing wall as you come down Nourse Street. The house is a double-storey on a promontory between Hillier and Albemarle[3] streets, with a beautiful panel of stained-glass sunshine to light the stairs and a second-storey balcony like the rounded prow of a riverboat.

For a while, the people who live in the Gandhi House, as we call it around here, kept a tree in their garden made entirely of metal, no doubt highly resistant to drought, with fanciful, curly branches like a candelabrum, where a cast-iron owl was perched. But it is gone now, dead of rust or carried away in the night by a scrap-metal dealer.

4 Proprieties

When they defined the boundary between Troyeville and Kensington, the town planners did not follow the suggestion of a street, which seems to be the norm; instead they drew a line behind the houses on the western side of Albemarle Street, where the back walls of the plots adjoin those of the houses behind them. Rather than meeting face to face, the two suburbs turn their backs on one another.

The recent history of the house at 22 Albemarle Street, strictly in Kensington, is nonetheless typical of the frontier suburb which Troyeville has become, a contested zone between inner-city suburbs like Fairview and New Doornfontein, which have evolved into black areas, and Kensington, which still holds on to its white identity.

The house is a renovation of the kind found in suburbs with a large Portuguese population (Troyeville and Bez Valley in the east, say, or Rosettenville and La Rochelle in the south). In a standard Portuguese renovation the structure is squared off, the fat pillars that once held up the veranda roof are replaced with angular, painted piping and the stoep and pathways are tiled; in more extreme versions, the entire façade may be tiled and the garden cemented over, with the occasional porthole provided for a scrawny rosebush to stick out its neck. In the Albemarle Street house, there is a low garden wall of brick topped with wrought-iron curlicues, a tiled path bisecting two squares of lawn, leading to glass doors in a rounded archway. The veranda has been closed in and provided with four lancet-arch windows, in pairs on either side of the doors. These windows are outlined in narrow panels of frosted glass as brown as a beer-bottle. Across the top of the flat façade is a single row of mosaic tiles.

The house was put up for sale in 1997. Perhaps the owner was frightened off when the old lady at 17 Blenheim Street was murdered. The murderers, surprised in the act by a neighbour, jumped over the back wall into the yard of the house behind, just a few doors up from No. 22, and escaped into Albemarle Street. After several months on the market and a string of show days, there were still no buyers, and for a time the house stood empty. Finally, it was put up for rent. The first black tenants moved in. It was around then that a sticker bearing the slogan of the anti-crime campaign – 'I don't do crime' – appeared on the glass door: either an appeal to the better nature of prospective burglars or an attempt by the new tenants (or their landlord) to reassure the neighbours.

For a while the new tenants stayed indoors. Then, as they grew more comfortable in the area, they became more visible. Soon there were children pushing toy cars on the pathway or playing soccer in the street. Tricycles and dolls lay on the lawn. Men lounged about on the steps or worked on cars at the kerbside, and women sat on upturned oildrums, catching the sun on a wintry afternoon.

What's wrong with these people? my brother Branko said during the last of our walking tours, just before he moved to Sandton. Why don't they stay inside like normal people? Why are they always lazing about in the yard? Have they got nothing better to do with their time than sit around in the sun?

But you're the one who's always complaining that there's no life on the streets, I said, and how terrible it is that people feel trapped in their own homes. Just last week you were remembering how we used to play cricket under the street lights at night after supper, when we were kids.

What's with the paint tins? he said grumpily. Can't they get proper garden furniture?

A few weeks later, Branko was insisting the place had been turned into a brothel. On his way down to see me one morning, he noticed a woman sitting on the kerb outside, with a towel draped over her shoulders that said 'Ambassador Hotel'. She was separating the strands of her thick braids so that they would dry in the sun, her fingers moving over her scalp as if she was working the fibres of some plant into matting. He slowed down to get a good look at her, he said, and she gave him a sly smile.

A brothel? It seemed possible. But the very next Sunday, as I was walking to the shops to fetch the paper, a black churchman, like a biblical prophet in his white cotton robes, came out of the house and made his way up the hill to Roberts Avenue ahead of me. The stick he carried in his right hand had been carved into a cross, and a Bible with golden edges stuck out of a pocket in his tunic. In the small of his back, carefully stitched to a broad red cummerbund, was a pure blue circle the size of a coaster.

Where would his congregation meet? In a clearing in the veld near the municipal dump in Elandsfontein, in a sealed room under the motorway in Newtown, filled with pitted wooden benches and the incense of exhaust fumes, beneath a tree on Langerman Kop?

As he walked he patted his hair with the palm of his left hand, and looked at the shadow of his head on the ground. Involuntarily I smoothed my own hair by combing it through with my fingers, and was reminded that we live differently in our bodies and our houses. But I had resolved not to pursue such difficult and divisive lines of thought, especially over weekends, and so I veered into Tile City in Op de Bergen Street for a chat with the hardware man.

5 The Madonna of Eleanor Street

The house at 18 Eleanor Street is another Portuguese modernization, but more restrained. It once had three notable features, all of them amulets against danger, but only one has survived. In the left-hand corner of the severely cropped lawn sat a life-size statue of a German shepherd dog, with painted fur and a grinning jaw. It looked like a large-scale version of the collection boxes the Society for the Prevention of Cruelty to Animals used to leave on shop counters. On the right-hand façade of the house, the second and third amulets were arranged symmetrically on either side of the central window (a bedroom, to judge by lacy curtains behind Spanish bars), like icons at an altar. On the left: a rectangular panel composed of six blue ceramic tiles, together depicting the Virgin Mary. On the right: a signboard, of exactly the same size and colour, declaring that the house was protected by the National Investigations and Security Systems (N.I.S.S.) armed response company.

This house has been sold to a coloured family, who apparently have no taste for Roman Catholic iconography. After a few months of tolerating her presence, they chiselled Mary off the wall: a patch of white plaster in the cream-coloured paintwork remains behind like a conscience. The dog is gone too, but the N.I.S.S. sign endures.

The spot where David Webster was shot dead is just across the road.

6 Carlton Centre I: Hawking the telephone dixie

When I was at high school, the father of one of my classmates invented the telephone dixie: a little desk-top cabinet for the tidy and convenient storage of telephone directories. The open-fronted box held three heavy-duty ledger files, hinged at the bottom so that they could be tilted out and opened flat. Using a simple mechanism of springy clasps, you could secure in these files the Yellow Pages and two directories of your choice – let's say Johannesburg and the West Rand – and they were guaranteed to stay spick and span through a year of regular use. It was a fine and necessary invention. There was an executive model, as I recall, in lightly padded vinyl, but even the plain metallic models were superbly made. I have forgotten the exact finishes, but the colour schemes of the day were culinary: mustard, burgundy, cream.

The school holidays came, and my friend and I were engaged as salesmen. For my friend, who lived in what is now Midrand, then known with more charm as Halfway House, 'town' was not Pretoria, as it was for me, but Johannesburg, and it was to that thrillingly unfamiliar city we went to do business. Every morning for a week, I tramped through the endless corridors of the Carlton Centre, in my school flannels and my father's tie, hawking the telephone dixie.

It was 1972 and the Carlton Centre had just been built. Colour scheme: orange. You could smell the paint on the walls and the latex adhesive on the wall-to-wall carpets. There was an air of supreme sophistication about the entire complex. One index of this was the colour-coded maps on shiny boards, showing the different blocks and shopping levels, and the numbers of individual shops, alongside the information booth, where a uniformed official sat ready to offer guidance if you lost your way. Surely such elaborate precautions had never been required before *inside* a building? They confirmed the vast and labyrinthine dimensions of the place.[4]

Then I had not yet read Frank Bettger's *How I Raised Myself from Failure to Success in Selling*,[5] which Dale Carnegie himself adjudged the most helpful and inspiring book on salesmanship he had ever read, and so I was lacking in expertise. My friend fared little better. But despite our evident lack of success, we laboured steadily up the floors of the office tower, my friend plying the even numbers and me plying the odd, demonstrating the virtues of the telephone dixie to anyone who would listen, and praying for orders. Our rise to the top took several days. Often I got no further than the receptionists, who sometimes made me wrestle with the spring-loaded clips for their own amusement. Occasionally I made it into the offices of junior managers and senior clerks. Here, with the whole city for a backdrop, every white person capable of sitting up straight behind a desk appeared to be a business magnate. Up we went, floor by floor. The higher we toiled, the more spectacular the views became. On a clear day, it was said, you could see Pretoria. I began to relish those moments when the person whose precious time I was wasting would leave the room to attend to more pressing concerns, so that I could stand before the window and look down at the immensity of the city, assured that even a hawker of telephone dixies could occupy the centre of it all. It was in these reflective moments that my sense of the unnatural beauty of Johannesburg was born and that I resolved to seek my fortune in these streets.

At the end of a busy morning, the sales team had lunch at the Pumpernickel on Level 200. The food was unlike anything we had ever seen. There were frankfurters with notches carved into their convex curves and skinny potato chips with corrugated edges. There were bangers wrapped in bacon and dribbled with melted cheese, all held together with toothpicks. The fruit juices had little umbrellas unfurled in them; the paper sleeves of the drinking straws had been teased into decorative ruffs. While we scoffed the only material rewards of our efforts, the demonstration dixies stood at heel beside our chairs like well-trained dogs.

7 Carlton Centre II: The vanishing parkade

Every month for the past fifteen years, on the second Thursday of the month to be precise, I have met my brother Branko for coffee at the Carlton Centre (to which he is also sentimentally attached, for reasons of his own). I could chart the life and death of this great complex by the sequence of coffee shops which came to serve as our regular meeting-place over the years: from the Koffiehuis, where the waitresses were got up as Dutch dairymaids in clogs and lace caps, to the Brazilian coffee shop, where the cups and saucers arrived and departed on a conveyor belt. But let me do it another way.

When we first began meeting, the parkade in Main Street, opposite the hotel, was always full. You would have to wind up the spiral ramp to the fourth or fifth floor to find a bay. Little arrows and neon signs saying 'Full' and 'Up', in red and green respectively, kept you circling higher until a floor would accept you. There were attendants too, the obligatory middlemen between motorists and machinery, waving you on. The shiny concrete gave unexpected squeals of delight beneath the tyres. When you finally came to rest, you had to memorize the colour of the floor and the number of the bay, or you would never find your way back. There were four lifts, large enough to park a Volkswagen in. Even here, in the parkade, the slightly unsettling smell of food, which came to circulate in the atmosphere of the entire centre once the paint fumes had worn off, reminded you that pleasurable consumption lay ahead.[6]

Then, in the mid-1990s, the parkade began to shrink. The demand for parking fell, level by level, like a barometer of change in the city centre. The people with cars were clearly going elsewhere. Suddenly you could find parking on the fourth floor, and after a while on the third, and then always on the second or first. Finally the illuminated arrows were switched off.

In May 1998 – it would have been Thursday the 14th – when I turned into Main Street, there was a chain slung across my usual entrance. The middleman, who was always there at the boom to catch the ticket the machine spat out and hand it to you through the window, was nowhere to be seen. Instead a sign urged me down an unfamiliar ramp into the basement. A long tunnel, with odd twists and turns in it, peculiar level landings and sudden lurching descents, took me down below the ground. I soon lost my sense of direction. Eventually I found myself in a crowded corner of the basement, where the cars were all huddled like refugees. An armed guard oversaw my arrival. I made my way to the nearest lift, but there was a label pasted across the crack between the doors, as if to prevent them from opening: Hotel Closed. It reminded me of a crime scene. The guard appeared at my shoulder and directed me to a distant lift, which brought me out in an unpopulated alley of the centre, which I had last ventured into with a telephone dixie in my hand.

As we sat drinking our espressos at the little counter in the office block, which somehow makes you feel like you're in New York, my brother told me that he would not be coming into the city any more. It was too far to travel, and too dangerous, and unpleasant anyway, what with empty shops and echoing corridors and the smell of urine in the doorways.

When I resurfaced into the chilly air a little later, a fierce white light caught my eye. Welders in overalls were sealing off the grand entrance to the Carlton Hotel behind a palisade fence.

8 The art lover

Sophie Calle's exhibition 'The Detachment' is on at the Johannesburg Art Gallery in Joubert Park.[7] She describes her way of working: 'I visited places from which symbols of the former East Germany have been effaced. I asked passers-by to describe the objects that once filled these empty spaces. I photographed the absence and replaced the missing monuments with their memories.' The photographs show empty niches, overturned pedestals, unscrewed plaques. In the accompanying texts, the citizens of East Berlin recollect the displaced memorials as best they can, accurately or not, with or without fondness; there are also photographs of the old times, when the symbols of power still occupied their places with confidence, and these allow us to stand in judgement on the veracity of the recorded memories.

The bell rings to signal that the gallery is about to close. I stop at the toilet in the basement on the way out. A streetchild, as filthy as a sweep, comes out of one of the cubicles with a length of toilet paper dangling from his pocket and starts to wash his face at one of the basins. While I'm wringing my hands under the dryer, a security guard bursts in, grabs the boy by his arm, and hustles him away.

I go out into the deserted gallery. On my left, set into the curved wall that discreetly screens the entrances into the toilets from the exhibition space, is a concrete ledge, and happening to glance down as I pass it, I see a grubby white sneaker sticking out. I bend down and look under the ledge. There is an oddly shaped recess I would never have noticed. Two small boys are crammed into it. They smell of woodsmoke and sweat. They draw in their legs and look at me with big eyes. Like a true art lover, I go on my way ambivalently, through the empty halls, past African crafts and 19th-century oils, and the security guard locks the door behind me.

E

9 Walking goodbye I: 'Hercules Cacti'

My friend Chas is going to live in Cape Town at the end of the year. For some months, ever since Branko abandoned me, I have been accompanying Chas on his goodbye walks, revisiting, recalling, and relinquishing the parts of the city he expects to miss despite himself. The city, we always agree, is no more than a mnemonic. Where do we go? Here and there. What do we talk about? This and that. What do we see?

In July, for instance, as we made our way along Empire Road through the S-bend at Helpmekaar Hoërskool, we discovered, atop a wall on the left, an innovative anti-scaling device known as 'Hercules Cacti'. Stepping gingerly through tangled ivy, and assuring ourselves first that the device was not electrified, we examined it in detail. 'Hercules Cacti' consisted of cylindrical segments, fiercely spiked and barbed all round with outgrowths like pineapple tops, apparently of metal but coated for durability, mounted horizontally on long axles affixed to the top of the wall. Ingenious, we said to one another, spinning a segment and watching it whirr. The thief hasn't been born who could get over here. More expensive than spikes, undoubtedly, but twice as effective. Probably more expensive than electric fencing too, but then there would be no running costs or maintenance. Looks indestructible. And quite natural, almost like thorn branches, especially in that drab olive-green. Then we backed away to the pavement, and went on, dusting the last sad traces of irony from the turn-ups of our trousers.

10 Walking goodbye II: The scent of eucalyptus

Further discoveries awaited us in Pieter Roos Park, where Victoria and Empire meet. In the south-western corner, the remains of a primitive outdoor gymnasium, from the heyday of jogging and Jane Fonda, with apparatus made of wooden posts for jumping over and hoisting oneself up on, all quite unfit for use. In the north-eastern corner, a metal sculpture, vaguely suggestive of a prehistoric bird, with two black men asleep in the shade of its belly. One opened an eye and glared at us balefully. The only other white men in the park appeared to be tramps.

In the middle, a grove of bluegums. The scent of eucalyptus reminded Chas of his boyhood home in Vereeniging, and that he is saying goodbye not just to Johannesburg but to the Transvaal, which no longer exists, to the Highveld, to the interior.

Then I too was reminded of my childhood, in a new suburb laid out in the veld on the edge of Pretoria. The houses were new, and in the American style, or so we thought, with their big glass windows and garages attached to one end; and the roads were long and straight and newly tarred, and littered with cow dung. In the mornings the herdboys would drive the cattle along Von Willich Avenue to graze in the veld on the edge of the suburb, and in the evenings they would bring them back again, to the whitewashed stalls of the smallholdings, where the bluegums shed long smooth curls of bark on which it was possible to write the life story of a marooned man. Electricity pylons marched to the east and west across the veld, and the Voortrekker Monument squatted on the distant horizon.

11 To the Café Europa

One afternoon in 1989, a retired proofreader by the name of Aubrey Tearle (the protagonist of one of my fictions) is supposed to have set out from his flat in Prospect Road, Berea, heading for the Café Europa, his Hillbrow haunt. For reasons too complicated to explain here, he is lugging with him a life's worth of papers in two shopping-bags. On the corner of O'Reilly and Fife, he chances upon an abandoned supermarket trolley, gratefully loads his bags into it, and goes speedily on to his destination. Having delivered the trolley into the hands of the security guard at the OK Bazaars in Twist Street, he ascends into the quiet interior of the Café Europa, where he takes his usual seat, arranges his papers about him and begins to work. Alas, the Café Europa has closed its doors. Like the Café Zürich and the Café de Paris, the Wien and the Pigalle, it endures as no more than a fiction of the remembered city.

12 Points of view

When I lived in Yeoville in the 1980s, I would go walking in Highlands to enjoy the view over Bez Valley. Highlands is one of those tiny suburbs most people don't even recognize, but I know someone who lived there as a child thirty years ago, in a block of flats on the very edge of the ridge.

On weekends, he once told me, there would be skokiaan parties on the slopes below, where women sold their home-brew among the bluegums, and a blend of dagga smoke and mbaqanga melodies would drift up on the breeze. Inevitably someone would call the police. The vans would arrive in Hunter Street with squealing tyres, and the cops would go chasing after people with their batons, while others lay in wait on Stewart's Drive for the fugitives. White policemen and black party-goers, crashing around in the veld, bawling and swearing. The balconies of the flats offered a grandstand view, and whole families would gather to watch, as if they were at the pantomime.

Once, one of the neighbours, vaulting over a couch in his haste to catch every minute of the entertainment, cracked his skull on the curve of an archway, and had to be taken away in an ambulance.

13 Murder

On a Saturday night in 1926, the writer Herman Charles Bosman shot dead his step-brother in the family home at 19 Isipingo Street, Bellevue.[8] The place was pointed out to me one day by my friend Louise, as we drove past on the way to my flat in Webb Street (the extension of Isipingo on the Yeoville side of Bezuidenhout Avenue). After that, I hardly ever passed by the house without being reminded of murder.

As an admirer of Bosman, I thought that people should be made aware of this historic site. I imagined a marker; nothing brassy, mind you, just a simple tablet, like those paving-stones that carry the impress of the manufacturer. And the spot marked on the tourist maps as a place of interest. Death by shooting was less common in those days, in my suburb at least, and seemed somehow more benign. And Bosman himself had given it a romantic sheen. Today I would want a map that is more complete, more representative, recording every violent death on the Witwatersrand, above ground and below, by axe and blade and bullet. What a title deed to despair it would be, this map of the city of the dead, cross-stitched in black, crumpling under the weight of sorrow as you struggle to unfold it on the dining-room table.

Louise finds this morbid. Why not a map of the living? she asks. Why not a map showing every room, in every house, in every street of this bursting city, where a life began?

14 Memory I: The Great Wall of Jeff

One night a couple of years ago, as we sat in the kitchen of Jeff's house in Rockey Street, drinking beer and eating prawn rolls from his uncle's restaurant in Chinatown, he shared with Branko and me the scheme for his next artistic project: a wall of remembrance.

The city is saturated with death, Jeff said, it is passing away even as we speak, and everyone in it, including ourselves. We must build to commemorate, while there is still time, not just the famous or the fallen, but ... everyone. Every person in the Greater Johannesburg area, identified by the voters' rolls, must be required to donate an object to the artist for use in the work. This object shall be no larger than a standard brick and shall be enclosed in due course in a transparent resin block of those very dimensions. These object-enclosing bricks shall be used in turn to construct a wall. The Great Wall of Jeff.

There and then, with a feverish sense of our own impending demise, we began to work out the costs. Or rather, because Branko insisted that we be realistic, the extent of the funds we would have to raise. Europe is awash with cash for installations and stuff like that, said Jeff. Asia unfortunately not. An input from the mainland would be good – but Taiwan is out of the question.

Let's say you manage to raise the money for a mountain of resin and a sea of glue, said Branko. The objects will still be a major headache. How on earth will you get people in this greedy town to give things away?

But we're not looking for diamond rings and krugerrands, said Jeff, although I'll bet we get a couple of them. We're looking for any little thing the donor can be induced to part with. It could be nothing more than a button or a piece of string. Everyone has something they could live without.

In the small hours we did the quantity surveying, totting up the number of bricks in a ten-metre length of wall, two metres high, two courses thick. Jeff fetched the calculator his brother sent him from Hong Kong for his birthday. Later we moved on to the likely numbers of everyday objects – keys, coins, pencil sharpeners. Even later we worked through the conventional body parts – appendixes, gallstones, wisdom teeth – and the run-of-the-mill fetishes.

I had started out thinking this was one of those artistic projects that would be easier to realize on paper than in the world. It had been on the tip of my tongue to offer to write it down, to work the idea up into a scrap of fiction, relieving Jeff of the responsibility of having to pretend that practical steps were necessary. But I came away convinced that the Great Wall of Jeff belonged in the city. I even had my eye on a patch of parkland in Bertrams for the construction site.

15 Memory II: The hyperama of sentimental value

The next morning Branko phoned to say that he had come to his senses and wanted nothing more to do with this mad scheme. Frankly, I was relieved. Once my sensible sibling, with his litany of costs and constraints, was out of the picture, we would be free to build as we pleased. And, indeed, the scheme immediately took an interesting new direction.

Calling it an artwork will create the wrong impression, I said to Jeff. People are so ill-disposed towards art. Let's make it a public works project.

What difference will that make?

We'll employ brick-makers, we'll create jobs, the whole thing will be voluntary and transparent. Instead of dictating to people, we'll ask them nicely to donate the materials: it will improve the quality of the objects. Anyone can be coerced into parting with a safety pin. But what's the point? Let 's say the whole initiative is aimed at those people who wish to be part of it, who have an active desire to be commemorated.

It was this line of thinking which introduced the question of values.

Jeff's idea: Why not have them donate an object that really means something to them. And let them put a price on it, an estimate of its worth, which we can etch upon the brick along with their names. This is the Golden City, after all, the capital of buying and selling. And what is a city if not a showcase of subjective attachments?

My idea: Why a wall? Half the city has already vanished behind walls. Even a semi-transparent one can only make things worse. Why not something useful?

At which point there arose before my mind's eye a building that owed something to the Crystal Palace, and something else to the Transvaal Museum in Church Street, Pretoria, and something more to the Hyperama in the Eastgate Mall. And I was walking along its shiny corridors, surrounded on all sides by a peculiarly impenetrable transparency, where objects hung suspended, attached by nothing but space to the names of the people who once loved them.

16 The poor man's purse

In the spring of 1991, I was walking up Viljoen Street in Lorentzville, when I saw a black man in overalls sitting on the kerb, taking off a pair of broken boots and putting on a brand-new pair of running shoes, which he had just finished lacing. I was reminded of Douglas Spaulding, the American kid in Ray Bradbury's Dandelion Wine,[9] who exchanged his winter shoes for a pair of Litefoot sneakers at Mr Sanderson's shoe store. Douglas cleverly persuaded the proprietor to try on a pair of Litefoots himself, to feel how quick and lively they rendered the wearer. Not only was the old man moved to give the boy the sneakers at a discount, he offered him a job selling shoes in his emporium. While I was recalling this, the black man finished lacing the shoes and walked quickly away, with a spring in his step, leaving the old boots side by side in the gutter. The whole episode seemed like a parable about the dignity of labour, the moving congruence of hard work rewarded by simple but intense pleasures. I went on my way with a lump in my throat.

A few blocks further on there was a commotion on the pavement outside Seedat's Outfitters in Kitchener Avenue. A passer-by had flung a brick through the plate-glass and snatched some goods from the window. The brick was still lying there among the dusty satin drapes, chrome-plated pedestals and handwritten price-tags. It was a wonderful brick, a model brick, with three round holes through it the size of one-rand coins, filled with chips of broken glass.

17 Double beds

In August, the tenants of the house at 32 Albemarle Street were evicted. The furniture piled on the pavement made it look like a forced removal. In passing, for the record, I counted ten double beds.

18 Brass

A previous owner of Marilyn's house was a DIY man and fond of wood. Her house is full of his handiwork. He must have been very tall, she says. Her feet don't touch the floor when she sits on the window seat, and the rails in the built-in cupboards are so high she can hardly reach. Even his little touches were large ones - the door handles were made for a heavyweight's fist, the window sills would hold a set of encyclopedias.

On the inside of the wall beside the front gate he installed a letter-box for a person with large appetites, someone capable of sustaining extensive correspondences and making extravagant purchases by mail order. On the outside was a brass slot, with a peak like a postman's cap for keeping out the rain, covering an aperture in the wall. That slot was generous enough to admit a rolled newspaper or a thickly stuffed A4 envelope.

A small letterbox is more than an inconvenience, it is the mark of a mean nature. But if Marilyn's letterbox had been smaller, if there had been less brass in it, it may have been less attractive to a thief. One night towards the end of May 1998 some scavenger after scrap stuck a crowbar under one edge of the slot and broke it out of the plaster. Now the box is filling up with dust and dead leaves. The hardware man at Tile City offered her a replacement in plastic, not as durable as brass but unlikely to be stolen. People had been coming in all day, he said, wanting plastic numbers for their gates.

Afterwards Marilyn and I took a walk through the neighbourhood, from one shadowy number of unvarnished wood to another of unpainted plaster, following the trail the thieves blazed up and down the blocks, breaking brass numbers off doors and walls.

In the front door of my own house is a slot, with a hinged flap marked 'Letters', left over from a time when the postman, unhindered by locks and barbs and security doors, could open the front gate, walk up the path, climb the steps, cross the stoep, and drop the letters through the slot onto the hallway floor.

When he explained why people searching for the Marymount always got lost on my corner, Branko unwittingly revealed something crucial about movement through the city. The way and the walker (and the driver, too, if he has time for such things) are in conversation. Ask a question of any intersection – say you are looking for company, the centre of things, water, the road less travelled – and it will answer, not always straightforwardly, allowing a quirk of the topography, the lie of the land, a glimpse of a prospect to nudge you one way or the other. This conversation is one of the things that makes city walking interesting, and one of the great masters of the art was Dickens.

Long before he invented London, Dickens knew that cities exist primarily so that we can walk around in them. The *Sketches by Boz*, his earliest published writings, collected for the first time in 1836, no less than the essays published thirty years later as *The Uncommercial Traveller*, were largely the products of such wanderings. In each of the books there is a piece devoted to walking in the city at night. 'The Streets – Night' starts with the declaration that the streets of London, 'to be beheld in the very height of their glory, should be seen on a dark, dull, murky winter's night',[10] and the descriptions that follow are confined largely to the savoury side of midnight, to muffin-men and kidney-pie merchants and playgoers. In the later piece, 'Night Walks', the insomniac author, in the figure of 'Houselessness', walks and walks and walks, from midnight to daybreak, and presents a fuller and more sombre picture of the city.

Yet even as he tells us how quiet and empty the streets are, when the last drunkards turned out by the publicans have staggered away, and the late piemen and hot-potato men have gone off trailing sparks, and even as he yearns for a sign of company, there seems to be life and light around every corner: the tollkeeper at his fire on Waterloo Bridge, the 'fire and light' of the Newgate turnkeys, a watchman with a lantern. In his most threatening encounters with other creatures – a furtive figure withdrawing into a shadowed doorway, a ragged beggar – they are as suspicious and frightened as he. In a coffee-room at Covent Garden, where there is toast and coffee to be had at an early hour, he comes across the most alarming figure of all: a man who produces a meat pudding from his hat, stabs it with his knife, tears it apart with his fingers and gobbles it down. It is enough to make one envious, that the darkest villains of the piece should be possessed of such extravagant habits and showy appetites.

When daylight comes, and the streets begin to fill with workmen and hawkers, Dickens admits what we have begun to suspect – that he and the streets have not just been conversing, but arguing, that it has taken him some effort, and given him some pleasure, to pursue his solitary way: 'And it is not, as I used to think, going home at such times, the least wonderful thing in London, that in the real desert region of the night, the houseless wanderer is alone there.' [11]

We are entitled to envy Dickens. He lived in a city which offered the walker 'miles upon miles of streets' in which to be lonely, and 'warm company' at every turn once his loneliness had been satisfied. He lived, moreover, in a city which collaborated enthusiastically in its own invention; we live in a city which resists our bravest efforts. Or have I misunderstood? Is the problem that we live in a fiction which unravels even as we grasp it? What would Dickens make of us, scurrying through these desperate streets, clutching at stones?

A stranger, arriving one evening in the part of Johannesburg I call home, would think it had been struck by some calamity, that every last person had fled. There is no sign of life. Behind the walls, the houses are ticking like bombs. The curtains are drawn tight, the security lights are glaring, the gates are bolted. Even the cars have hidden themselves. Our stranger, passing fearfully through the streets, whether in search of someone with open hands of whom he might ask directions or merely of someone to avoid in the pursuit of solitude, finds no one at all.

◂B2 ◂D10

House Martienssen
Jo Ractliffe

'Architects' houses tend to be interesting not because they inevitably exceed either on practical or aesthetic grounds the work done in the normal way, but because they are in a sense snatches of autobiography. The autobiographical note can, of course, creep into a house designed for a client just as it does in the work of a novelist like André Gide when he purports to be writing a novel. But it still remains a general proposition that the artistic or technical stock-in-trade of the architect – that which enables him to solve a specific problem in terms of possessed equipment – is something a little external to his own core, his own centre of self expression. The very definition of architecture, the aspect which distinguishes it so sharply from the personal arts, poetry, music, sculpture and painting, necessitates this aloofness, this method which is the exploitation of an elaborate technique rather than the direct and simple outpouring of a creative spirit.

...

Now the formulation of one's own problems has little similarity to the recording and digesting of externally generated conditions or problems. There is a tendency towards blurring and confusion since the statement of the problem (specifically in the design of an architect's own house) and the available theoretical technique are offshoots of the same personality.'

R. Martienssen, 'Evolution of an architect's house',
South African Architectural Record, February (1942).

FUJI RDPII
I 9
RDPII 10

JJI RDPII
RDPII 137
RDPII 11

E

FUJI RDPII
RDPII 17
RDPII

FUJI RDPII
RDPII 19

Take
your
body
where it has
never
been before

In the nowhere city which is Jo'burg we, the people of the leisured classes, always seem to be taking our bodies to where they've been before.

Along the bleak, billboard-encrusted thoroughfares and freeways of this city we take them to safe places, walled or otherwise enclosed, implicitly or explicitly exclusive, places which provide the flattering illusion of meaningful being and dwelling. We travel in our burglar- and bullet-proof cars from our walled and wired houses to the well-patrolled labyrinths of Westgate, Eastgate, Northgate, all those lookalike bunker-faced shopping malls. Or, if we consider ourselves too cool for trolleys, we take our bods out to some leafy suburb or other, to a carefully preserved villagey street, where we cling to our tables in cutesy coffee bars or linger in second-hand bookshops before they disappear, like countless others before them, into even safer neighbourhoods. We'll follow them there too and protect them all over again for as long as they last, sipping our sidewalk cappuccinos, sheltering behind our newspapers and our cellphones. And so we try to shut out the beggars and the parking attendants gesturing to us endlessly with bland knowingness from the margins of our guarded field of vision.

There is no 'there' in the nowhere city. Gertrude Stein's comment about the American urban dystopias holds for Johannesburg too, a city that for its own economic and political reasons increasingly lacks a natural and organic centre with its own irresistible magnetism for an indwelling community. And so, in this sprawling placeless place where glittering affluence and abject wretchedness are chained together like dead and living bodies, we are always en route, we always have places to go. The urban health club is one of these places, guarded and exclusive like all our favourite destinations. But it promises, in pulsating neon writing, something entirely unique, a chance to take our bodies where they've never been before. We suspend our disbelief and we keep on going back, again and again, to take our bodies to that where.

What an ambitious challenge it would be to analyse the contemporary Jo'burg gym the way Walter Benjamin, in his famous essay, analysed the 19th-century Parisian arcade.[1] Through a close-up focus on this specific phenomenon he aimed to uncover a more general social and cultural logic. Benjamin himself could be seen prowling the arcades like some sort of tramp, obsessively sniffing out the evasive habits of the *flâneur*, the relaxed and skilful connoisseur for whom the city was a free field of stimulus and adventure. Here in the arcades, according to his analysis, the new modern culture of the commodity emerged, a culture of disjunct movement where the senses are relentlessly bombarded by stimuli, a mobile, swirling landscape marked by chance encounter, fast transaction, the frenetic circulation of money, goods and bodies.[2]

Merely contemplating a comparable project daunts the writer. For the roughshod architectural and social amalgam of Jo'burg seems to resist and deplete the imagination, the faculty par excellence that is libidinally charged by cities like Paris and New York. As Cyril Connolly says: 'If Paris is the setting for a romance, New York is the perfect city in which to get over one, to get over anything. Here the lost "douceur de vivre" is forgotten and intoxication of living takes its place.'[3] Young Jo'burg, squirming in its constant itchy entropy of fast money and still faster guns, more often than not seems to be the one place where it would be appropriate to stop the world and get off. Perhaps that is the steady reminder emitted by its only distinguishing landmarks, the broadcasting towers of Brixton and Hillbrow.

With envy one recalls those famous commemorative lines by Baudelaire in his poem *Le Cygne*. 'Paris changes!' he declares ... but new buildings, old neighbourhoods, 'all turn into allegory and my dearest / memories weigh more than a stone'.[4] Although he is lamenting the demolition and

F

reconstruction of Paris in the 19th century under Baron Haussmann, the city embodies a cultural and architectural history that authorizes the weight of lyrical mourning.

Even more enviously one remembers Whitman in Crossing Brooklyn Ferry celebrating New York's glories 'strung like beads on my smallest sights and hearings, on the walk in the street and the passage over the river'. At the end of this paean he describes the buildings ringing the water as 'dumb, beautiful ministers' and addresses them as useful, lovable things, with perfection in them ... 'Great or small, you furnish your parts toward the soul.'[5]

In stark contrast to these melancholy, celebratory poetic gestures towards beloved cities, Jo'burg has provided scant hold to the imagination. Belief in its 'integrity' seems to be lacking – exactly the kind of belief that made the minds so abundant in the previous two examples. To the poet Wilma Stockenström, Jo'burg offers merely the bleak fantasy of its projected repeated rise and fall, greedy and without grandeur, again and again, on the inexhaustible bed of inland gold that brought it into being. Unlike other sunken cities, she laments, it will not flounder dreamily at the bottom of a sea. It will simply cave in over its own excavated foundations, and feed grimly on the remains of generations of slaving miners until it is ready to be exploited once again.[6]

Nonetheless, it appears that city life, however unglamorous the city, challenges us to incessant narrative, to chronicle the past of our environment in order to make sense of it in the present. Focusing on the gym as a social space exemplary of at least one aspect of the urban social style of Johannesburg, such a narrative would ideally include a vertical projection, seeking out its prefigurations from the times of 'randlords and rotgut', to use Charles van Onselen's phrase; and a horizontal one, listing concurrent social spaces. As for the latter projection, at one extreme we might posit the little cement arenas of the open-air Zionist meeting places dotted all over the city in the interstices where grass and rock remain; and at the other, the rave venues of a whiter kind of ecstasy.

For the time being, however, I ask you to join me on a little reconnaissance trip to where you and I might well have been before with our bodies.

Reading the phenomenon of the modern urban gymnasium is an exercise in complicit critique. The institution does not reveal itself fully to those who have not participated in it in a literally heartfelt way, and a critique is therefore both a confession and an act of myth-making. Only sworn accomplices can absolve one through their understanding and supportive testimony. And perhaps some little grace may be harvested from this – the grace of community, albeit the uneasy kind of community whose members can smirk at their own myth while upholding it religiously. For, between those regular members of the health club who have come to share a pittance of critical consciousness regarding their addiction, a moment of mutual recognition might be exchanged on entering through the turnstiles or on inserting the body into the machines of the toning circuit: we are here for life! Or on leaving, passing out through the glass doors, greeting the guard and staying upwind of the vagrants, filled with gratified exhaustion, a towel slung around the neck like a wreath of wilted laurel, their eyes might meet furtively to admit: we've had our fix, a habit through which we shield ourselves, a slight protective veneer that has to be reapplied, preferably every day, like an anti-death deodorant.

Travelling from afar on one of the anonymous arteries connecting the random parts of the metropolis, the regular gym-goer has a chance to contemplate her goal from a distance. To begin with: a stylized brand name on a standardized display board in a readily recognizable colour scheme – those interchangeable features that lend this kind of gym the same paradoxical character as Kentucky Fried Chicken and Steers fast-food outlets all over the city. The brand livery both marks and un-marks place and cause in the traveller, producing an uneasy sense of disorientation in which every neighbourhood might be mistaken for another. The building itself is nearly always executed in a distinctive postmodern style, combining concrete, corrugated iron, pert little gables, pillars and pastel colours. It is built to display and entice, its business is visible, especially at night, when, in the brightly lit interior, the plethora of rhythmically pumping limbs and davening torsos, strangely framed and miniaturized by the vast glass windows all around, causes an association to arise ghostlike in the mind ... 'In Xanadu did Kubla Khan / A stately pleasure-dome decree.' From the outside at night the gym indeed looks like a sanctuary for slightly transgressive fun, finely tuned pleasures indulged in by a group of privileged participants. But a fogged-up section in the row of glass windows also draws the attention: the play of vague figures engaged in the languid gestures of ablution, grooming and dressing, evokes the image of a sanatorium, its gaunt spaces fraught with doubtful waters and vapours, its sounds muffled by an endless supply of towels and bathrobes. At this point a slight apprehension of possible disease, tenuous health and curative strictures might grip the throat of our traveller. A final turn is added to her anticipation as she approaches the entrance on foot across the parking lot. She becomes aware of a low continuous hum emanating from an ominously intestinal array of air-conditioning pipes, screened from the world by a sturdy, industrial metal grid. Steam hisses around her feet from the manholes in the paving. A hot smell envelops her. It is a heady compound of blow-dried hair, disinfectants, chloride, and various cosmetic scents and perfumes. And then invariably it is hell that blazes forth in her imagination. As she enters the foyer, where the disco beat vibrates in the marble underfoot, she knows: there is no turning back from this place and its unholy promise of pleasure, health and self-flagellation. In fact, it is a message that burns there in unrelenting pink neon, not 'All hope abandon, ye who enter here', but something similar: 'Take your body where it has never been before.'

In this insidiously persuasive sentence we find the three relationships which rule, in specifically configured forms, the social space of the upmarket health club: the relationship of the self with its own body, the relationship of the self with the immediately sensed surroundings, and, in the cajoling voice that utters the invitation, the relationship with the other.

These three relationships coincide more or less with Freud's delineation of the three major threats feared by human beings. 'We are threatened with suffering from three directions: from our own body, which is doomed to decay and dissolution and which cannot even do without pain and anxiety as warning signals; from the external world, which may rage against us with overwhelming and merciless forces of destruction; and finally from our relations to other men.'[7]

Looming large behind all three is the threat of the end, the sudden and final end beyond which there is no fresh start, the threat called death. In order to live with the fears embodied in these relationships we tinker at them incessantly, adjusting them and improvising with them in ways that are all basically ineffective and powerless. For we cannot change anything fundamental in the existential facticity of our creatureliness.

F

The fashionable health clubs of our day show some of the ways in which upper middle-class urban dwellers in South Africa invest tinkering-energy and tinkering-time to stave off and cover up the dangers lurking in the body, in its world and in other bodies.

These three relationships have one thing in common in the confines of the gym. On the surface they exhibit a fullness, a kind of showy plenitude. On closer inspection, however, they appear conspicuously devoid of meaning. And so the gym turns into a travesty of all its promises: it is a pleasure-dome where the richness of the sensurround can never gratify the senses, a sanatorium where health and fitness are in the final analysis out of reach, a hell where we are thrust together, always side by side with the other, without ever encountering them in the mode that Levinas calls 'being-for'. And all these disillusionments are permanently amplified by the sometimes subtle, sometimes brutal, but always palpable social pressures from which we are constantly trying to flee, the pressures that keep the upper classes on the move and going places. The pressure of the poor, the pressure of the murderously resentful, the pressure of unthinkable dangers lurking in the empty lots and on the dark sidewalks as we rush past in our locked cars.

Always having come in from the cold of the nowhere city, we always have to turn ourselves out again, taking our bodies back from where they've been to where they've been before – vulnerable, shootable, lootable, rape-able first-world bodies suspended for ever in a multiple-stop flight from safety to safety with nowhere in between.

It is this added dimension of fear characterizing life in the city that lends extra poignancy to the highly artificial and privatized social space in which the pseudo-community of body-maintainers tinker away at their fitness and longevity programmes.

Here a double optics of panorama and reflection flatters the gaze of the insecure. The windows offer an almost all-round view of the city; the mirrors in between cast back the images of the inmates. And so the gym is at the same time a safe and cosy nest, closed in on itself, and an open but safe vantage point from which to take in the cityscape. The narcissistic command of the view alternates with the narcissistic confirmation offered by the mirror.

The immediate and simultaneous availability of two of the strongest of visual seductions works like an anaesthetic to soothe the ache of dreary exercise routines. These seductions offer distraction from that other visual ego trip of the gym – the electronic screen attached to the aerobic machines flashing the kilometres you've run or rowed or cycled, the kilojoules you've worked off, the watts you're generating. There is no space here for reverie, for the eyes to rest or linger: they are constantly bounced off mirroring surfaces or sucked into an obligatory overview. The space in a modern gym is quite the opposite of the space in a tree, which is in it the way honey is in a comb. The space in a health club seems to be incessantly raked and rubbed into a multitude of sensory stimuli. It is tailor-made, it would seem, to satisfy the frenzy of small claims brought to it by people suffering from the huge irredeemable fears of the unsafe nowhere of the city.

The soundscape of the gym is answerable to the very same claims. Like many of the cars pulling into the parking lot outside, the gym itself is a capsule filled with an all-pervasive pulsation of disco music. The health-kickers immerse themselves in this throb as in a kind of oblivion. Most use the beat as a pace-setter while pumping away on the Stairmaster or the four-pedalled Schwinn Aerodyne. Add to this the twang of the sprung chains of the rowing machines, the hum of the air-conditioning, the clanging of weights, the bleeps indicating the end and beginning of drill sequences, the manic shouting of aerobic trainers, and you have no less than an infernal din. Every now and again this racket recedes into insignificance as announcements are made and staff and members hailed through the super-loud intercom system. The total effect is of a kind of airport where all manner of urgencies and high-priority, precision manoeuvres are afoot. It is truly a place where only the last of the melancholic eavesdropper angels would pick up the sounds that really matter: the perilously accelerated heartbeats, the fiery host of rasping breaths, the zing of stretched tendons producing a dark timbre in the bone, the squelching of contracting muscles. For here, let it be said, the body is seen but not heard. It is generally not smelt either in this deodorized, reodorized environment. Here a smelly body is likely to get you filthy looks. Helen Keller it was (to be nostalgic for a moment) who professed that she seldom found lively or entertaining those who lacked a distinctive personal odour. 'In the odour of young men there is something elemental, as of fire, storms and salt sea. It pulsates with buoyancy and desire.'[8] There is a whole chapter to be written on the deodorized male of the gym and the unsniffable quality of his prowess.

In our specific time and place, there opens up before our eyes an entire field of research into the altered states of the black male body in the gym space. In a country where the half-naked bodies of black men have always been associated in white minds with back-breaking roadworks and other forms of public labour (tainted to this day by the demeaning aura of penal servitude that they acquired under apartheid), and where black male bodies are strongly marked in the olfactory memory of white people by the smell of 'black sweat', it is interesting to note the beginnings of a tentative reassessment in the facial expressions of white women.

The act of working out within arm's length of a black man with a stereotypically athletic physique, now also impeccably deodorized, may produce in a white woman a new stereotypical reaction of inversely racist admiration for the ultimately desirable black-and-beautiful body. In turn, these groomed black bodies harden into the gestural behaviour that is generally acceptable in the gym. The loud talking and easy touching between black men disappear when they don their Nikes and sporty vests to mount the treadmills.

As for the tactile dimension, the health club provides a space where self-fondling is licensed, and even obligatory. One is asked to be considerate and not drip and spatter all over the place. And so the gym becomes a veritable laboratory where the rats have learnt to gentle themselves. The index of this activity is the sweat towel, the standard gesture that of wiping the face, the head and the neck – only one's own, of course (and the unfeeling limbs of the machines). But in the presence of so much bodily proximity, the possibility of mutual stroking, so intensely suggested by exposed surfaces of skin all around, provokes little tell-tale gestures betraying our physiological needs for touching. The face lowered into the towel stays there a bit longer than necessary, the neck gets towelled with a lingering hand. It is said that the most significant difference between human and animal primate tactility is that the animal primates primarily touch others, while the human primates touch themselves, and especially their heads. Desmond Morris suggests that 'the main reason we have for touching our heads is one of obtaining comfort from unconsciously mimed acts of being touched by someone else'.[9] Michael Argyle, in a similar vein, says: 'Perhaps touching the self is a kind of emotional equivalent of talking to oneself.'[10] We human primates, a little lonely and emotionally bereft, must stroke ourselves because no one else will.

It takes only a slight overdrawing of the picture to recognize that the various harsh sensory modulations of this club environment are greedily but vainly appropriated because of the sorely needed frisson they seem to provide. Only a slight adjustment of perspective allows us a vision of the gym as a sad, slow-motion traction ward where the invalids, arms stretched, legs splayed, prostrate or strung up, are suspended in a kind of hypnosis of heavily mediated self-service. They pull and push and swing the handles of the toning appliances as though they want to infuse the reluctant limbs of squeaky mechanical lovers with some enthusiasm of their own. The only result is that these heavy, mechanically hinged arms and legs move in taunting tandem with their own limbs.

One consequence of this compulsive mock intimacy is the chafing and grazing of the skin that commonly results from vigorous workouts. The need to be soothed is self-perpetuating, and another product is presented to assuage the hopeless hunger. It is called a dermoprotector and it is advertised, part of the enchantment kit offered by the club, on posters bearing full-colour close-ups of perfectly groomed and toned male and female torsos: 'Skin friendly, dermatologically approved, unisex, scientifically formulated, moisturizing, pH balanced, alcohol free, keeps skin healthy.' Now one begins to understand the anxiety of neglect, the wistful interest with which creams and oils are applied to the freshly steamed and showered bodies in the cloakroom.

The self-touching behaviour shown by the predominantly white (and typically non-tactile) population of the gym stands in stark contrast to the way in which the cleaners in the cloakrooms disinterestedly lean against each other during their breaks, arms flung about each other's bodies, hands casually touching. It jars even more with the way in which the three little beggars at the entrance huddle closely together as they whisper in unison for bread from the fat-burners. The poor are not credible in this environment. The over-stimulated senses do not even register these vague black forms. They are treated with less interest than the knobs of the shower tap. Labour and survival, we could remind ourselves, impinge on the body in ways very different from the workout and recreation. Above the poverty line, the needs of the body are seen in a totally different light: the well-fed body is a consuming one first and foremost, and the measure of its proper condition is the capacity to consume what the consumer society has to offer.

So much for the relationship between the self and space as it is tinkered with in the gym. For the relationship between the self and the body, we will seek guidance in Zygmunt Bauman's Life in Fragments.[11]

Contrary to the discipline and coercion forced upon the body of the soldier and the producer by the external authorities of the state and industrial capitalism in modernist times, the postmodern body is now subject only to internal vigilance. The aim is no longer health in order to fight or work, but fitness in order to tirelessly absorb new sensations, new pleasures, new experiences. The fear is no longer that one will be penalized for deviance. The fear now is that one will be penalized for inadequate self-realization, for failing, in the words of Bauman, to acquire the shape and form one wished to acquire, whatever those might have been.

Project Body is strictly do-it-yourself, involving self-improvement and self-formation, but there is support from the health and fitness commodities industry. The industry provides the means, the tests, the measurements, the indexes and the sculpting instruments towards self-supporting, self-scrutinizing and self-teaching on the road to maximum fitness. Advertisements for these products play on the notions that a sagging body is a sign of moral laxness and that fitness is an index of worthiness in a person. A fit body is

> a highly sensitive, finely tuned instrument of pleasure, any pleasure, whether sexual, gastronomic or derived from mere physical exercise and demonstration of fitness. It is not so much the performance of the body that counts, as the sensations the body receives in the course of the performance, those sensations must be deep and deeply gratifying – 'thrilling', 'ravishing', 'enrapturing', 'ecstatic'. The state of unfitness stands for languor, apathy, listlessness, dejection, a lackadaisical response to stimuli, for a shrinking or just 'below average' capacity for and interest in new sensations and experiences. To be 'depressed' means to be unwilling to go out and 'enjoy oneself', to 'have fun'. The most popular and frightening 'disorders' are, one way or the other, consumption disorders – to keep the body fit means to keep it ready to absorb and to be stimulated.[12]

The search for the truly fit body, Bauman continues, is plagued by anxiety, for maximum fitness is an end that can never be reached. How will one ever know whether one's own sensations 'match the standard'? Even more poignantly, whether one has reached the peak that others are capable of? 'However deeply experienced, sensations can always be deeper and thus never deep enough ... there is a sliding and ascending and infinite scale of rapture which, when applied to the actually experienced, casts on every experience a deep shadow of "malfunction". The sliding scale of pleasure turns into a sliding scale of dysfunction, and spells endless disaffection and restlessness forever.'[13]

Products advertised on the walls of the gym invariably play on 'rapture' and 'ecstasy'. One such poster shows a tiny, perfectly shaped female figure in a bathing costume diving gracefully into a green void. She is deliciously miniaturized next to the enlarged close-up of a vineleaf from which a drop of water is suspended, barely held up by a liquid filament. Fitness, this image suggests, will even guarantee sensations on the ravishing microscopic level of secret vegetable life. Whoever cannot reach into these depths of sensation does not pass the fitness test.

The fitness test, however, can never measure the desired end result or indicate on an integrated scale the measure of progress towards the final goal. The exercises in the gym fragment the body. The tests do not run along a totalizing curve but are radically episodic; they are run in trivial units of time that seem to belie the unfolding of life within the span of 'longevity'. While insight into your progress towards the final goal is refused, you may cherish instead the details of the short term as measured on clocks, all bearing the brand name 'World Time Machine'. Or you can monitor the separate results of pulling or pushing weight on the instruments labelled 'Challenger'. Passing from Challenger 1 to Challenger 18, you can successfully tone the quadriceps, the triceps, the biceps, the rhomboids, the inner and outer hip abductors, and the post and anterior deltoids. You can gentle your latissimus dorsi on the Challenger of lateral pull-down, or revel in the lying-down leg-curl while suspended on the bench of Challenger 3. God is in the detail, even in the gym, and the relationship with the segments of your body occludes the relationship with the integrated projection of the fit and perfected self. This chimes with Jonathan Raban's shrewd perceptions of contemporary urban life in *Soft City*: 'In this search for the disappearing self, the physical body becomes a central symbol; the stomach, intestines, and organs of reproduction are solemnly attended to, as vessels in which the precious self is contained.' The zealots of macrobiotic cookery (one of the urban sects Raban skilfully analyses) 'create themselves over gas rings, feeding their immaculate insides on harmoniously balanced amounts of yin and yang foods ... Serious, narcissistic, terrifyingly provident, like all fanatics they brim with latent violence; when they exclude and condemn, they do so with a ringing stridency … They are miniaturists in their talented cultivation of themselves.'[14]

There is assistance available in the gym for this grasping of one's own body and its maintainable parts. It is called the personal trainer. He is the God of the detail. He details your fat with an adjustable fat-clamp, measuring the deposits on the arm, the midriff, the calf. He presses his knuckles knowingly into your brachioradialis and delicately fingers your erector spinae when you flex. His touch is professional, his role is the breakdown of your vital functions. And although his interaction with his client is watched with envy by those who have to service themselves without outside assistance, they search in vain for signs of true communication. For he is trained, like all the other club members, in the art of civil inattention, studied indifference, polite evasion. This constitutes their relationship to each other.

Of course, the attitude of inattention is familiar to city dwellers all over the world. But in the gym it gains a specific poignancy, for here, in such close and intense proximity with the other, the glance and the gaze have to guard more than ever against looking into the exposed particulars of flesh dressed to exercise: moles, muscle dimples, small or large deformities, aberrations of the gut or posture – all must go unnoticed or be noticed without flinching. The face of the other is scanned by eyes glazed with neutrality and intent on carrying off a successful mismeeting.

In South Africa now, the equilibrium of the guarded gaze is threatened by the emergence of the upper middle-class black woman as a gym-goer, and especially the kind of woman who still bears the signs of a traditional or working-class diet in bosom and buttocks. Like her housewifely white counterpart, the overweight black woman wears an explicit, almost ostentatiously nonplussed expression as a form of self-defence when she heaves herself on to the spindly seat of one or other exercise contraption. The glances exchanged between black and white in this category are full of subtle meanings. Apart from the recognition that they share a rung low down on the health club's ladder of presentability, and a slightly aggressive acknowledgement of racist power relationships, there is the possibility of an entirely new register of shared emotion: the gentle irony and humour of knowing that they are locked in a defiant but compromised stand against the ruling male demand: 'Woman, be thin!'

The gym is not for the innocent or the artless. To be caught out openly admiring the hot body on the Ergo machine is to be framed as the most uncool dumb-bell in the joint. Still this type of interaction provides the perfect camouflage for what is known as 'cruising'. But here the focus is on the other primarily as an object of aesthetic interest, as a source of sensation, rather than an instance of moral appeal. Erotic encounters cultivated in the gym are generally episodic affairs conducted by a carefully composed selection of the presentable self. To be 'committed' would be as tasteless as it is to be fat.

In his analysis of the social behaviour of postmodernist society, Bauman distinguishes between several forms of togetherness.[15] So many aspects of this are apparent in the gym that it stands revealed as a veritable hyperama of togethernesses. With the mobile togetherness of the busy street the gym shares the behaviour of steering safely between or avoiding collision with others who are on the same trajectory as ourselves. Encounters are a nuisance or a delay. We cannot escape being beside each other, but we try hard not to be *with* each other. The same goes for the unavoidable, relatively stationary togetherness of the locker room. This space, which has something in common with the aircraft cabin or the waiting room, is a site of refrigerated encounters. We spread ourselves and our stuff out as widely as possible on the little benches in the locker room to avoid closeness, just as we put our raincoats or umbrellas on the seat next to ours in the doctor's waiting room.

In some respects gym togetherness also works like the tempered togetherness of an office building, where the design of space enables structured encounters and disables unstructured ones. People in the free-weight section, in the judo studios and on the squash courts project a certain cliquishness because of this. In the aerobic classes, in the step and high-impact gatherings, all of them areas of even more concentration than the gym space in general, one recognizes something of the manifest togetherness of a protest march or a football crowd: 'The higher than usual physical density gestates a similar density of sensual impressions; the overflow of sights and sounds, a higher than usual level of sensual stimulation.'[16] What is noticeable here is the monotonous homogeneity of stimuli: the same twists and twirls gone through by a uniform mass of bodies clad in similar satiny, body-hugging outfits. A kind of mechanical solidarity, where there are no selves capable of meeting others. The gym even provides space for what Bauman calls 'the postulate togetherness of shadowy and abstruse dream-communities'.[17] Postulated togetherness, he says, 'is always a work of imagination spurred by homesickness, the urge to feel at home, to recognize one's surroundings and belong there.' So, in the space set aside for refreshments, I have noticed a coterie of ex-bodybuilders, bodybuilders gone to flab, with the same thick necks, the same wide-armed waddle and uncomfortably overdeveloped thighs. They have turned the juice bar into a private lounge where they huddle in a collective aftermath of glory. Slowly and deliberately they feed themselves on the high-energy snacks provided by the club's canteen. They no longer build their bodies, but they dream of starting again. They need each other to keep that dream alive. I see them leaving, alone, when the lights are dimmed and the plastic cover is pulled over the pool for the night.

Some gym-goers behave as though the entire club is a scene of meta-togetherness, like a pub or a holiday beach, specifically designed for encounters. Meta-togetherness is above all a land of endless experiment, of trial and error without any binding force. There are the people one always sees breaking through the polite distance barriers with strange pushy attitudes and fixation in their eyes. They are repulsed often, it seems, for they are always with different partners.

In the end, these are but slight variations in a space that belongs more or less to the affluent, which in our country means an even smaller proportion of the population than usual. The health club privatizes social spacing and upholds its own forms of exclusion and subtle oppression. This is a community that collectively retreats into generalized conformity and a shared resentment of strangers and oddballs – such as the dwarf and his assistant who came in one night, or the sado-masochistic couple in search of public thrills, whose deviant behaviour didn't go down too well among the regulars. The space of the gym is designed to provide relief from the gaze of the hungry, encountered at almost every red traffic-light on the way there. It provides an asylum and a cure for those suffering from the indifference that has come to be known as 'compassion fatigue'. In the gym they can celebrate their indifference in a safely structured and sanctioned way.

What are the specific ways in which South African gyms deviate from those in say New York or Paris? That would be a grateful field for some patient urban anthropologist who is also an accomplished club member. For the time being, one might merely speculate, in a slightly hopeful vein, that the gym as a place that sanctions the tentative, experimental glance between black and white augurs the possibility of a new, intelligent, self-critical mutual awareness and openness, alive to the historical overdeterminations which cling to the complex of colour and class in this country.

Perhaps the gym here keeps open a protean space, a distorted and painfully aberrant offspring of the parks in European metropolises, of the traditional market places in African towns, where more or less the same people regularly converge for semi-public, semi-intimate togetherness, a seminal form of the multicultural bonhomie prematurely dubbed by politicians and pop stars alike 'the rainbow nation'.

It is as though the gym space in South Africa, cast in its undecided hybrid architecture reminiscent of warehouses and hyperamas, cannot be formally 'completed' in the way it might be in a culturally satiated, socially homogeneous and stable first-world situation. The neutrality that would characterize a metropolitan gym is prevented from settling here by the filigree tremors of the historical revolution fulfilling itself – tremors of revenge and entitlement, of suppressed disgust and secret desire, of power greedily gained and reluctantly lost, tremors which assert themselves even through the noisy pretences of the fitness industry.

In this sense the South African gym might even be conceived of as a kind of 'nursery' for the tenuous insights that arise from a literally exposed, shared creatureliness. The new South African gym only partly succeeds in consolidating the understanding of 'us inside' – safe, civilized and affluent – over against 'them outside' – dangerous, endangered, brutish and poor. The manifold 'othernesses' increasingly thrown together between its walls would undermine any attempt at a conspiracy of the like-minded. By dint of its own inner alterities, the South African gym keeps on referring to the differences and contradictions of society at large.

It is certain that some things could only happen in this South African space.

One evening I spotted a strange visitor, a redundant body, left over from an era when weightlifting had nothing to do with fitness and everything to do with wily skills and a metaphysical quarrel with gravity.

He had a fierce neck, covered in permanently distended veins and tendons, betraying some uncontrolled habit of straining. The effect was very unlike that produced by the carefully monitored exertions of the regular bodybuilder. Mumbling excuses, swaggering extravagantly, he bustled his way to the free-weight section. Here, with a great sense of purpose, he selected several flat, round weights. Then he lay down on his stomach and motioned someone to come and stack them on his back. He started to do push-ups, shuddering violently, embarrassing everybody, implying with his behaviour that there is a world where notions of 'burden', 'feat', 'struggle' and 'trick' still involve solid and resistant entities.

I went up to him after his workout where he hung over the balustrade, gaunt with some incredibly old-fashioned sorrow.

'You don't come to the gym often,' I ventured.

He looked at me with the childlike candour that some rough men of old still possess and readily confessed. He had the blues. He needed to pull some weight. He used to be a horse-lifter with Boswell & Wilkie's circus, in a wrestling suit with tiger-stripes and black leather leggings laced up to the knee. But then the SPCA complained.

He used to lift a horse hanging in a harness, backstepping up a suspended rope ladder, the horse hanging from a leather strap over his right shoulder.

'That was more than lifting a weight,' he said. That was about balance and timing, I gathered, and about whispering sweet nothings to an airborne horse, pleading for self-induced lightness, for slow, regular horsebreaths. That was about having an accomplice with delicate ears conspiring with one against the deadly pull of the sawdusted earth below.

'That kept me humble,' he said, 'although I was a hero. There were trumpets and spotlights and rounds of applause. When I got down I mounted her and she carried me in a trot around the ring. I deserved that. And so did she. Why should horses always carry men? And not the other way around? It happened just where we're standing now, when this was still an empty lot. The tent used to be pitched right here where they came and built the gym.'

F

◄E11

Building and self-reliance

Iain Low

> There Shall Be Houses, Security And Comfort!
> All people shall have the right to live where they choose, to be decently housed, and to bring up their families in comfort and security.
>
> From *The Freedom Charter*, 1955

As the end of its first five-year period in government approaches, the African National Congress (ANC) has formulated Growth, Employment and Redistribution (Gear) as a primary strategy to facilitate the economic and social transformation of South Africa. Yet this strategy, with its emphasis on the formation of public-private partnerships, seems limited, lacking the creative stance which might harness and promote the plurality and imagination that the post-apartheid condition demands. It appears that Gear favours the established private sector whilst 'absolving' the public sector of its traditional responsibilities to build a civil society and protect the common interest. More importantly, it lacks an explicit programme for the radical redress of apartheid's major legacy – the social injustice experienced by countless numbers of urban and rural poor. The previously disenfranchised want social goods and services and they want them immediately. Housing and the built environment are the central needs.

The ANC's Reconstruction and Development Programme (RDP), formulated before the election, imaginatively interpreted the promises contained in the Freedom Charter to present a cogent strategy for providing social services to the disadvantaged. However, as early as 1995 the RDP was surprisingly abandoned and absorbed into the offices of the Ministry of Finance and the Deputy President. The move says much about the dangers of the centralization of power. Despite a great deal of justificatory political and economic rhetoric to the contrary, it is apparent that the dissolution of the RDP had an extremely negative effect on government's ability to meet its goals in the provision of services. The target of creating one million jobs and one million houses before the next election in 1999 has rapidly receded into the realms of fantasy.

In place of a concrete programme we now have a paper industry run largely by the planning professionals. A spate of policy papers – both 'green' and 'white' – have set out a host of frameworks within which the reconstruction and development of various sectors may be negotiated. Notwithstanding the necessity for a regulatory framework within which to operate, this approach has concentrated effort at the level of theorizing and delayed the necessary action on the ground.

Despite this, South Africa has witnessed real changes. For the most part this change is hidden, or more accurately goes unrecognized, because it occurs in the 'informal sector'. The minibus taxi industry provides an example. The industry emerged in the apartheid era to redress the absence of comfortable, affordable, accessible and reliable public transport between the outlying townships and places of employment. Over the years this local response to a lack in the formal system has grown and developed into a crucial part of the transport sector. Other areas of the 'informal sector' are developing in the same way today.

Underlying such initiatives is the concept and indeed the practice of 'self-reliance'. People are taking responsibility for their own lives, acting to meet their direct needs, and succeeding despite incredibly limited means and practically no resource base whatsoever. In this way they are contributing not only to their own individual well-being, but more importantly to the collective production of a vital force which is helping to transform our cities into living environments.

Object lessons

Informal selling – Mealie vendors and urban nomads, Hillbrow

By now it should be obvious that informal economic activities in Hillbrow and other inner-city areas of Johannesburg are neither random nor autonomous. Tents, trolleys, telephones and tomatoes are all part of a system linking the members of a new class of 'urban nomads' who have begun to inhabit the city.

In the inner city and other parts of Johannesburg, a strong and flexible business system which defies conventional economic classification is rapidly emerging. The supply of goods and services – coal fires for the roasting of mealies (corn on the cob), live chickens for sale to those who do not yet own refrigerators, fresh fruit and vegetables for daily consumption, the safe storage of goods overnight – is organized by countless unseen negotiations which together constitute an informal economy. Sophisticated 'hubs and networks' of association are developing to support these activities. Arising out of cooperation in the face of adversity, such activities generate support systems with peculiar and 'invisible' spatializations which no conventional formal-sector consultant could ever read, let alone predict. Their central feature is the common ground of shared experience gained through direct engagement in the world. The absence of state or other interventions speaks volumes for the capacity of people and communities to operate self-reliantly within limited means (a fact

Hillbrow.

the 'paper industry' scarcely acknowledges). At the same time, it is clear that these efforts, which rely mainly on agreements between individuals, have the potential to merge eventually into organized structures with immense bargaining power.

To outsiders, the roasting and selling of mealies seems like a haphazard trade. In fact, it depends on sophisticated systems of delivery. Coal is delivered to strategic sites throughout the city, where fires are prepared in tin braziers. These sites are usually in the inner reaches of abandoned city blocks, so that others are not inconvenienced by the fumes. By mid-morning, when the coals are glowing and the fires have lost their smoke, the braziers are delivered by squads of pedestrian couriers to the city's numerous 'street restaurants'. Here vendors roast and sell fresh mealies (also delivered to them through a supply network) as a healthy staple meal. The mealie vendors of the inner city, far from being disconnected individuals each eking out a living on their own, are linked by patterns of support, delivery and spatial regulation.

These new patterns are clearly evident in Hillbrow, Johannesburg's most densely populated neighbourhood. Despite the verbose protestations of the guardians of civic order, the area is merely undergoing a cycle of revolution. It has always been a home to migrants. In previous decades, numerous European migrants in search of work and the fruits of the apartheid economy, treated Hillbrow as an arrival centre. Their 'hubs and networks' were expressed in a dense café society. Now establishments like the Café Wien and the Café de Paris have given way to new forms, as European migrants are replaced by Africans, whether local people from the countryside or foreigners. In the insecure position they occupy, these people often resort to what they know best, which is exchange at the most basic and everyday level.

Hillbrow, possessing the only true urbanity in South Africa, provides a constructive 'maidan' where outsiders may find a place and establish an identity in an emerging and transforming society. Despite the normal economic rivalries, there is growing coexistence between people of radically different backgrounds, as a new economic class emerges. These urban nomads, in addition to being living proof of the possibility of a harmonious, non-racial society, provide an example of economic initiative that is self-reliant, imaginative and in tune with the environment.

Building houses – Victoria Mxenge and People's Dialogue, Philippi

The Victoria Mxenge housing development in Philippi on the outskirts of Cape Town, which already boasts more than twenty homes, is an initiative which originated outside the formal sector and government. People's Dialogue, a community-based service organization, now provides technical assistance. The project gathers together women and families who fall outside both the conventional bank mortgage system and the government's subsidy system, which favour the provision of housing by the formal sector, and has as its central feature a housing savings scheme. The participants are some of the poorer families in Philippi, with an average income of R790 (about $130) per month.[1] Yet within these severe constraints, they have achieved a quality dwelling of 55 square metres at a cost of R12,000 (about $2,000).[2]

How do they do it? In Victoria Mxenge the provision of housing has been re-envisioned as a development tool. Self-reliant production methods are employed. By placing the means of production in the hands of the homeowner, 'losses' in the form of contractor's profits have been severely reduced. This allows subsidy monies and other savings to be retained and spent directly on building materials. Having to make collective decisions, run the savings scheme and manage the construction and contracting also develops organizational, financial and managerial skills. The project is as much about building community as about building houses, and each step in the production of a house is valued for its potential to build capacity and transfer skills. Through a system of 'counterparting', skills are transferred from woman to woman, and gradually a resilient community is being established which has real capacity to deal with present and future conflict and change.

It is interesting that women have taken the lead in this project. In Africa it is not uncommon to find women as the heads of households. Women, perhaps because they desire the best for their

children, often seem to have broader horizons than men. In housing initiatives men tend to focus on the house as an investment or commodity, concerning themselves with selling or preparing materials, selling their labour in the conventional way, or even 'selling' plots for settlement on state or unoccupied land. By contrast, women seem to focus on the qualitative aspects, on the value of a house as a 'home', on how it will enrich the long-term future of the family. A number of the women at Victoria Mxenge speak of pursuing 'comfort' rather than mere possession.

The Victoria Mxenge project, like other housing associations now developing throughout the country, is employing self-reliant building methods to turn shack dwellers into homeowners.

Taking our bearings

The question prompted by these object lessons is how the substantial economic potential shown by ordinary people in their daily lives can be incorporated into and supported by government policy and strategy. The formulation of 'Land Development Objectives', required by legislation, is intended to facilitate community participation on such matters in the 'new' South Africa. However, having one's views heard and recorded at a meeting is one thing; having them interpreted and acted upon in the contested political realm is another, and the discrepancy between the two unfortunately adds weight to the claim that South Africa's new democracy is only skin-deep. The failure to meaningfully involve the millions of ordinary citizens who daily demonstrate their capacity to build and develop for themselves does incalculable damage to the country's transformation.

South Africa's critical moment of 1994 is well past. For us it is perhaps not just a matter of changing Gear, or even of getting into Gear, but of changing vehicles. Self-reliance represents an alternative for transformation and development. As a strategy of empowerment, it seeks to locate the means of production in the local domain, and to reinforce and maintain energy and effort at the lowest levels in the economic hierarchy, in order to benefit those who are most in need.

The principle of self-reliance

For urban dwellers in the contemporary world the concept of 'self-reliance' appears somewhat remote. Most of what we do is mediated by secondary powers and conditions, and we acquire less and less through direct experience. Material culture and technology, and especially the notion of the 'latest', have become both an obsession and the measure of all progress. In addition, we suffer

Victoria Mxenge housing project, Philippi.

from a 'tyranny of the eye', whereby vision and the surface of the image are privileged above the deeper and more complex aspects of human interaction. Life has been vitiated by our reliance upon things outside our own control. One corollary of this condition is a neglect of the past. We have an acute predilection for immediate gratification, and are directed toward the potential and measurable future benefits from anything 'new'. History, memory and tradition hold little interest for us, and we turn away from them at significant loss to what is local or particular to our unique circumstances.

A counterpoint to this may be found in conditions of origins, where a culture of 'self-reliance' predominated. As a matter of economic necessity, this culture still persists in many developing countries, and their productions continue to encapsulate qualities of life that have been lost in the 'progressive' project. Consequently, artefacts produced through self-reliant modes tend to engender great nostalgia in modern subjects. Here we find embodied the qualities that we have been deprived of by modernity in our own 'advanced' cultures. Of more significance to us should be the economic utility imbued in these artefacts: they possess a dimension of guaranteed economic empowerment, which is automatically transferred to a craftsperson through their ownership and control of the means of production.

A grasp of the economic conditions which govern everyday life is fundamental to an understanding of 'self-reliance', and to its reinterpretation in a more positive light. While it may not be a developing country's first choice of strategy, its claims are strong in circumstances where choices are limited or absent. This has immense relevance for Southern Africa in the light of the present euphoria around globalization. In South Africa, apartheid presented a sophisticated form of capitalism which controlled and directed every aspect of the economy to the advantage of the few. The choices to which the white élite became so accustomed will never be available to the majority, and we cannot realistically hope to achieve even an average GDP in relation to the developed world. Despite the political and legislative dismantling of apartheid, the effects of three centuries of exploitation will be difficult to eradicate.

The conditions we face in Africa are different not merely because of colonial imperialism, but more simply because we are Africans. This difference, those qualities indigenous to the places and communities within which we live and work, should be made integral to any process of development. Africans have been known as prodigious builders,[3] and this skill above all has relevance for national reconstruction and development, particularly under conditions of extreme poverty. More particularly, it has relevance for architecture conceived of as both a social and an economic practice.

The Training for Self-Reliance Project, Lesotho

The history of the project

The Training for Self-Reliance Project (TSRP) was initiated by the government of Lesotho and the World Bank's International Development Agency (IDA) in the early 1970s. The founding aim of this parastatal project was to upgrade education throughout the Kingdom of Lesotho, and it was therefore linked to the Education Planning Unit of the Ministry of Education. The architectural component of the project involves upgrading and adding to existing schools, extending them by adding kitchens, toilets and other facilities, and constructing some new schools. As a less developed country, Lesotho qualifies for credit from the World Bank on favourable terms, and it is the TSRP's task to implement such 'soft' loan agreements in the pursuit of its aims.

Lesotho is geographically and economically enclaved by South Africa, and has long been dependent upon South Africa for its survival. Since the founding of the nation under Moshoeshoe, the country's boundaries have been threatened from the surrounding territory, a threat which became extreme during the 1980s when Prime Minister Leabua Jonathan overtly supported the ANC. Lesotho's economic fragility has also been heightened by its extreme dependency upon migrant labour to the South African mines. In response to this dependency, the country has historically adopted a generic

The building system

Setting out of the pad foundation.

Ring beam at ground level joins adjacent stub columns, saving on undersurface masonry and providing a datum to work from.

Window and door infill fits exactly between columns.

Small building prototype provides an excellent learning model for the acquisition of a range of building skills.

Experimental fibreglass window.

Office store.

Double-storey building on a tight site allows space to be retained for play areas and introduces more complex construction techniques.

Open-framed classroom before infill.

rging gable wall with ring beam providing additional
-term stability.

Local community effort to infill an open-framed classroom.

y resource rooms.

Grabbing morning sun for the cold winter.

Classroom showing roof structure and infill walls.

F

oti' brick.

Concrete block produced on site.

Typical stone quarried on site.

F

'development philosophy', through which it actively seeks development opportunities and tries to promote local independence.

The establishment of the TSRP as a parastatal reflected two complementary aspects of the national development ethic. Firstly, the project would be a relatively autonomous entity parallel to government. Secondly, it would seek to promote national independence through training and work. The notions of upgrading education and of furthering development and self-reliance were inextricably linked in the very conception of the project. It is aimed at capacity building – and therefore at 'nation building' – across the different levels of society, and as such may hold some valuable lessons for architecture in South Africa.

It could be said that the TSRP is a project with a memory. Various traditional cultural and political forms, which have their origins in Moshoeshoe's founding of the nation, have been taken up in the project. One of these is the pitso or public meeting, the primary forum of democratic debate, which allows the valued individual voice to filter up from each village under the local chief, through the districts, to gatherings of the nation under the King or Paramount Chief. Pitsos allow for direct and immediate participation in decision-making; they also produce a collective vision and resilient consensus which readily translate into sustainable projects. Whether the specific TSRP project involves construction, maintenance, or some other input, the scope of responsibility is agreed upon with the community at the outset and informs the design.

The complexity of architecture makes speculative research almost impossible. However, 'thinking through making' is a kind of experimentation, and the work produced by the TSRP may be regarded as 'built research'. The continued pursuit of the programme by various governments over more than two decades bears witness to its developmental capability. This was especially notable in the 1980s, when the architectural component resonated powerfully with other scales and areas of development.

In the early 1980s, the architectural unit embarked on a phase of 'built experimentation'. Drawing on shared knowledge about materials, siting, local customs, the preferences of the authorities, and so on, a number of prototypical schools were built as 'tests' at various locations in one district. On the basis of these experiments a building system was devised which could respond to a variety of conditions. The system had to be specific enough to be practicable, but open enough to respond to and further a necessary plurality and difference. Not being subject to the usual 'project cycle' which defines a conventional building programme, the architects were able to reflect upon and improve their designs with each new school by omitting, adding or adjusting various elements. In time, trombe passive solar-heating walls, roof lighting, double-storey construction, pit latrines, and rural

Kingdom of Lesotho.

kitchens were all incorporated, enriching the diversity of the work and allowing for the upgrading of education facilities throughout Lesotho. To date, some 300 schools have been built or upgraded.

Skill and empowerment

The social aspect of the project was enhanced by an openness to other learning processes. By gradually maintaining most of the technical assistance 'in house', the project built up a team of local Basotho who took charge of various aspects of the work. All the decision-making, from the initial *pitso* consultation with the village, through siting and orientation, to site supervision was gradually entrusted to younger members of the team, who in turn empowered contractors and supervisors, thus providing the country with a robust infrastructure to support the education sector. Today the TSRP is managed entirely by Basotho.

In Lesotho, the ownership of skill, the exercise of labour and the idea of community itself are woven into the very fabric of the built environment. People build their own homes and villages, and are often unfamiliar with the divisions of labour we take for granted. Villagers have unique skills for the making of shelter in their particular circumstances – the quarrying and dressing of *in situ* sandstone, the working and crafting of wood, and so on. These skills are hereditary and resistant to external influence, yet they may be enhanced through organized building programmes. This not only maintains capital and skill within the village economy, but can develop the capacity of contractors and allow some villagers to enter into the formal building sector.

The local technical institute, the Lerotli Polytechnic, trains architectural technicians, but besides the private sector, the Ministry of Works and a small number of other government departments there is not much architectural employment on offer in Lesotho. The building system developed by the TSRP, with its accumulation of repetitive elements, lends itself to computer-aided design. However, the labour-intensive individual production of project drawings and documentation allows for a more direct skill transfer and is therefore favoured for its developmental advantages. Given the lack of employment opportunities, the TSRP provides ideal in-service training for students. Site and construction supervision also lend themselves to in-service training. The TSRP has thus radically enhanced the local contracting industry, and both construction foremen and architectural technicians have gone on to establish their own construction firms.

Architectural design 'at the drawing board' is never neutral. It predetermines a set of relations around production. By incorporating 'counterparting' and the transfer of skills into complex architectural processes, the TSRP has helped to establish and maintain a vibrant construction industry in Lesotho. The project continues to serve the educational needs of the country. At the outset the project relied heavily on foreign consultants; today practically the entire staff is Basotho. Rainbow Construction, a local contracting firm initiated and nurtured through the project, has gone on to compete in the Highlands Water Scheme on tenders that run to millions of rands. The director of the firm, Thabo Makakole, is a Mosotho whose career began at Lerotli Polytechnic and the TSRP. These firms continue to use stone and other traditional techniques, and now provide a model for individual interpretation by others. Local is holding its own against global.[4]

Building as manifesto: Lessons for South Africa

> The establishment of order in a mutable and finite world is the ultimate purpose of all man's thought and action.
>
> Alberto Perez-Gomez[5]

Architecture is an applied art, which is best practised through the asking of thoughtful questions in relation to a given set of circumstances. In South Africa today, in a context of transformation, architects need to ask whose interests they should be serving and by what means.

Architects here have been reluctant activists. By their passivity or by more active collusion, many helped to translate apartheid policies into built form. Architects and their colleagues, the planners, have a great deal to answer for. Yet today many of these 'professionals' busily court the new government, not with imaginative development plans but by paying obeisance to 'the public-private partnership'.

The legacy of apartheid is indelibly etched on our cities, in separation and in emptiness. Johannesburg and its surroundings are symptomatic. The economic powerhouse of the country lays claim to 'global city' status, and yet it often appears to be no more than a mining town. Architects are increasingly marginalized, while project managers and developers, pursuing economic efficiency and utilitarian function, direct the creation of the new landscape. Reductive analysis is shaping the city in ways that echo the apartheid era. How will Johannesburg and other cities reinvent themselves without a genuine shift in thinking?

Architectural research becomes meaningful when its uncovers new ground. To this end, we need rigorous and critical analysis, and we need to arrive at conclusions which can be applied and tested within a particular architectural setting. Each building should be a manifesto, a declaration of what is possible. A crucial element of this is to establish the grounds for new productive relations by conceptualizing 'community participation' and 'economic empowerment' meaningfully. The prevalent abdication of professional responsibility in this regard trivializes the capacities of ordinary people. By not exploring alternatives, by not experimenting and taking risks, architects are failing to learn by doing, and once again running the risk of producing landscapes of monotony, constructed in the interests of capital rather than comfort.

Economic empowerment of the poor should be the starting point of every project. And self-reliance can be a primary development tool, especially in circumstances where the poor have been grossly and consistently neglected. The transformation of the society demands that we look back to establish and restore what has been lost, and that we look forward to ensure the vigorous empowerment of the disadvantaged. Too often, those who are being 'empowered' in the new South Africa have already enjoyed an education and other advantages.

The poorest of the poor, frequently the homeless, are already demonstrating self-reliance in countless ways, but most of these, being classified as 'informal', go unrecognized and have no effect on official policy. In squatter settlements, in nomadic urban commercial culture, in more recently formalized projects of the Homeless People's Federation and the People's Dialogue, whole communities are taking charge of their own development. These projects demonstrate a realistic alternative

Pitso with local community to discuss the new school and community participation.

framework for transformation and development in which external support is merely complementary.

Looking to the experience of other countries in the region may perhaps be considered an aspect of 'self-reliance' in itself. The TSRP in Lesotho provides a workable model of an architecture participating productively in national development, by placing community participation and indigenous methods and materials at the centre of its practice. In South Africa, resistance to these challenges still needs to be overcome. Policy and practice need to find a more constructive dialogue, specifically by directing their attention to the capacities of ordinary citizens.

◄E7 ►G6

Steinkopf community centre
Angela Buckland

The Steinkopf community centre was built in 1978. It was designed by the architect Roelof Uytenbogaardt and was one of the first community buildings in the country. Steinkopf is a remote town in the Western Cape, 500 kilometres from Cape Town. It has 6,000 inhabitants.

COLT

9

Undisciplined practices: Architecture in the context of freedom

Hannah le Roux

> We therefore, through our freely elected representatives, adopt this Constitution as the supreme law of the Republic so as to –
> Heal the divisions of the past and establish a society based on democratic values, social justice and fundamental human rights;
> Lay the foundations for a democratic and open society in which government is based on the will of the people and every citizen is equally protected by law;
> Improve the quality of life of all citizens and free the potential of each person; and
> Build a united and democratic South Africa able to take its rightful place as a sovereign state in the family of nations.
>
> From the Preamble, Constitution of the Republic of South Africa[1]

Shifting grounds

The preamble to the Constitution seems an odd place to look for a definition for emergent architectural practices. But in its construction as a collaborative document, in its awkward attempt to simultaneously recognize and overcome historical categories, and in its metaphoric allusions to building, it might be closer to an exemplary space than anything yet set in concrete.

From within it, a new subject for architecture emerges. These citizens begin to replace the restricted bodies defined by apartheid's plans and laws. Individuals and communities are released by the removal of restrictions on travel, association and property. Liberated from a terrain demarcated into areas of prescription, these citizens now have the right to form new relationships with and within space.

It could be said that the uncoordinated actions of these newly positioned citizens have precipitated many of the briefs of any architecture that might be classified as post-apartheid. The actions of street vendors, the use of public space for gatherings of workers and community groups, land invasions by the homeless, and the claiming of heritage and environmental rights have provoked a reassessment

Aerial photograph of Meadowlands East, Zone 3, Soweto, 16 April 1993.

of space – its appearance and representation. Contested or neglected spaces have been established as the sites for key projects: the Union Buildings, Robben Island, the Fort, Alexandra's East Bank, Durban's Warwick Triangle, Johannesburg city pavements and library lawns, Kliptown, Qunu.

The forecourt of the Union Buildings, in the past a site for mass gatherings to protest against apartheid, was chosen as the setting for the inauguration of Nelson Mandela as state president in 1994. The unusually large number of people allowed to gather there for the occasion altered the meaning of the site. In an analogous way the negative associations of Robben Island and the Fort as spaces of confinement for political prisoners have been challenged by proposals for their reuse as the homes for new democratic institutions. The more everyday transformation of urban public space in Durban and Johannesburg brought about in recent years by the appearance of street traders has culminated in urban renewal projects.

Clearly, a new terrain for architecture is opening up. Yet the means to bring about form within this emergent context is less apparent: what moves need to be made, by whom, in what order, to bring about a construction that will both allow for and sustain the emergence of freed human potential?

Left, right: The polarities of disciplined practice

> ... recognitions of lived spatialities threaten a priori formal categories of architecture and surface irreconcilable tensions within its disciplinary boundaries.
>
> Gülsüm Nalbantoğlu[2]

The new sites and subjects of practice appear to have unsettled the profession of architecture. The widespread dissolution or symbolic renaming of professional alliances in the 1990s is symptomatic of the reordering of the discipline. The names of the professional institutes, the regulatory body, and several large practices have been changed in this period, and these shifts show how political change has disturbed prior orders.

Crudely, it could be said that two opposing positions characterized the significant practices of architects towards the end of apartheid: those who would not build because of politics, set against those who would not admit to the political for the sake of building. Left, right: together and apart they marched forward with some notion of direction for their practices. Militant refusal defined the limits of their discourse, allowing them to construct and practise disciplined modes of architecture in a period of struggle.

Discussion of student projects at the University of Natal Town Planning School, c. 1964.

On the left, the refusal to bring into being anything solid without the prior creation of an equitable context emerged as the ethical position favoured by activists and theoreticians. Whether from direct involvement in trying to secure built resources for disenfranchised communities, or from a position of observation, they reached the conclusion that a just built architecture was impossible. Architecture as the production of spatialized political demands, utopian visions, and representations without permanence took its place.

Alternative modes of engagement were attempted. Planact, an interdisciplinary collective including architects, was formed by young graduates involved in advocacy planning for the residents of Westbury township.[3] Their work entailed consulting with the community to draw up alternatives to government proposals for new housing. The design and production of The People's Workbook by the Environmental Development Agency around 1980,[4] and the establishment of practices such as Akanani in Venda attended to the situation of the rural poor.

Some students and lecturers used the universities as a productive space for theoretical research and the dissemination of new approaches. Student theses such as Stanley Saitowitz's 'A Dissertation' (1976),[5] which examined the interrelationships between human agency and building, suggested an imaginative alternative to apartheid space. Similar themes emerged in the Metropolis and University of Cape Town student conferences of 1986 and 1987, which brought together practitioners from neighbouring countries, theoreticians and students. Project offices and interdisciplinary discussion groups, such as those that resulted in the formation of Planact, were led by student architects.

The work done towards the creation of this alternative architecture brought into play some significant techniques, such as brief formation through collective contributions, and the recognition of process and the temporal as areas for discussion. The collective work which these projects involved encouraged the pursuit of organizational and interdisciplinary approaches to project management, while the ethos of the conferences and discussion groups provoked practitioners to share their work and experiences in a critical, discursive forum.

On the right, the position struck by architects was a refusal to speak. In a period of increasingly brutal and complicated spatial repression, most architects favoured by the state to design its infrastructure kept quiet and did their work. Where they were involved in monumental works too significant to evade representation in the media, such as the seats of homeland governments, these architects tried to neutralize any consideration of their immediate contexts.

Drawing on conservative interpretations of phenomenology and formalism, architects on the right argued that spatial experience and form were realities that transcended their temporal context. The history that produced the buildings of this era would be overcome by their ability to endure. Writing of their design for the square in front of the building that housed the tricameral parliament of 1984, the architects Munnik Visser and Black explained: 'Obelisks, statues, and flagpoles furnish areas and emphasize the relationship between sections of the square and its buildings.'[6] Their description presented the architecture as a closed system of formal arrangements and remained silent about the symbolism of these elements for the African majority, who were still excluded from power under the tricameral system. Bannie Britz advanced a similar definition of an architectural approach, exemplified in the Bophuthatswana parliamentary complex, that would converse with itself and its setting, and presumably transcend the need to make sense to the homeland regime's current victims.[7]

In the struggle to establish legitimacy for their practices, at the time of apartheid's crisis, both sides adopted a disciplined approach to their work. Whether it was constituted as attachment to a cause or as detachment in the name of production, the militarism common to the tactics of both sides might be evident. Left and right, propagandists and sappers, the left articulating a collective will and the right delivering infrastructure with efficiency, they were separated by their choice of opposing sides rather than by their shared belief in an exemplary professional identity. In a sense, both left and right were fighting for survival in a situation that they knew was about to be transformed.

NE 51/9 type house showing breakdown of brickwork into panels.

Yet neither position can claim to have produced an authentic architecture for the post-apartheid period. In the wake of the negotiated settlement, these positions, like those of former armed forces, have been hybridized rather than emerging clearly as victor and vanquished. Their uneasy combination, the new relationship between left and right in the new walk forward, makes for an unsteady movement.

Breaking ranks: Emergent positions

> What is seemingly transitory and ephemeral, processual and only a body of images, is often, by its illusion of stability, more durable than our eroding stone monuments.
>
> Labelle Prussin[8]

The meeting of citizens and architects under conditions of freedom may be said to lead to a new kind of architectural movement, which unlike its predecessors – modern, regionalist and postmodern – centres on types of actions rather than forms. It is a movement of inventive movements: tentative gestures and exploratory stances generated by the new position of client and architect on an unstable terrain.

For most architects this is the first encounter with previously disenfranchised clients as citizens: the first admission of black demands in a white space. As the power of architects to speak for or plan for their subjects is suspended, the placing of material to make space becomes an act of negotiation between parties. The relationships between the architect and the subject of the design become more complex, redefining the binary roles played before: maker/user, planner/subject, controller/controlled. Now architecture could be said to emerge from a negotiable space, one defined in flexible processes and materials, as a preliminary stage to the fixed spaces of built work.

The formulation of flexible strategies, the ability to move to and fro between positions, between empathetic and authoritative modes, characterize the journey undertaken in the few exemplary projects that have emerged since apartheid.

Among these strategies are new ways of seeing the social and spatial landscape. Techniques of observation, which intersect the architect's distanced, panoptic view of the site with the view from the ground, have opened up an understanding of place which is revelatory for both clients and planners.

Durban's Warwick Triangle, a spatially complex area of intense informal trading that is packed between major transport terminals and highway flyovers, is the site for an exemplary work in progress. In carrying out their brief to locate a market for medicine traders, the architects Erik Orts Hansen, Andrew Makin and Janina Masojada, in their collaborative identity as the Design Workshop, have mimicked the subversive movements of their once marginalized clients. Their project follows on the traders' location of stalls, storage and private space on sites below, across and temporarily within those spaces that actually appear on plan as circulation routes. They accordingly retrieve those spaces which were not planned, and hence not zoned. This process of observation and engagement on site, as an adjunct to mapping or viewing from above, produces an intersection of lived and disciplinary representations.

In translation to building, this strategy liberates lost space. By opening up connections with significant nodes, it serves to empower a community that was previously condemned to a marginal position on the site. In this aspect, through the intervention of architects in collaboration with public authorities, the design has the scope of the master plan. Yet the vision of the site carried through into the design simultaneously confounds the tradition of the master plan as a dominating, unwieldy form. Instead, a fragmented web of spatial relationships is constructed on top of existing complexity without erasing it.

Holding back form is another strategy. Here the architect defers design by allowing users to construct, at least in part, spaces of significant identity and value through their own suggestion or

Warwick Triangle medical traders' market, Durban.

physical involvement. The idea of the open or unfinished project is central. This approach relies on an understanding of space as a temporal realm, capable of flexible and layered configurations. The principles of nomadic architecture, where the permanence of a community is constructed by a common image of space, enacted in ritual or motion, rather than the physical structures of the village, seem to apply to the spaces which emerge.

In the provision of housing, this approach is common in theory and scarce in practice.[9] Perhaps, as participants grapple with new roles, their fears of losing control of the process limit the emergence of the shared vision that is necessary for an open project to achieve closure. In some cases, the construction of a community of users takes priority over the construction of form in order to guarantee some stability of vision for the project. This has been the approach of architects such as Paul Mikula of Architects' Collaborative and Carin Smuts, whose time has been divided between organizational work within a potential client group and architectural work in making the resultant structures.

Prior to the construction of street-trading spaces in inner-city Johannesburg, Eddie Tsepe and Anthony Philbrick, the partners of Informal Sector Architects, located meeting spaces for the hawker community they were to serve.[10] Through gathering together this otherwise dispersed group some sort of progress could be made towards designing trading space within the city. In Kliptown, hawkers consulted about their needs made a similar demand for a meeting hall.[11] Demands like these compel us to recognize that communities may be simultaneously unified and dispersed, and that the appropriate architectural responses may therefore be fragmented and arranged across a broad territory, contrary to the conception of architecture as form enclosing discrete spaces. Where the one approach is present and not working, the other might be needed.

Many of the buildings constructed for this new context are, or claim to be, temporary structures. An important aspect of this is the use of flexible materials that allow users to be physically involved in constructing and adjusting space. The Mansel Road traders in Durban, who had formed a settlement from plastic drums and sheeting, presented a self-built environment that responded materially both to their insecure position on a public road and to their means of livelihood as sellers of the drums. In the design for their new permanent location, Rodney Harber worked from the dimensions of the existing settlement.[12] The new built structures effectively 'hold' an open courtyard, which ensures that the users can repeat their strategy of tailoring space with material at hand and which becomes the most remarkable space in an otherwise tough and functional domain. Unseen from the outside and hence free from institutional control or public scrutiny, the courtyards have become highly personalized spaces, constructed by the women to serve a rich – and probably illegal – mixture of economic and private uses.

As bodies are freed up, spaces that were formerly confining are redefined. Typologies of control become the matrix for actions of demolition, alteration and possession which transform space with strategic but often minimal physical effect. Some of the earliest projects envisaged for transforming apartheid space concerned hostels and worker facilities.

Protekon, a service organization within the national port authority, has been charged with redesigning dock and station areas to meet the demands of increasingly powerful trade unions.

Design Workshop, Hawker Bridge, Durban, 1998. Project in progress.

The policies promoted by the organization, such as the encouragement of worker representation in planning, have attracted young architects with a background of resistance to apartheid.

One of Protekon's ongoing projects is the creation and upgrading of workers' messes in Durban harbour. The new threshold of Hlanganani workers' mess at Maydon Wharf is inscribed with the signatures of its makers alongside that of the project architect, Jeremy Steere.[13] As an alteration work to an existing office building shared between workers and management, this project relies on gestural moments such as this to reverse the usual hierarchies carried within architectural convention and the built structure itself. The scale of the built intervention is relatively modest, but the lived experience of the building, through the reordering of the threshold and its presentation as a collaborative work, has been transformed.

The work of Martin Mitchell, who spent his year 'in training' as a guerrilla architect working without the usual prerequisites of a brief, a site, or a professional qualification, presents a more radical strategy.[14] His projects involve the construction and installation of street furniture for public settings in Johannesburg. Working in two modes, installing 'kitchens' and 'dining-room suites' by night as gifts for marginalized inhabitants of the city, and organizing the video recording of his projects for national television, he confounds the conventional separation of building and event.

Undisciplined practices

... real architecture can only start now.

Paul Mikula[15]

Emergent practices which flout the proper disciplinary modes can serve to renew architecture through being aberrant. They are distanced from the belief that another architecture, constructed from more authentic forms or practices, might be retrieved. Instead, they interrogate the habitual modes of making architecture by following, intermittently, paths set out by new users of space. At these moments of departure from the disciplinary norm, the possibility of other forms of practice emerges.

The lack of formal similarities among these new works is striking. Rather, the guiding threads are the identity of the architect, which is in crisis or flux, and the identity of the user as it emerges in the wake of political change. What is given and received, what is negotiated and settled, and what is fixed in material adjacent to the free body of the new user is the story of these projects.

Mansel Road drum sellers, Durban.

One might hope that these undisciplined practices will bring about a liberating architecture, in which unforeseen intersubjectivities continue to undermine the historical power relationships between architect and user. It would be an architecture through which the given roles of race, gender and cultural affiliation in the shaping of space would be shaken up. It would be an architecture without orders, without a naturalized set of values vested in a priori forms or procedures.

Following Gülsüm Nalbantoğlu's observation of architects' responses to illegal settlements in Turkey, one might spell out the transformational role these practices could play within their disciplinary context: 'If the meaning and symbols of culture have no primordial unity or fixity, a focus on the processes of negotiation in the immediacy of spatial practice may provide openings to liberate the discipline of architecture from its primary closures.'[16]

The image of an open architecture is an intriguing one. A space constructed through negotiations, transformed by use and resisting formal closure could be seen as the antithesis of architecture in any monumental sense. As a disciplinary response to the construction of a new constitution, its appearance might then be fleeting. Its hope for survival may be to remain on the run, as a movement of undisciplined practices.

◄E8 ◄E10 Stills from the video invisible architecture.

Apartheid and the death of South African cities

Achmat Dangor

It is quite unfashionable these days to use apartheid as a reference point when trying to find the roots of South Africa's economic and political problems. In the name of reconciliation, a blanket amnesia is being imposed on South Africans: what you forget you forgive, and what you forgive you reconcile yourself to. The only problem with this rather generous approach to history is that there are lessons to be learned from the past. This somewhat utilitarian fact aside, there is something distinctly sad about losing one's past, however bitter one might feel about some of it.

Let us consider how the decline of South Africa's major city, Johannesburg, is the direct result of politicians and planners choosing to forget or to ignore its history. Since remembering is something very intimately human, this history is perhaps best recalled through personal testimony.

I grew up in the 1950s, in a suburb called Fordsburg, located on the western edge of the city. From my grandmother's corrugated-iron and wood house, which dated back to Fordsburg's old mining days, I could walk to school, to the market, to the cinemas, the sports fields, the dairy, the shops, to the mosque or any number of Christian churches if I so wished. There were even safe places in which to play truant from school.

The house itself had a front stoep that shaded the entrance and served to extend the living area. In warm climates, being able to relax 'outside' while still feeling held in the safe embrace of your property, lends a sense of spaciousness even to the humblest of homes. You stepped through the front door into the living room, a large open space which the carpet divided neatly into two zones, one for 'lounging' and the other for eating. Two ornate doorways led to the cooking, cleaning and sleeping areas: bathroom, toilet and kitchen to the left, bedrooms to the right.

I don't mean to romanticize the architecture. This was a modest house: in size, construction and cost. Yet it provided a lifestyle that a working class family could afford. And its location within a 'community' of services made a difficult life bearable. Here a rather bookish boy, his arthritic grandmother and two young aunts (who spent much of their teens working in clothing factories) found comfort and stimulation. A quality of life that was unostentatious but satisfying. There was the time and the inclination to read, to listen to music.

One day a man in a grey suit came to the door and told my grandmother that she and her family had to move. She was a 'Malay' living in an 'Indian' group area. 'What's the difference?' she asked him. 'It's the law,' he said. 'In any case, your house is a slum dwelling.'

That night over supper my grandmother told her daughters that we had to move and that it was no use arguing or resisting. This kind of thing was happening all over the city, in Mayfair, Vrededorp, Malaycamp. People were being forced out and their houses razed to the ground. Time would be better spent looking for another place. 'What did the man mean when he said our house was a slum?' I wanted to know. They laughed at my innocence. Thank goodness I was too young to really understand, or the ranks of bomb-planting 'terrorists' might have had another youthful recruit.

When I look back now, I realize that we were living through a nightmare in slow, sequential motion. The apartheid policy of 'separate equalities' was being applied with ruthless logic. In this distorted understanding, the country was made up of different 'nations' who had to live in separate areas for the sake of 'racial peace'. The enforced separation had to begin in the cities, where huge numbers of people of all kinds lived together, not as a matter of choice but because of the pressure of space. Here your neighbour's race was a secondary consideration, even if you seethed inwardly that a black or a white or an Indian had moved in next door. You resented and then you adapted. That is the dynamic that governs the functioning of cities the world over. Apartheid was determined to reverse this immutable process.

'My grandmother's house in the early 1950s.'

The state had developed a whole arsenal of laws to help it achieve the unimaginable: people of different races living in separate, pre-planned ghettos. These laws ranged from the Slum Clearance Act to the much blunter Group Areas Act. In my grandmother's case, her perfectly good – even beautiful – house was declared a slum because it had been built before 1920 and was not constructed of brick and mortar.

In more difficult cases, where for legal reasons an abode could not be declared a slum dwelling, or where no alternative housing was provided, pressure was applied by destroying all the local amenities – cinemas, schools, clinics, recreation centres, sports fields. In the new, racial group areas to which people were relocated, social amenities were concentrated at central points. These became the nerve centres of the separate local governments. Euphemistically called 'community centres', they housed the bureaucrats who controlled the lives of local residents, determining who was 'legal' and who not. What followed was corruption and patronage on a scale comparable only to the old Soviet Union (I am told). We still live with that legacy today.

Apartheid, I see now with hindsight, involved the slow destruction of Johannesburg as a city of communities. Separate, inherently unequal townships were built at a distance from the city to accommodate the various segregated 'population groups'. The new houses were built to a uniform National Housing Standard pattern. One strong feature of this design was the way people walked into their 'homes' right off the street. The stoep, that simple, long-established way of enhancing a small house, was abolished. A space-to-occupation formula was devised, which in theory allowed for the separation of sexes and a density of no more than three people per room. The fact that it was impossible to achieve this perversely noble goal – in later years, bathrooms and kitchens were counted as 'rooms' to obscure the fact that actual occupation in most township houses exceeded the legal limit – is beside the point.

What is tragically pertinent is that Johannesburg's death was planned, probably inadvertently, in the 1950s. Thanks to the schemes devised then and pursued with such brutal single-mindedness in the following decades, most of the city's citizens now live far from the central business district and other centres of commerce and employment. Millions must be spent to sustain hastily designed and inefficient mass transit systems; minibuses pollute the atmosphere and clog the roads, while conflict in the taxi industry is the cause of much violence in Johannesburg.

In the townships, nearly all the architecture is too rudimentary to allow for any significant upgrading. Add-on structures usually provide little more than additional sleeping space. Services such as water, sanitation and electricity were designed to cope with artificially reduced population statistics: the apartheid government, and even the former liberal Johannesburg City Council, for a long time refused to acknowledge that Soweto had more than a million citizens – as if black people and their needs might be conjured away by playing with figures. As a consequence, the services are fragmented and inefficient, and need to be heavily subsidized.

But let us accept that all of this is just another historical consequence of apartheid, that in the spirit of reconciliation we need to forgive the perpetrators (who include some of today's more vociferous liberal politicians) and get on with our lives. Well, perhaps I'm oversimplifying, but in our desire to forget and forgive, we seem to be repeating the same mistakes our erstwhile masters made.

Housing estates built under the Reconstruction and Development Programme (the RDP) are mushrooming on the peripheries of the city. These houses have the same 'Housing Standard' feel as the old apartheid 'matchboxes', except that they're even smaller because of a lack of funds and the great number of people who need shelter. The lack of infrastructure and amenities, so characteristic of the past, continues to be a feature of these settlements. No clinics, no schools, not even a patch of veld cleared to offer some compensatory sense of leisure. It seems that being relatively poor – I say 'relatively' because to obtain such a house you must at least have an income – condemns you to that relentless blandness that apartheid perfected.

Is there an alternative? (Policy-makers always seem to demand of their critics the solutions they themselves were elected to find.) Let's begin by remembering that, in the name of urban planning, people were driven out of the cities, into dormitory townships that today require costly subsidies merely to keep on being inefficient and inadequate. Would one answer not be to establish new housing complexes much closer to the city? The vast tracts of unused or underused land will strike anyone who travels around Johannesburg.

Another answer might be to develop the inner city itself. Instead of building more pondoks (shacks) in the veld, fifteen or twenty kilometres outside the city, spend that money to rehabilitate areas such as Doornfontein, Hillbrow, Bertrams and many other traditionally 'white' suburbs, which are crumbling under the weight of illegal occupation, bank red-lining, and other problems. Of equal importance: ensure that the rehabilitation does not lead to the large-scale destruction of city architecture, some of which is quite unique. And create financing and legal systems that allow for significant joint or group ownership. The cooperative experiments in Toronto and some parts of New York come to mind.

Of course, this will require investment from the private sector. And business people always have a whole string of pre-emptive complaints up their sleeves. 'What about the crime?' they will say. 'What about people not paying for services?' One of the peculiarities of modern urban civilization is the power of what Americans call 'critical mass'. Get enough people to live together in dwellings that are not just shelters, in an environment where leisure and cultural stimulation are a safe walk away, give them the means of owning the dwellings and the environment – and they will pay their way.

Funny isn't it? There is less crime in Killarney, where the 'larnies' live in great and intimate numbers, than in Hillbrow, where mostly black people live. The crime in Killarney is opportunistic, whereas in Hillbrow it is endemic. What's the difference? Look at the architecture, examine the vastly different patterns of ownership. In Killarney there is something worth keeping, and keeping in good shape. It is yours, or it can be. Hillbrow is a place in perpetual transition. You move in because you have to, you move out as quickly as you can. Soon this will happen to those RDP matchbox towns as well.

Who cares that a drug dealer has just set up shop (sometimes quite literally) on the corner? Who cares if electrical wiring is being stolen? Or if the house next door or the flat above is being used as an overpriced doss-house for exploiting illegal immigrants? Not me, says the transient citizen, no matter how upstanding he or she may be. I'll be out of here as soon as I can.

I remember people saying the very same thing over a beer in a township backyard twenty years ago. It makes me think Apartheid is alive and well: he's just acquired an RDP house and his children have moved to Hillbrow.

Achmat Dangor is writing here in his personal capacity and his views do not necessarily reflect those of the Independent Development Trust.

◀E6 ▶G10

Carletonville
Jodi Bieber

1 Khutsong.

2 Blyvooruitzicht Mine.

3 Hostel, Khutsong.

4 Hostel, Blyvooruitzicht Mine.

5 Dutch Reformed Church.

6

Settlements, change and planning in South Africa since 1994
David Dewar

The first democratic election of 1994 was an extraordinary moment in South Africa. With the advent of democracy, many of us who had long been urging fundamental change in the practice of urban planning and management in the country felt that a corner had been turned.

For the first time there was a government in power which had as its main concern the well-being of the majority of the population, and as its central policy a vigorous reconstruction and development programme, aimed at making rapid, visible improvements in the lives of the urban poor. It seemed as if the time of those professions involved in the making of the built environment had arrived: the moment called for innovation, for creative professional leadership and for rapid advances and new ways of doing.

After four years, it is apposite to reflect on our progress since that hopeful beginning, and such reflection forms the basis of this essay.

In principle and in practice

Overall, the last four years have been marked by deep disappointment, and in many quarters by disillusionment.

The period might have been an urban planner's dream. The human needs crying out for attention were immense, and for the first time there was the political will to deal with them. New legislation, the Development Facilitation Act of 1995, sought to place a humanistic and environmentally sound set of normative principles at the heart of the planning system, calling for settlements that are more compact and integrated, promote mixed uses and are environmentally sustainable. This legislation, along with the Local Government Transition Act of 1996, requires all local authorities to develop integrated development plans which deal with spatial, environmental, economic, social and institutional issues holistically, and to link their plans to budgets.

However, while the intentions have changed for the better, in practice it has been business as usual. South African towns and cities are mainly growing in two ways. First, there are low-cost housing schemes. These mass schemes are largely monofunctional. They are undertaken on disconnected parcels of land and characterized by a low-density, undifferentiated blanket of free-standing housing shells. Social and commercial facilities and other vibrant urban activities are notable mainly by their absence; the local market is so thinly spread that there are not sufficient thresholds to support a wide range of goods and services. Public transport is woefully inadequate for the same reason, and life is appallingly inconvenient and expensive in these places. A striking feature is the almost total lack of spatial cohesion: nothing is contained or enclosed. Buildings are isolated events in a sea of space; they do not contribute to bounding space, or to defining streets or public areas. The results are environments which are overtly hostile to pedestrians, made instead to suit the motor car – even though the vast majority of inhabitants have no real prospect of owning one – and offering no shade, no cover, no features of interest or stimulation, no short cuts. It is usually impossible to discern any social, economic or environmental concerns in the making of these schemes, which seem to have been ordered simply by questions of engineering efficiency.

The second way the cities are growing is through land invasions: the illegal occupation, mainly of public land, and the establishment of informal or shack settlements. Spatially, these are frequently superior to the pre-planned settlements, for their layouts are at least informed by pedestrian needs, and the relationship between housing units is usually the result of negotiated compromises on issues

Uytenbogaardt and Rozendal with Architects Associated, Springfield Terrace, Cape Town, 1992.

such as light, air, fire-making, and the keeping of chickens and other livestock. Their great inadequacies, however, are that they are seldom integrated with larger urban systems, they lack utility services, there is no higher order of spatial structure, and tenure is insecure.

While the Development Facilitation Act calls for integration and compaction, in reality the dominant spatial patterns continue to be fragmentation, separation and sprawl, and qualities of urbanity are inevitably lacking. To make things worse, the provision of housing and social and utility services is cumbersome and slow, and the backlogs continue to grow.

Why is vigorous and beneficial change not occurring? Why, when for the first time there is a high degree of coincidence between the desires of politicians, planners and large numbers of the population, are these aspirations not being met? Why is planning not flourishing and giving positive direction?

The planning environment as an obstacle to change

The climate of planning and development has contributed to the lack of progress.The legislative framework of planning has become increasingly fragmented and distorted. Nationally, this has been a time of frenetic policy-making and planning, but it has largely occurred within discrete national line-function departments, with little reference to the activities in other departments. Critical components of spatial planning such as transport, water, the environment, housing and land all have their own policy frameworks and planning procedures. Worse, these policies are often in direct conflict with each other. An example which is of considerable importance for spatial planning can be found in the conflicting policies of the Department of Housing and the Department of Land Affairs, which is the statutory home of the planning profession. On the one hand, the Department of Land Affairs calls for compact, integrated and sustainable settlements. On the other, the Department of Housing discourages the granting of housing subsidies for plots smaller than 300 to 400 square metres, thereby contributing very significantly to sprawl and making the achievement of compact, integrated settlements an impossibility.

There have also been intense turf battles between departments. Of particular importance to planners is the struggle between the Department of Constitutional Development, which has local government as part of its portfolio, and the Department of Land Affairs, the current home of the planning profession, for control over the system of municipal planning. On the one hand, the Department of Land Affairs, through the Development Facilitation Act, makes it a statutory requirement for local authorities to articulate 'Land Development Objectives'. On the other, the Department of Constitutional Development, through the Transitional Local Government Act, requires local authorities to produce 'Integrated Development Plans' which are tied to municipal budgets, and it is busy making this a statutory requirement too. While there are overlaps between the two products, there are also significant differences.

What are the consequences of these dynamics? Firstly, the planning system is confused, and professionals and land developers alike are finding it very difficult to work with. Secondly, the system has become increasingly cumbersome: the delays in getting projects approved are increasing significantly, and this is encouraging people to act outside of the law. Thirdly, and perhaps most importantly, conflicting policies make it almost impossible to achieve the normative principles which now theoretically lie at the heart of the planning system.

For public authorities the watchword has been 'transformation'. Everything has been changing at once, and especially for local government in larger cities. In Greater Cape Town, for example, 56 municipalities have been transformed into six. Officials have been transferred across authority boundaries and many have been retrenched as the overall staffing levels of local authorities were reduced. At the same time their responsibilities have increased dramatically. Vigorous policies of affirmative action have led to some people being promoted beyond their levels of competence.

All of this has resulted in low morale, growing despondency and falling levels of energy in the public sector. There has also been a lowering of capacity, particularly in the professional and skilled sectors. A new generation of planning and design professionals is struggling to shift from the rhetoric of protest to the practice of development, and finding that it is much more difficult to make things happen than to prevent them from happening.

The issue of capacity extends into the arena of political decision-making. Local decision-making forums are now dominated by people who, because of the previous political system, have little or no experience in local government and whose sense of possibilities has been shaped and limited by their own, highly inadequate urban living experiences.

For the private planning sector it is largely business as usual. Most of the work is undertaken by precisely the same people who unproblematically shaped the urban landscape under apartheid. Computer programmes set up in the past to produce standardized layout responses continue to operate unchanged. A new, more developmental rhetoric shrouds the old practices and, in the process, devalues the currency of the developmental argument. Professional planners are providing little real leadership for processes of change.

The public at large tends to respond in one of two ways. Amongst historically disadvantaged communities there is growing disillusionment and anger at the pace of delivery. Expectations are unrealistically high and there is an entrenched culture of entitlement. The professions concerned with the built environment face increasing hostility from the very people whom they are ethically bound to serve. Amongst middle-class and more affluent communities there is considerable political resistance to change. The Nimby attitude – 'Not in my back yard' – is especially prevalent when it comes to the close integration of living areas for the poor with the major systems of the cities.

Problems in land development: The case of Springfield Terrace

Although aspects of the broader climate have contributed to the lack of progress, institutional issues associated with land development projects at the local level are even more important, for settlements grow largely through the cumulative effects of local projects.

The crux of the problem is that the institutional frameworks and mindsets which are still in place were developed over many years to support a very different model of development from that called for in the Development Facilitation Act. The system is based on a reactive, controlling form of planning which supports the separation of uses, a suburban model of housing and the strict separation of the functions of public and private sectors.

To illustrate the difficulties that this disjuncture creates for development in practice, let us look at the Springfield Terrace housing project in Cape Town.

Springfield Terrace is a high-density infill housing scheme consisting of 133 units, both simplex and duplex, in the form of three- and four-storey walk-ups. It is located in Woodstock, an old inner-city area within walking distance of the central business district, and was completed in 1992. It was the first relatively large inner-city infill project in South Africa with a non-racial basis, aimed at the lower income market and utilizing state housing subsidies. It was intended as a pilot project to demonstrate a number of necessary innovations.

The most important of these was an infill approach to urban development. This involves accommodating new housing on well-located, underused land within the existing urban fabric – as opposed to building on the urban peripheries – in order to compact settlements. This has a number of advantages: there are large savings in transport and energy costs; historical investments in social and utility infrastructure are put to maximum use; vibrant local markets are created for small service industries, and higher thresholds ensure higher levels of support for social and commercial facilities, thereby increasing convenience.

The scheme also hoped to show how small parcels of well-located, publicly owned land – of which there is a great deal in South African towns and cities – can be used strategically, and how high-density housing can result in highly liveable environments, if the public space is properly designed. (Gross densities of 156 dwelling units per hectare and net densities of 257 dwelling units per hectare were achieved.)

Additional aims were to demonstrate the working of a public-private partnership in housing, and to show how cross-subsidization can lower the entry price of housing for low-income households.

The primary developer was Headstart Developments, which was registered as a not-for-profit housing utility company. Headstart was funded by a number of large national corporations as part of their social responsibility programmes, but was a separate legal entity and had its own board of directors. The intention was to undertake the project on a partnership basis, involving Headstart, the Cape Town City Council and the local community.

The site identified was well located in relation to public transport (rail, bus and taxis) and to existing, but in some cases underutilized, social facilities. Two of these, a church and the Rahmaniyeh Institute, a Muslim community centre, flanked the site.

The issue of land assembly was central to the project. The site was made up of two land parcels, totalling 8,038 square metres. The smaller one (1,515 square metres) consisted of some vacant plots and seventeen badly dilapidated cottages, most of which were subsequently condemned, housing 25 tenant households. This parcel was purchased on the open market, with an undertaking to rehouse the tenant households, preferably in the scheme.

The second parcel (6,523 square metres) was residual land left over from land expropriated to construct the Eastern Boulevard freeway. This land was under the control of the city council, who donated it at nominal cost to the scheme as its contribution to the partnership. The two sites were then consolidated.

For economic reasons, and for logistical reasons associated with mobilizing state subsidies, the scheme was undertaken as a totality using one main builder. Vigorous attempts to mobilize a consortium of small builders to do the work came to nothing. Completed units were sold into private ownership under sectional title legislation.

In order to mobilize national housing subsidies, and to achieve a wide demographic mix, a variety of accommodation types was designed, ranging from bedsitters of 27 square metres to two- and three-bedroom units of 72 square metres.

The project was aimed at three segments of the housing market. Buyers in two of these would qualify for different forms of state subsidy, while those in the third would be drawn from the open market. The aim was to sell units in the open category for the highest possible price and use the profits thus generated to subsidize the entry price to the lowest level possible.

On the face of it, the project was successful: it produced a living environment which is popular with its residents, and its central public space has become a community meeting place. It won a merit award from the South African Institute of Architects, and the local authority often shows it off to national and international visitors. In fact, many of the urban objectives which Headstart sought to demonstrate have become part of public policy.

However, some significant objectives were not achieved. An active partnership with the council never materialized. The project overran the budget by 11.5 per cent and took more than three years to complete. The cross-subsidization initiative also fell through. Some of the reasons for these failures throw light on the more general structural problems in the planning system.

Weak partnerships

Successful public-private partnerships require socially responsible developers and entrepreneurially-minded authorities. There must be trust between the partners and clarity about their respective roles. The Springfield Terrace project met none of these conditions.

It was the first time the local authority had entered into a partnership with a private sector, non-profit organization in the area of land and housing. Some local politicians and officials were suspicious of the relationship. Since Headstart was funded by large corporations, some felt, entirely mistakenly, that the 'non-profit' motive was somehow a front. They could not overcome the distrust of the private sector that comes so readily to public officials.

The absence of sound partnerships led to a series of functional breakdowns. Every time the project suffered a political setback the council ran for cover.

There was also a lack of clarity about the different roles and responsibilities. The financing of the public courts and spaces around which the housing was organized are a case in point. It was Headstart's position that quality public spaces were central to successful lower-income housing. They argued that the value of these spaces impacted on the entire community, not just on the participating households, and that the local authority should therefore be responsible for both capital and maintenance costs in this regard. Further, they argued that these costs should be recovered from general taxes, rather than from the buyers through the purchase price, to avoid burdening the very people the project was meant to assist. The local authority, on the other hand, took the position that the costs should be built into the unit prices.

The dispute contributed to delays which forced up holding costs. Eventually, Headstart decided to act as a benevolent local authority: it absorbed capital costs of some half a million rand to plant and pave the public spaces, but did not pass these on to end-users. This added to the budget overruns.

The lack of clarity about roles also caused confusion and delay in the approval process, with the council trying to act as both player and referee.

Cumbersome approval processes

The approval process was protracted. It took a staggering nineteen and a half months from the time that sketch plans were submitted – by which point much discussion and negotiation had already taken place with the council – to the granting of final approvals. This increased overall costs drastically through the holding costs of the land, the rapidly escalating prices of building materials, and sharply rising interest rates.

Why did the process take so long? Firstly, the scheme was complex, requiring various approvals of different kinds. This raised a problem of sequencing. For example, the council would not proceed with the rezoning application until a decision had been made in principle about the disposal of public open space. Then again, building plans could not be scrutinized until zoning waivers had been granted.

Secondly, the problem of sequencing was compounded by the number of different authorities involved in the negotiations. For example, both the city council and the provincial administration needed to approve the change of status of the site from public open space to subdivided land, and to approve the rezoning. However, submissions could only be made to the provincial administration after the council had made a recommendation. Similarly, the council was reluctant to process the proposal for subdivision until the Housing Board had agreed to provide bridging finance. The board, in turn, required an expression of support from the council. And so it went on.

Thirdly, and most importantly, the scheme challenged many of the generally accepted tenets of a number of departments and ran into problems around the fragmentation of line-functions. On the one hand, officials in the planning department were excited about the project. They accepted that it was based on different principles to those which underlay the regulations, and that innovation was called for. They offered to set up an interdepartmental team to fast-track the decision-making.

On the other hand, they failed to convince other departments, such as those concerned with roads, traffic, fire, cleansing and so on, to participate in the innovation. The fast-tracking team did not work. The actual process was one of drawn-out negotiations with different departments, each viewing the problem from a different perspective, all trying to maximize the operation of their own sphere of competence rather than optimize the scheme as a whole. The main public court, for example, had to be larger than the designers intended, because the department responsible for garbage removal would not budge from their demand that a garbage truck be able to turn around in it unhindered.

Inadequate institutional support

A serious problem was the lack of institutional support necessary to tackle the project as a totality. The issue of rental accommodation provides a telling example.

Initially, the project intended to provide a certain amount of rental accommodation. It was considered important to offer various types of tenure so that there would be a measure of choice, and analyses had revealed that there was considerable demand for rental in the inner city. It was also assumed that subsidized rental housing would be cheaper. This was very important in relation to the 25 households in the cottages that were to be demolished, as a commitment had been made to accommodate them in the scheme if possible. However, many of them were only erratically employed, and few of them either wished to own their own dwelling or could afford to do so.

But the whole idea proved to be problematic. The first difficulty concerned costs. Tenants who rented would be unlikely to invest large amounts of their own resources to improve finishes, and so the quality of finishes in rental accommodation would have to be reasonably high from the outset. But this increased the costs per unit of space. If units were to be affordable they would therefore have to be very small, raising the spectre of overcrowding, which might discourage buyers. Alternatively, the higher costs would place the units beyond the qualifying limits for subsidies, rendering them unaffordable to low-income households.

This difficulty was finally overcome by making rooms the focus of subsidy rather than units. Rooms, sharing facilities such as bathrooms and kitchens, were arranged flexibly so that they could be organized and reorganized at very little additional cost into one-, two- or three-bedroom units. For example, if the household consisted of four adults, say a married couple and two female single parents, the married couple would qualify for a room subsidy, as would each of the other adults. Depending on family circumstances, each could then choose how many rooms they wanted or could afford. The Housing Board accepted this proposal for subsidy purposes, and 64 rooms of this kind were included in the initial scheme.

This raised a second difficulty: the institutional capacity to administer the rental accommodation. Headstart's task was to experiment and innovate, and it was never conceived as a long-term administrator. Some other institution would have to be found to administer and maintain the rental accommodation on an on-going basis. The logical choice was the Cape Town City Council, which had its own rental stock and was willing in principle to take on the task. However, the sale of public rental stock in South African cities over the last decade, a course of action promoted by government, has meant that high administrative costs have fallen on a decreasing number of units. This has led in turn to excessively high rents.

As there was no alternative non-governmental agency with the capacity to supply this service in the inner city at the time, the rental option fell away.

The institutional positioning of housing

In South Africa, the provision of low-income housing is a local authority responsibility, and local authorities are politically controlled. Housing is therefore highly politicized. In the Springfield Terrace project, steps had to be taken to evict two of the original tenant families for antisocial behaviour and for failure to pay their heavily subsidized rents. A party-political representative, who was not even from the immediate community, picked up the cause of these families and set about making highly publicized political capital of it. This put strain on the partnership, as the council sought cover, and lengthy delays resulted. The problem disappeared immediately once the new residents themselves supported Headstart's actions.

A question of class

Although this is not a matter the housing authorities can control, it is clear that the concept of cross-subsidization failed largely because of deeply rooted class attitudes. Many prospective buyers of the more expensive units, who really liked the accommodation and the scheme, were put off by the lower-income status of the surrounding areas. If cross-subsidization is to be pursued, it will have to occur over a much larger area, or between different uses, rather than within relatively small housing schemes.

Demonstrating an alternative

Although Springfield Terrace was built in the early 1990s, the general operating climate remains the same today. It is clear that the rapid production of better-quality urban housing on a large scale, as called for in the new policy, will not occur until the institutional problems associated with housing provision are dealt with. It is not possible to introduce a new model of development while continuing to use the old instruments.

Change will be difficult, but it is by no means impossible. What is required in the short term is a series of pilot projects to explore and demonstrate an alternative and to learn from it.

What qualities should such pilot projects have?

They should be large enough to result in high-intensity, mixed-use urban environments and not just housing estates. They should be located on sites which have a strategic importance in the broader structure of towns and cities, thus enabling them to have significant structural knock-on effects and contributing towards greater urban efficiency.

The projects should be undertaken in partnership with industrial, commercial and housing developers, local authorities, transport and environmental authorities, and provincial education and health departments. They should be run by interdisciplinary teams of professionals, made up of the best minds available and drawn from both the public and the private sectors.

The public finance for the projects should be the same as that normally allocated to urban developments, but should not come in predetermined line-function forms (so much for roads, so much for clinics, and so on). There must be sufficient scope to think innovatively about the form and function of urban elements and how their service can best be improved in the face of the reality of scarce resources.

The existing planning and control regulations and approval procedures should be suspended in relation to the pilot project sites, so that these processes themselves may be re-examined.

Finally, the state should establish a network through which the lessons learned in different projects across the country can be rapidly disseminated.

There is little risk in any of this. Given the amount of finance now effectively being wasted as far as investment in the built environment is concerned, there is absolutely nothing to lose.

G

▶H8

Environmental portraits
Zwelethu Mthethwa

1 Langa.
2 Siyanda.

3 Nyanga.
4 Siyanda.
5 Mooi River.
6 Guguletu.

7 Umlazi.
8 Umlazi.
9 Umlazi.
10 Mooi River.

11 Nyanga.
12 Mooi River.
13 Howick.
14 Umlazi.

8

G

8

G

8

G

F3433-3440

ANT TOUCH
THIS

8

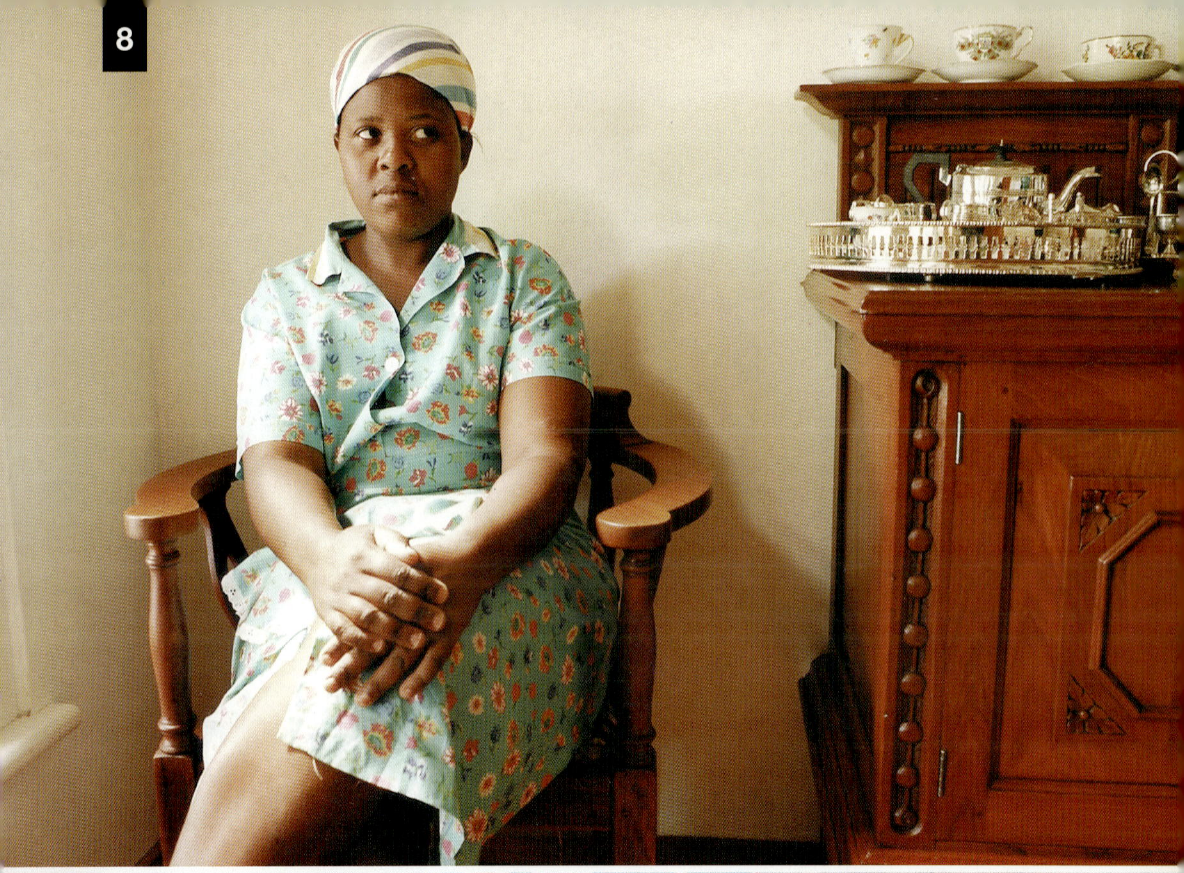

G

Interiors, District Six, c. 1950

Shamil Jeppie

It struck me that our history is contained in the homes we live in, that we are shaped by the ability of these simple structures to resist being defiled. There, in the heart of Salaam's house ... the scene had been set for the inevitable drama of our lives.

Achmat Dangor, *Kafka's Curse*[1]

The undisputed heart of Cape Town, for its working-class inhabitants at least, was District Six. In 1966 the apartheid government declared that everyone would have to move out of the area to make way for new housing for whites. Despite public protests, the long-settled residents were forced to evacuate the neighbourhood, and virtually all the buildings, except churches and mosques, were steadily razed to the ground.[2]

This forced removal of thousands of families marked a new chapter in the history of Cape Town. A distinctive space was wrenched from the heart of the city. That space, renamed Zonnebloem, was never even half-filled by its intended settlers. Even today it remains a scar on the slopes of Table Mountain.

The poor people, who made up most of the more than 50,000 who were removed, were given new living quarters in low-cost blocks of flats – small and basic, appropriate to their dormitory purpose – in what is known as the Cape Flats. Most of the middle-class residents went to the suburbs. The dry and sandy Flats had been known snobbishly as *buite* (outside, beyond, distant) by the people of inner-city Cape Town; but it was there, far from the centre, that they had to begin a new life in unfamiliar surroundings. District Six became an 'old world' which could never be revisited except in memory.

On the Cape Flats the new apartments and the newcomers from the inner city did not fit together well. The stable, neighbourly relationships, cultural formations and lifestyles of the settled inner city, which the forced removal had disrupted, could not be reproduced in the modern and quite desolate setting of planned townships with alien names such as Bontheuwel and Manenberg. The destruction of District Six was thus about far more than the reduction of buildings to rubble and dust. These structures were homes and dwellings, carrying intimate and layered histories often stretching back into the middle of the 19th century. Individual houses or blocks also represented whole ethnic or class subcultures, as well as the depths of family experience and personal memory. If bulldozed walls could speak ...

Professional photographers and newspaper reporters captured very little of the material culture or lived interior world of District Six's razed buildings. While the area did have a vibrant public life, existence began in the enclosed spaces and closeness of home and hearth. As Gaston Bachelard observed about home and being: 'Life begins well, it begins enclosed, protected, all warm in the bosom of the house ... it is the human being's first world ... the house is a large cradle.'[3] The interior life of District Six is the subject of this essay.

Many Capetonians who lived outside District Six viewed it as a slum; insiders sometimes shared this perception, especially after they had managed to move up and out of the area. Mobility shapes perspective. Richard Rive, the well-known author of novels such as 'Buckingham Palace', District Six, recalled growing up in a neighbourhood that was 'damp, dirty and dank'.[4] Undoubtedly, this alliterative description fitted many of the private and public spaces of District Six; contemporary photographic images, in their visual selectiveness and imaginative partiality, support the view. But whereas Rive judged the area with a certain aloofness, an earlier writer strove to give his judgement a more directly felt content. In his novella A Walk in the Night, Alex La Guma combines the skills of a painter and a poet to craft a classic image of the slum:

> He turned down another street, away from the artificial glare of Hanover [Street], between stretches of damp, battered houses with their broken-ribs of front-railings; cracked walls and high tenements that rose like the left-overs of a bombed area in the twilight; vacant lots and weed-grown patches where houses had once stood; and deep doorways resembling the entrances to deserted castles. There were children playing in the street, darting among the overflowing dustbins and shooting at each other with wooden guns. In some of the doorways people sat or stood, murmuring idly in the fast-fading light like wasted ghosts in a plague-ridden city.[5]

Rive is correct to remind us that 'it is notoriously easy to romanticize about slum life and sentimentalize it'.[6] But our appreciation of District Six space is not a choice between mushy sentimentalism and blunt condemnation. Among both insiders and outsiders there are nuances in consciousness, contradictory memories, and varieties of spatial perception and experience which we must approach with the appropriate care. 'District Six was a slum ...' Such generality flattens the history and diversity of the place, collapses its class and status divisions, permits no distinction between hallowed private and battered public spaces. It affords no value to individual experience or popular memory or collective constructions of space. More pertinently, it obscures the ways in which residents arranged their interior spaces; how they organized and made habitable the only homes and dwellings they had ever known.

District Six's residential buildings – whether the ageing Victorian ones or those constructed in the 1930s such as Bloemhof Flats – were homes and dwellings, in the rich double sense of the latter term: they provided material cover and protective shelter, and they also articulated a structure of feeling, a cultural system and a way of living.[7] District Six dwelling was both artefact and process, shelter and life itself.

Family and home, as in other places and times, were intertwined. Moral values, principles and dispositions were essentially 'systematized', shaped and negotiated – incorporated, rejected, transformed – in the home.[8] In materialist terms, home was the vital location of reproduction. But this is to limit a full appreciation of the richness and complexity of 'home'. In various ways homes were not dark, except from the outside, but often comparatively bright; not completely dirty but not completely wholesome either; not damp but secure and comforting.

House and home. 'House' stands only for the structure, for a building. 'Home' is richer, it brings together ideas of the physical space itself and the broader notion of household, signifying refuge and intimacy, dwelling and ownership, warmth and belonging. A home does not need to be a building, it may be as little as a fire beneath a bridge: the space marked by that fire will be a focus, a centre, a starting point from which all else proceeds. Afrikaans has only one word, 'huis' (also formed as 'tuis') to carry these different meanings. In the working-class Afrikaans of the inner city, 'huis' was home, house, dwelling. And it is here that we should start when looking at District Six.

Formal housing was never in abundance; affordable living space was in constant demand, not only in the District but throughout the Cape Town area. The Social Survey of Cape Town conducted in the early forties found that more than two-thirds of coloured households were crowded or over-crowded.[9] Housing supply in the Cape Peninsula was a persistent problem for local and national governments.[10] Professor Edward Batson's research for the Social Survey found that only a fifth of coloured households were not crowded. Two out of three homes were crowded or overcrowded, whereas only one in thirty white households was in that condition.[11] In 1950 the municipal Housing Supervisor stated:

> Almost every house in the districts where the Coloured people live is packed tight. Children grow up and marry and in turn have children and are unable to find a place of their own. A family is turned out of an overcrowded house and finds shelter with friends for a few days – which grow into weeks, months, years. They sleep in living rooms, in kitchens, in passages, in garages ...[12]

The racialization of the phenomenon was unfortunate. The category 'coloured' was so broad and unspecific as to be meaningless sociologically. The people of the inner city were from every ethnic, linguistic, religious, regional and racial background. But the dominant discourse relied on the language of race to speak of urban problems, preferring to deal with some nebulous 'coloured' rather than the poor, often recently urbanized city dweller in search of a job and a decent place to stay.

The number of rooms and amount of floor space depended on the quality and type of house. There were tenement flats and semi-detached row houses of a better quality. Whatever their design, most of the District's houses shared a characteristic 'low-grade' status with other working-class housing in areas such as Woodstock and the Bokaap. These properties had a market value of less than £2,000 each. A very small proportion of 'non-Europeans', some 3 to 5 per cent, were housed in 'medium-grade' properties valued at between £2,000 and £5,000.[13] These were obviously larger detached units. 'High-grade' housing was an extreme rarity.

In the ubiquitous tenements and row houses of the District, residents and their worldly possessions were packed closely into each unit. Multiple generations met and mingled amidst an assortment of tightly arranged heirlooms, newly acquired furnishings, and other belongings. A family's goods, whether inherited pieces of furniture or wares valued for their modern functions, were a collection of treasures. Very little was ever discarded. Rather, what could be accumulated, stored or recycled was saved. But home was not about things. Private household space was pre-eminently collective family space, although the idea of family was elastic and open.

There were some nuclear families, but they were not pervasive. Yet the ideal of one nuclear family in each unit of housing was what must have motivated the architects of the city's working-class quarters. Some residents may have shared such an ideal or hope at one time or another. A house was certainly meant neither for an individual nor for a group living together, but for a family. The latter was understood firstly to mean a man, his wife and their offspring. Then other blood relatives would be accommodated, beginning with the parents of either the husband or wife. A newly-married couple might also initially take up residence with the husband's family, or more rarely with the wife's. Finally, strangers might be taken in as an act of kindness. Monogamy was the norm, but men had mistresses (in the parlance of the District a mistress was a hou-vrou, a kept woman), and polygamy was practised, at least among a small number of audacious Muslims. The rate of births out of wedlock was high, and because it often fell to women to raise the children, matricentral families were not uncommon. Nearly every family type lived at some point in what the Social Survey classified as 'crowded conditions'.

In its discussion of the classic anthropological concerns of kinship and residence, one study in the 1950s found that 'there are no fixed residence rules, and the residential group varies according to economic situation and personal wishes in each case. In most urban areas this haphazard diversity has been further intensified by an acute housing shortage.'[14]

A single household probably went through a series of kinship arrangements. By the 1950s it seems that the nuclear family, even among those for whom it had once been a reality, was a distant memory. Traditional kinship ties were valued, but they were also extended to incorporate co-residents and neighbours. Home was where family and kinship ties were cemented, and thus where strangers could become part of the family. Not only did additional family members (grandparents, aunts, cousins, nephews) come to share one house, but rooms were rented out to newly-married couples who were not relations, desperate families recommended by friends, or complete strangers prepared to pay for accommodation. 'Eleven people lived in our house in Tyne Street,' Linda Fortune says in the opening lines of her memoir of the District.[15] Fatima Karriem lived in one room with four of her children before moving to larger quarters, which even then were not big enough. Despite her cramped circumstances she had thirteen pregnancies in all, but only seven babies survived.[16] There is evidence that lobbies were used as living space by really desperate families. One resident remembers the passage of an apartment on the corner of Harrington and Albertus streets being occupied without the permission of the owners, who bumped, with obvious bewilderment, into the additional occupants one morning.[17] But experiences like this were exceptional.

Galiema Albertyn grew up in a two-storey apartment on Selkirk Street.[18] The ground floor had two rooms: her mother and father slept in the front one, and the five children in the other. Although they were renters themselves, her parents sub-let an upstairs room; another one on the second floor was occupied by her grandmother and an aunt. Fatima Karriem recalls moving into one such room: 'Toe kry ek 'n kamer in Selkirk Straat, in daai pad. Toe gaat ek daar bly met vier kinners.' ('So I got a room in Selkirk Street, in that road. So I went to live there with four children.') Gradually she and her husband purchased household essentials: ''n Kas gekoep, dressing tafel gekoep, die en daai.' ('Bought a cupboard, a dressing table, this and that.') She concludes ironically: 'Toe het ek 'n double-storey huis vol goed van soebat.' ('Then I had a double-storey house full of stuff from nagging.')[19]

The few photographers who came close to entering District Six homes captured only the short passageway from the front door. Whether photographers really wanted to cross the threshold and depict the interior world of the houses is another question. Perhaps there was usually very little of interest within to document for the wider world, except evidence of hardship and poverty. These conditions were already represented and could always be conveyed well enough through street scenes and panoramic shots of the area – general views that captured scrawny kids and the peeling façades of dilapidated Victorian buildings.

Houses were compact places. Given that they were mainly single-storey semi-detached houses or double-storey row houses, they were long and narrow rather than square and spacious, giving them a sense of depth from the stoep or front entrance. A net curtain was very often hung at the end of the lobby, cutting off either the kitchen or the sitting room from the street. The curtain represented an internal frontier between private and public. It symbolically protected the intimate domestic space and kept the world at bay. Behind it, women could be less concerned with their appearance, a family's real class – in the colloquial sense – could be hidden or revealed, and arguments settled without the rest of the neighbourhood watching.

If home was the heart of the private sphere, the immediate neighbourhood – usually the families on either side – came next in degree of closeness. These neighbours could go beyond the net curtain

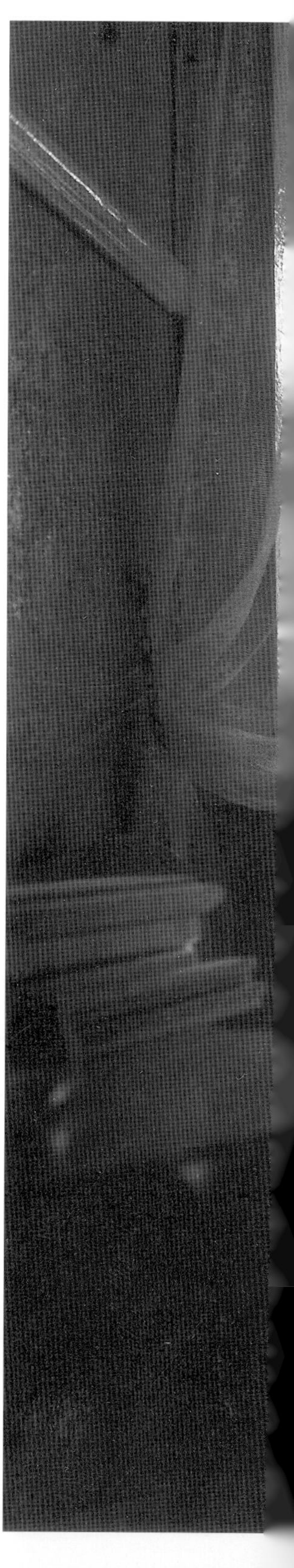

Interior, District Six.
Photograph by Jansje Wissema.

at most times. On special occasions the house might allow a freer flow of insiders and outsiders from the wider neighbourhood. Christmas or the Muslim labarang, a christening or doekmal, and an engagement or wedding reception provided opportunities when the sanctuary could be breached. Members of the community active in public associations of all kinds, ranging from sports teams to choirs and church groups to political parties, often also had to make their sitting rooms available for meetings or rehearsals. Then the space came to feel like collective property. The net curtain was ignored, the two halves were tightly pulled aside or the entire thing taken down. During New Year's celebrations the reverse happened: the house was brought onto the street, as benches and chairs were placed on the front stoep and pavement, and special food was prepared for enjoyment on the street while watching the passing Malay choirs and coon troupes.

The curtain made it easier to see the outside from within than the other way round. Open doors, like open windows and shutters, allowed in sunlight and fresh air, so necessary in old and crowded dwellings, but did not permit strangers a view of the full domestic space, especially the kitchen. The architectural photographer, Jansje Wissema, has two shots of lobbies from the inside out, showing the heavily painted walls hung with photographic portraits of family members and pictures in frames, and the customary linoleum which was easy to replace when it wore out.[20]

If the contemporary photographer was ill-placed or conceptually ill-equipped to portray the interior worlds of District Six houses, then the novelist serves us better. La Guma takes us beyond the lace curtain.

> The front of the house was in darkness but beyond the dangling lace curtain at the end of the passageway light glared in the sitting-room. The floor was covered with bright linoleum decorated with geometrical designs, and there was a low table with a large clay vase containing coloured paper flowers held up in a piece of netting-wire. A big new radiogram stood against one wall and a sideboard displayed a pair of vases and a glass-covered tea tray with pictures of the Royal Family behind the glass. The wallpaper was old, but there was still colour in the pattern of cabbage-like flowers and ribbons. A brocaded divan stood against another wall and its armchairs across two corners.[21]

Usually two bedrooms branched off from the lobby. Linda Fortune describes her family house in Tyne Street, which was like so many others where the 'long, wide passage ran from the front door to the kitchen. Two big rooms led off it, both to the left.'[22] At the end was the heart of the house, the kitchen.

Individual rooms were essentially for sleeping – with men and women separated, except of course for married couples – but they also served other purposes. Apartments were too small to set spaces aside for special occasions, such as a hall to receive visitors or a lounge for entertaining them, and apart from the kitchen and toilet every room was usually occupied. Although the amount of space obviously depended on the size of the family, rooms served multiple purposes – lounges, for instance, would be transformed into bedrooms at bedtime. People slept on mattress-beds, sofas, even on cushions spread on the wooden floors. Besides the beds, the rooms were crammed with wardrobes, dressers, chairs. Every nook and cranny would be filled with someone's belongings – on top of cupboards, under beds, behind dressing tables or sideboards – while a piece of equipment such as a sewing machine might be set up somewhere if a family member was doing private tailoring work. Houses were full of things, but the atmosphere was by no means comfortably bourgeois or snug. In La Guma's frank and unsentimental terms, this was the 'cramped world of poverty'.[23]

The Social Survey, in its drier prose, stated that 'one-third of all Coloured households in Cape Town occupied enough rooms, but not enough bedrooms, to reach the minimum accommodation for sleeping'. A substantial percentage 'did not even occupy enough rooms to reach this minimum'.[24] But the size of a house is not a neutral category; it is experienced and lived, and memory also plays with the certitudes of quantification. Omar Albertyn recalls his family's Roger Street home in a characterization which is fairly typical of the District's row houses: 'Dit was een kamer en dan was dit nog 'n kamer en dan kry jy die kombuis. En dan nog 'n kamer.' ('There was one room and then another one and then you had the kitchen. And then another room.')[25] But as if to assure us that these two brief sentences abbreviate the size of his childhood home, he hastily adds: 'Maar dit was groot kamers.' ('But they were big rooms.') And he goes on: 'En even die Bokaapse huise is ook groot kamers, groot kamers. En dan groot ceilings, hoe ceilings.' ('And even the Bokaap houses were also big rooms, big rooms. And also big ceilings, high ceilings.') A resident of the corner of Pontac and Lee streets, Margaret Abrahams, lived like Omar Albertyn and others in 'dat white houses in a row'. She remembered the shape of the space similarly but its size differently: 'Not big, just two rooms – two rooms and the passage, no dining room, and just through the kitchen was another little room.'[26]

The kitchen was small. It would usually have a small table in the centre where people ate their meals, and shelves covered with fancy paper rather than cupboards for storing kitchenware. Piles of firewood and coal had regularly to be delivered to the kitchen for the coal stove. Electrical appliances were steadily entering homes in the 1930s and '40s, but by the '50s the reliable coal stove had not yet been displaced by the new and probably fashionable electrical one. The City Council started a domestic electrification campaign in 1932, and initially even offered free wiring of houses to get people to use electricity. Alongside this it promoted the sale of electrical appliances on hire purchase or rented them to consumers. Thus stoves, refrigerators, washing machines, water-heaters and other household appliances were advertised by the council as safer, more efficient and cleaner alternatives to coal.[27]

In many cases, though, the turn to electricity for household lighting did not signal the end of the coal stove, which continued to serve many vital purposes. Apart from being cheap to run, the coal stove provided hot water while meals were being cooked (and it could carry more pots than its electrical competitor). It also heated the house very well and this was especially appreciated in the city's wet winters. A 'Dover' or another kind of coal stove, with its imposing size, the warmth it generated, and the multiple functions it fulfilled, was the heart of the kitchen and perhaps of the house itself.

Because toilets, which also served as bathrooms, stood in the back yard, separated from the main living quarters, children were washed in basins on the kitchen floor – hot water was always available from the coal stove. Washing rules established particular family rituals: first the boys would wash and then the girls, or the youngest then the eldest, every alternate night, or Sundays before or after lunch, or however individual family time and values dictated.

Whatever property was occupied, it was immediately personalized, 'domesticated' and 'possessed' by its inhabitants. A new location was made to feel like home – perhaps a home the family had lived in before. Wedding photographs, personal memorabilia and ornaments would be put out on dressers or in display cabinets. Religious paintings or icons, a Christian cross or the framed Arabic calligraphy of the attributes of Allah called a rakam, would be placed high up on walls, especially near the front door. These images, or talismans prepared by the area's holy men or women and hidden away above the door, would bless the space, keeping away the devil or bad jinn (spirits), and marking religious identity.

Furniture might be rearranged or combined in novel ways from time to time to create different ambiences. Pushing the bed to the opposite side, for instance, might break the boredom of the arrangements. The matrimonial bed and bedroom would literally be 'dressed up' for the new couple. The new bedcovers and curtains, among other things, could be relied upon for a long time afterwards to give the main bedroom a special touch when it was needed.

House cleaning was a major part of a family's weekly routine. Floors had to be scrubbed and polished and furniture shined regularly. Each member of a household would usually be assigned a special task. For big occasions when visitors were expected, cleaning and polishing were vital: the intensity with which this was done was an index of a family's respectability.

District Six interiors were not styled from decor magazines: they simply developed organically. Despite the monotony of the physical layouts, each house had its own individual sensibility, its own colours and textures, its own smell. Home was a corner of the world that families owned, even if they were perpetual renters.

At the other end of the scale, beyond the boundaries of the District, stood houses which may as well have been at the other end of the earth. Zubeida Booley was raised in an élite Cape Town household, at 7 Buitensingel Street, not at all far from District Six, indeed within easy walking distance, yet very remote in all other respects. This was an 'old Dutch house ... typically Dutch', she says, in its architectural aspect, with a long stoep, spacious garden and balcony.[28] The house was apparently so impressive that it was once the subject of an amateur painter's creative efforts. When the family finally sold the place it was converted into a wholesaler's warehouse.

Its interior dimensions were thoroughly bourgeois and decorated with care. Rooms were set aside for guests, there was a billiards room, and visitors were received in the sitting room. A piano demonstrated the value placed on 'serious music'. Many important local and overseas visitors came to stay with the family in their huge dwelling, including Mahatma Gandhi when he visited the city before the First World War. The Gool family owned and lived in the house, including the son Goolam, who became a medical doctor and a political radical active in Cape Town's fractious left-wing movements.[29] The house was so huge that Zubeida Booley had trouble recalling the exact number of rooms:

> You came into a little entrance hall. There were two rooms opposite. Then from the entrance hall they had a glass door like that. You opened the glass door and you went into a huge dining room. Then off the dining room were two bedrooms and a small room – like a little passage. And from there, there was a winding staircase to the room at the top.
> So now you have counted an entrance hall – which you don't have to count – but on each side were two rooms. The dining room which was a huge room, that was two bedrooms ... three, four, five. Then this room, you went up a small staircase and into a passage. Now in that passage we've got six rooms already. There was six, seven, eight, nine, ten, and eleven. Then there was another staircase coming down. And there was what my parents called the children's dining room – twelve![30]

This house boasted an inside bathroom with a wood-burning cylinder to heat water. Surprisingly, the kitchen was rather small: 'Our kitchen was a small dark hole at the end of the house.' It was a 'poky little room'. The Gools were quick to adopt electricity and acquire all the new appliances – an electric stove and a refrigerator, for instance – for which the kitchen was expanded, taking over what was known as the children's dining room. But the heart of the house remained the main dining room because it was big and 'everyone could sit comfortably at the table'. The kitchen held little attraction for the family and it was simply a place to prepare meals. There the family's domestic help was based. The help may well have come from District Six, as the women of the area would undertake casual work in the homes of the wealthy citizens of Cape Town. In these homes they saw expensive ornaments from all over the world, which they could never have imagined in their District Six dwellings, and brought back some of the tastes, and ways of keeping their own homes appropriately respectable.

As long ago as the late 1960s, the first richly illustrated books on District Six appeared, and the procession which followed shows no sign of letting up.[31] All these books have been preoccupied with the public face of the area. Forced removals called attention to the District as a vanishing setting in the inner city. A place became an image, a grubby photographic still life. But a spatial ensemble with a complex history which gathers together diverse experiences and memories cannot be captured by a distant camera.

Looked at from the outside, as they are in these photographs, the homes of District Six appear as rows of inert buildings. Where there is life to be seen it is on the streets. Undoubtedly, there was lively public space in the District. But the life of its people began and ended inside, in interior spaces and interior voices, and that is where our retelling of its past ought to locate itself. Houses start out on the drawing boards of architects and planners, and end up as physical structures in the world. But homes are lived spaces made and remade by the people who dwell in them, shaped by their histories, dispositions and notions of domesticity.

The work of historical reconstruction is always difficult, and it is bound to be imperfect and uneven. But in the case of District Six the problems are magnified, because the place itself was literally wiped from the face of the earth. Here memory assumes a particular importance and poignancy, opening a way for us into those bright interiors behind the faded image.

◀F10 ▶G11

'My porzie, my zla, my koesta' *
Rafs Mayet

These pictures were taken in two townships in Durban, Chatsworth to the south and Phoenix to the north. These are South African Indian areas. You can find similar buildings in most townships around Durban.

Chatsworth was established in 1960. People were moved there from areas that had been rezoned (like Cato Manor), from shack settlements that were being demolished and from the old Magazine Barracks near the city centre. Approximately 22,000 units were built to accommodate more than 250,000 people. There were 18 different plan types for single dwelling units, semi-detached units and blocks of flats. Plot sizes ranged from 209 to 250 square metres, with people on the corners having larger pieces of land.

Most of the pictures of Chatsworth are from Units One and Two, which are known as Havenside and Bayview. These were among the first units completed. People here still complain that the city council has not fixed things like the verges and pavements.

Phoenix was established in 1975 and the houses were first occupied the following year. People were moved to Phoenix from various areas around Durban, such as the Warwick Avenue Triangle and Clairwood. By 1986 more than 35,300 houses had been built and occupied; 14,600 of these are semi-detached, with two to four bedrooms, and they house about 102,000 persons. The average plot size is 200 square metres.

Most of the Phoenix pictures are from the Stanmore and Grove End Units, which were among the last to be completed.

* my house

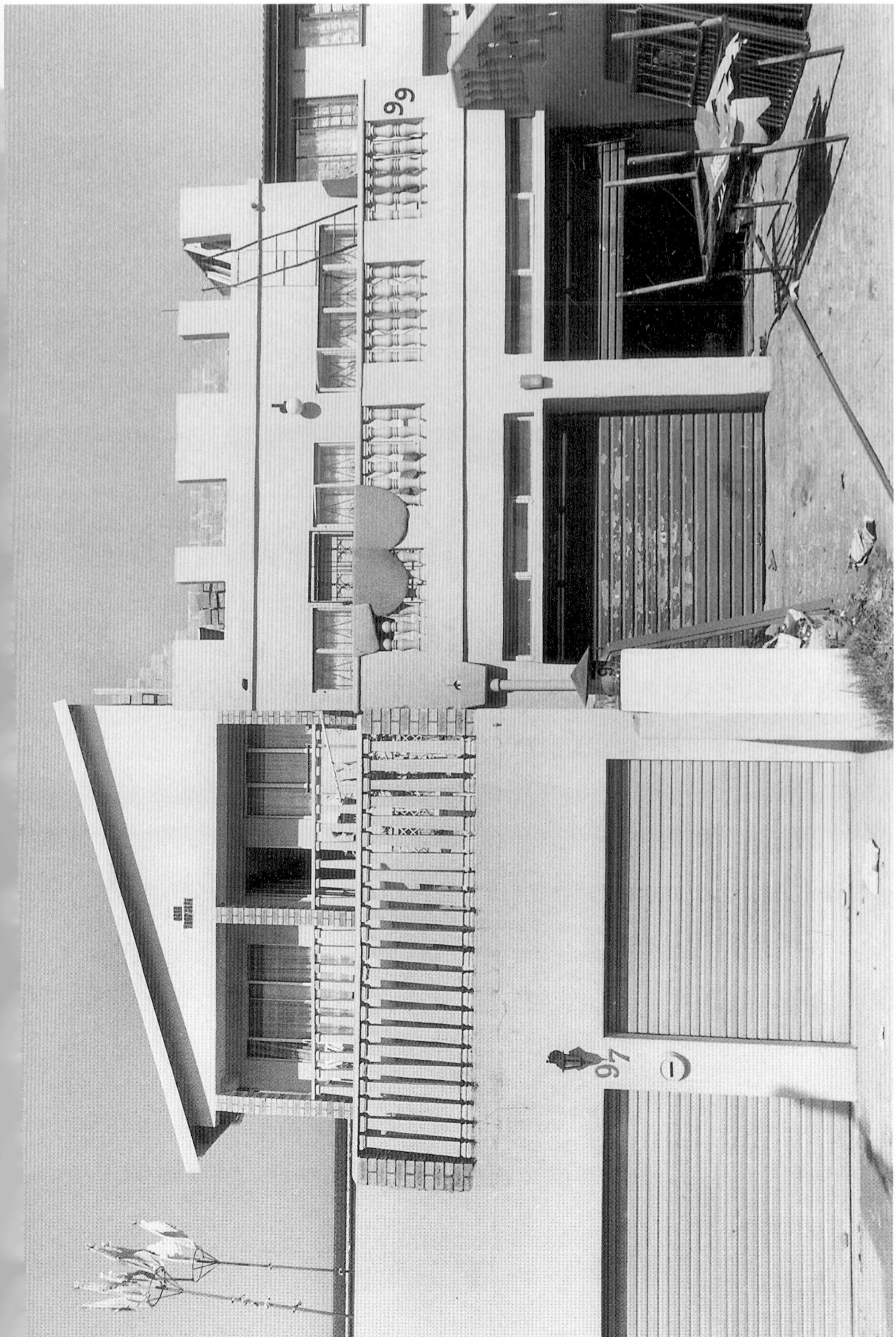
99
97

15

11

G

Modernism at the margins

Daniel Herwitz

I

We begin at the centre in order to understand the periphery. If the cultures of modernism are to be divided into margin and centre, it is because the modern art and architecture which arose in the cosmopolitan centres of Europe and America arose in the context of robust artworlds, and the art and architecture at the margins did not. In the first instance, the form of life which gave rise to the European modernisms and avant-gardes was urban. Critics, journalists, novelists, and private citizens conversing over endless coffees and bottles of Pernod spread the news and fomented public opinion. The bourgeoisie grazed, sampled and consumed. The institutions of production (the painter's studio, the architect's office, the craftsperson's atelier) produced, the institutions of exhibition (the museum, the gallery, the Salon des Refusés) exhibited. All were part of a larger pattern of spectacle, speed, commodification, urbanization, nationalism and industrial capitalization which constituted Parisian – and global – modernity. For better and worse, Paris was traversed too by a system of gazes: museum-goers gazing with a sense of ownership at objects taken from the colonies, the bourgeoisie watching itself and sampling the goods on offer in the newly created department stores on the newly created boulevards, men turning an appraising eye on the city's many prostitutes. These placed art at the cusp of pleasure, ownership and commodification.

Modernism in art and architecture arises and dwells at the centre of this urban world. The critical paintings of Edouard Manet could only have arisen because a web of museums, exhibitions, critics, bourgeois interests, buying and selling was in place in Paris, 'capital of the nineteenth century'.[1] Similarly, Le Corbusier could only have conceived the intention to revolutionize Paris by razing it to the ground and replacing it with rows of urban high-rises, because the city remained fragrant and ebullient in a world which, in the minds of the avant-garde architects, required radical

Martienssen Fassler and Cooke, House Stern, Houghton, Johannesburg, 1934-5.

reconstruction. By existing in the cosmopolitan form in which it did, within the wider context of modernity, Paris itself helped to occasion those ideals of architectural and social progress. The city allowed for a form of life within which Le Corbusier's utopian desire to 'bite off the hand that fed him so as to make a radically better one' could take on avant-garde meaning.

It is worth belabouring these points because they sharpen the question of modernism at the margins: What is it like to produce architecture, cities, 'modern spaces' at the margins of those cosmopolitan worlds, outside the geographical circuits of Paris, Moscow, Berlin, Milan, London, New York, and far from modernity's lively circulation of cultural phenomena? How does modernism get itself invented where urbanization is fragmentary; patterns of intellectual, cultural, economic and political dependency remain colonial; institutions, criticism, nationalist ideologies and the fetish of cultural commodities exist haphazardly if at all; the circle of artists is small; populations are split between subaltern and élite; economies are rudimentary, and life is stultified by the colonial yoke and the repression of indigenous traditions? Since a great deal of modernist history has happened under such conditions – from China and India to South Africa and Brazil – the question is hardly marginal to global self-understanding. And yet, for the most part, the emergence and experience of modernism in architecture and art in the various corners of the world have still to be explored and presented.

In considering this matter ourselves, we might ask: If modernism originates in the first instance out of a specific form of life, then what does it mean for it to originate elsewhere, where that form of life is largely absent or minimal? In South Africa for example? The easy answer, and one it is in the interest of the centre to give (for it confirms the centrality of the centre and the marginality of the margin), is that it is impossible for anything authentically new in the field of modernism to be invented in such backwaters. These stagnant places are condemned to live in a state of endless imitation of the centres, waiting for the good news of the avant-garde future to trickle down in the form of day-old newspapers, discount merchandise and fading opera singers. Always behind the times – so the answer goes – those at the margins are lucky to have made the occasional pilgrimage to the centres, so that they might bring back something of modernity to their ordinary lives in the form of memory and new cultural routine. We hear the accents of colonialist condescension in the answer too, arguing that the colony – as enclosed cultural museum, as land of childhood – is inherently incapable of inventing modernity.

However, the answer contains a germ of truth (which it converts into a lie in order to disempower): the achievement of modernism at the margins takes place in the shadow of an ongoing dependency on the colonial centre or its neo-colonial successor, and in order for something new to be achieved this dependency must be endured, accommodated, and at best worked through and converted into an opportunity. Lacking a robust artworld of its own, the marginal location must depend on that of the centre. Moreover, modernism at the margins tends to arise in situations of colonial or neo-colonial dependency, where the marginal culture has been cut off from its own vital past and abjectly follows the master in all things. In the first instance, modernism at the margins is usually imitative of new creations radiating out from the centre. Marginal artists or architects must depend on metropolitan models which are never quite their own, never quite capable of bringing their culture, society, aspirations and context to expression, never quite able to enter the fabric of the world of culture which is also theirs. Thus the blanket claim that modernism at the margins is inherently imitative turns a complex social condition into a defining state, a difficult creative starting point into an essential lack or inferiority. In any event, the originality and interest of the art and culture of modernity produced at the margins (that is, in most of the world), even in a 'settler society' like South Africa, simply belie the claim. This art has sometimes returned to captivate the centre, but it is often excluded from the vigorous circulation it deserves. It is in the interest of the centre to perform this act of exclusion, since it keeps the centre from being 'decentred' – a condition which finally happens anyway, but less overwhelmingly than is often thought.

The case of South Africa is especially interesting, since one way of understanding Eurocentrism there is to see it as the very desire to continue this state of dependency, to rest assured of one's identity by sustaining oneself as an adjunct of European culture. Conceived of not as dependency but as a badge of identity (European rather than 'native' or indigenous), Eurocentrism in South Africa expresses the settler's desire to claim cultural difference from the native and hegemony over him. It is the refusal to take on the project of remaking one's culture in a way that reflects essentially new conditions of existence which are neither European nor 'native' but something as yet to be defined. It is the refusal of the sublime possibility of becoming a new subject, as yet unrepresentable to oneself or one's tribe. In these circumstances, and in response to these pressures, Europe becomes a tribe; the colonial is the European become tribal. One can see this in the way colonials band together in groups, and in the way their architecture fiercely attaches itself to European models and refuses assimilation with the locality.

Of course, no settler group is this stereotypical, and counter-tendencies of all kinds will always be found. Irma Stern, the great South African artist of the 1920s and '30s, was active in the German avant-garde and exhibited with Die Brücke, until the outbreak of the First World War sent her rushing home. For her, home was a provincial prison, with few galleries, little interest in new forms of representation and little space for a creative woman to 'be herself'. Increasingly estranged and reclusive, she disappeared into her exoticizations of 'the native'. No doubt Stern is Eurocentric enough, as one might expect of a first-generation settler of German-Jewish extraction who emerged as a painter among the European avant-gardes.[2] She felt instinctively attuned to the German expressionist desire to find utopia in the vibrant and unbridled colours of the 'primitive', and was a direct descendant of the exoticizing line which runs from Gauguin to Max Pechstein, her mentor. However, she had also grown up on African soil among African people, and her work goes far beyond exoticism in its poignant attachment to and identification with its idealized subjects. She portrays these 'natives' as locals, with a degree of genuine subjectivity, foregrounding them where the viewer must engage with them directly (whereas Pechstein, say, would consign his figures to the landscape in the background). A drama between exoticization (about being distant) and locality (about being close) is played out in her work, a drama central to her identity as artist and woman. Stern felt the burden of living at the margins, caught between cultures, between being settled and unsettled, and though this hardly made her life as a creative artist any easier, it made her and her work more genuine, less tribal and less contented.

The settler's splitting-off of European allegiance from African intuition and likeness – a split no doubt worthy of deconstruction, since it serves to sustain 'logocentric' oppositions along racial lines – is one which Stern manages only in a highly ambivalent way, and it produces her personal and artistic drama. However, Eurocentrism is but one form that modernism (and modernity generally) at the margins takes, even in South Africa, and it is but one response to the split self of late colonialism.[3] As the century advances, colonial subjects throughout the world find themselves divided in various ways between attachment to their localities and to the colonial centres which rule them. These rifts in their identities require new forms of representation to be acknowledged or worked through, which means that the impetus to modern representation is internal to the specific conditions of late colonial existence, and different from its impetus in the world of Manet or Le Corbusier (where flâneurship or avant-garde radicalism are more central determinants of innovation than any split in the self). In the colony, it is from states of uncertainty, of ambivalence, of fragmentation in identity, of life between the poles of attachment to Europe and submission to 'creolization', that modern architecture and art, novels and poems tend to arise. If art is going to speak to those conditions and so acknowledge the people who live them, it had better be different from the European models it inherits. Such art therefore hovers between imitation of the given and assertion of difference, as it remakes the models in the name of another identity – African, Indian, Japanese, and so on.

When colonies are ready to strike out in the adventure of modernism, their desire is often to find ways of recovering the expression of their difference by recovering a past. As Frantz Fanon states:

'Colonialism is not satisfied merely with hiding a people in its grip ... By a kind of perverted logic, it turns to the past of the oppressed people and distorts, disfigures and destroys it. This work of devaluing pre-colonial history takes on a dialectic significance today.'[4] The recovery of this past goes beyond the rhetoric of difference because it is a way for a dispossessed colonial self to regain an identity, a set of traditions, which the colonizer's hand has crushed. However, resurrecting the past, and the image of the self invested in its recovery, is no easy task. The modern artist or architect may end up fetishizing this past (along with the subaltern subjects who are taken to be its living emblem); or 'museumizing' it in works which 'copy' from the historical sites and vitrines. Or the artist may endow some emblematic aspect of past styles with magical qualities, so that it gives the appearance of being able to make the modern artefact redolent with 'the essence of past and people', so that a people might again 'be itself'.

But what is that, 'to be again oneself'? Evidently it requires the acknowledgement that one is irreducibly different than one was, for the effects of modernity are one's own, just as the form of life and set of traditions trampled under the colonizer's boot are one's own; and eventually art and culture come to understand – however imperfectly or ambivalently – that their modernist condition is one of being irreducibly different from what they might once have been (and even that is uncertain); and then nostalgia, fundamentalism and essentialism give way to the perception that the past can only be recovered by remaking the entire field of the self, split as it is, thus converting fragmentation into opportunity. In many colonial cultures, the recovery of intricate visual traditions, texts, oral narratives and the like is a driving force of nationalism, since the aspiration to repossess the past can represent the will to find again the signs of one's group identity.

However, contemporary life cannot be revitalized by simply returning traditions to the people; for one has learned to view one's own past as if in a museum, and one's own people as if they are figments of the colonial imagination. New forms of regard and representation must be invented, which means that becoming oneself and producing modernism at the margins are finally two sides of the same historical adventure. In order to reanimate the past, in order to bring out those aspects of the self buried under the weight of splitting, repression or habits of displacement, everything must be remade. The West provides the materials through which late colonial artists or architects might revisit their own past, just as the art of West Africa provided a stimulant for early modernists in Europe. In a global culture, the new makes possible the rediscovery of the old, and the deformations produced by models from the centre are transmuted into stimulants for innovation. Some forms of expression have already asserted their presence in one, and these must be brought into line with the contours of the self generally. Others are searched for and then put to use. Imitation, which prevents this process of recovery, is thereby overcome, and materials from the centre are viewed for their experimental possibilities (as models, suggestions, hints, paths of possibility). But it takes some time for a culture at the margins to come to understand and practise this Nietzschean art of empowerment, especially given the states of dependency and inferiority which trouble the starting point.

Now, Irma Stern's work is important because it shows by contrast how little early South African modernism, created as it was by white settlers and their descendants, was motivated to recover African tradition, a form of life which was finally not its own. And her work also shows how the early gestures of reaching out to Africa were deeply implicated in exoticism, however much they rose above it. For later artists it would be different. The art made in resistance to apartheid would have little about it that was exotic. Later still, in the wake of the demise of apartheid, artists would experience a heady moment of freedom, in which the yearning for contact with other cultures and styles might be fulfilled, in which identity might be a matter of experimentation. African painters would appropriate abstract expressionism, recasting it with the patterns of Ndebele wall paintings, Zulu pots or the landscape of the bush; young sculptors whose parents were immigrants from Europe but who grew up in this world of snakes, red earth and the sublime violence of nature would find West African forms natural – thus confirming the thought that they too were African.

II

In South African architecture, this cultural and stylistic intermingling has yet to take place. Indeed, modern architecture here hardly went through the phase of exoticized exploration, although it would surely have been enriched by the plethora of magnificent pre-modern styles that presented themselves – from Ndebele houses and Zulu kraals to Cape Dutch homesteads and Karoo houses. Yet South African cityscapes show a diversity of building styles: Durban's Indian market, with its Indo-Victorian pleasantries and crowds and somewhat dilapidated bustle, gives way along the main streets of the city to an admixture of Victorian and art deco styles and 1950s department stores, which culminate in turn in a clearly colonial Victorian city square, with a cathedral, city hall and post office. If this city, like all other South African cities, lacks public spaces, it is because these were a threat to colonial notions of divide and rule, and even more so to apartheid laws of separation. But the city remains a paean, in its crowded and dirty way, to the hybridization which was explicitly ruled out. We shall return to this point in due course, for it shows that in spite of everything, South African cities are varied and complex in ways which speak of people commingling in the whirl of modernity. The Indian market, and those excellent imitations of metropolitan buildings with which it clashes, and the clash itself, are part of the history of modernity in architecture in this corner of the world.

The production of architecture at the margins is different to painting, writing or sculpting. Modern architecture is defined by international models in a very specific sense. Since these international currencies radiate out from European (and also American) centres, architecture at the margins is in this specific sense Eurocentric. The International Style would have found this 'Eurocentrism' perfectly acceptable, since it rejected the very concept of imitation. How could a style which strove to be universal, be imitated? By definition it could simply be expanded into new areas of application. Insofar as the International Style was a truly international movement, considered by architects of the centre and the margins alike as the only progressive course, architects did not regard the lack of modernist reinvention in the local domain as a loss: their work was of a different order of avant-garde reality, more like a science than an art, and therefore less concerned with issues of diversity and locality. The International Style – Eurocentric too insofar as it arose in relation to specific problems which were not exactly those of the margins – was also part of an international capitalism which was essentially homogenizing (in spite of the movement's Marxist pretensions). The style did have its sophistications fine-tuned by certain 'third-world architects' (Oscar Niemeyer and Lúcio Costa of Brazil, Charles Correa of India, Kunio Mayekawa and Kenzo Tange of Japan, Hassan Fathy of Egypt); and the style, which had in fact evolved into a collection of related styles, was finally decentred – like the flow of international capital generally. But it was only with the birth of post-modernism in architecture that locality and variety came to the fore again. And only recently has it become important to remake models from the centre in diverse ways at the periphery – now better conceived of as a host of decentred multiplicities.

Nationalist sentiment and new global wealth have seen to it that commissions for new architectural forms that are suitably referential and expressive of locality – at least as such things are conceived of by international corporate capitalism – now abound. But there has always been far less scope for variety and invention in architecture than in the more socially autonomous arts like painting and writing. Overcoming imitation in this field is no easy task. Where the desire to resist imitating the centre has arisen, the tasks of recovering 'traditional modes of dwelling' for a modernizing society or significantly remaking international models in the light of local geographies and cityscapes have been beset by a host of stylistic and economic concerns. In many of the other arts there is room for individuals and groups to experiment, to make mistakes, to chance upon solutions. Architects do not have this space, except in abstraction on the drawing board: the city is not a blank canvas or a page, and this imposes both a conservatism and a radicalism on their work, making the slow process through which international models are absorbed and reshaped more difficult.

At the centre (it has been noted often enough), postmodernism took up recovery under the guise of mere play. The remaking of modernist models in the light of a deeper spirit of place and people has been the exception rather than the rule. Japan might be regarded as the pre-eminent exception – but note why. Japanese modular construction was a central influence on modern architecture in the first place (Frank Lloyd Wright, Mies van der Rohe), as central as the African mask in the origins of cubist and expressionist painting (Picasso, Kirchner). And in Japanese culture, nationalism is deeply invested in shared styles of representation, so there has been cultural capital to be gained from building in a 'Japanese spirit' and – until recently at least – the financial capital to do it with. Japan has produced an architecture capable of inflecting international styles of steel and curtain wall with refined geometrical abstraction, a minimalist, efficient spirituality consonant both with contemporary Japanese society and with pre-modern design. Here the eternal return has a vivifying effect, in the same way that the Japanese house with its simple modularity, open plan, efficient use of space and natural setting, is reshaped by the global modern design influences it first stimulated. Architects in other parts of the world, lacking this special relationship, may not find it quite so easy to invest global models with the traces of a reanimated self. Some traditions are simply harder to blend with what the modern world offers than others – even where there is the will and the money to make the attempt.

The International Style was not simply the shared ideology of a group of architects; it became the currency of builders, and this is very important for modern construction at the margins. As much as the style suited the unctuous few who wished to make buildings of the expensive sleekness appropriate to big capital, so its principles – applied in the crudest possible way with the cheapest possible materials – suited the unscrupulous many who wished to find cheap solutions to rapid urban construction. It is a harsh irony that a style which arose in the name of avant-garde Marxist 'radical social planning and construction through new design' should have ended up delivering exactly what was required for profitable mass construction, the bleak and corroded products of which now stretch endlessly from São Paulo to Mexico City to Detroit to Warsaw to Rome to Johannesburg to Durban to Shanghai. In South Africa, as in other marginal societies, the cities have frequently been ruled by builders rather than architects. One may see more than enough evidence of this in Durban, in the cheap, tasteless and ill-kept 1950s curtain wall which bursts out around the Indian market, in the gaps between the Victoriana and the dirty-brown replicas of petit bourgeois English originals (preserved in the Birminghams of the builders' memories, one supposes). Other South African cities, even glorious Cape Town, fare no better. Nor do Rome, Caracas, Newark. In this respect, South Africa is not distinctive: it is set apart rather by its almost total lack of appreciation for local landscape.

Before we pursue this point, another irony of the circulation of the International Style is worth noting: the utopian schemes of the architects and planners at the centre were actually put into practice at the margins. Although these visionaries aimed to raze the cities and towns of the metropolitan centres themselves, the powerful would not indulge them. Le Corbusier never rebuilt Paris; instead, Niemeyer and Costa built Brasilia. Mies was given a chance to build the Illinois Institute of Technology south of the Chicago city centre; Wright more or less filled a relatively open suburb of Chicago known for its many oak trees with his little masterpieces. But in general, when cities destroyed in the Second World War were being rebuilt, or when American suburbs were being citified with big buildings, the tune was called by the corporate builder, who wanted to build quickly, conservatively and for maximum profit. Only in the colonies, with their open veld and relatively undeveloped cities, could the modern architect realize his dream of the city constructed from scratch. The third world, rather than the first, became the site of utopian design: Brasilia, Chandigarh and Dhaka; not Paris, Rome and New York.[5] Similarly, modernism could infest the 'second world', with its war-ravaged cities and technocratic five-year plans: from Moscow to Budapest, lives would be lived in freezing conformity in massive, unornamented apartment blocks, warmed only by excesses of vodka.

Thus Eurocentric postures different to those that affect the other arts obtain in the creation of architecture at the margins. We have touched on two of these: firstly, cheap versions of the International Style – which originates in the European and American avant-gardes in response to conditions specific to their artworlds – spring up throughout the world; and secondly, the margins become a laboratory of utopian practices. A third form of Eurocentrism originates in the third world itself, and is endemic to settler societies. In South Africa, it combines with the other two varieties to configure the entire landscape of building. This Eurocentrism is the satisfaction and complacency that come with remaining a dependent satellite of the metropolitan centre. The Eurocentric modernist claims ownership over the colony by retaining the sense – or illusion – of ownership of the means of cultural production. By remaining a producer of what he thinks of as European modernism, he remains European rather than indigenous in his own eyes. Alienated from the South African landscape, unwilling to become one with people he views as wholly other in character and as no more than the material for his workforce, attached to an identity formed in another country across the seas, the Eurocentric modernist views the South African colony without any sustained aspiration to set it free in the field of culture by inventing new cultural forms to give its difference expression and resolve the splits in a self. The Eurocentric modernist has few such splits, or at any rate prefers to preserve them (splitting off his love of the veld, say, or fluency in Zulu from his capacity as a modernist creator). This is why Eurocentrism tends to be a more powerful force in settler societies like South Africa than in those where modernization is achieved by indigenous peoples: it is the settler who defines himself (as often as not) as a transplant whose real cultural home lies elsewhere.

Central to the history of modern construction in South Africa is a split between public and private building. Some South African bourgeois homes are marvellously comfortable with their own hybrid identities. In Johannesburg, Herbert Baker built the grand homes of the 'randlords' out of the beautiful, whitish-brown stone of the Highveld, and did so with an airy, Victorian grandeur worthy of mining magnates and craggy hills, effortlessly harmonizing dwelling and landscape (even if pylons, enormous mine-dumps, gritty industrial spaces and bleak corrugated-iron shanty towns tell another story of brutal and rapacious capitalism). Having arrived in South Africa fresh from a grand tour of the classical sites, his Palladian and English-country instincts taught him to blend site with stone, park and garden into one harmonious whole (unfortunately his Mediterranean impetus was confined to the building of private spaces). The houses of the Durban Berea, on the other hand, blend French Caribbean balustrades with English stone construction in idiosyncratic formulations which are nothing short of romantic. The Natal midlands home, sporting a traditional thatched roof overhanging French doors to provide an open, airy space covered from sun and rain and trellised with roses, is a colonial gem.

Public space is another matter, and there the freedom to invent disappears. White South Africans apparently had little taste for the creation of hybrid public spaces: public life was regulated, even before the rule of apartheid, by a severe Eurocentrism in design and mission. Although there is sunlight and warmth in many South African cities nearly all year round, precious little is made of it in urban public space. Only rarely did the builder or planner of public space recast European models and blend them with existing architectural and spatial forms; instead it was designed to divide and rule, to incorporate the privileged into 'European' culture and exclude all others. And 'European' often meant northern Europe and Britain rather than the Mediterranean. Thus public space was park rather than piazza, domesticated landscape in the city rather than open meeting or dwelling space in streets and squares along the lines of, say, Italy or Spain. Baker's 'Edwardian villa' remained a private indulgence.

This refusal to open space to an urban colloquy which would have tangled the rules of division is part of the reason why South Africa is relatively empty of representational forms. This point must be sketched with the right degree of subtlety, for it is not that South Africa is not drenched in the representational forms of its various peoples: that would be an absurd idea, since culture is almost by definition a system of signs, and no culture could be free of public representation. However,

South Africa lacks representation in that its culture of museums and galleries and so on was purposely underdeveloped and remained purposely exclusive. The story is fairly simple. In Europe and America, cultures arose which were dedicated to the institutions of representation in the name of the nation. These were produced in Europe by the history of monarchy (with its spectacles of power and elaborate palaces) and in America by the growth of a business culture which revelled in the thought that its contribution to the national good, and its hegemonic position, depended on its establishment of culture. The Rockefellers built the University of Chicago and the Museum of Modern Art, and collected a host of masterpieces which they Americanized through ownership. American capitalism came of age in the era of nationalism, and took its business to be that of proving that what is good for business is good for the nation. One means to this end was the gifting of culture to the nation, through museums, foundations, and the like. By contrast, South African business developed in a colonial context, when the country was not even a nation but a possession to drain and plunder. South African business was too busy making profits and investing them safely to contribute to those institutions that produce what Lefebvre calls 'the space of representations'.[6] Apartheid, as I have said, was terrified of intermingling, of persons as much as cultures, and sought to rule out this possibility by building no spaces in which it might occur. There was little room for active participation in the public sphere except through a culture of opposition. South Africans were denied the opportunity to become more like one another through their shared use of public institutions and the conversations which naturally accrue to such places. For as people come to share public space, their styles of representation grow gradually more alike and blend subtly into each other, thus making public conversation possible.

Representation of the past has been scant. Museums entrusted with the task have reduced the past to a few dissociated objects from some family collection, imbued with local sentimentality, drained of life like specimens behind glass in a museum of natural history. Crucial archives remain buried, inaccessible or even corrupted (by humidity or neglect), a sign not merely of a government strapped for cash – there is always money to be found for such projects – but unaccustomed to valuing the institutions of representation for their cultivation of public discourse, memory and morally acute citizenship. In recent years museums have at last begun to fulfil this task, while the Truth and Reconciliation Commission has enabled us to hear the first haunting, faltering exchanges in a new public conversation.

III

The history of public building in Johannesburg is largely a history of reception: internationalism received from the position of the 'internationalist at the margins' whose internationalism is a form of Eurocentrism. It is also a history of cannibalization: the discovery of gold here in the late 19th century produced a tidal wave of immigrants willing to work hard and ready to strike it rich, and the city grew with astonishing rapidity. This rough-and-tumble excitement, the violent expansion of the resources of production, the formation of a city whose desires were as raw as its resources, required the immediate importation of style: style in which the captains of industry could celebrate their triumphal conquests of man and mineral; style in which the hordes of immigrants could inhabit the growing city; style in which capital could confirm its glory. Hence the Edwardian mansions, the colonnaded and domed banking houses, the skyscrapers from New York and Chicago. If Johannesburg arose in the marginal playing fields of capitalism, it also arose with the wild energy of a hyperactive infant.

Now what Johannesburg clearly lacked, in the first flush of its infancy, was the kind of robust artworld, the cosmopolitan framework of life, which allows modernism to dwell at the cusp of modernity. Moreover, this was not something the infant temporarily lacks but will develop as it matures: at the margins of modernity, surrounded by complex currents of Eurocentrism and dependency, the state of attachment to the cosmopolitan centre is more or less permanent. This attachment, which prevented Johannesburg from ever becoming 'The Second Greatest City After Paris' (as the artist William Kentridge ironically denotes it), had complex reasons, some of which we have discussed – the rule of the International Style, for example, and its refusal of individual variation except at relatively superficial levels. What is important to note is that the Eurocentrism which rested content with a dependency on modernist models from the centre – in the belief that these would make Johannesburg a little piece of Europe rather than an extension of Africa – combined with the specifically architectural attachment to the International Style to confine architectural experiments in localization and local identification largely to *private* space. The public/private divide became paramount, and remains so to this day.

From the outset, whatever variations Johannesburg architects gave to the models imported from Europe and America were fairly minimal. The history begins early: the first high-rise buildings had arrived in the city by 1902. In his book *Johannesburg Style*, Clive Chipkin points out that the American high-rise appeared in Johannesburg even before it did in London. 'This reveals, too, a new cultural factor, a growing New York-Johannesburg axis.'[7] There soon developed a similar communication between Chicago and Johannesburg – 'the one as originator, the other as recipient' – although with this difference: 'While the Chicago buildings are light and airy structures, Johannesburg's Edwardian architecture is massive and weighty – a celebratory financial style that is related to the City, or, where blocked inset columns occur, to the contemporary reconstruction of Regent Street in London.'[8] It is not as if there is no variation whatsoever on imported models: Johannesburg is after all a city with its own form of get-rich-quick materialism, its own brand of instant urbanism, its own mix of people, its own stone and geography, and its own architects and builders, and it would be odd to find a complete absence of local inflection. But very quickly the city understood itself to share deep likenesses with New York and Chicago, as well as London and the cities of the European North. And its desire was to create itself in the image of these cities.

The 'Transvaal Group' of architects, formed in the early 1930s, was named as such by Le Corbusier himself, and revolved around an important disciple of his, Rex Martienssen. Martienssen had spent significant amounts of time studying Le Corbusier's buildings (and those of other European modernists, especially the German expressionist, Erich Mendelsohn). The Transvaal Group constructed modernist houses in the wealthy Johannesburg suburb of Houghton and blocks of modernist flats and high-rises in the city. The influence of the master can be seen in House Stern of 1934, by Martienssen Fassler and Cooke, which is clearly modelled on Le Corbusier's famous Villa Stein at Garches in France. Chipkin, who highlights the lines of influence in features such as the external staircase with its powerful diagonal, the paved first-floor terrace 'floating as an idea', curved walls and other elements, puts it unequivocally: 'Le Corbusier is everywhere.'[9]

In the design of his own house in the Johannesburg suburb of Greenside, Martienssen reveals his personal love of the Italian Renaissance – especially through his subtle way of configuring abstract forms in glass and brick, with small Renaissance-Mannerist windows, highly asymmetrically placed, punctuating a serenely proportioned façade-like front that announces its solidity even as it promises access to the space within. Moreover, the house commands the site in the manner of a *palazzo*, rather than being open to it in the manner of a 'glass box': this is achieved by raising the structure slightly, on what is otherwise a fairly flat and open site, and by running a low white wall across the front of it, with a set of stairs which must be climbed in the approach from 'below'. However, Martienssen's love of southern architectural styles is confined – as Baker's was before him – to the realm of private design.

As editor, writer, teacher and builder, Martienssen became the centre of modernist dissemination. Fully internationalized, he and his associates conceived of themselves as part of a worldwide aesthetic and cultural revolution, of which Johannesburg was simply a local 'city-site'. In this view, shared by the likes of Niemeyer and Costa, questions of locality were simply misplaced. 'There are no problems of form, only problems of building,' Mies had famously remarked, meaning that context posed no questions for the general theory of architectural form, but merely for its application in a particular place. Of course, Mies's principles of the steel and glass box with its open plan were not the same as Le Corbusier's, announced in Vers une Architecture (which Martienssen had read before going to Paris in 1933). So form in fact remained an issue for the modernists, as their contending allegiances demonstrate. However, Mies's open plan, which was capable of infinite variation in modular subdivision, and Le Corbusier's 'plan libre' or 'free plan', which separated design from load-bearing structure, thus allowing freedom in the shape and skin of the building, were close enough in kind to allow for a mentality or 'style' – the International Style.

Martienssen and his group produced their own manifesto in 1933, which included these words: 'The contemporary spirit is abroad ... we should regard ourselves as drawing near to a remote future rather than receding from a historic past – indeed all living art is the history of the future.'[10] The two rather different meanings of the word 'abroad' are interesting here, as they suggest that the contemporary spirit is both 'present everywhere', 'in circulation' all around them, and 'overseas', 'in a foreign country'. This captures the marginal position of these architects perfectly: they are abreast of the international trends, and yet they are also grasping at what is distant from them, so that their city might catch up with the contemporary, with the centre, and truly live. Thus, while their manifesto, declaring its intention to erase the past and harness the teeming, utopian energies of the future, is avant-gardism at its most authentic,[11] they have (I repeat) no Paris to scandalize, no Paris to raze. They find themselves in what is still little more than a mining town, surrounded by the recently constructed Edwardian and art deco buildings of the earlier generation. This urban radicalism, existing in a still empty and unformed marginal space, must announce itself as arising both from here and from elsewhere; the full thrust of its radical attack is directed at a world which lies at a distance, in Europe, even if that world is also continuous in some ways with the immediate one, South Africa.

From first to last, every modernist style imaginable found representation in Johannesburg, from Victoriana to art deco. This openness to influence sometimes produced those delicious ironies which lend the study of history its peculiar pleasures. Chipkin, for instance, describes the 'temporary fascination' of some businessmen and architects of the 1920s with the 'Fascist house style', a blend of modernized classicism and futurism which reached Johannesburg as an 'irradiation from Mussolini's Rome ... either directly or indirectly via centres like New York'.[12] Many of those who had fallen under the spell of this rhetoric later fought against the Fascists during the Second World War.

An offshoot of the Transvaal Group took modernism into the next generation with a critique of Le Corbusier and his South African disciples. This group of Johannesburg architects included Norman Hanson and Gordon McIntosh, both associated with Martienssen earlier on, as well as John Fassler and Roy Kantorowich (Martienssen himself died prematurely in 1942). This new 'group' sought to extend and refine international models of European origin by softening Le Corbusier's philosophy of construction. Although they always denied that they were part of a 'movement', Julian Cooke has argued that they shared a deep concern with a set of ideas developed in Europe from the 1930s onwards, which he summarizes as 'a new classicism, vernacular traditionalism, and a revised and softened functionalism',[13] and that they took the European buildings generated by these ideas as their models.

Cooke also describes the group's interest in shifts in European architecture, such as the revival of 'National Romanticism' in Sweden, and how the South Africans adopted similar strategies to make architecture 'warmer and more approachable': 'The minimal range of materials of heroic modernism, detailed to almost nothing, was replaced by a larger palette: facebrick, terrazzo, mosaic, travertine, random rubble stonework, timber, wrought iron – a far cry from painted steel windows and glass.' They also returned to decoration, which the Transvaal Group had despised, and 'abstract forms were softened with texture, wide eaves, gently pitched roofs and pergolas'.[14]

While we have focused on private dwellings, it would be wrong to think that there was no attempt at all to hybridize the public sphere. In the late 1950s and early 1960s, the architect Norman Eaton

went furthest towards imbuing his buildings – including his public buildings – with a feeling for African life and design. Eaton travelled extensively throughout Africa and incorporated design features based on Zanzibar buildings, North African texture patterns and Ndebele façades. Exoticizing Africa, in the manner of Irma Stern, as a vast oneness, and also in love with its light, open space and red earth, and its design patterns, Eaton blended these elements with his 'Mediterraneanism' to incorporate marvellous wall murals, striking chevron brick and tiled floor designs, and 'Africanized' circular forms in the concrete 'parks' around his buildings. Eaton's designs are exceptional in their attempt to hybridize modernist and local styles. And this exceptionality brings us back to the main argument: modernism here is sufficiently purist and constricted to prevent a more pervasive hybridization.

IV

The group associated with Hanson and Kantorowich, taking their cue from recent tendencies in the International Style, included local materials and ornamentation in their designs in order to reduce the severity of pristine modernism. If 'nationalism' meant anything to them, it was simply the idea of favouring the local environment as a source of materials and ornaments. The architecture of the apartheid regime pursued a more exacting political definition of the term, concerning itself with who comprised the South African nation and how it would live, with the rules of identity and citizenship.

While much of the architecture of apartheid was thoroughly provincial in outlook and scale,

Willie Meyer with Jan van Wijk, Rand Afrikaans University, Johannesburg. Opening ceremony, May 1976.

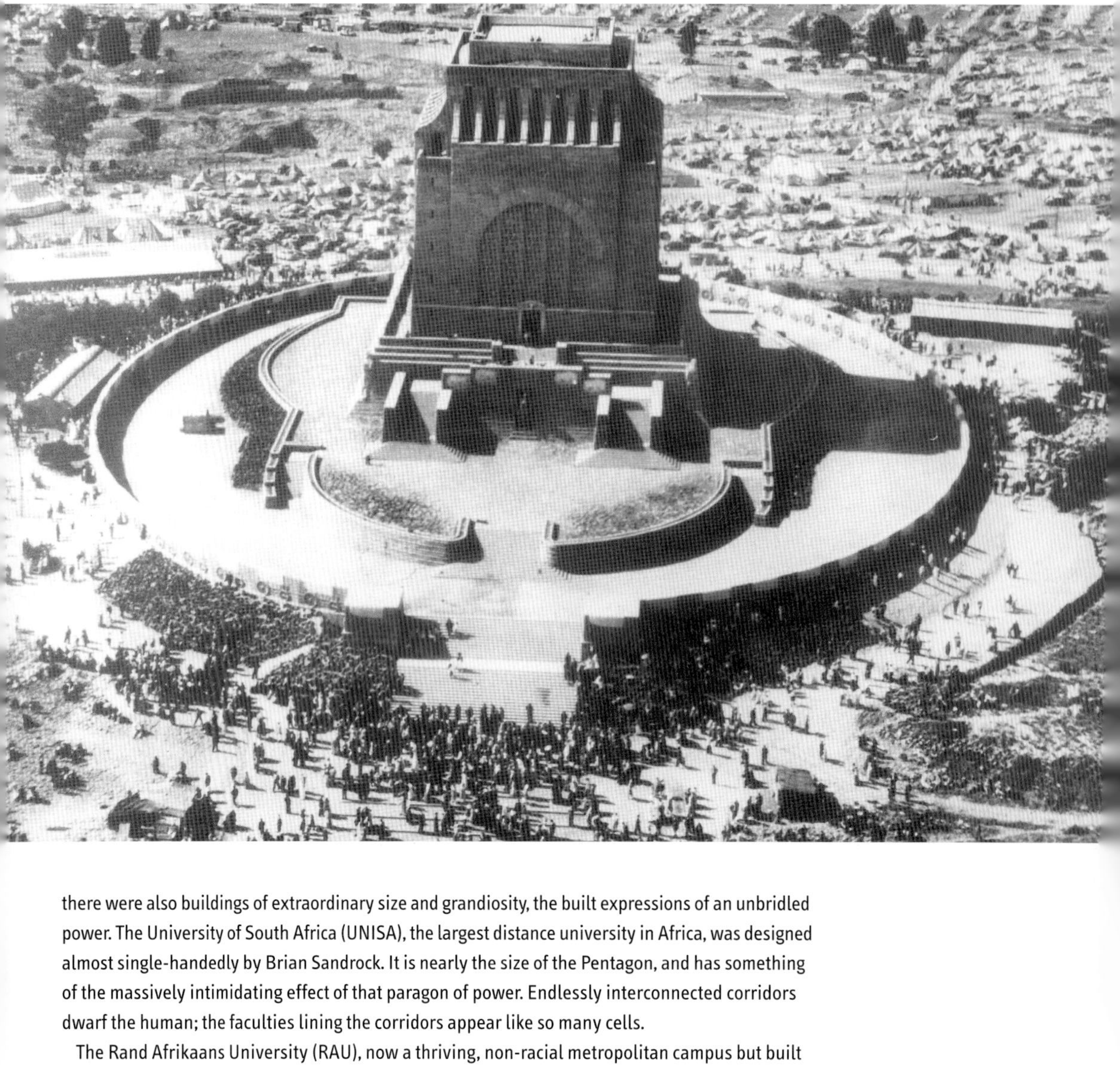

there were also buildings of extraordinary size and grandiosity, the built expressions of an unbridled power. The University of South Africa (UNISA), the largest distance university in Africa, was designed almost single-handedly by Brian Sandrock. It is nearly the size of the Pentagon, and has something of the massively intimidating effect of that paragon of power. Endlessly interconnected corridors dwarf the human; the faculties lining the corridors appear like so many cells.

The Rand Afrikaans University (RAU), now a thriving, non-racial metropolitan campus but built originally as a bulwark of Afrikaner culture, exhibits the principles of apartheid construction to a T. The university was designed by Willie Meyer in association with Jan van Wijk. A series of 'blocks' surrounds a vast amphitheatre. Students are meant to assemble here but they seldom do, for one feels dwarfed by the encircling structure and watched from every window. Perhaps the amphitheatre with its Roman references encouraged a sense of embattled but secure identity among the white, Afrikaans-speaking students who daily traversed it in earlier years. The construction is intricate, indeed excellent, with a vast downward spiral of buildings reaching completion in the dramatic stage of the amphitheatre. The floors of the buildings are of wholly unornamented concrete. One's location is defined in terms reminiscent of a prison: 'D Ring, Level 4' and so on. Each faculty branching off from the ring attains a measure of 'privacy', but the larger effect is to make the faculties themselves disappear into insignificance: it is the great ring that matters, not its individual elements. This is grandiose architecture, and it is an irony that the architect was a pupil of Louis Kahn. Here Kahn has been imported to the periphery to legitimate Afrikaner nationalist identity. His meditative, elemental spaces have been rendered panoptic and larger-than-life.

Gerard Moerdyk, Voortrekker Monument, Pretoria. Opening ceremony, 16 December 1949.

On the whole, the modernist public architecture of apartheid, unlike that of Italian Fascism or the German Reich, leaves little room for Wagnerian mythological referencing. The RAU campus is allowed a reference which is crucial for Afrikaner nationalism: the circular arrangement of the buildings and the tightly enclosed interior space are not simply panoptic, they also reproduce the image of the laager. The Voortrekkers, the Afrikaner pioneers who first colonized the interior of the country in the 1800s, would draw their ox-wagons into a protective circle as a defence against attack. The impenetrable laager came to represent an implacable resistance against all outsiders, as well as a contained gathering place for the volk, for the people, and the RAU amphitheatre surely carries these meanings. One might have expected the grand buildings of apartheid to resonate with the architectural glories of Afrikaner history. After all, the Cape Dutch homestead with its whitewashed walls and French balustrades is a masterpiece of simple elegance; while the little Karoo house with its tin roof shading the front stoep against the desert heat has an apt and delicate beauty of its own. But such references are almost entirely absent. When nationalism demanded a return to mythic origins, it was almost invariably to the Great Trek and the laager. By obsessively mythologizing the Trek as the founding event of the nation, the means through which the land was truly occupied and conquered, the nationalists claimed ownership of South Africa and asserted their entitlement to rule. The black South Africans who were there before them were reduced both to a vanquished enemy and to a mere aspect of the landscape itself (like the flora and fauna). These two contradictory images deprived the 'native' of a founding role in the identity of the nation.

The Voortrekker Monument near Pretoria is the major commemoration of the Trek. It was designed by Gerard Moerdyk, who drew his inspiration from Bruno Schmitz's Völkerschlacht Memorial in Leipzig.[15] Both the enclosing wall with its ox-wagon reliefs and the circular interior echo the form of the laager. From the upper floor, with its 'history paintings', the visitor looks down upon the cenotaph where an eternal flame is burning (for the time being at least). In the domain of public building, the spareness of modern architectural style tends to preclude massive ornamentation and referentiality; but in the realm of monuments, the level of creative play with symbols, signs, references and styles can be intensified – and with it the level of kitsch. The result in this case is a graphic illustration of one of the operations of modernism at the margins. The monument takes art deco forms and renders them as ornament, hardening their fluid lines, imposing a religious severity and overstated indomitability. The kitsch resides in the tension between the deco elements and the memorializing purpose: the building looks like a deco radio tower made to do duty as church or bunker. Here models from the cosmopolitan centre have been stylized and twisted to a purpose finally at odds with their 'intrinsic' force, with no attempt to work them through or render them appropriate.

V

We have seen that apartheid sought to prevent the intermingling that is a mark of the modern. Yet this intermingling persisted. Sometimes the incipient rhythms of modernity were so powerful that the only way of disrupting them was to obliterate an entire city quarter. This was the fate of the Johannesburg suburb of Sophiatown.

By the 1930s Sophiatown – less a suburb perhaps than a para-city at the periphery of a city at the margins of modernity – had already outgrown its identity as a shanty town filled with violence and poverty (which it surely was) to become the slowly emerging centre of a new form of life produced by the urbanized black people who called it home. American influences – Harlem music, Hollywood film – went into a lively, hybridized cultural life of shebeens, jazz, dancing. The painter Gerard Sekoto found his genius in these winding streets, by attending to the brilliant refractions of colour and hard shadows which the dry, transparent light produced on corrugated iron and crumbling plaster.

Paris, where he made his home soon after the institution of apartheid, would finally cripple his talent: without this place, this light, this colour he was finished. In the 1950s, Sophiatown became the seedbed for a new generation of African intellectuals and artists, flâneurs whose gazes, when directed to the white world of the city (from which black people were excluded by law), could not help but become politicized. Moreover, the cultural forums of the Sophiatown era – most notably the equally famous Drum magazine, which provided a livelihood for some of these writers and photographers – were themselves places where the constructed and divided 'races' of apartheid mingled and melded.

It is no coincidence that the Defiance Campaign of 1952, the first mass mobilization against unjust laws in the country's history, gestated in areas like Sophiatown. It was only because of the new identities, forms of flâneurship and contiguities (spatial, intellectual, recreational) which the para-cities engendered that resistance could emerge out of a racially mixed conglomeration of people from all walks of life: politicians, professionals, intellectuals, workers. James Holston has argued in an eloquent essay that cities are perhaps the central sites where pressure is placed on the dispensation of formal rights (to vote, to move freely, to receive procedural justice) and substantive rights (freedom of work, economic justice, health and welfare, equal education, cultural expression and identification, and the like) by new, dispossessed or marginal populations. Since this apportionment of formal and substantive rights is in effect the apportionment of citizenship, cities are the central site (often if not always) where citizenship is passionately and tumultuously questioned and finds itself inexorably changing.[16] To break up the forms of resistance and, more than that, the new identities being created in Sophiatown, it was essential that the para-city itself be destroyed. The history of anti-Semitism in Europe had already shown that even when forced into ghettos, Jews would seep back into the textures of the city as a whole over time, through assimilation, hybridization, intermarriage, economic embroilment and shared forms of life that must of necessity arise in contiguous urban environments. A tour of the Prague Ghetto clearly shows the movement of Jewish ownership, of Jewish capital and life, out of the Ghetto and into the rest of the city in the early 20th century. This urban embroilment brought pressure for change to bear on the system of rights, unequally apportioned to Christian and Jew, change that was brutally curtailed in 1939. Similarly, Sophiatown (later Cato Manor, and District Six) had to be destroyed. What the apartheid state required was that a physical gap be opened up between para-city and city proper, so that the latter might retain its pure integrity. Forced removals, by rending the very urban fabric through which new identities could be woven, deprived a generation of its language. An entire spectrum of African identities at the margins of the margins, a uniquely cosmopolitan set of identities and their now unimaginable potentials, were killed off. When resistance finally re-emerged in the mid-1970s, steeped in the brutalities of apartheid and the impoverished rhetoric of the Eastern bloc, in anger and exile, it spoke a more violent and intolerant language whose echoes are still heard today.

And yet even in the confrontational years of the late 1970s, public space evolved which rejected the strictures of apartheid: in the Newtown area of Johannesburg, in the old fruit and vegetable market and the surrounding buildings, a dynamic zone of non-racial culture developed. At the hub of it was the Market Theatre itself, where some of the most renowned anti-apartheid theatre was developed and performed, and there were also galleries, restaurants, bars, music venues, art schools, flea markets. The area has a chaotic informality that is distinctively Southern African. Nearby, the modernist skyscrapers of downtown Johannesburg, towers of unadorned concrete and reflective glass, remind us that we are on a peculiar frontier where the first world meets the third.

So we return to the theme of a city whose urbanism, whose juxtapositions of form and personality, whose inflections, interminglings and gaps bespeak a complex, convoluted modernity which neither colonial nor apartheid rules could prevent or undo. Johannesburg (like Durban and Cape Town), defined by strict rules of public construction which sought to prevent the natural intermingling which is part and parcel of urbanized modernity everywhere, remains vibrant with difference. Despite the poverty, despite the crime, it is the kind of city Baudelaire extolled – one whose contingencies, fragmentations, paths of intermingling and shifting processes of life cannot be theorized from any single angle, but instead require the work of witnessing, enjoyment and fascination which is that of the modern painter.

Johannesburg should always have cultivated the modernist work of free-floating fascination and critique. But can we imagine Baudelaire's 'painter of modern life' here, can we imagine a Manet of the Highveld? This mythical genius would have had to reinvent himself, finding a new position, working his Parisianisms through in order to give representation to a different kind of city, one of unadulterated capitalism and desperate poverty, a city of lively Sophiatowns and barren squatter camps, a city both excited by the opportunity it offers and bored by its remoteness from the centre. This reinvention would also have displaced him, since South Africa's grave history would not easily have accepted the light touch of the *flâneur*. And if this genius were to arise today? Perhaps he would find the lack of a robust, cosmopolitan artworld in South Africa less of a problem than the global trade in installations and biennales, flowing in the well-worn channels from centre to margin, with its postmodern image-speak which drains locality as surely as the International Style ever did.

From one perspective, South African spaces are built to order, to survey, to administer, to facilitate mining, industry and work, to exemplify essentialized distinctions between colonizer and colonized, to reflect a 'European' taste which is coloured by the exotic and responds to local climate. From another, South African spaces exhibit the hybridities of immigrant cities, where diverse people arrive and amalgamate, where identities are shed and new ones taken on, where streets, neighbourhoods and suburbs collide in the formation of a modernity that contains its own chaotic pile-up of meanings and styles of life.

VI

New forms of public space are developing in the highly imitative, postmodern malls of South African cities. The malls always amaze tourists, who fly in to 'see Africa' (meaning animals, vast empty spaces, unspoilt beaches and native peoples) only to find themselves in spaces which are virtually indistinguishable from those of New York, and probably fancier and bigger than those of Rome or London. The Pavilion, located outside Durban just off the freeway, is a veritable monument to global capitalism. In this, one of the largest malls in Africa, the vast interior spaces of modern department stores meet the Crystal Palace and Brighton Beach. The glaring fake-Victorian structure, whose glassy green and golden domes can be seen – like Chartres Cathedral – from a distance of fifty miles, recalls English colonial style with a nostalgia worthy of KwaZulu-Natal's Anglophile tendencies and celebrates late capitalist consumption with a brashness worthy of Los Angeles or the 'home shopping channel'.

The mall pours with crowds at all times, for it is safe (something rare in this crime-ridden country) and unique (something even rarer in a shrinking world). In addition to the history of global capitalism according to which the mall gets invented, the entire history of South African space, constructed on the principle of 'divide and rule', must enter into the genealogy of the South African mall, which through a vast irony becomes one of the few genuinely *public* spaces in an underpopulated country and a rare melting pot for races who continue to live highly separate lives. Television, if we concede that it is 'public space', might be another arena where the 'rainbow nation' of the New South Africa begins to exist. The new malls – like the new clubs, bars, gyms, shops – commingle a new interracial middle class predicated on shared yuppiedom and shared pleasure in consumption, a rainbow class formed in the image of late capitalist liberalism. The members of this new class are not (yet) as absorbed in consumerism as their American counterparts, just as the spaces they occupy are not (yet) as corrupted by the excesses of late capitalism, and it remains to be seen what relationships their new proximity will produce.

The marvellous range of pre-modern architectural forms which graces South African space has yet to be absorbed into new forms of public (as well as private) building and design. This project of assimilation has happened in America, but it took time. Consider that in the late eighteenth century, Thomas Jefferson in his design for the University of Virginia incorporated copies of key European architectural masterpieces, which he believed every student requiring Bildung or cultivation – and certainly every student wanting to design the then new and open America – would perforce have to study. To him it was clear that America, empty of all but the 'native' – whose dwellings would hardly have been thought capable of serving the new settlers well – and lacking cities and traditions, other than those imported from Europe, could progress to a 'culture' of its own only through copying examples and using them as models. And since most Americans of his generation would never see Europe, he would bring Europe to them as best he could. It took many years before American architecture began to do more than bow before the altar of these copies and transcended its position as a 'copier of copies' (the degraded position which Plato believed was common to all art, but which we now associate with specifically dependent art). However, even at the moment when Jefferson was designing his university, there were already originals (in every sense of the word) which had been made in America and bore the stamp of its unique future: Shaker furniture, plain-spoken clapboard houses, perhaps even Jefferson's own Monticello. America began to give the world models for the new, built in accordance with its own sense of ideality and integrity, its sense of its people, their dwelling and destiny – the Chicago skyscraper, the Chrysler Building, the houses and factories of Frank Lloyd Wright – once its place in the flow of international capital had been secured in the late 19th century, capital always being a condition of building. And once it began to look inward and conceive of itself as a new land requiring a new form of self-articulation. The thought that the newness of America required new forms of articulation in line with American life, so that America, being new, could achieve an identity out of 'what it was already', this Nietzschean notion of an America created through return (to the street corner and the American on it), this project of thinking the identity of America into existence by acknowledging an America already (incipiently) there, of course required architecture. Cities with an American face had to be made so that American life would have a place in which to happen. While originating in the American transcendentalists (Emerson, Thoreau and the Alcotts), while carried forward into Whitman, the inheritance of this project of creation-by-return in architectural form is what produced the America which gifted the city of Johannesburg with new forms of building in which, to a degree, the middle-class and mostly white inhabitants of that city could recognize themselves. Architecture in modernity has always been a place in which to dream, fantasize, authorize what a people is: Johannesburg, and indeed the world, was gifted with the American vision of this project. Current American globalizations are perhaps less welcome.

The gift of the Chicago Style to a particular segment of white South Africa has now become a gift to all citizens, as the new nation rewrites its entire past in a new colloquy. The Zulu kraal, the Cape Dutch and Karoo house, the Victorian building on the Durban embankment, the cave, the Ndebele mural – these are now potentially the cultural legacy of the entire nation, which is finally ready to accept them as its own and entitled by law and spirit to do so. This re-imagining of a formerly divided cultural 'patrimony' will also produce new buildings, as architecture opens itself to all the country's citizens and acknowledges their differential claims – granted space, will and capital. Furthermore, postmodernism, for all its defects, has opened up an immense space in which stylistic fusion can occur. It is now possible for South Africa, in postmodern times, to engage in the modernist project of taking models from the centre and working them through in the light of the local. South Africans should not rest content with the postmodern preference for the copy and the postmodern pleasure of referential game-playing; they should seek also to know again (for the first time) the original, so that the return might lead to the making of something new in line with what the place actually is. And what it is includes the history of modernism, but also much more. When South African architecture recites and recasts the life of the street corner, the field, the rural village and town, and also the life of the mall with its fake Italianate piazza, it will become original. It must seek to know these forms without political correctness, which means firmly appreciating their difficulties and limitations as well as their hidden beauties. Then it will be prepared to engage with the eternal return, to find again those forms of dwelling and give them what Heidegger calls an 'outlook' or a face.[17] Then the country will speak differently to its former landlords.

►H6

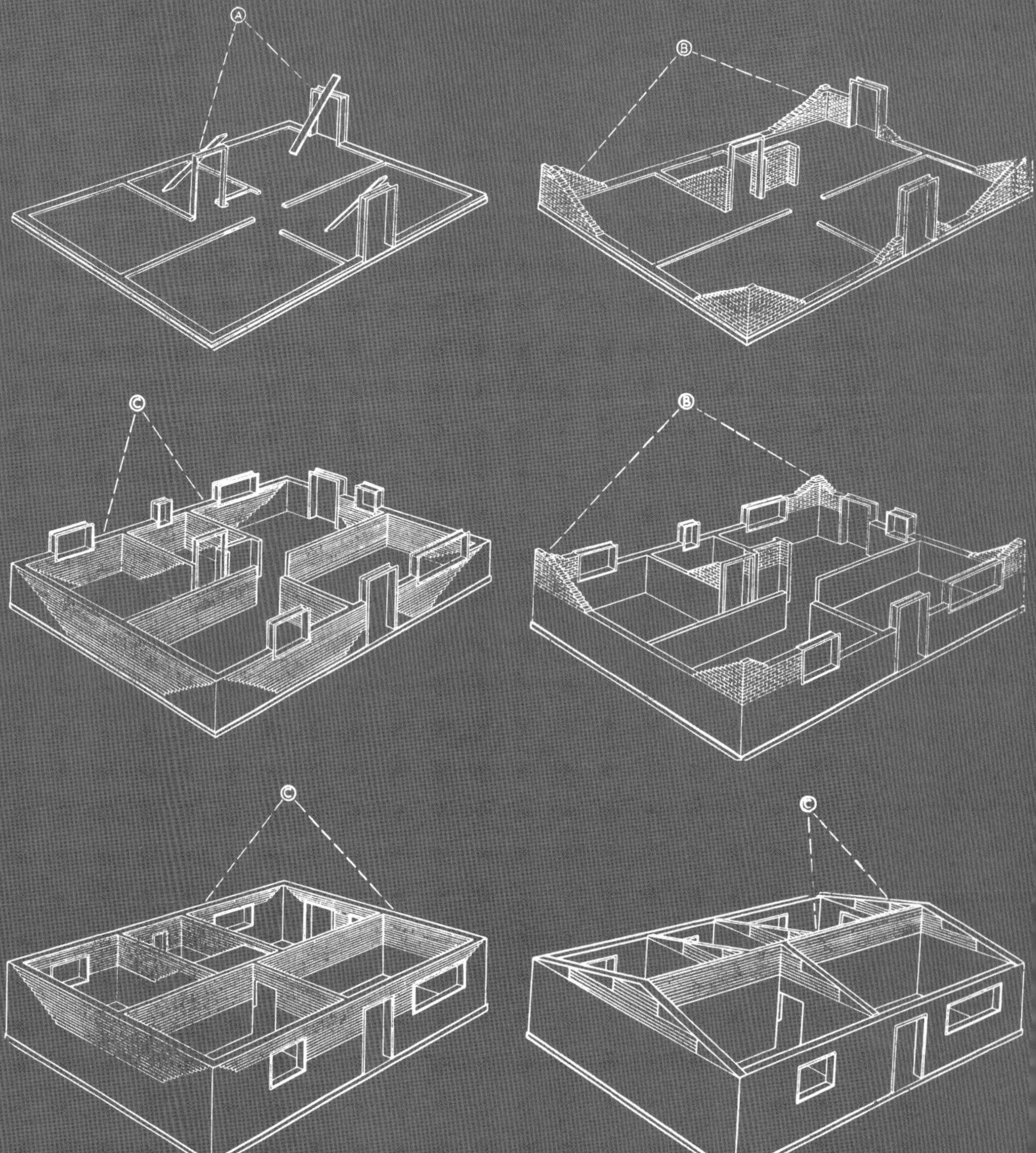
A
B
C
B
C
C

The social programme of the South African Modern Movement[1]
Derek Japha

Introduction

In 1951 the National Building Research Institute (NBRI) began work on experimental housing projects at Witbank and KwaThema. For three previous decades the attempts by the South African state to control the supply of urban housing for Africans had been relatively ineffectual. The Urban Areas Act of 1923 had placed the responsibility for providing such housing on local authorities, but many of them built little or nothing; and those that did build, used different standards and different planning constructs. From time to time a particular project would be described as a 'model location'. What this meant was that it was considered an example of best practice, to be emulated if desired. The experimental projects at Witbank and KwaThema were models of an entirely different kind, which were to have a far more pervasive impact. They were the first tangible signs of a new political will to take control of the national process of housing provision, and they prepared the ground for what was soon to become a massive, state-sponsored building programme. The projects provided a rigorously theorized planning framework for the 'native township' of the 1950s and '60s that did so much to define the form and character of the apartheid city, as well as providing designs for the houses in them and practical demonstrations of the technical methods that had been devised for their realization.

That this impetus to provide urban houses for black people, unparalleled in scale in South Africa before or in any comparable country at the time, should have come from the Department of Native Affairs after it had been taken over by Verwoerd is sufficiently curious to have interested historians before. Following analyses of similar state 'welfare' projects by revisionist historians elsewhere, local scholars have offered various explanations for this government intervention: that it served the economic interests of large building companies; that it was required for the reproduction of labour for commerce and industry; that it was the spatial matrix of the 'power of apartheid', creating the physical conditions for surveillance and the preconditions for the implementation of influx control and the Group Areas Act.[2]

But no one has yet explored the fact that the Witbank and KwaThema projects were also the culmination of a long housing research programme initiated many years earlier by prominent architect members of the alignment called the South African Modern Movement, whose efforts were prompted by concerns similar to those which had made the problem of social housing central to European modernism.

Like the state housing programme of the 1950s, the South African Modern Movement was sufficiently distinctive to have attracted previous scholarly attention. As is well known, its nucleus was a small group of exceptionally able architects, whose talents made them valued members of the international architectural avant-garde. The Transvaal Group, as this nucleus came to be called, was respected for the intellectual contribution of its leader, Rex Martienssen, who turned a stuffy and parochial architectural journal, the South African Architectural Record (SAAR) into an imaginative and intellectually challenging publication with a global audience. The Group's reputation rested also on the dazzling Corbusian buildings and designs of the Martienssen partnership and the possibly even more gifted Norman Hanson, works which, while few in number, were the equal of practically any contemporary modernist buildings in the world.

It is widely accepted that the South African Modern Movement was a formalist movement. Although the social mission of architecture and planning was one of the defining features of modernist discourse, and although South African modernism developed in parallel with a housing crisis of considerable dimensions, the members of the Transvaal Group initially appropriated modernist

NE 51/9 type house showing the six brickwork tasks.

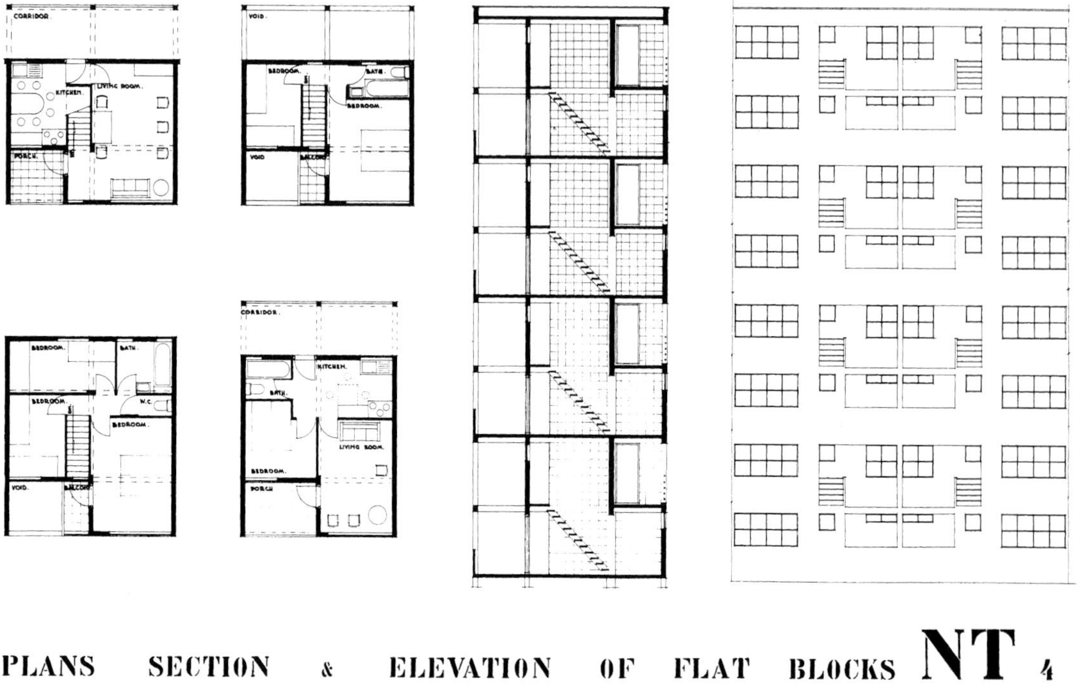

aesthetics and technics with little interest in their application to social problems. This essay begins with the first signs of a change in this attitude in the late 1930s. These signs were noticed by the authoritative historian of the South African Modern Movement, Gilbert Herbert, who discussed them briefly at the end of his book,[3] but he made clear his view that the Movement was all but over when they appeared. The interpretation offered in this essay is different. I shall try to show that when these signs of change appeared, the South African Modern Movement was only just beginning. The issue at stake is not the question of dates, but the nature of modernism.

Developing the social programme

By 1937 students at the School of Architecture at the University of the Witwatersrand were beginning to challenge the nature of the relationship between local modernism and its European sources and, in the process, to insist that the hitherto neglected field of planning was a core modernist activity and that housing was an architectural problem of critical importance. The prime mover in the development of this new consciousness was Kurt Jonas, a Marxist whose intellect and design talents had taken him into the inner circle of the Transvaal Group while he was still a student leader.

His critique of the Group's formalism was first expressed in an address delivered in 1938 to the Student Society at the Witwatersrand School.[4] In this address he deplored the aestheticism of the Transvaal Group as the product of an unacceptably narrow definition of architecture, one which avoided the question of 'whether it is really worth while to produce luxury commodities only, or whether there is not a bigger task ... the task of altering and designing the living conditions of the large masses'.[5] Jonas made clear his belief that it was incumbent on South African modernists to recover the lost political dimension of European modernism and to work actively for social transformation, but he recognized the difficulties that would face progressive architects confronting this challenge in capitalist societies. While not alluding directly to the South African context of racism and exploitation, he went so far as to conclude that working within the system was pointless,

Plans, section and elevation of flat blocks, 1939.

because 'it is a fallacy to believe that society could be changed by architecture'.[6] Realizing progressive architectural solutions to social problems, he said, depended on prior social change; in the absence of such change, the architect could aspire to be no more than a polemicist making 'paper architecture' and helping to engender a progressive spirit.[7]

When it came to models for such action, his polemicist of choice was less radical than might have been the case. He merely attempted to construct a political justification for the Transvaal Group's favoured icon, Le Corbusier, by presenting his work as an illustration of scientific modernism and the logical product of sociological, psychological and technical analysis. Corbusian town-planning schemes, in his view, could never be implemented in a capitalist state because they were unprofitable and would 'change the mental make up of their inhabitants [since] ... if people moved from slums to towns such as those designed by Le Corbusier, there ... would be an end to capitalist society'.[8] Behind this curiously self-contradictory mixture of naive determinism, pessimism about the social mission of architecture and the attempt to situate Le Corbusier within the radical tradition,[9] lay the perennial dilemma of the architect seeking to politicize his or her practice, the desire for the activist engagement of the discipline, but the fear that its efforts would be perverted by the context in which it was forced to operate.

It was a dilemma to which Jonas was unable to respond by following his own advice to the Student Society. In fact, the interests that his lecture articulated had already found expression in practical action in which a different concept of engagement was postulated. In 1938 Jonas undertook the organization of a congress on town planning, with the primary objective, we may surmise, of exposing local modernists to the lacunae in their understanding of modernism. In his introduction to the congress, which he chaired, Jonas suggested that the possibilities for a significant professional contribution, even in an unacceptable social and political dispensation, should not be underrated, and that, even if architects could not immediately attain the objective of a transformative architecture, they could nevertheless 'give the impetus to some betterment to man's surroundings, and show what could be done, without Utopian premises, simply by applying the resources of contemporary economics, science and art'.[10]

Even before the congress, a group of students employing this concept of engagement and led by Jonas had selected 'native housing' as a thesis topic, and invested sufficient thought and energy in their work for it to have been published as a book that was favourably reviewed in the international architectural press.[11] This thesis work was presented to the congress as one of two demonstrations of sharp-end planning practice. Apart from a competition in 1931 for the design of a location at Orlando,[12] it was perhaps the first significant intervention by architects in African housing, and certainly the first from an overtly modernist perspective. The thesis consisted in the design of a satellite town for 20,000 people, with proposals for housing and various community facilities. The layout of the scheme owed a great deal to the redent blocks of the Ville Radieuse and the apartments and community buildings, while not entirely Corbusian in style, were also influenced strongly by his work. The thesis was intended as a practical demonstration of the three necessary phases for a rational and non-utopian approach to the problem of housing and urbanism that Jonas had identified in his opening address to the congress: 'a scientific theory, a logical programme, and a practical line of action.'[13] What this implied was the accurate analysis of the existing context and the development of solutions capable of being implemented within it. Consequently, although many negative structural features of the South African context as they applied to housing for Africans were identified and strongly criticized by the student team, they were accepted as constraints for the design. For instance, the concept of the satellite township for African housing was accepted in spite of the serious reservations they expressed about urban segregation, and the subsidization of rentals, however desirable in principle, was rejected on the grounds that it was an impediment to the realization of African housing schemes.[14]

The thesis and Jonas's presentation to the congress implied that notwithstanding negative contextual features, substantial achievements were still possible in the newly identified core fields of

planning and housing. This was so partly because of the existence of a purely technical field of operation for the discipline, unaffected by politics; partly because of the capabilities of design to mitigate adverse contextual features; and partly because of the inherent and potentially subversive effect of architecture on popular consciousness. This rationale for architectural engagement therefore contained a hidden agenda in political and environmental terms, one which substituted a utopia of unrealizable intentions for the utopia of the unrealizable plan. This thinking was to set the pattern for the work of the following years.

The concern with housing problems was at first relatively isolated within the Witwatersrand School of Architecture, but then spread rapidly through the profession in the early 1940s, fuelled by an international climate in which programmes for post-war reconstruction were a common obsession, by the belief that a similar programme would be inevitable locally and by the increasingly visible housing crisis on the Witwatersrand and elsewhere.[15] Thus far the town planning congress of 1938 had been the only significant contribution towards defining a response to these problems; but in spite of the claims to the contrary, the ideas about housing that had been illustrated were obviously unrealistic, and in any case were rapidly superseded by the local manifestations of an international crisis in the Modern Movement precipitated by the war.

In 1941 one of the members of the 'native housing' thesis group, Roy Kantorowich, published a recantation, in which he extended Jonas's critique of utopianism by pointing out that it applied perfectly to Le Corbusier. According to Kantorowich, the City of Tomorrow and the Ville Radieuse, which he and his colleagues had previously seen as the progressive exemplars of a future society, were in fact impractical, ideologically contaminated schemes of social regeneration, the products of Le Corbusier's infatuation with the myth of 'the Architect as Hero' and of his belief in environmental determinism. Kantorowich suggested that as a result Le Corbusier had completely misread the impetus of contemporary capitalism and the consequent scope available to architects to effect social change.[16]

Three-dimensional view of flat blocks, 1939.

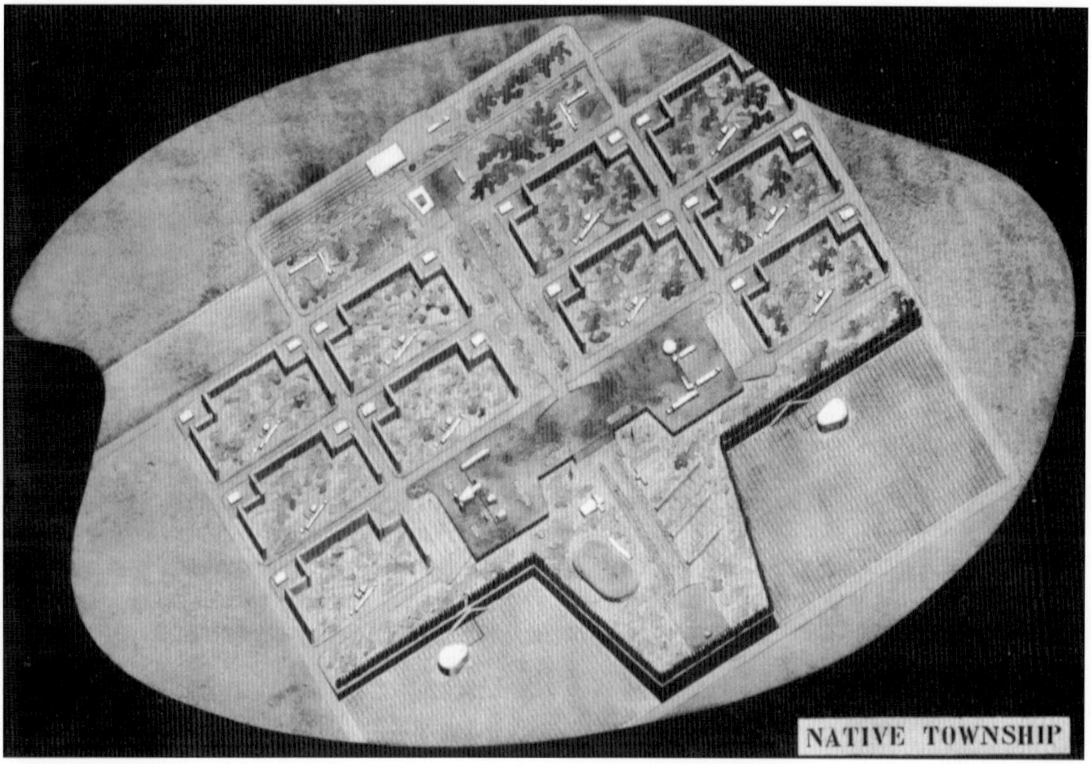

This article provoked an extensive and acrimonious correspondence between the detractors and supporters of Le Corbusier,[17] ending with an important contribution from Norman Hanson.[18] Hanson's letter clearly shows his dissatisfaction with what he evidently had come to see as the formalist tendencies in his own early work, and his growing belief in the necessity for a social and political practice within the discipline, as advocated by Jonas. The letter was his first public manifesto speaking to these new concerns, written just when his position had been consolidated as the leading figure in South African modernism after the death of Martienssen. He was also a leading member of the Transvaal Provincial Institute, its chief spokesman on housing issues and the prime mover in the further engagement of architects in the housing programme.

While falling short of rejecting Le Corbusier's architecture, Hanson agreed with Kantorowich's critique of Corbusian politics and planning and supported his argument for the political engagement of the discipline by returning to and elaborating the themes that had earlier absorbed Jonas. An architect, Hanson wrote, was 'decisively conditioned by his time' and must 'ally himself with progressive forces if he wants to avoid being drawn ... into the camp of social reaction'.[19] This alliance could best be made by contributing to the development of a better and less exploitative distribution of resources in the built environment, which in turn could be achieved only by a realist rather than idealistic architectural practice, rooted in a just social organization.[20] For Hanson, realism meant involvement, within the terms of the discipline, in the 'struggle for making tolerable the material conditions of the lives of all people by the planned and equitable use of human and material resources'.[21]

Hanson's contribution to this interchange was unequivocal about the need for disciplinary engagement and for a scientific housing programme based on social research. But the rejection of Corbusian planning required the development of a new formal paradigm to fill the void. This was attempted in the work leading up to the ambitious and influential 'Rebuilding South Africa' exhibition of 1943,[22] sponsored by the Transvaal Provincial Institute and compiled together with the Witwatersrand

Site plan of native township, 1939.

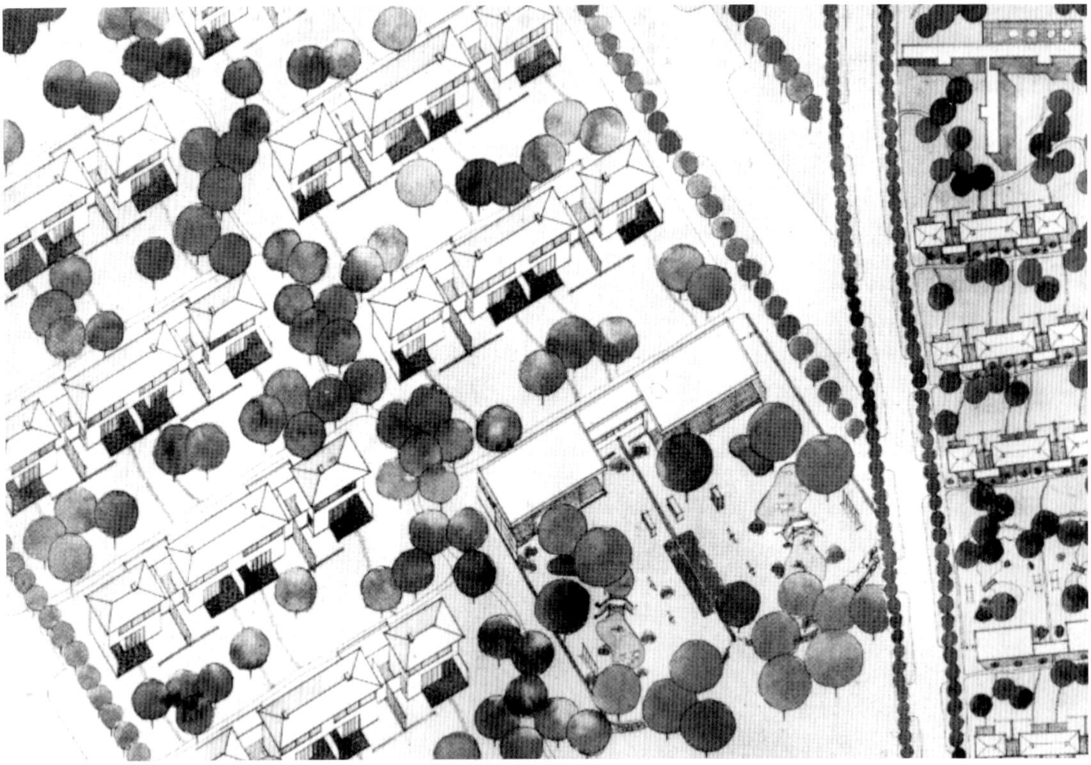

School. The intellectual impetus for the project probably came from Hanson, who was the main organizer and delivered one of the keynote papers to the accompanying conference.[23] The exhibition aimed to offer a new set of planning ideas more in tune with the concept of realist engagement with South African environmental problems, including the housing crisis. These ideas were developed from diverse sources, such as Soviet planning, American New Towns policy, German Rationalism of the 1920s, the writing of Lewis Mumford and the post-war work of Walter Gropius.

Of these, the last two were probably the most significant. After the publication of The Culture of Cities, Mumford became an almost inevitable source for South African architects disenchanted with Le Corbusier.[24] Although Mumford's hostility, expressed then more by lack of interest than by overt criticism, was not yet as developed as it would later become, the tenor of his book was utterly at variance with Corbusian urbanism.[25] Mumford was not an anti-modernist, but by virtue of his attacks on internationalism and pleas for regionalism his writing incorporated into the body of modernist thinking ideas to which the internationalists had for the most part been hostile.[26] The Culture of Cities, however, also argued for the continuation of some aspects of modernist practice, and therefore must have seemed to offer the possibilities of both continuity and regeneration; the recovery of 'authentic modernism' rather than its loss.

One of the reasons for the impact of the book was that it was not couched purely in generalities that were hard to apply. Mumford directed attention to appropriate formal models for his favoured 'organic' approach, by relating the concepts of regionalism, the Garden City as defined by Howard, and the neighbourhood unit as defined by Perry and implemented by Stein and Wright at Radburn and elsewhere.[27] All these were projected as the planning devices for establishing a new regionalist consciousness which would 'sustain the richest types of human culture [and offer] a home to every type of character and disposition and human mood' and provide a 'habitat [forming] a continuous background to the delicately shaded scale of human feelings and values [as] the prime requisite of a cultivated life'.[28] It was an iconography difficult to resist.

Aerial view showing portion of super-block housing units, 1939.

Gropius was an equally obvious reference for South African modernists who had lost their taste for Le Corbusier. He was widely regarded as particularly responsive to social issues, published important papers on housing,[29] consistently argued against an architecture predicated only on stylistic preconceptions, his work was widely considered a practical demonstration of 'objective scientific method' within the discipline and, after leaving Germany for America shortly before the war, he himself had tried to come to terms with the complex of ideas extolled by Mumford.

The 1943 exhibition was a direct reflection of these new influences. It was presented as a development of the 1938 town planning congress, but in fact it was a radical departure, even if this was openly admitted only by a participant sociologist, who claimed that underlying the later conference was a philosophy 'that would make Le Corbusier choke in his Vichy waters'.[30] As this observer obviously saw, Le Corbusier's internationalist vision, which had dominated the work of 1938, was decisively abandoned in favour of a Mumfordian regionalism, considered to be more realistic, democratic and locally relevant, and therefore better able to achieve wide social, environmental and aesthetic goals. In this new programme, the proposed model for the spatial organization of the residential environment became the neighbourhood unit.[31]

The one link between the 1938 congress and the 1943 exhibition, however, was the concept of 'science-based practice', and the 1943 work tried to advance this concept from mere polemic to fact. The exhibition reflected not only Mumford's theories, but also the first three stages of his recommended method, based on linear, inductive design procedures: the topographical and historical survey, the critical outline of needs and activities in terms of social ideals and purposes, and the imaginative reconstruction and projection into the plan. The exhibition was arranged to suggest that the scientific status of the discipline rested not only on its command of technical issues, but on a design method in which the act of design would be directed by objective analyses from the disciplines of economics, sociology and psychology.[32]

Regionalism, however, is in essence response to context; and in South Africa the pairing of

Plan of a neighbourhood unit, 1939.

regionalism and the neighbourhood unit offered very specific possibilities for physically reinforcing South African patterns of urban segregation. In his paper to the 1943 conference, Hanson showed that he was aware of some of the dangers, and argued vigorously against the use of these new planning models to intensify economic inequality. Stating that 'territorial splitting up may ... tend towards sectionalism or worse, towards a vicious form of segregation', he went on to say that

> for the basic requirements of life all sections of the population have an equal claim. The non-European community cannot be discriminated against when such fundamentals as health and housing minima are being established. The fact remains that the community pattern is possible only when there is equal participation of all the people in the growth of the city, when the benefits of social and health services and civic amenities are enjoyed equally, when similar and corresponding rights in property and local management prevail within each community unit and when the living conditions of none fall below scientifically determined social and physical minima.[33]

Provided that equal standards were achieved and 'vicious segregation' avoided, Hanson seems to have considered separation potentially beneficial, in that there was some 'margin for differentiation' in the 'difficult field of race characteristics, where the expression of cultural and social habits and traditions must find a place'.[34] Thus, regionalism and neighbourhood planning, he suggested, offered a solution to the 'vital question of the residential segregation of non-European from European races', which could be achieved through the 'extension of community planning from the regional to the urban sphere'.[35] What he meant by this was explained by a statement earlier in the paper that

> The points of resemblance between regional and urban problems are ... illustrated most strikingly in the controversial field of racial segregation. The relation of a native reserve or region to adjacent regions and the totality of regions is not unlike subsisting relationships between the location or native township and the entire structure of the town. The community pattern in both cases carries the hope of a reasonable settlement of present differentiation.[36]

And again: 'Like regionalism on the national scale, the community pattern of the town offers the possibility of a balanced distribution of the economic and social advantages of urban life.'[37] By this argument, what for Jonas had been an unpalatable necessity had now become a virtue.

Implementation

Given the development of this broad planning programme in the early 1940s, it is not surprising that the Institute of South African Architects (ISAA), at Hanson's instigation, began to address another of the key items on Mumford's list, the 'absorption of the plan by the community and its translation into action through the appropriate political and economic agencies'. The moment was opportune. As the housing problem in the country's urban areas grew steadily into a full-scale crisis,[38] it became more and more obvious that drastic reorganization of the state housing agencies was imminent. This held out the prospect of dealing with a fluid bureaucracy particularly susceptible to influence.

The first overtures from the profession regarding the housing issue had been made in 1941, but were inconclusive.[39] After the 1943 exhibition, the profession again approached the Minister of Health and the Directorate of Housing,[40] and Hanson was appointed to the advisory National Housing Council in 1944 and to the National Housing and Planning Commission (NHPC) in 1945. He continued to hold this latter position until 1963, serving on the executive committee from 1947 onwards.

At first the NHPC's efforts were restricted purely to housing for ex-servicemen. Throughout 1946 and most of 1947 the organization showed as little sign of coming to terms with the African housing crisis as had its predecessor. In the first years after Hanson's appointment the ideas of the 1943 exhibition thus had little impact on official policy. But by the time that Hanson became disillusioned with the abilities of the NHPC to confront the planning problems facing it, a new possibility for exerting influence had presented itself in the rapidly developing field of housing research.

This research followed inevitably from the expanding role of the state in the provision of housing, but at first it was uncertain what direction the research would take and who would control it. In 1945 the NHPC wrote to Dr Schönland, the Scientific Advisor to the Prime Minister, to argue for the establishment of a housing research programme, but were told that their efforts had been pre-empted by the formation of a Building Research Unit by the Department of Commerce and Industries.[41] This body was to become the NBRI.

Since the research focus of the new institute had not yet been formalized, a Building Research Advisory Committee was established to 'formulate the questions to be asked'. The ISAA was offered representation on this committee, and naturally nominated Hanson for the position. He was therefore involved with policy formulation for the NBRI from the very beginning, and by virtue of his membership of the NHPC was uniquely qualified to connect the interests of the two organizations. The tentative brief set out before a preparatory meeting of the Advisory Committee in 1945 was for technical research not specifically oriented to housing problems, such as studies of the properties of building materials and the scientific study of the design and efficiency of buildings.[42] By 1946, however, probably as a result of Hanson's intervention, an architectural division had been established, with a brief which included the organization of field experiments around housing for the NHPC in collaboration with the ISAA and the universities, and 'the study of Non European urban and rural housing to discover means of providing [housing] in sufficient quantity to relieve the acute shortage; and of improving the standards of accommodation'.[43] The Architectural Research Officer appointed for this work was Paul Connell, one of the joint authors of the 1938 thesis.

The establishment of scientifically determined social and physical space minima became the obvious focus of the research, uniting as it did sociological and technical problems and involving a return to well-trodden modernist ground. By early 1947 the issue of standards was firmly on the agenda of the NHPC. After a tentative and unsuccessful attempt from within the organization to deal with the issue, the Council for Scientific and Industrial Research (CSIR), within which the NBRI was situated, was appointed to undertake and coordinate all work on housing standards and a major research project was initiated to pursue this task.[44] Following an official CSIR invitation to the ISAA, members of the South African Modern Movement were well represented on the various subcommittees.[45]

This project resulted in the publication of the interim reports of eight subcommittees and the main committee on minimum standards of accommodation in 1949.[46] The reports had two main aims. The first was to develop the basis for a non-racial, scientific minimum standard of space for housing in South Africa and to delineate the further research required to implement it. The second was to enshrine the neighbourhood planning concepts of the 1943 exhibition in local housing practice, and to define the standards of open space and facilities necessary to make them work.[47] These documents represented the culmination of the process initiated in 1943.

Although this work was executed at the behest of the NHPC, the reports, like the earlier congress and exhibition, were still largely the products of a professional and academic discourse isolated from the practical realities of implementation, and their most important concepts can be traced to international influence: the belief in the possibility of an objective science of the environment informed by sociology, psychology and economics, the pursuit of standard-setting as a key activity, and the pairing of regionalism and the neighbourhood unit as the formal model for housing development. As the *Interim Report of the Main Committee* indicates, this relative isolation was to some extent intentional.[48] But it was possible only in the context of the governing United Party's inability to frame a coherent 'native policy', as a result of which little African housing was built while the research was undertaken, and the research programme was not forced to confront issues realistically. Nor indeed were its objectives dictated officially by the NHPC.

While vacillation in the NHPC allowed some latitude for pursuing the liberal intentions reflected in the research reports, it also gave rise to frustration at the lack of action on the ground. As early as 1946 Hanson had reported to the ISAA as follows:

> I will not summarize or comment on the effectiveness of [my work in the NHPC] except to state that what is revealed in all its nakedness is the confused and uncoordinated approach to planning problems which is characteristic of physical development in South Africa. In this respect the Commission possesses powers which thus far it has not exercised to do regional planning and to co-ordinate town planning. These powers are somewhat vague and inadequate and measures far more dynamic and far-reaching will have to be taken before the rudiments of planned development can be attempted in South Africa.[49]

By the middle of 1948 this situation was little changed. Thus the advent of the new government, however unwelcome in some respects, may well have seemed a prelude to exactly the measures yearned for. Shortly after the National Party's election victory, the ISAA took steps to maintain the relationships which it had established with the housing agencies under the United Party administration. The new minister, A.J. Stals, was asked to receive a deputation to discuss the 'national housing question', bearing in mind the past achievements of architects in the NHPC and in the field, and the ISAA's desire to 'continue to assist, in fact to render greater assistance to the Government on an issue of such national importance at such a critical juncture'.[50]

The minister agreed to a meeting, and a memorandum and a further letter were prepared and presented to him when it took place in July 1948. The letter voiced Hanson's frustrations of several years before. It argued that the organization of the NHPC was basically sound and capable of carrying out a large building programme, that the results thus far were only a fraction of what the profession could achieve, and that, in order for national housing to proceed more rapidly and productively 'in the first instance and in contrast to past practice, a more scientific definition of the housing programme should now be undertaken [because] lack of such definition has prevented a clear statement of the problem'.[51] Although the hope of more extensive professional involvement was to remain unfulfilled, the minister was reportedly 'impressed' and the profession's representation on the NHPC and in the NBRI was unaffected by the change in government.

The final and most important of the recommendations of the 1949 interim reports concerned the need for further research 'to study ways and means of ensuring the provision of the recommended standards in all future housing [and] to consider every promising avenue by which its object could be attained'. This included the investigation of methods of construction, sources of labour and material, the production of building material and the possibilities of more efficient organization in building.[52] The immediate consequence of this recommendation was the formation of further committees to review the standards recommended in the interim reports and to examine in depth the problem of the costs of 'native housing'.

These new committees developed fully the elements of the 'native township' of the apartheid state, as applied for the first time in Witbank and KwaThema. The final phase of this research was, of course, carried out in parallel with the increasingly coherent formulation of urban 'native' policy by the new government. It was a formulation that led, as Wilkinson has shown,[53] to the systematic instrumentalization of housing policy to achieve a number of objectives which were stated unambiguously by Eiselen, the Secretary for Native Affairs, and by Verwoerd himself. Both saw quite clearly that the implementation of apartheid depended on the development of a successful urban housing programme. As they put it, 'Orderly housing is a prerequisite of proper control, whereby vagrants and parasites who always flourish in slum conditions can be cut out. This scheme to house all workers under control, co-ordinated with the control of influx, which must be made effective by means of the labour bureaux ... will radically improve the conditions of the Native populations of the towns.'[54]

The appropriation of the profession's research into housing to serve these political objectives

became a matter of course. It was made possible by the easy congruence of the regional planning/neighbourhood unit pairing with the desired spatial organization of the apartheid city and the distribution of resources within it. This easy congruence can be illustrated by considering the proposed forms, development procedures and rhetoric associated with a project for a new town developed by Gropius in the early 1940s at Harvard University.[55] In addition to traditional Garden City measures like communal landownership and local self-government, the project dealt with the evolution of legal, financial and administrative instruments to enable planners to conceive and implement master plans for resettlement.

> Such a policy [resettlement of people in new townships] calls for transferring endangered production as well as purchasing power from a sore spot in the old city area to a sound new city, resettling those inhabitants of the old city who cannot be gainfully employed and have hence become a serious cause of blight and congestion. This transfer of idle labour would relieve the sick body of the old city ... Simultaneously the stranded workers could be reclaimed for production at a much lower cost per capita than the old town had to pay for slum clearance on expensive land ... By transplanting idle labour from cities as well as rural regions, both the townsman and the farmer will be helping to build new settlements. These 'reception basins' for uprooted people could take over functions which neither our big cities nor the open country can fulfil.[56]

The planning mode which this project exemplifies was ideally suited to the perpetuation of townships as urban islands, to the demarcation not only of separate racial areas but of separate ethnic areas, and to the concentration of poverty where it would be invisible. All of these practices except ethnic (as opposed to racial) segregation had existed before, but the research programme systematized them and made them scientific. The increasingly reductionist approach to the analysis of housing problems also allowed for the appropriation of the research to the problem of making townships

Aerial view of KwaThema new native township, Springs, c. 1955.

H

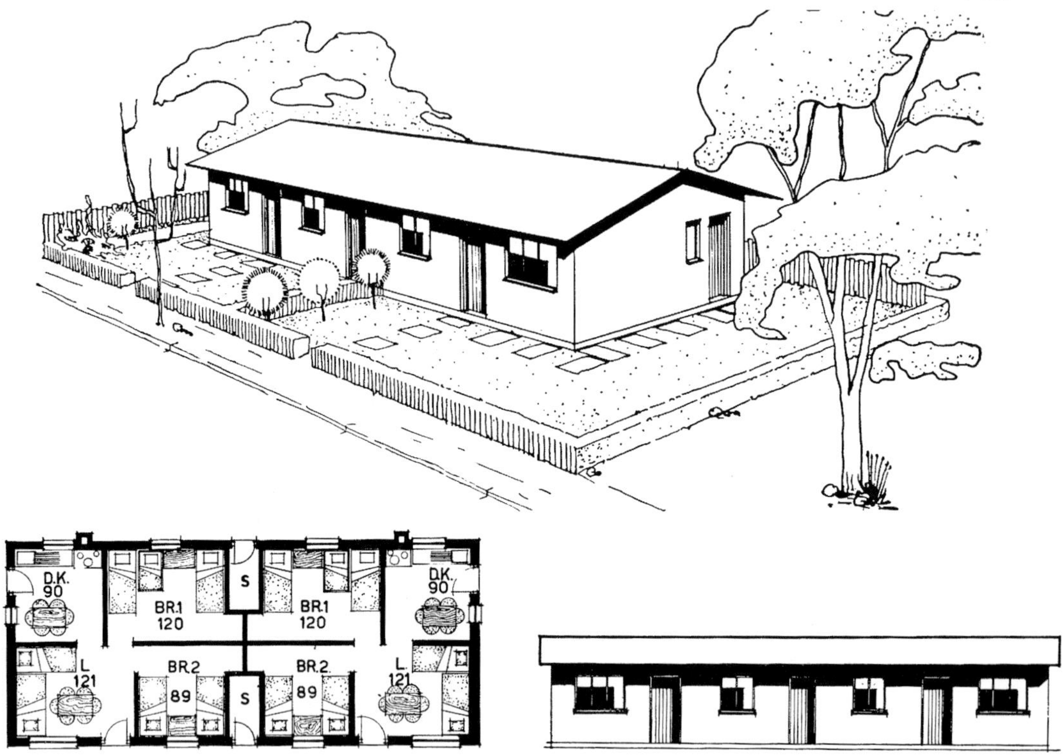

'economic', a term which was official shorthand for the elimination of subsidy. The question of responsibility for losses sustained on African housing schemes had long been a point of conflict between the state, local authorities and the commercial and industrial lobby and none of the various state formulas to distribute this loss had provided a solution acceptable to all parties.[57] This had led to two problems from the perspective of the NHPC. One was that some local authorities built no housing at all. The other was that some attempted to build up substantial capital assets at sub-economic rates, by providing what was considered to be 'lavish' accommodation, particularly with respect to community facilities.[58] This had been partially curbed by placing a ceiling on permissible annual losses per house, but the NHPC considered it possible to reduce the figure substantially.[59]

With the accession to power of the Nationalists, the programme for the reduction of losses became a programme for the elimination of loss.[60] This in turn became a cornerstone of the African housing policy emanating from the Department of Native Affairs, and was identified as such by Verwoerd himself: 'It must be realized that one cannot get a housing campaign on a national scale started as long as it is founded on uneconomic building methods, that is to say the unsound position: every additional house for a non-European means an additional burden to the European Community.'[61] The measure of success of the policy to eliminate subsidized housing is that in 1950/1 20 per cent of housing funds allocated were for economic housing and 80 per cent for sub-economic; by 1953/4 the proportion was approximately equal; by 1954/5 it had been inverted; and by 1961 only R22,472 out of R10,760,299 allocated for African housing was for housing that was subsidized (0.2 per cent).[62] It was a situation that enabled W. Mocke, Senior Urban Areas Commissioner, to claim with evident satisfaction in 1956 that the cost of housing had 'ceased to be an ever increasing burden on both the central Government and local authorities'.[63]

This was a policy of the utmost significance to the further development of the housing research programme. Under the direction of a new generation of architects trained at the Witwatersrand School, principally Douglas Calderwood, the chief planner of KwaThema and author of the book

Plan, elevation and perspective of three-roomed semi-detached house NE 51/8, 1951.

Native Housing in South Africa,[64] the research became directed more and more to achieving only this single objective. While claims continued to be made that the programme was based on meaningful social enquiry and was achieving real gains in relation to the environmental quality of African housing,[65] these became little more than platitudes in the face of an increasingly technicist practice, as the programme began to focus almost exclusively on the rationalization of the individual house as the unit of production.[66]

Since the precondition for any detailed technical work on costs was the finalization of the question of space standards, the first priority was to bring to a conclusion the preliminary investigations of the 1949 research committees. To this end a joint committee of the Department of Native Affairs, the NHPC and the NBRI was established to review the 1949 reports. These reports had tried to strike some kind of balance between biologically defined minima and economic realism, but had been opposed to the establishment of a minimum standard on the criterion of cost or race.[67] However, in recognizing the 'special problems' pertaining to urban African housing and in conceding that they had no real objection to an 'austerity approach' or to the reduction, in an emergency, of the recommended standards, the authors were tacitly admitting the futility of their own stated position.[68]

The standards they had established were modified by the review committee in two respects. They were made racially applicable and they were drastically reduced. This reduction amounted to an average of about 30 per cent if one compares room sizes only, but was greater if projected occupancies are taken into account. If these revised standards are compared with housing standards prior to 1949, it becomes clear that the entire standard-setting exercise did little more than rationalize accommodation standards at levels approximately equivalent to already current practice. The new standards implied some design improvements and were slightly better in some cases, but in others they were worse and on average they made little difference,[69] except that they now had scientific sanction, as the products of a long and systematic process of research.[70] They were published in 1951 as Minimum Standards of Accommodation for Non-Europeans, and were used as the template for all subsequent state-funded housing and as the basis for the designs of the NE 51/ series of houses by the architectural branch of the NBRI.

The completion of these designs meant that type plans were now available which could be used for further rationalization to reduce costs. Several possible avenues were open and all were explored, using the NE 51/9 house as the basis for the research. The point of departure was that, while it would be impossible to achieve substantial savings on any single item,[71] the minute examination of every aspect of the buildings and their procurement would yield significant results. Accordingly, committees were set up to investigate the technical elements of building, labour employed on construction, materials, overheads and profits, and unorthodox construction methods.

The effectiveness of this approach can be measured by a simple comparison: in 1944 the Director of Housing had given the National Housing Council a figure of £400 as the cost of a house.[72] The cost of an equivalent house in KwaThema, after ten intervening years of inflation, was between £227 and £310.[73] In its own terms, this was an extraordinary achievement, even if it had been achieved largely by substituting poorly paid black artisans for the white artisans whose activities, even in the field of 'native housing', had previously been protected by law.

Thus the scheme at KwaThema, described as 'the interpretation of sociological findings into bricks and mortar',[74] brought together the products of a ten-year programme of 'objective technical research', the regional planning of African housing, the neighbourhood unit as the spatial model for its organization, the rationalized house constructed according to a space standard believed to constitute a workable basis by which family life may be safeguarded',[75] and a concept of rational labour utilization for this construction.

In the face of this progressively technicist approach, the spatial aims underlying the planning constructs used in KwaThema and Witbank are difficult to detect in the featureless landscapes of the realized housing estates, except at the abstract level of the plan. The organization of KwaThema conforms in almost every respect to the classic definition of the neighbourhood by Perry.

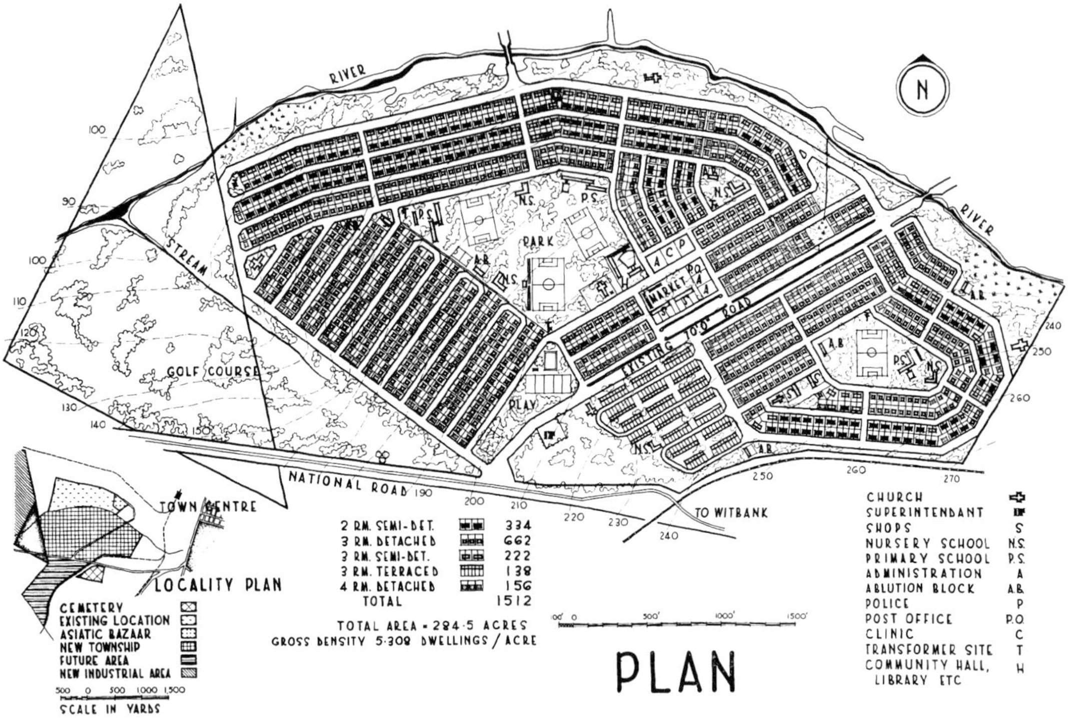

Built for about 6,000 people, it has boundaries separating the neighbourhood from the body of the town, an internal street system, and a school and community centre as the nuclei around which 'local democracy' could evolve. In such a neighbourhood responsible citizens could live and be formed.

Conclusion

I am not suggesting that architects created the 'native township' single-handed, nor do I wish to overemphasize their influence. Space and bricks were just two of numerous elements that came together to organize the 'native township' as a site of power, and architects had little to do with many of them. I am also aware that the mobility of social meaning makes the interpretation of episodes like this less than straightforward. It is surely one of the more distinctive ironies of the present that the NE 51/9, the basic four-roomed house of the 1950s, has now come to seem to so many people in the shacks and overcrowded rooms of what are still apartheid cities both so desirable and so unattainable within the framework of present policy. It is also the case that, in the face of contemporary globalization, regionalism has recently resurfaced as a pressing theoretical issue in architectural discourse.

My interest here is mainly in the role of a certain type of modernist discourse in the creation of the knowledge bases for sites where power can be exercised. In this narrative, I have tried to show that a number of prominent members of the alignment called the South African Modern Movement set out in the late 1930s to correct what they saw as the unacceptable formalism of the movement's origins by recovering the missing social dimension of international modernism. To do this they initiated a chain of logically consequent actions to develop a programme for African housing and to take that programme into the appropriate state agencies, where the positions of responsibility and influence they achieved cannot often have been matched by architects of similar stature. And from these agencies, they took their programme into the space of South African cities, to Witbank

Final layout of Witbank's new native township, c. 1950.

and KwaThema and the countless townships modelled on them, populated with the ubiquitous NE series of houses that they invented as standards.

But my case that in 1939 the South African Modern Movement was just beginning rather than ending is based less on this continuity of personae and programme, than on the proposition that the entire enterprise seems in so many ways a quintessential modernist project. Its key concepts were the need for rigorous studies of the urban neighbourhood, the importance of standard-setting exercises about space and meticulous technical investigations of standardized houses, and the general claim that the work should be seen as the practical implementation of an objective science of the environment. The congruence between this complex of propositions and the surveillance planning of apartheid came, not so much because a naive, liberal programme was co-opted by a ruthless regime, but from the association of two modernisms: the modernism of apartheid social engineering and the modernism of the creation of subjects through science.

Paul Rabinow has identified what he calls two archaeological moments in modernist planning: 'techno-cosmopolitanism' and 'middling modernism'. He tells us that they shared the imperatives of industrialization and welfare, the project to regulate society through art and science. Techno-cosmopolitanism was regionalist modernism, blending the universal technical imperatives of modern planning with the particularities of local sites, customs, traditions, and social and cultural institutions. Techno-cosmopolitan modernism, therefore, embraced the possibility of a universal core of planning actions complemented by specificity on the fringes. It was modernism tailored to the local context. Middling modernism operated instead on a universal human subject, whose needs could be discovered, analysed and formalized. Middling modernism sought to create 'New Men' purified and liberated to pursue the new forms of sociality that would inevitably arise from the creation of healthy spaces and forms. Science would define humanity's needs and technical planners would meet them.[76]

The social programme of the South African Modern Movement began as a middling modernist project, but was transformed into a peculiarly South African techno-cosmopolitan project which never quite lost the imprint of its middling modernist roots, one which was culture-specific without traditional iconography. This transformation occurred with the substitution of Mumford for Le Corbusier, the region and the neighbourhood for the general community of man. The middling modernist project, as Jonas correctly predicted in his 1938 address to the Student Society, would have been impossible to implement in South Africa, the environment above all others where culture counted, where the primary definer of difference was race, and where, whatever social science could purport to measure, it was certainly not abstract human need.

◄H3 ►H8

Interpreting the 1994 African township landscape

Owen Crankshaw and Susan Parnell

Pictures of urban life under apartheid are familiar even to non-South Africans. In the past the monotonous image of endless ranks of 'matchbox' houses spoke of the state's regimentation of African townships. A favourite technique of film-makers and journalists was to contrast this Orwellian township scene with the freedom and individualism of white suburbia. Although this imagery exaggerated the extent of state control, it nonetheless captured the National Party's model of the high apartheid city, which aimed not only to segregate residents by race but also to ensure that urban Africans would not rise above their designated role as servants to the needs of white society. To this end, the state intervened in a host of ways to regulate and control life in both African and white residential areas.

By 1994, the restrictions which framed this image of South African cities had been abolished. The visible effect that the post-apartheid transformation in urban policy has had on the cities is uneven: the old white residential areas look fundamentally the same, even though an increasing number of the residents are now black. In the old African townships, however, the regulated and monotonous landscape has been overturned. As we shall see, however, this change pre-dates the political settlement and was set in motion by political resistance, government reform and the changing social structure of the urban African population.

High apartheid

The uniformity of African townships was largely a result of state provision of and control over housing during the 1950s and '60s. The irregular landscape of black middle-class housing, slums and shanty towns which characterized the period immediately after the Second World War was systematically destroyed by state demolitions, forced removals and mass rehousing. By the end of the 1960s, almost all housing stock in African townships had been built by the state during the preceding two decades. These low-cost houses and hostels were all constructed to a standardized set of architectural designs and in the same range of materials.

The well-known matchbox house came in two versions, detached and semi-detached, but in every other respect the four-roomed structures were virtually identical. Viewed from the street, the matchbox presented a symmetrical façade: a central front door flanked by two small windows. The walls were made of unplastered stock brick and the roofs of unpainted asbestos sheeting. The front door opened into a living room, and three doors led directly off that into two bedrooms and a kitchen. The kitchen was at the rear of the house, with a door leading to the backyard and the outside toilet. Water was supplied by a single outside tap next to the back door, and there was usually no inside bathroom.

In many ways the early hostel units resembled the matchbox houses: they were also detached, single-storey structures built with the same stock brick and asbestos roofs. The hostel interior, however, was quite different. The single external door led into a central kitchen area, and two doors on either side of the kitchen led into the dormitories, which usually held eight beds each. Toilets and showers were in separate ablution buildings. Originally the dormitories were partitioned with room dividers, but the residents would also use curtains and blankets. The hostel units were usually arranged in serried ranks separated by bare earth or lawns.

The early township landscape was not only monotonous, it was austere. Post-war building shortages, the introduction of reinforced-concrete technology and the predominance of modern functionalist aesthetics help to explain its harshness.

But the homogeneity of the townships extended beyond bricks and mortar. The apartheid state

Meadowlands, 1954 and RDP project, Middelburg Township, Eastern Cape, 1998.

gradually withdrew freehold and leasehold property rights from the African middle class, so that by the late 1960s every urban African was a state tenant. Regardless of income or status, African residents were provided with the same level of services. These generally included running water, sewage and refuse removal but did not extend to domestic electricity, telephone lines or street postal services. Similarly, all streets were unpaved, and lacked kerbstones, drains, street names, road signs, pavement trees and street lights. The only residential variation in the township landscape was between family units and shared, single-sex hostels, although even then the building materials and design were similar, as we've already noted. This uniformity was perpetuated well into the 1970s by strict municipal control over squatting, sub-letting and domestic renovations.

In addition to these direct controls, the state achieved its ends indirectly through the pass laws, which were used to control urbanization. Under these laws, rural-born Africans were prevented from living anywhere in the cities except as migrant workers in single-sex hostels, while family housing in matchbox units was granted only to Africans who had either been born in urban areas or who had qualified for residence there by long periods of urban employment. The pass laws were therefore an additional means of controlling squatting and sub-letting, and thus of maintaining the apartheid model of African urban settlement.

The state sought to control every aspect of African urban life. Transport to and from work was exclusively by state-owned bus and train services. Recreation and leisure facilities were also provided solely by the state. Private enterprises in the form of restaurants, music venues and bars were illegal. Illegal shebeens flourished, but were hidden behind the façades of ordinary matchbox houses. The only non-residential buildings on the township streetscape were churches and a few small retail outlets and official beerhalls. The limited commercial development in the townships was a direct consequence of restrictive state policy, and it forced Africans to do much of their shopping in white-owned businesses in the far-off city centres. In contrast to the restrictions on private commerce, official beerhalls proliferated. The municipal monopoly over the brewing and distribution of beer in the townships was used to raise revenues which paid for services in African townships. In this way the state ensured that revenues raised from rates and taxes on white residential and commercial properties would not be spent on African areas.

However, this landscape of high apartheid is now only remembered by older township residents. The younger generation grew up in a much more heterogeneous environment because, from the early 1980s onwards, social and political forces began to reshape the cities.

The decline of apartheid

Townships no longer bear the marks of state control. Instead of the homogeneous landscape of official design, African townships are now as varied as the freehold settlements they once replaced. Nowadays, almost every backyard hosts sub-tenants who live in shacks or formal outbuildings. These backyard shacks, which are designed and built by the residents themselves, are made of wood or zinc, or even of plastic and canvas sheeting. With their variety of materials, design, position and orientation, they stand in stark contrast to the ranks of uniform matchbox houses. No shelters are ever built in front yards and so the clean lines of the streetscape are untouched. However, from the vantage point of even a small hill, the densely packed roofs of the backyard shacks are clearly evident. From the air, the visual impact of this informal building is even greater, and its sheer volume creates the impression of a residue of formal houses floating in a sea of shacks.

Shacks have also sprung up on vacant land in the townships and on the urban fringes. Like their counterparts in the backyards, the structures in these shanty towns or 'squatter camps' are built by the residents themselves from a wide variety of materials. Depending on the city, and therefore on the supply of materials, the shacks may be made primarily of wood or of corrugated-iron sheets. The street layouts are also very different to the planned townships of earlier years. The camps of the mid-1980s grew incrementally and under constant threat of removal, and as a result they are densely and haphazardly settled. Access is more likely to be along narrow and winding footpaths than by road. The more recent settlements were often bold statements of political resistance and feature large stands and wide roads laid out on a gridiron plan.

Built outside the law, these settlements are vividly opposed to the order and regularity of state-built formal housing and, within the constraints of poverty, they reflect the individual aspirations and styles of the residents. Cattle and goats are often left to roam in the streets, a clear sign of the rural origins of many inhabitants. There are spaza shops on every corner, and it is not uncommon to find traditional healers plying their trade.

In many respects, these shanty towns are similar to the site-and-service settlements and low-cost housing schemes built since the 1980s. Reforms in housing policy during the late apartheid period reversed the government ban on urban housing provision. However, these new policies did not entail state provision of housing but rather the provision of serviced sites where residents had to build their own homes. Although the new democratically elected government does provide residents with a one-off subsidy, this is usually insufficient to pay for both a serviced site and a formal house, with the result that most of the new housing stock is of a much lower standard than even the matchbox houses of the 1950s and '60s.

In contrast to the shanty towns and site-and-service schemes, new middle-class neighbourhoods have been developed in most African townships, and the houses there are indistinguishable from their counterparts in the white suburbs. Although mass-produced by large property developers, these family homes are varied in their position, orientation and finish to cater for individual tastes. By comparison with the small, four-roomed matchbox units, such privately owned houses are large, usually having three bedrooms, a separate bathroom and a garage. They are also better finished than council stock, with roofs of clay or concrete tiles instead of asbestos, and walls of painted plaster or face brick instead of stock brick or concrete blocks. The stands are larger, and sport manicured lawns and flower beds.

The transformation of the township landscape has not only been about the construction of new and different housing stock. Often the original matchbox houses have also been altered, sometimes beyond recognition. Common renovations include the installation of larger windows, smart front doors and garden walls. Occasionally extra rooms are built onto the original house, while only rarely are extra floors added.

These dramatic changes to the original houses have been accompanied by fundamental changes in the quality of infrastructure and the use of public space. State reforms which lifted prohibitions on both formal and informal trading in townships have resulted in significant changes in land use. By day, township streets are now characterized by hawkers, new retail outlets (especially fast-food chains), modern shopping malls and taxi services. By night, serviced districts are now illuminated by street lights and advertisements for public 'taverns'. Although coal smoke, darkness and dust are still features of township life, they are largely restricted to the shanty towns.

We have described two quite distinct township landscapes. The first, associated with high apartheid, was characterized by monotony, regulation and control. The second, associated with the

Backyard shacks, Tokoza, 1998.

decline of apartheid, was characterized by heterogeneity, resistance and reform. While considerable attention has been given to interpreting the urban landscape of high apartheid, we know relatively little about the changes wrought by apartheid's decline.

Interpreting the changing urban landscape

The roots of this new urban landscape can be traced to popular resistance to apartheid, to reforms in official urban policy and to changes in the occupational structure of the urban African population, which all acted in concert to break the high-apartheid mould of regimented township life. In the first two decades of apartheid, the homogeneity of the township landscape corresponded to the lack of class differentiation in urban African society, whereas the changes evident in the built environment over subsequent decades reflected increasing social inequality.

The first sign that the apartheid state was losing its grip on African townships came with the proliferation of backyard shacks as families spilled out of their overcrowded houses. This overcrowding was a direct result of the government's strategy to prevent African urbanization. From 1968 onwards the government tried to displace African urbanization from the white cities by restricting all new housing construction to the far-flung 'homelands'. The natural growth of the urban African population and in-migration soon outstripped the existing supply of state housing. The housing shortage continued to grow throughout the 1970s and '80s, until there were more people living in backyards than in the official houses.

During the 1970s, the nationally appointed administration boards ruled the townships with an iron fist. Where backyard shacks were tolerated their numbers were controlled and squatters were summarily evicted. However, with the abolition of the administration boards and the creation of autonomous black local authorities, a new kind of patron-client politics emerged in which African councillors sometimes gave the go-ahead for squatter settlements on selected tracts of government land. During the popular uprisings of the mid-1980s, the community councils lost control of the townships and squatter camps proliferated, as civic and youth organizations led land invasions in open defiance of the state.

In reaction to these widespread protests, the government embarked upon racial reforms to win the support of a black élite. One prong of this strategy was to give back urban property rights to African residents who could afford to pay for them. At first the government tried to woo the African middle class with leasehold rights of 99 years, but when this met with a lukewarm response the popular demand for freehold rights was conceded. This reform opened the way for property developers to build new tracts of middle-class housing in African townships for the minority who could afford it. If it had not been for the de facto collapse of racial residential segregation from the early 1980s onwards, middle-class Africans would have been trapped in the townships and the extent of these élite residential developments would have been much greater.

Growing class inequality also helped to change the township landscape. Since the mid-1970s urban African society has become relatively polarized by upward occupational mobility on the one hand, and rising unemployment on the other. The economic boom of the 1960s had given rise to chronic

Alexandra Township, 1996.

shortages of white artisans, clerks, cashiers, sales people and nurses. Under pressure to meet employers' demands for skilled and white-collar workers, the government introduced far-reaching educational and labour reforms, as a direct result of which many Africans moved upwards into jobs that were previously filled by whites (see Figure 1). Over the same period, however, unemployment amongst unskilled and poorly educated Africans rose steadily. By 1995, fully one-third of the African workforce was unemployed. The contrast between urban African society in the early and the late apartheid periods could not be more stark. Whereas in the 1950s most African workers were employed full-time in poorly paid and unskilled jobs, in the 1990s African workers have been increasingly polarized into a class of unemployed and unskilled workers on the one hand, and a class of relatively well-paid skilled and white-collar workers on the other.

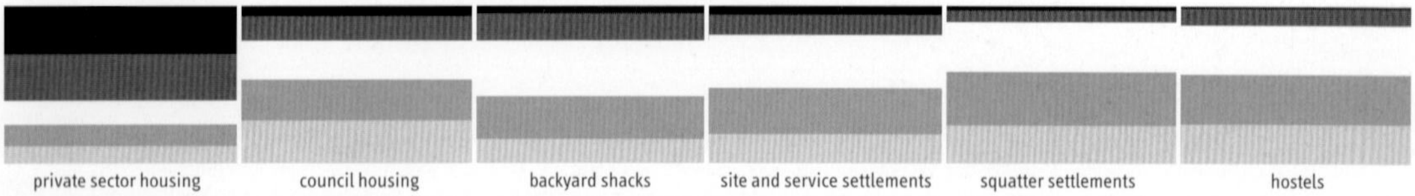

This growing inequality has corresponded to and reinforced the differentiated township landscape of the 1990s. Whereas the state had provided subsidized and low-cost rental housing for urban Africans during the early apartheid period, in the 1980s it turned to the private sector to deal with the housing shortage. As a result, formal housing was restricted to only those Africans who could afford to buy their own homes, and the new, privately built houses of the 1980s were bought and occupied by people employed in relatively well-paid jobs or eligible for housing subsidies. The residents in these new areas are typically supervisors, artisans, technicians, personnel officers, schoolteachers, nurses and police officers (see Figure 2). By contrast, the failure of the state to provide low-cost housing for urban Africans since the late 1960s meant that the poor were left homeless. The residents of shanty towns are therefore mostly unskilled and semi-skilled workers, and there are relatively high rates of unemployment.

Distribution of housing types/labour:
- managers, professionals, semi-professionals and technicians
- clerks, salespersons, rank-and-file security and protection workers
- skilled and semi-skilled manual workers
- unskilled manual workers
- never employed

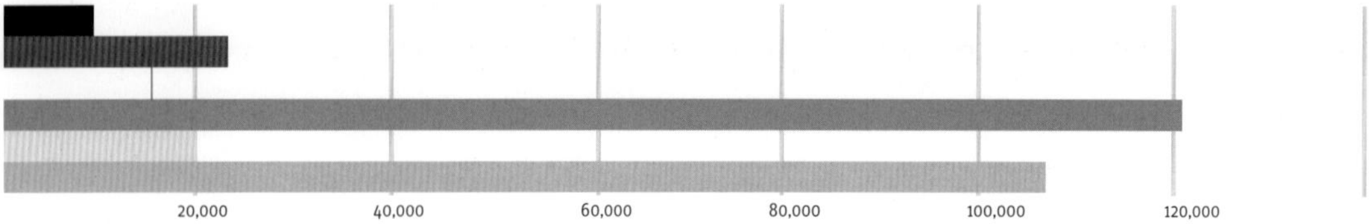

On 27 April 1994, when South Africans went to the voting booths to participate in the country's first democratic elections, African townships were the focus of international media attention once again. The street scenes that provided the backdrop to the long queues outside the polling booths on that day testified to the distorted society that apartheid had made. However, in interpreting this township landscape we must acknowledge that it was produced not just by apartheid at its height, but by its reform and decline.

Distribution of accommodation type:
- site and service settlements
- hostels
- squatter settlements
- backyard shacks and rooms
- private sector housing
- council housing

◄G6 ◄G8

The Dead Zone: The confined space of political conflict, Tokoza township

Greg Marinovich

28° 08' 11'' E
26° 20' 10'' S

I return to the cracked concrete square where these coordinates meet: the petrol station at 6024 Khumalo Street, Tokoza. It surprises me to see workers busily renovating this vandalized, looted place. It is four years since the final large-scale battle was fought in Tokoza's Dead Zone, and eight years since the hostilities first began.

My last memory of the garage is of watching a friend lay a bunch of wild flowers on this spot, her long hair hiding her face; it was the first anniversary of the death of photographer Ken Oosterbroek, shot dead here in 1994 on a day of bloody skirmishes. Then the weeds and wild grasses had been rampant, forcing their way through every crevice and gap. A political poster from a forgotten local election, articulately defaced with a blade, had fluttered on a wall. The yellow-and-blue mobile police station that had been posted to the area in an attempt to keep the peace seemed hopelessly too small. Now it is no longer needed, and traffic moves freely past the garage. The hostel has been refurbished, and people are cautiously moving back into some of the deserted houses.

The forecourt of this petrol station is the epicentre of what was once a war. Tokoza, a black township sixteen kilometres south-east of Johannesburg, is a small, nondescript place, yet a bitter and prolonged conflict raged here between 1990 and 1994. The war was between Inkatha members based in migrant workers' hostels and African National Congress supporters living in the surrounding township houses. The migrants were all Zulu-speakers and mainly from rural KwaZulu-Natal; the residents had a variety of ethnic backgrounds. Hostel dwellers versus householders. The conflict recurred in every township on the Reef – that swath of gold-mining towns with Johannesburg at its centre – and so it was dubbed the 'Hostel War'.

In Tokoza, the Dead Zone where the fighting took place was no larger than a neighbourhood, but it had the highest death toll during the four years preceding South Africa's first democratic election in 1994. In the first ten days of conflict on the Reef in August of 1990 more than 500 people died, most of them in Tokoza, where just one day's death toll was 143.[1]

As a photographer, I passed through the Dead Zone countless times during that period, sometimes casually, sometimes scared witless, and sometimes all fired up with adrenalin while chasing pictures. Running through the heart of the Zone was the notorious Khumalo Street. If you stand with the garage to your left, facing north-east, the tarred surface of Khumalo Street runs straight into the section nicknamed Ulundi. The original Ulundi is the rural capital of the KwaZulu homeland, the seat of power of Inkatha, the traditionalist Zulu movement (reconstituted in 1990 as the Inkatha Freedom Party). Tokoza's Ulundi was, and still is, a Zulu stronghold – or a besieged last redoubt, depending on your point of view. Ulundi consists of the sprawling hostel complex on the left-hand side of Khumalo Street and the little 'matchbox' houses opposite, which the Zulus forcibly occupied when the conflict flared. The area was feared and hated by non-Inkatha members, who would not dare to set foot there, just as a visit to the township was deadly for hostel Zulus. At the beginning of the war, it was possible to drive through Ulundi and even to enter the hostel but, as the conflict deepened and attitudes hardened, that stretch of Khumalo Street became a no-go area, though occasionally we would brave a run along it, sinking low into the car seats, racing past the stop signs, hoping no one would shoot. To venture into the hostels during the first year of the war was a scary tightrope act. One day it was fine to go in, meet the induna (headman) and get permission to work, talk to people, share a beer, photograph. On other days, when the hostility was high, you would soon meet with aggression. Later, it was out of the question.

In the opposite direction, Khumalo Street leads south-west into the territory controlled by residents owing their allegiance to the African National Congress. From this mid-point, if you look east, you can still see deserted and derelict houses – the no man's land that was the focal point of the Dead Zone.

The Dead Zone was an almost perfect, though offset triangle. The longest side was less than 2,000 metres and the shortest about 900 metres. It was bordered in the west by the railway line and in the east by Letsoho Road, also Tokoza's border with neighbouring Katlehong. The apex of the Dead Zone slipped almost exactly into the apex of another, much larger triangle formed by Katorus, the collective name for the contiguous townships of Katlehong, Tokoza and Vosloorus. On the far eastern edge, the N3 highway stops Vosloorus pushing out any further, while Vereeniging Road and the railway line close Tokoza in from the west.

The roots of Tokoza's conflict lay inside the fortress-like municipal hostels lining the western pavement of Khumalo Street. The furthest of these dormitory compounds, barely discernible in the distance, is Madala ('The Old One'). The middle hostel is Khuthuze ('to be pick-pocketed'), while the southernmost one, adjacent to the petrol station, is 'Angola' – as the graffito on its bullet-scarred wall confirms. This was the name given to it by the Zulu warriors within as a salute to a seemingly never-ending war. The allusion to such a ruined country is unfortunate, but less so than its official name which appears on maps – Mshaya'zafe, a Zulu phrase meaning 'beat him to death'.

Municipal hostels are found throughout the Reef. Historically, they were designed to be occupied temporarily by black migrants from the rural areas, whose movement, employment and rights to residence were controlled by a series of laws from the 1920s onwards. Hostels were for 'single men'. This is not to say that the men who lived there were necessarily unmarried, but simply that they were not allowed to bring their wives or families to live with them. They had been given temporary permission to stay in urban areas as long as they were gainfully employed. When their labour was no longer needed, they had to return to their 'homelands' as stipulated by various Acts of Parliament and enforced by the pass laws. It is estimated that more than seventeen million black people were prosecuted under the pass laws from 1916 to 1981.[2]

The hostels are basically bisected quadrangles surrounded by contiguous single-storey concrete-block quarters. Enter a typical hostel, and the dirt and neglect assault your senses. Raw sewage from blocked and broken pipes spills on to the ground, uncollected garbage and dead dogs rot unattended. The communal ablution blocks have not been maintained and broken toilets rise from reeking pools in stalls that never had doors. The cold-water showers have no doors either, so that those shitting can pass the time by watching those washing. There is no heating, although temperatures drop to below freezing in winter. In summer, the poorly ventilated rooms are stifling and the stench unbearable.

A dormitory has a central room, about four metres square and equipped with a concrete table, which serves as a communal dining room, living room, shared space. Most of the window panes are missing and are covered with plastic, cardboard or zinc. To each side a door leads into an open-plan sleeping room. Each room is meant to be shared by four men, but often as many as sixteen are crammed in; each person has about 1.8 by 1.5 metres of space in which to sleep, and overcrowding sometimes sees beds occupied in shifts. Hostel dwellers usually hang their clothes from a length of wire strung above their beds, and use the grey steel lockers to store food, pots and a few smaller items. There are no ceilings, just a corrugated-iron or asbestos roof, often in disrepair. During the war, many Zulu-speakers sought refuge in the hostels, and entire families moved in from the townships, adding to the overcrowding and unhygienic conditions.

Each hostel has only one entrance, and no provision is made for entertainment – unless one counts the ubiquitous beerhall run by the municipality. There is generally a rough stall from which an entrepreneur is selling parts of an animal slaughtered somewhere in the hostel, while others try to make a living by converting their rooms into shebeens or informal taverns where beer in quart bottles and sorghum beer in paper cartons is sold and consumed. Drunkenness is common. Selling the celebrated variety of marijuana grown in KwaZulu-Natal offers another source of income, and in the early days of the war some township youths would risk a potentially deadly visit to buy dagga or insangu. I once came across the bodies of two young boys who had been burnt to death in a hostel courtyard, their hands bound with wire. 'ANC spies,' the warriors told me, but another Zulu man whispered that the boys had simply come in search of dagga. The hostels of Khumalo Street are austere structures, neglected by the municipality and by the tenants; their architecture imposes a claustrophobic proximity within, and isolation and distance without.

At the time of the war, the social alienation of the hostel dwellers had been exacerbated by their exclusion from most political activities planned and initiated by township residents. The sporadic strikes, stay-aways and boycotts called from 1976 onwards to force political change or protest against living conditions were almost always organized without consulting the migrants, who were not seen as a permanent or integral part of the community. The hostel dwellers were thus often caught unawares by civic action, which they neither understood nor supported. For them a strike or a stay-away simply lost them money by keeping them from work – their sole reason for being in the townships. They had no real stake in the community.

Then, as now, most township residents regarded the hostel dwellers as strangers who contributed nothing to the community, as backward country bumpkins. In tsotsitaal, the urban slang that sets city sophisticates apart from their country cousins, the hostel dwellers are referred to as 'stupids'. More insultingly, they are mdlwembe – wild dogs – from the Zulu adage which says that once a domestic dog has left the kraal or homestead and gone into the bush, it becomes wild and can never be domesticated again. On their side, Inkatha supporters often refer to their ANC opponents as izazi or 'clevers' – deceitful city slickers.

After the pass laws were abolished in 1986, many former migrants began moving into shack settlements in the cities and bringing their families to live with them. But others, and especially conservative Zulus, continued to see life in the townships as a temporary sojourn. Their wives and families stayed on in the rural areas and the men went home for visits when work and money allowed. The system of land control in KwaZulu supported this choice: unless land remains in use by a family, it can be taken by the chief and reallocated. People are also strongly attached to traditional lands where their ancestors are buried and where their spirits reside. Zulus who die in the cities are rarely buried there; their bodies are taken home. One consequence of these strong rural ties was that the hostels came to be increasingly dominated by Zulus. Another was that clan feuds – a feature of rural Zulu life – were pursued in the towns, and regular feuding ensured that hostel Zulus were permanently prepared for conflict. Traditional Zulu militarized social units, consisting of amaButho or warrior groups under the control of an induna, were also activated in the hostels.

These were the forces unleashed repeatedly in 1990 and 1991, when thousands of Zulus, wearing red headbands and carrying spears, shields, machetes and the occasional hidden assault rifle, would surge out of the hostels and down Khumalo Street, a sea of chanting aggression. At first they inflicted heavy casualties in the township, until the formation of neighbourhood Self-Defence Units, made up of youths who received training and weapons from the ANC, evened the scales. By then the 'comrades' had renamed their neighbourhoods. The three sections surrounding the hostels, and thus most involved in the conflict, would now be known as Slovo section, in honour of the Communist Party leader, Joe Slovo; Lusaka section, with a nod to the Zambian capital where many exiled ANC leaders found a home; and Mandela section. The map of Tokoza had been redrawn: Ulundi on one side, Slovo on the other. And between them the Dead Zone.

The ferocity of the fighting that engulfed townships on the Reef surprised many. Various factors contributed to a volatile situation. After the release of Nelson Mandela in February 1990 and the unbanning of the liberation movements, including the ANC, the Pan-Africanist Congress and the Communist Party, political competition intensified. Inkatha's decision to transform itself from a 'cultural movement' into a registered political party – the Inkatha Freedom Party – heaped fuel on the fire. The long, drawn-out process of negotiations towards a new dispensation provided ample opportunity for manipulating these oppositions.

In Tokoza's Slovo section (formerly Penduka), the launch of the IFP coincided with the rise of a gang of petty thieves called the Bad Boys. They were tsotsis – muggers, small-time thugs, car thieves – who were becoming more brazen and dangerous. One day they tried to rob the driver of a truck delivering milk to a neighbourhood store, owned by a Zulu businessman and founder of a small 'Zionist' Christian sect, Bishop Mbhekiseni Khumalo. The bishop ran out of his store with his newly acquired handgun and fired at the fleeing tsotsis. But the shot hit a woman bystander, killing her. The bishop claimed that the Bad Boys had killed her, but there were many eyewitnesses to the shooting, and the neighbourhood started to turn against him. He remained unrepentant and increasingly belligerent.

At this time, the IFP had begun a recruitment drive and the bishop sought their protection in return for 'promoting' membership. The bishop and his well-armed thugs became known as the Khumalo Gang and led a campaign of terror to force people to join the IFP or leave the area. The decade-old political conflict between Inkatha and the ANC in rural KwaZulu-Natal, along with its intolerance of political opponents, was imported into Tokoza. Some non-Zulus chose not to leave their homes and stayed on in Ulundi, but were continually suspected of being spies. Most fled. ANC supporters collected funds to buy guns and prepared to defend themselves. The area around the hostel was primed for the war that would follow within days.

Elements in the white security forces helped to spark the dangerously flammable tinder that lay between the opposing sides by supplying weapons to the IFP. After decades of government propaganda demonizing the liberation movements as part of an anti-Christian, Communist 'total onslaught' against white South Africa, it is perhaps not surprising that the average white policeman (like the average citizen) was antipathetic to the supporters of the ANC. And the antipathy was mutual. Comrades would glare at the police and insult them, and on occasion resort to stones, petrol bombs and guns.

Relations between the police and the IFP were a different matter. It was not uncommon to see a Zulu migrant raise his hands in a show of deference or call a white policeman 'inkosi' – my lord. A bearded white journalist, who might have been mistaken for a policeman on a bad day, told me how he had come across a Zulu castrating a dead Xhosa in the aftermath of a battle in Tokoza in 1990. The man with the knife had turned to him and said, 'Please, my colonel, let me finish just this one!'

The strategies employed by the government in townships like Tokoza were not new. In many ways Namibia had been a dry run in illegitimate pre-electoral manipulation. To those familiar with the convoluted underworld of covert operations it is clear that the South African government, faced with the inevitability of democratic elections in Namibia, set about fomenting communal violence in the hope of disrupting the elections and preventing a SWAPO landslide. Now the same authorities would stop at nothing – from gun-running and assassination to unlawful funding and crooked justice – to ensure that Inkatha defeated or weakened the ANC enough to upset their electoral chances.

There were widespread allegations of 'third force' involvement in the conflict that racked the Reef. While some of this may have been a smokescreen, an attempt by the newly unbanned organizations to deflect criticism for aggressions of their own or a lack of political control over militant and even criminal structures, it has since become clear that government or 'parastatal' forces instigated and perpetrated violence at critical periods. This was especially noticeable whenever a breakthrough in the national political negotiations appeared likely: periods of calm would be violated by an attack or massacre that was sure to spark further hostilities.

In the Dead Zone, Khumalo Street took on the name 'Sniper Alley' for a while, adopted from the street in Sarajevo notorious for its hidden assassins. But before long it reverted simply to Khumalo Street. The mention of its real name was far more chilling than a reference to some far-off war that no one in Tokoza gave a damn about.

The hostels became purely Inkatha bases, after purges to drive out or kill anyone who wasn't Zulu: ethnic cleansing before the phrase gained currency. The houses nearest the hostels were invaded and became Inkatha territory too. Refugees fleeing the fighting could be seen carrying bundles on their heads or using wheelbarrows to cart off what they could ahead of the attacks. For Zulu-speakers in the townships, life became very difficult. Now they had to prove they were not Inkatha supporters. Many were killed simply because they spoke Zulu, especially if they had a rural accent, betrayed by the characteristic 'l' instead of 'r'. A suspected Inkatha member would be shown a one-rand coin and asked what it was: to answer 'iRandi' would save him, whereas 'iLandi' was a death sentence.

In the houses close to the Zulu area of Tokoza, residents' lives were tossed about like flotsam on an unruly sea by political machinations. The war advanced street by street, encroaching further into previously safe sections. Homes were burnt, windows broken, everything of value looted. Gardens that had once been carefully tended were trampled flat and overgrown with weeds. These houses became front-line bases from which opposing sides sniped at each other, until you could hardly find a wall, iron gate or fence on Khumalo, Tshabalala and Mdakana streets that did not have a bullet hole in it.

Slovo section, the area just south of Ulundi, was the home of SDU bases one to five, and these would be moved as circumstances demanded. Early one winter morning, on the edge of no man's land in Mdakana Street, the teenage fighters heard a knock on the door of their base, and a voice outside hailed them, using all the correct slang and greetings. The boys opened the door. But instead of the comrades they expected, they found Inkatha fighters, who charged in firing. Three of the youths died. The survivors dragged their mortally wounded comrades back into a safer area, leaving behind a trail of blood smeared along the walls, and a woollen balaclava filled with brain matter and gore. A leather cap lay on the ground, with the bullet hole in it still smoking.

One of the dead boys was laid out in a yard deeper in ANC territory, his tackies placed neatly next to his feet. In the cold morning air, on a plastic chair, his mother sat vigil over the body. She did not cry. Her face, as she stared at the blanket-covered shape that had been her son, was rigid with grief and anger. What hopes had she cherished for this boy?

An overweight white policeman carrying an automatic rifle entered the yard. The circle of youths silently ringing the body parted resentfully to let him pass. He spoke to the mother in Afrikaans, asking for her name and address.

'I do not speak that language,' she answered. 'English or Tswana, whatever you prefer.'

He knew that she must have learned Afrikaans at school. He repeated his question again in Afrikaans. She ignored him. The boys around the body began to hiss menacingly.

Realizing that he would not win this battle of wills, he angrily switched to English: 'What is your address?'

'I have no address, I am a refugee,' she answered, still not looking at him. She knew that there was no point, that the police would never investigate the death or try to find the killers, that they were just looking for information they could use to track down the SDUs and confiscate their weapons.

In Mandela section, a tiny cluster of homes in the northernmost corner of the Dead Zone, a hardened group of young fighters somehow resisted the Inkatha impis (Zulu warriors). The SDU there was led by a man in his early twenties who shared a nickname with one of the enemy hostels: 'Madala', they called him – 'The Old One.' He had been given the name by his fighters, none of them out of their teens and most trying to balance schoolwork with warfare. From one of their bases in a deserted house on the front line they would keep watch through a hole in the wall made by removing two bricks. The hole was large enough to fire out of, but small enough to present a minimal target for opposing snipers. This safe house was in the second street behind the front. An ordinary four-roomed 'matchbox' abandoned by its owners, it was now shared by a dozen teenage fighters and their younger 'camp followers' – even younger children who ran errands and assisted during combat. The yard would be swept clean most days when they were not fighting, they washed their own clothes and cooked their own meals. Racy girls would appear, especially for parties, but they were excluded from the mainstream of the fighters' lives. Contributions from the residents enabled them to buy the food they needed, although some SDUs took to crime to supplement the donations – Coca-Cola trucks would be hijacked when the boys needed money. It was groups of children like these who fought the war, who lived in the Dead Zone. Brutalized by the violence they had witnessed or suffered, few had the opportunity to escape to a better life. One of the SDU leaders in Slovo section was a young man called Rastaman, who joined the unit after his entire family was wiped out by attackers. He had survived by hiding under a bed.

The SDUs earned a loyal following. In Lusaka section the fighters wore headscarves and black T-shirts with 'Lusaka Section SDU' printed on them. They were extremely proficient, using hand signals to communicate and moving like soldiers in Vietnam war movies. They could strip and reassemble the battered old AK-47s they used in a matter of seconds while under fire, and they had young boys to carry ammunition clips for them. The idea was to keep the spare ammunition separate from the 'big machines' in case they got picked up by the police or army. The scarce ammunition was more valuable than the rifles themselves.

In late 1993 and early 1994 the death toll accelerated again; after a night of running battles the police would pick up as many as sixty bodies. There were so many casualties that the residents complained that the police left corpses lying in the streets most of the day. Dogs left behind by residents who had fled formed ravenous packs and survived by eating from the corpses. Mourners spoke fearfully of these dogs shadowing funeral cortèges on their way to the cemetery.

In the month before the 1994 election there was another marked increase in violence but, despite both sides being better organized and better armed, non-combatant casualties were lower. People had grown more adept at avoiding danger areas, and the massive impi attacks of 1990 and 1991 no longer occurred. The SDUs even had a mortar, which they fired at the hostel during an all-out assault just days before the election. On the day Ken Oosterbroek was shot dead, and Judah Ngwenya and I wounded by security forces on the forecourt of the garage in Khumalo Street, the combatants took over the township, and the country looked likely to follow Tokoza into civil war. My colleagues tell me that the following day was even worse. The security forces abandoned Tokoza to its own devices as hundreds of ANC fighters stormed the hostel and were driven back by volleys of automatic fire. Dozens died. Who knows where it would have ended? But then the IFP did a complete turnabout. Mangosuthu Buthelezi announced that his party would take part in the elections after all. The violence ceased immediately. In a news broadcast, Nelson Mandela, soon to be president, mentioned Ken and said he hoped that he would be the last casualty of the war.

Four years on, the Dead Zone is no more, though the dead still cast a shadow on the living. One half of Mshaya'zafe hostel has been renovated and people can live there without relinquishing their human dignity. But the rent has been increased from around R15 to R80, and so the freshly painted rooms are empty, boycotted by the hostel dwellers who say they are too expensive. The rest of the hostels are full, and as squalid as ever. The Inkatha people who once occupied the homes abandoned by fleeing residents have been forced to leave, and the original owners are slowly moving back in, repairing and cleaning. Interior walls have been blackened by cooking fires and ceilings rotted by leaking water. The shops on the corner of Madondo and Khumalo streets are still burnt-out shells, but at the petrol station they are stacking bricks and mixing concrete.

Bodies out of place: Crossroads and the landscapes of exclusion
Steven Robins

> To me there appears little difficulty in administering the Code of Native Law in an urban area to which the Act may refer. Under the Code it is not possible for a Native to become detribalised. Every Native must acknowledge allegiance to a Chief, otherwise it strikes at the root of Native Government of the Province.
>
> Native Economic Commission, 1930[1]

Throughout the century, South African administrators, planners and scholars have made repeated attempts to draw precise boundaries between rural and urban African spaces and identities. However, these divides have been notoriously unstable and difficult to sustain in the face of complex social realities. The response of colonial and apartheid authorities was an anxious repetition of stereotypes about rural traditionalists and urban degenerates. Although colonial and apartheid discourses sought to straitjacket rural Africans in unchanging 'tribal' or traditional identities, the divide between tradition and modernity has also always been unstable and contested.

This essay investigates how apartheid securocrats drew on stereotypes of rural and urban Africans in ways that exacerbated conflict in the informal settlement of Crossroads in Cape Town during the mid-1980s. The apartheid state's complicity in the Crossroads conflict, through an alliance with Xhosa traditionalists, was corroborated in a Supreme Court finding in 1988, and again more recently in Truth and Reconciliation Commission hearings into the Crossroads violence. The analysis presented here suggests ways of understanding how spatialized practices of violence in Crossroads stabilized what had been elusive and fluid rural and urban identities, and anchored previously shifting and blurred boundaries.

In the early 1980s, there was growing conflict in Crossroads (as in many other townships) between militant youth and conservative older leaders, including headmen and community councillors. The 'amaqabane' or 'comrades', rejected what they regarded as the collaborationist stance of their elders: they wanted the headman system abolished and council structures boycotted. This rejection of authority led increasingly to violent confrontation. The 'Fathers', as the conservative contingent became known, sought protection and support from the apartheid securocrats.

The apartheid authorities regarded the comrades as a dangerous, alien presence in Crossroads. For a combination of reasons, including the necklace murders of 'collaborators', the Fathers and their security-force allies agreed to purge Crossroads of these subversive youth activists. While this violent expulsion had a practical purpose, in that it enabled the area to be defended against the comrades' attacks, it also allowed for stable identity formation. It created a homogeneous social space, a place exclusive to Xhosa traditionalists, and allowed Crossroads to be characterized as a rural enclave in the city.

Although many commentators have dealt with the socio-economic and cultural-ideological origins of the bloody conflicts in Crossroads in 1986, and indeed with those of the clashes between hostel migrants and township residents in other parts of the country from the mid-1970s onwards, few have analysed the nature of the violence itself. In most accounts, violence has been treated as a mere epiphenomenon, a psychological by-product and surface effect of 'deeper' structural and cultural-ideological factors. But what such perspectives fail to acknowledge are the complex ways in which new subject positions are constructed through violent acts: 'Novel subject positions are constructed and construed by violent performances, and this mutation of agency renders formal ideological rationale and prior contextual motivation unstable and even secondary.'[2] Violence may play a significant role in shaping socio-spatial structures, boundaries and identities.

J

April 1986, Old Crossroads residents attack the satellite camps.

The 'great divide' between rural and urban Africans

With the onset of industrialization and urbanization, an imagined 'great divide' between town and country, the modern and the traditional, began to shape how Africans were represented in colonial discourse, popular culture and literature. Whereas the 'town native' was associated with disorder and disease, the rural African villager was often portrayed as living in an idyllic pastoral space of social stability, ethnic purity and cultural authenticity. It is therefore hardly surprising that colonial (and apartheid) administrators came to view 'tribal' village elders as a conservative bulwark against the militancy of the younger generation of modernizing urban Africans. Whereas these traditionalists could be accommodated within the paternalistic British colonial administrative framework of 'indirect rule', and later within apartheid's Bantustan policies, the urban progressives tended to gravitate towards militant African nationalist struggles against racial domination.

Since the early decades of the century, public health discourse pathologized the urban African who was seen to be ill-equipped to cope with city life. It was believed that the exposure of 'detribalized' Africans to the alien urban environment would result in physical, moral, cultural and psychological decline and degeneration. Urban Africans were thought to be especially susceptible to syphilitic or tubercular infection, for instance, and it was widely held that the urban environment encouraged 'impulsive' sexual behaviour and aggression amongst Africans.[3] In addition to these sanitary and behavioural dangers, urbanization was seen to place the actual physiology of the African body at risk. For instance, up until the 1960s it was widely accepted amongst public health practitioners that rural Zulus registered lower blood pressure than city dwellers. It was also generally accepted that urbanization placed Africans at risk in relation to a range of conditions including diabetes, ulceration, headaches and 'psychosomatic' conditions affecting the skin, stomach and bowel.[4] On a different level, it was thought that the cities rendered Africans susceptible to alien communist ideologies and African nationalist influences. By contrast, the traditional rural African was perceived as the 'good native', physically, culturally and psychologically healthy and well adjusted.

Numerous scholars contributed towards the ideological reproduction of an imagined 'great divide' between rural traditionalists and urban progressives. In the early decades of this century, advocates of segregationist policies, including scholars, expressed concern about what they saw as processes of cultural dislocation and 'detribalization' experienced by urban Africans. Anthropologists advised colonial administrators and policy-makers to preserve 'tribal' institutions through the creation of special reserves. There was widespread agreement that it would be detrimental to allow Africans to become thoroughly 'Westernized', and the urban areas were portrayed as especially dangerous and alien environments for Africans. These ideas played a significant role in legitimizing the segregationist ideas of the 1920s and '30s that culminated in apartheid. By mid-century, a consensus had emerged amongst scholars and administrators that 'detribalized', urban Africans were becoming increasingly dysfunctional victims of the corrosive social forces of the city. Given the dangers of cultural and psychological 'degeneration', the rural reserves were viewed as the most appropriate places for salvaging a threatened African cultural identity and heritage.

Apartheid ideologues and policy-makers were especially wary of the urban 'ethnic melting pot' and sought to prevent the 'detribalization' of Africans through influx control and Bantustan legislation. Representations of city space under apartheid were profoundly shaped by imagery on the dangers of impurity and contamination. This discourse formed the cornerstone of segregationist urban planning, which culminated in the slum clearance legislation used to justify the demolition and forced removal of multiracial working class neighbourhoods such as District Six and Sophiatown.

Anthropological literature also tried to clarify the cultural and sociological dimensions of the town and country divide. For example, Philip and Iona Mayer's Townsmen or Tribesmen,[5] a study of the East London area published in 1961, portrayed two groups of Africans with different orientations: 'school people' were 'detribalized', urban individuals who were educated and Christian;

'red people' (from the custom of decorating body and clothes with ochre) were traditionalists who resisted the lure of urban 'Western' culture and continued to maintain strong ties to their rural homelands. Because of their cultural assimilation and embrace of modern urban life, the 'school people' were more integrated into the cities and had more social mobility than the traditionalists. So, although urban-based Africans participated in many different worlds – work, the rural home, the hostel, the township – their orientation was seen to be either towards town or countryside.

Anthropologists have tended to be particularly sympathetic towards the plight of the 'red people', who were seen to be resisting cultural incorporation into Western society. The retention of 'tribal' traditions by 'red people' was often interpreted as an admirable sign of their refusal to become the 'civilized' clones of Europeans. This bipolar logic reproduced a chain of associated binaries: modern/traditional, urban/rural, educated/unschooled, Christian/pagan, progressive/ conservative, and so on.

The complex issue of urban and rural consciousness has been a particularly well-documented area of anthropological research in South Africa. In recent years, anthropologists have pointed out that the retention of certain 'traditional' practices amongst African migrant workers is not so much a sign of cultural conservatism as a creative response to the harsh and exploitative conditions of their incorporation into the capitalist system. They argue that these expressions of cultural continuity should not be interpreted as a manifestation of some pristine and timeless rural African culture, but rather as a strategic response to proletarianization.[6] In other words, these are hybridized responses that are historically produced during traumatic encounters with modernity and capitalism.[7] During the 1970s, Magubane[8] and Mafeje[9] launched similar critiques of essentialist representations of timeless African cultures. They also blamed earlier anthropologists such as Philip Mayer for failing to adequately situate 'tribal' consciousness and the notion of the 'tribe' within the context of racial capitalism, the migrant labour system and processes of exploitation and class differentiation. In a recent article, Mafeje yet again challenges the artificial divide by drawing attention to the complex, hybrid character of African identities.[10]

Crossroads squatter camp residents retrieve their possessions after witdoeke burn down the camp.

Hybridity and subversion

Post-structuralist theory has provided a particularly powerful analytical framework for conceptualizing, and perhaps subverting, the binary logic that structures colonial discourses on the rural/urban divide. For instance, it allows us to understand how the culturally hybrid, 'Westernized' urban African threatens to destabilize the established Self/Other binary. As Homi Bhabha has noted, the hybrid Other who mimes the Master produces an anxiety and ambivalence in the colonizer that destabilizes the binary order of Self/Other; an excess or uncontainable surplus is produced that slips outside of the binary order, resulting in an anxious repetition of the stereotypes which promise mastery. According to Bhabha, this ambivalence of colonialism destabilizes the certainty of colonial power.[11] A safe stereotype that is seen to pose no threat to the Self/Other binary is of course that of the 'good rural native'.

Jane Jacobs reminds us that Bhabha's notion of hybridity is not simply a mixing together: 'It is a dialogic dynamic in which certain elements in dominant cultures are appropriated by the colonized and rearticulated in subversive ways. In Bhabha's words, hybridity is about the "seizure of the sign ... a contestation of the given symbols of authority." '[12] This subversive reading of cultural hybridity allows us to recognize the creative agency of urbane and savvy African bricoleurs like the Drum writers of the 1950s, who shrugged off straitjacketing notions of the 'good rural native'. Writers like Can Themba, Nat Nakasa, Lewis Nkosi, Bloke Modisane and Es'kia Mphahlele sought instead to celebrate black urban culture. They were passionate about black American jazz and the writers of the Harlem Renaissance, they took up the dress and style of Chicago and New York, elaborating a rich transatlantic cultural style. This hybrid black culture was seen as subversive by apartheid functionaries, reinforcing their belief that alien urban influences were responsible for corrupting authentic rural African culture. Can Themba recalled how the urban sophisticates of Sophiatown directly challenged apartheid thinking:

> We were not the calm dignified Africans that the Church so admires (and fights for); not the unspoiled rural Africans the Government so admires, for they tell no lies, they do not steal, and above all, they do not try to measure up to the white man ... We were those sensitive might-have-beens who had knocked on the door of white civilization (at the highest levels that South Africa could offer) and had heard a gruff 'No' or a 'Yes' so shaky and insincere that we withdrew our snail horns at once.[13]

The celebration of the cultural hybridity and diversity of Sophiatown was not something unique in the history of South Africa. Neither were the Drum writers the first to embrace transatlantic black urban identities and cultural styles. Instead, these expressions were part of an ongoing process of cultural invention and bricolage that began with African urbanization and the discovery of gold on the Reef in the 1880s and continues today.

Yet stereotypes about rural and urban African identities persist. It was precisely the power and tenacity of these stereotypes that allowed apartheid securocrats to mobilize traditionalism as a conservative political force in the Crossroads conflict of the 1980s.

'Those who return home'

In his recent work, Mafeje reminds us that the divide between hostel migrants and township residents was spatially reinforced through segregated accommodation. In Langa, as in other townships, the

Funeral of satellite camp resident killed during fighting with Old Crossroads residents.

migrants or amagoduka ('those who return home') lived in hostels, whereas permanently urbanized people or abantu baselokishini ('the people of the location') lived in houses. Mafeje shows that the correlations between factors like education and conservatism or rural orientation are far more complex than the conventional 'red' and 'school' division acknowledges, and that differences in this regard have to do with social differentiation and class formation rather than 'detribalization'.[14] These are complexities which severely enforced spatial divisions have tended to obscure.

Since the 1920s, as part of the official policy of curbing African urbanization, migrant workers from the rural areas were prevented from bringing their wives and families to the cities. Legislation ensured that migrants were temporary urban residents who would return to the rural areas once their contracts expired or they retired, became ill or were retrenched. The mine-owners and the state built mine compounds and township hostels to segregate these temporary migrants spatially from urban Africans. In these grim, overcrowded places migrants could be sealed off from the broader political currents prevailing in the townships, and especially those regarded as militant. The hostels were ethnically segregated and under the authority of neo-traditional leaders known as izibonda (headmen). They were meant to be 'total institutions' (to use Goffman's term), centres of surveillance and control that would reproduce a docile African workforce.

In trying to account for the violent conflict between militant youth and the Fathers in Crossroads, a religious counsellor who worked in the hostels referred to the long-standing tensions and cultural differences between hostel dwellers and township residents. He had observed the social distance between rural migrants and their township neighbours; hostel dwellers, he said, were 'a small island in a huge urban community'. The relationship between rural migrants in Crossroads and residents of the surrounding townships of Nyanga and Guguletu was very similar.

> They were looked upon with contempt by most of the township people. They were regarded as illiterate rural people lacking in any urbane manners and sophistication. They were looked upon as people who had strange ways, spoke Xhosa with a peculiar accent, dressed slovenly, and were unfamiliar with basic hygiene ... The hostel dwellers never felt that they had any responsibility to the larger community.[15]

Despite the state's determination to insulate rural migrants from township residents there was always interaction across the divides. However, during the periods of extreme political crisis in 1976 and from the early 1980s onwards, violent conflict erupted between the two groups in Cape Town and elsewhere. These clashes inscribed very clear socio-spatial boundaries between the hostels and the townships. What had previously been 'mixed' residential spaces with blurred and porous boundaries allowing for daily interaction suddenly became homogeneous spaces with clear and dangerous boundaries – until the crises were over and interaction resumed again.

In Crossroads in 1986, the socio-spatial divide was not between the hostels and the townships, but between areas analogous to these in some ways: the 'traditionalist' stronghold of Crossroads and the surrounding ANC aligned townships and satellite squatter camps of Nyanga Bush (Esangeni), Nyanga Extension (Emavundleni) and Portland Cement.

Crossroads: The Place of the Fathers

A brief history

Today, massive shanty towns such as Crossroads, KTC and Khayelitsha continue to bear witness to decades of apartheid planning. Dr. W. S. Eiselen, one of Prime Minister Verwoerd's chief architects of apartheid, stated in 1955 that, since the Western Cape constituted a 'Coloured Labour Preference Area', black people – meaning Africans – would eventually all have to be 'repatriated' to the Xhosa 'homelands' of the Transkei and Ciskei. Eiselen's statement formed the basis of influx control policies that attempted to curb black urbanization (until the scrapping of the pass laws in 1986). These policies also drew on the Stallard Doctrine of 1923, which stated that the presence of Africans in 'white' cities would be tolerated only in so far as they served to 'minister to the needs of the white man'.

The apartheid state used pass law arrests, forced removals and 'deportation' to prevent Africans from Transkei and Ciskei from settling permanently in the Western Cape. To qualify for a permanent hold in Cape Town (in terms of Section 10 of the Urban Areas Act) Africans had to show proof of both permanent employment and long-term residence in the city. However, for hundreds of thousands of people from the chronically impoverished rural dumping grounds, living 'illegally' in squatter settlements was the only escape from hunger and destitution.

Crossroads is a shanty town on the outskirts of Cape Town near the airport. The first families arrived in the mid-1970s, and over the following decade tens of thousands of Xhosa-speaking people from Transkei and Ciskei settled there. The settlement consisted of thousands of corrugated-iron and wood shacks on a strip of land of roughly one square mile. By the mid-1980s, it had an estimated population of somewhere between forty and eighty thousand.

Despite persistent police harassment, arrests and imprisonment, the people who found their way to Crossroads (and to other squatter camps around Cape Town) in the late 1970s refused to be 'repatriated' to the rural areas. Their plight and their resistance to the efforts of the state to demolish their homes received national and international media attention and led eventually to the official recognition of Crossroads as a permanent settlement. With the effective collapse of influx control in the 1980s, largely as a result of concerted resistance and mass mobilization, large numbers of Africans moved into Crossroads.

During the late 1970s and early '80s, Crossroads was represented in the media and to the international community as a highly cohesive and heroic community struggling against a repressive regime. By the mid-1980s, however, struggles over access to housing and development resources contributed towards violent leadership tussles that revealed deep fissures in the community.

One aspect of this leadership struggle involved the youth. As opposition to apartheid intensified, youth activists aligned with the United Democratic Front, a broad national alliance of anti-apartheid organizations with its roots in the African National Congress, came to play a prominent role in local community politics. In their attempts to render the townships ungovernable, militant activists targeted community councillors and others regarded as apartheid collaborators. This led to a series of bloody conflicts between the comrades and the Fathers.

The 'witdoeke' – as the Fathers became known thanks to the white headscarves and armbands they wore when they went into battle – were under the leadership of Johnson Ngxobongwana and Sam Ndima. Ngxobongwana, an enigmatic former UDF leader who had fallen out with his one-time allies, led a drive to force the comrades and their supporters out of Crossroads. From about March of 1986, thousands of people were hounded out of the community. They proceeded to rebuild shacks on adjacent land in what became known as the satellite camps of Nyanga Bush, Nyanga Extension and Portland Cement. A series of tit-for-tat killings of witdoek and comrade leaders and supporters ensued. These killings precipitated three weeks of fighting in May and June 1986 that left 57 people dead and tens of thousands homeless.

During the fighting the comrades and their supporters were violently expelled from the satellite camps too. In the process, Mahobe Drive, the road separating Crossroads from the townships of Nyanga and Guguletu, was transformed into a rigid boundary line, and it was on this frontier that some of the most violent incidents occurred. Finally the shacks in the satellite camps were burnt to the ground by witdoeke assisted by the police and army. Numerous witnesses testified that they had seen heavily armed police escorting the witdoeke into battle. Having burnt down the satellite camps, the witdoeke barricaded Mahobe Drive, thereby preventing refugees from collecting their belongings and rebuilding their homes. Meanwhile the military cordonned off the area and surrounded the former satellite camps with barbed wire. An estimated fifty thousand people from these settlements ended up seeking refuge in Nyanga, Guguletu and the newly established township of Khayelitsha.

The role of the state and the police

Most journalists who covered the conflict in Crossroads concurred on one issue: it had been manipulated by the apartheid state.

The state had manipulated intergenerational tensions between sons and fathers, between comrades and witdoeke, to achieve one of the most brutal and effective forced removals in South Africa's history. In the early 1980s there had been militant and concerted resistance to resettlement in Khayelitsha ('New Home'), which was even further from the 'white' city. Now, through the orchestration of conflict in Crossroads, not only had the state succeeded in destroying what had become an ANC stronghold and no-go area for the police, but it had also managed to relocate thousands of 'unruly' squatters to a more distant and more effectively policed township.

The Cape Times, a mainstream liberal newspaper, gave special prominence to the role of the police and military in fuelling the flames of conflict. Journalist Chris Bateman made the point that those who had taken refuge in the satellite camps had been both largely beyond the control of police and a threat to Ngxobongwana's power. Bateman went on: 'In March 1986 two policemen were killed in the satellite camps. Nine of Ngxobongwana's men died in clashes with radicals. It was in both Ngxobongwana's and the police's interests to get rid of the camps ... once and for all. That, simply, is the lead-up to the shattering events of May 1986.'[16]

Another Cape Times journalist, Tony Weaver, had no doubt that the police, military and Crossroads administrators had deliberately exacerbated divisions and tensions in the community.

Ngxobongwana's own home guard, responsible for purging Crossroads of radical elements, was a 'quasi-military unit'. In addition to the threat to Ngxobongwana's 'almost tribal stronghold', as Weaver put it, he was also 'coming under pressure from the police to "maak skoon" (clean up) his area'.[17]

The liberal press were not alone in attributing the conflict to the manipulations of the state and its security forces. Community activists like Josette Cole argued that militant youth and women posed a threat to the political hegemony of traditional patriarchal leadership. The state had taken advantage of the tensions generated by this threat to recruit Ngxobongwana, Ndima and their headmen as willing partners in crushing the UDF.[18]

Clerics, NGO and development workers, and numerous residents claimed that police had told the witdoeke they should not allow their 'children' to usurp political control through people's courts, consumer boycotts, petrol bombs and necklacings. In 1986, Nicholas Haysom of the Centre for Applied Legal Studies concluded that these militant strategies played into the hands of the security forces. 'Fathers against Sons. There has been a dramatic emergence in 1985 of the incidence of intergenerational hostility. Tensions between parents and children have been founded on a resentment of the

J

May 1986, residents salvage their belongings as government bulldozers move into Old Crossroads.

prominent role the youth play in formulating strategies and making decisions for the community coupled with increasing disrespect for their parents.' This last aspect, Haysom argued, and especially acts like the flogging of adults at people's courts and the theft of goods by youths manning roadblocks during boycotts, gave the witdoeke sufficient justification for teaching the children a lesson.[19] In 1986, Sam Ndima himself said of the comrades: 'We will not allow them to beat and punish their own people.'[20]

The use of the terms 'Fathers' and 'comrades' by the press reinforced a dangerous divide within Crossroads. However, not all 'Fathers' were elderly, conservative or rural-oriented men, and neither were all youths supporters of the 'comrades'. In addition, not all township residents supported the 'comrades', and not all Crossroads squatters supported the 'witdoeke'. Yet the uncritical use of these terms helped to solidify rigid boundaries between what had once been quite fluid social categories and identities.

One other element in the conflict should concern us here. The simmering tensions which the state was able to exploit to achieve its own counter-revolutionary objectives were not just the outcome of struggles over political leadership and ideology but over access to material resources. One of these was housing. In December 1985, in return for ridding Crossroads of the comrades, the Fathers were offered a R2 million housing upgrading scheme. The added incentive the Fathers had for cleaning up the satellite camps was that this area had been earmarked for Phase 3 of the housing scheme. According to Weaver, the Crossroads leadership under Ngxobongwana claimed that the satellite squatters had no right to occupy land which had been set aside for upgrading. After the witdoeke burned down the shacks there, tens of thousands of homeless refugees were forced to relocate to Khayelitsha and other townships. The witdoeke had thus helped the state to achieve two important aims: they had eliminated the growing UDF influence and activity in the Western Cape; and they had undermined more than a decade of resistance to the government's attempts to eliminate uncontrolled urbanization and 'illegal' squatting around Cape Town.

Widespread media and public allegations of police collusion with the witdoeke were later corroborated in over three thousand affidavits – from reporters, clerics, social welfare workers, doctors and squatters – collected by the Legal Resources Centre in Cape Town. Following a protracted court case the Minister of Police was ordered to pay R5 million in compensation to victims of police and witdoek violence. Police collusion would be corroborated again ten years later in hearings before the Truth and Reconciliation Commission.

Killing in the name of the Fathers

The Truth and Reconciliation Commission's hearings into the violence in Crossroads and KTC in 1986 took place over a period of four days in May 1997 at St. Gabriel's Roman Catholic Church in Guguletu. Although many members of these shattered communities came to the hearings, Johnson Ngxobongwana and his followers were conspicuously absent. Ngxobongwana, who was forcibly

June 1986, KTC, police teargas residents defending their homes.

expelled from Crossroads himself in 1990, ignored a subpoena to appear before the Commission. Now a National Party Member of Parliament in the Western Cape provincial legislature, Ngxobongwana accused the Commission of being biased in favour of the ANC.

However, Ngxobongwana's lieutenant, Sam Ndima, did testify, as did many clerics, health workers, journalists, lawyers, security force personnel, administrators, residents and victims of the violence. One of the key witnesses, Ulrich Schelhase, a senior administrator in Crossroads in the 1980s, openly acknowledged that the security forces had fomented conflict in the area. After four days of evidence it was clear that the Commissioners had come to regard the violence as a product of covert 'third force' military operations. In this account, Ngxobongwana, Ndima and their followers were portrayed as victims manipulated by white puppet masters in the apartheid security structures. This Truth Commission narrative seemed to offer the possibility for reconciliation between Crossroads residents on both sides of the divide.

I first encountered administrator Schelhase in May 1987, a year after the devastating violence in Crossroads. Schelhase's perspective on the conflict then revealed the ideological and strategic thinking that lay behind the military's decision to enter into an alliance with the Fathers. In my interview with him, Schelhase extolled patriarchal traditionalism and indicted the youth for their lack of discipline and respect. Citing the instance of the flogging of adults by children, Schelhase drew a clear distinction between two sets of 'modern black youth'. On the one hand, there were children who had grown up in hostels, exposed to drink and drugs and other negative influences: 'The migrant labour system was responsible for creating a segment of black youth who are confused ... Because they have had no traditional upbringing and no family life, they have no discipline and they become susceptible to communist ideologies.' On the other hand, there were the children of Crossroads, who lived with their parents and were subject to the positive influences of family life. The youth from the satellite camps, Schelhase said,

> ... tried to corrupt the youth of Crossroads ... The satellite youth became so radical and politicized that they started to make inroads into the moral fibre of the Crossroads youth. That is one of the reasons that the Crossroads traditional authorities came into revolt against this infiltration of what they call the *maqabane* or comrades ... who didn't support the system. This is alien to the traditional system ... The comrades youth are wild. They have lost parental discipline.[21]

Schelhase's testimony to the Truth Commission makes it clear that the securocrats saw the 'tribal' rural areas as places of social and political conservatism and stability. By contrast, the cities were hotbeds of youthful militancy and political instability. And by extension, Crossroads, the Place of the Fathers, came to be seen as a rural enclave within the city.

Schelhase revealed that the daily administration of Crossroads in the 1980s involved close cooperation between the security establishment and the provincial and local administration boards. State supporters and informers were identified and instructed to infiltrate 'the enemy' – that is, the UDF. Crossroads was approached as an occupied territory, with counter-insurgency strategies shaping planning and administration. The country was under a State of Emergency and the police and army found themselves unable to patrol certain zones in Crossroads and the adjacent townships. In this 'revolutionary climate' the *witdoeke* emerged as the natural allies of the apartheid state in its war against militant subversives.

An exchange between Commissioner Ramashala and Schelhase around the military's 'cleaning up operation', which culminated in a *witdoek* attack on comrade strongholds in KTC, revealed the thinking behind this counter-revolutionary strategy. Schelhase explained the operation of the 'oil spot' strategy, which was based on the work of American Marine Colonel John McEwan and provided theoretical guidelines for dealing with 'revolutionary situations': 'It was a model in which we had to operate. And if the model dictates that we have to reward people, communities or sections of communities that are non-violent and that collaborate with the system, then that section or that community, their needs must be answered to. If they have got specific needs we must provide those needs.' In Crossroads, apparently, the non-violent, cooperative section of the community was the witdoeke, and the reward came in the form of urban development and a housing upgrading scheme.

Later, Commissioner Ramashala referred to a document which established a direct link between the security system and the administration of Crossroads.

Ramashala: Sir, I'd like to refer you to a document, with the stamp 'Secretariat of the State Security Council'. It is WPGBS/22/7/2. Now I can't speak Afrikaans but ...

Schelhase: I can help you ... Paragraph 9 reads: 'Brigadier de Jager is of the opinion that the older people – the actions of the older people against the comrades necessitates support, although it is on a covert manner. He will mention this to the Development Board so that they can convey the possibility of support to the Fathers ...'

Ramashala: Now you say you didn't know about the term 'witdoeke' but you are aware of the term 'Fathers'?

Schelhase: ... It was more the military people who referred to the Fathers and some referred to the conservatives and there were various descriptions of a faction or a mindset within the community ... I think the 'Fathers' thing is probably something that was an offspring of the 1976 situation, and that it was just continued as a father/youth issue ...

The challenge to the patriarchal power of the Fathers posed by militant youth and women was met by a violent defence of existing generational and gender hierarchies. It also created the conditions for an alliance between the Fathers and the securocrats. This convergence of interests was revealed at the Truth Commission hearings, where State Security Council documents were made public for the first time.

The picture that emerges in these documents, as Roger Friedman wrote afterwards, reveals such a morbid fascination with Crossroads as to suggest that it was perceived as an experiment in social engineering. In March 1986, for instance, security police headquarters informed the Joint Security Staff that the South African Defence Force in the Western Province was already working clandestinely 'to bring the fathers into conflict with the comrades'. On 21 May the Western Province Joint Management Council reported to the State Security Council Secretariat that about seven hundred huts had been burnt in the satellite camps around Crossroads and that people were being moved to Khayelitsha. 'Fathers are well-disposed towards the security forces and are not a security risk as they want law and order. Fathers cannot be openly supported due to the hostility of the leftist press.' On 9 June, the day on which the destruction of KTC began, the Management Council reported that there would be 'a victory feast for the witdoeke in the form of the slaughter of cattle. The cost has not been finalized, but it is estimated at about R3,000.'[22]

Army chaplains distribute Bibles in Old Crossroads.

'How can you dance while a person is burning?'

In his appearance before the Truth Commission, Sam Ndima, the former witdoek leader and veteran of the Crossroads war, spoke of his horror at seeing the comrades singing and dancing around the burning bodies of alleged informers: 'There were people who were dancing around this burning person, so I said, "How could you dance around a person who is dying?" Then they said, "You ought to be necklaced yourself." They said, "Come." So I decided to keep quiet ...' It was scenes like this, he said, that prompted the witdoeke to enter into an alliance with the police.

The Fathers adopted and mimicked some of the state's methods of repression, but without the burden of legal constraints or policing procedures, minimal as those were. As state surrogates the Fathers were able to unleash the most vicious and brutal violence upon their opponents, even as the comrades pursued their own gruesome killings of collaborators. It could be argued that in their barbaric 'pre-modern' methods of violence they acted out the repressed desires of the modern apartheid state.

The Fathers set up their own 'Pollsmoor' – the original Pollsmoor is one of the largest prisons in the Western Cape – where comrades were held, beaten and killed: 'We agreed with the policemen that when someone has disobeyed or broken the law, we must arrest them and take them [to our prison].' Questioned about the people who had died in this 'halfway station', Ndima assured the Commission that he personally had saved some of those who were supposed to be killed.

The Commissioners' reading of the alliance in Crossroads was rather different to Ndima's: the elders and the securocrats had arrived at a marriage of convenience, whereby the police and army would help the witdoeke to expel the comrades from Crossroads. When this objective had been achieved, the witdoeke would be rewarded with a housing scheme.

While the idea of a third force operation planned at senior levels in the state is certainly corroborated by documents produced at the hearing, it does not adequately explain the actual mechanisms through which practices of violence constituted the categories and inscribed the boundaries between witdoeke and comrades. It is only once we recognize the spatialized character of the violence in Crossroads that it becomes clear how incontestable boundaries were drawn between insiders and outsiders.

The Red Sea

The Truth Commission heard evidence from Ruth Kebisela, a victim of witdoek violence. Kebisela and five friends were caught in a roadblock at the entrance to Crossroads in 1986.

> We were going to a party in Vuyani's car. On our way, on the main road to Khayelitsha ... we found the road was blocked. There was a pile of tyres piled up across the road. The stones were thrown at our car. Then we got shocked, 'What's happening, what's happening here?' ... An old man was hiding behind this pile of tyres. He said, 'Stop, stop your car.' And then the car was stopped. Then he said, 'Get out, we want the driver.' Then they opened the door. And then we asked, 'What is happening?' He said, 'Yes, you are comrades, you are the Guguletu comrades, what do you want here?' We said, 'No, we are going to Khayelitsha, we are not comrades, we don't know what is happening ...' They said, 'Yes, you kids of prostitutes, we have got you now. We are going to show you ...'

After some dispute, two of the young men were dragged away. The rest were taken to the 'Red Sea', a dam adjacent to Crossroads.

> We stood next to the Red Sea. Then when we looked we saw a head floating in the water, and the lower part of the body ... We could see some heads floating and headless bodies floating. We apologized, and asked, 'What have we done?' Then they said, 'You will see.' Then they were arguing. One said, 'This one deserves a tyre, this one deserves a tyre.' Then they hit us. 'What

size tyre do you wear? What size do you wear?' ... Then they were putting tyres around our necks, the three of us. Then came a big tin of paraffin. Then there was some argument. They disagreed on what to do with us ... One old man, who was apparently sympathetic, said to the people, 'We are going to fight with Khayelitsha, because these people are not from Guguletu. They say they are going to Khayelitsha. So if you kill these kids, there will be problems with Khayelitsha people ...'

The two youths who had been singled out were hacked to death. The four survivors were taken to 'Pollsmoor', the witdoeke's makeshift prison. Later they appeared before a witdoek 'court', where they were interrogated and beaten by old men who took on the roles of interrogators, magistrates, policemen, detectives and so on. Again, while the 'accused' stood on a raised platform as if in the dock, it was alleged that they had been sent by Guguletu comrades to attack the Fathers. The bizarre mimicking of both the state terror of police interrogations and the formalized legality of the judicial system revealed the affinities and convergences between the institutions and practices of violence of the witdoeke and the state. So not only was Crossroads spatially organized into wards under 'tribal' headmen, it was also modelled on apartheid institutions of repression and social control, without any of the tenuous statutory limits. We may speculate too that in some way these proceedings were a response to the 'people's courts' run by the comrades.

From Kebisela's evidence it is clear that in the eyes of the witdoek elders, if you were young and came from Guguletu you were definitely a comrade. And as a 'township outsider' you were a legitimate target. The spatialization of violence left no room to negotiate identity; your place of residence defined who you were and which side of the fence you were on. Had Kebisela been able to furnish a name and address in Crossroads, or produce a kinship or clan tie to a Crossroads resident, she may have been able to step out of this lethal socio-spatial binary.

Spatializing violence, stabilizing identity

Colonial discourses which pathologized urban African identity were incorporated into segregationist ideologies that culminated in apartheid's homelands and migrant labour policies. It has been argued here that this line of ideas was perpetuated by counter-revolutionary strategists in the 1980s. As the interview with Schelhase reveals, in Crossroads administrators and securocrats drew on notions of the friendly 'rural native' and the 'tribal elder' to position the Fathers as the custodians of a conservative order. Crossroads came to be seen as a disciplined, quasi-rural enclave within an anarchic, corrupt urban space.

In colonial and apartheid discourses the city was a space of danger, contamination and impurity. Dirt, as anthropologist Mary Douglas reminds us, is 'matter out of place'.[23] Social boundaries are constantly being drawn to distinguish between those who belong and those who, because of some perceived cultural difference, are deemed to be out of place and the source of pollution.[24] In South Africa during the early decades of this century, an artificial divide was drawn between rural and urban Africans which implied that black bodies were out of place in white cities. This led in time to the clearest articulation of the 'race problem' in the apartheid city, with the attempt to construct homogeneous black identities and confine them safely in spatially segregated townships.

The barriers between these racialized spaces were drawn both through routine bureaucratic procedures and everyday spatial practices. Under apartheid, vibrant mixed urban areas such as Sophiatown and District Six were destroyed in the name of 'slum clearance'. The denial of urban residential rights to millions of black South Africans had at root the idea that the proper place of the 'native' was in the rural areas, where authentic African cultures could be preserved. Despite a long legacy of colonial discourse on rural and urban African identities, the binaries it proposed tended to collapse under the pressure of contemporary urban realities, as they did in Crossroads in the early 1980s. The violent conflict there redrew the boundaries around complex and shifting political and social identities in a clear and unambiguous way.

The state also tapped into the gendered and generational nature of traditional power and authority. The militant politics of youth and women activists was seen by both the Fathers and the state to have violated and inverted traditional age and gender hierarchies. By violently expelling the comrades it was believed that the naturalized order of African patriarchal authority would be restored.

During 1976, and again in the 1980s, Crossroads experienced socio-spatial cycles of residential mixing and segregation that were in many ways similar to the residential patterns produced through urban violence in divided cities such as Belfast. Murray and Boal[25] and Feldman[26] write about the complex ways in which previously mixed residential areas in North Belfast undergo a process of spatial rigidification that culminates in the expulsion of 'outsiders' and the production of ethnically homogeneous spaces with ossified boundaries. The prior situation of fluid social boundaries is replaced with one in which communities are barricaded in highly segregated neighbourhoods.

> Within an urban system ... violence can be seen as an important factor in shaping spatial structure. The periodic outbreaks of sectarian violence in Belfast and the enduring memory of them have been a powerful force maintaining high levels of ethnic segregation and territoriality ... During years of peace, the relaxation of tensions results in hundreds of families venturing out of segregated districts and thus increasing the degree of residential mixing. When strife occurs, however, these households are among the first victims; direct attacks or intimidation forces the local minority to flee to the security of their co-religionists. In this context the control of space is of crucial importance for the securities it offers and opportunities it provides, violence becomes a deliberate tool of social engineering. It is used, as in the case of North Belfast, both to defend space against invasion and to gain new territory ... it is a means of ensuring social homogeneity.[27]

In his attempt to understand urban violence on the East Rand in the 1990s, Mahmood Mamdani[28] has explored the position of Inkatha-aligned migrants in the townships, hostels and shanty towns. Mamdani questions the explanatory power of various accounts, whether these focus on violence as a product of third force sponsorship and instigation, the alienation experienced by hostel dwellers in the cities, or the strategies deployed by marginalized migrants seeking access to scarce resources. Although he concedes that there may be an element of truth in each of these arguments, he questions their failure to take agency and political choice into proper consideration. Even in circumstances of dire material need, he argues, political choice does exist; Zulu tradition was not simply imposed on migrants 'from above', it was also voluntarily reproduced 'from below'. The ANC and the UDF failed to take the specific needs and aspirations of migrants into account, failed to present them with a viable alternative, and this made it considerably easier for Inkatha and the apartheid state to recruit migrants.[29] Moreover, the threat to their urban base posed by the ANC's demand that

Vigilante in satellite camp.

hostels be turned into family units made this move almost inevitable.

While Mamdani's analysis provides insights into the conditions and constraints that shaped individual political choices, it does not tell us much about how relatively fluid identities were suddenly fixed as a series of lethal binaries: Zulu and non-Zulu, rural and urban, traditionalist and progressive, hostel dweller and township resident, Inkatha and ANC. What actual mechanisms produced these ethnicized identities and social boundaries? The Crossroads conflict reveals how they were produced through spatialized practices of violence.

The barricades and roadblocks erected along Mahobe Drive and at the entrances into Crossroads provide the clearest physical markers of this process. It was on this interface, the very place where Ruth Kebisela's friends were hacked to death, that the boundaries between 'inside' and 'outside' were drawn in blood.

In post-apartheid South Africa, the idealization of rural space as the site of authentic African culture continues to find expression in the booming tourist industry of ethnic villages such as Shakaland and Namastad. At the same time, the globalization of multicultural tourism in the 1990s has meant that South African cities have also come to be celebrated as authentic African spaces. In recent years, while urban planners were seeking out vernacular architectural forms and African aesthetics, township tours have begun taking international visitors to shebeens and spaza shops to experience 'authentic' African urban life.

However, the landscapes of inclusion and exclusion have not simply evaporated. Although the permanence of blacks in the cities has finally been accepted, in Cape Town the racial grids of separation continue to divide the white, middle-class inner city and the leafy southern suburbs from the impoverished coloured and African townships of the Cape Flats. While the Cape Flats are clearly not what we would call 'rural', this is nonetheless a peri-urban space separated from the historically white areas by various barriers – buffer strips, highways, railway lines. And though these racially segregated spaces are no longer legislated, they are now sustained by a combination of the 'invisible hand of the market' and white fear of black criminality and violence. The advent of more or less exclusive shopping and entertainment malls in the white suburbs has intensified the polarization. In some parts of the city, for some people, black bodies are still out of place.

Photographs by Guy Tillim and Dave Hartman.

◄A12 ◄D11

Notes

Crime and the emerging landscape of post-apartheid Johannesburg

B2 Lindsay Bremner

1 M. Varder, 'Reliving a long day's journey into Johannesburg's night', *Mail & Guardian*, 16-22 January 1998 (Johannesburg), pp. 18, 19.

2 C. van Onselen, *Studies in the Social and Economic History of the Witwatersrand, 1886-1914* (2 vols, Johannesburg, Ravan, 1982), vol. 1, *New Babylon*, p. 23.

3 J. Robinson, 'Power, space and the city: Historical reflections on apartheid and post-apartheid urban orders' in D. Smith (ed.), *The Apartheid City and Beyond* (Johannesburg, Witwatersrand University Press, 1992), p. 294.

4 W.J.P. Carr, *Soweto: Its Creation, Life and Decline* (Johannesburg, South African Institute of Race Relations, 1990).

5 S. Oppler, 'Partners against crime' in *Policing the Transformation* (Halfway House, Institute for Security Studies, 1997), p. 53.

6 Varder, 'Reliving a long day's journey'.

7 M. Shaw, 'Crime in transition' in *Policing the Transformation*, p. 14.

8 Shaw, 'Crime in transition' in *Policing the Transformation*, p. 23.

9 Shaw, 'Crime in transition' in *Policing the Transformation*, p. 10.

10 Shaw, 'Crime in transition' in *Policing the Transformation*, p. 10.

11 Shaw, 'Crime in transition' in *Policing the Transformation*, p. 10.

12 Shaw, 'Crime in transition' in *Policing the Transformation*, p. 8.

13 L. Bremner, 'Development and resistance: The lessons for the planners of Phola Park', *Urban Forum*, 5:1 (1994), pp. 23-44.

14 J. May, 'Experience and perceptions of poverty in South Africa', Data Research Africa working paper (1996), p. 80, quoted in A. Louw and M. Shaw, *Stolen Opportunities: The Impact of Crime on South Africa's Poor* (Johannesburg, Institute for Security Studies, 1997).

15 Varder, 'Reliving a long day's journey'.

16 Greater Johannesburg Metropolitan Council, Planning, Urbanization and Environment Management Cluster (Johannesburg, GJMC, 1997).

17 D. Rodney, 'Terror teams pillaging Jo'burg suburbs', *Star*, 20 March 1997 (Johannesburg), p. 1.

18 C. Jacobs, 'Locking out the criminals', *Sunday Times* (Metro), 10 May 1998 (Johannesburg).

19 L. Madywabe, 'Soweto, where the only barrier between people and criminals is the front door', *Sunday Independent*, 18 May 1997 (Johannesburg), p. 11.

20 M. Shaw and L. Camera, *Policing the Transformation? New Issues in South Africa's Crime Debate* (Johannesburg, Institute for Defence Policy, 1996), p. 24.

21 D. Ehlers, I. Hirshfeld and C. Schutte, *Perceptions of Current Sociopolitical Issues in South Africa* (Pretoria, Human Sciences Research Council, 1996).

22 C. Marriott, 'Great Wall of suburbia keeps robbers out and owners in', *Star*, 2 May 1997 (Johannesburg), p. 9.

23 Shaw, 'Crime in transition' in *Policing the Transformation*, p. 20.

24 Oppler, 'Partners against crime' in *Policing the Transformation*, p. 59.

25 Ehlers et al., *Perceptions of Current Sociopolitical Issues*.

26 Louw and Shaw, *Stolen Opportunities*, p. 16; Madywabe, 'Soweto'.

27 R. Simmonds, 'Row over road closure', *North Eastern Tribune*, 5 June 1998 (Johannesburg), p. 1.

28 D. Shapshak, 'Close our street', *North Eastern Tribune*, 16 August 1996 (Johannesburg), p. 1.

29 G. Collins, 'Back to the laager for Jo'burg's rich suburbs', *Metro*, 19 May 1996 (Johannesburg), p. 3.

30 Collin Gregor, Managing Director, SBV (a cash-in-transit company).

31 See, for instance, C. Hani, 'Waiting for the next order', *Mayibuye*, 4 (1991), pp. 10-12; R. Kasrils, 'Kasrils on Umkhonto', *Work in Progress*, 68:8 (1990), pp. 7-10.

32 R. Williams, 'Changing the guard?', *Work in Progress*, 84:9 (1992), pp. 15-7.

33 Shaw, 'Crime in transition' in *Policing the Transformation*, p. 25.

34 D. Beresford, 'S.A. crime is getting organised', *Mail & Guardian*, 1998 (Johannesburg).

35 S. Grobbelaar, 'I set up the heists', *Star*, 7 March 1998 (Johannesburg), p. 1; S. Naidoo, '"Deep Throat" links police to cash heists', *Saturday Star*, 23 May 1998 (Johannesburg), p. 2.

36 D. Rodney, 'How deadly Heist Gang was born', *Star*, 28 January 1998 (Johannesburg), p. 1.

37 Simmonds, 'Row over road closure', p. 1.

38 X. Mangcu, 'Seeking common national values', *Mail & Guardian*, 5-11 June 1998 (Johannesburg), p. 28.

Homesteads and headrests

B11 Rayda Becker

1 P. Harries, 'Labour migration from Mozambique to South Africa; with special reference to the Delagoa Bay hinterland, c. 1862 to 1897', Ph.D. thesis (London, University of London, 1983), p. 110.

2 See P. Harries, *Work, Culture, and Identity: Migrant Labourers in Mozambique and South Africa, c. 1860-1910* (Johannesburg, Ravan Press, 1994).

3 R. Sieber, *African Furniture and Household Objects* (Bloomington and London, Indiana University Press, 1980), p. 17.

4 Sieber, *African Furniture*, p. 17.

5 A. Wanless, 'Headrests in the Africana Museum', Parts 1-9, *Africana Notes and News*, 26:6, 26:7, 27:2, 27:5, 27:8, 28:3, 28:7, 29:2, 29:4 (1985-90); Parts 10-11, unpublished.

6 Wanless No. 327 (79/565) and No. 340 (65/5255).

7 Harries, 'Labour migration', p. 154.

8 See E. Schneider, *Ndebele*, The Heritage Library of African People (New York, Rosen Publishing, 1997), p. 50; and Harries, *Work, Culture, and Identity*, pp. 208-9.

9 Sandra Klopper observes that Zulu headrests are found at Mai-Mai, but the two statements are not necessarily contradictory: whatever other social changes are indicated by the availability of headrests at an urban market, it may also be a sign precisely that headrests are still being left at migrants' rural homes. See S. Klopper, 'The art of Zulu-speakers in Northern Natal-Zululand: An investigation of the history of beadwork, carving and dress from Shaka to Inkatha', Ph.D. thesis (Johannesburg, University of the Witwatersrand, 1992), p. 118, note 34.

10 I. Powell, *Ndebele: A People and their Art* (Cape Town, Struik, 1995).

11 See, for instance, M. Courtney-Clarke, *Ndebele: The Art of an African Tribe* (New York, Rizzoli, 1986).

Whited sepulchres: On the reluctance of monuments

C4 David Bunn

1 K. Blixen, *Out of Africa* (Harmondsworth, Penguin, 1979 (1937)), p. 304.

2 Blixen, *Out of Africa*, p. 307.

3 J. Young, *The Texture of Memory: Holocaust Memorials and Meaning* (New Haven, Yale University Press, 1993), p. 2.

4 Blixen, *Out of Africa*, p. 308.

5 See, for instance, D. Greig, *Herbert Baker in South Africa* (Cape Town, Purnell, 1970), and D. Picton-Seymour, *Historical Buildings in South Africa* (Cape Town, Struikhof, 1989).

6 Two important articles by Peter Merrington have helped to undermine the myths of foundation attached to Baker by architectural historians. Amongst others, see P. Merrington, 'Pageantry and primitivism: Dorothea Fairbridge and the "Aesthetics of Union"', *Journal of Southern African Studies*, 21:4 (December 1995), pp. 643-56; and 'Masques, monuments, and masons: The 1910 Pageant of the Union of South Africa', *Theatre Journal*, 49:1 (March 1997), pp. 1-14. For a concise overview of Baker's Arts and Crafts influences, see M. Attwell and A. Berman, 'Arts and Crafts and Baker's Cape style', *Architecture SA*, July/August (1992), pp. 27-9.

7 Quoted in F. Bird, 'Herbert Baker in hindsight: Why cast him in bronze?', *Architecture SA*, July/August (1992), p. 25.

8 Cathy Mills cites this quotation from the *Church Chronicle* of 1905 in her 'Sir Herbert Baker's early churches at the Cape', *Architecture SA*, July/August (1992), p. 34.

9 Sir H. Rider Haggard, *She, King Solomon's Mines, Allan Quatermain* (New York, Dover, 1951), p. 48.

10 For a good account of this tour see H. Wittenberg, 'Rhodes Memorial: Imperial aesthetics and the politics of prospect', paper presented at a Centre for African Studies seminar, University of Cape Town, 20 March 1996, pp. 6-7.

11 Quoted in M. Keith, *Herbert Baker: Architecture and Idealism, 1892-1913* (Gibraltar, Ashanti, 1990), p. 30.

12 Haggard, *She, King Solomon's Mines, Allan Quatermain*, p. 327.

13 Quoted in L. McNay, *Foucault: A Critical Introduction* (Cambridge, Polity Press, 1994), p. 120.

14 H. Bhabha, *The Location of Culture* (London, Routledge, 1993), p. 248.

15 J. Laband, *Rope of Sand* (Johannesburg, Jonathan Ball, 1995), p. 381.

16 C. Hamilton, 'Theophilus Shepstone and the making of Rider Haggard's Shaka', paper presented at a Centre for African Studies seminar, University of Cape Town, September 1995.

17 N. Cope, *To Bind the Nation: Solomon kaDinizulu and Zulu Nationalism 1913-1933* (Pietermaritzburg, University of Natal Press, 1993), pp. 258-61.

18 André du Toit was almost single-handedly responsible for challenging this 'Calvinist paradigm' of Afrikaner history. See his 'No chosen people: The myth of the Calvinist origins of Afrikaner nationalism and racial ideology', *American Historical Review*, 88 (1983), pp. 920-52.

19 J.J. Oberholster, *The Historical Monuments of South Africa* (Cape Town, Rembrandt Van Rijn Foundation, 1972), pp. 197-8.

20 Imperialist wars such as the South African War completely transformed the landscape of rural districts. Hundreds of miles of barbed-wire fences were erected to control Boer commandos, and chains of blockhouses built to guard bridges and railroads. For a provocative account of fencing and the transformation of the South African landscape, see I. Hofmeyr, *'We Spend Our Years as a Tale That Is Told': Oral Historical Narrative in a South African Chiefdom* (Johannesburg, Witwatersrand University Press, 1993), Chapter 3.

21 S. Žižek, *The Sublime Object of Ideology* (London, Verso, 1989), p. 87.

22 One of the best descriptions of this epic saga is in A. McClintock, *Imperial Leather* (London, Routledge, 1995), pp. 370-9.

23 McClintock, *Imperial Leather*, p. 373.

24 C. Rassool and L. Witz, 'The 1952 Jan van Riebeeck Tercentenary Festival: Constructing and contesting public national history in South Africa', *Journal of African History*, 34 (1993), p. 449.

25 Quoted in E. Delmont, 'The Voortrekker Monument: Monolith to myth', paper presented at the Myths, Monuments, Museums Conference, University of the Witwatersrand History Workshop, Johannesburg, 16 July 1992, p. 10.

26 D. O'Meara, *Forty Lost Years: The Apartheid State and the Politics of the National Party, 1948-1994* (Athens, Ohio, Ohio University Press, 1996), p. 173.

27 See 'Head Office, Training and Distribution Centre, BMW', 1984 Project Awards, *Architecture SA*, November/December (1984), pp. 38-41.

28 Federasie van Afrikaanse Kultuurvereniginge (FAK), *Afrikanerbakens* (Johannesburg, FAK, 1989).

29 FAK, *Afrikanerbakens*, p. 30.

30 FAK, *Afrikanerbakens*, p. 30.

31 *Architect and Builder*, June (1962), p. 3.

32 FAK, *Afrikanerbakens*, p. 30.

33 Jane Carruthers offers the most comprehensive explanation of this process. See also my meditations on the neighbouring game reserve, Mala Mala, in 'Comparative barbarism: Game reserves, sugar plantations, and the modernization of South African landscape' in K. Darian-Smith, L. Gunner and S. Nuttall (eds.), *Text, Theory, Space* (London, Routledge, 1996), pp. 37-52.

34 U. De V. Pienaar, *Neem Uit die Verlede* (Pretoria, National Parks Board, 1990), pp. 534-5.

35 *Sunday Times*, 14 August 1968.

36 *Die Burger*, 28 November 1968.

37 The following sequence partly summarizes a far fuller description in my article 'The sleep of the brave: Graves as sites and signs in the colonial Eastern Cape', forthcoming in P. Landau (ed.), *Images and Empires* (New Haven, Yale University Press, 1998).

38 There are several good studies of Ntaba ka Ndoda, including J.B. Peires, 'Ethnicity and pseudo-ethnicity in the Ciskei' in L. Vail (ed.), *The Creation of Tribalism in South Africa* (Los Angeles, University of California Press, 1989), pp. 395-413; M.G. Whisson and C.W. Manona, 'Maqoma and Ciskeian politics today' in N. Charlton (ed.), *Ciskei: Economics and Politics of Dependence in a South African Homeland* (London, Croom Helm, 1980), pp. 214-27; and others.

39 *Daily Dispatch*, 12 April 1982.

40 J. Rushmere, 'Ntaba ka Ndoda: A concept', East London, Erasmus Rushmere Reid, n.d.

41 Rushmere, 'Ntaba ka Ndoda'.

42 I am thinking here of Žižek's description of the recourse to nationalism in Eastern Europe after the disappearance of the 'vanishing mediator' of Soviet communism (*The Sublime Object*, pp. 231-7).

43 C. Crais, *The Making of the Colonial Order: White Supremacy and Black Resistance in the Eastern Cape, 1770-1865* (Johannesburg, Witwatersrand University Press, 1992); J. Comaroff and J. Comaroff, *Of Revelation and Revolution Volume 2* (Chicago, University of Chicago Press, 1997), p. 309.

44 C.A. Harrop-Allin, *Norman Eaton: Architect* (Cape Town, Struik, 1975), pp. 69-70.

45 Harrop-Allin, *Norman Eaton*, p. 68.

46 M. Hutton-Squire, 'Mmabatho, capital of Bophuthatswana: Its planning and development', *Architecture SA*, Autumn (1981), p. 39.

47 Hutton-Squire, 'Mmabatho', p. 41.

48 Hutton-Squire, 'Mmabatho', p. 44.

49 Mallows himself refers to Haussmann's Paris as an ideal example of a 'strong visual overall design statement'. See E.W.N. Mallows, 'Mmabatho – A reply', *Architecture SA*, August (1981), p. 43.

50 M. Hall, 'The legend of the Lost City; Or, the man with golden balls', *Journal of Southern African Studies*, 21:2 (June 1995), pp. 179-99.

'Ons bou vir die Bank': Nationalism, architecture and Volkskas Bank

D3 Melinda Silverman

1 *'Ons bou vir die Bank'* is the title of a reference work published internally by Volkskas documenting the buildings occupied by each branch of the bank since its inception in 1934 until 1964 – the date of publication. The two embossed and leather-bound volumes that constitute the work were assembled by Carl Engelbrecht, manager of the property division of Volkskas. Reporting to the sixth managers' conference in 1964, Engelbrecht explained that his work could equally have been entitled *Die Ideale Bank*, but because the *Groot Afrikaanse Woordeboek* did not include the bank building itself in its definition of the word 'bank', he had to rely on another title: *'Ons sê mos: ons bou 'n bank as ons 'n gebou vir die Bank oprig'* ['After all, we say we are building a bank when we erect a building for the bank']. Or more evocatively, *'Ons bou vir die Bank, U bou aan die Bank, maar saam bou ons Volkskas, die Bank'* ['We are building *for* the Bank, you are building *up* the Bank, but together we are building Volkskas, the Bank'] (Sesde Bestuurders Konferensie, Bloemfontein, 1964). The title of this essay acknowledges the importance ascribed to the bank buildings as expressions of the bank's ideals. In addition to the sources below, the essay draws on interviews conducted in 1998 with Carl Engelbrecht, Volkskas archivist and erstwhile property manager; Dr Piet Snyman, ABSA Group heritage consultant; and Gawie Fagan.

2 *'Die monument versinnebeeld ons eiendomsreg op hierdie land.'* ['The monument symbolizes our right of ownership to this land.'] Gerard Moerdyk, architect of the Voortrekker Monument, in *Huisgenoot*, 25 November 1949.

3 C. Engelbrecht, *Die Bank van Oom Bossie* [Uncle Bossie's Bank] (Pretoria, Volkskas, 1978) and *Van Akker tot Eik* [From Acorn to Oak] (Pretoria, Volkskas, 1981).

4 Engelbrecht, *'Ons bou vir die Bank'*, epigraph.

5 D. O'Meara, *Volkskapitalisme: Class, Capital and Ideology in the Development of Afrikaner Nationalism, 1934-1948* (Johannesburg, Ravan Press, 1983), p. 55.

6 Quoted in O'Meara, *Volkskapitalisme*, p. 65.

7 O'Meara, *Volkskapitalisme*, p. 71.

8 P. De V. Pienaar, *Kultuurgeskiedenis van die Afrikaner* (Cape Town, Nasionale Boekhandel, 1968), p. 130 (quote originally in Afrikaans).

9 *Volkshandel*, June 1947.

10 O'Meara, *Volkskapitalisme*, p. 102.

11 In a 1936 article entitled *'Die boukuns as faktor in ons kultuurstryd'* ['Architecture as a factor in our cultural struggle'] Moerdyk made a strident call for an architecture produced *'deur mense besiel met die Afrikaanse ideaal van 'n aparte Afrikaanse kultuur ...'* ['by people inspired by the Afrikaans ideal of a separate Afrikaans culture']. *Die Burger*, 24 September 1936.

12 *'Die ontwikkeling van eie Suid-Afrikaanse boustyl: Uitheemse invloede werk dit sterk teen'* ['The development of a South African architecture: Foreign influences work strongly against it'], *Die Vaderland*, 17 September 1932.

13 *Die Burger*, 10 April 1933.

14 'J.A. Smith commented at length on the Cape Dutch style of architecture which the board would like applied to bank buildings. He has doubts about the desirability of applying the style.' Quoted (in Afrikaans) in Engelbrecht, *'Ons bou vir die Bank'*.

15 *Huisgenoot*, 25 November 1949.

16 'Hoggenheimer was the Semitic-featured caricature of *Die Burger*'s cartoons, the racist symbol for monopoly capital in all its forms. The term was also used interchangeably with "Imperialism" ... It is a corruption of the name of the "Hochenheimer" estate of arch-imperialist mining magnate Sir Percy Fitzpatrick.' O'Meara, *Volkskapitalisme*, p. 258.

17 C. Chipkin, *Johannesburg Style: Architecture & Society 1880s-1960s* (Cape Town, David Philip, 1993), p. 281.

18 Chipkin, *Johannesburg Style*, p. 281.

19 D. Posel, 'Modernity and measurement: Further thoughts on the apartheid state', paper presented to the Institute for Advanced Social Research, University of the Witwatersrand, 1996, p. 13. And see Posel's essay in this volume.

20 Posel, 'Modernity and measurement', p. 13 (footnote).

21 Quoted by Tim Clynick in 'A *boerevolk* for a *boerestand*?: *Broedertwis* and two manuscripts of platteland modernity, c. 1959', paper presented to the Institute for Advanced Social Research, University of the Witwatersrand, 1994, p. 6.

22 Clynick, 'A *boerevolk* for a *boerestand*?', p. 2.

23 See the comment about cooperation with 'our English friends' in Engelbrecht, *Van Akker tot Eik*, p. 59.

24 An article from *Die Oosterlig*, 9 September 1958, entitled *'Bantoe kry eie bank'* ['Bantu get their own bank'] quoted in Engelbrecht, *Van Akker tot Eik*, p. 65, mentions *'die naturelle-inwoners van Natalspruit wat 'n geweldige groot koopkrag het'* ['the native residents of Natalspruit who have enormous buying power'].

25 Notwithstanding considerable efforts to develop an industrial and hence an urban base, 83 per cent of Volkskas branches were still in the platteland in 1965 (Engelbrecht, *Van Akker tot Eik*, p. 434).

26 R. Fisher and S. le Roux, *Architecture of the Transvaal* (Pretoria, UNISA, 1998).

27 In a speech entitled 'Ons geboue' [Our buildings] delivered in 1968, Hurter, in reviewing the bank's architectural project, articulated his reservations about the possibility of modernizing the Cape Dutch style: *'Ek vind dit jammer dat daar in ons land nie 'n eie Suid-Afrikaanse boustyl ontwikkel het wat sakegeboue betref nie. In die verlede het die Bank self probeer om die Kaaps-Hollandse boustyl te moderniseer maar sonder oortuigende*

resultate.' ['I find it a pity that a South African national style of architecture hasn't developed in our country as far as commercial buildings are concerned. In the past the Bank itself tried to modernize the Cape Dutch style but without convincing results.'] Engelbrecht, *Van Akker tot Eik*, p. 214.

28 Fisher, 'The third vernacular'.

29 D. Japha, 'The birth of the state housing policy', seminar presented at the Architecture Student Conference, University of the Witwatersrand, 1986.

30 G. Herbert, *Martienssen and the International Style: The Modern Movement in South African Architecture* (Cape Town and Rotterdam, A.A. Balkema, 1975), p. 152.

31 S. Giedion, *Space, Time and Architecture: The Growth of a New Tradition* (Cambridge, Mass., Harvard University Press, 1947), p. 392.

32 G. Fagan, 'Regionalism', seminar presented at the Architecture Student Conference, University of Cape Town, 1985, p. 5.

33 Interview with Carl Engelbrecht.

34 Fisher, 'The third vernacular'.

35 Engelbrecht, *Van Akker tot Eik*, p. 124.

36 Engelbrecht, *Van Akker tot Eik*, p. 124.

37 Fagan, 'Regionalism', p. 1.

38 Fagan, 'Regionalism', p. 2.

39 Eaton, quoted by Fagan, 'Regionalism', p. 2.

40 Fagan, 'Regionalism', p. 6.

41 See 'Standard plan for a post office', 1914, by P. Eagle for the Public Works Department of the Union of South Africa. National Archive, Pretoria, S262.

42 Interview with Barbara Conradie, Chief Archivist for the Standard Bank, Johannesburg, 1998.

43 Sesde Bestuurders Konferensie, Bloemfontein, 1964.

44 O'Meara, *Volkskapitalisme*, p. 254.

45 Engelbrecht, *Van Akker tot Eik*, p. 319.

46 Engelbrecht, *Van Akker tot Eik*, p. 320.

47 Engelbrecht, *Van Akker tot Eik*, p. 320.

48 Engelbrecht, *Van Akker tot Eik*, p. 320.

49 Engelbrecht, *Van Akker tot Eik*, p. 343.

Personal traits: The work of Eaton and Biermann in Durban

D5 Tony Morphet

1 Recent revelations at the Truth and Reconciliation Commission hearings into the programme for chemical and biological weapons show that these fantasies remained active right into the eighties.

2 The background and details of the crisis, as well as the way in which it was tackled, are given in P. Wilkinson, 'A discourse of modernity: The Social and Economic Planning Council's fifth report on Regional and Town Planning, 1944', *African Studies*, 55:2 (1996), pp. 141-81.

3 For details on the career of the famous Cape Dutch architect, Thibault, see B. Biermann, *Boukuns in Suid-Afrika* (Cape Town and Amsterdam, A.A. Balkema, 1955); and for Sir Herbert Baker and the school which developed under his direction see C.A. Harrop-Allin, *Norman Eaton: Architect* (Cape Town, Struik, 1975).

4 The standard work on Martienssen is the published doctoral thesis by G. Herbert, *Martienssen and the International Style: A Case Study in the Dissemination of the Modern Movement in Architecture* (Pretoria, University of South Africa, 1969). Herbert gives a full account of the close relation between Martienssen and Le Corbusier.

5 Le Corbusier quoted in F. Demissie, 'Modern architecture and the design of "native housing" in South Africa, 1925-1955', paper presented at the Displacements Conference, Northwestern University, Evanston, 1995.

6 Kurt Jonas, Roy Kantorowich and Norman Hanson were important participants in the debates. Details of the positions they took can be found in Derek Japha's essay in this volume, 'The social programme of the South African Modern Movement'. I am indebted to this essay (first presented at a Centre for African Studies seminar at the University of Cape Town in 1986) and to the paper by Peter Wilkinson noted above for information on the modern movement.

7 See Japha, 'The social programme'; and L. Mumford, *The Culture of Cities* (London, Secker and Warburg, 1938).

8 B. Biermann, *Boukuns in Suid-Afrika*.

9 B. Biermann, 'Diversity and interaction as the South African lifestyle', paper presented at the Fifth Annual Conference of the South African Association of Art Historians, Durban, 17-19 July 1989.

10 A. Preller, 'Foreword' in Harrop-Allin, *Norman Eaton*, p. 9.

11 P. Melvin, 'Barrie Biermann: The active contemplative', *Natal Institute of Architecture Journal*, 2 (1992), p. 2.

12 See the letters between Eaton and Hendricks quoted in R. Fisher, 'Norman Eaton: Some influences on his insights', *Journal of Cultural History*, 11:2 (November 1997), p. 82.

13 Lord Holford, 'An appreciation', *South African Architectural Review* (February 1967), p. 17.

14 J. Barnett, 'Save Barrie's house', *Natal Institute of Architecture Journal*, 2 (1992), p. 1.

15 Melvin, 'Barrie Biermann', p. 2.

16 Biermann, 'Diversity and interaction', p. 2.

17 Potchefstroom (1940), Pietermaritzburg (1941-3), Kroonstad (1943-4) and Ermelo (1944).

18 N. Eaton, 'Pretoria of the future', *South African Architectural Record* (November 1963), p. 22.

19 The details of the history of the Netherlands Bank are in S. Jones, *Financial Enterprise in South Africa since 1950* (Basingstoke, Macmillan, 1992).

20 The original design and structure took the screen round the four sides, the back of the building being laid out as a courtyard. The courtyard has since been lost as a result of further development on the site. For details see Harrop-Allin, *Norman Eaton*, p. 111.

21 B. Biermann, 'An appreciation', *South African Architectural Record* (February 1967), p. 21.

22 See details of the correspondence between Biermann and Willem Visser in C. Polwarth, 'A study of the influence of Barrie Biermann on the architectural culture of southern Africa', M.Arch. thesis (Durban, University of Natal, 1994).

23 B. Biermann, *Red Wine in South Africa* (Cape Town, Buren, 1971).

24 A. Verster, 'Planting palms in the desert', *Natal Institute of Architecture Journal*, 2 (1992), p. 7.

25 Holford, 'An appreciation', p. 16.

26 Harrop-Allin, *Norman Eaton*, p. 114.

27 A. Tzonis and L. Lefaivre, 'Critical regionalism' in M. Speaks (ed.), *The Critical Landscape* (Rotterdam, 010 Publishers, 1996), p. 134.

(Im)mobilizing space – dreaming of change

D7 Jennifer Robinson

1 Z. Mda, *Ways of Dying* (Cape Town, Oxford, 1995), p. 46.

2 Mda, *Ways of Dying*, p. 100.

3 Mda, *Ways of Dying*, p. 115.

4 Mda, *Ways of Dying*, p. 115.

5 A. Escobar and S. Alvarez (eds.), *The Making of Social Movements in Latin America: Identity, Strategy and Democracy* (Boulder, Westview Press, 1992).

6 A. Escobar, 'Culture, economics and politics in Latin American social movements theory and research' in Escobar and Alvarez, *The Making of Social Movements*, p. 69.

7 R. Behar, 'Rage and redemption: Reading the life story of a Mexican marketing woman', *Feminist Studies*, 16:2 (1990), p. 230, quoted in Escobar, 'Culture, economics and politics', p. 77.

8 A. Askew and W. Logan (eds.), *Cultural Identity and Urban Change in Southeast Asia: Interpretive Essays* (Geelong, Victoria, Deakin University Press, 1994); J. Comaroff and J. Comaroff (eds.), *Modernity and Its Malcontents: Ritual and Power in Postcolonial Africa* (Chicago, University of Chicago Press, 1993).

9 T.A. Simone, *In Whose Image? Political Islam and Urban Practices in Sudan* (Chicago, University of Chicago Press, 1994), p. 128.

10 H. Lefebvre, *The Production of Space* (Oxford, Basil Blackwell, 1991).

11 Lefebvre, *The Production of Space*, p. 326; D. Harvey, *The Urban Experience* (Oxford, Basil Blackwell, 1989).

12 Lefebvre, *The Production of Space*, p. 332.

13 See S. Pile, *The Body and the City* (London, Routledge, 1996), which establishes this reading of *The Production of Space*.

14 Lefebvre, *The Production of Space*, p. 39.

15 Pile, *The Body and the City*, p. 148.

16 Lefebvre, *The Production of Space*, p. 51.

17 Lefebvre, *The Production of Space*, p. 349.

18 S. Pile, 'Human agency and human geography revisited: A critique of "new models" of the self', *Transactions of the Institute of British Geographers*, 18 (1993), pp. 122-39; Pile, *The Body and the City*.

19 Lefebvre, *The Production of Space*, pp. 41-2.

20 See, for example, D. Cornell, *Beyond Accommodation: Ethical Feminism, Deconstruction and the Law* (London, Routledge, 1991).

21 S. Freud, *The Interpretation of Dreams* (London, Penguin, 1991 (1900)), p. 247.

22 Freud, *The Interpretation of Dreams*, p. 700.

23 Freud, *The Interpretation of Dreams*, p. 381.

24 Freud, *The Interpretation of Dreams*, p. 417.

25 Freud, *The Interpretation of Dreams*, p. 419.

26 See S. Pile, 'Freud, dreams and imaginative geographies' in A. Elliot (ed.), *Freud 2000* (Oxford, Polity Press, 1998).

27 See H. Nast and S. Pile (eds.), *Places through the Body* (London, Routledge, 1998), pp. 413-4.

28 J. Jacobs, *Edge of Empire: Postcolonialism and the City* (London, Routledge, 1995).

29 Lefebvre, *The Production of Space*, p. 52.

30 Lefebvre, *The Production of Space*, p. 54.

31 Lefebvre, *The Production of Space*, p. 317.

32 D. Dewar, 'The urban question in South Africa: The need for a planning paradigm shift', *Third World Planning Review*, 14:4 (1995), pp. 407-20.

33 A. Mabin, 'Conceptualizing, making and governing the Witwatersrand', paper presented at the Africa's Urban Past Conference, SOAS, London, June 1996.

34 J. Western, *Outcast Cape Town* (Berkeley, University of California Press, 1996 (1981)), p.xix.

35 D. Massey, J. Allen and S. Pile (eds.), *City Worlds* (London, Routledge, forthcoming 1999).

36 See Massey et al., *City Worlds*.

Globalization and the identity of African urban practices

D8 AbdouMaliq Simone

1 See in particular E.A. Swynegedoux, 'The Mammon quest: "Glocalisation", interspatial competition and monetary order – The construction of new spatial scales' in M. Dunford and G. Kafkalas (eds.), *Cities and Regions in the New Europe: The Global-Local Interplay and Spatial Development Strategies* (London, Belhaven, 1992), pp. 39-67; S. Sassen, *Cities in a World Economy* (Thousand Oaks, Pine Forge Press, 1994); K. Robins, 'Prisoners of the city: Whatever could a postmodern city be?' in E. Carter, J. Donald and J. Squires (eds.), *Space and Place* (London, New Formations/Lawrence and Wishart, 1993); E. Soja, 'Six discourses on the postmetropolis' in S. Westwood and J. Williams (eds.), *Imagining Cities: Scripts, Signs, Memory* (London and New York, Routledge, 1997); S. Sassen, 'Urban impacts of economic globalization' in J. Brotchie, M. Batty, E. Blakely, P. Hall and P. Newton (eds.), *Cities in Competition: Productive and Sustainable Cities for the 21st Century* (Melbourne, Longman Australia, 1995).

2 C. Monga, *The Anthropology of Anger: Civil Society and Democracy in Africa* (Boulder, Lynne Reinner, 1996); A. Appadurai, *Modernity at Large: Cultural Dimensions of Globalization* (Minneapolis, University of Minnesota Press, 1997); A. Bayat, 'Uncivil society: The politics of the "informal people"', *Third World Quarterly*, 18:1 (1997), pp. 53-72.

3 G. O'Tuathail and T. Luke, 'Present at the (dis)integration: Deterritorialization and reterritorialization in the new wor(l)d order', *Annals of the Association of American Geographers*, 84 (1994), pp. 381-98.

4 J. MacGaffey, *Entrepreneurs and Parasites: The Struggle for Capitalism in Zaïre* (Cambridge, Cambridge University Press, 1987); E. Aryeetey, 'Formal and informal economic activities' in S. Ellis (ed.), *Africa Now: People, Policies, and Institutions* (The Hague, DGIS, 1995).

5 A. Gupta and J. Ferguson, 'Beyond culture: Space, identity and the politics of difference', *Cultural Anthropology*, 7:1 (1992), pp. 6-24; M. Banya, 'Transnationalism', *Current Sociology*, 41:3 (1993), pp. 1-95; A. Appadurai, 'The production of locality' in R. Fardon (ed.), *Counterworks: Mapping the Diversity of Knowledge* (London, Routledge, 1995); M. Watts, 'A new deal in emotions' in J. Crush (ed.), *Power of Development* (London and New York, Routledge, 1995).

6 M. Keith, 'Conclusion: A changing space for a changing time' in S. Pile and M. Keith (eds.), *Geographies of Resistance* (London and New York, Routledge, 1997).

7 I. Amundsen, 'Afropessimism: A response from below?' in A. Ofstad and A. Wiig (eds.), *Development Theory: Recent Trends*, Proceedings of the NFU Annual Conference, Report 6 (Bergen, Chr. Michelsen Institute, 1993); J-C. Williame, L. Hugues and P. Rosenblum, 'Zaïre: Predicaments and prospects: A report to the Minority Rights Group', *Peaceworks*, 11 (1997).

8 I. Albert, J. Adisa, T. Agbola and G. Herault, *Urban Management and Urban Violence in Africa*, Proceedings of the International Symposium held at Ibadan, Nigeria, 7-11 November 1994 (Ibadan, Institut français de recherche en Afrique, 1994).

9 T.A. Simone, *In Whose Image Political Islam and Urban Practices in Sudan* (Chicago, University of Chicago Press, 1994).

10 E. Wamba dia Wamba, 'The struggles for the second independence in Congo' in P. Anyang'Nyong'o (ed.), *Popular Struggles for Democracy in Africa* (London, Zed, 1987); A. Kenz, 'Youth and violence' in Ellis, *Africa Now*; M. Diouf, 'Urban youth and Senegalese politics: Dakar 1988-1994', *Public Culture*, 8:2 (1996), pp. 225-49.

11 A. Mbembe and J. Roitman, 'Figures of the subject in times of crisis' in P. Yaegar (ed.), *The Geography of Identity* (Ann Arbor, University of Michigan Press, 1996).

12 Monga, *Anthropology of Anger*.

13 J. Bibangambah, 'Macro-level constraints and the growth of the informal sector in Uganda' in J. Baker and P. Pedersen (eds.), *The Rural-Urban Interface in Africa* (Uppsala, Scandinavian Institute of African Studies, 1992); J. Dawson and B. Oyeyinka, 'Structural adjustment and the urban informal sector in Nigeria', International Labour Organization Working Paper 65 (Geneva, 1993); J. MacGaffey and G. Windsperger, 'The endogenous economy', Background Paper for the Long-Term Prospectives Study for Sub-Saharan Africa: Institutional and Sociopolitical Issues (Washington, DC, World Bank).

14 Aryeetey, 'Formal and informal economic activities' in Ellis, *Africa Now*.

15 Simone, *In Whose Image*.

16 R. Tomlinson, R. Hunter, M. Jonker, C. Rogerson and J. Rogerson, 'Johannesburg inner-city strategic development framework: Economic analysis', Greater Johannesburg Transitional Metropolitan Council (Johannesburg, 1995).

17 O. Crankshaw and C. White, 'Survey of the Johannesburg central city', Group for Human Resources, Human Sciences Research Council (Pretoria, 1992).

18 S. Berry, 'Social institutions and access to resources', *Africa*, 59:1 (1988), pp. 40-55.

19 S. Barnes, *Patrons and Power: Creating a Political Community in Metropolitan Lagos* (Manchester, Manchester University Press, 1986).

20 Mbembe and Roitman, 'Figures of the subject'.

21 For a description of some of these dynamics see Cinergie, 'The real economy of the West African region: Retrospective analysis 1960-1990 and alternative visions for 2020', RESADOC, Sahel Institute Working Paper 2 (Bamako, 1994).

'Corpses behind screens': Native space in the city

D11 Gary Minkley

This essay draws extensively on material in the Cape Archives (CA), and especially on the East London municipal holdings (ELN). The notes also refer to the East London Municipality archive (ELM) held by the City Council; and the Border Chamber of Industries archive (BCI) in East London.

1 Interviews with residents of Mdantsane, Duncan Village and East London, two City Councillors, and a Meld representative, 6-15 July 1998, East London.

2 See photograph of East Bank Location from 1910 postcard, East London Museum. In the 1890s, when East Bank Location was established, black residents in East London were also segregated into a number of smaller locations including Fingo, Seaside, Newsam's Town, Wesleyan, West Bank and Cambridge. From about 1900, East Bank, West Bank and Cambridge locations survived, and East Bank (later called Duncan Village) became the largest and most significant.

3 See K. Tankard, 'The labyrinth of East London lore', 1997 (www.ru.ac.za/el/history) for images of what has come to be signified as the 'traditional Xhosa round hut'.

4 In colonial writing, 'primitive' African architecture, associated with imagined traditional, tribal and rural identities, was often characterized as 'wattle and daub'.

5 See also correspondence of Town Clerk, R.E. Dowding, and Minutes of Committee 'A' chaired by Cr M.T. Fleming, 21 September – 20 November 1917.

6 See also G. Minkley, 'Border dialogues: Race, class and space in the industrialization of East London, 1902-1963', Ph.D. thesis (Cape Town, University of Cape Town, 1994).

7 The squatter settlement became a determining concern in the Cape during the 1940s. In the Western Cape squatters were defined as people who lived in self-built housing on private land and paid rent for the occupied sites, or who occupied municipal and state land but in areas not designated as locations. These settlements and the self-built 'shackyard' sections of official locations became integrally linked, so that any one term – pondokkie, shack dweller, slum, tin town, shanty, hovel, overcrowding, and so on – tended to imply all the others. All the terms refer to the same object, namely the native and native space in the city, 'share the same style and support a strategy, a common institutional or political drift and pattern' (M. Cousins and A. Hussain, *Michel Foucault* (London, Macmillan, 1984), pp. 84-5).

8 See, for example, the Britten, Slarke and Cauldwell Reports for Cape Town, and the Thornton and Welsh Commissions for East London; and also the series of reports associated with the Fagan Commission of Enquiry. For a discussion of space as lived, perceived and conceived, see H. Lefebvre, *The Production of Space* (Oxford, Blackwell, 1991), p. 67; S. Pile, *The Body and the City, Psychoanalysis, Space and Subjectivity* (London, Routledge, 1996); and E. Soja, *Thirdspace: Journeys to Los Angeles and Other Real-and-Imagined Places* (Cambridge and Oxford, Blackwell, 1996).

9 See G. Minkley and N. Rousseau, 'The native crisis in the 1940s: Life histories, official representation and academic discourse', paper presented at the South African Historical Society Conference, Rhodes University, Grahamstown, July 1995; as well as Minkley, 'Border dialogues'.

10 See S.L. Foster, 'Introduction' in S.L. Foster (ed.), *Corporealities* (London, Routledge, 1996), pp. xi-xvii.

11 See Pile, *The Body and the City*, an enormously important work from which I draw with unstated acknowledgement, and especially Chapter 6. See also P. Stallybrass and A. White, *The Politics and Poetics of Transgression* (Ithaca, Cornell University Press, 1986), especially pp. 125-48.

12 See Pile, *The Body and the City*, pp. 174-81.

13 CA, 3/ELN, 918 reflects the way that Cr Taylor's statement (quoted above) about forcing overcrowding underground was also part of a discourse of moral degradation associated with the nature and presence of slum dwellers as native and tribal.

14 This quote from the Britten Report, p. 6, applies to the argument more generally, and is echoed in the Thornton and Welsh Reports on East London.

15 The term is taken from the official archive, particularly CA, 3/ELN, Boxes 1150-56, Correspondence, Location, General, 1947-56, but seems to have been drawn initially from meetings and correspondence with Cape Town City Council and Native Affairs staff. It means literally 'to become a kaffir', or 'to be made into a kaffir'.

16 Photographs in the municipal archives, and subsequently in P. and I. Mayer, Townsmen or Tribesmen: Conservatism and the Process of Urbanization in a South African City (Cape Town, Oxford University Press, 1961) demonstrate the associated 'picture theories'.

17 The term is from Doreen Massey, A Place in the World (Oxford, Open University/Oxford University Press, 1995). I use it in relation to the model township to suggest the double meanings of and routes to such a 'vision', and to reflect on the spatial ambiguities drawn out in Massey's formulation.

18 This is explored in some detail in my thesis 'Border dialogues'.

19 M. Hunter, Reaction to Conquest (London, Oxford University Press, 1936), pp. 446-7.

20 This paragraph draws on M. Vaughn, Curing Their Ills: Colonial Power and African Illness (Cambridge, Cambridge University Press, 1991); see also A. Ashforth, The Politics of Official Discourse in Twentieth Century South Africa (Oxford, Clarendon Press, 1990).

21 More generally Minkley, 'Border dialogues', pp. 198-231.

22 Mayer, Townsmen or Tribesmen, p. 46.

23 Minkley, 'Border dialogues', pp. 198-231. Although I am concerned here with how the location was perceived and conceived within a local power geometry, it goes without saying that the imposed distinctions were transgressed and contested. Let us hear just one dissenting voice, from a letter written by a resident to the City Council in the 1950s: '... there is more going on here than you can ever know. The Location is never silent and obedient, it does not only listen to you, and I see things you cannot.'

24 J. Robinson, 'The power of apartheid: Territoriality and state power in South African cities – Port Elizabeth, 1923-1972', Ph.D. thesis (Cambridge, Cambridge University, 1990).

25 More generally see Minkley, 'Border dialogues', Chapters 5 and 8.

26 See Minkley, 'Border dialogues', Chapter 8; and E. Nel, 'The spatial planning of racial residential segregation in East London, 1948-1973', MA thesis (Johannesburg, University of the Witwatersrand, 1990).

27 See Minkley, 'Border dialogues', pp. 310-31.

28 Hunter, Reaction to Conquest, pp. 446-7.

29 Various sections of the township had unofficial names, which later found their way into official discourse. One section was ironically named New Brighton (after the new Port Elizabeth municipal township), Tulandivile ('Keep quiet, I have understood'), Maxambeni (after sugar pockets hidden during police liquor raids) and Gomorra or Gommora ('Place of sin').

30 These terms are drawn almost at random from the official archive, particularly CA, 3/ELN, and the Daily Dispatch, and reflect the dominant representations at the time. See Minkley, 'Border dialogues', especially Chapters 5 and 8.

31 See also Minkley, 'Border dialogues', Chapter 5.

32 D. Haraway, Modest Witness – @Second – Millennium: Feminism and Technoscience (New York and London, Routledge, 1997), pp. 135-6.

33 See P. Rabinow, Essays on the Anthropology of Reason (Princeton, Princeton University Press, 1996), pp. 59-79. On the South African planning nexus around 'new men' and 'township spaces' see Costs of Urban Bantu Housing (Pretoria, Council for Scientific and Industrial Research, 1954), which extends the ideas in A Guide to the Planning of Non-European Townships (Pretoria, National Housing Office, 1951) and Minimum Standards of Accommodation for Non-Europeans (Pretoria, National Housing Office, 1951).

34 Rabinow, Essays, p. 77. There have been important explanatory discussions of this moment in urban planning and subsequent developments. Amongst others, Mabin and Smit deal with the wider social and political-economic impetuses and the bureaucratic, investigative and internal workings (institutional presences) of the various state departments; Parnell and Mabin with relationships and differences between local and central state, and the influences of 'modernism'; and Bozzoli with the subsequent emergence of what she calls 'high racial modernism' and its effect on township rule and experience from the 1960s onwards. See A. Mabin and D. Smit, 'Reconstructing South Africa's cities: The making of urban planning 1900-2000', Planning Perspectives, 12:2 (1997), pp. 193-223; S. Parnell and A. Mabin, 'Rethinking urban South Africa', Journal of Southern African Studies, 21:1 (1995), pp. 39-61; B. Bozzoli, 'From governability to ungovernability: Power, class, and authority in South Africa's black cities', paper presented at the Africa seminar, University of Cape Town, 25 September 1996.

35 A. Mabin, 'Bureaucracy, class and design: The planning of the "townships" from the forties to the nineties – an outline', paper presented at the Work, Class and Culture Symposium, University of the Witwatersrand, Johannesburg, 28-30 June 1993, pp. 1-15; subsequently developed in Mabin and Smit, 'Reconstructing South Africa's cities' and Parnell and Mabin, 'Rethinking urban South Africa'.

36 Rabinow, Essays, pp. 74-8.

37 Calderwood was Senior Research Officer in the Architectural Division of the Institute.

38 Rabinow, Essays, p. 74.

39 Haraway, Modest Witness, p. 15.

40 F.R. Rodseth, F. van Heerden and J.E. Jennings, 'Native housing research in South Africa', National Building Research Institute Bulletin, 6 (June 1951), pp. 7-15. Rodseth was the Under-Secretary (Administration) of the Native Affairs Department, Van Heerden the Secretary of the National Housing Office and Jennings the Director of the National Building Research Institute.

41 Connell was then Professor of Architecture at the University of Natal.

42 Rabinow, Essays, p. 77.

43 For a fuller discussion of this period see Minkley, 'Border dialogues', Chapter 8 and Nel, 'The spatial planning of racial residential segregation'.

44 Bantu, May 1976. The descriptions can be found in a range of places. I have drawn on G. Cook and J. Opland (eds.), Mdantsane: Transitional City (Grahamstown, Institute for Social and Economic Research, Rhodes University, 1980); M. Nash and N. Charton (eds.), An Empty Table? (Athlone, South African Council of Churches, 1981); J. Lelyveld, Move Your Shadow (Johannesburg, Jonathan Ball, 1986); the Quail Report of the Ciskei Commission, 1980; and Ciskei Information Service, Land of Opportunity, Ciskei (East London, CIS, 1975).

45 For more details on the Bantustan policies and on the Ciskei, see SPP Report, The Eastern Cape.

46 T. Gordon, 'Mdantsane: The evolution of a dependency' in Cook and Opland, Mdantsane, p. 10.

47 Gordon, 'Evolution of a dependency', pp. 1-26.

48 Gordon, 'Evolution of a dependency', p. 11.

49 See Lelyveld, Move Your Shadow, pp. 156-7. Lelyveld explains that when the Ciskei became 'independent' and disappeared from South African references, in the telephone book, for example, Mdantsane became an 'international city', and Ciskei was classified between China (Taiwan) and Cyprus.

50 See Gordon, 'Evolution of a dependency', p. 15; also interviews with Mdantsane residents conducted by the author in December 1990 to January 1991 and in 1993/4.

51 E. Joubert, The Long Journey of Poppie Nongena (Johannesburg, Jonathan Ball/Southern Books, 1981), pp. 200-1, 205.

52 See N. Haysom, Ruling with the Whip (Braamfontein, Development Studies Group, Southern African Research Service, 1983), pp. 1-90; Interviews with residents, 1990-4, pp. 47-8.

53 These comments on the location build on my 'Border dialogue', Chapters 5-8; and in general terms also on Bozzoli, 'From governability'. The arguments about Mdantsane are significantly shaped by interviews conducted in 1990-4.

54 M. de Certeau, The Practice of Everyday Life (Berkeley, Los Angeles and London, University of California Press, 1984), pp. 115-30.

55 Joubert, Poppie Nongena, p. 225. For a discussion of this 'fiction', which contains significant elements of Nongena's own life history, see A. McClintock, Imperial Leather (London, Routledge, 1995).

56 D.R. Matravers, 'It's all in a day's work' in Cook and Opland, Mdantsane, pp. 45-6.

57 Interviews with residents, 1990-4.

58 See N. Haysom, Ruling with the Whip.

59 Interviews with residents, 1990-4.

60 Interview with resident, December 1991.

61 For a richly suggestive comparative work, on which I have drawn extensively here, see D. Taylor, Disappearing Acts: Spectacles of Gender and Nationalism in Argentina's Dirty War (Durham and London, Duke University Press, 1997), Chapter 5.

62 The term is loosely borrowed from Soja, Thirdspace, where it is borrowed in turn from Lefebvre, The Production of Space.

63 These stories may be traced in newspaper reports, political and official documents, biographies and interviews of the 1980s, and also in contemporary stories told before the Truth and Reconciliation Commission. An Umgqkomo lorry is a municipal vehicle, especially one of the old square police vans.

64 See I. de Kok, 'Cracked heirlooms: Memory on exhibition' in S. Nuttall and C. Coetzee (eds.), The Making of Memory in South Africa (Cape Town, Oxford University Press, 1998), p. 69.

65 See De Kok, 'Cracked heirlooms', p. 70.

66 See De Kok, 'Cracked heirlooms', p. 70.

67 See Taylor, Disappearing Acts, p. 139: 'Much like the corpse, empty of its soul, representations of death refer to an absence of full meaning by signalling the presence of meaning elsewhere ... both conceal and reveal at the same time; both are doubled in that they point to what is absent and to their own act of representing.'

68 De Certeau, The Practice of Everyday Life, p. 123.

The native heart: The architecture of the University of Pretoria campus

E2 Roger Fisher

1 For information on the University of Pretoria this essay draws on C.H. Rautenbach (ed.), Ad Destinatum: Gedenkboek van die Universiteit van Pretoria, 1910-1960 (Johannesburg, Voortrekkerpers, 1960); and F.J. Spies and D.H. Heydenrych, Ad Destinatum II: 'n Geskiedenis van die Universiteit van Pretoria, 1960-1982 (Pretoria, University of Pretoria, 1987). Biographical information on South African figures is from the Dictionary of South African Biography (5 volumes, Pretoria, Human Sciences Research Council, 1968-87); and

information on architects is from an electronic database by J. Walker, *Biographies of South African Architects until 1940* (Pietermaritzburg, National Monuments Council, 1995).
2 F.L. Cachet, *De Worstelstrijd de Transvalers; aan het volk van Nederland verhaald* (Amsterdam, Kruyt, 1882).
3 *South African Architectural Record*, 43:6 (1958), p. 40. The obituary read: 'We regret to record the death of Dr G.L.P. Moerdyk late of 65, Saambou Buildings, Andries St, Pretoria.'
4 J. Hambidge, *The Elements of Dynamic Symmetry* (New York, Dover, 1967 (1919)).
5 See G. Herbert, *Martienssen and the International Style: The Modern Movement in South African Architecture* (Cape Town, Balkema, 1975), p. 184.
6 W.D. Howie (ed.), 'Die argitektuur van Pretoria', *South African Architectural Record*, 50:12 (1965), pp. 45-56.
7 N. Pevsner, 'Johannesburg: The development of a contemporary vernacular', *Architectural Review*, 113:678 (1953), pp. 361-82.
8 O. Groats, 'Modern shell roof structures in South Africa', *South African Architectural Record*, 35:4 (1950), pp. 75-8.

Does size matter? The apartheid state's powers of penetration
E3 Deborah Posel
1 C. Chipkin, *Johannesburg Style: Architecture & Society 1880s-1960s* (Cape Town, David Philip, 1993), p. 278.
2 Chipkin, *Johannesburg Style*, p. 279.
3 P.A. Brynard, 'Administrative reform' in S.X. Hanekom, R. Rowland and E. Bain (eds.), *Key Aspects of Public Administration* (Johannesburg, Macmillan, 1986), p. 221.
4 Z. Baumann, *Modernity and the Holocaust* (Cambridge, Polity Press, 1989), p. 113.
5 Union of South Africa, *Social and Economic Planning Council: Report No. 3 – Aspects of Public Service Organisation and Employment* (Pretoria, Government Printer, 1944), UG 15-44, paragraph 4.
6 Union of South Africa, *Social and Economic Planning Council*, paragraph 5.
7 *House of Assembly Debates*, 1964, volume 11, column 5944.
8 Addressing parliament, one United Party MP referred to figures cited by 'a University of South Africa professor' to the effect that between 1937 and 1966 'the number of civil service employees has increased by 276% [at the same time as] ... the white population increased by only 70%'. *House of Assembly Debates*, 1969, volume 26, column 4457.
9 The idea of the 'public service' encompasses the civil service, but also includes those agencies and workers directly involved in the provision of services – nurses, educators, police and prison personnel, and so on. The 'civil service' refers more narrowly to those agencies and workers directly engaged in the running of government departments and implementing government policy decisions.
10 Republic of South Africa, *Public Services Commission: 50th Annual Report*, RP 26/1962, annexure A.
11 Republic of South Africa, *Public Services Commission: 56th Annual Report*, RP 39/1968, annexure A. Note that statistics compiled by the PSC after 1967 use a different basis of measurement, so that it is not possible to make coherent comparisons before and after 1967.
12 According to these figures, the most dramatic rate of expansion of the permanent establishment occurred prior to 1951 – an increase of 110% from 1938. However, the data cited in the next paragraph, which take temporary appointees into account, produce a different picture, showing the decade of 1950-60 to have been the period of most accelerated growth in the public service.
13 These figures are not entirely compatible with the data from the Public Services Commission cited in the previous paragraph; when the numbers of temporary appointees are excluded, the data used here still measure a larger permanent establishment than the PSC – a reminder that all these statistics need to be treated with caution.
14 See A. Seegers, 'The head of government and the executive' in R. Schrire (ed.), *Malan to De Klerk: Leadership in the Apartheid State* (London, Hurst and Co., 1994), p. 42. These figures exclude the administrations of self-governing states.
15 B. Roux, 'The central administration, provincial and local authorities, and the judiciary' in D. Worrall (ed.), *South Africa: Government and Politics* (Pretoria, Van Schaik, 1971), p. 82.
16 See D. O'Meara, *Forty Lost Years: The Apartheid State and the Politics of the National Party, 1948-1994* (Johannesburg, Ravan, 1996), p. 61.
17 See D. Posel, *The Making of Apartheid, 1948-1961* (Oxford and Cape Town, Clarendon Press, 1991 and 1997), p. 70.
18 'English-speaking customs collector bowler-hatted', *Star*, 1 August 1959 (Johannesburg).
19 'Ons opname tel koppe', *Rapport*, 26 May 1974 (Johannesburg).
20 'Few English in top jobs', *Star*, 12 December 1976.
21 'Address of the retiring president, Mr D. van Wyk', *The Public Servant*, July 1943 and April 1944.
22 'Staff shortage is critical', *Star*, 19 April 1961.
23 Central Archives Depot, SAB K262 99/G/37/9, part 4, Committee on Administrative Training for the South African Public Service, 1970, 'Die konferensie van hoofde van departemente'.
24 'No pay rise yet for civil servants', *Sunday Express*, 14 January 1965 (Johannesburg).
25 'Staff shortage no better', *Rand Daily Mail*, 2 April 1965 (Johannesburg).
26 'Call for public service probe', *Rand Daily Mail*, 22 February 1968.
27 'All-out bid for state workers', *Rand Daily Mail*, 24 October 1968.
28 *House of Assembly Debates*, 1969, volume 26, column 4454.
29 Quoted in 'Public service facing crisis', *Rand Daily Mail*, 19 March 1969.
30 'Calls for public service probe', *Rand Daily Mail*, 22 February 1968.
31 Secretary of the Treasury, quoted in 'Shattering staff shortage', *Rand Daily Mail*, 15 August 1969.
32 *House of Assembly Debates*, 1969, volume 26, column 4457.
33 Cited in G. Adler, 'Skills, control and "careers at work"', *South African Sociological Review*, 5:2 (1993), p. 51.
34 Republic of South Africa, *Public Service Commission: 56th Annual Report*, RP 39/1968, p. 5.
35 *House of Assembly Debates*, 1964, volume 11, column 5932.
36 *House of Assembly Debates*, 1969, volume 27, column 7170; Republic of South Africa, *Public Service Commission: 56th Annual Report*, RP 39/1968, annexure F(1), p. 21.
37 'Top level checkup on state pay', *Rand Daily Mail*, 22 May 1968.
38 Republic of South Africa, *Public Service Commission: 61st Annual Report*, RP 97/1973, p. 34.
39 Republic of South Africa, *Public Service Commission: 59th Annual Report*, RP 43/1971, p. 12.
40 'Mulder warns on scramble for staff', *Rand Daily Mail*, 7 January 1975.
41 'Address of the retiring president, Mr D. van Wyk', *The Public Servant*, July 1943.
42 See D. Posel, 'Van der Merwe's office: Whiteness and work in the apartheid civil service', *Journal of Southern African Studies*, forthcoming 1998.
43 One of the indices of this is the extent to which the English, and to a lesser but nonetheless significant extent the Afrikaans, press gave prominent coverage to bunglings of various kinds in the civil service (hence my frequent reference to newspaper sources).
44 'Plea for more pay in public service', *Rand Daily Mail*, 17 October 1964.
45 'Inquiry urged into image of government workers', *Rand Daily Mail*, 20 October 1967.
46 'Many public servants unqualified', *Rand Daily Mail*, 20 October 1967.
47 'Shattering staff shortage', *Rand Daily Mail*, 15 August 1969.
48 'Cabinet staff crisis', *Sunday Express*, 20 December 1970.
49 'Public service crisis', *Star*, 26 February 1976.
50 For details on these changes, see Posel, 'Van der Merwe's office'.
51 *House of Assembly Debates*, 1969, volume 26, column 4454.
52 'Calls for change in recruit methods', *Rand Daily Mail*, 21 May 1969.
53 'Public service takes notice of bonus days', *Sunday Express*, 21 September 1975.
54 'Public service crisis', *Star*, 26 February 1976.
55 In fact, during the 1960s the Cabinet's reaction to reports of an incompetent, inefficient or oversized public service was defensive and accusatory; such talk, it was said, 'was peddling a crisis-mindedness' ('Public servants shortage', *Rand Daily Mail*, 17 June 1969).
56 'Revamping the public service – key is speed', *Star*, 17 September 1979.
57 'Super-sekretarisse met nuwe bedeling', *Beeld*, 19 November 1979 (Johannesburg).
58 O'Meara, *Forty Lost Years*, pp. 283-5.
59 O'Meara, *Forty Lost Years*, p. 279.
60 This was reflected in figures released by the Department of Statistics, published in 'Public sector spends more', *Rand Daily Mail*, 17 September 1980.
61 'No civil servants will lose their jobs', *Rand Daily Mail*, 8 December 1979.
62 Republic of South Africa, *Commission for Administration Annual Report 1980-81*, RP 36/1982, p. 11.
63 'The civil service crisis', *Star*, 25 February 1981.
64 'Tortoise remark upsets public servants', *Rand Daily Mail*, 16 July 1980.
65 'Manpower wasted in public service', *Rand Daily Mail*, 30 August 1968.
66 See, for example, D. Davis and D. Fine, *Beyond Apartheid: Labour and Liberation in South Africa* (Johannesburg, Ravan Press, 1990); Posel, *The Making of Apartheid*.
67 Cited in 'Shattering staff shortage', *Rand Daily Mail*, 15 August 1969.
68 See Posel, 'Van der Merwe's office'.

The great apartheid building boom: The transformation of Johannesburg in the 1960s
E4 Clive Chipkin
1 See C. Chipkin, *Johannesburg Style: Architecture & Society 1880s-1960s* (Cape Town, David Philip, 1993).
2 A.R. Colquhoun, *The Afrikander Land* (London, John Murray, 1906), pp. 395-6.
3 C. Dunn, 'A world fit for whites', *Observer*, 20 July 1969 (London), p. 21.
4 D. Hobart Houghton, 'Economic development' in M. Wilson and L. Thompson (eds.), *The Oxford History of South Africa* (Oxford, Oxford University Press, 1971), p. 39.
5 J. Davenport, 'The only real industrial complex south of Milan', *Fortune* magazine, December 1966, p. 181.

6 J.D.F. Jones, 'Strength in isolation', Financial Times, 25 September 1967 (London), p. 9.
7 J.G. Ward, 'Central city property development in South Africa', Data, September 1972 (Johannesburg), p. 9.
8 E.W.N. Mallows, 'A new image for Johannesburg', Optima, December 1973 (Johannesburg), p. 172.
9 A. Bush-Brown, Skidmore, Owings & Merrill: Architecture and urbanism 1973-1983 (Stuttgart, Verlag Gerd Hatje, 1984).
10 'People in architecture', Northwards Bulletin (March 1989), p. 1.
11 R. Fee, 'Tall buildings in South Africa', Architecture SA, March/April (1991), p. 17.
12 Interviewed at 44 Main Street, Johannesburg, 21 May 1996.
13 E.W.N. Mallows in discussion with S. Zar, April 1998.
14 See E. Hobsbawm, Art and Power: Europe under the Dictators, 1930-45 (London, Thames & Hudson, 1996).
15 M. Tafuri, Architecture and Utopia: Design and Capitalist Development (Cambridge, Mass., MIT Press, 1980), p. 3.
16 I. McCallum, Architecture USA (London, Architectural Press, 1959), p. 136.
17 Architects: Colyn and Meiring, Cape Town, 1968.
18 D. O'Meara, Volkskapitalisme: Class, Capital and Ideology in the Development of Afrikaner Nationalism, 1934-1948 (Johannesburg, Ravan Press, 1983).
19 J. Jones, 'Sanlam leads the break out of the laager', Business Day, 6 September 1996 (Johannesburg), p. 11.
20 E.W.N. Mallows and J. Beinart, 'Planning in the CBD: The potential of the periphery', Traffic Quarterly, April (1966), p. 189.
21 S. Zar, unpublished research paper (1986). To record some of the engineers: Braamfontein – A.S. Joffe; Faraday – Ove Arup; Bridge 6 – Hawkins Hawkins and Osborn, with German consultant Bauburo Grassl.
22 W. Pryce-Rosser papers, quoted in Zar, unpublished paper.
23 Zar, unpublished paper.
24 Le Corbusier and F. de Pierrefeu, The Home of Man (London, Architectural Press, 1948).
25 In recent years some of these have been converted into mosques or Hindu temples.
26 Architect and Builder, March (1968).
27 I. Wilkins and H. Strydom, The Super Afrikaners (Johannesburg, Jonathan Ball, 1978), p. 3.
28 Die Eike was so inconspicuous that few could have known it was the Broederbond's headquarters before that fact was revealed in a BBC documentary of the 1980s. Needless to say the film was banned in South Africa.
29 Wilkins and Strydom, The Super Afrikaners, p. 368.
30 E. van der Westhuizen, 'W.O. Meyer: Architect and philosopher', Lantern, 42:3 (1993), p. 18.
31 Van der Westhuizen, 'W.O. Meyer'.
32 Van der Westhuizen, 'W.O. Meyer'.
33 W.O. Meyer, interviewed by P. Goldsmid, Johannesburg, August 1996, for the film Johannesburg Style (SABC, 1997).
34 'Wilhelm O. Meyer and Partners: Buildings and Projects, 1967 to 1978' (Practice profile).
35 Van der Westhuizen, 'W.O. Meyer'.
36 'RAU success story', Star, 8 May 1973 (Johannesburg), p. B1.
37 A. Kuper, 'Objects of desire', Times Literary Supplement, 8 May 1998 (London), p. 7.
38 M. Swilling, R. Humphries and K. Shubane (eds.), Apartheid City in Transition (Cape Town, Oxford University Press, 1991).
39 A.J.P. Taylor, The Course of German History (London, Hamish Hamilton, 1945), p. 88.
40 Rand Daily Mail, 12 August 1971 (Johannesburg).
41 D. Pallister, S. Stewart and I. Lepper, South Africa Inc: The Oppenheimer Empire (Johannesburg, Media House, 1987).
42 See, for instance, Star, 6 and 7 August 1964; Sunday Times, 26 March 1967.
43 H. Oppenheimer, 'Suzman the economist', Business Day, 5 June 1990 (Johannesburg), leader page.
44 K. Owen, Business Day (Johannesburg).
45 D. Yudelman, The Emergence of Modern South Africa (Cape Town, David Philip, 1984), p. 285.

Reconstruction and the making of urban planning in 20th-century South Africa
E6 Alan Mabin

1 This argument is elaborated in A. Mabin and D. Smit, 'Reconstructing South Africa's cities: The making of urban planning 1900-2000', Planning Perspectives, 12:2 (1997), pp. 193-223.
2 P. Wilkinson, 'A discourse of modernity: The Social and Economic Planning Council's fifth report on Regional and Town Planning, 1944' in Planning History Study Group, Proceedings of the Symposium on South African Planning History (Pietermaritzburg, PHSG, 1993), pp. 239-79.
3 The initial planning for the Foreshore Scheme was done in the late 1930s and early '40s, but the final plan was developed after the War and published in 1947.
4 D. O'Meara, Forty Lost Years: The Apartheid State and the Politics of the National Party, 1948-1994 (Johannesburg, Ravan Press, 1996), Chapter 14.
5 J. Rantete, The Third Day of September (Johannesburg, Ravan Press, 1984); O'Meara, Forty Lost Years, pp. 248, 264.
6 P. Hendler, 'Living in apartheid's shadow: Residential planning for Africans in the PWV region 1970-1990', Urban Forum, 3:2 (1992).
7 A. Morris, 'The desegregation of Hillbrow, Johannesburg, 1978-82', Urban Studies, 31:6 (1994), pp. 821-35.
8 P. Gordhan, panellist, in Proceedings of the SAITRP Conference on Planning and the New Constitution (Durban, SAITRP, 1985), pp. 71-2.
9 J. McCarthy, 'Urban reconstruction and South Africa's future', Richard Turner Memorial Lecture, University of Natal, Pietermaritzburg, 29 May 1991; D. Dewar and R. Uytenbogaardt, South African Cities: A Manifesto for Change (Cape Town, Urban Problems Research Unit, 1992).
10 A. Mabin, 'On the problems and prospects of overcoming segregation, fragmentation and surveillance in southern Africa's cities in the post-modern era' in S. Watson and K. Gibson (eds.), Postmodern Cities and Spaces (Oxford, Blackwell, 1995), pp. 187-98.
11 I. Turok, 'Restructuring or reconciliation? South Africa's Reconstruction and Development Programme', International Journal of Urban and Regional Research, 19:2 (1995), pp. 305-18.
12 Department of Constitutional Development, White Paper on Local Government, April 1998.
13 J. Robinson, 'Power, space and the city: Historical reflections on apartheid and post-apartheid urban orders' in D.M. Smith (ed.), Urbanisation in Contemporary South Africa (London, Routledge, 1992).

Rival futures: Struggle visions, post-apartheid choices
E8 Mark Swilling

1 I was a co-founder of Planact in 1985 and occupied various positions on the Executive over the following years. From September 1990 to September 1993 I was employed as a full-time project worker. I have served on the Board since 1997 and was elected Chairperson in 1998.
2 G. O'Donnell, P. Schmitter and D. Whitehead, Transitions from Authoritarian Rule (Baltimore and London, Johns Hopkins University Press, 1986).
3 J. Rantete, The African National Congress and the Negotiated Settlement in South Africa (Johannesburg, Van Schaik, 1998).
4 See M. Swilling and D. Wooldridge, 'Policy and institutional prospects and challenges' in A.P.J. Burger, F. Theron and A. van Rooyen, Challenges in Change (Stellenbosch, University of Stellenbosch, 1996); C. de Koning and J. Fick, 'A development perspective on policy management: From analysis to process facilitation', mimeo, Development Bank of Southern Africa (Midrand, 1995); and C. Heymans, 'Policy support for strategic management in the public sector: Some international perspectives', mimeo, Development Bank of Southern Africa (Midrand, 1995).
5 See White Paper on Urban Development Strategy.
6 This analysis differs considerably from the more teleological explanations which ascribe the conservative orientation of housing policy to the dominance of business in the policy process from the outset. In my view, more effective strategies could have countered the relatively strong position of business and other vested interests, as happened in other sectors such as land, water affairs and health.
7 In other words, what national legislation is only now making compulsory, the CWMC had begun to formulate as far back as 1993!

Street addresses, Johannesburg
E11 Ivan Vladislavić

1 C. Dickens, A Christmas Carol (London, Collins, 1932 (1843)), pp. 4-5.
2 M. de Paravicini, 'Toll the last bell', Sunday Times (Metro), 28 June 1998 (Johannesburg), p. 4.
3 Misspelt on the map as 'Albermarle', but correct on the street-signs and kerbstone markings.
4 The total floor area was 3.5 million square feet, of which 1.9 million square feet were below street level (Public information boards, Level 200).
5 F. Bettger, How I Raised Myself from Failure to Success in Selling (Kingswood, The World's Work, 1913).
6 The smell of food in the parking garages presumably has to do with the ventilation system, a crucial part of a complex with 50,000 square metres of shopping space entirely underground. Ventilation was a major challenge during the underground construction, and 18 tons of air a minute had to be drawn into the basement for the workers. Strangely enough for a project that made such a strong vertical statement, the early construction must have seemed more like mining than building (Public information boards, Level 200).
7 First shown at the Galerie Arndt, Berlin. See also S. Calle, The Detachment/Die Entfernung - A Berlin Travel Guide (Amsterdam, Gordon & Breach, forthcoming).
8 See B. Sachs, Herman Charles Bosman as I Knew Him (Johannesburg, Golden Era, 1974). Bosman was a great walker. For an amusing account of the night streets of Johannesburg in the 1940s, and the difficulties of writing about anything that happens after midnight, see 'Talk of the town' in A Sip of Jerepigo (Johannesburg, Dassie Books, 1957).

9 R. Bradbury, Dandelion Wine (London, Corgi, 1969), pp. 16-8.
10 C. Dickens, 'The Streets – Night' in Sketches by Boz (London, Caxton, 1910 (1836)), p. 244.
11 C. Dickens, 'Night Walks' in The Uncommercial Traveller (London, Everyman, 1969 (1860)), p. 135.

'Take your body where it has never been before'
F4 Marlene van Niekerk
1 W. Benjamin, Charles Baudelaire: A Lyric Poet in the Era of High Capitalism (London, New Left Books, 1973).
2 C. Prendergast, 'Framing the city: Two Parisian windows' in M.A. Caws (ed.), City Images: Perspectives from Literature, Philosophy and Film (New York, Gordon and Beach, 1991), p. 181.
3 Quoted by A. Kazim, 'The New York writer and his landscape' in Caws, City Images, p. 139.
4 'Paris change! Mais rien dans ma mélancolie / N'a bougé! palais neufs, échafaudages, blocs / Vieux faubourgs, tout pour moi devient allégorie / Et mes chers souvenirs sont plus lourds que des rocs'. From The Flowers of Evil: A Selection edited by Marthiel and Jackson Mathews (New York, New Directions, 1958), p. 80.
5 From Leaves of Grass (New York, Signet, 1960), p. 149.
6 Weg van die deernis van meer of see / verrys 'n stad wat mettertyd kraak / in die son om steierend te val / soos opvulling en dolomiet meegee ... Eendag sal die boor 'n rif raak / sy punt sidderend druk in sagte / motvlerke, ru indringend om weer / 'n goudgod vir nog 'n stad te maak. From Spieël van Water (Cape Town, Human & Rousseau, 1973).
7 S. Freud, Civilization and its Discontents (London, Hogarth Press, 1973), p. 14.
8 Quoted in A. Synnot, The Body Social: Symbolism, Self and Society (London, Routledge, 1993), p. 188.
9 D. Morris, Gestures (New York, Stein and Day, 1979), p. 188.
10 M. Argyle, Bodily Communication (London, Methuen, 1978), p. 265.
11 Z. Bauman, Life in Fragments: Essays in Postmodern Morality (Oxford, Blackwell, 1995), p. 116 ff.
12 Bauman, Life in Fragments, p. 116.
13 Bauman, Life in Fragments, p. 117.
14 J. Raban, Soft City (London, Collins Harvill, 1988), pp. 174-5.
15 Bauman, Life in Fragments, p. 44 ff.
16 Bauman, Life in Fragments, p. 47.
17 Bauman, Life in Fragments, p. 40.

Building and self-reliance
F7 Iain Low
1 People's Dialogue, Building Houses, Building People: The Story of the First 130 Houses Built by Women in the Savings Schemes of the South African Homeless People's Federation (Cape Town, People's Dialogue, 1995). People's Dialogue, PO Box 34639, 7937 Groote Schuur, Cape Town.
2 People's Dialogue, 1997.
3 B. Rudofsky, The Prodigious Builders (New York, Secker and Warburg, 1977).
4 My grateful thanks to Thabo Makakole, Ignatius Lefa Monese, Karabo Letele, Germa Sehlolo, Mphethi Morojele, Ernest Kolobe, A.S. Sivam, Donald Cromer, M'e Patience Molapo at TSRP; the construction firms Rainbow, Nqaka, Monahali, Maseru, and D & S; the Ministry of Education Planning Unit; M'e Motselebane; the people of the Kingdom of Lesotho.
5 A. Perez-Gomez, Architecture and the Crisis of Modern Science (MIT Press, Cambridge, Mass., 1987), p. 3.

Undisciplined practices: Architecture in the context of freedom
F9 Hannah le Roux
1 Republic of South Africa, Constitution of the Republic of South Africa (Pretoria, Government Printer, 1996), p. 1.
2 G.B. Nalbantoğlu, 'Limits of (in)tolerance: The carved dwelling in the architectural and urban discourse of modern Turkey', in G.B. Nalbantoğlu and C.T. Wong (eds.), postcolonial space(s) (Princeton, Princeton Architectural Press, 1997), p. 11.
3 See J. Noble, 'Before we could build', Spazio e Societa, 77 (1997), pp. 88-97.
4 Environmental Development Agency, R. Berold (ed.), The People's Workbook (Johannesburg, Environmental Development Agency, 1981).
5 S. Saitowitz, 'A dissertation', B.Arch. thesis (Johannesburg, University of the Witwatersrand, 1976).
6 International Union of Architects, H. Beck (ed.), UIA, 8 (1985).
7 B. Britz, 'Is a South African architecture possible?', Architecture SA, November/December (1982), pp. 66-68.
8 L. Prussin, African Nomadic Architecture: Space, Place and Gender (Washington and London, Smithsonian Institution Press, 1995), p. xvi.
9 See, for example, the proposals for social housing in a recent competition in H. Tilman (ed.), Integration or Fragmentation: The Housing Generator Competition for South African Cities (Rotterdam, NAi Publishers, 1997).
10 H. le Roux, 'Five Johannesburg architects', Spazio e Societa, 77 (1997), pp. 110-111.
11 Documented in the All School Architecture Project, Department of Architecture (Johannesburg, University of the Witwatersrand, February 1998).
12 R. Harber, 'Return of the urban poor man – Mansel Road bus facility', KZ-NIA Journal, 4 (1997), pp. 6-7.
13 KZ-NIA Journal, 3 (1997), p. 7.
14 M. Mitchell, 'Urban architecture survival kit', student project including video insert, Department of Architecture (Johannesburg, University of the Witwatersrand, 1997).
15 C. Slessor (ed.), 'Complexities and contradictions', The Architectural Review, CXCVII: 1177 (March 1995), p. 49.
16 Nalbantoğlu, 'Limits of (in)tolerance', p. 100.

Interiors, District Six, c. 1950
G10 Shamil Jeppie
1 A. Dangor, Kafka's Curse (Cape Town, Kwela Books, 1997), p. 35.
2 For background on District Six see S. Jeppie and C. Soudien (eds.), The Struggle for District Six: Past and Present (Cape Town, Buchu Books, 1990).
3 G. Bachelard, The Poetics of Space (Boston, Beacon Press, 1962), p. 7.
4 R. Rive, 'Buckingham Palace', District Six (Cape Town, David Philip, 1987). The phrase is from Rive's essay 'I remember District Six' in M. Mutloatse (ed.), Umhlaba Wethu: A Historical Indictment (Skotaville, Braamfontein, 1987), p. 90.
5 A. La Guma, A Walk in the Night (London, Heinemann, 1962), p. 21.
6 Rive, 'I remember District Six', p. 90.
7 See M. Heidegger, 'Building dwelling thinking' in D.F. Krell (ed.), Martin Heidegger: Basic Writings (San Francisco, Harper, 1977), pp. 323-39.
8 See P. Bourdieu, Outline of a Theory of Practice (Cambridge, Cambridge University Press, 1977), especially his discussions of habitus and house.
9 See report in The Sun, 22 October 1943 (Cape Town).
10 See UG 18/43, Report of a Committee of Enquiry Appointed to Enquire into Conditions Existing on the Cape Flats and Similarly-Affected Areas in the Cape Division.
11 E. Batson, Social Survey of Cape Town (Cape Town, University of Cape Town, 1942), No. 21, p. 9.
12 Cape Times, 20 June 1950.
13 P. Scott, 'Cape Town: A multi-racial city', Geographical Journal, 121 (1955), pp. 149-57.
14 The quote and some of the points in this paragraph are drawn from S. Patterson, Colour and Culture in South Africa (London, Routledge and Kegan Paul, 1953), p. 148.
15 L. Fortune, The House on Tyne Street: Childhood Memories of District Six (Cape Town, Kwela Books, 1996), p. 2.
16 Interview with Mrs. F. Karriem, Western Cape Oral History Project (WCOHP) transcript, Manuscripts Division, University of Cape Town (UCT), pp. 12-19.
17 Anecdote told by a Guguletu couple to S. Prosalendis and staff of the District Six Museum.
18 Interview with Mrs. G. Albertyn, WCOHP transcript, Manuscripts Division, UCT, p. 13.
19 Interview, Karriem.
20 J. Wissema, District Six (Linden, Fontein Publishing, 1986), p. 39.
21 La Guma, Walk in the Night, p. 49.
22 Fortune, The House on Tyne Street, p. 2.
23 La Guma, Walk in the Night, p. 48.
24 Batson, Social Survey, No. 24, p. 3.
25 Interview with Mr. O. Albertyn, WCOHP transcript, Manuscripts Division, UCT, p. 15-16.
26 Interview with Mrs. M. Abrahams, WCOHP transcript, Manuscripts Division, UCT, p. 3.
27 See any Annual Report of the City Electrical Engineer from 1932 onwards.
28 Interview with Mrs. Z. Booley, WCOHP transcript, Manuscripts Division, UCT, p. 17.
29 See G. Lewis, Between the Wire and the Wall: A History of 'Coloured' Politics (Cape Town, David Philip, 1987).
30 Interview, Booley, p. 20.
31 For just one recent example, see C. Breytenbach, The Spirit of District Six (Cape Town, Human and Rousseau, 1997).

Modernism at the margins
H3 Daniel Herwitz
1 For a reading of Manet's work against the transformations of Paris and the flow of capital in the nineteenth century, see T.J. Clark, The Painting of Modern Life: Paris in the Art of Manet and his Followers (New York, Knopf, 1984).
2 For a measured approach to Irma Stern's exoticizing gaze see the introduction to N. Dubow (ed.), Paradise: The Journals and Letters of Irma Stern, 1917-1933 (Diep River, Chameleon Press, 1991).

3 The idea of the split subject was first formulated by Frantz Fanon and has been developed by Homi Bhabha. See F. Fanon, Black Skin, White Masks (London, Pluto, 1986 (1952)), and the Introduction to that book by H. Bhabha, 'Remembering Fanon'.
4 F. Fanon, 'On national culture' in P. Williams and L. Chrisman (eds.), Colonial Discourse and Post-Colonial Theory (New York, Columbia University Press, 1994), p. 37.
5 For a fascinating discussion of the Brasilia project and its subversion by local populations see J. Holston, The Modernist City: An Anthropological Critique of Brasilia (Chicago and London, Chicago University Press, 1989).
6 H. Lefebvre, The Production of Space (Oxford, Basil Blackwell, 1984).
7 C. Chipkin, Johannesburg Style: Architecture & Society 1880s-1960s (Cape Town, David Philip, 1993), p. 44.
8 Chipkin, Johannesburg Style, p. 49.
9 Chipkin, Johannesburg Style, p. 168.
10 'zerohour', quoted in Chipkin, Johannesburg Style, p. 89.
11 For discussion of the mentality underpinning the avant-garde pronouncement and its ideas of starting from scratch in the name of a utopian future, see M. Perloff, The Futurist Movement: Avant-Garde, Avant-Guerre, and the Language of Rupture (Chicago and London, Chicago University Press, 1986); and D. Herwitz, Making Theory/Constructing Art: On the Authority of the Avant-Garde (Chicago and London, Chicago University Press, 1993).
12 Chipkin, Johannesburg Style, p. 75.
13 J. Cooke, 'Shifts after the thirties', Architecture SA, July and August 1993, pp. 24-5.
14 Cooke, 'Shifts after the thirties', pp. 26-7.
15 Chipkin, Johannesburg Style, p. 280.
16 See J. Holston and A. Appadurai, 'Cities and citizenship', Public Culture, 8:2 (1996).
17 M. Heidegger, The Origin of the Work of Art (New York, Harper and Row, 1975), pp. 40-5.

The social programme of the South African Modern Movement
H6 Derek Japha

1 This essay is a revised version of my paper 'The social programme of the South African movement in architecture', presented at a Centre for African Studies seminar, University of Cape Town, 1986.
2 See P. Wilkinson, 'Out of sight ... out of mind? The development of African housing policy in Johannesburg and the genesis of Soweto, 1902-1953', unpublished manuscript; and P. Wilkinson, 'Providing "adequate shelter": The South African state and the "resolution" of the African housing crisis, 1948-1954' in D. Hindson (ed.), Working Papers in Southern African Studies Volume 3 (Johannesburg, Ravan Press, 1983). See also J. Robinson, The Power of Apartheid: State Power and Space in South African Cities (Oxford, Butterworth-Heinemann, 1996). The term 'the power of apartheid' is hers.
3 G. Herbert, Martienssen and the International Style: The Modern Movement in South African Architecture (Cape Town and Rotterdam, A.A. Balkema, 1975).
4 Published as K. Jonas, 'The architect and the social system', South African Architectural Record (SAAR), 1938, p. 204 ff.
5 Jonas, 'The architect and the social system', p. 213.
6 Jonas, 'The architect and the social system', p. 214.
7 Jonas, 'The architect and the social system', pp. 213-4.
8 Jonas, 'The architect and the social system', p. 214.
9 Presented in obvious ignorance of the authoritarian syndicalism underlying the Ville Radieuse. For a discussion of Le Corbusier and syndicalism, see R. Fishman, Urban Utopias in the Twentieth Century: Ebenezer Howard, Frank Lloyd Wright and Le Corbusier (New York, Basic Books, 1977), p. 226 ff.
10 K. Jonas, 'Introduction to the town planning congress', SAAR, 1938, p. 268.
11 P. Connell, C. Irvine-Smith, K. Jonas, R. Kantorowich and F. Wepener, Native Housing (Johannesburg, Witwatersrand University Press, 1939). In an unsigned review article in the Royal Institute of British Architects Journal, January (1944), p. 67, it was described as the only work of its kind, of significance to the 'entire colonial housing problem'.
12 Won by Furner's Partnership, with Martienssen second. See 'The Klipspruit planning competition', SAAR, 1931, p. 86.
13 Jonas, 'Introduction to the town planning congress', p. 269.
14 'The main argument against subsidized rents [for 'native' housing] lies in the fact that as long as the immoral principle of fiscal segregation and the social pariahdom of the Bantu proletariat persists as social realities, so long will no municipality or public body in South Africa provide decent living conditions for the Natives if that requires subsidization from general revenue. The harsh reality is that the ruling European population of South Africa gives presents to the Natives only by miscalculation ... In the long run the Bantu proletariat cannot expect to get better housing accommodation than it can pay for. Therefore, to suggest improvements on the present housing schemes resulting in sub-economic rents is to cherish Utopian illusions.' Connell et al., Native Housing, p. 43.
15 This was reflected in a dramatic increase in the number of articles on housing published in the SAAR during the war. In addition to other sources quoted below, see, for instance, M. Bryer, 'Housing or holocaust', 1940, p. 415 ff., B. Spence, 'Native housing', 1940, p. 387 ff. and 'The problem of the location: A report of housing conditions in the Transvaal', 1943, p. 25 ff.; the entire June and July issues of 1943; and N. Hanson, 'The problem of housing now and after the war', 1944, p. 191 ff.
16 R. Kantorowich, 'The modern theorists of planning: Le Corbusier, Frank Lloyd Wright, etc.', SAAR, 1942, p. 6 ff.
17 See H. Martienssen, 'Le Corbusier and the USSR', SAAR, 1942, p. 84 ff.; R. Kantorowich, letter to SAAR, 1942, p. 178 ff.; and A. Stewart, letter to SAAR, 1942, p. 291 ff.
18 N. Hanson, letter to SAAR, 1942, pp. 298-9.
19 Hanson, letter to SAAR, p. 298.
20 Hanson, letter to SAAR, pp. 298-9.
21 Hanson, letter to SAAR, p. 299.
22 The exhibition itself and the entire proceedings of the accompanying congress were published in the SAAR in the September and October issues, 1943.
23 N. Hanson, 'Community planning', SAAR, October (1943), p. 228 ff.
24 L. Mumford, The Culture of Cities (New York, Harcourt, Brace & World, 1938). I am accentuating the role of Mumford because his work was crucial to the development of the American urban policy of the New Deal which was so influential in South Africa and because the literature by Hanson and others makes constant reference to The Culture of Cities. But Mumford's work was, of course, only one element in a wide range of 'regionalist' influences which appeared before and after the war. Others include the Tennessee Valley Authority Project, as the 'most significant example of regionalism achieved under a capitalist economy', Soviet regional planning, the publication of the Wright Report on regional planning for New York State, the Barlow Report, the work of the Regional Planning Association of America and the work of Perry, Wright and Stein reflected in American New Towns.
25 In The Culture of Cities he criticized early schemes like the City for Three Million People and Algiers, but called the Ville Radieuse a marked ideological improvement and Nemours 'one of the best rational layouts that has yet appeared' (p. 414). But by 1963 Mumford was describing Le Corbusier as a 'menace'. See the letter to Osborn quoted in R. Walden, 'Introduction' in R. Walden, (ed.), The Open Hand – Essays on Le Corbusier (Cambridge, Mass. and London, MIT Press, 1977), p. 1.
26 The connection between the Garden City concept and such landmarks in Modern Movement housing practice as the work of Ernst May, not entirely obvious on the surface, had been correctly pointed out by Mumford (The Culture of Cities, p. 399). Mumford made this connection vivid by juxtaposing Greenbelt, Maryland with Römerstadt on opposite sides of Plate IX. What he did not point out was that May had actually worked for Unwin, although there is, of course, no trace of Unwin's nostalgic neo-medievalism in May's Frankfurt Siedlungen.
27 In South Africa, the feature of planning practice often attributed to the influence of the Garden City concept is the geographically isolated township in the form of a dormitory suburb, surrounded by arterial roads or a green space/buffer strip, in which low-rise, low-density housing and local community facilities are located along a characteristically irregular pattern of internal roads. This owes nothing to Howard, whose ideas were predicated neither on the dormitory suburb, nor on such low densities, nor on the subdivision of urban districts at a scale smaller than that of the town as a whole. Whatever the demerits of the Garden City model, failures in South African housing design cannot be attributed to its use. Unwin's Hampstead Garden Suburb is more relevant (itself a departure from Howard), as are his writings on density, including the famous pamphlet 'Nothing gained by overcrowding' and the paper 'Higher building in relation to town planning', both republished in W. Creese (ed.), The Legacy of Raymond Unwin: A Human Pattern for Planning (Cambridge, Mass. and London, MIT Press, 1967). However, it is the neighbourhood concept (for a review of the literature see G. Herbert, 'The neighbourhood unit principle and organic theory', Sociological Review, July (1963), p. 165 ff.) not the Garden City concept which is particularly pertinent to the planning of African housing in South Africa. This was originally formulated by Perry, subsequently popularized by Mumford and practised in a range of examples which is extraordinarily diverse, both formally and ideologically. Densities and plan forms vary considerably among these different applications, but the constant is the idea of the geographically isolated, self-contained residential neighbourhood. This idea is reflected as much in applications like the Siedlungen built in Frankfurt and Berlin and the micro-districts of Soviet planning practice, as it is in American examples like Radburn.
28 Quoted in A. Stewart, 'Man and nature', SAAR, 1939, p. 393 ff.
29 See, for instance, 'The sociological premises of the minimum dwelling' and 'Houses, walk-ups or high rise', republished in W. Gropius, Scope of Total Architecture (London, Allen and Unwin, 1956).
30 L. Silberman, 'The social postulates of planning', SAAR, 1943, p. 216.
31 None of these ideas was entirely new in South Africa. Arguments for neighbourhood planning had appeared sporadically at congresses and in the professional journals. The concept had been discussed briefly but not by name in S. Biesheuvel, 'The psychological

approach to planning', SAAR, 1938, p. 291 (paper to the 1938 congress). Regionalism had already been advocated as well. But these concepts were unsystematic and untheorized until the exhibition, where their application was advanced for the time, even in international terms.
32 See N. Hanson, 'Vote of thanks to G Ballenden', SAAR, July 1942, pp. 145-6. The preconditions for planning are stated as a comprehensive survey to determine demand, capacity level of production, socio-economic conditions, overcrowding, income levels, occupations, the economic growth of the 'native', demographic trends, factors affecting regional planning, the structure of the building industry, relationships between building costs and wage levels, appropriate building materials, etc. The implicit assertion in the passage that these issues can be objectively interrogated to provide planning constraints is an illustration of the reduction of political questions to technical questions characteristic of this type of discourse.
33 Hanson, 'Community planning', pp. 231, 234.
34 In this respect, Hanson quoted Stalin: 'to ... create closer spiritual ties between the centre of Russia and the border regions, we must develop local national schools, national theatres and national education institutions and must raise the cultural level of the people of the border regions. Nobody will deny that [the] border regions, since they are striving for the cultural and material prosperity of the masses, must have their own native schools, courts, administration and government bodies recruited from among the native people.' (J. Stalin, 'The policy of the Soviet government on the national question in Russia' in A. Fineberg (ed.), Marxism and the National and Colonial Question: A Collection of Articles and Speeches (Moscow and Leningrad, Co-operative Publishing Society of Foreign Workers in the USSR, 1935), quoted in 'Community planning', p. 230.) Hanson appears to have believed that initial differentiation in that way would create the conditions for integration later: 'The principles in community planning at both regional and urban levels are of particular significance to South Africa, where the integration of communities is a process awaiting realization.' (Hanson, 'Community planning', p. 234.)
35 Hanson, 'Community planning', p. 233.
36 Hanson, 'Community planning', p. 232.
37 Hanson, 'Community planning', p. 234.
38 In 1944 the Directorate of Housing estimated that 440,000 houses would be required over the next ten years. Minutes of National Housing Council meeting, 11/12 December 1944, GES 2434 P15, National Archives, Pretoria (hereafter NA).
39 Late in 1941 an ISAA delegation met J.H. Hofmeyer to recommend the inclusion of a complete scheme of regional planning in the national planning programme and the establishment of a Planning Commission with broad terms of reference. This objective was to be satisfied by the formation of the Social and Economic Planning Council in 1943, and on the advice of its future Chairman, J.H. van Eck, from 1942 onwards the ISAA began to concentrate on housing in its representations to the state. ISAA Central Council (CC) Minutes, 26 January 1942.
40 These exchanges are recorded in CC Minutes, 20 September 1943, 21 July 1944, 7 October 1944; letter dated 5 June 1945 appended to CC Minutes, 18 June 1945; ISAA Executive Committee Minutes, 22 August 1944, 11 May 1945.
41 Letter Schönland to Secretary for Public Health, 23 March 1945, GES 2520 PH 11, NA.
42 Minutes of Meeting, 15 March 1945, GES 2520 PH 11, NA.
43 Hanson suggested that he had initiated the NBRI programme of housing research by convincing the CSIR that, if the NBRI was to become effectively involved in housing, it would have to conduct research of a kind not normally undertaken by building research institutes, namely social research. Personal communication, October 1985.
44 Hanson claimed to have originated the project himself, but I have been unable to verify this independently. He also suggested that he considered the reports to be his major contribution to South African housing. Personal communication, 1985.
45 For a list of members see DS 9, Interim Report of the Main Committee (NBRI, Pretoria, 1949), Appendix I. Hanson was chairman of the main committee, Douglass Cowin chairman of the subcommittee on house design, Gordon McIntosh a member of the subcommittee on estate planning, Kantorowich a corresponding member, and Connell secretary for the entire project. Other membership was diverse, including representatives of the housing agencies, state departments, the Institute of Race Relations, and even some African members, including Dr A.B. Xuma, President of the African National Congress.
46 See NBRI series DS 1-9 (Pretoria, 1949).
47 See DS 4, Interim Report of the Sub Committee on Estate Planning, p. 13 ff. This report was singled out by the main committee as one of the most significant, as indeed it is.
48 'The ... task of the Committee would be ... to make recommendations based on the need to protect the health, comfort, convenience, and welfare of the population' and it would attend to the practical issues of implementation 'only after the basic standards had been laid down' (emphasis in original), pp. 2-3.
49 N. Hanson, ISAA Executive Committee (or CC?) Minutes, 24 April 1946.
50 ISAA Executive Committee Minutes, 15 July 1948.
51 CC Minutes, 30 September 1948.
52 DS 9, p. 37.
53 Wilkinson, 'Providing "adequate shelter"', p. 78 and passim.
54 See Wilkinson, 'Providing "adequate shelter"', p. 78 and H. Verwoerd, Speech to Senate, 30 May 1952, reprinted in A. Pelzer (ed.), Verwoerd Speaks: Speeches 1948-1966 (Johannesburg, APB Publishers, 1966), p. 45.
55 See W. Gropius and M. Wagner, 'A program for city reconstruction', The Architectural Forum, July (1943), pp. 76-7. This paper should be read in conjunction with W. Gropius, 'Organic neighbourhood planning' (1949) reprinted in Gropius, Scope of Total Architecture; and W. Gropius, Rebuilding Our Communities (Chicago, P. Theobald, 1945). I refer to these ideas in detail because they were undoubtedly known to South African housing researchers. Calderwood, for example, quoted from the latter book in an address to the Institute of Race Relations on 'native housing' in 1952.
56 Gropius and Wagner, 'A program for city reconstruction', pp. 78, 79.
57 See Wilkinson, 'Providing "adequate shelter"', p. 74 ff.
58 See, for example, the memorandum entitled 'Extension of national housing schemes with special reference to native housing needs' attached to a letter from Gluckman to Hofmeyer, 9 January 1948, GES 2533 PH 38, NA.
59 See undated memorandum with the same title as that in the previous note, identified as 'First Memo' GES 2533 PH 38. It contained the argument that the NHPC could substantially reduce losses on 'native housing', then fixed at £30 per annum per house.
60 Wilkinson, 'Providing "adequate shelter"', p. 76.
61 Speech to Senate, 30 May 1952, reprinted in Pelzer, Verwoerd Speaks.
62 See UG 78 '64, p. 4.
63 W. Mocke, 'The Native Services Levy Act No. 64 of 1952', Bantu, February (1956), p. 36.
64 D.M. Calderwood, Native Housing in South Africa (Johannesburg, Witwatersrand University Press, 1953).
65 Calderwood, Native Housing, p. 12 and passim.
66 In a paper delivered in 1951, the Director of the NBRI gave the objects of housing as the maintenance of health, social validity (design in such a way as to eliminate 'social malpractices'), the elimination of maintenance, and as far as possible the elimination of subsidy. By far the greatest percentage of research actually produced by the NBRI after about 1946 was devoted to the last of these.
67 DS 9, Interim Report of the Main Committee, pp. 2, 18.
68 DS 9, Interim Report of the Main Committee, p. 37.
69 This assertion rests on an analysis of 14 pre-standards plans taken mainly from P.H. Connell, Sub Economic Housing Practice in South Africa (Pretoria, CSIR (NBRI), 1947). Seven were larger than the approved minimum standard by between 2 and 36 per cent, and seven were smaller, by between 2 and 13 per cent.
70 See D.M. Calderwood and P.H. Connell, 'Minimum standards of accommodation for the housing of non-Europeans in South Africa' in CSIR, Research Studies on the Costs of Urban Bantu Housing (Pretoria, CSIR (NBRI), 1954), Appendix B, pp. 1-2.
71 In fact, there was one area where substantial reductions were possible, and that was in the substitution of cheap black labour for more expensive white labour. Since this idea had been mooted already in the mid-1940s it did not evolve in the NBRI, but the NBRI research did quantify its effects and devise methods for its rational implementation. Whereas so called 'native craft workers' were 77 per cent as productive as skilled labour, the comparative rates of pay were 2s 2p as opposed to 7s 4p per hour, that is, 29.5 per cent, which could result in overall cost savings of 13 per cent of the prime cost of building, since skilled labour represented 25 per cent of the total prime cost. See A. Glen, 'Time studies of labour employed on the building of urban Bantu houses, using Native workers on a craft basis' in CSIR, Costs of Urban Bantu Housing, Appendix B.
72 National Housing Council Minutes, 11 December 1944, GES 2434 PH 15.
73 These costs were then correlated with 'capacity to pay' in a more rigorous way than had been attempted before. The NBRI produced a paper to highlight what its Director called 'several fundamental misconceptions in the present approach to the Native housing problem in South Africa' (J. Jennings, 'The role of housing research in the provision of housing for the urban Bantu', CSIR (Pretoria, 1952), reprinted from Municipal Affairs, XVIII:205/6). This paper divided prospective tenants statistically, according to set criteria, into those who could pay economic rentals, those requiring subsidized rentals, and those unable to pay rent at all. This provided the argument used by Verwoerd that there was no need for a subsidized housing programme because only 12.9 per cent of the sample surveyed fell into the sub-economic category, with the remainder divided into those who could pay economic rentals (40 per cent) and those unable to pay rental at all (46.7 per cent), who could be catered for only by site-and-service schemes. See H. van Beinum, 'Study of the socio-economic status of Native families in the Payneville Location, Springs', National Building Research Institute Bulletin, 8 (June 1952), p. 8.
74 Calderwood, Native Housing, p. 188.
75 CSIR, Costs of Urban Bantu Housing, p. 2.
76 Much of this paragraph is a rearrangement of sentences and phrases from Rabinow's text

'Colonialism, modernity: The French in Morocco' in N. AlSayyad (ed.), *Forms of Dominance: On the Architecture and Urbanism of the Colonial Enterprise* (Aldershot, Avebury, 1992), pp. 167, 168.

The Dead Zone: The confined space of political conflict, Tokoza township
J10 Greg Marinovich

1 A. Minaar, 'Hostels and violent conflict on the Reef' in A. Minaar (ed.), *Communities in Isolation: Perspectives on Hostels in South Africa* (Pretoria, Human Sciences Research Council, 1993).
2 M. Wentzel, 'Historical origins of hostels in South Africa: Migrant labour and compounds' in Minaar, *Communities in Isolation.*

Bodies out of place: Crossroads and the landscapes of exclusion
J12 Steven Robins

1 See M. Lacey, *Working for Boroko: The Origins of a Coercive Labour System in South Africa* (Johannesburg, Ravan Press, 1981), p. 106.
2 A. Feldman, *Formations of Violence: The Narrative of the Body and Political Terror in Northern Ireland* (Chicago, University of Chicago Press, 1991), p. 26.
3 R.A. Butchart, 'On the anatomy of power: Bodies of knowledge in South African socio-medical discourse', Ph.D. thesis (Pretoria, University of South Africa, 1995), p. 304.
4 Butchart, 'On the anatomy of power', p. 305.
5 P. Mayer and I. Mayer, *Townsmen or Tribesmen: Conservatism and the Process of Urbanization in a South African City* (Cape Town, Oxford University Press, 1971 (1961)).
6 J. Comaroff, *Body of Power, Spirit of Resistance: The Culture and History of a South African People* (Chicago and London, University of Chicago Press, 1985); D. Coplan, 'The emergence of an African working class culture' in S. Marks and R. Rathbone (eds.), *Industrialisation and Social Change in South Africa: African Class Formation, Culture and Consciousness 1870-1930* (London, Longman, 1982).
7 During the 1950s and '60s, researchers at the Rhodes Livingstone Institute also challenged the logic of rural/urban binaries by showing the complex ways in which African miners adapted to the urban compounds of Copperbelt mines in what was then Northern Rhodesia (Zambia). Migrants from rural areas became involved in trade unions and forged complex and creative adaptations to their working environments. They were not straitjacketed by traditional identities and cultural practices.
8 B. Magubane, 'The "Xhosa" in town revisited: Urban social anthropology – A failure in method and theory', *American Anthropologist*, 75 (1973), pp. 1701-14.
9 A. Mafeje, 'Ideology of tribalism', *Journal of Modern African Studies*, 4:2 (1971).
10 A. Mafeje, 'Who are the makers and objects of anthropology? A critical comment on Sally Falk Moore's "Anthropology and Africa"', *African Sociological Review*, 1:1 (1997), pp. 1-15. Referring to his well-known study of Langa township written with Monica Wilson, *A Study of Social Groups in an African Township: Langa* (Cape Town, Oxford University Press, 1963), Mafeje notes that even then the distinction between 'school' and 'red' was becoming blurred, for instance with regard to the correlation between Christian conversion and a desire for modern education.
11 J. Jacobs, *Edge of Empire: Postcolonialism and the City* (London and New York, Routledge, 1996), p. 28.
12 Jacobs, *Edge of Empire*, p. 28.
13 C. Themba, *The Will to Die* (Cape Town, David Philip, 1972), p. 110, quoted in U. Hannerz, 'Sophiatown: The view from afar' in U. Hannerz, *Transnational Connections: Culture, People and Places* (London and New York, Routledge, 1996), p. 188.
14 Mafeje, 'Who are the makers and objects of anthropology?', pp. 9-10.
15 Interview with M.T., May 1987, Cape Town. See S. Robins, 'Comrades, vigilantes and "divide and rule": A study of African resistance and cooption in Crossroads, South Africa', M.A. thesis (New York, Columbia University, 1988).
16 C. Bateman, 1986, from an unpublished MS by T. Weaver and C. Bateman.
17 Interview by Craig Matthew and Vernon Matzopolous, World Television News, 1986.
18 J. Cole, *The Politics of Reform and Repression 1976-1986* (Cape Town, David Philip, 1987).
19 N. Haysom, 'Mabangalala: The rise of right-wing vigilantes in South Africa', Centre for Applied Legal Studies Occasional Paper No. 10 (Johannesburg, University of the Witwatersrand, 1986), pp. 104-22.
20 Haysom, 'Mabangalala', p. 111.
21 Interviewed in Cape Town, 1986.
22 R. Friedman, 'Victory feast reward planned for Witdoek', *Cape Times*, 12 June 1997.
23 M. Douglas, *Purity and Danger: An Analysis of the Concepts of Pollution and Taboo* (London, Routledge, 1966).
24 D. Sibley, 'Outsiders in society and space' in K. Anderson and F. Gale (eds.), *Inventing Place: Studies in Cultural Geography* (London, Longman, 1992), pp. 107-22.
25 R. Murray and F.W. Boal, 'The social ecology of urban violence' in D.T. Herbert and D.M. Smith (eds.), *Social Problems and the City: Geographical Perspectives* (Oxford, Oxford University Press, 1979), pp. 139-57.
26 Feldman, *Formations of Violence.*
27 Murray and Boal, 'Social ecology of urban violence', pp. 153-4.
28 M. Mamdani, *Citizen and Subject: Contemporary Africa and the Legacy of Late Colonialism* (Cape Town, David Philip, 1996).
29 Mamdani, *Citizen and Subject*, p. 284.

Image credits

Aircraft Operating Company 350
Architecture SA, January/February (1990) 28
Barrow, J., An Account of Travels into the Interior of Southern Africa in the Years 1797 and 1798 (2 vols, London, T. Cadell and W. Davies, 1806) 36
Bieber, Jodi 12 (Hadebe)
Bogaert, A., Historische reizen... (1711) 39
Bremner, Lindsay 58
Bunn, David 112
Calderwood, D.M, Native Housing in South Africa (Johannesburg, Witwatersrand University Press, 1953) 433, 434, 436
Cape Institute of Architects, Jansje Wissema Photographic Collection 388
Clan paths re-creating the order of village settlements during Babona in Doufitoukou 176
Community Arts Project/Mediaworks, Cape Town 297
Connell, P.H., C. Irvine-Smith, K. Jonas, R. Kantorowich and F. Wepener, Native Housing: A Collective Thesis (Johannesburg, Witwatersrand University Press, 1939) 424, 426, 427
Dainfern Golf Estate and Country Club brochure 48
Dangor, Achmat, photograph courtesy of 358
Deckler, Thorsten and Shiuan-Wen Chu 63
Department of Architecture, University of Natal, Durban 147, 150, 152, 154
Dullaart, Thys 11 (Bieber)
East London Museum 202
Engelbrecht, C., Die Bank van Oom Bossie (Pretoria, Volkskas, 1978) 128, 131
Engelbrecht, C., 'Ons bou vir die Bank' (2 vols, Pretoria, Volkskas, 1964) 135 - 140
Fairbridge, D., Historic Farms of South Africa (London, Oxford University Press, 1931) 31
Goddard, Graeme 14 (Mayet)
Goje, Sandile, Meeting of two cultures, 1993 80
Goldblatt, David 101, 102, 144, 145, 232, 242, 252, 253, 260
Hadebe, Themba 441
Hamblyn, Adèle 17 (Van Niekerk)
Hallen, Hans 105, 107
Hammerl, Anton 53
Harber, Rodney 356
Harold Strange Library of African Studies, Greater Johannesburg Metropolitan Library Services 23
Hartman, Dave 456, 464
Headstart, photograph courtesy of 368
Hentrich, H., Standard Bank Centre (Johannesburg, Standard Bank Investment Corporation, 1970) 256
Hutton-Squire, M., 'Mmabatho, capital of Bophuthatswana: Its planning and development', Architecture SA, Autumn (1981) 26
invisible architecture directed by Karen Schoonbee 357
Le Roux, Hannah 354
Lewis, R.B., 'A "city" within a city – The creation of Soweto', address delivered at the University of the Witwatersrand, Johannesburg, 6 September 1966 24
Low, Iain 330 - 342
Makin, Andrew 355
Martienssen, R., 'Evolution of an architect's house', South African Architectural Record, February (1942) 344
Massa farmhouse enclosure 184
Matakam homestead 172
Mayibuye Centre, Cape Town 266, 293
Molenaar, Kitty 438
Morojele, Mphethi 278 - 283
Morris, P., Soweto: A Study by the Transvaal Region of the Urban Foundation (Johannesburg, Urban Foundation, 1980) 51
Motau, Ruth 196, 197
MuseumAfrica, Johannesburg 20, 50, 272
Musgum family enclosure 180
National Archives Pretoria 109, 236, 264, 415, 416
NBRI, Costs of Urban Bantu Housing Series DR 10 (Pretoria, Council for Scientific and Industrial Research, 1954), Section U 353, 422
Nel, P.G., J H Pierneef – His Life and his Work (Cape Town, Perskor, 1990) 27
'Netherlands Bank, Durban', Architect and Builder, 16 (1966) 158, 160
Penny, P., 'Property', South Africa: An Investor Chronicle and Stock Exchange Gazette Survey, November (1968) 251
Pisani, Almaro, Alvise Louis, 'Carta Geografica de Africa del Capo de Bon esperanze sino al regno et Imperio Monamotapo ...', 1793, private collection of Dr. I. Norwich. 118
Picturesque Voyage to India, 1810, MuseumAfrica, Johannesburg 35
Plan SA, 4 (1964) 352
Planact Archive 284, 442
Planning, Urbanization and Environmental Management Cluster (Greater Johannesburg Metropolitan Council, July 1997) 55
Private Collection, Johannesburg 78
Rand Daily Mail, 15 September 1962. Times Media Collection, MuseumAfrica, Johannesburg 258
Rautenbach, C.H. (ed.), Ad Destinatum: Gedenkboek van die Universiteit van Pretoria, 1910-1960 (Johannesburg, Voortrekkerpers, 1960) 223
'Rebuilding South Africa', supplement to South African Architectural Record, October (1943) 428, 429
Sack, Monty 248
Sagalyn, Adine 15, 17 (Ndebele, Vladislavić)
Samson, Trevor, Times Media Ltd 61
Schumacher, J., The Cape in 1776-77: Aquarelles by Johannes Schumacher from the Swellengreble Collection at Breda (The Hague, Stols, 1951) 33
Screen Training Project, Johannesburg 295
South African Library, Cape Town 94, 97, 98
Soweto in Transition Project, Sociology Department, University of the Witwatersrand, Johannesburg 443
Spies F.J., and D.H. Heydenrych, Ad Destinatum II: 'n Geskiedenis van die Universiteit van Pretoria, 1960-1982 (Pretoria, University of Pretoria, 1987) 223
Standpunt, Beeld, reproduced in Plan, 54:1 (1969) 92, 110
Summary of the Report of the Commission for the Socio-economic Development of the Bantu Areas within the Union of South Africa (Pretoria, Government Printer, 1955) 21
Swanepoel, François, University of Pretoria School of Architecture Archives 224, 229, 330, 231
The South African Council for Atomic Energy (Pretoria, Heer Drukkers, 1964) 24
Thompson, F.L., and L.W. Thornton White, Report of the Town Planning Advisers on the Cape Town Foreshore Scheme (Pretoria, Government Printer, 1940) 268
Tillim, Guy 459, 460, 463, 466, 469
Times Media Collection, MuseumAfrica, Johannesburg 438
Truscott, S.J., The Witwatersrand Goldfields Banket and Mining Practice (London, Macmillan, 1898) 25
University of Pretoria School of Architecture Archives 146, 220, 222, 225, 226, 228, 229, 234
University of the Witwatersrand (Standard Bank Collection) 82
University of the Witwatersrand Architecture Collection 404
Vesty, Jo 14 (Marinovich)
Volkskas Archive 132, 133, 143
Walton, J., African Village (Pretoria, J.L. van Schaik, 1956) 29
West Rand Administration Board (Technical Department) 30
'Wilhelm O. Meyer and Partners: Buildings and Projects, 1967 to 1978' (Practice profile) 263
Yellow Pages, Johannesburg 1996/7 (Telkom SA Ltd) 57

Colophon

This book has been produced on the occasion of 'South African Seasons', a year of exhibitions and activities on South Africa in Rotterdam, and the exhibition 'blank____' in the Netherlands Architecture Institute, Rotterdam, from 16 December 1998 to 30 March 1999.

editors Hilton Judin (Cape Town), Ivan Vladislavić (Johannesburg)
design Kitty Molenaar (Amsterdam, Cape Town)
image research Jenny Sandler (Cape Town)
research Marianne de Klerk (Pretoria), Joanne Lees (Durban), Noeleen Murray (Cape Town), Melinda Silverman (Johannesburg)
copy editors Ivan Vladislavić (Johannesburg), Andrew May (Amsterdam), Colin Underwood (Amsterdam)
scanning Scan Shop (Cape Town)
printing SSP (Amsterdam)
typeface FF Info
publisher Simon Franke
production Paula Vaandrager, Astrid Vorstermans

special thanks to Nina Cohen, Minky Schlesinger and Floris van Luin

'South African Seasons' was made possible through the support of:

the Netherlands
Ministry of Development Cooperation; Ministry of Education, Culture and Science; Ministry of Foreign Affairs; Ministry of Housing, Spatial Planning and Environment; Embassy of South Africa; National Committee for International Cooperation and Sustainable Development (NCDO); City of Rotterdam; Dirk Scherpenzeel Stichting; EFL Stichting; VSB Foundation; Van Puffelen Publicity Company

Rotterdam
Alliance Française; Dunya Foundation; HR&O-Rotterdam Academy of Architecture and Urban Design; International Film Festival Rotterdam; Kunsthal Rotterdam; Maritiem Museum Prins Hendrik; Museum Boijmans Van Beuningen; Natural History Museum Rotterdam; Nederlands Foto Instituut; Netherlands Institute for Southern Africa; Poetry International Rotterdam; Rotterdam Arts Council; Rotterdam Public Library; Rotterdamse Schouwburg (Municipal Theatre of Rotterdam); Via Kunst – Institute for Contemporary Street Art; Witte de With Center for Contemporary Art; Youth Theatre Group Het Waterhuis; Zaal de Unie; Netherlands Architecture Institute: Kristin Feireiss, Annemieke de Kler, Brigitte van der Sande, Angeli Poulssen, Francien van Westrenen, Billy Nolan

South Africa
District Six Museum; Carl Engelbrecht; Hans Hallen; Rodney Harber; Clinton Harrop-Allin; Mayibuye Centre; Ministry of Arts, Culture, Science and Technology; Ministry of Housing; MuseumAfrica; National Archives; National Arts Council; Walter Peters; Planact; Royal Embassy of the Netherlands in South Africa; Piet Snyman; South African Library; Volkskas

Published in Southern Africa by David Philip Publishers (Pty) Ltd, 208 Werdmuller Centre, Newry Street, Claremont 7708, South Africa, tel. 21-644136, fax 21-643358.

Available in North, South and Central America through D.A.P./ Distributed Art Publishers Inc, 155 Sixth Avenue 2nd Floor, New York, NY 10013-1507, tel. 212 627.1999, fax 212 627.9484.

Available in the United Kingdom and Southern Ireland through Art Data, 12 Bell Industrial Estate, 50 Cunnington Street, London W4 5HB, tel. 181-747 1061, fax 181-742 2319.

Printed and bound in the Netherlands
isbn 90-5662-092-4 (NAi Publishers, the Netherlands)
isbn 0-86486-394-2 (David Philip Publishers, South Africa)